Visual Basic 2005 Recipes

A Problem-Solution Approach

Todd Herman, Allen Jones,
Matthew MacDonald, and
Rakesh Rajan

Apress®

Visual Basic 2005 Recipes: A Problem-Solution Approach

Copyright © 2007 by Todd Herman, Allen Jones, Matthew MacDonald, Rakesh Rajan

ISBN-13 (pbk): 978-1-59059-852-8

ISBN-10 (pbk): 1-59059-852-0

Printed and bound in the United States of America 9 8 7 6 5 4 3 2 1

Lead Editor: Ewan Buckingham
Technical Reviewer: Damien Foggon
Editorial Board: Steve Anglin, Ewan Buckingham, Gary Cornell, Jonathan Gennick, Jason Gilmore, Jonathan Hassell, Chris Mills, Matthew Moodie, Jeffrey Pepper, Ben Renow-Clarke, Dominic Shakeshaft, Matt Wade, Tom Welsh
Project Manager: Beth Christmas
Copy Edit Manager: Nicole Flores
Copy Editor: Marilyn Smith
Assistant Production Director: Kari Brooks-Copony
Production Editor: Ellie Fountain
Compositor: Susan Glinert
Proofreader: Liz Welch
Indexer: John Collin
Artist: Kinetic Publishing Services, LLC
Cover Designer: Kurt Krames
Manufacturing Director: Tom Debolski

Distributed to the book trade worldwide by Springer-Verlag New York, Inc., 233 Spring Street, 6th Floor, New York, NY 10013. Phone 1-800-SPRINGER, fax 201-348-4505, e-mail orders-ny@springer-sbm.com, or visit http://www.springeronline.com.

For information on translations, please contact Apress directly at 2855 Telegraph Avenue, Suite 600, Berkeley, CA 94705. Phone 510-549-5930, fax 510-549-5939, e-mail info@apress.com, or visit http://www.apress.com.

The source code for this book is available to readers at http://www.apress.com in the Source Code/Download section.

This book is for my incredible wife and best friend Amy, as well as
my son Aidan and daughter Alaina. Without them I wouldn't be the man
I am today and this book may not have been possible.
—Todd Herman

Contents at a Glance

Contents

■CHAPTER 3 Application Domains, Reflection, and Metadata 77

■CHAPTER 4 Threads, Processes, and Synchronization 111

■CHAPTER 5   Files, Directories, and I/O 161

About the Authors

TODD HERMAN works for Northrop Grumman developing software for the Department of State. He has been programming since he received his first computer, a Commodore 64, on his eleventh birthday. His experience ranges from developing data-entry software in FoxPro for a water research laboratory to writing biometric applications in Visual Basic for NEC. He currently lives in Virginia with his wife and children, and spends his free time programming, playing games, and watching the Sci-Fi channel.

ALLEN JONES has 15 years of experience covering a wide range of IT disciplines in a variety of sectors; however, his true passion has always been software development. Allen is currently Director of Product Development at Smith-Bayes, a UK-based firm that develops high-end, strategic-decision-support software derived from technology used in Formula 1 motor racing.

MATTHEW MACDONALD is an author, educator, and Microsoft MVP. He is a regular contributor to programming journals and the author of more than a dozen books about .NET programming, including *Pro .NET 2.0 Windows Forms and Custom Controls in C#*, *Pro ASP.NET 2.0*, and *Pro WPF* (each published by Apress). In a dimly remembered past life, he studied English literature and theoretical physics.

RAKESH RAJAN coauthored an earlier book on which this book is based (*Visual C# 2005 Recipes*, Apress, 2006). Sadly, Rakesh passed away in 2006. He was a Microsoft MVP in C# and an MCSD in .NET. As a software engineer from India, Rakesh worked with US Technology at Technopark, Trivandrum in Kerala.

About the Technical Reviewer

DAMIEN FOGGON is a freelance programmer and technical author based in Newcastle, England. He is technical director of Thing-E Ltd., a company specializing in the development of dynamic web solutions for the education sector, and founder of Littlepond Ltd. He started out working for BT in the UK before moving on to progressively smaller companies, finally founding his own company. Now he can work on all the cool new technologies, rather than the massive monolithic developments that still exist out there.

Damien is the author of *Beginning ASP.NET 2.0 Databases: From Novice to Professional* (Apress, 2006). He can be reached at http://www.littlepond.co.uk.

Acknowledgments

I first want to thank Richard Guidorizzi for reaffirming my thoughts regarding writing a book. Furthermore, I must thank Ewan Buckingham for seeing something in my e-mail and offering me the opportunity to write this. Finally, I must also extend my thanks and appreciation to Damien Foggon, my technical reviewer. His comments and suggestions forced me to dig deeper into myself and the material to make this a book to be proud of.

Todd Herman

Introduction

Attempting to learn all there is to know about developing VB .NET applications using the Microsoft .NET Framework would be an incredibly daunting task. For most of us, the easiest and best approach is to dive in and start writing code. We learn through testing and experimentation, and when we run into the unknown, we search the Internet or grab a book to assist with the current subject.

Visual Basic 2005 Recipes is not a book that attempts to teach you about the inner workings of a specific subject. It is a resource book that should sit near you as you program, where you can quickly use it to reference what you need.

As you are settled in front of your computer working, you will inevitably run into a situation where you need a little guidance, as all of us do from time to time. The subject matter in this book is so comprehensive that you are bound to find at least one recipe that will fit the bill whenever you need that nudge in the right direction.

This book will not teach you everything you need know about developing VB .NET applications in Visual Studio 2005, but it will be invaluable as a stepping stone. Use the recipes as you need them, to help move your development projects along or to give you a starting point for your own experimentation.

Note This book is based on a previously published book called *Visual C# 2005 Recipes*. All the contents were converted to Visual Basic and updated to reflect some VB-specific features and functionality. While the recipes all target .NET Framework 2.0, many of the recipes will still work on .NET Framework 1.1. Where a recipe uses functionality specific to .NET Framework 2.0, comments were added to present possible alternatives for using .NET Framework 1.1. Furthermore, as we are on the cusp of a new version of the .NET Framework (3.5) and Visual Studio (code-named Orcas), Chapter 15 covers a new and remarkable feature known as Language Integrated Query (LINQ).

■ ■ ■

CHAPTER 1

Application Development

This chapter covers some of the fundamental activities you will need to perform when developing your Visual Basic .NET (VB .NET) solutions. The recipes in this chapter describe how to do the following:

- Use the VB .NET command-line compiler to build console and Windows Forms applications (recipes 1-1 and 1-2)

- Create and use code modules and libraries (recipes 1-3 and 1-4)

- Access command-line arguments from within your applications (recipe 1-5)

- Use compiler directives and attributes to selectively include code at build time (recipe 1-6)

- Access program elements built in other languages whose names conflict with VB .NET keywords (recipe 1-7)

- Give assemblies strong names and verify strong-named assemblies (recipes 1-8, 1-9, 1-10, and 1-11)

- Sign an assembly with a Microsoft Authenticode digital signature (recipes 1-12 and 1-13)

- Manage the shared assemblies that are stored in the global assembly cache (recipe 1-14)

- Make your assembly more difficult to decompile (recipe 1-15)

- Manipulate the appearance of the console (recipe 1-16)

- Compile and embed a string resource file (recipe 1-17)

Note All the tools discussed in this chapter ship with the Microsoft .NET Framework or the .NET Framework software development kit (SDK). The tools that are part of the .NET Framework are in the main directory for the version of the framework you are running. For example, they are in the directory C:\WINDOWS\Microsoft.NET\Framework\v2.0.50727 if you install version 2.0 of the .NET Framework to the default location. The .NET installation process automatically adds this directory to your environment path.

The tools provided with the SDK are in the Bin subdirectory of the directory in which you install the SDK, which is C:\Program Files\Microsoft Visual Studio 8\SDK\v2.0 if you chose the default path during the installation of Microsoft Visual Studio 2005. This directory is *not* added to your path automatically, so you must manually edit your path in order to have easy access to these tools or use the shortcut to the command prompt installed in the Windows Start ➤ Programs menu of Visual Studio that calls vcvarsall.bat to set the right environment variables.

Most of the tools support short and long forms of the command-line switches that control their functionality. This chapter always shows the long form, which is more informative but requires additional typing. For the shortened form of each switch, see the tool's documentation in the .NET Framework SDK.

1-1. Create a Console Application from the Command Line

Problem

You need to use the VB .NET command-line compiler to build an application that does not require a Windows graphical user interface (GUI) but instead displays output to, and reads input from, the Windows command prompt (console).

Solution

In one of your classes, ensure you implement a Shared method named Main with one of the following signatures:

```
Public Shared Sub Main()
End Sub
Public Shared Sub Main(ByVal args As String())
End Sub
Public Shared Function Main() As Integer
End Sub
Public Shared Function Main(ByVal args As String()) As Integer
End Sub
```

Build your application using the VB .NET compiler (vbc.exe) by running the following command (where HelloWorld.vb is the name of your source code file):

```
vbc /target:exe HelloWorld.vb
```

■**Note** If you own Visual Studio, you will most often use the Console Application project template to create new console applications. However, for small applications, it is often just as easy to use the command-line compiler. It is also useful to know how to build console applications from the command line if you are ever working on a machine without Visual Studio and want to create a quick utility to automate some task.

How It Works

By default, the VB .NET compiler will build a console application unless you specify otherwise. For this reason, it's not necessary to specify the /target:exe switch, but doing so makes your intention clearer, which is useful if you are creating build scripts that will be used by others or will be used repeatedly over a period of time.

To build a console application consisting of more than one source code file, you must specify all the source files as arguments to the compiler. For example, the following command builds an application named MyFirstApp.exe from two source files named HelloWorld.vb and ConsoleUtils.vb:

```
vbc /target:exe /main:HelloWorld /out:MyFirstApp.exe HelloWorld.vb ConsoleUtils.vb
```

The /out switch allows you to specify the name of the compiled assembly. Otherwise, the assembly is named after the first source file listed—HelloWorld.vb in the example. If classes in both the

HelloWorld and ConsoleUtils files contain `Main` methods, the compiler cannot automatically determine which method represents the correct entry point for the assembly. Therefore, you must use the
compiler's /main switch to identify the name of the class that contains the correct entry point for your
application. When using the /main switch, you must provide the fully qualified class name (including
the namespace); otherwise, you will get a BC30420 compilation error: "'Sub Main' was not found in
'HelloWorld'."

If you have a lot of VB .NET code source files to compile, you should use a response file. This
simple text file contains the command-line arguments for vbc.exe. When you call vbc.exe, you give
the name of this response file as a single parameter prefixed by the @ character. Here is an example:

```
vbc @commands.rsp
```

To achieve the equivalent of the previous example, commands.rsp would contain this:

```
/target:exe /main:HelloWorld /out:MyFirstApp.exe HelloWorld.vb ConsoleUtils.vb
```

For readability, response files can include comments (using the # character) and can span
multiple lines. The VB .NET compiler also allows you to specify multiple response files.

The Code

The following code lists a class named `ConsoleUtils` that is defined in a file named ConsoleUtils.vb:

```
Imports System

Namespace Apress.VisualBasicRecipes.Chapter01
    Public Class ConsoleUtils

        ' This method will display a prompt and read a response from the console.
        Public Shared Function ReadString(ByVal message As String) As String

            Console.Write(message)
            Return Console.ReadLine

        End Function

        ' This method will display a message on the console.
        Public Shared Sub WriteString(ByVal message As String)

            Console.WriteLine(message)

        End Sub

        ' This method is used for testing ConsoleUtils methods.
        ' While it is not good practice to have multiple Main
        ' methods in an assembly, it sometimes can't be avoided.
        ' You specify in the compiler which Main subroutine should
        ' be used as the entry point. For this example, this Main
        ' routine will never be executed.
        Public Shared Sub Main()

            ' Prompt the reader to enter a name.
            Dim name As String = ReadString("Please enter a name:   ")
```

```
        ' Welcome the reader to Visual Basic 2005 Recipes.
        WriteString("Welcome to Visual Basic 2005 Recipes, " & name)

    End Sub

  End Class
End Namespace
```

The HelloWorld class listed next uses the ConsoleUtils class to display the message "Hello, World" to the console (HelloWorld is contained in the HelloWorld.vb file):

```
Imports System

Namespace Apress.VisualBasicRecipes.Chapter01
    Public Class HelloWorld

        Public Shared Sub Main()

            ConsoleUtils.WriteString("Hello, World")

            ConsoleUtils.WriteString(vbCrLf & "Main method complete. Press Enter.")
            Console.ReadLine()

        End Sub
    End Class
End Namespace
```

Usage

To build HelloWorld.exe from the two source files, use the following command:

```
vbc /target:exe /main:Apress.VisualBasicRecipes.Chapter01.HelloWorld ➥
/out:HelloWorld.exe ConsoleUtils.vb HelloWorld.vb
```

1-2. Create a Windows-Based Application from the Command Line

Problem

You need to use the VB .NET command-line compiler to build an application that provides a Windows Forms–based GUI.

Solution

Create a class that inherits from the System.Windows.Forms.Form class. (This will be your application's main form.) In one of your classes, ensure you implement a Shared method named Main. In the Main method, create an instance of your main form class and pass it to the Shared method Run of the System.Windows.Forms.Application class. Build your application using the command-line VB .NET compiler, and specify the /target:winexe compiler switch.

■Note If you own Visual Studio, you will most often use the Windows Application project template to create new Windows Forms–based applications. Building large GUI-based applications is a time-consuming undertaking that involves the correct instantiation, configuration, and wiring up of many forms and controls. Visual Studio automates much of the work associated with building graphical applications. Trying to build a large graphical application without the aid of tools such as Visual Studio will take you much longer, be extremely tedious, and result in a greater chance of bugs in your code. However, it is also useful to know the essentials required to create a Windows-based application using the command line in case you are ever working on a machine without Visual Studio and want to create a quick utility to automate some task or get input from a user.

How It Works

Building an application that provides a simple Windows GUI is a world away from developing a full-fledged Windows-based application. However, you must perform certain tasks regardless of whether you are writing the Windows equivalent of Hello World or the next version of Microsoft Word, including the following:

- For each form you need in your application, create a class that inherits from the System. Windows.Forms.Form class.

- In each of your form classes, declare members that represent the controls that will be on that form, such as buttons, labels, lists, and textboxes. These members should be declared Private or at least Protected so that other program elements cannot access them directly. If you need to expose the methods or properties of these controls, implement the necessary members in your form class, providing indirect and controlled access to the contained controls.

- Declare methods in your form class that will handle events raised by the controls contained by the form, such as button clicks or key presses when a textbox is the active control. These methods should be Private or Protected and follow the standard .NET event pattern (described in recipe 13-10). It's in these methods (or methods called by these methods) where you will define the bulk of your application's functionality.

- Declare a constructor for your form class that instantiates each of the form's controls and configures their initial state (size, color, position, content, and so on). The constructor should also wire up the appropriate event handler methods of your class to the events of each control.

- Declare a Shared method named Main—usually as a member of your application's main form class. This method is the entry point for your application, and it can have the same signatures as those mentioned in recipe 1-1. In the Main method, call Application.EnableVisualStyles to allow XP theme support, create an instance of your application's main form, and pass it as an argument to the Shared Application.Run method. The Run method makes your main form visible and starts a standard Windows message loop on the current thread, which passes the user input (key presses, mouse clicks, and so on) to your application form as events.

The Code

The Recipe01_02 class shown in the following code listing is a simple Windows Forms application that demonstrates the techniques just listed. When run, it prompts a user to enter a name and then displays a message box welcoming the user to Visual Basic 2005 Recipes.

```vb
Imports System
Imports System.Windows.Forms

Namespace Apress.VisualBasicRecipes.Chapter01

    Public Class Recipe01_02
        Inherits Form

        ' Private members to hold references to the form's controls.
        Private Label1 As Label
        Private TextBox1 As TextBox
        Private Button1 As Button

        ' Constructor used to create an instance of the form and configure
        ' the form's controls.
        Public Sub New()
            ' Instantiate the controls used on the form.
            Me.Label1 = New Label
            Me.TextBox1 = New TextBox
            Me.Button1 = New Button

            ' Suspend the layout logic of the form while we configure and
            ' position the controls.
            Me.SuspendLayout()

            ' Configure Label1, which displays the user prompt.
            Me.Label1.Location = New System.Drawing.Size(16, 36)
            Me.Label1.Name = "Label1"
            Me.Label1.Size = New System.Drawing.Size(155, 16)
            Me.Label1.TabIndex = 0
            Me.Label1.Text = "Please enter your name:"

            ' Configure TextBox1, which accepts the user input.
            Me.TextBox1.Location = New System.Drawing.Point(172, 32)
            Me.TextBox1.Name = "TextBox1"
            Me.TextBox1.TabIndex = 1
            Me.TextBox1.Text = ""

            ' Configure Button1, which the user clicks to enter a name.
            Me.Button1.Location = New System.Drawing.Point(109, 80)
            Me.Button1.Name = "Button1"
            Me.Button1.TabIndex = 2
            Me.Button1.Text = "Enter"
            AddHandler Button1.Click, AddressOf Button1_Click

            ' Configure WelcomeForm, and add controls.
            Me.ClientSize = New System.Drawing.Size(292, 126)
            Me.Controls.Add(Me.Button1)
            Me.Controls.Add(Me.TextBox1)
            Me.Controls.Add(Me.Label1)
            Me.Name = "Form1"
            Me.Text = "Visual Basic 2005 Recipes"
```

```
            ' Resume the layout logic of the form now that all controls are
            ' configured.
            Me.ResumeLayout(False)

        End Sub

        Private Sub Button1_Click(ByVal sender As Object, ➥
ByVal e As System.EventArgs)

            ' Write debug message to the console.
            System.Console.WriteLine("User entered: " + TextBox1.Text)

            ' Display welcome as a message box.
            MessageBox.Show("Welcome to Visual Basic 2005 Recipes, " + ➥
TextBox1.Text, "Visual Basic 2005 Recipes")

        End Sub

        ' Application entry point, creates an instance of the form, and begins
        ' running a standard message loop on the current thread. The message
        ' loop feeds the application with input from the user as events.
        Public Shared Sub Main()
            Application.EnableVisualStyles()
            Application.Run(New Recipe01_02())
        End Sub

    End Class
End Namespace
```

Usage

To build the Recipe01_02 class into an application, use this command:

```
vbc /target:winexe Recipe01-02.vb
```

The /target:winexe switch tells the compiler that you are building a Windows-based application. As a result, the compiler builds the executable in such a way that no console is created when you run your application. If you use the /target:exe switch instead of /target:winexe to build a Windows Forms application, your application will still work correctly, but you will have a console window visible while the application is running. Although this is undesirable for production-quality software, the console window is useful if you want to write debug and logging information while you're developing and testing your Windows Forms application. You can write to this console using the Write and WriteLine methods of the System.Console class.

Figure 1-1 shows the WelcomeForm.exe application greeting a user named John Doe. This version of the application is built using the /target:exe compiler switch, resulting in the visible console window in which you can see the output from the Console.WriteLine statement in the button1_Click event handler.

Figure 1-1. *A simple Windows Forms application*

1-3. Create and Use a Code Module from the Command Line

Problem

You need to do one or more of the following:

- Improve your application's performance and memory efficiency by ensuring the runtime loads rarely used types only when they are required.
- Compile types written in VB .NET to a form you can build into assemblies being developed in other .NET languages.
- Use types developed in another language and build them into your VB .NET assemblies.

Solution

Build your VB .NET source code into a module by using the command-line compiler and specifying the /target:module compiler switch. To incorporate existing modules into your assembly, use the /addmodule compiler switch.

How It Works

Modules are the building blocks of .NET assemblies and should not be confused with the Module object type block. Modules consist of a single file that contains the following:

- Microsoft Intermediate Language (MSIL) code created from your source code during compilation
- Metadata describing the types contained in the module
- Resources, such as icons and string tables, used by the types in the module

Assemblies consist of one or more modules and an assembly manifest. An *assembly manifest* is metadata that contains important information (such as the name, version, culture, and so on) regarding the assembly. If the assembly contains a single module, the module and assembly manifest are usually built into a single file for convenience. If more than one module exists, the assembly represents a logical grouping of more than one file that you must deploy as a complete unit. In these situations, the assembly manifest is either contained in a separate file or built into one of the modules. Visual Studio includes the MSIL Disassembler tool (Ildasm.exe), which lets you view the raw MSIL code for any assembly. You can use this tool to view an assembly manifest.

By building an assembly from multiple modules, you complicate the management and deployment of the assembly, but under some circumstances, modules offer significant benefits:

- The runtime will load a module only when the types defined in the module are required. Therefore, where you have a set of types that your application uses rarely, you can partition them into a separate module that the runtime will load only if necessary. This can improve performance, especially if your application is loaded across a network, and minimize the use of memory.

- The ability to use many different languages to write applications that run on the common language runtime (CLR) is a great strength of the .NET Framework. However, the VB .NET compiler can't compile your Microsoft C# or COBOL .NET code for inclusion in your assembly. To use code written in another language, you can compile it into a separate assembly and reference it. But if you want it to be an integral part of your assembly, you must build it into a module. Similarly, if you want to allow others to include your code as an integral part of their assemblies, you must compile your code as modules. When you use modules, because the code becomes part of the same assembly, members marked as `Friend` or `Protected Friend` are accessible, whereas they would not be if the code had been accessed from an external assembly.

Usage

To compile a source file named ConsoleUtils.vb (see recipe 1-1 for the contents) into a module, use the command `vbc /target:module ConsoleUtils.vb`. The result is the creation of a file named ConsoleUtils.netmodule. The netmodule extension is the default extension for modules, and the filename is the same as the name of the VB .NET source file.

You can also build modules from multiple source files, which results in a single file containing the MSIL and metadata (the assembly manifest) for all types contained in all the source files. The command `vbc /target:module ConsoleUtils.vb WindowsUtils.vb` compiles two source files named ConsoleUtils.vb and WindowsUtils.vb to create the module named ConsoleUtils.netmodule. The module is named after the first source file listed unless you override the name with the /out compiler switch. For example, the command `vbc /target:module /out:Utilities.netmodule ConsoleUtils.vb WindowsUtils.vb` creates a module named Utilities.netmodule.

To build an assembly consisting of multiple modules, you must use the /addmodule compiler switch. To build an executable named MyFirstApp.exe from two modules named WindowsUtils. netmodule and ConsoleUtils.netmodule and two source files named SourceOne.vb and SourceTwo.vb, use the command `vbc /out:MyFirstApp.exe /target:exe /addmodule:WindowsUtils.netmodule, ConsoleUtils.netmodule SourceOne.vb SourceTwo.vb`.

This command will result in an assembly that is composed of the following components:

- MyFirstApp.exe, which contains the assembly manifest as well as the MSIL for the types declared in the SourceOne.vb and SourceTwo.vb source files

- ConsoleUtils.netmodule and WindowsUtils.netmodule, which are now integral components of the multifile assembly but are unchanged by this compilation process

---

■**Caution** If you attempt to run an assembly (such as MyFirstApp.exe) without any required netmodules present, a `System.IO.FileNotFoundException` is thrown the first time any code tries to use types defined in the missing code module. This is a significant concern because the missing modules will not be identified until runtime. You must be careful when deploying multifile assemblies.

1-4. Create and Use a Code Library from the Command Line

Problem

You need to build a set of functionality into a reusable code library so that multiple applications can reference and reuse it.

Solution

Build your library using the command-line VB .NET compiler, and specify the `/target:library` compiler switch. To reference the library, use the `/reference` compiler switch when you build your application, and specify the names of the required libraries.

How It Works

Recipe 1-1 showed you how to build an application named MyFirstApp.exe from the two source files ConsoleUtils.vb and HelloWorld.vb. The ConsoleUtils.vb file contains the `ConsoleUtils` class, which provides methods to simplify interaction with the Windows console. If you were to extend the functionality of the `ConsoleUtils` class, you could add functionality useful to many applications. Instead of including the source code for `ConsoleUtils` in every application, you could build it into a library and deploy it independently, making the functionality accessible to many applications.

Usage

To build the ConsoleUtils.vb file into a library, use the command `vbc /target:library ConsoleUtils.vb`. This will produce a library file named ConsoleUtils.dll. To build a library from multiple source files, list the name of each file at the end of the command. You can also specify the name of the library using the `/out` compiler switch; otherwise, the library is named after the first source file listed. For example, to build a library named MyFirstLibrary.dll from two source files named ConsoleUtils.vb and WindowsUtils.vb, use the command `vbc /out:MyFirstLibrary.dll /target:library ConsoleUtils.vb WindowsUtils.vb`.

Before distributing your library, you might consider strong naming it so that no one can modify your assembly and pass it off as being the original. Strong naming your library also allows people to install it into the global assembly cache (GAC), which makes reuse much easier. (Recipe 1-9 describes how to strong name your assembly, and recipe 1-14 describes how to install a strong-named assembly into the GAC.) You might also consider signing your library with an Authenticode signature, which allows users to confirm you are the publisher of the assembly. (See recipe 1-12 for details on signing assemblies with Authenticode.)

To compile an assembly that relies on types declared within external libraries, you must tell the compiler which libraries are referenced using the /reference compiler switch. For example, to compile the HelloWorld.vb source file (from recipe 1-1) if the ConsoleUtils class is contained in the ConsoleUtils.dll library, use the command vbc /reference:ConsoleUtils.dll HelloWorld.vb. Remember these four points:

- If you reference more than one library, separate each library name with a comma or semi-colon, but don't include any spaces. For example, use /reference:ConsoleUtils.dll, WindowsUtils.dll.

- If the libraries aren't in the same directory as the source code, use the /libpath switch on the compiler to specify the additional directories where the compiler should look for libraries. For example, use /libpath:c:\CommonLibraries,c:\Dev\ThirdPartyLibs.

- Note that additional directories can be relative to the source folder. Don't forget that at runtime, the generated assembly must be in the same folder as the application that needs it, except if you deploy it into the GAC.

- If the library you need to reference is a multifile assembly, reference the file that contains the assembly manifest. (For information about multifile assemblies, see recipe 1-3.)

1-5. Access Command-Line Arguments

Problem

You need to access the arguments that were specified on the command line when your application was executed.

Solution

Use a signature for your Main method that exposes the command-line arguments as a String array. Alternatively, access the command-line arguments from anywhere in your code using the Shared members of the System.Environment class.

How It Works

Declaring your application's Main method with one of the following signatures provides access to the command-line arguments as a string array:

```
Public Shared Sub Main(ByVal args As String())
End Sub
Public Shared Function Main(ByVal args As String()) As Integer
End Sub
```

At runtime, the args argument will contain a string for each value entered on the command line after your application's name. The application's name is not included in the array of arguments.

If you need access to the command-line arguments at places in your code other than the Main method, you can process the command-line arguments in your Main method and store them for later access. However, this is not necessary since you can use the System.Environment class, which provides two Shared members that return information about the command line: CommandLine and GetCommandLineArgs.

The CommandLine property returns a string containing the full command line that launched the current process. Depending on the operating system on which the application is running, path information might precede the application name. Microsoft Windows 2003, Windows NT 4.0, Windows 2000, and Windows XP don't include path information, whereas Windows 98 and Windows ME do. The GetCommandLineArgs method returns a String array containing the command-line arguments. This array can be processed in the same way as the String array passed to the Main method, as discussed at the start of this section. Unlike the array passed to the Main method, the first element in the array returned by the GetCommandLineArgs method is the filename of the application.

The Code

To demonstrate the access of command-line arguments, the Main method in the following example steps through each of the command-line arguments passed to it and displays them to the console. The example then accesses the command line directly through the Environment class.

```
Imports System

Namespace Apress.VisualBasicRecipes.Chapter01
    Public Class Recipe01_05

        Public Shared Sub Main(ByVal args As String())

            ' Step through the command-line arguments
            For Each s As String In args
                Console.WriteLine(s)
            Next

            ' Alternatively, access the command-line arguments directly.
            Console.WriteLine(Environment.CommandLine)

            For Each s As String In Environment.GetCommandLineArgs()
                Console.WriteLine(s)
            Next

            ' Wait to continue
            Console.WriteLine(vbCrLf & "Main method complete.  Press Enter.")
            Console.ReadLine()

        End Sub

    End Class
End Namespace
```

Usage

If you execute the Recipe01-05 example using the following command:

```
Recipe01-05 "one \"two\"   three" four 'five    six'
```

the application will generate the following output on the console:

```
one "two"    three
four
'five
six'
"C:\Programming\Visual Basic 2005 Recipes\Chapter01\Recipe01-05\bin\Debug\Recipe
01-05.vshost.exe" "one \"two\"    three" four 'five    six'
C:\Programming\Visual Basic 2005 Recipes\Chapter01\Recipe01-05\bin\Debug\Recipe0
1-05.vshost.exe
one "two"    three
four
'five
six'
```

Notice that the use of double quotes (") results in more than one word being treated as a single argument, although single quotes (') do not. Also, you can include double quotes in an argument by escaping them with the backslash character (\). Finally, notice that all spaces are stripped from the command line unless they are enclosed in double quotes.

1-6. Include Code Selectively at Build Time

Problem

You need to selectively include and exclude sections of source code from your compiled assembly.

Solution

Use the #If, #ElseIf, #Else, and #End If preprocessor directives to identify blocks of code that should be conditionally included in your compiled assembly. Use the System.Diagnostics. ConditionalAttribute attribute to define methods that should be called conditionally only. Control the inclusion of the conditional code using the #Const directive in your code, or use the /define switch when you run the VB .NET compiler from the command line.

How It Works

If you need your application to function differently depending on factors such as the platform or environment on which it runs, you can build runtime checks into the logic of your code that trigger the variations in operation. However, such an approach can bloat your code and affect performance, especially if many variations need to be supported or many locations exist where evaluations need to be made.

An alternative approach is to build multiple versions of your application to support the different target platforms and environments. Although this approach overcomes the problems of code bloat and performance degradation, it would be an untenable solution if you had to maintain different source code for each version, so VB .NET provides features that allow you to build customized versions of your application from a single code base.

The #If, #ElseIf, #Else, and #End If preprocessor directives allow you to identify blocks of code that the compiler should include or exclude in your assembly at compile time. This is accomplished by evaluating the value of specified symbols. Since this happens at compile time, it may result in multiple executables being distributed.

Symbols can be any literal value. They also support the use of all standard comparison and logical operators or other symbols. The #If..#End If construct evaluates #If and #ElseIf clauses only until it finds one that evaluates to true, meaning that if you define multiple symbols (winXP and win2000, for example), the order of your clauses is important. The compiler includes only the code in the clause that evaluates to true. If no clause evaluates to true, the compiler includes the code in the #Else clause.

You can also use logical operators to base conditional compilation on more than one symbol. Use parentheses to group multiple expressions. Table 1-1 summarizes the supported operators.

Table 1-1. *Logical Operators Supported by the #If.. #End If Directive*

Operator	Example	Description
NOT	#If NOT winXP	Inequality. Evaluates to true if the symbol winXP is not equal to True. Equivalent to #If NOT winXP.
AND	#If winXP AND release	Logical AND. Evaluates to true only if the symbols winXP and release are equal to True.
AndAlso	#If winXP AndAlso release	Logical AND. Works the same as the AND operator, except that the second expression (release) is not evaluated if the first expression (winXP) is False.
OR	#IF winXP OR release	Logical OR. Evaluates to true if either of the symbols winXP or release is equal to True.
OrElse	#IF winXP OrElse release	Logical OR. Works to the same as the OR operator, except that the second expression (release) is not evaluated if the first expression (winXP) is True.
XOR	#IF winXP XOR release	Logical XOR. Evaluates to true if only one of the symbols, winXP or release, is equal to True.

■**Caution** You must be careful not to overuse conditional compilation directives and not to make your conditional expressions too complex; otherwise, your code can quickly become confusing and unmanageable—especially as your projects become larger.

To define a symbol, you can either include a #Const directive in your code or use the /define compiler switch. Symbols defined using #Const are active until the end of the file in which they are defined. Symbols defined using the /define compiler switch are active in all source files that are being compiled. All #Const directives must appear at the top of your source file before any code, including any Imports statements.

If you only need to determine if a symbol has been defined, a more elegant alternative to the #If preprocessor directive is the attribute System.Diagnostics.ConditionalAttribute. If you apply ConditionalAttribute to a method, the compiler will ignore any calls to the method if the symbol specified by ConditionalAttribute is not defined, or set to False, at the calling point.

Using ConditionalAttribute centralizes your conditional compilation logic on the method declaration and means you can freely include calls to conditional methods without littering your code with #If directives. However, because the compiler literally removes calls to the conditional method from your code, your code can't have dependencies on return values from the conditional method. This means you can apply ConditionalAttribute only to subroutines.

The Code

In this example, the code assigns a different value to the local variable platformName based on whether the winXP, win2000, winNT, or Win98 symbols are defined. The head of the code defines the win2000 symbol. In addition, the ConditionalAttribute specifies that calls to the DumpState method should be included in an assembly only if the symbol DEBUG is defined during compilation. The DEBUG symbol is defined by default in debug builds.

```vb
#Const win2000 = True

Imports System
Imports System.Diagnostics

Namespace Apress.VisualBasicRecipes.Chapter01

    Public Class Recipe01_06

        ' Declare a string to contain the platform name
        Private Shared platformName As String

        <Conditional("DEBUG")> _
        Public Shared Sub DumpState()
            Console.WriteLine("Dump some state...")
        End Sub

        Public Shared Sub Main()

            #If winXP Then              ' Compiling for Windows XP
                platformName = "Microsoft Windows XP"
            #ElseIf win2000 Then        ' Compiling for Windows 2000
                platformName = "Microsoft Windows 2000"
            #ElseIf winNT Then          ' Compiling for Windows NT
                platformName = "Microsoft Windows NT"
            #ElseIf win98 Then          ' Compiling for Windows 98
                platformName = "Microsoft Windows 98"
            #Else                       ' Unknown platform specified
                platformName = "Unknown"
            #End If

            Console.WriteLine(platformName)

            ' Call the conditional DumpState method
            DumpState()

            ' Wait to continue...
            Console.WriteLine(vbCrLf & "Main method complete.  Press Enter.")
            Console.Read()

        End Sub

    End Class
End Namespace
```

Usage

To build the example and define the symbol `winXP`, use the command `vbc /define:winXP ConditionalExample.vb`. If you compile this sample without defining the `winXP` symbol, the `win2000` symbol will be used since it was defined directly in the code.

Notes

You can apply multiple `ConditionalAttribute` instances to a method in order to produce logical OR behavior. Calls to the following version of the `DumpState` method will be compiled only if the `DEBUG` or `TEST` symbols are defined:

```
<Conditional("DEBUG"), Conditional("TEST")> _
Public Shared Sub DumpState()
    ...
End Sub
```

Achieving logical AND behavior is not as clean and involves the use of an intermediate conditional method, quickly leading to overly complex code that is hard to understand and maintain. You should be cautious with this approach, as you may end up with code in your assembly that is never called. The following is a quick example that requires the definition of both the `DEBUG` and `TEST` symbols for the `DumpState` functionality (contained in `DumpState2`) to be called:

```
<Conditional("DEBUG")> _
Public Shared Sub DumpState()
    DumpState2()
End Sub

<Conditional("TEST")> _
Public Shared Sub DumpState2()
    ...
End Sub
```

It's important to remember that you are not limited to Boolean values for your symbols. You can define a symbol with a string value, like this:

```
#Const OS = "XP"
```

You could also do this using the command `vbc /define:OS=\"XP\" ConditionalExample.vb`. You must escape quotation marks using the \ character.

To use this new symbol, the preprocessor `#If..#End If` construct must be changed accordingly:

```
#If OS = "XP" Then            ' Compiling for Windows XP
    platformName = "Microsoft Windows XP"
#ElseIf OS = "2000" Then      ' Compiling for Windows 2000
    platformName = "Microsoft Windows 2000"
#ElseIf OS = "NT" Then        ' Compiling for Windows NT
    platformName = "Microsoft Windows NT"
#ElseIf OS = "98" Then        ' Compiling for Windows 98
    platformName = "Microsoft Windows 98"
#Else                         ' Unknown platform specified
    platformName = "Unknown"
#End If
```

> ▨**Note** The Debug and Trace classes from the System.Diagnostics namespace use ConditionalAttribute on many of their methods. The methods of the Debug class are conditional on the definition of the symbol DEBUG, and the methods of the Trace class are conditional on the definition of the symbol TRACE.

1-7. Access a Program Element That Has the Same Name As a Keyword

Problem

You need to access a member of a type, but the type or member name is the same as a VB .NET keyword.

Solution

Surround all instances of the identifier name in your code with brackets ([ ]).

How It Works

The .NET Framework allows you to use software components developed in other .NET languages from within your VB .NET applications. Each language has its own set of keywords (or reserved words) and imposes different restrictions on the names programmers can assign to program elements such as types, members, and variables. Therefore, it is possible that a programmer developing a component in another language will inadvertently use a VB .NET keyword as the name of a program element. Using brackets ([ ]) enables you to use a VB .NET keyword as an identifier and overcome these possible naming conflicts.

The Code

The following code fragment creates the new Operator (perhaps a telephone operator) class. A new instance of this class is created, and its Friend property is set to True—both Operator and Friend are VB .NET keywords:

```
Public Class [Operator]
    Public [Friend] As Boolean
End Class

'  Instantiate an operator object
Dim operator1 As New [Operator]

'  Set the operator's Friend property
operator1.[Friend] = True
```

1-8. Create and Manage Strong-Named Key Pairs

Problem

You need to create public and private keys (a key pair) so that you can assign strong names to your assemblies.

Solution

Use the Strong Name tool (sn.exe) to generate a key pair and store the keys in a file or cryptographic service provider (CSP) key container.

■**Note** A CSP is an element of the Win32 CryptoAPI that provides services such as encryption, decryption, and digital signature generation. CSPs also provide key container facilities, which use strong encryption and operating system security to protect any cryptographic keys stored in the container. A detailed discussion of CSPs and CryptoAPI is beyond the scope of this book. All you need to know for this recipe is that you can store your cryptographic keys in a CSP key container and be relatively confident that it is secure as long as no one knows your Windows password. Refer to the CryptoAPI information in the platform SDK documentation for complete details.

How It Works

To generate a new key pair and store the keys in the file named MyKeys.snk, execute the command sn -k MyKeys.snk. (.snk is the usual extension given to files containing strong name keys.) The generated file contains both your public and private keys. You can extract the public key using the command sn -p MyKeys.snk MyPublicKey.snk, which will create MyPublicKey.snk containing only the public key. Once you have this file in hand, you can view the public key using the command sn -tp MyPublicKeys.snk, which will generate output similar to the (abbreviated) listing shown here:

```
Microsoft (R) .NET Framework Strong Name Utility  Version 2.0.50727.42
Copyright (C) Microsoft Corporation. All rights reserved.

Public key is
07020000002400005253413200040000010001002b4ef3c2bbd6478802b64d0dd3f2e7c65ee
6478802b63cb894a782f3a1adbb46d3ee5ec5577e7dccc818937e964cbe997c12076c19f2d7
ad179f15f7dccca6c6b72a

Public key token is 2a1d3326445fc02a
```

The public key token shown at the end of the listing is the last 8 bytes of a cryptographic hash code computed from the public key. Because the public key is so long, .NET uses the public key token for display purposes and as a compact mechanism for other assemblies to reference your public key. (Recipes 11-14 and 11-15 discuss cryptographic hash codes.)

As the name suggests, you don't need to keep the public key (or public key token) secret. When you strong name your assembly (discussed in recipe 1-9), the compiler uses your private key to generate a digital signature (an encrypted hash code) of the assembly's manifest. The compiler embeds the digital signature and your public key in the assembly so that any consumer of the assembly can verify the digital signature.

Keeping your private key secret is imperative. People with access to your private key can alter your assembly and create a new strong name—leaving your customers unaware they are using modified code. No mechanism exists to repudiate compromised strong name keys. If your private key is compromised, you must generate new keys and distribute new versions of your assemblies that are strong named using the new keys. You must also notify your customers about the compromised keys and explain to them which versions of your public key to trust—in all, a very costly exercise in terms of both money and credibility. You can protect your private key in many ways; the approach you use will depend on several factors:

- The structure and size of your organization

- Your development and release process

- The software and hardware resources you have available

- The requirements of your customer base

▉Tip Commonly, a small group of trusted individuals (the *signing authority*) has responsibility for the security of your company's strong name signing keys and is responsible for signing all assemblies just prior to their final release. The ability to delay sign an assembly (discussed in recipe 1-11) facilitates this model and avoids the need to distribute private keys to all development team members.

One feature provided by the Strong Name tool to simplify the security of strong name keys is the use of CSP key containers. Once you have generated a key pair to a file, you can install the keys into a key container and delete the file. For example, to store the key pair contained in the file MyKeys.snk to a CSP container named StrongNameKeys, use the command sn -i MyKeys.snk StrongNameKeys. You can install only one set of keys to a single container. (Recipe 1-9 explains how to use strong name keys stored in a CSP key container.)

An important aspect of CSP key containers is that they include user-based containers and machine-based containers. Windows security ensures each user can access only his own user-based key containers. However, any user of a machine can access a machine-based container.

By default, the Strong Name tool uses machine-based key containers, meaning that anyone who can log on to your machine and who knows the name of your key container can sign an assembly with your strong name keys. To change the Strong Name tool to use user-based containers, use the command sn -m n, and to switch to machine-based stores, use the command sn -m y. The command sn -m will display whether the Strong Name tool is currently configured to use machine-based or user-based containers.

To delete the strong name keys from the StrongNameKeys container (as well as delete the container), use the command sn -d StrongNameKeys.

1-9. Give an Assembly a Strong Name

Problem

You need to give an assembly a strong name for several reasons:

- So it has a unique identity, which allows people to assign specific permissions to the assembly when configuring code access security policy

- So it can't be modified and passed off as your original assembly

- So it supports versioning and version policy
- So it can be installed in the GAC and shared across multiple applications

Solution

When you build your assembly using the command-line VB .NET compiler, use the /keyfile or /keycontainer compiler switches to specify the location of your strong name key pair. Use assembly-level attributes to specify optional information such as the version number and culture for your assembly. The compiler will strong name your assembly as part of the compilation process.

Note If you are using Visual Studio, you can configure your assembly to be strong named by opening the project properties, selecting the Signing tab, and checking the Sign the Assembly box. You will need to specify the location of the file where your strong name keys are stored—Visual Studio does not allow you to specify the name of a key container.

How It Works

To strong name an assembly using the VB .NET compiler, you need the following:

- A strong name key pair contained either in a file or in a CSP key container. (Recipe 1-8 discusses how to create strong name key pairs.)

- Compiler switches to specify the location where the compiler can obtain your strong name key pair:

  - If your key pair is in a file, use the /keyfile compiler switch, and provide the name of the file where the keys are stored. For example, use /keyfile:MyKeyFile.snk.

  - If your key pair is in a CSP container, use the /keycontainer compiler switch, and provide the name of the CSP key container where the keys are stored. For example, use /keycontainer:MyKeyContainer.

- Optionally, specify the culture that your assembly supports by applying the attribute System.Reflection.AssemblyCultureAttribute to the assembly. (You can't specify a culture for executable assemblies because executable assemblies support only the neutral culture.)

- Optionally, specify the version of your assembly by applying the attribute System.Reflection.AssemblyVersionAttribute to the assembly.

Note If you are using .NET Framework 1.0 or 1.1, the command-line VB .NET compiler does not support the /keyfile and /keycontainer compiler switches. Instead, you must use the AssemblyKeyFileAttribute and AssemblyKeyNameAttribute assembly-level attributes within your code to specify the location of your strong name keys. Alternatively, use the Assembly Linker tool (al.exe), which allows you to specify the strong name information on the command line using the /keyfile and /keyname switches. Refer to the Assembly Linker information in the .NET Framework SDK documentation for more details.

The Code

The executable code that follows (from a file named Recipe01-09.vb) shows how to use the optional attributes (shown in bold text) to specify the culture and the version for the assembly:

```
Imports System
Imports System.Reflection

<Assembly:AssemblyCulture("")>
<Assembly:AssemblyVersion("1.1.0.5")>

Namespace Apress.VisualBasicRecipes.Chapter01

    Public Class Recipe01_09

        Public Shared Sub main()
            Console.WriteLine("Welcome to Visual Basic 2005 Recipes")

            ' Wait to continue...
            Console.WriteLine(vbCrLf & "Main method complete.  Press Enter.")
            Console.Read()
        End Sub

    End Class
End Namespace
```

Usage

To create a strong-named assembly from the example code, create the strong name keys and store them in a file named MyKeyFile using the command sn -k MyKeyFile.snk. Then install the keys into the CSP container named MyKeys using the command sn -i MyKeyFile.snk MyKeys. You can now compile the file into a strong-named assembly using the command vbc /keycontainer:MyKeys Recipe01-09.vb. If you are not using a CSP container, you can specify the specific key file using the command vbc /keyfile:MyKeyFile.snk Recipe01-09.vb.

Notes

If you use Visual Studio 2005, you may not be able to include the optional AssemblyVersion attribute in your code. This is because the attribute may already exist for the assembly. By default, Visual Studio automatically creates a folder called MyProject. This folder stores multiple files, including AssemblyInfo.vb, which contains standard assembly attributes for the project. These can be manually edited or edited through the Assembly Information dialog box (see Figure 1-2), accessible from the Application tab of the project properties. Since the AssemblyInfo.vb file is an efficient way to store information specific to your assembly, it is actually good practice to create and use a similar file, even if you are not using Visual Studio to compile.

Figure 1-2. *The Assembly Information dialog box*

1-10. Verify That a Strong-Named Assembly Has Not Been Modified

Problem

You need to verify that a strong-named assembly has not been modified after it was built.

Solution

Use the Strong Name tool (sn.exe) to verify the assembly's strong name.

How It Works

Whenever the .NET runtime loads a strong-named assembly, the runtime extracts the encrypted hash code that's embedded in the assembly and decrypts it with the public key, which is also embedded in the assembly. The runtime then calculates the hash code of the assembly manifest and compares it to the decrypted hash code. This verification process will identify whether the assembly has changed after compilation.

If an executable assembly fails strong name verification, the runtime will display an error message or an error dialog box (depending on whether the application is a console or Windows application). If executing code tries to load an assembly that fails verification, the runtime will throw a System. IO.FileLoadException with the message "Strong name validation failed," which you should handle appropriately.

As well as generating and managing strong name keys (discussed in recipe 1-8), the Strong Name tool allows you to verify strong-named assemblies. To verify that the strong-named assembly Recipe01-09.exe is unchanged, use the command sn -vf Recipe01-09.exe. The -v switch requests the Strong Name tool to verify the strong name of the specified assembly, and the -f switch forces strong name verification even if it has been previously disabled for the specified assembly. (You can disable strong name verification for specific assemblies using the -Vr switch, as in sn -Vr Recipe01-09.exe; see recipe 1-11 for details about why you would disable strong name verification.)

If the assembly passes strong name verification, you will see the following output:

```
Microsoft (R) .NET Framework Strong Name Utility  Version 2.0.50727.42
Copyright (C) Microsoft Corporation. All rights reserved.

Assembly 'Recipe01-09.exe' is valid
```

However, if the assembly has been modified, you will see this message:

```
Microsoft (R) .NET Framework Strong Name Utility  Version 2.0.50727.42
Copyright (C) Microsoft Corporation. All rights reserved.

Failed to verify assembly --
Strong name validation failed for assembly 'Recipe01-09.exe'.
```

1-11. Delay Sign an Assembly

Problem

You need to create a strong-named assembly, but you don't want to give all members of your development team access to the private key component of your strong name key pair.

Solution

Extract and distribute the public key component of your strong name key pair. Follow the instructions in recipe 1-9 that describe how to give your assembly a strong name. In addition, specify the /delaysign switch when you compile your assembly. Disable strong name verification for the assembly using the -Vr switch of the Strong Name tool (sn.exe).

■**Note** If you are using Visual Studio, you can configure your strong-named assembly to be delay signed by opening the project properties, selecting the Signing tab, and checking the Delay Sign Only box. Doing so will prohibit your project from being run or debugged. You can get around this by skipping verification using the -Vr switch of the Strong Name tool.

How It Works

Assemblies that reference strong-named assemblies contain the public key token of the referenced assemblies. This means the referenced assembly must be strong named before it can be referenced. In a development environment in which assemblies are regularly rebuilt, this would require every developer and tester to have access to your strong name key pair—a major security risk.

Instead of distributing the private key component of your strong name key pair to all members of the development team, the .NET Framework provides a mechanism named *delay signing* with which you can partially strong name an assembly. The partially strong-named assembly contains the public key and the public key token (required by referencing assemblies) but contains only a place-holder for the signature that would normally be generated using the private key.

After development is complete, the signing authority (who has responsibility for the security and use of your strong name key pair) re-signs the delay-signed assembly to complete its strong name. The signature is calculated using the private key and embedded in the assembly, making the assembly ready for distribution.

To delay sign an assembly, you need access only to the public key component of your strong name key pair. No security risk is associated with distributing the public key, and the signing authority should make the public key freely available to all developers. To extract the public key component from a strong name key file named MyKeyFile.snk and write it to a file named MyPublicKey.snk, use the command sn -p MyKeyFile.snk MyPublicKey.snk. If you store your strong name key pair in a CSP key container named MyKeys, extract the public key to a file named MyPublicKey.snk using the command sn -pc MyKeys MyPublicKey.snk.

Once you have a key file containing the public key, you build the delay-signed assembly using the command-line VB .NET compiler by specifying the /delaysign compiler switch. For example, to build a delay-signed assembly, using the MyPublicKey.snk public key, from a source file named Recipe01-11.vb, use this command:

```
vbc /delaysign /keyfile:MyPublicKey.snk Recipe01-11.vb
```

When the runtime tries to load a delay-signed assembly, the runtime will identify the assembly as strong named and will attempt to verify the assembly, as discussed in recipe 1-10. Because it doesn't have a digital signature, you must configure the runtime on the local machine to stop verifying the assembly's strong name using the command sn -Vr Recipe01-11.exe. Note that you need to do so on every machine on which you want to run your application.

■**Tip** When using delay-signed assemblies, it's often useful to be able to compare different builds of the same assembly to ensure they differ only by their signatures. This is possible only if a delay-signed assembly has been re-signed using the -R switch of the Strong Name tool. To compare the two assemblies, use the command sn -D assembly1 assembly2.

Once development is complete, you need to re-sign the assembly to complete the assembly's strong name. The Strong Name tool allows you to do this without changing your source code or recompiling the assembly; however, you must have access to the private key component of the strong name key pair. To re-sign an assembly named Recipe01-11.exe with a key pair contained in the file MyKeys.snk, use the command sn -R Recipe01-11.exe MyKeys.snk. If the keys are stored in a CSP key container named MyKeys, use the command sn -Rc Recipe01-11.exe MyKeys.

Once you have re-signed the assembly, you should turn strong name verification for that assembly back on using the -Vu switch of the Strong Name tool, as in sn -Vu Recipe01-11.exe. To enable verification for all assemblies for which you have disabled strong name verification, use the command sn -Vx. You can list the assemblies for which verification is disabled using the command sn -Vl.

■**Note** If you are using .NET Framework 1.0 or 1.1, the command-line VB .NET compiler does not support the /delaysign compiler switch. Instead, you must use the System.Reflection.AssemblyDelaySignAttribute assembly-level attributes within your code to specify that you want the assembly delay signed. Alternatively, use the Assembly Linker tool (al.exe), which does support the /delaysign switch. Refer to the Assembly Linker information in the .NET Framework SDK documentation for details.

1-12. Sign an Assembly with an Authenticode Digital Signature

Problem

You need to sign an assembly with Authenticode so that users of the assembly can be certain you are its publisher and the assembly is unchanged after signing.

Solution

Use the Sign Tool (signtool.exe) to sign the assembly with your software publisher certificate (SPC).

■Note Versions 1.0 and 1.1 of the .NET Framework provided a utility called the File Signing tool (signcode.exe) that enabled you to sign assemblies. The File Signing tool is not provided with .NET Framework 2.0 and has been superseded by the Sign Tool discussed in this recipe.

How It Works

Strong names provide a unique identity for an assembly as well as proof of the assembly's integrity, but they provide no proof as to the publisher of the assembly. The .NET Framework allows you to use Authenticode technology to sign your assemblies. This enables consumers of your assemblies to confirm that you are the publisher, as well as confirm the integrity of the assembly. Authenticode signatures also act as evidence for the signed assembly, which people can use when configuring code access security policy.

To sign your assembly with an Authenticode signature, you need an SPC issued by a recognized *certificate authority* (CA). A CA is a company entrusted to issue SPCs (along with many other types of certificates) for use by individuals or companies. Before issuing a certificate, the CA is responsible for confirming that the requesters are who they claim to be and also for making sure the requesters sign contracts to ensure they don't misuse the certificates that the CA issues them.

To obtain an SPC, you should view the Microsoft Root Certificate Program Members list at `http://msdn.microsoft.com/library/default.asp?url=/library/en-us/dnsecure/html/rootcertprog.asp`. Here you will find a list of CAs, many of whom can issue you an SPC. For testing purposes, you can create a test SPC using the process described in recipe 1-13. However, you can't distribute your software signed with this test certificate. Because a test SPC isn't issued by a trusted CA, most responsible users won't trust assemblies signed with it.

Once you have an SPC, you use the Sign Tool to Authenticode sign your assembly. The Sign Tool creates a digital signature of the assembly using the private key component of your SPC and embeds the signature and the public part of your SPC in your assembly (including your public key). When verifying your assembly, the consumer decrypts the encrypted hash code using your public key, recalculates the hash of the assembly, and compares the two hash codes to ensure they are the same. As long as the two hash codes match, the consumer can be certain that you signed the assembly and that it has not changed since you signed it.

Usage

The Sign Tool provides a graphical wizard that walks you through the steps to Authenticode sign your assembly. To sign an assembly named MyAssembly.exe, run this command:

```
signtool signwizard MyAssembly.exe
```

Click Next on the introduction screen, and you will see the File Selection screen, where you must enter the name of the assembly to Authenticode sign (see Figure 1-3). Because you specified the assembly name on the command line, it is already filled in. If you are signing a multifile assembly, specify the name of the file that contains the assembly manifest. If you intend to both strong name and Authenticode sign your assembly, you must strong name the assembly first. (See recipe 1-9 for details on strong naming assemblies.)

Figure 1-3. *The Sign Tool's File Selection screen*

Clicking Next takes you to the Signing Options screen (see Figure 1-4). If your SPC is in a certificate store, select the Typical radio button. If your SPC is in a file, select the Custom radio button. Then click Next.

Assuming you want to use a file-based certificate (like the test certificate created in recipe 1-13), click the Select from File button on the Signature Certificate screen (see Figure 1-5), select the file containing your SPC certificate, and then click Next.

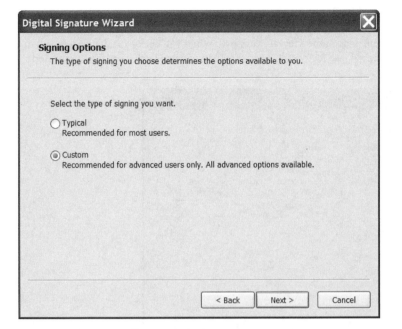

Figure 1-4. *The Sign Tool's Signing Options screen*

Figure 1-5. *The Sign Tool's Signature Certificate screen*

The Private Key screen allows you to identify the location of your private keys, which will either be in a file or in a CSP key container, depending on where you created and stored them (see Figure 1-6). The example assumes they are in a file named PrivateKeys.pvk. When you click Next, if you selected to use a file, you will be prompted (see Figure 1-7) to enter a password to access the file (if required).

Figure 1-6. *The Sign Tool's Private Key screen*

Figure 1-7. *Prompt for password to private key*

You can then select whether to use the sha1 or md5 hash algorithm (see Figure 1-8). The default is sha1, which is suitable for most purposes. On the Hash Algorithm screen, pick an algorithm, and then click Next.

Figure 1-8. *The Sign Tool's Hash Algorithm screen*

Click Next to leave the default values on the Additional Certificates screen, the Data Description screen, and the Timestamping screen. Finally, click Finish. If you are using a file-based private key that is password protected, you will once again be prompted to enter the password, after which the Sign Tool will Authenticode sign your assembly.

■**Note** The Sign Tool uses capicom.dll version 2.1.0.1. If an error occurs when you run signtool.exe that indicates capicom is not accessible or not registered, change to the directory where capicom.dll is located (which is C:\Program Files\Common Files\Microsoft Shared\CAPICOM by default), and run the command `regsvr32 capicom.dll`.

1-13. Create and Trust a Test Software Publisher Certificate

Problem

You need to create an SPC to allow you to test the Authenticode signing of an assembly.

Solution

Use the Certificate Creation tool (makecert.exe) to create a test X.509 certificate and the Software Publisher Certificate Test tool (cert2spc.exe) to generate an SPC from this X.509 certificate. Trust the root test certificate using the Set Registry tool (setreg.exe).

How It Works

To create a test SPC for a software publisher named Todd Herman, create an X.509 certificate using the Certificate Creation tool. The command makecert -n "CN=Todd Herman" -sk MyKeys TestCertificate.cer creates a file named TestCertificate.cer containing an X.509 certificate and stores the associated private key in a CSP key container named MyKeys (which is automatically created if it does not exist). Alternatively, you can write the private key to a file by substituting the -sk switch with -sv. For example, to write the private key to a file named PrivateKeys.pvk, use the command makecert -n " CN=Todd Herman" -sv PrivateKey.pvk TestCertificate.cer. If you write your private key to a file, the Certificate Creation tool will prompt you to provide a password with which to protect the private key file (see Figure 1-9).

Figure 1-9. *The Certificate Creation tool requests a password when creating file-based private keys.*

The Certificate Creation tool supports many arguments, and Table 1-2 lists some of the more useful ones. You should consult the .NET Framework SDK documentation for full coverage of the Certificate Creation tool.

Table 1-2. *Commonly Used Switches of the Certificate Creation Tool*

Switch	Description
-e	Specifies the date when the certificate becomes invalid.
-m	Specifies the duration—in months—that the certificate remains valid.
-n	Specifies an X.500 name to associate with the certificate. This is the name of the software publisher that people will see when they view details of the SPC you create.
-sk	Specifies the name of the CSP key store in which to store the private key.
-ss	Specifies the name of the certificate store where the Certificate Creation tool should store the generated X.509 certificate.
-sv	Specifies the name of the file in which to store the private key.

Once you have created your X.509 certificate with the Certificate Creation tool, you need to convert it to an SPC with the Software Publisher Certificate Test tool (cert2spc.exe). To convert the certificate TestCertificate.cer to an SPC, use the command `cert2spc TestCertificate.cer TestCertificate.spc`. The Software Publisher Certificate Test tool doesn't offer any optional switches.

The final step before you can use your test SPC is to trust the root test CA, which is the default issuer of the test certificate. The Set Registry tool (setreg.exe) makes this a simple task with the command `setreg 1 true`. You can now Authenticode sign assemblies with your test SPC using the process described in recipe 1-12. When you have finished using your test SPC, you must remove trust of the root test CA using the command `setreg 1 false`.

1-14. Manage the Global Assembly Cache

Problem

You need to add or remove assemblies from the GAC.

Solution

Use the Global Assembly Cache tool (gacutil.exe) from the command line to view the contents of the GAC as well as to add and remove assemblies.

■**Note** The Global Assembly Cache tool was included with earlier versions of the .NET Framework. Microsoft has since designated it as a developer-specific tool and removed it from .NET Framework 2.0. It is now part of the SDK and is installed with Visual Studio 2005.

How It Works

Before you can install an assembly in the GAC, the assembly must have a strong name. (See recipe 1-9 for details on how to strong name your assemblies.) To install an assembly named SomeAssembly.dll into the GAC, use the command `gacutil /i SomeAssembly.dll`. You can install different versions of the same assembly in the GAC to meet the versioning requirements of different applications.

To uninstall the SomeAssembly.dll assembly from the GAC, use the command `gacutil /u SomeAssembly`. Notice that you don't use the .dll extension to refer to the assembly once it's installed in the GAC. This will uninstall all assemblies with the specified name. To uninstall a particular version, specify the version along with the assembly name; for example, use `gacutil /u SomeAssembly,Version=1.0.0.5`.

To view the assemblies installed in the GAC, use the command `gacutil /l`. This will produce a long list of all the assemblies installed in the GAC, as well as a list of assemblies that have been precompiled to binary form and installed in the native image (ngen) cache. To avoid searching through this list to determine whether a particular assembly is installed in the GAC, use the command `gacutil /l SomeAssembly`.

■**Note** The .NET Framework uses the GAC only at runtime; the VB .NET compiler won't look in the GAC to resolve any external references that your assembly references. During development, the VB .NET compiler must be able to access a local copy of any referenced shared assemblies. You can either copy the shared assembly to the same directory as your source code or use the `/libpath` switch of the VB .NET compiler to specify the directory where the compiler can find the required assemblies.

1-15. Make Your Assembly More Difficult to Decompile

Problem

You want to make sure that people cannot decompile your .NET assemblies.

Solution

The *only* way to ensure that your assembly cannot be decompiled is by not making it directly accessible. This can be accomplished using a server-based solution. If you must distribute assemblies, you have *no* way to stop people from decompiling them. The best you can do is use obfuscation and components compiled to native code to make your assemblies more difficult to decompile.

How It Works

Because .NET assemblies consist of a standardized, platform-independent set of instruction codes and metadata that describes the types contained in the assembly, they are relatively easy to decompile. This allows decompilers to generate source code that is close to your original code with ease, which can be problematic if your code contains proprietary information or algorithms that you want to keep secret.

The only way to ensure people can't decompile your assemblies is to prevent them from getting your assemblies in the first place. Where possible, implement server-based solutions such as Microsoft ASP.NET applications and Web services. With the security correctly configured on your server, no one will be able to access your assemblies, and therefore they won't be able to decompile them.

When building a server solution is not appropriate, you have the following two options:

- Use an obfuscator to make it difficult to understand your code once it is decompiled. Some versions of Visual Studio include the Community Edition of an obfuscator named Dotfuscator. Obfuscators use a variety of techniques to make your assembly difficult to decompile; principal among these techniques are renaming of `Private` methods and fields in such a way that it's difficult to read and understand the purpose of your code, and inserting control flow statements to make the logic of your application difficult to follow.

- Build the parts of your application that you want to keep secret in native DLLs or COM objects, and then call them from your managed application using P/Invoke or COM Interop. (See Chapter 12 for recipes that show you how to call unmanaged code.)

Neither approach will stop a skilled and determined person from reverse engineering your code, but both approaches will make the job significantly more difficult and deter most casual observers.

■**Note** The risks of application decompilation aren't specific to VB .NET or .NET in general. Determined people can reverse engineer any software if they have the time and the skill.

1-16. Manipulate the Appearance of the Console

Problem

You want to control the visual appearance of the Windows console.

Solution

Use the Shared properties and methods of the System.Console class.

How It Works

Version 2.0 of the .NET Framework dramatically enhances the control you have over the appearance and operation of the Windows console. Table 1-3 describes the properties and methods of the Console class that you can use to control the console's appearance.

Table 1-3. *Properties and Methods to Control the Appearance of the Console*

Member	Description
Properties	
BackgroundColor	Gets and sets the background color of the console using one of the values from the System.ConsoleColor enumeration. Only new text written to the console will appear in this color. To make the entire console this color, call the method Clear after you have configured the BackgroundColor property.
BufferHeight	Gets and sets the buffer height in terms of rows. Buffer refers to the amount of actual data that can be displayed within the console window.
BufferWidth	Gets and sets the buffer width in terms of columns. Buffer refers to the amount of actual data that can be displayed within the console window.
CursorLeft	Gets and sets the column position of the cursor within the buffer.
CursorSize	Gets and sets the height of the cursor as a percentage of a character cell.
CursorTop	Gets and sets the row position of the cursor within the buffer.
CursorVisible	Gets and sets whether the cursor is visible.
ForegroundColor	Gets and sets the text color of the console using one of the values from the System.ConsoleColor enumeration. Only new text written to the console will appear in this color. To make the entire console this color, call the method Clear after you have configured the ForegroundColor property.
LargestWindowHeight	Returns the largest possible number of rows based on the current font and screen resolution.
LargestWindowWidth	Returns the largest possible number of columns based on the current font and screen resolution.
Title	Gets and sets text shown in the title bar.
WindowHeight	Gets and sets the physical height of the console window in terms of character rows.

Table 1-3. *Properties and Methods to Control the Appearance of the Console (Continued)*

Member	Description
WindowWidth	Gets and sets the physical width of the console window in terms of character columns.
Methods	
Clear	Clears the console.
ResetColor	Sets the foreground and background colors to their default values as configured within Windows.
SetWindowSize	Sets the width and height in terms of columns and rows.

The Code

The following example demonstrates how to use the properties and methods of the Console class to dynamically change the appearance of the Windows console:

```
Imports System

Namespace Apress.VisualBasicRecipes.Chapter01
    Public Class Recipe01_16

        Public Shared Sub Main(ByVal args As String())

            ' Display the standard console.
            Console.Title = "Standard Console"
            Console.WriteLine("Press Enter to change the console's appearance.")
            Console.ReadLine()

            ' Change the console appearance and redisplay.
            Console.Title = "Colored Text"
            Console.ForegroundColor = ConsoleColor.Red
            Console.BackgroundColor = ConsoleColor.Green
            Console.WriteLine("Press Enter to change the console's appearance.")
            Console.ReadLine()

            ' Change the console appearance and redisplay.
            Console.Title = "Cleared / Colored Console"
            Console.ForegroundColor = ConsoleColor.Blue
            Console.BackgroundColor = ConsoleColor.Yellow
            Console.Clear()
            Console.WriteLine("Press Enter to change the console's appearance.")
            Console.ReadLine()

            ' Change the console appearance and redisplay.
            Console.Title = "Resized Console"
            Console.ResetColor()
            Console.Clear()
            Console.SetWindowSize(100, 50)
            Console.BufferHeight = 500
            Console.BufferWidth = 100
```

```
            Console.CursorLeft = 20
            Console.CursorSize = 50
            Console.CursorTop = 20
            Console.CursorVisible = False
            Console.WriteLine("Main method complete.  Press Enter.")
            Console.ReadLine()

        End Sub

    End Class
End Namespace
```

1-17. Embed a Resource File in an Assembly

Problem

You need to create a string-based resource file and embed it into an assembly.

Solution

Use the Resource Generator (resgen.exe) to create a compiled resource file. You then use the /resource switch of the compiler to embed the file into the assembly.

█Note The Assembly Linker tool (al.exe) also provides functionality for working with and embedding resource files. Refer to the Assembly Linker information in the .NET Framework SDK documentation for details.

How It Works

If you need to store strings in an external file and have them accessible to your assembly, you can use a resource file. Resources are some form of data (a string or an image, for example) that is used by an application. A resource file is a repository of one or more resources that can be easily accessed.

If you need to store only strings, you can create a simple text file that contains one or more key/value pairs in the form of *key=value*. You cannot create image resources starting from a text file.

Once you have your text file, you compile it using the Resource Generator (resgen.exe). Using this utility, you can convert the text file into either of two types:

- An .resx file, which is an XML resource file. This file is fully documented and can be edited manually. It is also capable of supporting image resources, unlike the text file. Consult the .NET Framework SDK documentation for more details on the .resx format.

- A .resource file, which is a compiled binary file and is required if you are embedding the file into your assembly using the command line compiler. You embed the .resource file into your assembly by using the /resource switch of the VB .NET compiler. The .resource file can be compiled from a .txt or an .resx file.

You access the contents of the resource file by instantiating a ResourceManager object. The GetString method is used to retrieve the value for the specified string. If you have stored something other than a string, such as an image, in your resource file, use the GetObject method and cast the return value to the appropriate type.

The Code

This example borrows the code from recipe 1-2. The dialog box titles and message prompt have been removed from the code and are now contained within an external resource file. The new program uses the `ResourceManager` object to access the resources.

```vb
Imports System
Imports System.windows.forms
Imports System.resources

Namespace Apress.VisualBasicRecipes.Chapter01

    Public Class Recipe01_17
        Inherits Form

        ' Private members to hold references to the form's controls.
        Private label1 As Label
        Private textbox1 As TextBox
        Private button1 As Button
        Private resManager As New ResourceManager("Recipe01_17.MyStrings", ➥
System.Reflection.Assembly.GetExecutingAssembly())

        ' Constructor used to create an instance of the form and configure
        ' the form's controls.
        Public Sub New()
            ' Instantiate the controls used on the form.
            Me.label1 = New Label
            Me.textbox1 = New TextBox
            Me.button1 = New Button

            ' Suspend the layout logic of the form while we configure and
            ' position the controls.
            Me.SuspendLayout()

            ' Configure label1, which displays the user prompt.
            Me.label1.Location = New System.Drawing.Size(16, 36)
            Me.label1.Name = "label1"
            Me.label1.Size = New System.Drawing.Size(155, 16)
            Me.label1.TabIndex = 0
            Me.label1.Text = resManager.GetString("UserPrompt")

            ' Configure textbox1, which accepts the user input.
            Me.textBox1.Location = New System.Drawing.Point(172, 32)
            Me.textbox1.Name = "textbox1"
            Me.textbox1.TabIndex = 1
            Me.textbox1.Text = ""

            ' Configure button1, which the user clicks to enter a name.
            Me.button1.Location = New System.Drawing.Point(109, 80)
            Me.button1.Name = "button1"
            Me.button1.TabIndex = 2
            Me.button1.Text = "Enter"
            AddHandler button1.Click, AddressOf button1_Click
```

```
            ' Configure WelcomeForm, and add controls.
            Me.ClientSize = New System.Drawing.Size(292, 126)
            Me.Controls.Add(Me.button1)
            Me.Controls.Add(Me.textbox1)
            Me.Controls.Add(Me.label1)
            Me.Name = "form1"
            Me.Text = resManager.GetString("FormTitle")

            ' Resume the layout logic of the form now that all controls are
            ' configured.
            Me.ResumeLayout(False)

        End Sub

        Private Sub button1_Click(ByVal sender As Object, ➡
    ByVal e As System.EventArgs)

            ' Write debug message to the console.
            System.Console.WriteLine("User entered: " + textbox1.Text)

            ' Display welcome as a message box.
            MessageBox.Show resManager.GetString("Message")  + textbox1.Text, ➡
    resManager.GetString("FormTitle"))

        End Sub

        ' Application entry point, creates an instance of the form, and begins
        ' running a standard message loop on the current thread. The message
        ' loop feeds the application with input from the user as events.
        Public Shared Sub Main()
            Application.EnableVisualStyles()
            Application.Run(New Recipe01_17())
        End Sub

    End Class
End Namespace
```

Usage

First, you must create the MyStrings.txt file that contains your resource strings:

```
;String resource file for Recipe01-17
UserPrompt=Please enter your name:
FormTitle=Visual Basic 2005 Recipes
Message=Welcome to Visual Basic 2005 Recipes,
```

You compile this file into a resource file by using the command resgen.exe MyStrings.txt Recipe01_17.MyStrings.resources. To build the example and embed the resource file, use the command vbc /resources:Recipe01_17.MyStrings.resources Recipe01-17.vb.

Notes

Using resource files from Visual Studio is a little different from using resource files from the command line. For this example, the resource file must be in the XML format (.resx) and added directly into the project. Instead of initially creating the .resource file, you can use the command `resgen.exe MyStrings.txt MyStrings.resx` to generate the .resx file required by Visual Studio.

CHAPTER 2

■ ■ ■

Data Manipulation

Most applications need to manipulate some form of data. The Microsoft .NET Framework provides many techniques that simplify or improve the efficiency of common data-manipulation tasks. The recipes in this chapter describe how to do the following:

- Manipulate the contents of strings efficiently to avoid the overhead of automatic string creation due to the immutability of strings (recipe 2-1)

- Represent basic data types using different encoding schemes or as byte arrays to allow you to share data with external systems (recipes 2-2, 2-3, and 2-4)

- Validate user input and manipulate string values using regular expressions (recipes 2-5 and 2-6)

- Create System.DateTime objects from string values, such as those that a user might enter, and display DateTime objects as formatted strings (recipe 2-7)

- Mathematically manipulate DateTime objects in order to compare dates or add/subtract periods of time from a date (recipe 2-8)

- Sort the contents of an array or an ArrayList collection (recipe 2-9)

- Copy the contents of a collection to an array (recipe 2-10)

- Use the standard generic collection classes to instantiate a strongly typed collection (recipe 2-11)

- Use generics to define your own general-purpose container or collection class that will be strongly typed when it is used (recipe 2-12)

- Serialize object state and persist it to a file (recipe 2-13)

- Read user input from the Windows console (recipe 2-14)

2-1. Manipulate the Contents of a String Efficiently

Problem

You need to manipulate the contents of a String object and want to avoid the overhead of automatic String creation caused by the immutability of String objects.

Solution

Use the System.Text.StringBuilder class to perform the manipulations and convert the result to a String object using the StringBuilder.ToString method.

How It Works

`String` objects in .NET are immutable, meaning that once they are created, their content cannot be changed. If you build a string by concatenating a number of characters or smaller strings, the common language runtime (CLR) will create a completely new `String` object whenever you add a new element to the end of the existing string. Here is an example:

```
Dim testString as String
testString="Hello"
```

At this point, you have a `String` object named `testString` that contains the value `"Hello"`. Since strings are immutable, adding the statement `testString=testString & " World"` will result in a new `String` object being created. The `testString` object's reference is changed to point to the newly generated string, which creates a new object that contains the value `"Hello World"`. This can result in significant overhead if your application performs frequent string manipulation.

The `StringBuilder` class offers a solution by providing a character buffer and allowing you to manipulate its contents without the runtime creating a new object as a result of every change. You can create a new `StringBuilder` object that is empty or initialized with the content of an existing `String` object. You can manipulate the content of the `StringBuilder` object using overloaded methods that allow you to insert and append string representations of different data types. At any time, you can obtain a `String` representation of the current content of the `StringBuilder` object by calling `StringBuilder.ToString`.

Two important properties of `StringBuilder` control its behavior as you append new data: `Capacity` and `Length`. `Capacity` represents the size of the `StringBuilder` buffer, and `Length` represents the length of the buffer's current content. If you append new data that results in the number of characters in the `StringBuilder` object (`Length`) exceeding the capacity of the `StringBuilder` object (`Capacity`), the `StringBuilder` must allocate a new buffer to hold the data. The size of this new buffer is double the size of the previous `Capacity` value. Used carelessly, this buffer reallocation can negate much of the benefit of using `StringBuilder`. If you know the length of data you need to work with, or know an upper limit, you can avoid unnecessary buffer reallocation by specifying the capacity at creation time or setting the `Capacity` property manually. Note that 16 is the default `Capacity` property setting. When setting the `Capacity` and `Length` properties, be aware of the following behavior:

- If you set `Capacity` to a value less than the value of `Length`, the `Capacity` property throws the exception `System.ArgumentOutOfRangeException`. The same exception is also thrown if you try to raise the `Capacity` setting above the value of the `MaxCapacity` property. This should not be a problem except if you want to allocate more than 2 gigabytes (GB).

- If you set `Length` to a value less than the length of the current content, the content is truncated.

- If you set `Length` to a value greater than the length of the current content, the buffer is padded with spaces to the specified length. Setting `Length` to a value greater than `Capacity` automatically adjusts the `Capacity` value to be the same as the new `Length` value.

The Code

The `ReverseString` method shown in the following example demonstrates the use of the `StringBuilder` class to reverse a string. If you did not use the `StringBuilder` class to perform this operation, it would be significantly more expensive in terms of resource utilization, especially as the input string is made longer. The method creates a `StringBuilder` object of the correct capacity to ensure that no buffer reallocation is required during the reversal operation.

```vb
Imports System
Imports System.Text

Namespace Apress.VisualBasicRecipes.Chapter02

    Public Class Recipe02_01

        Public Shared Function ReverseString(ByVal str As String) As String

            ' Make sure we have a reversible string.
            If str Is Nothing Or str.Length <= 1 Then
                Return str
            End If

            ' Create a StringBuilder object with the required capacity.
            Dim revStr As StringBuilder = New StringBuilder(str.Length)

            ' Convert the string to a character array so we can easily loop
            ' through it.
            Dim chars As Char() = str.ToCharArray()

            ' Loop backward through the source string one character at a time and
            ' append each character to the StringBuilder.
            For count As Integer = chars.Length - 1 To 0 Step -1
                revStr.Append(chars(count))
            Next

            Return revStr.ToString

        End Function

        Public Shared Sub Main()
            Console.WriteLine(ReverseString("Madam Im Adam"))

            Console.WriteLine(ReverseString("The quick brown fox jumped ➡
    over the lazy dog."))

            ' Wait to continue
            Console.WriteLine(vbCrLf & "Main method complete.  Press Enter.")
            Console.ReadLine()

        End Sub

    End Class
End Namespace
```

2-2. Encode a String Using Alternate Character Encoding

Problem

You need to exchange character data with systems that use character-encoding schemes other than UTF-16, which is the character-encoding scheme used internally by the CLR.

Solution

Use the System.Text.Encoding class and its subclasses to convert characters between different encoding schemes.

How It Works

Unicode is not the only character-encoding scheme, nor is UTF-16 the only way to represent Unicode characters. When your application needs to exchange character data with external systems (particularly legacy systems) through an array of bytes, you may need to convert character data between UTF-16 and the encoding scheme supported by the other system.

The MustInherit class Encoding and its concrete subclasses provide the functionality to convert characters to and from a variety of encoding schemes. Each subclass instance supports the conversion of characters between the instance's encoding scheme and UTF-16. You obtain instances of the encoding-specific classes using the Shared factory method Encoding.GetEncoding, which accepts either the name or the code page number of the required encoding scheme.

Table 2-1 lists some commonly used character-encoding schemes and the code page number you must pass to the GetEncoding method to create an instance of the appropriate encoding class. The table also shows Shared properties of the Encoding class that provide shortcuts for obtaining the most commonly used types of encoding objects.

Table 2-1. *Character-Encoding Classes*

Encoding Scheme	Class	Create Using
ASCII	ASCIIEncoding	GetEncoding(20127) or the ASCII property
Default (current Microsoft Windows default)	Encoding	GetEncoding(0) or the Default property
UTF-7	UTF7Encoding	GetEncoding(65000) or the UTF7 property
UTF-8	UTF8Encoding	GetEncoding(65001) or the UTF8 property
UTF-16 (Big Endian)	UnicodeEncoding	GetEncoding(1201) or the BigEndianUnicode property
UTF-16 (Little Endian)	UnicodeEncoding	GetEncoding(1200) or the Unicode property

Once you have an Encoding object of the appropriate type, you convert a UTF-16 encoded Unicode string to a byte array of encoded characters using the GetBytes method. Conversely, you pass a byte array of encoded characters (such as UTF-8) to the GetString method, which will produce a UTF-16 encoded Unicode string.

The Code

The following example demonstrates the use of some encoding classes.

```vbnet
Imports System
Imports System.IO
Imports System.Text.Encoding

Namespace Apress.VisualBasicRecipes.Chapter02

    Public Class Recipe02_02

        Public Shared Sub Main()

            ' Create a file to hold the output.
            Using output As New StreamWriter("output.txt")
                ' Create and write a string containing the symbol for pi.
                Dim srcString As String = String.Format("Area = {0}r^2", ➥
ChrW(&H3A0))
                output.WriteLine("Source Text:  " & srcString)

                ' Write the UTF-16 encoded bytes of the source string.
                Dim utf16String As Byte() = Unicode.GetBytes(srcString)
                output.WriteLine("UTF-16 Bytes: {0}", ➥
BitConverter.ToString (utf16String))

                ' Convert the UTF-16 encoded source string to UTF-8 and ASCII.
                Dim utf8String As Byte() = UTF8.GetBytes(srcString)
                Dim asciiString As Byte() = ASCII.GetBytes(srcString)

                ' Write the UTF-8 and ASCII encoded byte arrays.
                output.WriteLine("UTF-8 Bytes:  {0}", ➥
BitConverter.ToString (utf8string))
                output.WriteLine("ASCII Bytes:  {0}", ➥
BitConverter.ToString (asciiString))

                ' Convert UTF-8 and ASCII encoded bytes back to UTF-16 encoded
                ' string and write to the output file.
                output.WriteLine("UTF-8 Text:  {0}", UTF8.GetString(utf8String))
                output.WriteLine("ASCII Text:  {0}", ASCII.GetString(asciiString))
            End Using

            ' Wait to continue
            Console.WriteLine(vbCrLf & "Main method complete.  Press Enter.")
            Console.ReadLine()

        End Sub

    End Class
End Namespace
```

Usage

Running the code will generate a file named output.txt. If you open this file in a text editor that supports Unicode, you will see the following content:

```
Source Text : Area =πr^2
UTF-16 Bytes: 41-00-72-00-65-00-61-00-20-00-3D-00-20-00-A0-03-72-00-5E-00-32-00
UTF-8  Bytes: 41-72-65-61-20-3D-20-CE-A0-72-5E-32
ASCII  Bytes: 41-72-65-61-20-3D-20-3F-72-5E-32
UTF-8  Text : Area = r^2
ASCII  Text : Area = πr^2
```

Notice that using UTF-16 encoding, each character occupies 2 bytes, but because most of the characters are standard characters, the high-order byte is 0. (The use of little-endian byte ordering means that the low-order byte appears first.) This means that most of the characters are encoded using the same numeric values across all three encoding schemes. However, the numeric value for the symbol pi (emphasized in bold in the preceding output) is different in each of the encodings. Representing the value of pi requires more than 1 byte. UTF-8 encoding uses 2 bytes, but ASCII has no direct equivalent and so replaces pi with the code 3F. As you can see in the ASCII text version of the string, 3F is the symbol for an English question mark (?).

■**Caution** If you convert Unicode characters to ASCII or a specific code page encoding scheme, you risk losing data. Any Unicode character with a character code that cannot be represented in the scheme will be ignored or altered.

Notes

The Encoding class also provides the Shared method Convert to simplify the conversion of a byte array from one encoding scheme to another without the need to manually perform an interim conversion to UTF-16. For example, the following statement converts the ASCII-encoded bytes contained in the asciiString byte array directly from ASCII encoding to UTF-8 encoding:

```
Dim utf8String As Byte() = Encoding.Convert(Encoding.ASCII, ➥
Encoding.UTF8, asciiString)
```

2-3. Convert Basic Value Types to Byte Arrays

Problem

You need to convert basic value types to byte arrays.

Solution

The Shared methods of the System.BitConverter class provide a convenient mechanism for converting most basic value types to and from byte arrays. An exception is the Decimal type. To convert a Decimal type to or from a byte array, you need to use a System.IO.MemoryStream object.

How It Works

The Shared method GetBytes of the BitConverter class provides overloads that take most of the standard value types and return the value encoded as an array of bytes. Support is provided for the Boolean, Char, Double, Short, Integer, Long, Single, UShort, UInteger, and ULong data types. BitConverter also provides a set of Shared methods that support the conversion of byte arrays to each of the standard value types. These are named ToBoolean, ToInt32, ToDouble, and so on. When using the BitConverter class, you may notice that some members include the values Int16, Int32, and Int64. These values are simply an alternate way of saying Short, Integer, and Long, respectively.

Unfortunately, the BitConverter class does not provide support for converting the Decimal type. Instead, write the Decimal type to a MemoryStream instance using a System.IO.BinaryWriter object, and then call the MemoryStream.ToArray method. To create a Decimal type from a byte array, create a MemoryStream object from the byte array and read the Decimal type from the MemoryStream object using a System.IO.BinaryReader instance.

The Code

The following example demonstrates the use of BitConverter to convert a Boolean type and an Integer type to and from a byte array. The second argument to each of the ToBoolean and ToInt32 methods is a zero-based offset into the byte array where the BitConverter should start taking the bytes to create the data value. The code also shows how to convert a Decimal type to a byte array using a MemoryStream object and a BinaryWriter object, as well as how to convert a byte array to a Decimal type using a BinaryReader object to read from the MemoryStream object.

```
Imports System
Imports System.IO
Namespace Apress.VisualBasicRecipes.Chapter02

    Public Class Recipe02_03

        ' Create a byte array from a decimal.
        Public Shared Function DecimalToByteArray(ByVal src As Decimal) As Byte()

            ' Create a MemoryStream as a buffer to hold the binary data.
            Using stream As New MemoryStream
                ' Create a BinaryWriter to write binary data to the stream.
                Using writer As New BinaryWriter(stream)
                    ' Write the decimal to the BinaryWriter/MemoryStream.
                    writer.Write(src)

                    ' Return the byte representation of the decimal.
                    Return stream.ToArray
                End Using
            End Using

        End Function

        ' Create a decimal from a byte array.
        Public Shared Function ByteArrayToDecimal(ByVal src As Byte()) As Decimal

            ' Create a MemoryStream containing the byte array.
            Using stream As New MemoryStream(src)
                ' Create a BinaryReader to read the decimal from the stream.
                Using reader As New BinaryReader(stream)
                    ' Read and return the decimal from the
                    ' BinaryReader/MemoryStream.
                    Return reader.ReadDecimal
                End Using
            End Using

        End Function
```

```
    Public Shared Sub Main()

        Dim b As Byte() = Nothing

        ' Convert a boolean to a byte array and display.
        b = BitConverter.GetBytes(True)
        Console.WriteLine(BitConverter.ToString(b))

        ' Convert a byte array to a boolean and display.
        Console.WriteLine(BitConverter.ToBoolean(b, 0))

        ' Convert an integer to a byte array and display.
        b = BitConverter.GetBytes(3678)
        Console.WriteLine(BitConverter.ToString(b))

        ' Convert a byte array to integer and display.
        Console.WriteLine(BitConverter.ToInt32(b, 0))

        ' Convert a decimal to a byte array and display.
        b = DecimalToByteArray(285998345545.563846696D)
        Console.WriteLine(BitConverter.ToString(b))

        ' Convert a byte array to a decimal and display.
        Console.WriteLine(ByteArrayToDecimal(b))

        ' Wait to continue
        Console.WriteLine(vbCrLf & "Main method complete.  Press Enter.")
        Console.ReadLine()

    End Sub

  End Class
End Namespace
```

■**Tip** The BitConverter.ToString method provides a convenient mechanism for obtaining a String representation of a byte array. Calling ToString and passing a byte array as an argument will return a String object containing the hexadecimal value of each byte in the array separated by a hyphen; for example, "34-A7-2C". Unfortunately, there is no standard method for reversing this process to obtain a byte array from a string with this format.

2-4. Base64 Encode Binary Data

Problem

You need to convert binary data into a form that can be stored as part of an ASCII text file (such as an XML file) or sent as part of a text e-mail message.

Solution

Use the Shared methods ToBase64CharArray and FromBase64CharArray of the System.Convert class to convert your binary data to and from a Base64-encoded Char array. If you need to work with the encoded data as a string value rather than as a Char array, you can use the ToBase64String and FromBase64String methods of the Convert class instead.

How It Works

Base64 is an encoding scheme that enables you to represent binary data as a series of ASCII characters so that it can be included in text files and e-mail messages in which raw binary data is unacceptable. Base64 encoding works by spreading the contents of 3 bytes of input data across 4 bytes and ensuring each byte uses only the 7 low-order bits to contain data. This means that each byte of Base64-encoded data is equivalent to an ASCII character and can be stored or transmitted anywhere ASCII characters are permitted. This process is not very efficient and can take a while to run on large amounts of data.

The ToBase64CharArray and FromBase64CharArray methods of the Convert class make it straightforward to Base64 encode and decode data. However, before Base64 encoding, you must convert your data to a byte array. Similarly, when decoding, you must convert the byte array back to the appropriate data type. (See recipe 2-2 for details on converting string data to and from byte arrays and recipe 2-3 for details on converting basic value types.) The ToBase64String and FromBase64String methods of the Convert class deal with string representations of Base64-encoded data.

The Code

The example shown here demonstrates how to Base64 encode and decode a Byte array, a Unicode String, an Integer type, and a Decimal type using the Convert class. The DecimalToBase64 and Base64ToDecimal methods rely on the ByteArrayToDecimal and DecimalToByteArray methods listed in recipe 2-3.

```
Imports System
Imports System.IO
Imports System.Text
Namespace Apress.VisualBasicRecipes.Chapter02

    Public Class Recipe02_04

        ' Create a byte array from a decimal.
        Public Shared Function DecimalToByteArray(ByVal src As Decimal) As Byte()

            ' Create a MemoryStream as a buffer to hold the binary data.
            Using stream As New MemoryStream
                ' Create a BinaryWriter to write binary data to the stream.
                Using writer As New BinaryWriter(stream)
                    ' Write the decimal to the BinaryWriter/MemoryStream.
                    writer.Write(src)

                    ' Return the byte representation of the decimal.
                    Return stream.ToArray
                End Using
            End Using

        End Function
```

```vbnet
' Create a decimal from a byte array.
Public Shared Function ByteArrayToDecimal(ByVal src As Byte()) As Decimal

    ' Create a MemoryStream containing the byte array.
    Using stream As New MemoryStream(src)
        ' Create a BinaryReader to read the decomal from the stream.
        Using reader As New BinaryReader(stream)
            ' Read and return the decimal from
            ' the BinaryReader/MemoryStream.
            Return reader.ReadDecimal
        End Using
    End Using

End Function


' Base64 encode a Unicode string
Public Shared Function StringToBase64(ByVal src As String) As String

    ' Get a byte representation of the source string.
    Dim b As Byte() = Encoding.Unicode.GetBytes(src)

    ' Return the Base64-encoded Unicode string.
    Return Convert.ToBase64String(b)

End Function

' Decode a Base64-encoded Unicode string.
Public Shared Function Base64ToString(ByVal src As String) As String

    ' Decode the Base64-encoded string to a byte array.
    Dim b As Byte() = Convert.FromBase64String(src)

    ' Return the decoded Unicode string.
    Return Encoding.Unicode.GetString(b)

End Function

' Base64 encode a decimal
Public Shared Function DecimalToBase64(ByVal src As Decimal) As String

    ' Get a byte representation of the decimal.
    Dim b As Byte() = DecimalToByteArray(src)

    ' Return the Base64-encoded decimal.
    Return Convert.ToBase64String(b)

End Function

' Decode a Base64-encoded decimal.
Public Shared Function Base64ToDecimal(ByVal src As String) As Decimal

    ' Decode the Base64-encoded decimal to a byte array.
    Dim b As Byte() = Convert.FromBase64String(src)
```

```vbnet
            ' Return the decoded decimal.
            Return ByteArrayToDecimal(b)

    End Function

    ' Base64 encode an integer.
    Public Shared Function IntToBase64(ByVal src As Integer) As String

            ' Get a byte representation of the integer.
            Dim b As Byte() = BitConverter.GetBytes(src)

            ' Return the Base64-encoded integer.
            Return Convert.ToBase64String(b)

    End Function

    ' Decode a Base64-encoded integer.
    Public Shared Function Base64ToInt(ByVal src As String) As Decimal

            ' Decode the Base64-encoded integer to a byte array.
            Dim b As Byte() = Convert.FromBase64String(src)

            ' Return the decoded integer.
            Return BitConverter.ToInt32(b, 0)

    End Function

    Public Shared Sub Main()

            ' Encode and decode a string
            Console.WriteLine(StringToBase64("Welcome to Visual Basic Recipes " & ➡
"from Apress"))
            Console.WriteLine(Base64ToString("VwBlAGwAYwBvAGOAZQAgAHQAbwA" + ➡
"gAFYAaQBzAHUAYQBsACAAQwAjACAAUgBlAGMAaQBwAGUAcwAgAGYAcgB" + ➡
"vAGOAIABBAHAAcgBlAHMAcwA="))

            ' Encode and decode a decimal.
            Console.WriteLine(DecimalToBase64(285998345545.563846696D))
            Console.WriteLine(Base64ToDecimal("KDjBUPO7BoEPAAAAAAAJAA=="))

            ' Encode and decode an integer.
            Console.WriteLine(IntToBase64(35789))
            Console.WriteLine(Base64ToInt("zYsAAA=="))

            ' Wait to continue
            Console.WriteLine(vbCrLf & "Main method complete.  Press Enter.")
            Console.ReadLine()

    End Sub

    End Class
End Namespace
```

> ■**Caution**   If you Base64 encode binary data for the purpose of including it as MIME data in an e-mail message, be aware that the maximum allowed line length in MIME for Base64-encoded data is 76 characters. Therefore, if your data is longer than 76 characters, you must insert a new line. For further information about the MIME standard, consult RFCs 2045 through 2049.

2-5. Validate Input Using Regular Expressions

Problem

You need to validate that user input or data read from a file has the expected structure and content. For example, you want to ensure that a user enters a valid IP address, telephone number, or e-mail address.

Solution

Use regular expressions to ensure that the input data follows the correct structure and contains only valid characters for the expected type of information.

How It Works

When a user inputs data to your application or your application reads data from a file, it's good practice to assume that the data is bad until you have verified its accuracy. One common validation requirement is to ensure that data entries such as e-mail addresses, telephone numbers, and credit card numbers follow the pattern and content constraints expected of such data. Obviously, you cannot be sure the actual data entered is valid until you use it, and you cannot compare it against values that are known to be correct. However, ensuring the data has the correct structure and content is a good first step to determining whether the input is accurate. Regular expressions provide an excellent mechanism for evaluating strings for the presence of patterns, and you can use this to your advantage when validating input data.

The first thing you must do is figure out the regular expression syntax that will correctly match the structure and content of data you are trying to validate. This is by far the most difficult aspect of using regular expressions. Many resources exist to help you with regular expressions, such as The Regulator (`http://regex.osherove.com/`) by Roy Osherove and RegExDesigner.NET by Chris Sells (`http://www.sellsbrothers.com/tools/#regexd`). The RegExLib.com web site (`http://www.regxlib.com/`) also provides hundreds of useful prebuilt expressions.

Regular expressions, which are case-sensitive, are constructed from two types of elements: *literals* and *metacharacters*. Literals represent specific characters that appear in the pattern you want to match. Metacharacters provide support for wildcard matching, ranges, grouping, repetition, conditionals, and other control mechanisms. Table 2-2 describes some of the more commonly used regular expression metacharacter elements. (Consult the .NET SDK documentation at `http://msdn2.microsoft.com/en-us/library/hs600312.aspx` for a full description of regular expressions.)

Table 2-2. *Commonly Used Regular Expression Metacharacter Elements*

Element	Description
.	Specifies any character except a newline character (\n)
\d	Specifies any digit
\D	Specifies any non-digit
\s	Specifies any whitespace character
\S	Specifies any non-whitespace character
\w	Specifies any word character
\W	Specifies any non-word character
^	Specifies the beginning of the string or line
\A	Specifies the beginning of the string
$	Specifies the end of the string or line
\z	Specifies the end of the string
|	Matches one of the expressions separated by the vertical bar; for example, AAA|ABA|ABB will match one of AAA, ABA, or ABB (the expression is evaluated left to right)
[abc]	Specifies a match with one of the specified characters; for example, [AbC] will match A, b, or C, but no other character
[^abc]	Specifies a match with any one character except those specified; for example, [^AbC] will *not* match A, b, or C, but will match B, F, and so on
[a-z]	Specifies a match with any one character in the specified range; for example, [A-C] will match A, B, or C
[^a-z]	Specifies a match with any one character *not* in the specified range; for example, [^A-C] will not match A, B, or C but will match B and F
( )	Identifies a subexpression so that it's treated as a single element by the regular expression elements described in this table
?	Specifies one or zero occurrences of the previous character or subexpression; for example, A?B matches B and AB, but not AAB
*	Specifies zero or more occurrences of the previous character or subexpression; for example, A*B matches B, AB, AAB, AAAB, and so on
+	Specifies one or more occurrences of the previous character or subexpression; for example, A+B matches AB, AAB, AAAB, and so on, but not B
{n}	Specifies exactly *n* occurrences of the preceding character or subexpression; for example, A{2} matches only AA and A{2}B matches only AAB
{n,}	Specifies a minimum of *n* occurrences of the preceding character or subexpression; for example, A{2,} matches AA, AAA, AAAA, and so on, but not A
{n, m}	Specifies a minimum of *n* and a maximum of *m* occurrences of the preceding character; for example, A{2,4} matches AA, AAA, and AAAA, but not A or AAAAA

The more complex the data you are trying to match, the more complex the regular expression syntax becomes. For example, ensuring that input contains only numbers or is of a minimum length is trivial, but ensuring a string contains a valid URL is extremely complex. Table 2-3 shows some examples of regular expressions that match against commonly required data types.

Table 2-3. *Commonly Used Regular Expressions*

Input Type	Description	Regular Expression
Numeric input	The input consists of one or more decimal digits; for example, 5 or 5683874674.	`^\d+$`
Personal identification number (PIN)	The input consists of four decimal digits; for example, 1234.	`^\d{4}$`
Simple password	The input consists of six to eight characters; for example, ghtd6f or b8c7hogh.	`^\w{6,8}$`
Credit card number	The input consists of data that matches the pattern of most major credit card numbers; for example, 4921835221552042 or 4921-8352-2155-2042.	`^\d{4}-?\d{4}-?\d{4}-?\d{4}$`
E-mail address	The input consists of an Internet e-mail address. The `[\w-]+` expression indicates that each address element must consist of one or more word characters or hyphens; for example, somebody@adatum.com.	`^[\w-]+@([\w-]+\.)+[\w-]+$`
HTTP or HTTPS URL	The input consists of an HTTP-based or HTTPS-based URL; for example, `http://www.apress.com`.	`^https?://([\w-]+\.)+[\w-]+(/[\w-./?%=]*)?$`

Once you know the correct regular expression syntax, create a new `System.Text.RegularExpressions.Regex` object, passing a string containing the regular expression to the `Regex` constructor. Then call the `IsMatch` method of the `Regex` object and pass the string that you want to validate. `IsMatch` returns a `Boolean` value indicating whether the `Regex` object found a match in the string. The regular expression syntax determines whether the `Regex` object will match against only the full string or match against patterns contained within the string. (See the `^`, `\A`, `$`, and `\z` entries in Table 2-2.)

The Code

The `ValidateInput` method shown in the following example tests any input string to see if it matches a specified regular expression.

```
Imports System
Imports System.Text.RegularExpressions
Namespace Apress.VisualBasicRecipes.Chapter02

    Public Class Recipe02_05
```

```
        Public Shared Function ValidateInput(ByVal expression As String, ➡
ByVal input As String) As Boolean

            ' Create a new Regex based on the specified regular expression.
            Dim r As New Regex(expression)

            ' Test if the specified input matches the regular expression.
            Return r.IsMatch(input)

        End Function

        Public Shared Sub Main(ByVal args As String())

            ' Test the input from the command line.  The first argument is the
            ' regular expression, and the second is the input.
            Console.WriteLine("Regular Expresion:  {0}", args(0))
            Console.WriteLine("Input:  {0}", args(1))
            Console.WriteLine("Valied = {0}", ValidateInput(args(0), args(1)))

            ' Wait to continue.
            Console.WriteLine(vbCrLf & "Main method complete.  Press Enter")
            Console.ReadLine()

        End Sub

    End Class
End Namespace
```

Usage

To execute the example, run Recipe02-05.exe and pass the regular expression and data to test as command-line arguments. For example, to test for a correctly formed e-mail address, type the following:

```
Recipe02-05 ^[\w-]+@([\w-]+\.)+[\w-]+$ myname@mydomain.com
```

The result would be as follows:

```
Regular Expression: ^[\w-]+@([\w-]+\.)+[\w-]+$
Input: myname@mydomain.com
Valid = True
```

Notes

You can use a Regex object repeatedly to test multiple strings, but you cannot change the regular expression tested for by a Regex object. You must create a new Regex object to test for a different pattern. This is because the ValidateInput method creates a new Regex instance each time it's called. A more suitable alternative, in this case, would be to use a Shared overload of the IsMatch method, as shown in the following variant of the ValidateInput method.

```
' Alternative version of the ValidateInput method that does not create
' Regex instances.
Public Shared Function ValidateInput(ByVal expression As String, ➥
ByVal input As String) As Boolean

    ' Test if the specified input matches the regular expression.
    Return Regex.IsMatch(input, expression)

End Function
```

2-6. Use Compiled Regular Expressions

Problem

You need to minimize the impact on application performance that arises from using complex regular expressions frequently.

Solution

When you instantiate the System.Text.RegularExpressions.Regex object that represents your regular expression, specify the Compiled option of the System.Text.RegularExpressions.RegexOptions enumeration to compile the regular expression to Microsoft Intermediate Language (MSIL).

How It Works

By default, when you create a Regex object, the regular expression pattern you specify in the constructor is compiled to an intermediate form (not MSIL). Each time you use the Regex object, the runtime interprets the pattern's intermediate form and applies it to the target string. With complex regular expressions that are used frequently, this repeated interpretation process can have a detrimental effect on the performance of your application.

By specifying the RegexOptions.Compiled option when you create a Regex object, you force the .NET runtime to compile the regular expression to MSIL instead of the interpreted intermediary form. This MSIL is just-in-time (JIT) compiled by the runtime to native machine code on first execution, just like regular assembly code. Subsequent calls to the same RegEx object will use the native version that was previously compiled. You use a compiled regular expression in the same way as you use any Regex object; compilation simply results in faster execution.

However, a couple downsides offset the performance benefits provided by compiling regular expressions. First, the JIT compiler needs to do more work, which will introduce delays during JIT compilation. This is most noticeable if you create your compiled regular expressions as your application starts up. Second, the runtime cannot unload a compiled regular expression once you have finished with it. Unlike as with a normal regular expression, the runtime's garbage collector will not reclaim the memory used by the compiled regular expression. The compiled regular expression will remain in memory until your program terminates or you unload the application domain in which the compiled regular expression is loaded. If you only plan to use a RegEx object once, there is no reason to compile it. Use compiling only for situations where a RegEx object is used frequently.

As well as compiling regular expressions in memory, the Shared Regex.CompileToAssembly method allows you to create a compiled regular expression and write it to an external assembly. This means that you can create assemblies containing standard sets of regular expressions, which you can use from multiple applications. To compile a regular expression and persist it to an assembly, take the following steps:

1. Create a `System.Text.RegularExpressions.RegexCompilationInfo` array large enough to hold one `RegexCompilationInfo` object for each of the compiled regular expressions you want to create.

2. Create a `RegexCompilationInfo` object for each of the compiled regular expressions. Specify values for its properties as arguments to the object constructor. The following are the most commonly used properties:

   • `IsPublic`, a `Boolean` value that specifies whether the generated regular expression class has `Public` visibility

   • `Name`, a `String` value that specifies the class name

   • `Namespace`, a `String` value that specifies the namespace of the class

   • `Pattern`, a `String` value that specifies the pattern that the regular expression will match (see recipe 2-5 for more details)

   • `Options`, a `System.Text.RegularExpressions.RegexOptions` value that specifies options for the regular expression

3. Create a `System.Reflection.AssemblyName` object. Configure it to represent the name of the assembly that the `Regex.CompileToAssembly` method will create.

4. Execute `Regex.CompileToAssembly`, passing the `RegexCompilationInfo` array and the `AssemblyName` object.

This process creates an assembly that contains one class declaration for each compiled regular expression—each class derives from `Regex`. To use the compiled regular expression contained in the assembly, instantiate the regular expression you want to use and call its method as if you had simply created it with the normal `Regex` constructor. (Remember to add a reference to the assembly when you compile the code that uses the compiled regular expression classes.)

The Code

This line of code shows how to create a `Regex` object that is compiled to MSIL instead of the usual intermediate form:

```
Dim reg As New Regex("[\w-]+@([\w-]+\.)+[\w-]+", RegexOptions.Compiled)
```

The following example shows how to create an assembly named MyRegEx.dll, which contains two regular expressions named `PinRegex` and `CreditCardRegex`.

```
Imports System
Imports System.Reflection
Imports System.Text.RegularExpressions

Namespace Apress.VisualBasicRecipes.Chapter02

    Public Class Recipe02_06

        Public Shared Sub Main()

            ' Create the array to hold the Regex info objects.
            Dim regexInfo(1) As RegexCompilationInfo
```

```
          ' Create the RegexCompilationInfo for PinRegex.
          regexInfo(0) = New RegexCompilationInfo("^\d{4}$", ➡
RegexOptions.Compiled, "PinRegex", "Apress.VisualBasicRecipes.Chapter02", True)

          ' Create the RegexCompilationInfo for CreditCardRegex.
          regexInfo(1) = New RegexCompilationInfo( ➡
"^\d{4}-?\d{4}-?\d{4}-?\d{4}$", RegexOptions.Compiled, "CreditCardRegex", ➡
"Apress.VisualBasicRecipes.Chapter02", True)

          ' Create the AssemblyName to define the target assembly.
          Dim assembly As New AssemblyName("MyRegEx")

          ' Create the compiled regular expression.
          Regex.CompileToAssembly(regexInfo, assembly)

      End Sub

    End Class
End Namespace
```

Usage

When you want to use your new assembly, you must first add a reference to it to your project. You can do this from within the Visual Studio interface or by using the /r:MyRegEx.dll option of the command-line compiler.

Once you have a reference to the assembly in your project, you can easily create a reference to the compiled regular expressions contained inside, as shown in this example:

```
Dim pinRegExp As New PinRegex
```

2-7. Create Dates and Times from Strings

Problem

You need to create a System.DateTime instance that represents the time and date specified in a string.

Solution

Use the Parse or ParseExact method of the DateTime class.

■**Caution** Many subtle issues are associated with using the DateTime class to represent dates and times in your applications. Although the Parse and ParseExact methods create DateTime objects from strings as described in this recipe, you must be careful how you use the resulting DateTime objects within your program. See the article titled "Coding Best Practices Using DateTime in the .NET Framework" (http://msdn.microsoft.com/netframework/default.aspx?pull=/library/en-us/dndotnet/html/datetimecode.asp) for details about the problems you may encounter.

How It Works

Dates and times can be represented as text in many different ways. For example, January 12 1975, 1/12/1975, and Jan-12-1975 are all possible representations of the same date, and 18:19 and 6:19 p.m. can both be used to represent the same time. The Shared DateTime.Parse method provides a flexible mechanism for creating DateTime instances from a wide variety of string representations.

The Parse method goes to great lengths to generate a DateTime object from a given string. It will even attempt to generate a DateTime object from a string containing partial or erroneous information and will substitute defaults for any missing values. Missing date elements default to the current date, and missing time elements default to 12:00:00 a.m. After all efforts, if Parse cannot create a DateTime object, it throws a System.FormatException exception.

The Parse method is both flexible and forgiving. However, for many applications, this level of flexibility is unnecessary. Often, you will want to ensure that DateTime parses only strings that match a specific format. In these circumstances, use the ParseExact method instead of Parse. The simplest overload of the ParseExact method takes three arguments: the time and date string to parse, a format string that specifies the structure that the time and date string must have, and an IFormatProvider reference that provides culture-specific information to the ParseExact method. If the IFormatProvider value is Nothing, the current thread's culture information is used.

The time and date must meet the requirements specified in the format string, or ParseExact will throw a System.FormatException exception. You use the same format specifiers for the format string as you use to format a DateTime object for display as a string. This means that you can use both standard and custom format specifiers.

The Code

The following example demonstrates the flexibility of the Parse method and the use of the ParseExact method. Refer to the documentation for the System.Globalization.DateTimeFormatInfo class in the .NET Framework SDK document for complete details on all available format specifiers.

```
Imports System

Namespace Apress.VisualBasicRecipes.Chapter02

    Public Class Recipe02_07

        Public Shared Sub Main(ByVal args As String())

            ' 1st January 1975 00:00:00
            Dim dt1 As DateTime = DateTime.Parse("Jan 1975")

            ' 12th January 1975 18:19:00
            Dim dt2 As DateTime = DateTime.Parse("Sunday 12 January 1975 18:19:00")

            ' 12th January 1975 00:00:00
            Dim dt3 As DateTime = DateTime.Parse("1,12,1975")

            ' 12th January 1975 18:19:00
            Dim dt4 As DateTime = DateTime.Parse("1/12/1975 18:19:00")

            ' Current Date 18:19
            Dim dt5 As DateTime = DateTime.Parse("6:19 PM")
```

```
          ' Display the converted DateTime objects.
          Console.WriteLine(dt1)
          Console.WriteLine(dt2)
          Console.WriteLine(dt3)
          Console.WriteLine(dt4)
          Console.WriteLine(dt5)

          ' Parse only strings containing LongTimePattern.
          Dim dt6 As DateTime = DateTime.ParseExact("6:19:00 PM", "h:mm:ss tt", ➥
Nothing)

          ' Parse only strings containing RFC1123Pattern.
          Dim dt7 As DateTime = DateTime.ParseExact("Sun, 12 Jan 1975 " + ➥
"18:19:00 GMT", "ddd, dd MMM yyyy HH':'mm':'ss 'GMT'", Nothing)

          ' Parse only strings containing MonthDayPattern.
          Dim dt8 As DateTime = DateTime.ParseExact("January 12", "MMMM dd", ➥
Nothing)

          ' Display the converted DateTime objects.
          Console.WriteLine(dt6)
          Console.WriteLine(dt7)
          Console.WriteLine(dt8)

          ' Wait to continue.
          Console.WriteLine(vbCrLf & "Main method complete.  Press Enter")
          Console.ReadLine()

      End Sub

   End Class
End Namespace
```

2-8. Add, Subtract, and Compare Dates and Times

Problem

You need to perform basic arithmetic operations or comparisons using dates and times.

Solution

Use the DateTime and TimeSpan structures, which support standard arithmetic and comparison operators.

How It Works

A DateTime instance represents a specific time (such as 4:15 a.m. on September 5, 1970), whereas a TimeSpan instance represents a period of time (such as 2 hours, 35 minutes). You may want to add, subtract, and compare TimeSpan and DateTime instances.

Internally, both DateTime and TimeSpan use *ticks* to represent time. A tick is equal to 100 nanoseconds. TimeSpan stores its time interval as the number of ticks equal to that interval, and DateTime stores time as the number of ticks since 12:00:00 midnight on January 1 in 0001 C.E. (C.E. stands for Common Era and is equivalent to A.D. in the Gregorian calendar.) This approach and the use of operator overloading makes it easy for DateTime and TimeSpan to support basic arithmetic and comparison operations. Table 2-4 summarizes the operator support provided by the DateTime and TimeSpan structures.

Table 2-4. *Operators Supported by DateTime and TimeSpan*

Operator	TimeSpan	DateTime
Assignment (=)	Because TimeSpan is a structure, assignment returns a copy and not a reference	Because DateTime is a structure, assignment returns a copy and not a reference
Addition (+)	Adds two TimeSpan instances	Adds a TimeSpan instance to a DateTime instance
Subtraction (-)	Subtracts one TimeSpan instance from another TimeSpan instance	Subtracts a TimeSpan instance or a DateTime instance from a DateTime instance
Equality (=)	Compares two TimeSpan instances and returns true if they are equal	Compares two DateTime instances and returns true if they are equal
Inequality (<>)	Compares two TimeSpan instances and returns true if they are not equal	Compares two DateTime instances and returns true if they are not equal
Greater than (>)	Determines if one TimeSpan instance is greater than another TimeSpan instance	Determines if one DateTime instance is greater than another DateTime instance
Greater than or equal to (>=)	Determines if one TimeSpan instance is greater than or equal to another TimeSpan instance	Determines if one DateTime instance is greater than or equal to another DateTime instance
Less than (<)	Determines if one TimeSpan instance is less than another TimeSpan instance	Determines if one DateTime instance is less than another DateTime instance
Less than or equal to (<=)	Determines if one TimeSpan instance is less than or equal to another TimeSpan instance	Determines if one DateTime instance is less than or equal to another DateTime instance
Unary negation (-)	Returns a TimeSpan instance with a negated value of the specified TimeSpan instance	Not supported
Unary plus (+)	Returns the TimeSpan instance specified	Not supported

The DateTime structure also implements the AddTicks, AddMilliseconds, AddSeconds, AddMinutes, AddHours, AddDays, AddMonths, and AddYears methods. Each of these methods, which accept a Double as opposed to a TimeSpan, allows you to add (or subtract using negative values) the appropriate element of time to a DateTime instance. These methods and the non-comparison operators listed in Table 2-4 do not modify the original DateTime; instead, they create a new instance with the modified value.

The Code

The following example demonstrates the use of operators to manipulate the DateTime and TimeSpan structures.

```
Imports System

Namespace Apress.VisualBasicRecipes.Chapter02

    Public Class Recipe02_08

        Public Shared Sub Main()

            ' Create a TimeSpan representing 2.5 days.
            Dim timespan1 As New TimeSpan(2, 12, 0, 0)

            ' Create a TimeSpan representing 4.5 days.
            Dim timespan2 As New TimeSpan(4, 12, 0, 0)

            ' Create a TimeSpan representing 1 week.
            Dim oneweek As TimeSpan = timespan1 + timespan2

            ' Create a DateTime with the current date and time.
            Dim now As DateTime = DateTime.Now

            ' Create a DateTime representing 1 week in the past.
            Dim past As DateTime = now - oneweek

            ' Create a DateTime representing 1 week in the future.
            Dim future As DateTime = now + oneweek

            ' Create a DateTime representing the next day using
            ' the AddDays method.
            Dim tomorrow As DateTime = now.AddDays(1)

            ' Display the DateTime instances.
            Console.WriteLine("Now      : {0}", now)
            Console.WriteLine("Past     : {0}", past)
            Console.WriteLine("Future   : {0}", future)
            Console.WriteLine("Tomorrow : {0}", tomorrow)

            ' Wait to continue.
            Console.WriteLine(vbCrLf & "Main method complete.  Press Enter")
            Console.ReadLine()

        End Sub

    End Class
End Namespace
```

2-9. Sort an Array or an ArrayList

Problem

You need to sort the elements contained in an array or an `ArrayList` structure.

Solution

Use the `ArrayList.Sort` method to sort `ArrayList` objects and the `Shared Array.Sort` method to sort arrays.

How It Works

The simplest `Sort` method overload sorts the objects contained in an array or `ArrayList` structure as long as the objects implement the `System.IComparable` interface and are of the same type. All of the basic data types implement `IComparable`. To sort objects that do not implement `IComparable`, you must pass the `Array.Sort` method an object that implements the `System.Collections.IComparer` interface. The `IComparer` implementation must be capable of comparing the objects contained within the array or `ArrayList`. (Recipe 13-3 describes how to implement both comparable types.)

The Code

The following example demonstrates how to use the `Sort` methods of the `ArrayList` and `Array` classes.

```
Imports System
Imports System.Collections

Namespace Apress.VisualBasicRecipes.Chapter02

    Public Class Recipe02_09

        Public Shared Sub Main()

            ' Create a new array and populate it.
            Dim array1 As Integer() = {4, 2, 9, 3}

            ' Sort the array.
            Array.Sort(array1)

            ' Display the contents of the sorted array.
            For Each i As Integer In array1
                Console.WriteLine(i.ToString)
            Next

            ' Create a new ArrayList and populate it.
            Dim list1 As New ArrayList(3)
            list1.Add("Amy")
            list1.Add("Alaina")
            list1.Add("Aidan")

            ' Sort the ArrayList.
            list1.Sort()
```

```
        ' Display the contents of the sorted ArrayList.
        For Each s As String In list1
            Console.WriteLine(s)
        Next

        ' Wait to continue.
        Console.WriteLine(vbCrLf & "Main method complete.  Press Enter")
        Console.ReadLine()

    End Sub

  End Class
End Namespace
```

2-10. Copy a Collection to an Array

Problem

You need to copy the contents of a collection to an array.

Solution

Use the ICollection.CopyTo method implemented by all collection classes. Alternatively, you can use the ToArray method implemented by the ArrayList, Stack, and Queue collections, as well as their respective generic versions List<T>, Stack<T>, and Queue<T>. Refer to recipe 2-12 for more information regarding generics.

How It Works

The ICollection.CopyTo method and the ToArray method perform roughly the same function: they perform a shallow copy of the elements contained in a collection to an array. The key difference is that CopyTo copies the collection's elements to an existing array, whereas ToArray creates a new array before copying the collection's elements into it.

The CopyTo method takes two arguments: an array and an index. The array is the target of the copy operation and must be of a type appropriate to handle the elements of the collection. If the types do not match, or no implicit conversion is possible from the collection element's type to the array element's type, a System.InvalidCastException exception is thrown. The index is the starting element of the array where the collection's elements will be copied. If the index is equal to or greater than the length of the array, or the number of collection elements exceeds the capacity of the array, a System.ArgumentException exception is thrown.

The ArrayList, Stack, and Queue classes and their generic versions (mentioned earlier) also implement the ToArray method, which automatically creates an array of the correct size to accommodate a copy of all the elements of the collection. If you call ToArray with no arguments, it returns an object() array, regardless of the type of objects contained in the collection. For convenience, the ArrayList.ToArray method has an overload to which you can pass a System.Type object that specifies the type of array that the ToArray method should create. (You must still cast the returned strongly typed array to the correct type.) The layout of the array's contents depends on which collection class you are using. For example, an array produced from a Stack object will be inverted compared to the array generated by an ArrayList object.

The Code

This example demonstrates how to copy the contents of an ArrayList structure to an array using the CopyTo method, and then shows how to use the ToArray method on the ArrayList object.

```
Imports System
Imports System.Collections
Namespace Apress.VisualBasicRecipes.Chapter02

    Public Class Recipe02_10

        Public Shared Sub Main()

            ' Create a new ArrayList and populate it.
            Dim list As New ArrayList(3)
            list.Add("Amy")
            list.Add("Alaina")
            list.Add("Aidan")

            ' Create a string array and use the ICollection.CopyTo method
            ' to copy the contents of the ArrayList.
            Dim array1(list.Count - 1) As String
            list.CopyTo(array1, 0)

            ' Use ArrayList.ToArray to create an object array from the
            ' contents of the collection.
            Dim array2 As Object() = list.ToArray()

            ' Use ArrayList.ToArray to create a strongly typed string
            ' array from the contents of the collection.
            Dim array3 As String() = DirectCast(list.ToArray(GetType(String)), ➥
String())

            ' Display the contents of the 3 arrays.
            Console.WriteLine("Array 1:")
            For Each s As String In array1
                Console.WriteLine(vbTab + "{0}", s)
            Next

            Console.WriteLine("Array 2:")
            For Each s As String In array2
                Console.WriteLine(vbTab + "{0}", s)
            Next

            Console.WriteLine("Array 3:")
            For Each s As String In array3
                Console.WriteLine(vbTab + "{0}", s)
            Next

            ' Wait to continue.
            Console.WriteLine(vbCrLf & "Main method complete.  Press Enter")
            Console.ReadLine()

        End Sub
```

```
      End Class
End Namespace
```

2-11. Use a Strongly Typed Collection

Problem

You need a collection that works with elements of a specific type so that you do not need to work with System.Object references in your code.

Solution

Use the appropriate collection class from the System.Collections.Generic namespace. When you instantiate the collection, specify the type of object the collection should contain using the generics syntax built into VB .NET 8.0.

How It Works

The generics functionality added to .NET Framework 2.0 and supported by specific syntax in VB .NET 8.0 make it easy to create type-safe collections and containers (see recipe 2-12). To meet the most common requirements for collection classes, the System.Collections.Generic namespace contains a number of predefined generic collections, including the following:

- Dictionary
- LinkedList
- List
- Queue
- Stack

When you instantiate one of these collections, you specify the type of object that the collection will contain by using the Of keyword with the type name in parentheses after the collection name; for example, Dictionary(Of System.Reflection.AssemblyName). As a result, all members that add objects to the collection expect the objects to be of the specified type, and all members that return objects from the collection will return object references of the specified type. Using strongly typed collections and working directly with objects of the desired type simplifies development and reduces the errors that can occur when working with general Object references and casting them to the desired type.

The Code

The following example demonstrates the use of generic collections to create a variety of collections specifically for the management of AssemblyName objects. Notice that you never need to cast to or from the Object type.

```
Imports System
Imports System.Reflection
Imports System.Collections.Generic
```

```vb
Namespace Apress.VisualBasicRecipes.Chapter02

    Public Class Recipe02_11

        Public Shared Sub Main()

            ' Create an AssemblyName object for use during the example.
            Dim assembly1 As New AssemblyName("com.microsoft.crypto, Culture=en, ➡
PublicKeyToken=a5d015c7d5a0b012, Version=1.0.0.0")

            ' Create and use a Dictionary of AssemblyName objects.
            Dim assemblyDictionary As New Dictionary(Of String, AssemblyName)

            assemblyDictionary.Add("Crypto", assembly1)

            Dim ass1 As AssemblyName = assemblyDictionary("Crypto")

            Console.WriteLine("Got AssemblyName from dictionary: {0}", ➡
CType(ass1, AssemblyName).ToString)

            ' Create and use a list of AssemblyName objects.
            Dim assemblyList As New List(Of AssemblyName)

            assemblyList.Add(assembly1)

            Dim ass2 As AssemblyName = assemblyList(0)

            Console.WriteLine(vbCrLf & "Got AssemblyName from list: {0}", ➡
CType(ass2, AssemblyName).ToString)

            ' Create and use a stack of AssemblyName objects.
            Dim assemblyStack As New Stack(Of AssemblyName)

            assemblyStack.Push(assembly1)

            Dim ass3 As AssemblyName = assemblyStack.Pop

            Console.WriteLine(vbCrLf & "Popped AssemblyName from stack: {0}", ➡
CType(ass3, AssemblyName).ToString)

            ' Wait to continue.
            Console.WriteLine(vbCrLf & "Main method complete.  Press Enter")
            Console.ReadLine()

        End Sub

    End Class
End Namespace
```

2-12. Create a Generic Type

Problem

You need to create a new general-purpose type such as a collection or container that supports strong typing of the elements it contains.

Solution

Use the generics functionality added to .NET Framework 2.0. Define your class using the generics syntax provided in VB .NET 8.0.

How It Works

You can leverage the generics capabilities of .NET Framework 2.0 in any class you define. This allows you to create general-purpose classes that can be used as type-safe instances by other programmers. When you declare your type, you identify it as a generic type by following the type name with a list of identifiers for the types used in the class, preceded by the `Of` keyword and enclosed in parentheses. Here is an example:

```
Public Class MyGeneric(Of T1, T2, T3)
End Class
```

This declaration specifies a new class named `MyGenericType`, which uses three generic types in its implementation (`T1`, `T2`, and `T3`). When implementing the type, you substitute the generic type names into the code instead of using specific type names. For example, one method might take an argument of type `T1` and return a result of type `T2`, as shown here:

```
Public Function MyGenericMethod(ByVal arg As T1) As T2
End Function
```

When other people use your class and create an instance of it, they specify the actual types to use as part of the instantiation. Here is an example:

```
Dim obj As New MyGenericType(Of String, System.IO.Stream, String)
```

The types specified replace `T1`, `T2`, and `T3` throughout the implementation, so with this instance, `MyGenericMethod` would actually be interpreted as follows:

```
Public Function MyGenericMethod(ByVal arg As String) As Stream
End Function
```

You can also include constraints as part of your generic type definition. This allows you to make specifications such as the following:

- Only value types or only reference types can be used with the generic type.
- Only types that implement a default (empty) constructor can be used with the generic type.
- Only types that implement a specific interface can be used with the generic type.
- Only types that inherit from a specific base class can be used with the generic type.
- One generic type must be the same as another generic type (for example, `T1` must be the same as `T3`).

For example, to specify that T1 must implement the System.IDisposable interface and provide a default constructor, that T2 must be or derive from the System.IO.Stream class, and that T3 must be the same type as T1, change the definition of MyGenericType as follows:

```
Public Class MyGenericType(Of T1 As {IDisposable}, T2 As {System.IO.Stream}, ➥
T3 As {T1})
End Class
```

The Code

The following example demonstrates a simplified bag implementation that returns those objects put into it at random. A *bag* is a data structure that can contain zero or more items, including duplicates of items, but does not guarantee any ordering of the items it contains.

```
Imports System
Imports System.Collections.Generic
Namespace Apress.VisualBasicRecipes.Chapter02

    Public Class Bag(Of T)
        '  A list to hold the bag's contents. The list must be
        '  of the same type as the bag.
        Private items As New List(Of T)

        '  A method to add an item to the bag.
        Public Sub Add(ByVal item As T)
            items.Add(item)
        End Sub

        '  A method to remove a random item from the bag.
        Public Function Remove() As T
            Dim item As T = Nothing

            If Not items.Count = 0 Then
                '  Determine which item to remove from the bag.
                Dim r As New Random
                Dim num As Integer = r.Next(0, items.Count)

                '  Remove the item.
                item = items(num)
                items.RemoveAt(num)
            End If

            Return item

        End Function

        '  A method to remove all items form the bag and return them
        '  as an array.
        Public Function RemoveAll() As T()

            Dim i As T() = items.ToArray()
            items.Clear()
            Return i

        End Function
```

```vb
    End Class

    Public Class Recipe02_12

        Public Shared Sub Main()

            ' Create a new bag of strings.
            Dim bag As New Bag(Of String)

            ' Add strings to the bag.
            bag.Add("Amy")
            bag.Add("Alaina")
            bag.Add("Aidan")
            bag.Add("Robert")
            bag.Add("Pearl")
            bag.Add("Mark")
            bag.Add("Karen")

            ' Take four strings from the bag and display.
            Console.WriteLine("Item 1 = {0}", bag.Remove())
            Console.WriteLine("Item 2 = {0}", bag.Remove())
            Console.WriteLine("Item 3 = {0}", bag.Remove())
            Console.WriteLine("Item 4 = {0}", bag.Remove())
            Console.WriteLine(vbCrLf)

            ' Remove the remaining items from the bag.
            Dim s As String() = bag.RemoveAll

            ' Display the remaining items.
            For i As Integer = 0 To s.Length - 1
                Console.WriteLine("Item {0} = {1}", i + 1.ToString, s(i))
            Next

            ' Wait to continue.
            Console.WriteLine(vbCrLf & "Main method complete.  Press Enter")
            Console.ReadLine()

        End Sub

    End Class
End Namespace
```

2-13. Store a Serializable Object to a File

Problem

You need to store a serializable object and its state to a file, and then deserialize it later.

Solution

Use a *formatter* to serialize the object and write it to a System.IO.FileStream object. When you need to retrieve the object, use the same type of formatter to read the serialized data from the file and deserialize the object. The .NET Framework class library includes the following formatter implementations for serializing objects to binary or SOAP format:

- System.Runtime.Serialization.Formatters.Binary.BinaryFormatter
- System.Runtime.Serialization.Formatters.Soap.SoapFormatter

How It Works

Using the BinaryFormatter and SoapFormatter classes, you can serialize an instance of any serializable type. (See recipe 13-1 for details on how to make a type serializable.) The BinaryFormatter class produces a binary data stream representing the object and its state. The SoapFormatter class produces a SOAP document. SOAP, which stands for Simple Object Access Protocol, is an XML-based protocol used to exchange messages over the network. SOAP is used as the primary mechanism for communicating with web services. Refer to recipes 10-13, 10-14, and 10-15 for more information about web services.

Both the BinaryFormatter and SoapFormatter classes implement the interface System.Runtime.Serialization.IFormatter, which defines two methods: Serialize and Deserialize. The Serialize method takes a System.IO.Stream reference and a System.Object reference as arguments, serializes the Object, and writes it to the Stream. The Deserialize method takes a Stream reference as an argument, reads the serialized object data from the Stream, and returns an Object reference to a deserialized object. You must cast the returned Object reference to the correct type.

■**Caution** To call the Serialize and Deserialize methods of the BinaryFormatter class, your code must be granted the SecurityPermissionFlag.SerializationFormatter permission. To call the Serialize and Deserialize methods of the SoapFormatter class, your code must be granted full trust, because the System.Runtime.Serialization.Formatters.Soap.dll assembly in which the SoapFormatter class is declared does not allow partially trusted callers. Refer to recipe 11-1 for more information about assemblies and partially trusted callers.

The Code

The example shown here demonstrates the use of both BinaryFormatter and SoapFormatter to serialize a System.Collections.ArrayList object containing a list of people to a file. The ArrayList object is then deserialized from the files and the contents displayed to the console. A reference to the System.Runtime.Serialization.Formatters.Soap assembly may need to be added to your project before it can be used.

```
Imports System
Imports System.IO
Imports System.Collections
Imports System.Runtime.Serialization.Formatters.Soap
Imports System.Runtime.Serialization.Formatters.Binary
```

```vbnet
Namespace Apress.VisualBasicRecipes.Chapter02

    Public Class Recipe02_13

        ' Serialize an ArrayList object to a binary file.
        Private Shared Sub BinarySerialize(ByVal list As ArrayList)

            Using str As FileStream = File.Create("people.bin")
                Dim bf As New BinaryFormatter()
                bf.Serialize(str, list)
            End Using

        End Sub

        ' Deserialize an Arraylist object from a binary file.
        Private Shared Function BinaryDeserialize() As ArrayList
            Dim people As ArrayList = Nothing

            Using str As FileStream = File.OpenRead("people.bin")
                Dim bf As New BinaryFormatter()
                people = DirectCast(bf.Deserialize(str), ArrayList)
            End Using
            Return people

        End Function

        ' Serialize an ArrayList object to a SOAP file.
        Private Shared Sub SoapSerialize(ByVal list As ArrayList)

            Using str As FileStream = File.Create("people.soap")
                Dim sf As New SoapFormatter()
                sf.Serialize(str, list)
            End Using

        End Sub

        ' Deserialize an Arraylist object from a SOAP file.
        Private Shared Function SoapDeserialize() As ArrayList
            Dim people As ArrayList = Nothing

            Using str As FileStream = File.OpenRead("people.soap")
                Dim sf As New SoapFormatter()
                people = DirectCast(sf.Deserialize(str), ArrayList)
            End Using
            Return people

        End Function

        Public Shared Sub Main()
```

```
    ' Create and configure the ArrayList to serialize.
    Dim people As New ArrayList
    people.Add("Alex")
    people.Add("Dave")
    people.Add("Jason")
    people.Add("Robb")

    ' Serialize the list to a file in both binary and SOAP format.
    BinarySerialize(people)
    SoapSerialize(people)

    ' Rebuild the lists of people form the binary and SOAP
    ' serializations and display them to the console.
    Dim binaryPeople As ArrayList = BinaryDeserialize()
    Dim soapPeople As ArrayList = SoapDeserialize()

    Console.WriteLine("Binary People:")
    For Each s As String In binaryPeople
        Console.WriteLine(vbTab & s)
    Next

    Console.WriteLine(vbCrLf & "SOAP People:")
    For Each s As String In soapPeople
        Console.WriteLine(vbTab & s)
    Next

    ' Wait to continue.
    Console.WriteLine(vbCrLf & "Main method complete.  Press Enter")
    Console.ReadLine()

  End Sub

 End Class
End Namespace
```

Usage

To illustrate the different results achieved using the BinaryFormatter and SoapFormatter classes, Figure 2-1 shows the contents of the people.bin file generated using the BinaryFormatter class, and Figure 2-2 shows the contents of the people.soap file generated using the SoapFormatter class.

```
0000h: 00 01 00 00 00 FF FF FF FF 01 00 00 00 00 00 00   .....ÿÿÿÿ......
0010h: 00 04 01 00 00 00 1C 53 79 73 74 65 6D 2E 43 6F   .......System.C
0020h: 6C 6C 65 63 74 69 6F 6E 73 2E 41 72 72 61 79 4C   llections.ArrayL
0030h: 69 73 74 03 00 00 00 06 5F 69 74 65 6D 73 05 5F   ist....._items._
0040h: 73 69 7A 65 08 5F 76 65 72 73 69 6F 6E 05 00 00   size._version..
0050h: 08 08 09 02 00 00 00 04 00 00 00 04 00 00 00 10   ...............
0060h: 02 00 00 00 04 00 00 00 06 03 00 00 00 04 41 6C   ..............Al
0070h: 65 78 06 04 00 00 00 04 44 61 76 65 06 05 00 00   ex......Dave...
0080h: 00 05 4A 61 73 6F 6E 06 06 00 00 00 04 52 6F 62   ..Jason......Rob
0090h: 62 0B                                             b.
```

Figure 2-1. *Contents of the people.bin file*

```
1    <SOAP-ENV:Envelope xmlns:xsi="http://www.w3.org/2001/XMLSchema-instance"
     xmlns:xsd="http://www.w3.org/2001/XMLSchema" xmlns:SOAP-ENC="
     http://schemas.xmlsoap.org/soap/encoding/" xmlns:SOAP-ENV="
     http://schemas.xmlsoap.org/soap/envelope/" xmlns:clr="
     http://schemas.microsoft.com/soap/encoding/clr/1.0" SOAP-ENV:encodingStyle="
     http://schemas.xmlsoap.org/soap/encoding/">
2    <SOAP-ENV:Body>
3    <a1:ArrayList id="ref-1" xmlns:a1="
     http://schemas.microsoft.com/clr/ns/System.Collections">
4    <_items href="#ref-2"/>
5    <_size>4</_size>
6    <_version>4</_version>
7    </a1:ArrayList>
8    <SOAP-ENC:Array id="ref-2" SOAP-ENC:arrayType="xsd:anyType[4]">
9    <item id="ref-3" xsi:type="SOAP-ENC:string">Alex</item>
10   <item id="ref-4" xsi:type="SOAP-ENC:string">Dave</item>
11   <item id="ref-5" xsi:type="SOAP-ENC:string">Jason</item>
12   <item id="ref-6" xsi:type="SOAP-ENC:string">Robb</item>
13   </SOAP-ENC:Array>
14   </SOAP-ENV:Body>
15   </SOAP-ENV:Envelope>
```

Figure 2-2. *Contents of the people.soap file*

2-14. Read User Input from the Console

Problem

You want to read user input from the Windows console, either a line or character at a time.

Solution

Use the Read or ReadLine method of the System.Console class to read input when the user presses Enter. To read input without requiring the user to press Enter, use the Console.ReadKey method.

How It Works

The simplest way to read input from the console is to use the Shared Read or ReadLine methods of the Console class. These methods will cause your application to block, waiting for the user to enter input and press Enter. In both instances, the user will see the input characters in the console. Once the user presses Enter, the Read method will return an Integer value representing the next character of input data, or –1 if no more data is available. Since Read reads only one character, it must be called repeatedly to continue capturing user input. The ReadLine method will return a string containing all the data entered, or an empty string if no data was entered.

.NET Framework 2.0 adds the ReadKey method to the Console class, which provides a way to read input from the console without waiting for the user to press Enter. The ReadKey method waits for the user to press a key and returns a System.ConsoleKeyInfo object to the caller. By passing true as an argument to an overload of the ReadKey method, you can also prevent the key pressed by the user from being echoed to the console.

The returned ConsoleKeyInfo object contains details about the key pressed. The details are accessible through the properties of the ConsoleKeyInfo class summarized in Table 2-5.

Table 2-5. *Properties of the ConsoleKeyInfo Class*

Property	Description
Key	Gets a value of the System.ConsoleKey enumeration representing the key pressed. The ConsoleKey enumeration contains values that represent all of the keys usually found on a keyboard. These include all the character and function keys; navigation and editing keys like Home, Insert, and Delete; and more modern specialized keys like the Windows key, media player control keys, browser activation keys, and browser navigation keys.
KeyChar	Gets a Char value containing the Unicode character representation of the key pressed. Special keys such as Insert, Delete, and F1 through F12 do not have a Unicode representation and will return Nothing.
Modifiers	Gets a bitwise combination of values from the System.ConsoleModifiers enumeration that identifies one or more modifier keys pressed simultaneously with the console key. The members of the ConsoleModifiers enumeration are Alt, Control, and Shift.

The KeyAvailable method of the Console class returns a Boolean value indicating whether input is available in the input buffer without blocking your code.

The Code

The following example reads input from the console one character at a time using the ReadKey method. If the user presses F1, the program toggles in and out of "secret" mode, where input is masked by asterisks. When the user presses Escape, the console is cleared and the input the user has entered is displayed. If the user presses Alt-X or Alt-x, the example terminates.

```
Imports System
Imports System.Collections.Generic

Namespace Apress.VisualBasicRecipes.Chapter02

    Public Class Recipe02_14
        Public Shared Sub Main()

            ' Local variable to hold the key entered by the user.
            Dim key As ConsoleKeyInfo

            ' Control whether character or asterisk is displayed.
            Dim secret As Boolean = False

            ' Character list for the user data entered.
            Dim input As New List(Of Char)
            Dim msg As String = "Enter characters and press Escape to see input." ➥
& vbCrLf & "Press F1 to enter/exit Secret mode and Alt-X to exit."

            Console.WriteLine(msg)
```

```vb
    ' Process input until the users enters "Alt-X" or "Alt-x".
    Do
        ' Read a key from the console. Intercept the key so that it is not
        ' displayed to the console. What is displayed is determined later
        ' depending on whether the program is in secret mode.
        key = Console.ReadKey(True)

        ' Switch secret mode on and off.
        If key.Key = ConsoleKey.F1 Then
            If secret Then
                ' Switch secret mode off.
                secret = False
            Else
                ' Switch secret mode on.
                secret = True
            End If
        End If


        If key.Key = ConsoleKey.Backspace Then
        ' Handle Backspace.
            If input.Count > 0 Then
                ' Backspace pressed remove the last character.
                input.RemoveAt(input.Count - 1)

                Console.Write(key.KeyChar)
                Console.Write(" ")
                Console.Write(key.KeyChar)
            End If


            ' Handle Escape.
        ElseIf key.Key = ConsoleKey.Escape Then
            Console.Clear()
            Console.WriteLine("Input:  {0}{1}{1}", New ➥
String(input.ToArray), vbCrLf)
            Console.WriteLine(msg)
            input.Clear()

            ' Handle character input.
        ElseIf key.Key >= ConsoleKey.A And key.Key <= ConsoleKey.Z Then
            input.Add(key.KeyChar)

            If secret Then
                Console.Write("*")
            Else
                Console.Write(key.KeyChar)
            End If

        End If
```

```vb
        Loop While Not key.Key = ConsoleKey.X Or Not key.Modifiers = ➥
ConsoleModifiers.Alt

        ' Wait to continue.
        Console.WriteLine("{0}{0}Main method complete.  Press Enter", vbCrLf)
        Console.ReadLine()

    End Sub

  End Class
End Namespace
```

■ ■ ■

CHAPTER 3

Application Domains, Reflection, and Metadata

The power and flexibility of the Microsoft .NET Framework is enhanced by the ability to inspect and manipulate types and metadata at runtime. The recipes in this chapter describe how to use application domains, reflection, and metadata. Specifically, the recipes in this chapter describe how to do the following:

- Control the loading of assemblies and the instantiation of types in local and remote applica-tion domains (recipes 3-1, 3-3, 3-4, and 3-7)

- Create application domains into which you can load assemblies that are isolated from the rest of your application (recipe 3-2)

- Create types that are guaranteed to be unable to cross application domain boundaries (recipe 3-5) and types that have the capability to cross application domain boundaries (recipe 3-6)

- Pass simple configuration data between application domains (recipe 3-8)

- Unload application domains, which provides the only means through which you can unload assemblies at runtime (recipe 3-9)

- Inspect and test the type of an object using a variety of mechanisms built into the VB .NET language and capabilities provided by the objects themselves (recipes 3-10 and 3-11)

- Dynamically instantiate an object and execute its methods at runtime using reflection (recipe 3-12)

- Create custom attributes (recipe 3-13), allowing you to associate metadata with your program elements, and inspect the value of those custom attributes at runtime (recipe 3-14)

■Note An excellent reference for detailed information on all aspects of application domains and loading assemblies is *Customizing the Microsoft .NET Framework Common Language Runtime* by Steven Pratschner (Microsoft Press, 2005).

3-1. Load an Assembly into the Current Application Domain

Problem

You need to load an assembly into the current application domain at runtime.

Solution

Use the `Shared Load` method or the `LoadFrom` method of the `System.Reflection.Assembly` class.

■Note The `Assembly.LoadWithPartialName` method has been deprecated in .NET Framework 2.0. Instead, you should use the `Assembly.Load` method described in this recipe.

How It Works

Unlike with Win32, where the referenced DLLs are loaded when the process starts, the common language runtime (CLR) will automatically load the assemblies referenced by your assembly only when the metadata for their contained types is required. However, you can also explicitly instruct the runtime to load assemblies. The `Load` and `LoadFrom` methods both result in the runtime loading an assembly into the current application domain, and both return an `Assembly` instance that represents the newly loaded assembly. The differences between each method are the arguments you must provide to identify the assembly to load and the process that the runtime undertakes to locate the specified assembly.

The `Load` method provides overloads that allow you to specify the assembly to load using one of the following:

- A `String` containing the fully or partially qualified *display name* of the assembly
- A `System.Reflection.AssemblyName` containing details of the assembly
- A `Byte` array containing the raw bytes that constitute the assembly

A fully qualified display name contains the assembly's text name, version, culture, and public key token, separated by commas (for example, `System.Data, Version=2.0.0.0, Culture=neutral, PublicKeyToken=b77a5c561934e089`). When using a fully qualified name, all four fields are mandatory. If you need to specify an assembly that doesn't have a strong name, use `PublicKeyToken=null`. You can also specify a partial display name, but as a minimum, you must specify the assembly name (without the file extension).

In response to the `Load` call, the runtime undertakes an extensive process to locate and load the specified assembly. The following is a summary of this process (consult the section "How the Runtime Locates Assemblies" in the .NET Framework SDK documentation for more details):

1. If you specify a strong-named assembly, the `Load` method will apply the version policy and publisher policy to enable requests for one version of an assembly to be satisfied by another version. You specify the version policy in your machine or application configuration file using `<bindingRedirect>` elements. You specify the publisher policy in special resource assemblies installed in the global assembly cache (GAC).

2. Once the runtime has established the correct version of an assembly to use, it attempts to load strong-named assemblies from the GAC.

3. If the assembly is not strong named or is not found in the GAC, the runtime looks for applicable `<codeBase>` elements in your machine and application configuration files. A `<codeBase>` element maps an assembly name to a specific file or a uniform resource locator (URL). If the assembly is strong named, `<codeBase>` can refer to any location including Internet-based URLs; otherwise, `<codeBase>` must refer to a directory relative to the application directory. If the assembly doesn't exist at the specified location, `Load` throws a `System.IO.FileNotFoundException`.

4. If no <codeBase> elements are relevant to the requested assembly, the runtime will locate the assembly using *probing*. Probing looks for the first file with the assembly's name (with either a .dll or an .exe extension) in the following locations:

- The application root directory

- Directories under the application root that match the assembly's name and culture

- Directories under the application root that are specified in the private binpath using the <privatePath> attribute.

The Load method is the easiest way to locate and load assemblies but can also be expensive in terms of processing if the runtime needs to start probing many directories for a weak-named assembly. The LoadFrom method allows you to load an assembly from a specific location. If the specified file isn't found, the runtime will throw a FileNotFoundException. The runtime won't attempt to locate the assembly in the same way as the Load method—LoadFrom provides no support for the GAC, policies, <codeBase> elements, or probing.

The Code

The following code demonstrates various forms of the Load and LoadFrom methods. Notice that unlike the Load method, LoadFrom requires you to specify the extension of the assembly file.

```
Imports System
Imports System.Reflection
Imports System.Globalization

Namespace Apress.VisualBasicRecipes.Chapter03

    Public Class Recipe03_01

        Public Shared Sub ListAssemblies()

            ' Get an array of the assemblies loaded into the current
            ' application domain.
            Dim assemblies As Assembly() = AppDomain.CurrentDomain.GetAssemblies()

            For Each a As Assembly In assemblies
                Console.WriteLine(a.GetName)
            Next

        End Sub

        Public Shared Sub Main()

            ' List the assemblies in the current application domain.
            Console.WriteLine("**** BEFORE ****")
            ListAssemblies()

            ' Load the System.Data assembly using a fully qualified display name.
            Dim name1 As String = "System.Data,Version=2.0.0.0," + ➥
"Culture=neutral,PublicKeyToken=b77a5c561934e089"
            Dim a1 As Assembly = Assembly.Load(name1)
```

```
              ' Load the System.Xml assembly using an AssemblyName.
              Dim name2 As New AssemblyName()
              name2.Name = "System.Xml"
              name2.Version = New Version(2, 0, 0, 0)
              name2.CultureInfo = New CultureInfo("")   ' Neutral culture.
              name2.SetPublicKeyToken(New Byte() {&HB7, &H7A, &H5C, &H56, ➥
&H19, &H34, &HE0, &H89})
              Dim a2 As Assembly = Assembly.Load(name2)

              ' Load the SomeAssembly assembly using a partial display name.
              Dim a3 As Assembly = Assembly.Load("SomeAssembly")

              ' Load the assembly named C:\shared\MySharedAssembly.dll.
              Dim a4 As Assembly = Assembly.LoadFrom("C:\shared\MySharedAssembly.dll")

              ' List the assemblies in the current application domain.
              Console.WriteLine("{0}{0}**** AFTER ****", vbCrLf)
              ListAssemblies()

              ' Wait to continue.
              Console.WriteLine(vbCrLf & "Main method complete.  Press Enter.")
              Console.ReadLine()

          End Sub

      End Class
End Namespace
```

3-2. Create an Application Domain

Problem

You need to create a new application domain.

Solution

Use the Shared method CreateDomain of the System.AppDomain class.

How It Works

The simplest overload of the CreateDomain method takes a single String argument specifying a human-readable name (friendly name) for the new application domain. Other overloads allow you to specify evidence and configuration settings for the new application domain. *Evidence* refers to information, such as a strong name or application path, that is used by the CLR when making security decisions. You specify evidence using a System.Security.Policy.Evidence object, and you specify configuration settings using a System.AppDomainSetup object.

The AppDomainSetup class is a container of configuration information for an application domain. Table 3-1 lists some of the properties of the AppDomainSetup class that you will use most often when creating application domains. These properties are accessible after creation through members of the AppDomain object. Some have different names, and some are modifiable at runtime; refer to the .NET

Framework's software development kit (SDK) documentation on the AppDomain class for a comprehensive discussion.

Table 3-1. *Commonly Used AppDomainSetup Properties*

Property	Description
ApplicationBase	The directory where the CLR will look during probing to resolve private assemblies. Recipe 3-1 discusses probing. Effectively, ApplicationBase is the root directory for the executing application. By default, this is the directory containing the assembly. This is readable after creation using the AppDomain.BaseDirectory property.
ConfigurationFile	The name of the configuration file used by code loaded into the application domain. This is readable after creation using the AppDomain.GetData method with the key APP_CONFIG_FILE. By default, the configuration file is stored in the same folder as the application.exe file, but if you set ApplicationBase, it will be in that same folder.
DisallowPublisherPolicy	Controls whether the publisher policy section of the application configuration file is taken into consideration when determining which version of a strong-named assembly to bind to. Recipe 3-1 discusses publisher policy.
PrivateBinPath	A semicolon-separated list of directories that the runtime uses when probing for private assemblies. These directories are relative to the directory specified in ApplicationBase. This is readable after application domain creation using the AppDomain.RelativeSearchPath property.

The Code

The following code demonstrates the creation and initial configuration of an application domain:

```
Imports System
Namespace Apress.VisualBasicRecipes.Chapter03

    Public Class Recipe03_02

        Public Shared Sub Main()

            ' Instantiate an AppDomainSetup object.
            Dim setupInfo As New AppDomainSetup

            ' Configure the application domain setup information.
            setupInfo.ApplicationBase = "C:\MyRootDirectory"
            setupInfo.ConfigurationFile = "MyApp.config"
            setupInfo.PrivateBinPath = "bin;plugins;external"

            ' Create a new application domain passing Nothing as the evidence
            ' argument. Remember to save a reference to the new AppDomain as
            ' this cannot be retrieved any other way.
            Dim newDomain As AppDomain = AppDomain.CreateDomain("My New " & ➥
```

```
"AppDomain, Nothing, setupInfo)

        ' Wait to continue.
        Console.WriteLine(vbCrLf & "Main method complete.  Press Enter.")
        Console.ReadLine()

    End Sub

End Class
End Namespace
```

> **Note** You must maintain a reference to the AppDomain object when you create it because no mechanism exists to enumerate existing application domains from within managed code.

3-3. Execute an Assembly in a Different Application Domain

Problem

You need to execute an assembly in an application domain other than the current one.

Solution

Call the ExecuteAssembly or ExecuteAssemblyByName (in .NET Framework 2.0) method of the AppDomain object that represents the application domain, and specify the filename of an executable assembly.

How It Works

If you have an executable assembly that you want to load and run in an application domain, the ExecuteAssembly or ExecuteAssemblyByName method provides the easiest solution. The ExecuteAssembly method provides four overloads. The simplest overload takes only a String containing the name of the executable assembly to run; you can specify a local file or a URL. Other ExecuteAssembly overloads allow you to specify evidence for the assembly (which affects code access security) and arguments to pass to the assembly's entry point (equivalent to command-line arguments).

The ExecuteAssembly method loads the specified assembly and executes the method defined in metadata as the assembly's entry point (usually the Main method). If the specified assembly isn't executable, ExecuteAssembly throws a System.MissingMethodException. The CLR doesn't start execution of the assembly in a new thread, so control won't return from the ExecuteAssembly method until the newly executed assembly exits. Because the ExecuteAssembly method loads an assembly using partial information (only the filename), the CLR won't use the GAC or probing to resolve the assembly. (See recipe 3-1 for more information.)

The ExecuteAssemblyByName method provides a similar set of overloads and takes the same argument types as ExecuteAssembly, but instead of just the filename of the executable assembly, it takes the display name of the assembly. (See recipe 3-1 for more information about the structure of assembly display names.) This overcomes the limitations inherent in ExecuteAssembly as a result of supplying only partial names. Here is an example of using this method:

```
Dim domain As AppDomain = AppDomain.CreateDomain("NewAppDomain")
domain.ExecuteAssemblyByName("Recipe03-06, Version=1.0.0.0, Culture=neutral, ➥
PublicKeyToken=null", Nothing, args)
```

The Code

The following code demonstrates how to use the ExecuteAssembly method to load and run an assembly. The Recipe03_03 class creates an AppDomain and executes itself in that AppDomain using the ExecuteAssembly method. This results in two copies of the Recipe03-03 assembly loaded into two different application domains.

```
Imports System
Namespace Apress.VisualBasicRecipes.Chapter03

    Public Class Recipe03_03

        Public Shared Sub Main(ByVal args As String())

            ' For the purpose of this example, if this assembly is executing
            ' in an AppDomain with the friendly name NewAppDomain, do not
            ' create a new AppDomain. This avoids an infinite loop of
            ' AppDomain creation.
            If Not AppDomain.CurrentDomain.FriendlyName = "NewAppDomain" Then
                ' Create a new application domain.
                Dim domain As AppDomain = AppDomain.CreateDomain("NewAppDomain")

                ' Execute this assembly in the new application domain and
                ' pass the array of command-line arguments.
                domain.ExecuteAssembly("Recipe03-03.exe", Nothing, args)

            End If

            ' Display the command-line arguments to the screen prefixed with
            ' the friendly name of the AppDomain.
            For Each s As String In args
                Console.WriteLine(AppDomain.CurrentDomain.FriendlyName + " : " + s)
            Next

            ' Wait to continue.
            If Not AppDomain.CurrentDomain.FriendlyName = "NewAppDomain" Then
                Console.WriteLine(vbCrLf & "Main method complete.  Press Enter.")
                Console.ReadLine()
            End If

        End Sub

    End Class
End Namespace
```

Usage

If you run Recipe03-03 using the following command:

```
Recipe03-03 Testing AppDomains
```

you will see that the command-line arguments are listed from both the existing and new application domains:

```
NewAppDomain : Testing
NewAppDomain : AppDomains
Recipe03-03.exe : Testing
Recipe03-03.exe : AppDomains
```

3-4. Avoid Loading Unnecessary Assemblies into Application Domains

Problem

You need to pass an object reference across multiple application domain boundaries; however, to conserve memory and avoid impacting performance, you want to ensure the CLR loads only the object's type metadata into the application domains where it is required (that is, where you will actually use the object).

Solution

Wrap the object reference in a System.Runtime.Remoting.ObjectHandle, and unwrap the object reference only when you need to access the object.

How It Works

When you pass a marshal-by-value (MBV) object across application domain boundaries, the runtime creates a new instance of that object in the destination application domain. This means the runtime must load the assembly containing that type metadata into the application domain. Passing MBV references across intermediate application domains can result in the runtime loading unnecessary assemblies into application domains. Once loaded, these superfluous assemblies cannot be unloaded without unloading the containing application domain. (See recipe 3-9 for more information.)

The ObjectHandle class allows you to wrap an object reference so that you can pass it between application domains without the runtime loading additional assemblies. When the object reaches the destination application domain, you can unwrap the object reference, causing the runtime to load the required assembly and allowing you to access the object.

The Code

The following code contains some simple methods that demonstrate how to wrap and unwrap a System.Data.DataSet using an ObjectHandle:

```
Imports System
Imports System.Data
Imports System.Runtime.Remoting

Namespace Apress.VisualBasicRecipes.Chapter03

    Public Class Recipe03_04
```

```
    ' A method to wrap a DataSet.
    Public Function WrapDataset(ByVal ds As DataSet) As ObjectHandle

        ' Wrap the DataSet.
        Dim objHandle As New ObjectHandle(ds)

        ' Return the wrapped DataSet.
        Return objHandle

    End Function

    ' A method to unwrap a DataSet.
    Public Function UnwrapDataset(ByVal handle As ObjectHandle) As DataSet

        ' Unwrap the DataSet.
        Dim ds As DataSet = CType(handle.Unwrap, DataSet)

        ' Return the DataSet.
        Return ds

    End Function

  End Class
End Namespace
```

3-5. Create a Type That Cannot Cross Application Domain Boundaries

Problem

You need to create a type so that instances of the type are inaccessible to code in other application domains.

Solution

Ensure the type is nonremotable by making sure it is not serializable (no Serializable attribute) and it does not derive from the MarshalByRefObject class.

How It Works

On occasion, you will want to ensure that instances of a type cannot transcend application domain boundaries. To create a nonremotable type, ensure that it isn't serializable and that it doesn't derive (directly or indirectly) from the MarshalByRefObject class. If you take these steps, you ensure that an object's state can never be accessed from outside the application domain in which the object was instantiated—such objects cannot be used as arguments or return values in cross-application domain method calls.

Ensuring that a type isn't serializable is easy because a class doesn't inherit the ability to be serialized from its parent class. To ensure that a type isn't serializable, make sure it does not have System.SerializableAttribute applied to the type declaration.

Ensuring that a class cannot be passed by reference requires a little more attention. Many classes in the .NET class library derive directly or indirectly from `MarshalByRefObject`; you must be careful you don't inadvertently derive your class from one of these. Commonly used base classes that derive from `MarshalByRefObject` include `System.ComponentModel.Component`, `System.IO.Stream`, `System.IO.TextReader`, `System.IO.TextWriter`, `System.NET.WebRequest`, and `System.Net.WebResponse`. (Check the .NET Framework SDK documentation on `MarshalByRefObject`. The inheritance hierarchy for the class provides a complete list of classes that derive from it.)

3-6. Create a Type That Can Be Passed Across Application Domain Boundaries

Problem

You need to pass objects across application domain boundaries as arguments or return values.

Solution

Use marshal-by-value (MBV) or marshal-by-reference (MBR) objects.

How It Works

The .NET Remoting system (discussed in Chapter 10) makes passing objects across application domain boundaries straightforward. However, to those unfamiliar with .NET Remoting, the results can be very different from those expected. In fact, the most confusing aspect of using multiple application domains stems from the interaction with .NET Remoting and the way objects traverse application domain boundaries.

All types fall into one of three categories: nonremotable, MBV, or MBR. Nonremotable types cannot cross application domain boundaries and cannot be used as arguments or return values in cross-application domain calls. (Recipe 3-5 discusses nonremotable types.)

MBV types are serializable types. When you pass an MBV object across an application domain boundary as an argument or a return value, the .NET Remoting system serializes the object's current state, passes it to the destination application domain, and creates a new copy of the object with the same state as the original. This results in a copy of the MBV object existing in both application domains. The content of the two instances are initially identical, but they are independent; changes made to one instance are not reflected in the other instance. This often causes confusion as you try to update the remote object but are actually updating the local copy. If you want to be able to call and change an object from a remote application domain, the object needs to be an MBR type.

MBR types are those classes that derive from `System.MarshalByRefObject`. When you pass an MBR object across an application domain boundary as an argument or a return value, in the destination application domain, the .NET Remoting system creates a *proxy* that represents the remote MBR object. To any class in the destination application domain, the proxy looks and behaves like the remote MBR object that it represents. In reality, when a call is made against the proxy, the .NET Remoting system transparently passes the call and its arguments to the remote application domain and issues the call against the original object. Any results are passed back to the caller via the proxy. Figure 3-1 illustrates the relationship between an MBR object and the objects that access it across application domains via a proxy.

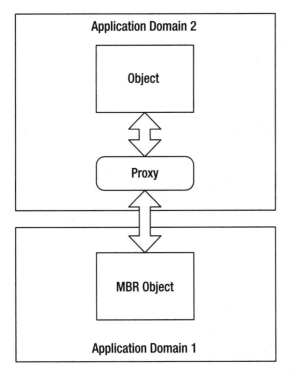

Figure 3-1. *An MBR object is accessed across application domains via a proxy.*

The Code

The following example highlights (in bold) the fundamental difference between creating classes that are passed by value (Recipe03_06MBV) and those passed by reference (Recipe03_06MBR). The code creates a new application domain and instantiates two remotable objects in it (discussed further in recipe 3-7). However, because the Recipe03_06MBV object is an MBV object, when it is created in the new application domain, it is serialized, passed across the application domain boundary, and deserialized as a new independent object in the caller's application domain. Therefore, when the code retrieves the name of the application domain hosting each object, Recipe03_06MBV returns the name of the main application domain, and Recipe03_06MBR returns the name of the new application domain in which it was created.

■**Note** This sample uses the CreateInstanceFromAndUnwrap method of the AppDomain class to create the instances of Recipe03_06MBV and Recipe03_06MBR in the new application domain. This method is covered in more detail in recipe 3-7.

```
Imports System
Namespace Apress.VisualBasicRecipes.Chapter03

    ' Declare a class that is passed by value.
    <Serializable()> _
    Public Class Recipe03_06MBV
```

```vb
        Public ReadOnly Property HomeAppDomain() As String
            Get
                Return AppDomain.CurrentDomain.FriendlyName
            End Get
        End Property

    End Class

    ' Declare a class that is passed by reference.
    Public Class Recipe03_06MBR
        Inherits MarshalByRefObject

        Public ReadOnly Property HomeAppDomain() As String
            Get
                Return AppDomain.CurrentDomain.FriendlyName
            End Get
        End Property

    End Class

    Public Class Recipe03_06
        Public Shared Sub Main(ByVal args As String())

            ' Create a new application domain.
            Dim newDomain As AppDomain = AppDomain.CreateDomain("My ➥
New AppDomain")

            ' Instantiate an MBV object in the new application domain.
            Dim mbvObject As Recipe03_06MBV = ➥
CType(newDomain.CreateInstanceFromAndUnwrap("Recipe03-06.exe", ➥
"Apress.VisualBasicRecipes.Chapter03.Recipe03_06MBV"), Recipe03_02MBV)

            ' Instantiate an MBR object in the new application domain.
            Dim mbrObject As Recipe03_06MBR = ➥
CType(newDomain.CreateInstanceFromAndUnwrap("Recipe03-06.exe", ➥
"Apress.VisualBasicRecipes.Chapter03.Recipe03_06MBR"), Recipe03_02MBR)

            ' Display the name of the application domain in which each of
            ' the objects is located.
            Console.WriteLine("Main AppDomain = {0}", ➥
AppDomain.CurrentDomain.FriendlyName)
            Console.WriteLine("AppDomain of MBV object = {0}", ➥
mbvObject.HomeAppDomain)
            Console.WriteLine("AppDomain of MBR object = {0}", ➥
mbrObject.HomeAppDomain)

            ' Wait to continue.
            Console.WriteLine(vbCrLf & "Main method complete.  Press Enter.")
            Console.ReadLine()

        End Sub

    End Class
End Namespace
```

Note Recipe 13-1 provides more details on creating serializable types, and recipe 10-16 describes how to create remotable types.

3-7. Instantiate a Type in a Different Application Domain

Problem

You need to instantiate a type in an application domain other than the current one.

Solution

Call the CreateInstance method or the CreateInstanceFrom method of the AppDomain object that represents the target application domain.

How It Works

The ExecuteAssembly method discussed in recipe 3-3 is straightforward to use, but when you are developing sophisticated applications that use application domains, you are likely to want more control over loading assemblies, instantiating types, and invoking object members within the application domain.

The CreateInstance and CreateInstanceFrom methods provide a variety of overloads that offer fine-grained control over the process of object instantiation. The simplest overloads assume the use of a type's default constructor, but both methods implement overloads that allow you to provide arguments to use any constructor.

The CreateInstance method loads a named assembly into the application domain using the process described for the Assembly.Load method in recipe 3-1. CreateInstance then instantiates a named type and returns a reference to the new object wrapped in an ObjectHandle (described in recipe 3-4). The CreateInstanceFrom method also instantiates a named type and returns an ObjectHandle-wrapped object reference; however, CreateInstanceFrom loads the specified assembly file into the application domain using the process described in recipe 3-1 for the Assembly.LoadFrom method.

AppDomain also provides two convenience methods named CreateInstanceAndUnwrap and CreateInstanceFromAndUnwrap that automatically extract the reference of the instantiated object from the returned ObjectHandle object; you must cast the returned Object to the correct type.

Caution Be aware that if you use CreateInstance or CreateInstanceFrom to instantiate MBV types in another application domain, the object will be created, but the returned Object reference won't refer to that object. Because of the way MBV objects cross application domain boundaries, the reference will refer to a copy of the object created automatically in the local application domain. Only if you create an MBR type will the returned reference refer to the object in the other application domain. (See recipe 3-6 for more details about MBV and MBR types.)

A common technique to simplify the management of application domains is to use a *controller class*. A controller class is a custom MBR type. You create an application domain and then instantiate your controller class in the application domain using CreateInstance. The controller class implements the functionality required by your application to manipulate the application domain and its contents. This could include loading assemblies, creating further application domains, cleaning up prior to deleting the application domain, or enumerating program elements (something you cannot normally do from outside an application domain). It is best to create your controller class in an assembly of its own to avoid loading unnecessary classes into each application domain. You should also be careful about which types you pass as return values from your controller to your main application domain to avoid loading additional assemblies.

The Code

The following code demonstrates how to use a simplified controller class named `PluginManager`. When instantiated in an application domain, `PluginManager` allows you to instantiate classes that implement the `IPlugin` interface, start and stop those plug-ins, and return a list of currently loaded plug-ins.

```
Imports System
Imports System.Reflection
Imports System.Collections
Imports System.Collections.Generic
Imports System.Collections.Specialized

Namespace Apress.VisualBasicRecipes.Chapter03

    ' A common interface that all plug-ins must implement.
    Public Interface IPlugin

        Sub Start()
        Sub [Stop]()

    End Interface

    ' A simple IPlugin implementation to demonstrate the PluginManager
    ' controller class.
    Public Class SimplePlugin
        Implements IPlugin

        Public Sub Start() Implements IPlugin.Start
            Console.WriteLine(AppDomain.CurrentDomain.FriendlyName & ➡
": SimplePlugin starting...")
        End Sub

        Public Sub [Stop]() Implements IPlugin.Stop
            Console.WriteLine(AppDomain.CurrentDomain.FriendlyName & ➡
": SimplePlugin stopping...")
        End Sub

    End Class

    ' The controller class, which manages the loading and manipulation
    ' of plug-ins in its application domain.
    Public Class PluginManager
        Inherits MarshalByRefObject
```

```vbnet
    ' A Dictionary to hold keyed references to IPlugin instances.
    Private plugins As New Dictionary(Of String, IPlugin)

    ' Default constructor.
    Public Sub New()

    End Sub

    ' Constructor that loads a set of specified plug-ins on creation.
    Public Sub New(ByVal pluginList As NameValueCollection)

        ' Load each of the specified plug-ins.
        For Each plugin As String In pluginList.Keys
            Me.LoadPlugin(pluginList(plugin), plugin)
        Next

    End Sub

    ' Load the specified assembly and instantiate the specified
    ' IPlugin implementation from that assembly.
    Public Function LoadPlugin(ByVal assemblyName As String, ➡
ByVal pluginName As String)

        Try
            ' Load the named private assembly.
            Dim assembly As Assembly = Reflection.Assembly.Load(assemblyName)

            ' Create the IPlugin instance, ignore case.
            Dim plugin As IPlugin = DirectCast(assembly.CreateInstance ➡
(pluginName, True), IPlugin)

            If Not plugin Is Nothing Then
                ' Add new IPlugin to ListDictionary
                plugins(pluginName) = plugin

                Return True
            Else
                Return False
            End If
        Catch
            ' Return false on all exceptions for the purpose of
            ' this example. Do not suppress exceptions like this
            ' in production code.
            Return False
        End Try

    End Function

    Public Sub StartPlugin(ByVal plugin As String)
```

```vbnet
        Try
            ' Extract the IPlugin from the Dictionary and call Start.
            plugins(plugin).Start()
        Catch
            ' Log or handle exceptions appropriately.
        End Try

    End Sub

    Public Sub StopPlugin(ByVal plugin As String)

        Try
            ' Extract the IPlugin from the Dictionary and call Stop.
            plugins(plugin).Stop()
        Catch
            ' Log or handle exceptions appropriately.
        End Try

    End Sub

    Public Function GetPluginList() As ArrayList

        ' Return an enumerable list of plug-in names. Take the keys
        ' and place them in an ArrayList, which supports marshal-by-value.
        Return New ArrayList(plugins.Keys)

    End Function

End Class

Public Class Recipe03_07

    Public Shared Sub Main(ByVal args As String())

        ' Create a new application domain.
        Dim domain1 As AppDomain = AppDomain.CreateDomain("NewAppDomain1")

        ' Create a PluginManager in the new application domain using
        ' the default constructor.
        Dim manager1 As PluginManager = CType(domain1.CreateInstanceAndUnwrap ➥
("Recipe03-07", "Apress.VisualBasicRecipes.Chapter03.PluginManager"), PluginManager)

        ' Load a new plugin into NewAppDomain1
        manager1.LoadPlugin("Recipe03-07", "Apress.VisualBasicRecipes." & ➥
"Chapter03.SimplePlugin")

        ' Start and stop the plug-in NewAppDomain1.
        manager1.StartPlugin("Apress.VisualBasicRecipes.Chapter03.SimplePlugin")
        manager1.StopPlugin("Apress.VisualBasicRecipes.Chapter03.SimplePlugin")

        ' Create a new application domain.
        Dim domain2 As AppDomain = AppDomain.CreateDomain("NewAppDomain2")
```

```
' Create a ListDictionary containing a list of plug-ins to create.
Dim pluginList As New NameValueCollection()
pluginList("Apress.VisualBasicRecipes.Chapter03.SimplePlugin") = ➡
"Recipe03-07"

' Create a PluginManager in the new application domain and
' specify the default list of plug-ins to create.
Dim manager2 As PluginManager = CType(domain1.CreateInstanceAndUnwrap ➡
("Recipe03-07", "Apress.VisualBasicRecipes.Chapter03.PluginManager", True, 0, ➡
Nothing, New Object() {pluginList}, Nothing, Nothing, Nothing), PluginManager)

' Display the list of plug-ins loaded into NewAppDomain2.
Console.WriteLine("{0}Plugins in NewAppDomain2:", vbCrLf)

For Each s As String In manager2.GetPluginList()
    Console.WriteLine(" - " & s)
Next

' Wait to continue.
Console.WriteLine(vbCrLf & "Main method complete.  Press Enter.")
Console.ReadLine()

    End Sub

End Class
End Namespace
```

Usage

If you run Recipe03-07, you should see the following:

```
NewAppDomain1: SimplePlugin starting...
NewAppDomain1: SimplePlugin stopping...

Plugins in NewAppDomain2:
 - Apress.VisualBasicRecipes.Chapter03.SimplePlugin
```

3-8. Pass Data Between Application Domains

Problem

You need a simple mechanism to pass general configuration or state data between application domains.

Solution

Use the SetData and GetData methods of the AppDomain class.

How It Works

You can pass data between application domains as arguments and return values when you invoke the methods and properties of objects that exist in other application domains. However, at times it is useful to pass data between application domains in such a way that the data is easily accessible by all code within the application domain.

Every application domain maintains a data cache that contains a set of name-value pairs. Most of the cache content reflects configuration settings of the application domain, such as the values from the AppDomainSetup object provided during application domain creation. (See recipe 3-2 for more information.) You can also use this data cache as a mechanism to exchange data between application domains or as a simple state storage mechanism for code running within the application domain.

The SetData method allows you to associate a string key with an object and store it in the application domain's data cache. The GetData method allows you to retrieve an object from the data cache using the key. If code in one application domain calls the SetData method or the GetData method to access the data cache of another application domain, the data object must support MBV or MBR semantics, or a System.Runtime.Serialization.SerializationException is thrown. (See recipe 3-6 for details on the characteristics required to allow objects to transcend application domain boundaries.)

When using the SetData or GetData methods to exchange data between application domains, you should avoid using the following keys, which are already used by the .NET Framework (refer to http://msdn2.microsoft.com/en-us/library/system.appdomain.getdata.aspx for more information):

- APP_CONFIG_FILE
- APP_NAME
- APPBASE
- APP_LAUNCH_URL
- LOADER_OPTIMIZATION
- BINPATH_PROBE_ONLY
- CACHE_BASE
- DEV_PATH
- DYNAMIC_BASE
- FORCE_CACHE_INSTALL
- LICENSE_FILE
- PRIVATE_BINPATH
- SHADOW_COPY_DIRS

The Code

The following example demonstrates how to use the SetData and GetData methods by passing a System.Collections.ArrayList between two application domains. After passing a list of pets to a second application domain for modification, the application displays the list. You will notice that the code running in the second application domain does not modify the original list because ArrayList is an MBV type, meaning that the second application domain has only a *copy* of the original list. (See recipe 3-6 for more details.)

```vbnet
Imports System
Imports System.Reflection
Imports System.collections

Namespace Apress.VisualBasicRecipes.Chapter03

    Public Class ListModifier

        Public Sub New()

            ' Get the list from the data cache.
            Dim list As ArrayList = CType(AppDomain.CurrentDomain.GetData("Pets"), ➡
ArrayList)

            ' Modify the list.
            list.Add("Turtle")

        End Sub

    End Class

    Public Class Recipe03_08

        Public Shared Sub Main()

            ' Create a new application domain.
            Dim domain As AppDomain = AppDomain.CreateDomain("Test")

            ' Create an ArrayList and populate with information.
            Dim list As New ArrayList
            list.Add("Dog")
            list.Add("Cat")
            list.Add("Fish")

            ' Place the list in the data cache of the new application domain.
            domain.SetData("Pets", list)

            ' Instantiate a ListModifier in the new application domain.
            domain.CreateInstance("Recipe03-08", "Apress.VisualBasicRecipes." & ➡
"Chapter03.ListModifier")

            ' Get the list and display its contents.
            For Each s As String In CType(domain.GetData("Pets"), ArrayList)
                Console.WriteLine(s)
            Next

            ' Wait to continue.
            Console.WriteLine(vbCrLf & "Main method complete.  Press Enter.")
            Console.ReadLine()

        End Sub

    End Class
End Namespace
```

3-9. Unload Assemblies and Application Domains

Problem

You need to unload assemblies or application domains at runtime.

Solution

You have no way to unload individual assemblies from a `System.AppDomain`. You can unload an entire application domain using the `Shared AppDomain.Unload` method, which has the effect of unloading all assemblies loaded into the application domain.

How It Works

The only way to unload an assembly is to unload the application domain in which the assembly is loaded. Unfortunately, unloading an application domain will unload all the assemblies that have been loaded into it. This might seem like a heavy-handed and inflexible approach, but with appropriate planning of your application domain, the assembly-loading structure, and the runtime dependency of your code on that application domain, it is not overly restrictive.

You unload an application domain using the `Shared AppDomain.Unload` method and passing it an `AppDomain` reference to the application domain you want to unload. You cannot unload the default application domain created by the CLR at startup.

The `Unload` method stops any new threads from entering the specified application domain and calls the `Thread.Abort` method on all threads currently active in the application domain. If the thread calling the `Unload` method is currently running in the specified application domain (making it the target of a `Thread.Abort` call), a new thread starts in order to carry out the unload operation. If a problem is encountered unloading an application domain, the thread performing the unload operation throws a `System.CannotUnloadAppDomainException`. Attempting to access the application domain after it has been unloaded will throw a `System.AppDomainUnloadedException`.

While an application domain is unloading, the CLR calls the finalization method of all objects in the application domain. Depending on the number of objects and nature of their finalization methods, this can take an arbitrary amount of time. The `AppDomain.IsFinalizingForUnload` method returns `True` if the application domain is unloading and the CLR has started to finalize contained objects; otherwise, it returns `False`.

The Code

This code fragment demonstrates the syntax of the `Unload` method:

```
' Create a new application domain.
Dim newDomain As AppDomain = AppDomain.CreateDomain("New Domain")

' Load assemblies into the application domain.
...

' Unload the new application domains.
AppDomain.Unload(newDomain)
```

3-10. Retrieve Type Information

Problem

You need to obtain a System.Type object that represents a specific type.

Solution

Use one of the following:

- The GetType operator
- The Shared GetType method of the System.Type class
- The Object.GetType method of an existing instance of the type
- The GetNestedType or GetNestedTypes method of the Type class
- The GetType or GetTypes method of the Assembly class
- The GetType, GetTypes, or FindTypes method of the System.Reflection.Module class

How It Works

The Type class provides a starting point for working with types using reflection. A Type object allows you to inspect the metadata of the type, obtain details of the type's members, and create instances of the type. Because of the type's importance, the .NET Framework provides a variety of mechanisms for obtaining references to Type objects.

One method of obtaining a Type object for a specific type is to use the GetType operator shown here:

```
Dim T1 As System.Type = GetType(System.Text.StringBuilder)
```

The type name is not enclosed in quotes and must be resolvable by the compiler (meaning you must reference the assembly). Because the reference is resolved at compile time, the assembly containing the type becomes a static dependency of your assembly and will be listed as such in your assembly's manifest.

Another method that returns a Type object is Object.GetType. This method returns the type of the object that calls it. The following is an example of its usage:

```
Dim myStringBuilder As New System.Text.StringBuilder
Dim myType As System.Type = myStringBuilder.GetType()
```

You can also use the Shared method Type.GetType, which takes a string containing the type name. Because you use a string to specify the type, you can vary it at runtime, which opens the door to a world of dynamic programming opportunities using reflection (see recipe 3-12). If you specify just the type name, the runtime must be able to locate the type in an already loaded assembly. Alternatively, you can specify an assembly-qualified type name. Refer to the .NET Framework SDK documentation for the Type.GetType method for a complete description of how to structure assembly-qualified type names. Table 3-2 summarizes some other methods that provide access to Type objects.

Table 3-2. *Methods That Return Type Objects*

Method	Description
Type.GetNestedType	Gets a specified type declared as a nested type (a type that is a member of another type) within the existing Type object.
Type.GetNestedTypes	Gets an array of Type objects representing the nested types declared within the existing Type object.
Assembly.GetType	Gets a Type object for the specified type declared within the assembly.
Assembly.GetTypes	Gets an array of Type objects representing the types declared within the assembly.
Module.GetType	Gets a Type object for the specified type declared within the module. (See recipe 1-3 for a discussion of modules.)
Module.GetTypes	Gets an array of Type objects representing the types declared within the module.
Module.FindTypes	Gets a filtered array of Type objects representing the types declared within the module. The types are filtered using a delegate that determines whether each Type should appear in the final array.

The Code

The following example demonstrates how to use the GetType operator and the Type.GetType method to return a Type object for a named type and from existing objects.

```
Imports System
Imports System.Text

Namespace Apress.VisualBasicRecipes.Chapter03

    Public Class Recipe03_10

        Public Shared Sub Main()

            ' Obtain type information using the GetType operator.
            Dim t1 As Type = GetType(StringBuilder)

            ' Obtain type information using the Type.GetType method.
            ' Case-sensitive, return Nothing if not found.
            Dim t2 As Type = Type.GetType("System.String")

            ' Case-sensitive, throw TypeLoadException if not found.
            Dim t3 As Type = Type.GetType("System.String", True)

            ' Case-insensitive, throw TypeLoadException if not found.
            Dim t4 As Type = Type.GetType("system.string", True, True)

            ' Assembly-qualified type name.
            Dim t5 As Type = Type.GetType("System.Data.DataSet,System.Data," & ➡
"Version=2.0.0.0,Culture=neutral,PublicKeyToken=b77a5c561934e089")
```

```
' Obtain type information using the Object.GetType method.
Dim sb As New StringBuilder
Dim t6 As Type = sb.GetType()

' Display the types.
Console.WriteLine("Type of T1:  {0}", t1.ToString)
Console.WriteLine("Type of T2:  {0}", t2.ToString)
Console.WriteLine("Type of T3:  {0}", t3.ToString)
Console.WriteLine("Type of T4:  {0}", t4.ToString)
Console.WriteLine("Type of T5:  {0}", t5.ToString)
Console.WriteLine("Type of T6:  {0}", t6.ToString)

' Wait to continue.
Console.WriteLine(vbCrLf & "Main method complete.  Press Enter.")
Console.ReadLine()

    End Sub

End Class
End Namespace
```

3-11. Test an Object's Type

Problem

You need to test the type of an object.

Solution

Use the inherited Object.GetType method to obtain a Type for the object. You can also use the TypeOf and Is operators to test an object's type.

How It Works

All types inherit the GetType method from the Object base class. As discussed in recipe 3-10, this method returns a Type reference representing the type of the object. The runtime maintains a single instance of Type for each type loaded, and all references for this type refer to this same object. This means you can compare two type references efficiently. For convenience, VB .NET provides the Is operator as a quick way to check whether an object is a specified type. In addition, Is will return True if the tested object is derived from the specified class. .NET Framework 2.0 includes the new IsNot operator for VB .NET. This operator is used to determine if an object is not a specified type. Furthermore, the Type.IsSubclassOf method can be used to determine if an object derives from the specified type.

When using the TypeOf, Is, and IsNot operators and the IsSubClassOf method, the specified type must be known and resolvable at compile time. A more flexible (but slower) alternative is to use the Type.GetType method to return a Type reference for a named type. The Type reference is not resolved until runtime, which causes a performance hit but allows you to change the type comparison at runtime based on the value of a string.

Finally, you can use the TryCast keyword to perform a safe cast of any object to a specified type. Unlike a standard cast that triggers a System.InvalidCastException if the object cannot be cast to the specified type, TryCast returns Nothing. This allows you to perform safe casts that are easy to verify, but the compared type must be resolvable at runtime.

■**Note** The runtime will usually maintain more than one instance of each type depending on how assemblies are loaded into application domains. Usually, an assembly will be loaded into a specific application domain, meaning a Type instance will exist in each application domain in which the assembly is loaded. However, assemblies can also be loaded by a runtime host in a domain-neutral configuration, which means the assembly's type metadata (and Type instances) is shared across all application domains. By default, only the mscorlib assembly is loaded in a domain-neutral configuration.

The Code

The following example demonstrates the various type-testing alternatives described in this recipe.

```
Imports System
Imports System.IO

Namespace Apress.VisualBasicRecipes.Chapter03

    Public Class Recipe03_11

        ' A method to test whether an object is an instance of a type.
        Public Shared Function IsType(ByVal obj As Object, ByVal myType ➥
As String) As Boolean

            ' Get the named type, use case-insensitive search, throw
            ' an exception if the type is not found.
            Dim t As Type = Type.GetType(myType, True, True)

            If t Is obj.GetType() Then
                Return True
            ElseIf obj.GetType.IsSubclassOf(t) Then
                Return True
            Else
                Return False
            End If

        End Function

        Public Shared Sub Main()

            ' Create a new StringReader for testing.
            Dim someObject As Object = New StringReader("This is a StringReader")

            ' Test if someObject is a StringReader by obtaining and
            ' comparing a Type reference using the TypeOf operator.
            If GetType(StringReader) Is someObject.GetType Then
                Console.WriteLine("GetType Is: someObject is a StringReader")
            End If
```

```
          ' Test if someObject is, or is derived from, a TextReader
          ' using the Is operator.
          If TypeOf someObject Is TextReader Then
              Console.WriteLine("TypeOf Is: someObject is a TextReader or a " & ➡
"derived class")
          End If

          ' Test if someObject is, or is derived from, a TextReader using
          ' the Type.GetType and Type.IsSubClassOf methods.
          If IsType(someObject, "System.IO.TextReader") Then
              Console.WriteLine("GetType: someObject is a TextReader")
          End If

          ' Use the TryCast keyword to perform a safe cast.
          Dim reader As StringReader = TryCast(someObject, StringReader)

          If Not reader Is Nothing Then
              Console.WriteLine("TryCast: someObject is a StringReader")
          End If

          ' Wait to continue.
          Console.WriteLine(vbCrLf & "Main method complete.  Press Enter.")
          Console.ReadLine()

      End Sub

   End Class
End Namespace
```

■**Tip** The Shared method GetUnderlyingType of the System.Enum class allows you to retrieve the underlying type of an enumeration.

3-12. Instantiate an Object Using Reflection

Problem

You need to instantiate an object at runtime using reflection.

Solution

Obtain a Type object representing the type of object you want to instantiate, call its GetConstructor method to obtain a System.Reflection.ConstructorInfo object representing the constructor you want to use, and execute the ConstructorInfo.Invoke method.

How It Works

The first step in creating an object using reflection is to obtain a Type object that represents the type you want to instantiate. (See recipe 3-10 for details.) Once you have a Type instance, call its GetConstructor method to obtain a ConstructorInfo representing one of the type's constructors.

The most commonly used overload of the GetConstructor method takes a Type array argument and returns a ConstructorInfo representing the constructor that takes the number, order, and type of arguments specified in the Type array. To obtain a ConstructorInfo representing a parameterless (default) constructor, pass an empty Type array (use the Shared field Type.EmptyTypes or new Type(0)); don't use Nothing, or GetConstructor will throw a System.ArgumentNullException. If GetConstructor cannot find a constructor with a signature that matches the specified arguments, it will return Nothing.

Once you have the desired ConstructorInfo, call its Invoke method. You must provide an Object array containing the arguments you want to pass to the constructor. If there are no arguments, pass Nothing. Invoke instantiates the new object and returns an object reference to it, which you must cast to the appropriate type.

Reflection functionality is commonly used to implement factories in which you use reflection to instantiate concrete classes that either extend a common base class or implement a common interface. Often both an interface and a common base class are used. The abstract base class implements the interface and any common functionality, and then each concrete implementation extends the base class.

No mechanism exists to formally declare that each concrete class must implement constructors with specific signatures. If you intend third parties to implement concrete classes, your documentation must specify the constructor signature called by your factory. A common approach to avoid this problem is to use a default (empty) constructor and configure the object after instantiation using properties and methods.

The Code

The following code fragment demonstrates how to instantiate a System.Text.StringBuilder object using reflection and how to specify the initial content for the StringBuilder (a String) and its capacity (an Integer):

```vbnet
Imports System
Imports System.Text
Imports System.Reflection

Namespace Apress.VisualBasicRecipes.Chapter03

    Public Class Recipe03_12

        Public Shared Function CreateStringBuilder() As StringBuilder

            ' Obtain the Type for the StringBuilder class.
            Dim type As Type = GetType(StringBuilder)

            ' Create a Type() containing Type instances for each
            ' of the constructor arguments - a String and an Integer.
            Dim argTypes As Type() = New Type() {GetType(System.String), ➥
GetType(System.Int32)}

            ' Obtain the ConstructorInfo object.
            Dim cInfo As ConstructorInfo = type.GetConstructor(argTypes)

            ' Create an Object() containing the constructor arguments.
            Dim argVals As Object() = New Object() {"Some string", 30}
```

```
        ' Create the object and cast it to a StringBuilder.
        Dim sb As StringBuilder = CType(cInfo.Invoke(argVals), StringBuilder)

        Return sb

    End Function

End Class
End Namespace
```

The following code demonstrates a factory to instantiate objects that implement the IPlugin interface (used in recipe 3-7):

```
Imports System
Imports System.Text
Imports System.Reflection

Namespace Apress.VisualBasicRecipes.Chapter03

    ' A common interface that all plug-ins must implement.
    Public Interface IPlugin

        Property Description() As String
        Sub Start()
        Sub [Stop]()

    End Interface

    ' An abstract base class from which all plug-ins must derive.
    Public MustInherit Class AbstractPlugIn
        Implements IPlugin

        ' Hold a description for the plug-in instance.
        Private m_description As String = ""

        ' Property to get the plug-in description.
        Public Property Description() As String Implements IPlugin.Description
            Get
                Return m_description
            End Get
            Set(ByVal value As String)
                m_description = value
            End Set
        End Property

        ' Declare the members of the IPlugin interface as abstract.
        Public MustOverride Sub Start() Implements IPlugin.Start
        Public MustOverride Sub [Stop]() Implements IPlugin.Stop

    End Class

    ' A simple IPlugin implementation to demonstrate the PluginFactory class.
    Public Class SimplePlugin
        Inherits AbstractPlugIn
```

```
        '  Implement Start method.
        Public Overrides Sub Start()
            Console.WriteLine(Description & ": Starting...")
        End Sub
        '  Implement Stop method.
        Public Overrides Sub [Stop]()
            Console.WriteLine(Description & ": Stopping...")
        End Sub

    End Class

    '  A factory to instantiate instances of IPlugin.
    NotInheritable Class PluginFactory

        Public Shared Function CreatePlugin(ByVal assembly As String, ➥
ByVal pluginName As String, ByVal description As String) As IPlugin

            '  Obtain the Type for the specified plug-in.
            Dim pluginType As Type = Type.GetType(pluginName & ", " & assembly)

            '  Obtain the ConstructorInfo object.
            Dim cInfo As ConstructorInfo = pluginType.GetConstructor ➥
(Type.EmptyTypes)

            '  Create the object and cast it to IPlugin.
            Dim plugin As IPlugin = TryCast(cInfo.Invoke(Nothing), IPlugin)

            '  Configure the new IPlugin.
            plugin.Description = description

            Return plugin

        End Function

        Public Shared Sub Main(ByVal args As String())

            '  Instantiate a new IPlugin using the PluginFactory.
            Dim plugin As IPlugin = PluginFactory.CreatePlugin("Recipe03-12", ➥
"Apress.VisualBasicRecipes.Chapter03.SimplePlugin", "A Simple Plugin")

            plugin.Start()
            plugin.Stop()

            '  Wait to continue.
            Console.WriteLine(vbCrLf & "Main method complete.  Press Enter.")
            Console.ReadLine()

        End Sub

    End Class
End Namespace
```

■Tip The System.Activator class provides two Shared methods named CreateInstance and CreateInstanceFrom that instantiate objects based on Type objects or strings containing type names. The key difference between using GetConstructor and Activator is that the constructor used by Activator is implied by the constructor arguments you pass to CreateInstance or CreateInstanceFrom. See the description of the Activator class in the .NET Framework SDK documentation for more details.

3-13. Create a Custom Attribute

Problem

You need to create a custom attribute.

Solution

Create a class that derives from the abstract (MustInherit) base class System.Attribute. Implement constructors, fields, and properties to allow users to configure the attribute. Apply the System. AttributeUsageAttribute attribute to your class to define the following:

- Which program elements are valid targets of the attribute
- Whether you can apply more than one instance of the attribute to a program element
- Whether the attribute is inherited by derived types

How It Works

Attributes provide a mechanism for associating declarative information (metadata) with program elements. This metadata is contained in the compiled assembly, allowing programs to retrieve it through reflection at runtime without creating an instance of the type. (See recipe 3-14 for more details.) Other programs, particularly the CLR, use this information to determine how to interact with and manage program elements.

To create a custom attribute, derive a class from the abstract (MustInherit) base class System. Attribute. Custom attribute classes by convention should have a name ending in Attribute (but this is not essential).

A custom attribute must have at least one Public constructor; the automatically generated default constructor is sufficient. The constructor parameters become the attribute's mandatory (or positional) parameters. When you use the attribute, you must provide values for these parameters in the order they appear in the constructor. As with any other class, you can declare more than one constructor, giving users of the attribute the option of using different sets of positional parameters when applying the attribute. Any Public non-constant writable fields and properties declared by an attribute are automatically exposed as named parameters. Named parameters are optional and are specified in the format of name-value pairs where the name is the property or field name. The following example will clarify how to specify positional and named parameters.

To control how and where a user can apply your attribute, apply the attribute AttributeUsageAttribute to your custom attribute class. AttributeUsageAttribute supports the one positional and two named parameters described in Table 3-3. The default values specify the value that is applied to your custom attribute if you do not apply AttributeUsageAttribute or do not specify a value for that particular parameter.

Table 3-3. *Members of the AttributeUsage Type*

Parameter	Type	Description	Default
ValidOn	Positional (required)	A member of the System.AttributeTargets enumeration that identifies the program elements on which the attribute is valid	None; you should set it to AttributeTargets.All
AllowMultiple	Named (optional)	Whether the attribute can be specified more than once for a single element	False
Inherited	Named (optional)	Whether the attribute is inherited by derived classes or overridden members	True

The Code

The following example shows a custom attribute named AuthorAttribute, which you can use to identify the name and company of the person who created an assembly or a class. AuthorAttribute declares a single Public constructor that takes a String containing the author's name. This means users of AuthorAttribute must always provide a positional String parameter containing the author's name. The Company property is Public, making it an optional named parameter, but the Name property is read-only—no Set accessor is declared—meaning that it isn't exposed as a named parameter.

```
Imports System
Namespace Apress.VisualBasicRecipes.Chapter03

    <AttributeUsage(AttributeTargets.Class Or AttributeTargets.Assembly, ➡
AllowMultiple:=True, Inherited:=True)> _
    Public Class AuthorAttribute
        Inherits System.Attribute

        Private m_Company As String    ' Author's company
        Private m_Name As String       ' Author's name

        ' Declare a public constructor.
        Public Sub New(ByVal name As String)
            Me.m_Name = name
            m_Company = ""
        End Sub

        ' Declare a property to get/set the company field.
        Public Property Company() As String
            Get
                Return m_Company
            End Get
```

```
            Set(ByVal value As String)
                m_Company = value
            End Set
        End Property

        ' Declare a property to get the internal field.
        Public ReadOnly Property Name() As String
            Get
                Return m_Name
            End Get
        End Property

    End Class
End Namespace
```

Usage

The following example demonstrates how to decorate types with `AuthorAttribute`:

```
Imports system

' Declare Todd as the assembly author. Assembly attributes
' must be declared after using statements but before any other.
' Author name is a positional parameter.
' Company name is a named parameter.
<Assembly: Apress.VisualBasicRecipes.Chapter03.Author("Todd", Company:="The" & ➥
"Code Architects")>
Namespace Apress.VisualBasicRecipes.Chapter03

    ' Declare a class authored by Todd.
    <Author("Todd", company:="The Code Architects")> _
    Public Class SomeClass
        ' Class implementation.
    End Class

    ' Declare a class authored by Kevin. Since the Company
    ' property is optional, we will leave it out for this test.
    <Author("Kevin")> _
    Public Class SomeOtherClass
        ' Class implementation.
    End Class
End Namespace
```

3-14. Inspect the Attributes of a Program Element Using Reflection

Problem

You need to use reflection to inspect the custom attributes applied to a program element.

Solution

All program elements, such as classes and subroutines, implement the System.Reflection. ICustomAttributeProvider interface. Call the IsDefined method of the ICustomAttributeProvider interface to determine whether an attribute is applied to a program element, or call the GetCustomAttributes method of the ICustomAttributeProvider interface to obtain objects representing the attributes applied to the program element.

How It Works

All the classes that represent program elements implement the ICustomAttributeProvider interface. This includes Assembly, Module, Type, EventInfo, FieldInfo, PropertyInfo, and MethodBase. MethodBase has two further subclasses: ConstructorInfo and MethodInfo. If you obtain instances of any of these classes, you can call the method GetCustomAttributes, which will return an Object array containing the custom attributes applied to the program element. The Object array contains only custom attributes, not those contained in the .NET Framework base class library.

The GetCustomAttributes method provides two overloads. The first takes a Boolean that controls whether GetCustomAttributes should return attributes inherited from parent classes. The second GetCustomAttributes overload takes an additional Type argument that acts as a filter, resulting in GetCustomAttributes returning only attributes of the specified type or those that derive from it.

Alternatively, you can call the IsDefined method. IsDefined provides a method that takes two arguments. The first argument is a Type object representing the type of attribute you are interested in, and the second is a Boolean that indicates whether IsDefined should look for inherited attributes of the specified type. IsDefined returns a Boolean indicating whether the specified attribute is applied to the program element and is less expensive than calling the GetCustomAttributes method, which actually instantiates the attribute objects.

The Code

The following example uses the custom AuthorAttribute declared in recipe 3-13 and applies it to the Recipe03_14 class. The Main method calls the GetCustomAttributes method, filtering the attributes so that the method returns only AuthorAttribute instances. You can safely cast this set of attributes to AuthorAttribute references and access their members without needing to use reflection.

```
Imports System
Namespace Apress.VisualBasicRecipes.Chapter03

    <Author("Kevin"), Author("Todd", Company:="The Code Architects")> _
    Public Class Recipe03_14

        Public Shared Sub Main()

            ' Get a Type object for this class.
            Dim myType As Type = GetType(Recipe03_14)

            ' Get the attributes for the type. Apply a filter so that only
            ' instances of AuthorAttributes are returned.
            Dim attrs As Object() = myType.GetCustomAttributes ➥
(GetType(AuthorAttribute), True)
```

```vbnet
            ' Enumerate the attributes and display their details.
            For Each a As AuthorAttribute In attrs
                Console.WriteLine(a.Name & ", " & a.Company)
            Next

            ' Wait to continue.
            Console.WriteLine(vbCrLf & "Main method complete.  Press Enter.")
            Console.ReadLine()

        End Sub

    End Class
End Namespace
```

CHAPTER 4

■ ■ ■

Threads, Processes, and Synchronization

One of the strengths of the Microsoft Windows operating system is that it allows many programs (processes) to run concurrently and allows each process to perform many tasks concurrently (using multiple threads). When you run an executable application, a new process is created. The process isolates your application from other programs running on the computer. The process provides the application with its own virtual memory and its own copies of any libraries it needs to run, allowing your application to execute as if it were the only application running on the machine.

Along with the process, an initial thread is created that runs your `Main` method. In single-threaded applications, this one thread steps through your code and sequentially performs each instruction. If an operation takes time to complete, such as reading a file from the Internet or doing a complex calculation, the application will be unresponsive (will *block)* until the operation is finished, at which point the thread will continue with the next operation in your program.

To avoid blocking, the main thread can create additional threads and specify which code each should start running. As a result, many threads may be running in your application's process, each running (potentially) different code and performing different operations seemingly simultaneously. In reality, unless you have multiple processors (or a single multicore processor) in your computer, the threads are not really running simultaneously. Instead, the operating system coordinates and schedules the execution of all threads across all processes; each thread is given a tiny portion (or *time slice*) of the processor's time, which gives the impression they are executing at the same time.

The difficulty of having multiple threads executing within your application arises when those threads need to access shared data and resources. If multiple threads are changing an object's state or writing to a file at the same time, your data will quickly become corrupted. To avoid problems, you must synchronize the threads to make sure they each get a chance to access the resource, but only one at a time. Synchronization is also important when waiting for a number of threads to reach a certain point of execution before proceeding with a different task and for controlling the number of threads that are at any given time actively performing a task—perhaps processing requests from client applications.

■Note Although it will not affect your multithreaded programming in VB .NET, it is worth noting that an operating system thread has no fixed relationship to a managed thread. The runtime host—the managed code that loads and runs the common language runtime (CLR)—controls the relationship between managed and unmanaged threads. A sophisticated runtime host, such as Microsoft SQL Server 2005, can schedule many managed threads against the same operating system thread or can perform the actions of a managed thread using different operating system threads.

This chapter describes how to control processes and threads in your own applications using the features provided by VB .NET and the Microsoft .NET Framework class library. Specifically, the recipes in this chapter describe how to do the following:

- Execute code in independent threads using features including the thread pool, asynchronous method invocation, and timers (recipes 4-1 through 4-6)

- Synchronize the execution of multiple threads using a host of synchronization techniques, including monitors, events, mutexes, and semaphores (recipes 4-7 and 4-11)

- Terminate threads and know when threads have terminated (recipes 4-12 and 4-13)

- Create thread-safe instances of the .NET collection classes (recipe 4-14)

- Start and stop running in new processes (recipes 4-15 and 4-16)

- Ensure that only one instance of an application is able to run at any given time (recipe 4-17)

As you will see in this chapter, delegates are used extensively in multithreaded programs to wrap the method that a thread should execute or that should act as a callback when an asynchronous operation is complete. As in VB .NET 1.1, the AddressOf operator is used to instruct the compiler to generate the necessary delegate instance.

4-1. Execute a Method Using the Thread Pool

Problem

You need to execute a task using a thread from the runtime's thread pool.

Solution

Declare a method containing the code you want to execute. The method's signature must match that defined by the System.Threading.WaitCallback delegate; that is, it must be a subroutine (not a function) and take a single Object argument. Call the Shared method QueueUserWorkItem of the System.Threading.ThreadPool class, passing it your method name. The runtime will queue your method and execute it when a thread-pool thread becomes available.

How It Works

Applications that use many short-lived threads or maintain large numbers of concurrent threads can suffer performance degradation because of the overhead associated with the creation, operation, and destruction of threads. In addition, it is common in multithreaded systems for threads to sit idle a large portion of the time while they wait for the appropriate conditions to trigger their execution. Using a thread pool provides a common solution to improve the scalability, efficiency, and performance of multithreaded systems.

The .NET Framework provides a simple thread-pool implementation accessible through the Shared members of the ThreadPool class. The QueueUserWorkItem method allows you to execute a method using a thread-pool thread by placing a work item into the queue. As a thread from the thread pool becomes available, it takes the next work item from the queue and executes it. The thread performs the work assigned to it, and when it is finished, instead of terminating, the thread returns to the thread pool and takes the next work item from the work queue.

Note If you need to execute a method with a signature that does not match the `WaitCallback` delegate, you must use one of the other techniques described in this chapter. See recipe 4-2 or 4-6.

The Code

The following example demonstrates how to use the `ThreadPool` class to execute a method named `DisplayMessage`. The example passes `DisplayMessage` to the thread pool twice: first with no arguments and then with a `MessageInfo` object, which allows you to control which message the new thread will display.

```vbnet
Imports System
Imports System.Threading

Namespace Apress.VisualBasicRecipes.Chapter04

    Class Recipe04_01
        ' A private class used to pass data to the DisplayMessage
        ' method when it is executed using the thread pool.
        Private Class MessageInfo
            Private m_Iterations As Integer
            Private m_Message As String

            ' A constructor that takes configuration settings for the thread.
            Public Sub New(ByVal iterations As Integer, ByVal message As String)

                m_Iterations = iterations
                m_Message = message

            End Sub

            ' Properties to retrieve configuration settings.
            Public ReadOnly Property Iterations() As Integer
                Get
                    Return m_Iterations
                End Get
            End Property

            Public ReadOnly Property Message() As String
                Get
                    Return m_Message
                End Get
            End Property

        End Class

        ' A method that conforms to the System.Threading.WaitCallback
        ' delegate signature. Displays a message to the console.
        Public Shared Sub DisplayMessage(ByVal state As Object)
            ' Safely case the state argument to a MessageInfo object.
            Dim config As MessageInfo = TryCast(state, MessageInfo)
```

```
            ' If the config argument is nothing, no arguments were passed to
            ' the ThreadPool.QueueUserWorkItem method; use default values.
            If config Is Nothing Then
                ' Display a fixed message to the console three times.
                For count As Integer = 1 To 3
                    Console.WriteLine("A thread pool example.")

                    ' Sleep for the purpose of demonstration. Avoid sleeping
                    ' on thread-pool threads in real applications.
                    Thread.Sleep(1000)
                Next
            Else
                ' Display the specified message the specified number of times.
                For count As Integer = 1 To config.Iterations
                    Console.WriteLine(config.Message)

                    ' Sleep for the purpose of demonstration. Avoid sleeping
                    ' on thread-pool threads in real applications.
                    Thread.Sleep(1000)
                Next
            End If
        End Sub

        Public Shared Sub Main()

            ' Execute DisplayMessage using the thread pool and no arguments.
            ThreadPool.QueueUserWorkItem(AddressOf DisplayMessage)

            ' Create a MessageInfo object to pass to the DisplayMessage method.
            Dim info As New MessageInfo(5, "A thread pool example with arguments.")

            ' Execute a DisplayMessage using the thread pool and providing an
            ' argument.
            ThreadPool.QueueUserWorkItem(AddressOf DisplayMessage, info)

            ' Wait to continue.
            Console.WriteLine("Main method complete.  Press Enter.")
            Console.ReadLine()

        End Sub
    End Class
End Namespace
```

Notes

Using the runtime's thread pool simplifies multithreaded programming dramatically; however, be aware that the implementation is a simple, general-purpose thread pool. Before deciding to use the thread pool, consider the following points:

- Each process has one thread pool, which supports by default a maximum of 25 concurrent threads per processor. You can change the maximum number of threads using the Shared ThreadPool.SetMaxThreads method, but some runtime hosts (IIS and SQL Server, for example) will limit the maximum number of threads and may not allow the default value to be changed at all.

- As well as allowing you to use the thread pool to execute code directly, the runtime uses the thread pool for other purposes internally. This includes the asynchronous execution of methods (see recipe 4-2), execution of timer events (see recipes 4-3 and 4-4), and execution of wait-based methods (see recipe 4-5). All of these uses can lead to heavy contention for the thread-pool threads, meaning that the work queue can become very long. Although the work queue's maximum length is limited only by the amount of memory available to the runtime's process, an excessively long queue will result in long delays before queued work items are executed. The Shared ThreadPool.GetAvailableThreads method returns the number of threads currently available in the thread pool. This can be useful in determining whether your application is placing too much load on the thread pool, indicating that you should increase the number of available threads using the ThreadPool.SetMaxThreads method.

- Where possible, avoid using the thread pool to execute long-running processes. The limited number of threads in the thread pool means that a handful of threads tied up with long-running processes can significantly affect the overall performance of the thread pool. Specifically, you should avoid putting thread-pool threads to sleep for any length of time.

- Thread-pool threads are background threads. You can configure threads as either foreground threads or background threads. Foreground and background threads are identical, except that a background thread will not keep an application process alive. Therefore, your application will terminate automatically when the last foreground thread of your application terminates.

- You have no control over the scheduling of thread-pool threads, and you cannot prioritize work items. The thread pool handles each work item in the sequence in which you add it to the work queue.

- Once a work item is queued, it cannot be canceled or stopped.

- Do not try to use thread-pool threads to directly update or manipulate Windows Forms controls, because they can be updated only by the thread that created them. For example, suppose that you have a form with a progress bar and a button that starts some action. When you click the button, a thread-pool thread is created to perform the action. Since the progress bar is part of the main application form, it exists on the main application's thread. Attempting to manipulate it from the thread-pool thread can cause unforeseen issues. The proper approach is to call delegate methods from the thread-pool threads and have them manipulate the interface for you.

4-2. Execute a Method Asynchronously

Problem

You need to start execution of a method and continue with other tasks while the method runs on a separate thread. After the method completes, you need to retrieve the method's return value.

Solution

Declare a delegate with the same signature as the method you want to execute. Create an instance of the delegate that references the method. Call the BeginInvoke method of the delegate instance to start executing your method. Use the EndInvoke method to determine the method's status as well as obtain the method's return value if complete.

How It Works

Typically, when you invoke a method, you do so synchronously, meaning that the calling code blocks until the method is complete. Most of the time, this is the expected, desired behavior because your code requires the operation to complete before it can continue. However, sometimes it is useful to execute a method asynchronously, meaning that you start the method in a separate thread and then continue with other operations.

The .NET Framework implements an asynchronous execution pattern that allows you to call any method asynchronously using a delegate. When you declare and compile a delegate, the compiler automatically generates two methods that support asynchronous execution: BeginInvoke and EndInvoke. When you call BeginInvoke on a delegate instance, the method referenced by the delegate is queued for asynchronous execution. BeginInvoke does not cause the code execution to wait, but rather returns immediately with an IAsyncResult instance. IAsyncResult is used when calling EndInvoke. The method referenced by BeginInvoke executes in the context of the first available thread-pool thread.

The signature of the BeginInvoke method includes the same arguments as those specified by the delegate signature, followed by two additional arguments to support asynchronous completion. These additional arguments are as follows:

- A System.AsyncCallback delegate instance that references a method that the runtime will call when the asynchronous method completes. The method will be executed by a thread-pool thread. Passing Nothing means no method is called, and you must use another mechanism (discussed later in this recipe) to determine when the asynchronous method is complete.

- A reference to an object that the runtime associates with the asynchronous operation for you. The asynchronous method does not use or have access to this object, but it is available to your code when the method completes, allowing you to associate useful state information with an asynchronous operation. For example, this object allows you to map results against initiated operations in situations where you initiate many asynchronous operations that use a common callback method to perform completion.

The EndInvoke method allows you to retrieve the return value of a method that was executed asynchronously, but you must first determine when it has finished. If your asynchronous method threw an exception, it will be rethrown so that you can handle it when you call EndInvoke. Here are the four techniques for determining whether an asynchronous method has finished:

- *Blocking* stops the execution of the current thread until the asynchronous method completes execution by calling EndInvoke. In effect, this is much the same as synchronous execution. However, you have the flexibility to decide exactly when your code enters the blocked state, giving you the opportunity to perform some additional processing before blocking.

- *Polling* involves repeatedly testing the state of an asynchronous method to determine whether it is complete by checking the IsCompleted property of the IAsyncResult returned from BeginInvoke. This is a simple technique and is not particularly efficient from a processing perspective. You should avoid tight loops that consume processor time; it is best to put the polling thread to sleep for a period using Thread.Sleep between completion tests. Because polling involves maintaining a loop, the actions of the waiting thread are limited, but you can easily update some kind of progress indicator.

- *Waiting* depends on the AsyncWaitHandle property of the IAsyncResult returned by BeginInvoke. This object derives from the System.Threading.WaitHandle class and is signaled when the asynchronous method completes. Waiting is a more efficient version of polling and also allows you to wait for multiple asynchronous methods to complete. You can specify time-out values to allow your waiting thread to notify a failure if the asynchronous method takes too long or if you want to periodically update a status indicator.

- A *callback* is a method that the runtime calls when an asynchronous operation completes. The calling code does not need to take any steps to determine when the asynchronous method is complete and is free to continue with other processing. Callbacks provide the greatest flexibility but also introduce the greatest complexity, especially if you have many asynchronous operations active concurrently that all use the same callback. In such cases, you must use appropriate state objects as the last parameter of BeginInvoke to match the completed methods against those you initiated.

■**Caution** Even if you do not want to handle the return value of your asynchronous method, you should call EndInvoke; otherwise, you risk leaking memory each time you initiate an asynchronous call using BeginInvoke.

The Code

The following code demonstrates how to use the asynchronous execution pattern. It uses a delegate named AsyncExampleDelegate to execute a method named LongRunningMethod asynchronously. LongRunningMethod simulates a long-running method using a configurable delay (produced using Thread.Sleep). The example contains the following five methods that demonstrate the various approaches to handling asynchronous method completion:

- The BlockingExample method executes LongRunningMethod asynchronously and continues with a limited set of processing. Once this processing is complete, BlockingExample blocks until LongRunningMethod completes. To block, BlockingExample calls the EndInvoke method of the AsyncExampleDelegate delegate instance. If LongRunningMethod has already finished, EndInvoke returns immediately; otherwise, BlockingExample blocks until LongRunningMethod completes.

- The PollingExample method executes LongRunningMethod asynchronously and then enters a polling loop until LongRunningMethod completes. PollingExample tests the IsCompleted property of the IAsyncResult instance returned by BeginInvoke to determine whether LongRunningMethod is complete; otherwise, PollingExample calls Thread.Sleep.

- The WaitingExample method executes LongRunningMethod asynchronously and then waits until LongRunningMethod completes. WaitingExample uses the AsyncWaitHandle property of the IAsyncResult instance returned by BeginInvoke to obtain a WaitHandle and then calls its WaitOne method. Using a time-out allows WaitingExample to break out of waiting in order to perform other processing or to fail completely if the asynchronous method is taking too long.

- The WaitAllExample method executes LongRunningMethod asynchronously multiple times and then uses an array of WaitHandle objects to wait efficiently until all the methods are complete.

- The CallbackExample method executes LongRunningMethod asynchronously and passes an AsyncCallback delegate instance (that references the CallbackHandler method) to the BeginInvoke method. The referenced CallbackHandler method is called automatically when the asynchronous LongRunningMethod completes, leaving the CallbackExample method free to continue processing. It's important to note that a reference to the AsyncExampleDelegate is passed to the BeginInvoke method via the DelegateAsyncState parameter. If you did not pass this reference, the callback method would not have access to the delegate instance and would be unable to call EndInvoke.

In VB .NET, it is not necessary to implicitly create a delegate instance, such as Dim longMethod As AsyncExampleDelegate = New AsyncExampleDelegate(AddressOf LongRunningMethod). Since the AddressOf operator does this automatically, the more efficient statement Dim longMethod As AsyncExampleDelegate = AddressOf LongRunningMethod is used instead.

■**Note** For the purpose of demonstrating the various synchronization techniques, the example performs several tasks that should be avoided when using the thread pool, including putting thread-pool threads to sleep and calling long-running methods. See recipe 4-1 for more suggestions on using the thread pool appropriately.

```vbnet
Imports System
Imports System.Threading
Imports System.Collections

Namespace Apress.VisualBasicRecipes.Chapter04

    Class Recipe04_02

        ' A utility method for displaying useful trace information to the
        ' console along with details of the current thread.
        Private Shared Sub TraceMsg(ByVal currentTime As DateTime, ➥
ByVal msg As String)

            Console.WriteLine("[{0,3}/{1}] - {2} : {3}", ➥
Thread.CurrentThread.ManagedThreadId, IIf(Thread.CurrentThread.IsThreadPoolThread, ➥
"pool", "fore"), currentTime.ToString("HH:mm:ss.ffff"), msg)

        End Sub

        ' A delegate that allows you to perform asynchronous execution of
        ' LongRunningMethod.
        Public Delegate Function AsyncExampleDelegate(ByVal delay As Integer, ➥
ByVal name As String) As DateTime

        ' A simulated long-running method.
        Public Shared Function LongRunningMethod(ByVal delay As Integer, ➥
ByVal name As String) As DateTime

            TraceMsg(DateTime.Now, name & " example - thread starting.")

            ' Simulate time-consuming process.
            Thread.Sleep(delay)

            TraceMsg(DateTime.Now, name & " example - thread stopping.")

            ' Return the method's completion time.
            Return DateTime.Now

        End Function

        ' This method executes LongRunningMethod asynchronously and continues
        ' with other processing. Once the processing is complete, the method
        ' blocks until LongRunningMethod completes.
        Public Shared Sub BlockingExample()

            Console.WriteLine(Environment.NewLine & "*** Running Blocking " & ➥
"Example ***")
```

```vb
    ' Invoke LongRunningMethod asynchronously. Pass Nothing for both the
    ' callback delegate and the asynchronous state object.
    Dim longMethod As AsyncExampleDelegate = AddressOf LongRunningMethod
    Dim asyncResult As IAsyncResult = longMethod.BeginInvoke(2000, ➥
"Blocking", Nothing, Nothing)

    ' Perform other processing until ready to block.
    For count As Integer = 1 To 3
        TraceMsg(DateTime.Now, "Continue processing until ready to block..")

        Thread.Sleep(300)
    Next

    ' Block until the asynchronous method completes.
    TraceMsg(DateTime.Now, "Blocking until method is complete...")

    ' Obtain the completion data for the asynchronous method.
    Dim completion As DateTime = DateTime.MinValue

    Try
        completion = longMethod.EndInvoke(asyncResult)
    Catch ex As Exception
        ' Catch and handle those exceptions you would if calling
        ' LongRunningMethod directly.
    End Try

    ' Display completion information.
    TraceMsg(completion, "Blocking example complete.")

End Sub

' This method executes LongRunningMethod asynchronously and then
' enters a polling loop until LongRunningMethod completes.
Public Shared Sub PollingExample()

    Console.WriteLine(Environment.NewLine & "*** Running Polling " & ➥
"Example ***")

    ' Invoke LongRunningMethod asynchronously. Pass Nothing for both the
    ' callback delegate and the asynchronous state object.
    Dim longMethod As AsyncExampleDelegate = AddressOf LongRunningMethod
    Dim asyncResult As IAsyncResult = longMethod.BeginInvoke(2000, ➥
"Polling", Nothing, Nothing)

    ' Poll the asynchronous method to test for completion. If not
    ' complete, sleep for 300ms before polling again.
    TraceMsg(DateTime.Now, "Poll repeatedly until method is complete.")

    While Not asyncResult.IsCompleted
        TraceMsg(DateTime.Now, "Polling...")
        Thread.Sleep(300)
    End While
```

```vb
    ' Obtain the completion data for the asynchronous method.
    Dim completion As DateTime = DateTime.MinValue

    Try
        completion = longMethod.EndInvoke(asyncResult)
    Catch ex As Exception
        ' Catch and handle those exceptions you would if calling
        ' LongRunningMethod directly.
    End Try

    ' Display completion information.
    TraceMsg(completion, "Polling example complete.")

End Sub

' This method executes LongRunningMethod asychronously and then
' uses a WaitHandle to wait efficiently until LongRunningMethod
' completes. Use of a time-out allows the method to break out of
' waiting in order to update the user interface or fail if the
' asynchronous method is taking too long.
Public Shared Sub WaitingExample()

    Console.WriteLine(Environment.NewLine & "*** Running Waiting " & ➥
"Example ***")

    ' Invoke LongRunningMethod asynchronously. Pass Nothing for both the
    ' callback delegate and the asynchronous state object.
    Dim longMethod As AsyncExampleDelegate = AddressOf LongRunningMethod
    Dim asyncResult As IAsyncResult = longMethod.BeginInvoke(2000, ➥
"Waiting", Nothing, Nothing)

    ' Wait for the asynchronous method to complete. Time-out after
    ' 300ms and display status to the console before continuing to
    ' wait.
    TraceMsg(DateTime.Now, "Waiting until method is complete.")

    While Not asyncResult.AsyncWaitHandle.WaitOne(300, False)
        TraceMsg(DateTime.Now, "Wait timeout...")
    End While

    ' Obtain the completion data for the asynchronous method.
    Dim completion As DateTime = DateTime.MinValue

    Try
        completion = longMethod.EndInvoke(asyncResult)
    Catch ex As Exception
        ' Catch and handle those exceptions you would if calling
        ' LongRunningMethod directly.
    End Try

    ' Display completion information.
    TraceMsg(completion, "Waiting example complete.")

End Sub
```

```vb
    ' This method executes LongRunningMethod asynchronously multiple
    ' times and then uses an array of WaitHandle objects to wait
    ' efficiently until all of the methods are complete. Use of a
    ' time-out allows the method to break out of waiting in order to
    ' update the user interface or fail if the asynchronous method
    ' is taking too long.
    Public Shared Sub WaitAllExample()

        Console.WriteLine(Environment.NewLine & "*** Running WaitAll " & ➡
"Example ***")

        ' An ArrayList to hold the IAsyncResult instances for each of the
        ' asynchonrous methods started.
        Dim asyncResults As New ArrayList(3)

        ' Invoke three LongRunningMethod asynchronously. Pass Nothing for
        ' both the callback delegate and the asynchronous state object. Add
        ' the IAsyncResult instance for each method to the ArrayList.
        Dim longMethod As AsyncExampleDelegate = AddressOf LongRunningMethod

        asyncResults.Add(longMethod.BeginInvoke(3000, "WaitAll 1", Nothing, ➡
Nothing))
        asyncResults.Add(longMethod.BeginInvoke(2500, "WaitAll 2", Nothing, ➡
Nothing))
        asyncResults.Add(longMethod.BeginInvoke(1500, "WaitAll 3", Nothing, ➡
Nothing))

        ' Create an array of WaitHandle objects that will be used to wait
        ' for the completion of all the asynchronous methods.
        Dim waitHandles As WaitHandle() = New WaitHandle(2) {}

        For count As Integer = 0 To 2
            waitHandles(count) = DirectCast(asyncResults(count), ➡
IAsyncResult).AsyncWaitHandle
        Next

        ' Wait for all three asynchronous methods to complete. Time-out
        ' after 300ms and display status to the console before continuing
        ' to wait.
        TraceMsg(DateTime.Now, "Waiting until all 3 methods are complete...")

        While Not WaitHandle.WaitAll(waitHandles, 300, False)
            TraceMsg(DateTime.Now, "WaitAll timeout...")
        End While

        ' Inspect the completion data for each method, and determine the
        ' time at which the final method completed.
        Dim completion As DateTime = DateTime.MinValue

        For Each result As IAsyncResult In asyncResults
            Try
                Dim completedTime As DateTime = longMethod.EndInvoke(result)
                If completedTime > completion Then completion = completedTime
            Catch ex As Exception
```

```
                    '  Catch and handle those exceptions you would if calling
                    '  LongRunningMethod directly.
                End Try
            Next

            '  Display completion information.
            TraceMsg(completion, "WaitAll example complete.")

        End Sub

        '  This method executes LongRunningMethod asnchronously and passes
        '  an AsyncCallback delegate instance. The referenced CallbackHandler
        '  method is called automatically when the asynchronous method
        '  completes, leaving this method free to continue processing.
        Public Shared Sub CallbackExample()

            Console.WriteLine(Environment.NewLine & "*** Running Callback" & ➡
        "Example ***")

            '  Invoke LongRunningMethod asynchronously. Pass an AsyncCallback
            '  delegate instance referencing the CallbackHandler method that
            '  will be called automatically when the asynchronous method
            '  completes. Pass a reference to the AsyncExampleDelegate delegate
            '  instance as asynchronous state; otherwise, the callback method
            '  has no access to the delegate instance in order to call EndInvoke.
            Dim longMethod As AsyncExampleDelegate = AddressOf LongRunningMethod
            Dim asyncResult As IAsyncResult = longMethod.BeginInvoke(2000, ➡
        "Callback", AddressOf CallbackHandler, longMethod)

            '  Continue with other processing.
            For count As Integer = 0 To 15
                TraceMsg(DateTime.Now, "Continue processing...")
                Thread.Sleep(300)
            Next

        End Sub

        '  A method to handle asynchronous completion using callbacks.
        Public Shared Sub CallbackHandler(ByVal result As IAsyncResult)
            '  Extract the reference to the AsyncExampleDelegate instance
            '  from the IAsyncResult instance. This allows you to obtain the
            '  completion data.
            Dim longMethod As AsyncExampleDelegate = DirectCast(result.AsyncState, ➡
        AsyncExampleDelegate)

            '  Obtain the completion data for the asynchronous method.
            Dim completion As DateTime = DateTime.MinValue

            Try
                completion = longMethod.EndInvoke(result)
            Catch ex As Exception
                '  Catch and handle those exceptions you would if calling
                '  LongRunningMethod directly.
            End Try
```

```
            ' Display completion information.
            TraceMsg(completion, "Callback example complete.")

        End Sub

        <MTAThread()> _
        Public Shared Sub Main()

            ' Demonstrate the various approaches to asynchronous method completion.
            BlockingExample()
            PollingExample()
            WaitingExample()
            WaitAllExample()
            CallbackExample()

            ' Wait to continue.
            Console.WriteLine(Environment.NewLine)
            Console.WriteLine("Main method complete. Press Enter.")
            Console.ReadLine()

        End Sub
    End Class
End Namespace
```

4-3. Execute a Method Periodically

Problem

You need to execute a method in a separate thread periodically.

Solution

Declare a method containing the code you want to execute periodically. The method's signature must match that defined by the System.Threading.TimerCallback delegate; in other words, it must be a subroutine (not a function) and take a single Object argument. Create a System.Threading. Timer object and pass it the method you want to execute, along with a state Object that the timer will pass to your method when the timer expires. The runtime will wait until the timer expires, and then call your method using a thread from the thread pool.

■Tip If you are implementing a timer in a Windows Forms application, you should consider using the System. Windows.Forms.Timer, which also provides additional support in Visual Studio that allows you to drag the timer from your Toolbox onto your application. For server-based applications where you want to signal multiple listeners each time the timer fires, consider using the System.Timers.Timer class, which notifies listeners using events.

How It Works

It is often useful to execute a method at regular intervals. For example, you might need to clean a data cache every 20 minutes. The System.Threading.Timer class makes the periodic execution of methods straightforward, allowing you to execute a method referenced by a TimerCallback delegate at specified intervals. The referenced method executes in the context of a thread from the thread pool. (See recipe 4-1 for notes on the appropriate use of thread-pool threads.)

When you create a `Timer` object, you specify two time intervals. The first value specifies the millisecond delay until the `Timer` first executes your method. Specify 0 to execute the method immediately, and specify `System.Threading.Timeout.Infinite` (which is –1) to create the `Timer` in an unstarted state. The second value specifies the interval in milliseconds; then the `Timer` will repeatedly call your method following the initial execution. If you specify a value of 0 or `Timeout.Infinite`, the `Timer` will execute the method only once (as long as the initial delay is not `Timeout.Infinite`). You can specify the time intervals as `Integer`, `Long`, `UInteger`, or `System.TimeSpan` values.

Once you have created a `Timer` object, you can modify the intervals used by the timer using the `Change` method, but you cannot change the method that is called. When you have finished with a `Timer` object, you should call its `Dispose` method to free system resources held by the timer. Disposing of the `Timer` object cancels any method that is scheduled for execution.

The Code

The `TimerExample` class shown next demonstrates how to use a `Timer` object to call a method named `TimerHandler`. Initially, the `Timer` object is configured to call `TimerHandler` after 2 seconds and then at 1-second intervals. The example allows you to enter a new millisecond interval in the console, which is applied using the `Timer.Change` method.

```
Imports System
Imports System.Threading

Namespace Apress.VisualBasicRecipes.Chapter04

    Class Recipe04_03

        Public Shared Sub Main()

            ' Create the state object that is passed to the TimerHandler
            ' method when it is triggered. In this case, a message to display.
            Dim state As String = "Timer expired."

            Console.WriteLine("{0} : Creating Timer.", ➥
DateTime.Now.ToString("HH:mm:ss.ffff"))

            ' Create a Timer that fires first after 2 seconds and then every
            ' second. The threadTimer object is automatically disposed at the
            ' end of the Using block.
            Using threadTimer As New Timer(AddressOf TimerTriggered, state, 2000, ➥
1000)
                Dim period As Integer

                ' Read the new timer interval from the console until the
                ' user enters 0 (zero). Invalid values use a default value
                ' of 0, which will stop the example.
                Do
                    Try
                        period = Int32.Parse(Console.ReadLine())
                    Catch ex As FormatException
                        period = 0
                    End Try
```

```
                        ' Change the timer to fire using the new interval starting
                        ' immediately.
                        If period > 0 Then threadTimer.Change(0, period)

                    Loop While period > 0
                End Using

                ' Wait to continue.
                Console.WriteLine("Main method complete. Press Enter.")
                Console.ReadLine()

        End Sub

        Private Shared Sub TimerTriggered(ByVal state As Object)
            Console.WriteLine("{0} : {1}", DateTime.Now.ToString("HH:mm:ss.ffff"), ➥
state)
        End Sub

    End Class
End Namespace
```

4-4. Execute a Method at a Specific Time

Problem

You need to execute a method in a separate thread at a specific time.

Solution

Declare a method containing the code you want to execute. The method's signature must match that defined by the System.Threading.TimerCallback delegate; that is, it must be a subroutine (not a function) and take a single Object argument. Create a System.Threading.Timer object, and pass it the method you want to execute along with a state Object that the timer will pass to your method when the timer expires. Calculate the time difference between the current time and the desired execution time, and configure the Timer object to fire once after this period of time.

How It Works

Executing a method at a particular time is often useful. For example, you might need to back up data at 1 a.m. daily. Although primarily used for calling methods at regular intervals, the Timer object also provides the flexibility to call a method at a specific time.

When you create a Timer object, you specify two time intervals. The first value specifies the millisecond delay until the Timer first executes your method. To execute the method at a specific time, you should set this value to the difference between the current time (System.DateTime.Now) and the desired execution time. The second value specifies the interval after which the Timer will repeatedly call your method following the initial execution. If you specify a value of 0, System.Threading.Timeout.Infinite, or TimeSpan(-1), the Timer object will execute the method only once. If you need the method to execute at a specific time every day, you can easily set this value using TimeSpan.FromDays(1), which represents the number of milliseconds in 24 hours.

The Code

The following code demonstrates how to use a `Timer` object to execute a method at a specified time. The `RunAt` method calculates the `TimeSpan` between the current time and a time specified on the command line (in RFC1123 format) and configures a `Timer` object to fire once after that period of time.

```
Imports System
Imports System.Threading
Imports System.Globalization

Namespace Apress.VisualBasicRecipes.Chapter04

    Class Recipe04_04
        Public Shared Sub RunAt(ByVal execTime As DateTime)

            ' Calculate the difference between the specified execution
            ' time and the current time.
            Dim waitTime As TimeSpan = execTime - DateTime.Now

            ' Check if a time in the past was specified. If it was, set
            ' the waitTime to TimeSpan(0) which will cause the timer
            ' to execute immediately.
            If waitTime < New TimeSpan(0) Then
                Console.WriteLine("A 'Past' time was specified.")
                Console.WriteLine("Timer will fire immediately.")
                waitTime = New TimeSpan(0)
            End If

            ' Create a Timer that fires once at the specified time. Specify
            ' an interval of -1 to stop the timer executing the method
            ' repeatedly.
            Dim threadTimer As New Timer(AddressOf TimerTriggered, ➥
"Timer Triggered", waitTime, New TimeSpan(-1))

        End Sub

        Private Shared Sub TimerTriggered(ByVal state As Object)
            Console.WriteLine("{0} : {1}", DateTime.Now.ToString("HH:mm:ss.ffff"), ➥
 state)
            Console.WriteLine("Main method complete. Press Enter.")
        End Sub

        Public Shared Sub Main(ByVal args As String())

            Dim execTime As DateTime

            ' Ensure there is an execution time specified on the command line.
            If args.Length > 0 Then
                ' Convert the string to a datetime. Support only the RFC1123
                ' DateTime pattern.
                Try
                    execTime = DateTime.ParseExact(args(0), "r", Nothing)
                    Console.WriteLine("Current time    : " & ➥
```

```
DateTime.Now.ToString("r"))
                    Console.WriteLine("Execution time   : " & ➥
execTime.ToString("r"))

                    RunAt(execTime)
            Catch ex As FormatException
                    Console.WriteLine("Execution time must be of the " & ➥
"format:{0}{1}{2}", ControlChars.NewLine, ControlChars.Tab, ➥
CultureInfo.CurrentCulture.DateTimeFormat.RFC1123Pattern)
            End Try

            ' Wait to continue.
            Console.WriteLine("Waiting for Timer...")
            Console.ReadLine()
        Else
            Console.WriteLine("Specify the time you want the method to " & ➥
"execute using the format :{0}{1} {2}", ControlChars.NewLine, ControlChars.Tab, ➥
CultureInfo.CurrentCulture.DateTimeFormat.RFC1123Pattern)
        End If
    End Sub
End Class

End Namespace
```

Usage

If you run Recipe04-04 using the following command:

Recipe04-04 "Sat, 24 Mar 2007 18:25:00 GMT"

you will see output similar to the following:

```
Current time    : Sat, 24 Mar 2007 18:24:25 GMT
Execution time  : Sat, 24 Mar 2007 18:25:00 GMT
Waiting for Timer...
18:25:00.0000 : Timer Triggered
Main method complete. Press Enter.
```

4-5. Execute a Method by Signaling a WaitHandle Object

Problem

You need to execute one or more methods automatically when an object derived from System.Threading.WaitHandle is signaled.

Solution

Declare a method containing the code you want to execute. The method's signature must match that defined by the System.Threading.WaitOrTimerCallback delegate. Using the Shared ThreadPool.

RegisterWaitForSingleObject method, register the method to execute and the WaitHandle object that will trigger execution when signaled.

How It Works

You can use classes derived from the WaitHandle class to trigger the execution of a method. Using the RegisterWaitForSingleObject method of the ThreadPool class, you can register a WaitOrTimerCallback delegate instance for execution by a thread-pool thread when a specified WaitHandle-derived object enters a signaled state. You can configure the thread pool to execute the method only once or to automatically reregister the method for execution each time the WaitHandle is signaled. If the WaitHandle is already signaled when you call RegisterWaitForSingleObject, the method will execute immediately. The Unregister method of the System.Threading.RegisteredWaitHandle object returned by the RegisterWaitForSingleObject method is used to cancel a registered wait operation.

The class most commonly used as a trigger is AutoResetEvent, which automatically returns to an unsignaled state after it is signaled. However, you can also use the ManualResetEvent, Mutex, and Semaphore classes, which require you to change the signaled state manually. AutoResetEvent and ManualResetEvent derive from the EventWaitHandle class, which in turn derives from WaitHandle.

The Code

The following example demonstrates how to use an AutoResetEvent to trigger the execution of a method named ResetEventHandler. (The AutoResetEvent class is discussed further in recipe 4-8.)

```vb
Imports System
Imports System.Threading

Namespace Apress.VisualBasicRecipes.Chapter04

    Class Recipe04_04

        ' A method that is executed when the AutoResetEvent is signaled
        ' or the wait operation times out.
        Private Shared Sub ResetEventHandler(ByVal state As Object, ByVal ➡
timedOut As Boolean)

            ' Display an appropriate message to the console based on whether
            ' the wait timed out or the AutoResetEvent was signaled.
            If timedOut Then
                Console.WriteLine("{0} : Wait timed out.", ➡
DateTime.Now.ToString("HH:mm:ss.ffff"))
            Else
                Console.WriteLine("{0} : {1}", ➡
DateTime.Now.ToString("HH:mm:ss.ffff"), state)
            End If

        End Sub

        Public Shared Sub Main()

            ' Create the new AutoResetEvent in an unsignaled state.
            Dim autoEvent As New AutoResetEvent(False)
```

```
        ' Create the state object that is passed to the event handler
        ' method when it is triggered. In this case, a message to display.
        Dim state As String = "AutoResetEvent signaled."

        ' Register the ResetEventHandler method to wait for the AutoResetEvent
        ' to be signaled. Set a time-out of 3 seconds and configure the wait
        ' operation to reset after activation (last argument).
        Dim handle As RegisteredWaitHandle = ➥
ThreadPool.RegisterWaitForSingleObject(autoEvent, AddressOf ResetEventHandler, ➥
state, 3000, False)

        Console.WriteLine("Press ENTER to signal the AutoResetEvent or enter" & ➥
"""CANCEL""" to unregister the wait operation.")

        While Not Console.ReadLine.ToUpper = "CANCEL"
            ' If "CANCEL" has not been entered into the console, signal
            ' the AutoResetEvent, which will cause the EventHandler
            ' method to execute. The AutoResetEvent will automatically
            ' revert to an unsignaled state.
            autoEvent.Set()
        End While

        ' Unregister the wait operation.
        Console.WriteLine("Unregistering wait operation.")
        handle.Unregister(Nothing)

        ' Wait to continue.
        Console.WriteLine("Main method complete. Press Enter.")
        Console.ReadLine()

    End Sub

    End Class
End Namespace
```

4-6. Execute a Method Using a New Thread

Problem

You need to execute code in its own thread, and you want complete control over the thread's state and operation.

Solution

Declare a method containing the code you want to execute. The method's signature must match that defined by the System.Threading.ThreadStart or System.Threading.ParameterizedThreadStart delegate. Create a new System.Threading.Thread object, and pass the method delegate as an argument to its constructor. Call the Thread.Start method to start the execution of your method.

How It Works

For maximum control and flexibility when creating multithreaded applications, you need to take a direct role in creating and managing threads. This is the most complex approach to multithreaded programming, but it is the only way to overcome the restrictions and limitations inherent in the approaches using thread-pool threads, as discussed in the preceding recipes. The Thread class provides the mechanism through which you create and control threads. To create and start a new thread, follow this process:

1. Define a method that matches the ThreadStart or ParameterizedThreadStart delegate. The ThreadStart delegate takes no arguments and must be a subroutine (not a function). This means you cannot easily pass data to your new thread. The ParameterizedThreadStart delegate must also be a subroutine but takes a single Object as an argument, allowing you to pass data to the method you want to run. (The ParameterizedThreadStart delegate is a welcome addition to .NET Framework 2.0.) The method you want to execute can be Shared or an instance method.

2. Create a new Thread object, and pass a delegate to your method as an argument to the Thread constructor. The new thread has an initial state of Unstarted (a member of the System. Threading.ThreadState enumeration) and is a foreground thread by default. If you want to configure it to be a background thread, you need to set its IsBackground property to True.

3. Call Start on the Thread object, which changes its state to ThreadState.Running and begins execution of your method. If you need to pass data to your method, include it as an argument to the Start call. If you call Start more than once, it will throw a System.Threading. ThreadStateException.

The Code

The following code demonstrates how to execute a method in a new thread and how to pass data to the new thread.

```
Imports System
Imports System.Threading

Namespace Apress.VisualBasicRecipes.Chapter04

    Class Recipe04_04

        ' A utility method for displaying useful trace information to the
        ' console along with details of the current thread.
        Private Shared Sub TraceMsg(ByVal msg As String)
            Console.WriteLine("[{0,3}] - {1} : {2}", ➥
Thread.CurrentThread.ManagedThreadId, DateTime.Now.ToString("HH:mm:ss.ffff"), msg)
        End Sub

        ' A private class used to pass initialization data to a new thread.
        Private Class ThreadStartData

            ' Member variables hold initialization data for a new thread.
            Private ReadOnly m_Iterations As Integer
            Private ReadOnly m_Message As String
            Private ReadOnly m_Delay As Integer

            Public Sub New(ByVal iterations As Integer, ByVal message As String, ➥
```

```vb
ByVal delay As Integer)
                m_Iterations = iterations
                m_Message = message
                m_Delay = delay
            End Sub

            ' Properties provide read-only access to initialization data.
            Public ReadOnly Property Iterations()
                Get
                    Return m_Iterations
                End Get
            End Property

            Public ReadOnly Property Message()
                Get
                    Return m_Message
                End Get
            End Property

            Public ReadOnly Property Delay()
                Get
                    Return m_Delay
                End Get
            End Property

        End Class

    ' Declare the method that will be executed in its own thread. The
        ' method displays a message to the console a specified number of
        ' times, sleeping between each message for a specified duration.
        Private Shared Sub DisplayMessage(ByVal config As Object)
            Dim data As ThreadStartData = TryCast(config, ThreadStartData)

            If Not data Is Nothing Then
                For count As Integer = 0 To data.Iterations - 1
                    TraceMsg(data.Message)

                    ' Sleep for the specified period.
                    Thread.Sleep(data.Delay)
                Next
            Else
                TraceMsg("Invalid thread configuration.")
            End If

        End Sub

        Public Shared Sub Main()

            ' Create a new Thread object specifying DisplayMessage
            ' as the method it will execute.
            Dim newThread As New Thread(AddressOf DisplayMessage)

            ' Create a new ThreadStartData object to configure the thread.
            Dim config As New ThreadStartData(5, "A thread example.", 500)
```

```
            TraceMsg("Starting new thread.")

            ' Start the new thread and pass the ThreadStartData object
            ' containing the initialization data.
            newThread.Start(config)

            ' Continue with other processing.
            For count As Integer = 0 To 12
                TraceMsg("Main thread continuing processing...")
                Thread.Sleep(200)
            Next

            ' Wait to continue.
            Console.WriteLine(Environment.NewLine)
            Console.WriteLine("Main method complete. Press Enter.")
            Console.ReadLine()

        End Sub

    End Class
End Namespace
```

4-7. Synchronize the Execution of Multiple Threads Using a Monitor

Problem

You need to coordinate the activities of multiple threads to ensure the efficient use of shared resources or to ensure several threads are not updating the same shared resource at the same time.

Solution

Identify an appropriate object to use as a mechanism to control access to the shared resource/data. Use the Shared method Monitor.Enter to acquire a lock on the object, and use the Shared method Monitor.Exit to release the lock so another thread may acquire it.

How It Works

The greatest challenge in writing a multithreaded application is ensuring that the threads work in concert. This is commonly referred to as *thread synchronization* and includes the following:

- Ensuring threads access shared objects and data correctly so that they do not cause corruption

- Ensuring threads execute only when they are meant to and cause minimum overhead when they are idle

The most commonly used synchronization mechanism is the System.Threading.Monitor class. The Monitor class allows a single thread to obtain an exclusive lock on an object by calling the Shared method Monitor.Enter. By acquiring an exclusive lock prior to accessing a shared resource or data, you ensure that only one thread can access the resource concurrently. Once the thread has finished with the resource, release the lock to allow another thread to access it. A block of code that enforces this behavior is often referred to as a *critical section*.

■Note Monitors are managed-code synchronization mechanisms that do not rely on any specific operating system primitives. This ensures your code is portable should you want to run it on a non-Windows platform. This is in contrast to the synchronization mechanisms discussed in recipes 4-8, 4-9, and 4-10, which rely on Win32 operating system–based synchronization objects.

You can use any object to act as the lock; it is common to use the keyword `Me` to obtain a lock on the current object, but it is better to use a separate object dedicated to the purpose of synchronization. The key point is that all threads attempting to access a shared resource must try to acquire the *same* lock. Other threads that attempt to acquire a lock using `Monitor.Enter` on the same object will block (enter a `WaitSleepJoin` state) and are added to the lock's *ready queue* until the thread that owns the lock releases it by calling the `Shared` method `Monitor.Exit`. When the owning thread calls `Exit`, one of the threads from the ready queue acquires the lock. We say "one of the threads" because threads are not necessarily executed in any specific order. If the owner of a lock does not release it by calling `Exit`, all other threads will block indefinitely. Therefore, it is important to place the `Exit` call within a `Finally` block to ensure that it is called even if an exception occurs. To ensure threads do not wait indefinitely, you can specify a time-out value when you call `Monitor.Enter`.

■Tip Because `Monitor` is used so frequently in multithreaded applications, VB .NET provides language-level support through the `Synclock` statement, which the compiler translates to the use of the `Monitor` class. A block of code encapsulated in a `Synclock` statement is equivalent to calling `Monitor.Enter` when entering the block and `Monitor.Exit` when exiting the block. In addition, the compiler automatically places the `Monitor.Exit` call in a `Finally` block to ensure that the lock is released if an exception is thrown.

Using `Monitor.Enter` and `Monitor.Exit` is often all you will need to correctly synchronize access to a shared resource in a multithreaded application. However, when you are trying to coordinate the activation of a pool of threads to handle work items from a shared queue, `Monitor.Enter` and `Monitor.Exit` will not be sufficient. In this situation, you want a potentially large number of threads to wait efficiently until a work item becomes available without putting unnecessary load on the central processing unit (CPU). This is where you need the fine-grained synchronization control provided by the `Monitor.Wait`, `Monitor.Pulse`, and `Monitor.PulseAll` methods.

The thread that currently owns the lock can call `Monitor.Wait`, which will release the lock and place that thread on the lock's *wait queue*. Threads in a wait queue also have a state of `WaitSleepJoin` and will continue to block until a thread that owns the lock calls either the `Monitor.Pulse` method or the `Monitor.PulseAll` method. `Monitor.Pulse` moves one of the waiting threads from the wait queue to the ready queue, and `Monitor.PulseAll` moves all threads. Once a thread has moved from the wait queue to the ready queue, it can acquire the lock the next time the lock is released. It is important to understand that threads on a lock's wait queue *will not* acquire a released lock; they will wait indefinitely until you call `Monitor.Pulse` or `Monitor.PulseAll` to move them to the ready queue.

So, in practice, when your pool threads are inactive, they sit in the wait queue. As a new work item arrives, a dispatcher obtains the lock and calls `Monitor.Pulse`, moving one worker thread to the ready queue, where it will obtain the lock as soon as the dispatcher releases it. The worker thread takes the work item, releases the lock, and processes the work item. Once the worker thread has finished with the work item, it again obtains the lock in order to take the next work item, but if there is no work item to process, the thread calls `Monitor.Wait` and goes back to the wait queue.

The Code

The following example demonstrates how to synchronize access to a shared resource (the console) and the activation of waiting threads using the Monitor.Wait, Monitor.Pulse, and Monitor.PulseAll methods. The example starts three worker threads that take work items from a queue and processes them. These threads initially have no work items and are put into a wait state using Monitor.Wait. When the user presses Enter the first two times, work items (strings in the example) are added to the work queue, and Monitor.Pulse is called to release one waiting thread for each work item. The third time the user presses Enter, Monitor.PulseAll is called, releasing all waiting threads and allowing them to terminate.

```
Imports System
Imports System.Threading
Imports System.Collections.Generic

Namespace Apress.VisualBasicRecipes.Chapter04

    Class Recipe04_04

        ' Declare an object for synchronization of access to the console.
        ' A shared object is used because you are using it in shared methods.
        Private Shared consoleGate As New Object

        ' Declare a Queue to represent the work queue.
        Private Shared workQueue As New Queue(Of String)

        ' Declare a flag to indicate to activated threads that they should
        ' terminate and not process more work items.
        Private Shared workItemsProcessed As Boolean = False

        ' A utility method for displaying useful trace information to the
        ' console along with details of the current thread.
        Private Shared Sub TraceMsg(ByVal msg As String)

            SyncLock consoleGate
                Console.WriteLine("[{0,3}/{1}] - {2} : {3}", ➥
Thread.CurrentThread.ManagedThreadId, IIf(Thread.CurrentThread.IsThreadPoolThread, ➥
"pool", "fore"), DateTime.Now.ToString("HH:mm:ss.ffff"), msg)
            End SyncLock

        End Sub

        ' Declare the method that will be executed by each thread to process
        ' items from the work queue.
        Private Shared Sub ProcessWorkItems()

            ' A local variable to hold the work item taken from the work queue.
            Dim workItem As String = Nothing

            TraceMsg("Thread started, processing items from the queue...")

            ' Process items from the work queue until termination is signaled.
            While Not workItemsProcessed
                ' Obtain the lock on the work queue.
                Monitor.Enter(workQueue)
```

```vb
        Try
            ' Pop the next work item and process it, or wait if none
            ' are available.
            If workQueue.Count = 0 Then
                TraceMsg("No work items, waiting...")

                ' Wait until Pulse is called on the workQueue object.
                Monitor.Wait(workQueue)
            Else
                ' Obtain the next work item.
                workItem = workQueue.Dequeue
            End If
        Catch
        Finally
            ' Always release the lock.
            Monitor.Exit(workQueue)
        End Try

        ' Process the work item if one was obtained.
        If Not workItem Is Nothing Then
            ' Obtain a lock on the console and display a series
            ' of messages.
            SyncLock consoleGate
                For i As Integer = 0 To 4
                    TraceMsg("Processing " & workItem)
                    Thread.Sleep(200)
                Next
            End SyncLock

            ' Reset the status of the local variable.
            workItem = Nothing
        End If
    End While

    ' This will be reached only if workItemsProcessed is true.
    TraceMsg("Terminating.")
End Sub

Public Shared Sub Main()

    TraceMsg("Starting worker threads.")

    ' Add an initial work item to the work queue.
    SyncLock workQueue
        workQueue.Enqueue("Work Item 1")
    End SyncLock

    ' Create and start three new worker threads running the
    ' ProcessWorkItems method.
    For count As Integer = 1 To 3
        Dim newThread As New Thread(AddressOf ProcessWorkItems)
        newThread.Start()
    Next
```

```
Thread.Sleep(1500)

' The first time the user presses Enter, add a work item and
' activate a single thread to process it.
TraceMsg("Press Enter to pulse one waiting thread.")
Console.ReadLine()

' Acquire a lock on the workQueue object.
SyncLock workQueue
    ' Add a work item.
    workQueue.Enqueue("Work Item 2.")

    ' Pulse 1 waiting thread.
    Monitor.Pulse(workQueue)
End SyncLock

Thread.Sleep(2000)

' The second time the user presses Enter, add three work items and
' activate three threads to process them.
TraceMsg("Press Enter to pulse three waiting threads.")
Console.ReadLine()

' Acquire a lock on the workQueue object.
SyncLock workQueue
    ' Add work items to the work queue, and activate worker threads.
    workQueue.Enqueue("Work Item 3.")
    Monitor.Pulse(workQueue)
    workQueue.Enqueue("Work Item 4.")
    Monitor.Pulse(workQueue)
    workQueue.Enqueue("Work Item 5.")
    Monitor.Pulse(workQueue)
End SyncLock

Thread.Sleep(3500)

' The third time the user presses Enter, signal the worker threads
' to terminate and activate them all.
TraceMsg("Press Enter to pulse all waiting threads.")
Console.ReadLine()

' Acquire a lock on the workQueue object.
SyncLock workQueue
    ' Signal that threads should terminate.
    workItemsProcessed = True

    ' Pulse all waiting threads.
    Monitor.PulseAll(workQueue)
End SyncLock

Thread.Sleep(1000)
```

```
        ' Wait to continue.
        TraceMsg("Main method complete. Press Enter.")
        Console.ReadLine()

    End Sub

  End Class
End Namespace
```

4-8. Synchronize the Execution of Multiple Threads Using an Event

Problem

You need a mechanism to synchronize the execution of multiple threads in order to coordinate their activities or access to shared resources.

Solution

Use the EventWaitHandle, AutoResetEvent, and ManualResetEvent classes from the System.Threading namespace.

How It Works

The EventWaitHandle, AutoResetEvent, and ManualResetEvent classes provide similar functionality. In fact, although the EventWaitHandle is new to .NET Framework 2.0, it is the base class from which the AutoResetEvent and ManualResetEvent classes are derived. (EventWaitHandle inherits from System.Threading.WaitHandle and allows you to create named events.) All three event classes allow you to synchronize multiple threads by manipulating the state of the event between two possible values: *signaled* and *unsignaled*.

Threads requiring synchronization call Shared or inherited methods of the WaitHandle abstract base class (summarized in Table 4-1) to test the state of one or more event objects. If the events are signaled when tested, the thread continues to operate unhindered. If the events are unsignaled, the thread enters a WaitSleepJoin state, blocking until one or more of the events become signaled or when a given time-out expires.

The key differences between the three event classes are how they transition from a signaled to an unsignaled state and their visibility. Both the AutoResetEvent and ManualResetEvent classes are local to the process in which they are declared. To signal an AutoResetEvent class, call its Set method, which will release only one thread that is waiting on the event. The AutoResetEvent class will then automatically return to an unsignaled state. The code in recipe 4-5 demonstrates how to use an AutoResetEvent class.

The ManualResetEvent class must be manually switched back and forth between signaled and unsignaled states using its Set and Reset methods. Calling Set on a ManualResetEvent class will set it to a signaled state, releasing all threads that are waiting on the event. Only by calling Reset does the ManualResetEvent class become unsignaled.

Table 4-1. *WaitHandle Methods for Synchronizing Thread Execution*

Method	Description
WaitOne	Causes the calling thread to enter a WaitSleepJoin state and wait for a specific WaitHandle derived object to be signaled. You can also specify a time-out value. The WaitingExample method in recipe 4-2 demonstrates how to use the WaitOne method.
WaitAny	A Shared method that causes the calling thread to enter a WaitSleepJoin state and wait for any one of the objects in a WaitHandle array to be signaled. You can also specify a time-out value.
WaitAll	A Shared method that causes the calling thread to enter a WaitSleepJoin state and wait for all the WaitHandle objects in a WaitHandle array to be signaled. You can also specify a time-out value. The WaitAllExample method in recipe 4-2 demonstrates how to use the WaitAll method.
SignalAndWait	A Shared method that causes the calling thread to signal a specified event object and then wait on a specified event object. The signal and wait operations are carried out as an atomic operation. You can also specify a time-out value. SignalAndWait is new to .NET Framework 2.0.

You can configure the EventWaitHandle class to operate in a manual or automatic reset mode, making it possible to act like either the AutoResetEvent class or the ManualResetEvent class. When you create the EventWaitHandle, you pass a value of the System.Threading.EventResetMode enumeration to configure the mode in which the EventWaitHandle will function; the two possible values are AutoReset and ManualReset. The unique benefit of the EventWaitHandle class is that it is not constrained to the local process. When you create an EventWaitHandle class, you can associate a name with it that makes it accessible to other processes, including nonmanaged Win32 code. This allows you to synchronize the activities of threads across process and application domain boundaries and synchronize access to resources that are shared by multiple processes. To obtain a reference to an existing named EventWaitHandle, call the Shared method EventWaitHandle.OpenExisting, and specify the name of the event.

The Code

The following example demonstrates how to use a named EventWaitHandle in manual mode that is initially signaled. A thread is spawned that waits on the event and then displays a message to the console—repeating the process every 2 seconds. When you press Enter, you toggle the event between a signaled and an unsignaled state. This example uses the Join keyword to cause the application's execution to wait until the thread terminates. Join is covered in more detail in recipe 4-12.

```
Imports System
Imports System.Threading

Namespace Apress.VisualBasicRecipes.Chapter04

    Class Recipe04_08

        ' Boolean to signal that the second thread should terminate.
        Public Shared terminate As Boolean = False

        '   A utility method for displaying useful trace information to the
```

```vbnet
    ' console along with details of the current thread.
    Private Shared Sub TraceMsg(ByVal msg As String)
        Console.WriteLine("[{0,3}] - {1} : {2}", ➡
Thread.CurrentThread.ManagedThreadId, DateTime.Now.ToString("HH:mm:ss.ffff"), msg)
    End Sub

    ' Declare the method that will be executed on the separate thread.
    ' The method waits on the EventWaitHandle before displaying a message
    ' to the console and then waits two seconds and loops.
    Private Shared Sub DisplayMessage()

        ' Obtain a handle to the EventWaitHandle with the name "EventExample".
        Dim eventHandle As EventWaitHandle = ➡
EventWaitHandle.OpenExisting("EventExample")

        TraceMsg("DisplayMessage Started.")

        While Not terminate
            ' Wait on the EventWaitHandle, time-out after two seconds. WaitOne
            ' returns true if the event is signaled; otherwise, false. The
            ' first time through, the message will be displayed immediately
            ' because the EventWaitHandle was created in a signaled state.
            If eventHandle.WaitOne(2000, True) Then
                TraceMsg("EventWaitHandle In Signaled State.")
            Else
                TraceMsg("WaitOne Time Out -- EventWaitHandle In" & ➡
"Unsignaled State.")
            End If
            Thread.Sleep(2000)
        End While

        TraceMsg("Thread Terminating.")
    End Sub

    Public Shared Sub Main()

        ' Create a new EventWaitHandle with an initial signaled state, in
        ' manual mode, with the name "EventExample".
        Using eventHandle As New EventWaitHandle(True, ➡
EventResetMode.ManualReset, "EventExample")
            ' Create and start a new thread running the DisplayMessage
            ' method.
            TraceMsg("Starting DisplayMessageThread.")
            Dim newThread As New Thread(AddressOf DisplayMessage)
            newThread.Start()

            ' Allow the EventWaitHandle to be toggled between a signaled and
            ' unsignaled state up to three times before ending.
            For count As Integer = 1 To 3
                ' Wait for Enter to be pressed.
                Console.ReadLine()
```

```
              ' You need to toggle the event. The only way to know the
              ' current state is to wait on it with a 0 (zero) time-out
              ' and test the result.
              If eventHandle.WaitOne(0, True) Then
                  TraceMsg("Switching Event To UnSignaled State.")

                  ' Event is signaled, so unsignal it.
                  eventHandle.Reset()
              Else
                  TraceMsg("Switching Event To Signaled State.")

                  ' Event is unsignaled, so signal it.
                  eventHandle.Set()
              End If
          Next

          ' Terminate the DisplayMessage thread, and wait for it to
          ' complete before disposing of the EventWaitHandle.
          terminate = True
          eventHandle.Set()
          newThread.Join(5000)

      End Using

      ' Wait to continue.
      Console.WriteLine(Environment.NewLine)
      Console.WriteLine("Main method complete. Press Enter.")
      Console.ReadLine()

    End Sub

  End Class
End Namespace
```

4-9. Synchronize the Execution of Multiple Threads Using a Mutex

Problem

You need to coordinate the activities of multiple threads (possibly across process boundaries) to ensure the efficient use of shared resources or to ensure several threads are not updating the same shared resource at the same time.

Solution

Use the System.Threading.Mutex class.

How It Works

The Mutex has a similar purpose to the Monitor discussed in recipe 4-7—it provides a means to ensure only a single thread has access to a shared resource or section of code at any given time. However, unlike the Monitor, which is implemented fully within managed code, the Mutex is a wrapper around an operating system synchronization object. This means you can use a Mutex to synchronize the activities of threads across process boundaries, even with threads running in nonmanaged Win32 code. You can use the OpenExisting method to open an existing, system-wide Mutex object.

Like the EventWaitHandle, AutoResetEvent, and ManualResetEvent classes discussed in recipe 4-8, the Mutex is derived from System.Threading.WaitHandle and enables thread synchronization in a similar fashion. A Mutex is in either a signaled state or an unsignaled state. A thread acquires ownership of the Mutex at construction or by using one of the methods listed earlier in Table 4-1. If a thread has ownership of the Mutex, the Mutex is unsignaled, meaning other threads will block if they try to acquire ownership. Ownership of the Mutex is released by the owning thread calling the Mutex. ReleaseMutex method, which signals the Mutex and allows another thread to acquire ownership. A thread may acquire ownership of a Mutex any number of times without problems, but it must release the Mutex an equal number of times to free it and make it available for another thread to acquire. If the thread with ownership of a Mutex terminates normally, the Mutex becomes signaled, allowing another thread to acquire ownership.

The Code

The following example demonstrates how to use a named Mutex to limit access to a shared resource (the console) to a single thread at any given time. This example uses the Join keyword to cause the application's execution to wait until the thread terminates. Join is covered in more detail in recipe 4-12.

```
Imports System
Imports System.Threading

Namespace Apress.VisualBasicRecipes.Chapter04

    Class Recipe04_09

        ' Boolean to signal that the second thread should terminate.
        Public Shared terminate As Boolean = False

        '   A utility method for displaying useful trace information to the
        '   console along with details of the current thread.
        Private Shared Sub TraceMsg(ByVal msg As String)
            Console.WriteLine("[{0,3}] - {1} : {2}", ➡
Thread.CurrentThread.ManagedThreadId, DateTime.Now.ToString("HH:mm:ss.ffff"), msg)
        End Sub

        '   Declare the method that will be executed on the separate thread.
        '   In a loop the method waits to obtain a Mutex before displaying a
        '   a message to the console and then waits one second before releasing
        '   the Mutex.
        Private Shared Sub DisplayMessage()

            ' Obtain a handle to the Mutex with the name MutexExample.
            ' Do not attempt to take ownership immediately.
            Using newMutex As New Mutex(False, "MutexExample")
                TraceMsg("Thread Started.")

                While Not terminate
                    ' Wait on the Mutex.
                    newMutex.WaitOne()
```

```vb
            TraceMsg("Thread owns the Mutex.")
            Thread.Sleep(1000)
            TraceMsg("Thread releasing the Mutex.")

            ' Release the Mutex.
            newMutex.ReleaseMutex()

            ' Sleep a little to give another thread a good chance of
            ' acquiring the Mutex.
            Thread.Sleep(100)
        End While
        TraceMsg("Thread terminating.")
    End Using

End Sub

Public Shared Sub Main()

    ' Create a new Mutex with the name MutexExample.
    Using newMutex As New Mutex(False, "MutexExample")
        TraceMsg("Starting threads -- press Enter to terminate.")

        ' Create and start three new threads running the
        ' DisplayMessage method.
        Dim thread1 As New Thread(AddressOf DisplayMessage)
        Dim thread2 As New Thread(AddressOf DisplayMessage)
        Dim thread3 As New Thread(AddressOf DisplayMessage)

        thread1.Start()
        thread2.Start()
        thread3.Start()

        ' Wait for Enter to be pressed.
        Console.ReadLine()

        ' Terminate the DisplayMessage threads, and wait for them to
        ' complete before disposing of the Mutex.
        terminate = True
        thread1.Join(5000)
        thread2.Join(5000)
        thread3.Join(5000)

    End Using

    ' Wait to continue.
    Console.WriteLine(Environment.NewLine)
    Console.WriteLine("Main method complete. Press Enter.")
    Console.ReadLine()

End Sub

    End Class
End Namespace
```

■**Note** Recipe 4-17 demonstrates how to use a named Mutex as a means to ensure only a single instance of an application can be started at any given time.

4-10. Synchronize the Execution of Multiple Threads Using a Semaphore

Problem

You need to control the number of threads that can access a shared resource or section of code concurrently.

Solution

Use the System.Threading.Semaphore class.

How It Works

The Semaphore is another synchronization class derived from the System.Threading.WaitHandle class. The Semaphore is new in .NET Framework 2.0, but it will be familiar to those with Win32 programming experience. The purpose of the Semaphore is to allow a specified maximum number of threads to access a shared resource or section of code concurrently.

As with the other synchronization classes derived from WaitHandle (discussed in recipes 4-8 and 4-9), a Semaphore is either in a signaled state or in an unsignaled state. Threads wait for the Semaphore to become signaled using the methods described earlier in Table 4-1. The Semaphore maintains a count of the active threads it has allowed through and automatically switches to an unsignaled state once the maximum number of threads is reached. To release the Semaphore and allow other waiting threads the opportunity to act, a thread calls the Release method on the Semaphore object. A thread may acquire ownership of the Semaphore more than once, reducing the maximum number of threads that can be active concurrently, and must call Release the same number of times to fully release it.

The Code

The following example demonstrates how to use a named Semaphore to limit access to a shared resource (the console) to two threads at any given time. The code is similar to that used in recipe 4-9 but substitutes a Semaphore for the Mutex. This example uses the Join keyword to cause the application's execution to wait until the thread terminates. Join is covered in more detail in recipe 4-12.

```
Imports System
Imports System.Threading

Namespace Apress.VisualBasicRecipes.Chapter04

    Class Recipe04_10

        ' Boolean to signal that the second thread should terminate.
        Public Shared terminate As Boolean = False
```

```vbnet
    ' A utility method for displaying useful trace information to the
    ' console along with details of the current thread.
    Private Shared Sub TraceMsg(ByVal msg As String)
        Console.WriteLine("[{0,3}] - {1} : {2}", ➥
Thread.CurrentThread.ManagedThreadId, DateTime.Now.ToString("HH:mm:ss.ffff"), msg)
    End Sub

    ' Declare the method that will be executed on the separate thread.
    ' In a loop the method waits to obtain a Semaphore before displaying a
    ' a message to the console and then waits one second before releasing
    ' the Semaphore.
    Private Shared Sub DisplayMessage()

        ' Obtain a handle to the Semaphore, created in main, with the name
        ' SemaphoreExample. Do not attempt to take ownership immediately.
        Using sem As Semaphore = Semaphore.OpenExisting("SemaphoreExample")
            TraceMsg("Thread Started.")

            While Not terminate
                ' Wait on the Semaphore.
                sem.WaitOne()

                TraceMsg("Thread owns the Semaphore.")
                Thread.Sleep(1000)
                TraceMsg("Thread releasing the Semaphore.")

                ' Release the Semaphore.
                sem.Release()

                ' Sleep a little to give another thread a good chance of
                ' acquiring the Semaphore.
                Thread.Sleep(100)
            End While
            TraceMsg("Thread terminating.")
        End Using

    End Sub

    Public Shared Sub Main()

        ' Create a new Semaphore with the name SemaphoreExample.
        Using sem As New Semaphore(2, 2, "SemaphoreExample")
            TraceMsg("Starting threads -- press Enter to terminate.")

            ' Create and start three new threads running the
            ' DisplayMessage method.
            Dim thread1 As New Thread(AddressOf DisplayMessage)
            Dim thread2 As New Thread(AddressOf DisplayMessage)
            Dim thread3 As New Thread(AddressOf DisplayMessage)

            thread1.Start()
            thread2.Start()
            thread3.Start()
```

```
        '  Wait for Enter to be pressed.
        Console.ReadLine()

        '  Terminate the DisplayMessage threads, and wait for them to
        '  complete before disposing of the Semaphore.
        terminate = True
        thread1.Join(5000)
        thread2.Join(5000)
        thread3.Join(5000)

    End Using

    '  Wait to continue.
    Console.WriteLine(Environment.NewLine)
    Console.WriteLine("Main method complete. Press Enter.")
    Console.ReadLine()

End Sub

End Class
End Namespace
```

4-11. Synchronize Access to a Shared Data Value

Problem

You need to ensure operations on a numeric data value are executed atomically so that multiple threads accessing the value do not cause errors or corruption.

Solution

Use the Shared members of the System.Threading.Interlocked class.

How It Works

The Interlocked class contains several Shared methods that perform some simple arithmetic and comparison operations on a variety of data types and ensure the operations are carried out atomically. Table 4-2 summarizes the methods and the data types on which they can be used. Note that the methods use the ByRef keyword on their arguments to allow the method to update the value of the actual value type variable passed in. If the operations you want to perform are not supported by the Interlocked class, you will need to implement your own synchronization using the other approaches described in this chapter.

■**Caution** Be aware, as of the time of this writing, the reliability of the 64-bit interlocked operations on a 32-bit platform is in question.

Table 4-2. *Interlocked Methods for Synchronizing Data Access*

Method	Description
Add	Adds two `Integer` or `Long` values and sets the value of the first argument to the sum of the two values.
CompareExchange	Compares two values; if they are the same, sets the first argument to a specified value. This method has overloads to support the comparison and exchange of `Integer`, `Long`, `Single`, `Double`, `Object`, and `System.IntPtr`.
Decrement	Decrements an `Integer` or `Long` value.
Exchange	Sets the value of a variable to a specified value. This method has overloads to support the exchange of `Integer`, `Long`, `Single`, `Double`, `Object`, and `System.IntPtr`.
Increment	Increments an `Integer` or `Long` value.

The Code

The following simple example demonstrates how to use the methods of the `Interlocked` class. The example does not demonstrate `Interlocked` in the context of a multithreaded program and is provided only to clarify the syntax and effect of the various methods.

```
Imports System
Imports System.threading

Namespace Apress.VisualBasicRecipes.Chapter04

    Class Recipe04_11

      Public Shared Sub Main()

          Dim firstInt As Integer = 2500
          Dim secondInt As Integer = 8000

          Console.WriteLine("firstInt initial value = {0}", firstInt)
          Console.WriteLine("secondInt initial value = {0}", secondInt)

          ' Decrement firstInt in a thread-safe manner. This is
          ' the thread-safe equivalent of firstInt = firstInt - 1.
          Interlocked.Decrement(firstInt)

          Console.WriteLine(Environment.NewLine)
          Console.WriteLine("firstInt after decrement = {0}", firstInt)

          ' Increment secondInt in a thread-safe manner. This is
          ' the thread-safe equivalent of secondInt = secondInt + 1.
          Interlocked.Increment(secondInt)

          Console.WriteLine("secondInt after increment = {0}", secondInt)
```

```
    ' Add the firstInt and secondInt values, and store the result
    ' in firstInt. This is the thread-safe equivalent of firstInt
    ' = firstInt + secondInt.
    Interlocked.Add(firstInt, secondInt)

    Console.WriteLine(Environment.NewLine)
    Console.WriteLine("firstInt after Add = {0}", firstInt)
    Console.WriteLine("secondInt after Add = {0}", secondInt)

    ' Exchange the value of firstInt with secondInt. This is the
    ' thread-safe equivalent of secondInt = firstInt.
    Interlocked.Exchange(secondInt, firstInt)

    Console.WriteLine(Environment.NewLine)
    Console.WriteLine("firstInt after Exchange = {0}", firstInt)
    Console.WriteLine("secondInt after Exchange = {0}", secondInt)

    ' Compare firstInt with secondInt, and if they are equal, set
    ' firstInt to 5000. This is the thread-safe equivalent of
    ' if firstInt = secondInt then firstInt = 5000.
    Interlocked.CompareExchange(firstInt, 5000, secondInt)

    Console.WriteLine(Environment.NewLine)
    Console.WriteLine("firstInt after CompareExchange = {0}", firstInt)
    Console.WriteLine("secondInt after CompareExchange = {0}", secondInt)

    ' Wait to continue.
    Console.WriteLine(Environment.NewLine)
    Console.WriteLine("Main method complete. Press Enter.")
    Console.ReadLine()

  End Sub

  End Class
End Namespace
```

4-12. Know When a Thread Finishes

Problem

You need to know when a thread has finished.

Solution

Use the IsAlive property or the Join method of the Thread class.

How It Works

The easiest way to test whether a thread has finished executing is to test the Thread.IsAlive property. The IsAlive property returns True if the thread has been started but has not terminated or been aborted. The IsAlive property provides a simple test to see whether a thread has finished executing, but commonly you will need one thread to wait for another thread to complete its processing. Instead of testing IsAlive in a loop, which is inefficient, you can use the Thread.Join method.

Join causes the calling thread to block until the referenced thread terminates, at which point the calling thread will continue. You can optionally specify an Integer or a TimeSpan value that specifies the time, after which the Join operation will time out and execution of the calling thread will resume. If you specify a time-out value, Join returns True if the thread terminated and returns False if Join timed out.

The Code

The following example executes a second thread and then calls Join (with a time-out of 2 seconds) to wait for the second thread to terminate. Because the second thread takes about 5 seconds to execute, the Join method will always time out, and the example will display a message to the console. The example then calls Join again without a time-out and blocks until the second thread terminates.

```
Imports System
Imports System.threading

Namespace Apress.VisualBasicRecipes.Chapter04

    Class Recipe04_12

        Private Shared Sub DisplayMessage()

            ' Display a message to the console 5 times.
            For count As Integer = 1 To 5
                Console.WriteLine("{0} : DisplayMessage thread", ➥
DateTime.Now.ToString("HH:mm:ss.ffff"))

                ' Sleep for 1 second.
                Thread.Sleep(1000)
            Next
        End Sub

        Public Shared Sub Main()

            ' Create a new Thread to run the DisplayMessage method.
            Dim newThread As New Thread(AddressOf DisplayMessage)

            Console.WriteLine("{0} : Starting DisplayMessage thread.", ➥
DateTime.Now.ToString("HH:mm:ss.ffff"))

            ' Start the DisplayMessage thread.
            newThread.Start()

            ' Block until the DisplayMessage thread finishes, or time-out after
            ' 2 seconds.
            If Not newThread.Join(2000) Then
                Console.WriteLine("{0} : Join timed out !!", ➥
DateTime.Now.ToString("HH:mm:ss.ffff"))
            End If
```

```
        ' Block again until the DisplayMessage thread finishes with
        ' no time-out.
        newThread.Join()

        ' Wait to continue.
        Console.WriteLine("Main method complete. Press Enter.")
        Console.ReadLine()

    End Sub

  End Class
End Namespace
```

4-13. Terminate the Execution of a Thread

Problem

You need to terminate an executing thread without waiting for it to finish on its own accord.

Solution

Call the Abort method of the Thread object you want to terminate.

How It Works

It is better to write your code so that you can signal to a thread that it should shut down and allow it to terminate naturally. Recipes 4-7, 4-8, and 4-9 demonstrate this technique (using a Boolean flag). However, sometimes you will want a more direct method of terminating an active thread.

Calling Abort on an active Thread object terminates the thread by throwing a System.Threading. ThreadAbortException in the code that the thread is running. You can pass an object as an argument to the Abort method, which is accessible to the aborted thread through the ExceptionState property of the ThreadAbortException. When called, Abort returns immediately, but the runtime determines exactly when the exception is thrown, so you cannot assume the thread has terminated by the Abort returns. You should use the techniques described in recipe 4-12 if you need to determine when the aborted thread is actually finished.

The aborted thread's code can catch the ThreadAbortException to perform cleanup, but the runtime will automatically throw the exception again when exiting the Catch block to ensure that the thread terminates. So, you should not write code after the Catch block because it will never execute. However, calling the Shared Thread.ResetAbort in the Catch block will cancel the abort request and exit the Catch block, allowing the thread to continue executing. Once you abort a thread, you cannot restart it by calling Thread.Start.

■**Note** An alternative to using the Abort method is to use a member variable. The thread should check the variable when appropriate. When you need to, set this variable to instruct the thread to end gracefully. This method offers a little more control than Abort.

The Code

The following example creates a new thread that continues to display messages to the console until you press Enter, at which point the thread is terminated by a call to `Thread.Abort`.

```vb
Imports System
Imports System.Threading

Namespace Apress.VisualBasicRecipes.Chapter04

    Class Recipe04_13

        Private Shared Sub Displaymessage()

            Try
                While True
                    ' Display a message to the console.
                    Console.WriteLine("{0} : DisplayMessage thread active", ➡
DateTime.Now.ToString("HH:mm:ss.ffff"))

                    ' Sleep for 1 second.
                    Thread.Sleep(1000)
                End While
            Catch ex As ThreadAbortException
                ' Display a message to the console.
                Console.WriteLine("{0} : DisplayMessage thread terminating - {1}", ➡
DateTime.Now.ToString("HH:mm:ss.ffff"), DirectCast(ex.ExceptionState, String))

                ' Call Thread.ResetAbort here to cancel the abort request.
            End Try

            ' This code is never executed unless Thread.ResetAbort is
            ' called in the previous catch block.
            Console.WriteLine("{0} : nothing is called after the catch block", ➡
DateTime.Now.ToString("HH:mm:ss.ffff"))

        End Sub

        Public Shared Sub Main()

            ' Create a new Thread to run the DisplayMessage method.
            Dim newThread As New Thread(AddressOf Displaymessage)

            Console.WriteLine("{0} : Starting DisplayMessage thread - press " & ➡
"Enter to terminate.", DateTime.Now.ToString("HH:mm:ss.ffff"))

            ' Start the DisplayMessage thread.
            newThread.Start()

            ' Wait until Enter is pressed and terminate the thread.
            System.Console.ReadLine()

            newThread.Abort("User pressed Enter")
```

```
'  Block again until the DisplayMessage thread finishes.
newThread.Join()

'  Wait to continue.
Console.WriteLine("Main method complete. Press Enter.")
Console.ReadLine()

    End Sub

    End Class
End Namespace
```

4-14. Create a Thread-Safe Collection Instance

Problem

You need multiple threads to be able to safely access the contents of a collection concurrently.

Solution

Use SyncLock statements in your code to synchronize thread access to the collection, or to access the collection through a thread-safe wrapper.

How It Works

By default, the standard collection classes from the System.Collections, System.Collections. Specialized, and System.Collections.Generic namespaces will support multiple threads reading the collection's content concurrently. However, if more than one of these threads tries to modify the collection, you will almost certainly encounter problems. This is because the operating system can interrupt the actions of the thread while modifications to the collection have been only partially applied. This leaves the collection in an indeterminate state, which could cause another thread accessing the collection to fail, return incorrect data, or corrupt the collection.

Note Using thread synchronization introduces a performance overhead. Making collections non-thread-safe by default provides better performance for the vast majority of situations where multiple threads are not used.

The most commonly used collections from the System.Collections namespace implement a Shared method named Synchronized; this includes only the ArrayList, Hashtable, Queue, SortedList, and Stack classes. The Synchronized method takes a collection object of the appropriate type as an argument and returns an object that provides a synchronized wrapper around the specified collection object. The wrapper object is returned as the same type as the original collection, but all the methods and properties that read and write the collection ensure that only a single thread has access to the initial collection content concurrently. You can test whether a collection is thread-safe using the IsSynchronized property. Once you get the wrapper, you should neither access the initial collection nor create a new wrapper; both result in a loss of thread safety.

The collection classes such as HybridDictionary, ListDictionary, and StringCollection from the System.Collections.Specialized namespace do not implement a Synchronized method. To provide thread-safe access to instances of these classes, you must implement manual synchronization using the `Object` returned by their `SyncRoot` property. This property and `IsSynchronized` are both defined by the `ICollection` interface that is implemented by all collection classes from `System.Collections` and `System.Collections.Specialized` (except `BitVector32`). You can therefore synchronize all your collections in a fine-grained way.

However, the new .NET Framework 2.0 classes in the `System.Collections.Generic` namespace provide no built-in synchronization mechanisms, leaving it to you to implement thread synchronization manually using the techniques discussed in this chapter.

■**Caution** Often you will have multiple collections and data elements that are related and need to be updated atomically. In these instances, you should not use the synchronization mechanisms provided by the individual collection classes. This approach will introduce synchronization problems, such as deadlocks and race conditions. You must decide which collections and other data elements need to be managed atomically and use the techniques described in this chapter to synchronize access to these elements as a unit.

The Code

The following code snippet shows how to create a thread-safe `Hashtable` instance.

```
' Create a standard Hashtable.
Dim hUnsync As New Hashtable

' Create a synchronized wrapper.
Dim hSync = Hashtable.Synchronized(hUnsync)
```

The following code snippet shows how to create a thread-safe `NameValueCollection`. Notice that the `NameValueCollection` class derives from the `NameObjectCollectionBase` class, which uses an explicit interface implementation to implement the `ICollection.SyncRoot` property. As shown, you must cast the `NameValueCollection` to an `ICollection` instance before you can access the `SyncRoot` property. Casting is not necessary with other specialized collection classes such as `HybridDictionary`, `ListDictionary`, and `StringCollection`, which do not use explicit interface implementation to implement `SyncRoot`.

```
' Create a NameValueCollection.
Dim nvCollection As New NameValueCollection

' Obtain a lock on the NameValue collection before modification.
SyncLock DirectCast(nvCollection, ICollection).SyncRoot
    ...
End SyncLock
```

4-15. Start a New Process

Problem

You need to execute an application in a new process.

Solution

Call one of the Shared Start method overloads of the System.Diagnostics.Process class. Specify the configuration details of the process you want to start as individual arguments to the Start method or in a System.Diagnostics.ProcessStartInfo object that you pass to the Start method.

How It Works

The Process class provides a managed representation of an operating system process and offers a simple mechanism through which you can execute both managed and unmanaged applications. The Process class implements five Shared overloads of the Start method, which you use to start a new process. All these methods return a Process object that represents the newly started process. Two of these overloads are methods that allow you to specify only the name and arguments to pass to the new process. For example, the following statements both execute Notepad in a new process.

```
' Execute notepad.exe with no command-line arguments.
Process.Start("notepad.exe")

' Execute notepad.exe passing the name of the file to open as a
' command-line argument.
Process.Start("notepad.exe", "SomeFile.txt")
```

Two other overloads allow you to specify the name of a Windows user who the process should run as. You must specify the username, password, and Windows domain. The password is specified as a System.Security.SecureString for added security. (See recipe 11-18 for more information about the SecureString class.) Here is an example:

```
Dim mySecureString As New System.Security.SecureString

' Obtain a password and place it in SecureString (see recipe 11-18).

' Execute notepad.exe with no command-line arguments.
Process.Start("notepad.exe", "Todd", mySecureString, "MyDomain")

' Execute notepad.exe passing the name of the file to open as a
' command-line argument.
Process.Start("notepad.exe", "SomeFile.txt", "Todd", mySecureString, "MyDomain")
```

The remaining Shared overload requires you to create a ProcessStartInfo object configured with the details of the process you want to run. Using the ProcessStartInfo object provides greater control over the behavior and configuration of the new process. Table 4-3 summarizes some of the commonly used properties of the ProcessStartInfo class.

It is also possible to create and view information on processes running on a remote computer. This is accomplished by creating an instance of a Process class and specifying the target computer name. You can also use the Shared methods GetProcessById, GetProcessByName and GetProcesses. Each method returns a Process object and has an overload that takes the name of the target computer.

When finished with a Process object, you should dispose of it in order to release system resources—call Close, call Dispose, or create the Process object within the scope of a Using statement.

■**Note** Disposing of a Process object does not affect the underlying system process, which will continue to run.

Table 4-3. *Properties of the ProcessStartInfo Class*

Property	Description
Arguments	The command-line arguments to pass to the new process.
Domain	A String containing the Windows domain name to which the user belongs.
ErrorDialog	If Process.Start cannot start the specified process, it will throw a System.ComponentModel.Win32Exception. If ErrorDialog is True, Start displays an error dialog box to the user before throwing the exception.
FileName	The name of the application to start. You can also specify any type of file for which you have configured an application association. For example, you could specify a file with a .doc or an .xls extension, which would cause Microsoft Word or Microsoft Excel to run.
LoadUserProfile	A Boolean indicating whether the user's profile should be loaded from the registry when the new process is started. This is used if you need to access information from the HKEY_CURRENT_USER registry key.
Password	A SecureString containing the password of the user.
UserName	A String containing the name of the user to use when starting the process.
WindowStyle	A member of the System.Diagnostics.ProcessWindowStyle enumeration, which controls how the window is displayed. Valid values include Hidden, Maximized, Minimized, and Normal.
WorkingDirectory	The fully qualified name of the initial directory for the new process.

The Code

The following example uses Process to execute Notepad in a maximized window and open a file named C:\Temp\file.txt. After creation, the example calls the Process.WaitForExit method, which blocks the calling thread until a process terminates or a specified time-out expires. This method returns True if the process ends before the time-out and returns False otherwise.

```
Imports System
Imports System.Diagnostics

Namespace Apress.VisualBasicRecipes.Chapter04

    Class Recipe04_15

        Public Shared Sub Main()

            ' Create a ProcessStartInfo object and configure it with the
            ' information required to run the new process.
            Dim startInfo As New ProcessStartInfo

            startInfo.FileName = "notepad.exe"
            startInfo.Arguments = "file.txt"
            startInfo.WorkingDirectory = "C:\Temp"
            startInfo.WindowStyle = ProcessWindowStyle.Maximized
            startInfo.ErrorDialog = True
```

```
    ' Declare a new process object.
    Dim newProcess As Process

    Try
        ' Start the new process.
        newProcess = Process.Start(startInfo)

        ' Wait for the new process to terminate before exiting.
        Console.WriteLine("Waiting 30 seconds for process to finish.")

        If newProcess.WaitForExit(30000) Then
            Console.WriteLine("Process terminated.")
        Else
            Console.WriteLine("Timed out waiting for process to end.")
        End If
    Catch ex As Exception
        Console.WriteLine("Could not start process.")
        Console.WriteLine(ex)
    End Try

    ' Wait to continue.
    Console.WriteLine(Environment.NewLine)
    Console.WriteLine("Main method complete. Press Enter.")
    Console.ReadLine()

    End Sub

    End Class
End Namespace
```

4-16. Terminate a Process

Problem

You need to terminate a process such as an application or a service.

Solution

Obtain a Process object representing the operating system process you want to terminate. For Windows-based applications, call Process.CloseMainWindow to send a close message to the application's main window. For Windows-based applications that ignore CloseMainWindow, or for non-Windows-based applications, call the Process.Kill method.

How It Works

If you start a new process from managed code using the Process class (discussed in recipe 4-15), you can terminate the process using the Process object that represents the new process. You can also obtain Process objects that refer to other currently running processes using the Shared methods of the Process class summarized in Table 4-4.

Table 4-4. *Methods for Obtaining Process References*

Method	Description
GetCurrentProcess	Returns a Process object representing the currently active process.
GetProcessById	Returns a Process object representing the process with the specified ID. This is the process ID (PID) you can get using Windows Task Manager.
GetProcesses	Returns an array of Process objects representing all currently active processes.
GetProcessesByName	Returns an array of Process objects representing all currently active processes with a specified friendly name. The friendly name is the name of the executable excluding file extension or path; for example, a friendly name could be notepad or calc.

As mentioned in recipe 4-15, you can obtain a Process object that refers to a process running on a remote computer. However, you can only view information regarding remote processes. The Kill and CloseMainWindow methods work only on local processes.

Once you have a Process object representing the process you want to terminate, you need to call either the CloseMainWindow method or the Kill method. The CloseMainWindow method posts a WM_CLOSE message to a Windows-based application's main window. This method has the same effect as if the user had closed the main window using the system menu, and it gives the application the opportunity to perform its normal shutdown routine. CloseMainWindow will not terminate applications that do not have a main window or applications with a disabled main window—possibly because a modal dialog box is currently displayed. Under such circumstances, CloseMainWindow will return False.

CloseMainWindow returns True if the close message was successfully sent, but this does not guarantee that the process is actually terminated. For example, applications used to edit data typically give the user the opportunity to save unsaved data if a close message is received. The user usually has the chance to cancel the close operation under such circumstances. This means CloseMainWindow will return True, but the application will still be running once the user cancels. You can use the Process.WaitForExit method to signal process termination and the Process.HasExited property to test whether a process has terminated. Alternatively, you can use the Kill method.

The Kill method simply terminates a process immediately; the user has no chance to stop the termination, and all unsaved data is lost. Kill is the only option for terminating Windows-based applications that do not respond to CloseMainWindow and for terminating non-Windows-based applications.

The Code

The following example starts a new instance of Notepad, waits 5 seconds, and then terminates the Notepad process. The example first tries to terminate the process using CloseMainWindow. If CloseMainWindow returns False, or the Notepad process is still running after CloseMainWindow is called, the example calls Kill and forces the Notepad process to terminate. You can force CloseMainWindow to return False by leaving the File Open dialog box open.

```vbnet
Imports System
Imports system.threading
Imports System.Diagnostics

Namespace Apress.VisualBasicRecipes.Chapter04

    Class Recipe04_16

        Public Shared Sub Main()

            ' Create a new Process and run notepad.exe.
            Using newProcess As Process = Process.Start("notepad.exe", ➥
 "C:\SomeFile.txt")
                ' Wait for 5 seconds and terminate the notepad process.
                Console.WriteLine("Waiting 5 seconds before terminating " & ➥
"notepad.exe.")
                Thread.Sleep(5000)

                ' Terminate notepad process.
                Console.WriteLine("Terminating Notepad with CloseMainWindow.")

                ' Try to send a close message to the main window.
                If Not newProcess.CloseMainWindow Then
                    ' Close message did not get sent - Kill Notepad.
                    Console.WriteLine("CloseMainWindow returned false - " & ➥
"terminating Notepad with Kill.")
                    newProcess.Kill()
                Else
                    ' Close message sent successfully. Wait for 2 seconds
                    ' for termination confirmation before resorting to kill.
                    If Not newProcess.WaitForExit(2000) Then
                        Console.WriteLine("CloseMaineWindow failed to " & ➥
"terminate - terminating Notepad with Kill.")
                        newProcess.Kill()
                    End If
                End If
            End Using

            ' Wait to continue.
            Console.WriteLine("Main method compelte. Press Enter.")
            Console.ReadLine()

        End Sub

    End Class
End Namespace
```

4-17. Ensure That Only One Instance of an Application Can Execute Concurrently

Problem

You need to ensure that a user can have only one instance of an application running concurrently.

Solution

Create a named `System.Threading.Mutex` object, and have your application try to acquire ownership of it at startup.

How It Works

The `Mutex` provides a mechanism for synchronizing the execution of threads across process boundaries and also provides a convenient mechanism through which to ensure that only a single instance of an application is running concurrently. By trying to acquire ownership of a named `Mutex` at startup and exiting if the `Mutex` cannot be acquired, you can ensure that only one instance of your application is running. Refer to recipe 4-9 for further information on the `Mutex` class.

The Code

This example uses a `Mutex` named `MutexExample` to ensure that only a single instance of the example can execute.

```
Imports System
Imports System.Threading

Namespace Apress.VisualBasicRecipes.Chapter04

    Class Recipe04_17

        Public Shared Sub Main()

            ' A Boolean that indicates whether this application has
            ' initial ownership of the Mutex.
            Dim ownsMutex As Boolean

            ' Attempts to create and take ownership of a Mutex named
            ' MutexExample.
            Using newMutex As New Mutex(True, "MutexExample", ownsMutex)
                ' If the application owns the Mutex it can continue to execute;
                ' otherwise, the application should exit.
                If ownsMutex Then
                    Console.WriteLine("This application currently owns the " & ➡
"mutex named MutexExample. Additional instances of this application will not " & ➡
"run until you release the mutex by pressing Enter.")
```

```
            Console.ReadLine()

            ' Release the mutex.
            newMutex.ReleaseMutex()
        Else
            Console.WriteLine("Another instance of this application " & ➥
"already owns the mutex named MutexExample. This instance of the application " & ➥
"will terminate.")
        End If
    End Using

    ' Wait to continue.
    Console.WriteLine("Main method complete. Press Enter.")
    Console.ReadLine()

    End Sub
End Class

End Namespace
```

■**Note** If you do not construct the `Mutex` in a `Using` statement and encapsulate the body of your application in the body of the `Using` block as shown in this example, in long-running applications, the garbage collector may dispose of the `Mutex` if it is not referenced after initial creation. This will result in releasing the `Mutex` and allowing additional instances of the application to execute concurrently. In these circumstances, you should include the statement `System.GC.KeepAlive(mutex)` to ensure the `Mutex` is not garbage collected. Thanks to Michael A. Covington for highlighting this possibility.

CHAPTER 5

■ ■ ■

Files, Directories, and I/O

The Microsoft .NET Framework I/O classes fall into two basic categories. First are the classes that retrieve information from the file system and allow you to perform file system operations such as copying files and moving directories. Two examples are the FileInfo and the DirectoryInfo classes. The second, and possibly more important, category includes a broad range of classes that allow you to read and write data from all types of streams. Streams can correspond to binary or text files, a file in an isolated store, a network connection, or even a memory buffer. In all cases, the way you interact with a stream is the same.

The primary namespace for .NET Framework I/O operations is System.IO; however, .NET Framework 2.0 offers VB .NET programmers another option in the form of the My object. My, located in the Microsoft.VisualBasic assembly, is a highly versatile object that encapsulates common functionality into several root classes. These classes provide quick and easy access to common functionality. Table 5-1 lists the main root classes of My.

Table 5-1. *Main Root Objects of My*

Object	Description
Application	Provides access to information and methods related to the current application.
Computer	Provides access to information and methods for various computer-related objects. This object contains the following child objects: Audio, Clipboard, Clock, FileSystem, Info, Keyboard, Mouse, Network, Ports, and Registry.
Forms	Provides access to information and methods related to the forms contained in your project.
Resources	Provides access to information and methods related to any resources contained in your project.
Settings	Provides access to information and methods related to your application settings.
User	Provides access to information and methods related to the current user.
WebServices	Provides access to information and methods related to any web services contained in your application.

The classes available to the My object are determined by the current project. For example, if you are creating a web control or web site, the My.Forms class will not be accessible. Refer to the .NET Framework software development kit (SDK) documentation for more details on the availability of My classes and for instructions on how this availability can be customized by using special compiler constants.

This chapter describes how to use the various file system and stream-based classes provided by the System.IO namespace and the My.Microsoft.VisualBasic.FileSystem class.

The recipes in this chapter describe how to do the following:

- Retrieve or modify information about a file, directory, or a drive (recipes 5-1, 5-2, 5-4, 5-5, and 5-17)

- Copy, move, and delete files and directories (recipe 5-3)

- Show a directory tree in a Microsoft Windows-based application and use the common file dialog boxes (recipes 5-6 and 5-18)

- Read and write text and binary files (recipes 5-7 and 5-8)

- Parse formatted text files (recipe 5-9)

- Read files asynchronously (recipe 5-10)

- Search for specific files and test files for equality (recipes 5-11 and 5-12)

- Work with strings that contain path information (recipes 5-13, 5-14, and 5-15)

- Create temporary files and files in a user-specific isolated store (recipes 5-16 and 5-19)

- Monitor the file system for changes (recipe 5-20)

- Write to COM ports (recipe 5-21)

- Generate random filenames (recipe 5-22)

- Retrieve or modify the access control lists (ACLs) of a file or directory (recipe 5-23)

5-1. Retrieve Information About a File, Directory, or Drive

Problem

You need to retrieve information about a file, directory, or drive.

Solution

Create a new System.IO.FileInfo, System.IO.DirectoryInfo, or System.IO.DriveInfo object, depending on the type of resource about which you need to retrieve information. Supply the path of the resource to the constructor, and then you will be able to retrieve information through the properties of the class.

How It Works

To create a FileInfo, DirectoryInfo, or DriveInfo object, you supply a relative or fully qualified path to the constructor. You can also use the GetFileInfo, GetDirectoryInfo, and GetDriveInfo Shared methods of the My.Computer.FileSystem. These methods return an instance of a FileInfo, DirectoryInfo, and DriveInfo object, respectively. You can retrieve information through the corresponding object properties. Table 5-2 lists some of the key members and methods of these objects.

Table 5-2. *Key Members for Files, Directories, and Drives*

Member	Applies To	Description
Exists	FileInfo and DirectoryInfo	Returns True or False, depending on whether a file or a directory exists at the specified location.
Attributes	FileInfo and DirectoryInfo	Returns one or more values from the System.IO. FileAttributes enumeration, which represents the attributes of the file or the directory.
CreationTime, LastAccessTime, and LastWriteTime	FileInfo and DirectoryInfo	Return System.DateTime instances that describe when a file or a directory was created, last accessed, and last updated, respectively.
FullName and Name	FileInfo and DirectoryInfo	Return a string that represents the full path, the directory, or the filename (with extension).
Extension	FileInfo	Returns a string representing the extension for the file.
IsReadOnly	FileInfo	Returns True or False, depending on whether a file is read-only.
Length	FileInfo	Returns the file size as a number of bytes.
DirectoryName and Directory	FileInfo	DirectoryName returns the name of the parent directory as a string. Directory returns a full DirectoryInfo object that represents the parent directory and allows you to retrieve more information about it.
Parent and Root	DirectoryInfo	Return a DirectoryInfo object that represents the parent or root directory.
CreateSubdirectory	DirectoryInfo	Creates a directory with the specified name in the directory represented by the DirectoryInfo object. It also returns a new DirectoryInfo object that represents the subdirectory.
GetDirectories	DirectoryInfo	Returns an array of DirectoryInfo objects, with one element for each subdirectory contained in this directory.
GetFiles	DirectoryInfo	Returns an array of FileInfo objects, with one element for each file contained in this directory.
DriveType	DriveInfo	Returns a DriveType enumeration value that represents the type of the specified drive; for example, Fixed or CDRom.
AvailableFreeSpace	DriveInfo	Returns a long that represents the free space available in the drive.
GetDrives	DriveInfo	Returns an array of DriveInfo objects that represents the logical drives in the computer.

The following are a few points to note while working with these objects:

- FileInfo and DirectoryInfo classes derive from the abstract FileSystemInfo class, which defines common methods like CreationTime, Exists, and so on. The DriveInfo class does not inherit from this base class, so it does not provide some of the common members available in the other two classes.

- The full set of properties FileInfo and DirectoryInfo objects expose is read the first time you interrogate any property. If the file or directory changes after this point, you must call the Refresh method to update the properties. However, this is not the case for DriveInfo; each property access asks the file system for an up-to-date value.

- Specifying an invalid path, directory, or drive when using the corresponding My.Computer. FileSystem methods will throw the appropriate exception. When using the FileInfo, DirectoryInfo, or DriveInfo classes directly, you will not encounter an error if you specify an invalid path. Instead, you will receive an object that represents an entity that does not exist— its Exists (or IsReady property for DriveInfo) property will be False. You can use this object to manipulate the entity. However, if you attempt to read most other properties, exceptions like FileNotFoundException, DirectoryNotFoundException, and so on will be thrown.

The Code

The following console application takes a file path from a command-line argument, and then displays information about the file, the containing directory, and the drive.

```
Imports System
Imports System.IO

Namespace Apress.VisualBasicRecipes.Chapter05

    Public Class Recipe05_01
        Public Shared Sub Main(ByVal args As String)

            If args.Length > 0 Then
                ' Display file information.
                Dim file As FileInfo = New FileInfo(args(0))

                Console.WriteLine("Checking file: " & file.Name)
                Console.WriteLine("File exists: " & file.Exists.ToString)

                If file.Exists Then
                    Console.Write("File created: ")
                    Console.WriteLine(file.CreationTime.ToString)
                    Console.Write("File last updated: ")
                    Console.WriteLine(file.LastWriteTime.ToString)
                    Console.Write("File last accessed: ")
                    Console.WriteLine(file.LastAccessTime.ToString)
                    Console.Write("File size: ")
                    Console.WriteLine(file.Length.ToString)
                    Console.Write("File attribute list: ")
                    Console.WriteLine(file.Attributes.ToString)
                End If
                Console.WriteLine()
```

```vbnet
        ' Display directory information.
        Dim dir As DirectoryInfo = file.Directory

        Console.WriteLine("Checking directory: " & dir.Name)
        Console.WriteLine("In directory: " & dir.Parent.Name)
        Console.Write("Directory exists: ")
        Console.WriteLine(dir.Exists.ToString)

        If dir.Exists Then
            Console.Write("Directory created: ")
            Console.WriteLine(dir.CreationTime.ToString)
            Console.Write("Directory last updated: ")
            Console.WriteLine(dir.LastWriteTime.ToString)
            Console.Write("Directory last accessed: ")
            Console.WriteLine(dir.LastAccessTime.ToString)
            Console.Write("Directory attribute list: ")
            Console.WriteLine(file.Attributes.ToString)
            Console.Write("Directory contains: ")
            Console.WriteLine(dir.GetFiles().Length.ToString & " files")
        End If
        Console.WriteLine()

        ' Display drive information.
        Dim drv As DriveInfo = New DriveInfo(file.FullName)

        Console.Write("Drive: ")
        Console.WriteLine(drv.Name)

        If drv.IsReady Then
            Console.Write("Drive type: ")
            Console.WriteLine(drv.DriveType.ToString)
            Console.Write("Drive format: ")
            Console.WriteLine(drv.DriveFormat.ToString)
            Console.Write("Drive free space: ")
            Console.WriteLine(drv.AvailableFreeSpace.ToString)
        End If

        ' Wait to continue.
        Console.WriteLine(Environment.NewLine)
        Console.WriteLine("Main method complete. Press Enter.")
        Console.ReadLine()

    Else
        Console.WriteLine("Please supply a filename.")
    End If

    End Sub

    End Class
End Namespace
```

Instead of explicitly creating the FileInfo, DirectoryInfo, and DriveInfo class instances, you can also use the appropriate Shared methods of the My.Computer.FileSystem class, as shown in the following examples.

```
'  Display file information.
Dim file As FileInfo = My.Computer.FileSystem.GetFileInfo(args(0))

'  Display directory information.
Dim dir As DirectoryInfo = ➡
My.Computer.FileSystem.GetDirectoryInfo(file.Directory.ToString)

'  Display drive information.
Dim drv As DriveInfo = My.Computer.FileSystem.GetDriveInfo(file.FullName)
```

Usage

If you execute the command Recipe05-01.exe c:\windows\win.ini, you might expect the following output:

```
Checking file: win.ini
File exists: True
File created: 8/23/2001 8:00:00 AM
File last updated: 1/11/2007 3:02:03 AM
File last accessed: 1/19/2007 2:24:23 PM
File size (bytes): 636
File attribute list: Archive

Checking directory: windows
In directory: c:\
Directory exists: True
Directory created: 6/13/2006 7:36:41 PM
Directory last updated: 1/19/2007 8:30:09 AM
Directory last accessed: 1/19/2007 3:34:32 PM
Directory attribute list: Archive
Directory contains: 204 files

Drive: c:\
Drive type: Fixed
Drive format: NTFS
Drive free space: 69418700800
```

■**Note**   Instead of using the instance methods of the FileInfo and DirectoryInfo classes, you can use the Shared File and Directory classes (note that a class corresponding to the DriveInfo class does not exist). The File and Directory methods expose most of the same functionality, but they require you to submit the filename or path with every method invocation. In cases where you need to perform multiple operations with the same file or directory, using the FileInfo and DirectoryInfo classes will be faster, because they will perform security checks only once. Also note that you could obtain the list of all logical drives in the computer by using the Shared DriveInfo.GetDrives method.

5-2. Set File and Directory Attributes

Problem

You need to test or modify file or directory attributes.

Solution

Create a `System.IO.FileInfo` object for a file or a `System.IO.DirectoryInfo` object for a directory and use the bitwise And, Or, and Xor operators to modify the value of the Attributes property.

How It Works

The `FileInfo.Attributes` and `DirectoryInfo.Attributes` properties represent file attributes such as archive, system, hidden, read-only, compressed, and encrypted. (Refer to the MSDN reference for the full list.) Because a file can possess any combination of attributes, the Attributes property accepts a combination of enumerated values. To individually test for a single attribute or change a single attribute, you need to use bitwise arithmetic.

Note The Attributes setting is made up (in binary) of a series of ones and zeros, such as 00010011. Each 1 represents an attribute that is present, while each 0 represents an attribute that is not. When you use a bitwise And operation, it compares each individual digit against each digit in the enumerated value. For example, if you bitwise And a value of 00100001 (representing an individual file's archive and read-only attributes) with the enumerated value 00000001 (which represents the read-only flag), the resulting value will be 00000001—it will have a 1 only where it can be matched in both values.

The Code

The following example takes a read-only test file and checks for the read-only attribute.

```
Imports System
Imports system.IO

Namespace Apress.VisualBasicRecipes.Chapter05

    Public Class Recipe05_02
        Public Shared Sub Main()

            ' This file has the archive and read-only attributes.
            Dim file As New FileInfo("data.txt")

            ' This displays the string "ReadOnly, Archive".
            Console.WriteLine(file.Attributes.ToString)
            Console.WriteLine(Environment.NewLine)

            ' This test fails, because other attributes are set.
            If file.Attributes = FileAttributes.ReadOnly Then
                Console.WriteLine("File is read-only (faulty test).")
            End If
```

```
              ' This test succeeds, because it filters out just the
              ' read-only attributes.
              If file.Attributes And FileAttributes.ReadOnly = ➥
FileAttributes.ReadOnly Then
                    Console.WriteLine("File is read-only (correct test).")
              End If

              ' Wait to continue.
              Console.WriteLine(Environment.NewLine)
              Console.WriteLine("Main method complete. Press Enter.")
              Console.ReadLine()

        End Sub

    End Class
End Namespace
```

When setting an attribute, you must use bitwise arithmetic, as demonstrated in the following example. In this case, it's needed to ensure that you don't inadvertently clear the other attributes.

```
' This adds just the read-only attribute.
file.Attributes = file.Attributes Or FileAttributes.ReadOnly

' This removes just the read-only attibute.
file.Attributes = file.Attributes Xor FileAttributes.ReadOnly
```

5-3. Copy, Move, or Delete a File or a Directory

Problem

You need to copy, move, or delete a file or directory.

Solution

You have two main options for manipulating files and directories. One option is to create a System.IO.FileInfo object for a file or a System.IO.DirectoryInfo object for a directory, supplying the path in the constructor. You can then use the object's methods to copy, move, and delete the file or directory. Alternatively, you can use the My.Computer.FileSystem class and its Shared methods.

How It Works

The FileInfo, DirectoryInfo, and My.Computer.FileSystem classes include a host of valuable methods for manipulating files and directories. Table 5-3 shows methods for the FileInfo class, Table 5-4 shows methods for the DirectoryInfo class, and Table 5-5 shows methods for the My.Computer.FileSystem class.

Table 5-3. *Key Instance Methods for Manipulating a FileInfo Object*

Method	Description
CopyTo	Copies a file to the new path and filename specified as a parameter. It also returns a new FileInfo object that represents the new (copied) file. You can supply an optional additional parameter of True to allow overwriting.
Create and CreateText	Create creates the specified file and returns a FileStream object that you can use to write to it. CreateText performs the same task, but returns a StreamWriter object that wraps the stream. For more information about writing files, see recipes 5-7 and 5-8.
Open, OpenRead, OpenText, and OpenWrite	Open opens a file and allows you to specify the mode (Open, Append, and so on), access type (Read, Write, and so on), and sharing options. OpenRead and OpenText open a file in read-only mode, returning a FileStream or StreamReader object. OpenWrite opens a file in write-only mode, returning a FileStream object. For more information about reading files, see recipes 5-7 and 5-8.
Delete	Removes the file, if it exists.
Encrypt and Decrypt	Encrypt/decrypt a file using the current account. This applies to NTFS file systems only.
MoveTo	Moves the file to the new path and filename specified as a parameter. MoveTo can also be used to rename a file without changing its location.
Replace	Replaces contents of a file by the current FileInfo object. This method could also take a backup copy of the replaced file.

Table 5-4. *Key Instance Methods for Manipulating a DirectoryInfo Object*

Method	Description
Create	Creates the specified directory. If the path specifies multiple directories that do not exist, they will all be created at once.
CreateSubdirectory	Creates a directory with the specified path in the directory represented by the DirectoryInfo object. If the path specifies multiple directories that do not exist, they will all be created at once. It also returns a new DirectoryInfo object that represents the last directory in the specified path.
Delete	Removes the directory, if it exists. If you want to delete a directory that contains files or other directories, you must use the overloaded Delete method that accepts a parameter named Recursive and set it to True.
MoveTo	Moves the directory (contents and all) to a new path. MoveTo can also be used to rename a directory without changing its location.

Table 5-5. *Key Shared Methods for Manipulating Files and Folders with the My.Computer.FileSystem Object*

Method	Description
CopyDirectory and CopyFile	Copy a directory (and all its contents) or a file to the new path specified.

Table 5-5. *Key Shared Methods for Manipulating Files and Folders with the My.Computer.FileSystem Object*

Method	Description
CreateDirectory	Creates a new directory with the specified name and path.
DeleteDirectory and DeleteFile	Delete the specified directory (and all its contents) or file. Both methods offer the Recycle parameter, which determines if files are deleted permanently or sent to the Recycle Bin. DeleteDirectory has a parameter named OnDirectoryNotEmpty to determine if all contents should be deleted.
MoveDirectory and MoveFile	Move a directory (and all its contents) or a file to the new path specified.
OpenTextFieldParser	Opens a file and returns a TextFieldParser object. The TextFieldParser class is contained in the Microsoft.VisualBasic.FileIO namespace and is used to parse the contents of a text file. For more information about parsing, see recipe 5-9.
OpenTextFileReader and OpenTextFileWriter	Open the specified file and return either a StreamReader or StreamWriter as appropriate. For more information about reading and writing files, see recipes 5-7 and 5-8.

The Code

One useful feature that is missing from the DirectoryInfo class is a copy method. The following example contains a helper function that can copy any directory and its contents.

```
Imports System
Imports system.IO

Namespace Apress.VisualBasicRecipes.Chapter05

    Public Class Recipe05_03

        Public Shared Sub Main(ByVal args As String())

            If args.Length = 2 Then
                Dim sourceDir As New DirectoryInfo(args(0))
                Dim destinationDir As New DirectoryInfo(args(1))

                CopyDirectory(sourceDir, destinationDir)

                ' Wait to continue.
                Console.WriteLine(Environment.NewLine)
                Console.WriteLine("Main method complete. Press Enter.")
                Console.ReadLine()
```

```
            Else
                Console.WriteLine("USAGE:   " & " Recipe05_03 [sourcePath] " & ➥
"[destinationPath]")
            End If

        End Sub

        Public Shared Sub CopyDirectory(ByVal source As DirectoryInfo, ➥
ByVal destination As DirectoryInfo)

            If Not destination.Exists Then
                destination.Create()
            End If

            ' Copy all files.
            Dim files As FileInfo() = source.GetFiles

            For Each file As FileInfo In files
                file.CopyTo(Path.Combine(destination.FullName, file.Name))
            Next

            ' Process subdirectories.
            Dim dirs As DirectoryInfo() = source.GetDirectories

            For Each dir As DirectoryInfo In dirs
                ' Get destination directory.
                Dim destinationDir As String = Path.Combine(destination.FullName, ➥
dir.Name)

                ' Call CopyDirectory recursively.
                CopyDirectory(dir, New DirectoryInfo(destinationDir))
            Next

        End Sub

    End Class
End Namespace
```

While the recipe contains examples of useful methods in the `FileInfo` and `DirectoryInfo` classes, you should use the new `Shared My.Computer.FileSystem.CopyDirectory` method. This would replace the entire preceding example with the following line of code.

```
My.Computer.FileSystem.CopyDirectory("SomeSourceDirectory", "SomeTargetDirectory")
```

5-4. Calculate the Size of a Directory

Problem

You need to calculate the size of all files contained in a directory (and, optionally, its subdirectories).

Solution

Examine all the files in a directory and add together their FileInfo.Length properties. Use recursive logic to include the size of files in contained subdirectories.

How It Works

The DirectoryInfo class does not provide any property that returns size information. However, you can easily calculate the size of all files contained in a directory using the FileInfo.Length property.

The Code

The following example calculates the size of a directory and optionally examines subdirectories recursively.

```
Imports System
Imports system.IO

Namespace Apress.VisualBasicRecipes.Chapter05

    Public Class Recipe05_04
        Public Shared Sub Main(ByVal args As String())

            If args.Length > 0 Then
                Dim dir As New DirectoryInfo(args(0))

                Console.WriteLine("Total size: " & ➥
CalculateDirectorySize(dir, True).ToString & " bytes.")

                ' Wait to continue.
                Console.WriteLine(Environment.NewLine)
                Console.WriteLine("Main method complete. Press Enter.")
                Console.ReadLine()

            Else
                Console.WriteLine("Please supply a directory path.")
            End If

        End Sub

        Public Shared Function CalculateDirectorySize(ByVal dir As DirectoryInfo, ➥
ByVal includeSubDirs As Boolean) As Long

            Dim totalSize As Long = 0

            ' Examine all contained files.
            Dim files As FileInfo() = dir.GetFiles

            For Each currentFile As FileInfo In files
                totalSize += currentFile.Length
            Next
```

```
            ' Examine all contained directories.
            If includeSubDirs Then
                Dim dirs As DirectoryInfo() = dir.GetDirectories

                For Each currentDir As DirectoryInfo In dirs
                    totalSize += CalculateDirectorySize(currentDir, True)
                Next
            End If

            Return totalSize

        End Function

    End Class
End Namespace
```

5-5. Retrieve Version Information for a File

Problem

You want to retrieve file version information, such as the publisher of a file, its revision number, associated comments, and so on.

Solution

Use the `Shared GetVersionInfo` method of the `System.Diagnostics.FileVersionInfo` class.

How It Works

The .NET Framework allows you to retrieve file information without resorting to the Windows API. Instead, you simply need to use the `FileVersionInfo` class and call the `GetVersionInfo` method with the filename as a parameter. You can then retrieve extensive information through the `FileVersionInfo` properties.

The Code

The `FileVersionInfo` properties are too numerous to list here, but the following code snippet shows an example of what you might retrieve.

```
Imports System
Imports system.Diagnostics

Namespace Apress.VisualBasicRecipes.Chapter05

    Public Class Recipe05_05
        Public Shared Sub Main(ByVal args As String())

            If args.Length > 0 Then
                Dim info As FileVersionInfo = ➡
FileVersionInfo.GetVersionInfo(args(0))
```

```
          ' Display version information.
          Console.WriteLine("Checking File: " & info.FileName)
          Console.WriteLine("Product Name: " & info.ProductName)
          Console.WriteLine("Product Version: " & info.ProductVersion)
          Console.WriteLine("Company Name: " & info.CompanyName)
          Console.WriteLine("File Version: " & info.FileVersion)
          Console.WriteLine("File Description: " & info.FileDescription)
          Console.WriteLine("Original Filename: " & info.OriginalFilename)
          Console.WriteLine("Legal Copyright: " & info.LegalCopyright)
          Console.WriteLine("InternalName: " & info.InternalName)
          Console.WriteLine("IsDebug: " & info.IsDebug)
          Console.WriteLine("IsPatched: " & info.IsPatched)
          Console.WriteLine("IsPreRelease: " & info.IsPreRelease)
          Console.WriteLine("IsPrivateBuild: " & info.IsPrivateBuild)
          Console.WriteLine("IsSpecialBuild: " & info.IsSpecialBuild)

          ' Wait to continue.
          Console.WriteLine(Environment.NewLine)
          Console.WriteLine("Main method complete. Press Enter.")
          Console.ReadLine()

      Else
          Console.WriteLine("Please supply a filename.")
      End If

  End Sub

End Class
End Namespace
```

Usage

If you run the command `Recipe05_05 c:\windows\explorer.exe`, the example produces the following output.

```
Checking File: c:\windows\explorer.exe
Product Name: Microsoftr Windowsr Operating System
Product Version: 6.00.2900.2180
Company Name: Microsoft Corporation
File Version: 6.00.2900.2180 (xpsp_sp2_rtm.040803-2158)
File Description: Windows Explorer
Original Filename: EXPLORER.EXE
Legal Copyright: c Microsoft Corporation. All rights reserved.
InternalName: explorer
IsDebug: False
IsPatched: False
IsPreRelease: False
IsPrivateBuild: False
IsSpecialBuild: False
```

5-6. Show a Just-in-Time Directory Tree in the TreeView Control

Problem

You need to display a directory tree in a TreeView control. However, filling the directory tree structure at startup is too time-consuming.

Solution

Fill the first level of directories in the TreeView control and add a hidden dummy node to each directory branch. React to the TreeView.BeforeExpand event to fill in subdirectories in a branch just before it's displayed.

How It Works

You can use recursion to build an entire directory tree. However, scanning the file system in this way can be slow, particularly for large drives. For this reason, professional file management software programs (including Windows Explorer) use a different technique. They query the necessary directory information when the user requests it.

The TreeView control is particularly well suited to this approach because it provides a BeforeExpand event that fires before a new level of nodes is displayed. You can use a placeholder (such as an asterisk or empty TreeNode) in all the directory branches that are not filled in. This allows you to fill in parts of the directory tree as they are displayed.

To use this type of solution, you need the following three ingredients:

- A Fill method that adds a single level of directory nodes based on a single directory. You will use this method to fill directory levels as they are expanded.

- A basic Form.Load event handler that uses the Fill method to add the first level of directories for the drive.

- A TreeView.BeforeExpand event handler that reacts when the user expands a node and calls the Fill method if this directory information has not yet been added.

The Code

The following shows the code for this solution. The automatically generated code for the form designer is not included here, but it is included with this book's downloadable code.

```
Imports System
Imports System.IO

'  All design code is stored in the autogenerated partial
'  class called DirectoryTree.Designer.vb. You can see this
'  file by selecting Show All Files in Solution Explorer.
Partial Public Class DirectoryTree

    Private Sub DirectoryTree_Load(ByVal sender As System.Object, ➥
ByVal e As System.EventArgs) Handles MyBase.Load
```

```
    ' Set the first node.
    Dim rootNode As New TreeNode("C:\")
    treeDirectory.Nodes.Add(rootNode)

    ' Fill the first level and expand it.
    Fill(rootNode)
    treeDirectory.Nodes(0).Expand()

End Sub

Private Sub treeDirectory_BeforeExpand(ByVal sender As Object, ➡
ByVal e As System.Windows.Forms.TreeViewCancelEventArgs) Handles ➡
treeDirectory.BeforeExpand

    ' If a dummy node is found, remove it and read the
    ' real directory list.
    If e.Node.Nodes(0).Text = "*" Then
        e.Node.Nodes.Clear()
        Fill(e.Node)
    End If

End Sub

Private Sub Fill(ByVal dirNode As TreeNode)

    Dim dir As New DirectoryInfo(dirNode.FullPath)

    ' An exception could be thrown in this code if you don't
    ' have sufficient security permissions for a file or directory.
    ' You can catch and then ignore this exception.

    For Each dirItem As DirectoryInfo In dir.GetDirectories
        ' Add a node for the directory.
        Dim newNode As New TreeNode(dirItem.Name)
        dirNode.Nodes.Add(newNode)
        newNode.Nodes.Add("*")
    Next

End Sub
End Class
```

Figure 5-1 shows the directory tree in action.

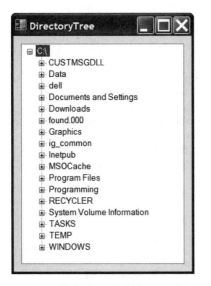

Figure 5-1. *A directory tree with the TreeView*

If you prefer to use the My object, you can replace the use of the DirectoryInfo class with the My.Computer.FileSystem class. The following replacement Fill method is an example of how to do this.

```
Private Sub Fill(ByVal dirNode As TreeNode)

    '  An exception could be thrown in this code if you don't
    '  have sufficient security permissions for a file or directory.
    '  You can catch and then ignore this exception.
    For Each dir As String In ➡
My.Computer.FileSystem.GetDirectories(dirNode.FullPath)
        '  Add a node for the directory.
        Dim newNode As New TreeNode(Path.GetFileName(dir))
        dirNode.Nodes.Add(newNode)
        newNode.Nodes.Add("*")
    Next

End Sub
```

5-7. Read and Write a Text File

Problem

You need to write data to a sequential text file using ASCII, Unicode (UTF-16), or UTF-8 encoding.

Solution

Create a new System.IO.FileStream object that references the file. To write the file, wrap the FileStream in a System.IO.StreamWriter and use the overloaded Write method. To read the file, wrap the FileStream in a System.IO.StreamReader and use the Read or ReadLine method. The File class also provides the Shared CreateText and OpenText methods for writing and reading UTF-8 files. Another alternative is to use the `OpenTextFileReader` and `OpenTextFileWriter` methods of the `My.Computer.FileSystem` class. These methods open a file and return a `StreamReader` or `StreamWriter`, respectively.

How It Works

The .NET Framework allows you to write or read text with any stream by using the `StreamWriter` and `StreamReader` classes. When writing data with the `StreamWriter`, you use the `StreamWriter.Write` method. This method is overloaded to support all the common VB .NET .NET data types, including strings, chars, integers, floating-point numbers, decimals, and so on. However, the `Write` and `WriteLine` methods always convert the supplied data to text. Unlike `Write`, the `WriteLine` method places each value on a separate line, so you should use it if you want to be able to easily convert the text back to its original data type.

The way a string is represented depends on the encoding you use. The most common encodings are listed in Table 5-6.

Table 5-6. *Common Encodings*

Encoding	Description	Represented By
ASCII	Encodes each character in a string using 7 bits. ASCII-encoded data cannot contain extended Unicode characters. When using ASCII encoding in .NET, the bits will be padded and the resulting byte array will have 1 byte for each character.	`ASCII` property of the `System.Text.Encoding` class
UTF-7 Unicode	Uses 7 bits for ordinary ASCII characters and multiple 7-bit pairs for extended characters. This encoding is primarily for use with 7-bit protocols such as mail, and it is not regularly used.	`UTF7` property of the `System.Text.Encoding` class
UTF-8 Unicode	Uses 8 bits for ordinary ASCII characters and multiple 8-bit pairs for extended characters. The resulting byte array will have 1 byte for each character (provided there are no extended characters).	`UTF8` property of the `System.Text.Encoding` class
Full Unicode (or UTF-16)	Represents each character in a string using 16 bits. The resulting byte array will have 2 bytes for each character.	`Unicode` property of the `System.Text.Encoding` class
UTF-32 Unicode	Represents each character in a string using 32 bits. The resulting byte array will have 4 bytes for each character.	`UTF32` property of the `System.Text.Encoding` class

The .NET Framework provides a class for each type of encoding in the `System.Text` namespace. When using `StreamReader` and `StreamWriter`, you can specify the encoding or simply use the default UTF-8 encoding.

When reading information, you use the `Read` or `ReadLine` method of `StreamReader`. The `Read` method reads a single character, or the number of characters you specify, and returns the data as an `Integer` that represents the character read or the number of characters read, respectively. The `ReadLine` method returns a string with the content of an entire line. The `ReadToEnd` method will return a string with the content starting from the current position to the end of the stream. An alternative to the

ReadToEnd method is the Shared ReadAllText method of the My.Computer.FileSystem and System.IO.File classes.

The Code

The following console application writes and then reads a text file.

```
Imports System
Imports System.IO
Imports System.Text

Namespace Apress.VisualBasicRecipes.Chapter05

    Public Class Recipe05_07
        Public Shared Sub Main()

            ' Create a new file.
            Using fs As New FileStream("test.txt", FileMode.Create)
                ' Create a writer and specify the encoding. The
                ' default (UTF-8) supports special Unicode characters,
                ' but encodes all standard characters in the same way as
                ' ASCII encoding.
                Using w As New StreamWriter(fs, Encoding.UTF8)

                    ' Write a decimal, string and char.
                    w.WriteLine(CDec(124.23))
                    w.WriteLine("Test string")
                    w.WriteLine("!"c)

                End Using
            End Using

            Console.WriteLine("Press Enter to read the information.")
            Console.ReadLine()

            ' Open the file in read-only mode.
            Using fs As New FileStream("test.txt", FileMode.Open)
                Using r As New StreamReader(fs, Encoding.UTF8)
                    ' Read the data and convert it to the appropriate data type.
                    Console.WriteLine(Decimal.Parse(r.ReadLine))
                    Console.WriteLine(r.ReadLine)
                    Console.WriteLine(Char.Parse(r.ReadLine))
                End Using
            End Using

            ' Wait to continue.
            Console.WriteLine(Environment.NewLine)
            Console.WriteLine("Main method complete. Press Enter.")
            Console.ReadLine()

        End Sub

    End Class
End Namespace
```

If you prefer to use the My object, you can use the OpenTextFileReader and OpenTextFileWriter methods of the My.Computer.FileSystem class. These methods do not require a FileStream object, which makes the code a little simpler, as shown in the following example.

```
' Open and write to a file.
Using w As StreamWriter = My.Computer.FileSystem.OpenTextFileWriter("test.txt", ➡
False, Encoding.UTF8)
    ' Write a decimal, string and char.
    w.WriteLine(CDec(124.23))
    w.WriteLine("Test string")
    w.WriteLine("!"c)
End Using

' Open and read from the file.
Using r As StreamReader = My.Computer.FileSystem.OpenTextFileReader("test.txt", ➡
Encoding.UTF8)
    ' Read the data and convert it to the appropriate data type.
    Console.WriteLine(Decimal.Parse(r.ReadLine))
    Console.WriteLine(r.ReadLine)
    Console.WriteLine(Char.Parse(r.ReadLine))
End Using
```

5-8. Read and Write a Binary File

Problem

You need to write data to a binary file, with strong data typing.

Solution

Create a new System.IO.FileStream object that references the file. To write the file, wrap the FileStream in a System.IO.BinaryWriter and use the overloaded Write method. To read the file, wrap the FileStream in a System.IO.BinaryReader and use the Read method that corresponds to the expected data type.

How It Works

The .NET Framework allows you to write or read binary data with any stream by using the BinaryWriter and BinaryReader classes. When writing data with the BinaryWriter, you use the Write method. This method is overloaded to support all the common VB .NET data types, including strings, chars, integers, floating-point numbers, decimals, and so on. The information will then be encoded as a series of bytes and written to the file. You can configure the encoding used for strings, which defaults to UTF-8, by using an overloaded constructor that accepts a System.Text.Encoding object, as described in recipe 5-7.

You must be particularly fastidious with data types when using binary files. This is because when you retrieve the information, you must use one of the strongly typed Read methods from the BinaryReader, unless you intend to read the file character by character. For example, to retrieve decimal data, you use ReadDecimal. To read a string, you use ReadString. (The BinaryWriter always records the length of a string when it writes it to a binary file to prevent any possibility of error.)

The Code

The following console application writes and then reads a binary file.

```
Imports System
Imports System.IO

Namespace Apress.VisualBasicRecipes.Chapter05

    Public Class Recipe05_08
        Public Shared Sub Main()

            ' Create a new file and writer.
            Using fs As New FileStream("test.bin", FileMode.Create)
                Using w As New BinaryWriter(fs)
                    ' Write a decimal, 2 strings and a char.
                    w.Write(CDec(124.23))
                    w.Write("Test string")
                    w.Write("Test string 2")
                    w.Write("!"c)
                End Using
            End Using
            Console.WriteLine("Press Enter to read the information.")
            Console.ReadLine()

            ' Open the file in read-only mode.
            Using fs As New FileStream("test.bin", FileMode.Open)
                Using sr As New StreamReader(fs)
                    ' Display the raw information in the file.
                    Console.WriteLine(sr.ReadToEnd)
                    Console.WriteLine()

                    ' Read the data and convert it to the appropriate data type.
                    fs.Position = 0
                    Using br As New BinaryReader(fs)
                        Console.WriteLine(br.ReadDecimal)
                        Console.WriteLine(br.ReadString)
                        Console.WriteLine(br.ReadString)
                        Console.WriteLine(br.ReadChar)
                    End Using
                End Using
            End Using

            ' Wait to continue.
            Console.WriteLine(Environment.NewLine)
            Console.WriteLine("Main method complete. Press Enter.")
            Console.ReadLine()

        End Sub

    End Class
End Namespace
```

5-9. Parse a Delimited Text File

Problem

You need to parse the contents of a delimited text file.

Solution

Create and configure a new `Microsoft.VisualBasic.FileIO.TextFieldParser` object that references the file you need to parse. Loop through the file until the `EndOfData` property is `True`. Use the `ReadFields` method to return an array of strings representing one row of parsed data from the file.

How It Works

The `TextFieldParser` class can be found in the `Microsoft.VisualBasic.FileIO` namespace. You can either use one of its constructors to create an instance directly or use the `Shared My.Computer.FileSystem.OpenTextFieldParser` method to return an instance. Some of the more important properties and methods of this class are listed in Table 5-7.

Table 5-7. *Key Properties and Methods of the TextFieldParser Class*

Property or Method	Description
CommentTokens	An array of strings that indicates which lines in the file are comments. Commented lines are skipped.
Delimiters	An array of strings that defines the delimiters used in the text file. TextFieldType must be set to FieldType.Delimited to use this property.
EndOfData	Returns True if there is no more data to be parsed.
ErrorLine	Returns the actual line in the file that threw the last MalformedLineException.
ErrorLineNumber	Returns the line number that threw the last MalformedLineException.
FieldWidths	An array of integers that defines the widths of each field. TextFieldType must be set to FieldType.FixedWidth to use this property.
HasFieldsEnclosedInQuotes	Indicates whether some fields are enclosed in quotation marks. This is True by default.
TextFieldType	Indicates the type of file (Delimited or FixedWidth) that is being parsed. This is set to Delimited by default.
ReadFields	Reads and parses all fields for the current row and returns the data as an array of strings. The pointer is then moved to the next row. If a field cannot be parsed, a MalformedLineException is thrown.

Table 5-7. *Key Properties and Methods of the TextFieldParser Class*

Property or Method	Description
SetDelimiters	Sets the Delimiters property to the value or values specified. The single parameter for this method is a parameter array, so you can supply a comma-separated list of values rather than an actual array.
SetFieldWidths	Sets the FieldWidths property to the value or values specified. The single parameter for this method is a parameter array, so you can supply a comma-separated list of values rather than an actual array.

Once you have an instance, you need to configure it according to the file you need to parse. If your file is delimited, set the TextFieldType property to Delimited and set the Delimiters property to the appropriate delimiters. If the file is fixed width, set the TextFieldType property to FixedWidth and set the FieldWidths property to the appropriate widths. Use the CommentTokens property to instruct the parser to skip rows that are comments and do not contain any data to be parsed.

Use the ReadFields method to parse the current row, return an array of strings containing each field parsed, and move the file pointer to the next row. If a field cannot be parsed, a MalformedLineException is thrown. You can then use the ErrorLine and ErrorLineNumber properties of the TextFieldParser class to obtain information about which line and field caused the exception.

The Code

The following example creates a sample comma-delimited log file. The file is then read and parsed, using the TextFieldParser class. The fields contained in the file are written to the console.

```
Imports System
Imports System.IO
Imports Microsoft.VisualBasic.FileIO

Namespace Apress.VisualBasicRecipes.Chapter05

    Public Class Recipe05_09

        Public Shared Sub Main()

            ' Create the sample log file.
            Using w As StreamWriter = ➡
My.Computer.FileSystem.OpenTextFileWriter("SampleLog.txt", ➡
 False, System.Text.Encoding.UTF8)

                ' Write sample log records to the file. The parser
                ' will skip blank lines. Also, the TextFieldParser
                ' can be configured to ignore lines that are comments.
                w.WriteLine("'In this sample log file, comments " & ➡
"start with a ""'"". The")
                w.WriteLine("'parser, when configured correctly, " & ➡
"will ignore these lines.")
                w.WriteLine("")
                w.WriteLine("{0},INFO,""{1}""", DateTime.Now, ➡
"Some informational text.")
                w.WriteLine("{0},WARN,""{1}""", DateTime.Now, ➡
```

```vb
                    "Some warning message.")
                            w.WriteLine("{0},ERR!,""{1}""", DateTime.Now, ➡
        "[ERROR] Some exception has occurred.")
                            w.WriteLine("{0},INFO,""{1}""", DateTime.Now, ➡
        "More informational text.")
                            w.WriteLine("{0},ERR!,""{1}""", DateTime.Now, ➡
        "[ERROR] Some exception has occurred.")

            End Using

            Console.WriteLine("Press Enter to read and parse the information.")
            Console.ReadLine()

            ' Open the file in and parse the data into a
            ' TextFieldParser object.
            Using logFile As TextFieldParser = ➡
        My.Computer.FileSystem.OpenTextFieldParser("SampleLog.txt")

                Console.WriteLine("Parsing text file.")
                Console.WriteLine(Environment.NewLine)

                ' Write header information to the console.
                Console.WriteLine("{0,-29} {1} {2}", "Date/Time in RFC1123", ➡
        "Type", "Message")

                ' Configure the parser. For this recipe, make sure
                ' HasFieldsEnclosedInQuotes is True.
                logFile.TextFieldType = FieldType.Delimited
                logFile.CommentTokens = New String() {"'"}
                logFile.Delimiters = New String() {","}
                logFile.HasFieldsEnclosedInQuotes = True

                Dim currentRecord As String()

                ' Loop through the file until we reach the end.
                Do While Not logFile.EndOfData
                    Try
                        ' Parse all the fields into the currentRow
                        ' array. This method automatically moves
                        ' the file pointer to the next row.
                        currentRecord = logFile.ReadFields

                        ' Write the parsed record to the console.
                        Console.WriteLine("{0:r} {1} {2}", ➡
        DateTime.Parse(currentRecord(0)), currentRecord(1), currentRecord(2))
                    Catch ex As MalformedLineException
                        ' The MalformedLineException is thrown by the
                        ' TextFieldParser anytime a line cannot be
                        ' parsed.
                        Console.WriteLine("An exception occurred attempting " & ➡
        "to parse this row:  ", ex.Message)
                    End Try
                Loop
            End Using
```

```
        ' Wait to continue.
        Console.WriteLine(Environment.NewLine)
        Console.WriteLine("Main method complete. Press Enter.")
        Console.ReadLine()

    End Sub

  End Class
End Namespace
```

The following is an example of the output you will see when you run this test.

```
Press Enter to read and parse the information.

Parsing text file.

Date/Time in RFC1123           Type  Message
Sat, 20 Jan 2007 13:34:32 GMT  INFO  Some informational text.
Sat, 20 Jan 2007 13:34:32 GMT  WARN  Some warning message such as watch
Sat, 20 Jan 2007 13:34:32 GMT  ERR!  [ERROR] Some exception has occurred.
Sat, 20 Jan 2007 13:34:32 GMT  INFO  More informational text.
Sat, 20 Jan 2007 13:34:32 GMT  ERR!  [ERROR] Some exception has occurred.
```

5-10. Read a File Asynchronously

Problem

You need to read data from a file without blocking the execution of your code. This technique is commonly used if the file is stored on a slow backing store (such as a networked drive in a wide area network).

Solution

Create a separate class that will read the file asynchronously. Start reading a block of data using the FileStream.BeginRead method and supply a callback method. When the callback is triggered, retrieve the data by calling FileStream.EndRead, process it, and read the next block asynchronously with BeginRead.

How It Works

The FileStream includes basic support for asynchronous use through the BeginRead and EndRead methods. Using these methods, you can read a block of data on one of the threads provided by the .NET Framework thread pool, without needing to directly use the threading classes in the System.Threading namespace.

When reading a file asynchronously, you choose the amount of data that you want to read at a time. Depending on the situation, you might want to read a very small amount of data at a time (for example, if you are copying it block by block to another file) or a relatively large amount of data (for example, if you need a certain amount of information before your processing logic can start). You specify the block size when calling BeginRead, and you pass a buffer where the data will be placed. Because the BeginRead and EndRead methods need to be able to access many of the same pieces of information, such as the `FileStream`, the buffer, the block size, and so on, it's usually easiest to encapsulate your asynchronous file reading code in a single class.

The Code

The following example demonstrates reading a file asynchronously. The `AsyncProcessor` class provides a public `StartProcess` method, which starts an asynchronous read. Every time the read operation finishes, the `OnCompletedRead` callback is triggered and the block of data is processed. If there is more data in the file, a new asynchronous read operation is started. `AsyncProcessor` reads 2 kilobytes (2,048 bytes) at a time.

```
Imports System
Imports System.IO
Imports System.Threading

Namespace Apress.VisualBasicRecipes.Chapter05

    Public Class AsyncProcessor

        Private inputStream As Stream

        ' The buffer that will hold the retrieved data.
        Private buffer As Byte()

        ' The amount that will be read in one block (2 kb).
        Private m_BufferSize As Integer = 2048

        Public ReadOnly Property BufferSize() As Integer
            Get
                Return m_BufferSize
            End Get
        End Property

        Public Sub New(ByVal fileName As String, ByVal size As Integer)

            m_BufferSize = size
            buffer = New Byte(m_BufferSize) {}

            ' Open the file, specifying true for asynchronous support.
            inputStream = New FileStream(fileName, FileMode.Open, FileAccess.Read, ➥
FileShare.Read, m_BufferSize, True)

        End Sub

        Public Sub StartProcess()

            ' Start the asynchronous read, which will fill the buffer.
            inputStream.BeginRead(buffer, 0, buffer.Length, ➥
AddressOf OnCompletedRead, Nothing)

        End Sub

        Private Sub OnCompletedRead(ByVal asyncResult As IAsyncResult)
```

```vb
            ' One block has been read asynchronously. Retrieve
            ' the data.
            Dim bytesRead As Integer = inputStream.EndRead(asyncResult)

            ' If no bytes are read, the stream is at the end of the file.
            If bytesRead > 0 Then
                ' Pause to simulate processing this block of data.
                Console.WriteLine("{0}[ASYNC READER]: Read one block.", ➥
ControlChars.Tab)
                Thread.Sleep(20)

                ' Begin to read the next block asynchronously.
                inputStream.BeginRead(buffer, 0, buffer.Length, ➥
AddressOf OnCompletedRead, Nothing)
            Else
                ' End the operation.
                Console.WriteLine("{0}[ASYNC READER]: Complete.", ControlChars.Tab)
                inputStream.Close()
            End If

        End Sub

    End Class
End Namespace
```

Usage

The following example shows a console application that uses `AsyncProcessor` to read a 2-megabyte file.

```vb
Imports System
Imports System.IO
Imports System.Threading

Namespace Apress.VisualBasicRecipes.Chapter05

    Public Class Recipe05_10

        Public Shared Sub Main(ByVal args As String())
            ' Create a 2 MB test file.
            Using fs As New FileStream("test.txt", FileMode.Create)
                fs.SetLength(2097152)
            End Using

            ' Start the asynchronous file processor on another thread.
            Dim asyncIO As New AsyncProcessor("test.txt", 2048)
            asyncIO.StartProcess()

            ' At the same time, do some other work.
            ' In this example, we simply loop for 10 seconds.
            Dim startTime As DateTime = DateTime.Now
```

```
            While DateTime.Now.Subtract(startTime).TotalSeconds < 10
                Console.WriteLine("[MAIN THREAD]: Doing some work.")

                ' Pause to simulate a time-consuming operation.
                Thread.Sleep(100)
            End While

            Console.WriteLine("[MAIN THREAD]: Complete.")
            Console.ReadLine()

            ' Remove the test file.
            File.Delete("test.txt")
        End Sub

    End Class
End Namespace
```

The following is an example of the output you will see when you run this test.

```
[MAIN THREAD]: Doing some work.
        [ASYNC READER]: Read one block.
        [ASYNC READER]: Read one block.
[MAIN THREAD]: Doing some work.
        [ASYNC READER]: Read one block.
        [ASYNC READER]: Read one block.
        [ASYNC READER]: Read one block.
        [ASYNC READER]: Read one block.
[MAIN THREAD]: Doing some work.
        [ASYNC READER]: Read one block.
        [ASYNC READER]: Read one block.
        [ASYNC READER]: Read one block.
        . . .
```

5-11. Find Files That Match a Wildcard Expression

Problem

You need to process multiple files based on a filter expression (such as *.dll or mysheet20??.xls).

Solution

Use the overloaded version of the System.IO.DirectoryInfo.GetFiles method that accepts a filter expression and returns an array of FileInfo objects. For searching recursively across all subdirectories, use the overloaded version that accepts the SearchOption enumeration.

How It Works

The DirectoryInfo and Directory objects both provide a way to search the directories for files that match a specific filter expression. These search expressions can use the standard ? and * wildcards. You can use a similar technique to retrieve directories that match a specified search pattern by using the overloaded DirectoryInfo.GetDirectories method. .NET Framework 2.0 offers a new overload of GetFiles for searching recursively using the SearchOption.AllDirectories enumeration constant.

As an alternative, you can also use the Shared GetFiles method of the My.Computer.FileSystem class. This method returns only strings representing the full path of the file, rather than FileInfo objects. As with the System.IO.DirectoryInfo.GetFiles method, you can use an overload to search recursively using the SearchOptions.SearchAllSubDirectories enumeration constant. This method also allows you to search for multiple file extensions at once.

The Code

The following example retrieves the names of all the files in a specified directory that match a specified filter string. The directory and filter expression are submitted as command-line arguments. The code then iterates through the retrieved FileInfo collection of matching files and displays the name and size of each one.

```
Imports System
Imports System.IO

Namespace Apress.VisualBasicRecipes.Chapter05

    Public Class Recipe05_11
        Public Shared Sub Main(ByVal args As String())

            If args.Length = 2 Then
                Dim dir As New DirectoryInfo(args(0))
                Dim files As FileInfo() = dir.GetFiles(args(1))

                ' Display the name of all the files.
                For Each file As FileInfo In files
                    Console.Write("Name: " & file.Name + " ")
                    Console.WriteLine("Size: " & file.Length.ToString)
                Next

                ' Wait to continue.
                Console.WriteLine(Environment.NewLine)
                Console.WriteLine("Main method complete. Press Enter.")
                Console.ReadLine()

            Else
                Console.WriteLine("USAGE:  Recipe05-11 [directory]" & ➥
"[filterExpression]")
            End If

        End Sub

    End Class
End Namespace
```

5-12. Test Two Files for Equality

Problem

You need to quickly compare the content of two files and determine if it matches exactly.

Solution

Calculate the hash code of each file using the `System.Security.Cryptography.HashAlgorithm` class, and then compare the hash codes.

How It Works

You might compare file content in a number of ways. For example, you could examine a portion of the file for similar data, or you could read through each file byte by byte, comparing each byte as you go. Both of these approaches are valid, but in some cases, it's more convenient to use a *hash code* algorithm.

A hash code algorithm generates a small (typically about 20 bytes) binary fingerprint for a file. While it's *possible* for different files to generate the same hash codes, that is statistically unlikely to occur. In fact, even a minor change (for example, modifying a single bit in the source file) has an approximately 50-percent chance of independently changing each bit in the hash code. For this reason, hash codes are often used in security code to detect data tampering. (Hash codes are discussed in more detail in recipes 11-14, 11-15, and 11-16.)

To create a hash code, you must first create a `HashAlgorithm` object, typically by calling the `Shared HashAlgorithm.Create` method. This defaults to using the sha1 algorithm but provides an overload allowing other algorithms to be provided. You can then call `HashAlgorithm.ComputeHash`, which returns a byte array with the hash data.

The Code

The following example demonstrates a simple console application that reads two filenames that are supplied as arguments and uses hash codes to test the files for equality. The hashes are compared by converting them into strings. Alternatively, you could compare them by iterating over the byte array and comparing each value. That approach would be slightly faster, but because the overhead of converting 20 bytes into a string is minimal, it's not required.

```
Imports System
Imports System.IO
Imports System.Security.Cryptography

Namespace Apress.VisualBasicRecipes.Chapter05

    Public Class Recipe05_12
        Public Shared Sub Main(ByVal args As String())

            If args.Length = 2 Then
                Console.WriteLine("comparing {0} and {1}", args(0), args(1))

                ' Create the hashing object.
                Using hashAlg As HashAlgorithm = HashAlgorithm.Create
                    Using fsA As New FileStream(args(0), FileMode.Open), ➡
fsB As New FileStream(args(1), FileMode.Open)
```

```
                  ' Calculate the hash for the files.
                  Dim hashBytesA As Byte() = hashAlg.ComputeHash(fsA)
                  Dim hashBytesB As Byte() = hashAlg.ComputeHash(fsB)

                  ' Compare the hashes.
                  If BitConverter.ToString(hashBytesA) = ➥
BitConverter.ToString(hashBytesB) Then
                      Console.WriteLine("Files match.")
                  Else
                      Console.WriteLine("No match.")
                  End If

              End Using

              ' Wait to continue.
              Console.WriteLine(Environment.NewLine)
              Console.WriteLine("Main method complete. Press Enter.")
              Console.ReadLine()

          End Using

      Else
          Console.WriteLine("USAGE:  Recipe05-12 [fileName] [fileName]")
      End If

    End Sub

  End Class
End Namespace
```

5-13. Manipulate Strings Representing Filenames

Problem

You want to retrieve a portion of a path or verify that a file path is in a normal (standardized) form.

Solution

Process the path using the System.IO.Path class. You can use Path.GetFileName to retrieve a filename from a path, Path.ChangeExtension to modify the extension portion of a path string, and Path.Combine to create a fully qualified path without worrying about whether your directory includes a trailing directory separation (\) character.

How It Works

File paths are often difficult to work with in code because of the many different ways to represent the same directory. For example, you might use an absolute path (C:\Temp), a UNC path (\\MyServer\\ MyShare\temp), or one of many possible relative paths (C:\Temp\MyFiles\..\ or C:\Temp\MyFiles\ ..\..\temp).

The easiest way to handle file system paths is to use the `Shared` methods of the `Path` class to make sure you have the information you expect. For example, here is how to take a filename that might include a qualified path and extract just the filename:

```
Dim filename As String = "..\System\MyFile.txt"
filename = Path.GetFileName(filename)

' Now filename = "MyFile.txt"
```

And here is how you might append the filename to a directory path using the `Path.Combine` method:

```
Dim filename As String = "..\..\myfile.txt"
Dim fullPath As String = "c:\Temp"

filename = Path.GetFileName(filename)
fullPath = Path.Combine(fullPath, filename)

' fullPath is now "c:\Temp\myfile.txt"
```

The advantage of this approach is that a trailing backslash (\) is automatically added to the path name if required. The `Path` class also provides the following useful `Shared` methods for manipulating path information:

- `GetExtension` returns just the extension of the file in the string. If there is no extension, an empty string is returned.

- `ChangeExtension` modifies the current extension of the file in a string. If no extension is specified, the current extension will be removed.

- `GetDirectoryName` returns all the directory information, which is the text between the first and last directory separators (\).

- `GetFileNameWithoutExtension` is similar to `GetFileName`, but it omits the extension.

- `GetFullPath` has no effect on an absolute path, and it changes a relative path into an absolute path using the current directory. For example, if C:\Temp\ is the current directory, calling `GetFullPath` on a filename such as test.txt returns C:\Temp\test.txt.

- `GetPathRoot` retrieves a string with the root (for example, "C:\"), provided that information is in the string. For a relative path, it returns `Nothing`.

- `HasExtension` returns `True` if the path ends with an extension.

- `IsPathRooted` returns `True` if the path is an absolute path and `False` if it's a relative path.

The `My.Computer.FileSystem` offers two `Shared` methods that also work with paths. The `CombinePath` method is the equivalent of `Path.Combine`. The `GetParentPath` method returns the path of the parent folder for the path specified.

■**Note** In most cases, an exception will be thrown if you try to supply an invalid path to one of these methods (for example, paths that include illegal characters). However, path names that are invalid because they contain a wildcard character (* or ?) will not cause the methods to throw an exception. You could use the `Path.GetInvalidPathChars` or `Path.GetInvalidFileNameChars` method to obtain an array of characters that are illegal in path or filenames, respectively.

5-14. Determine If a Path Is a Directory or a File

Problem

You have a path (in the form of a string), and you want to determine whether it corresponds to a directory or a file.

Solution

Test the path with the `Directory.Exists` and `File.Exists` methods.

How It Works

The `System.IO.Directory` and `System.IO.File` classes both provide an `Exists` method. The `Directory.Exists` method returns `True` if a supplied relative or absolute path corresponds to an existing directory, even a shared folder with an UNC name. `File.Exists` returns `True` if the path corresponds to an existing file.

As an alternative, you can use the `Shared FileExists` and `DirectoryExists` methods of the `My.Computer.FileSystem` class. These methods work in the same way as the `System.IO.Directory` and `System.IO.File` methods.

The Code

The following example demonstrates how you can quickly determine if a path corresponds to a file or directory.

```
Imports System
Imports System.IO

Namespace Apress.VisualBasicRecipes.Chapter05

    Public Class Recipe05_14
        Public Shared Sub Main(ByVal args As String())

            For Each arg As String In args
                Console.Write(arg)

                If Directory.Exists(arg) Then
                    Console.WriteLine(" is a directory.")
                ElseIf File.Exists(arg) Then
                    Console.WriteLine(" is a file.")
                Else
                    Console.WriteLine(" does not exist.")
                End If
            Next

            ' Wait to continue.
            Console.WriteLine(Environment.NewLine)
            Console.WriteLine("Main method complete. Press Enter.")
            Console.ReadLine()

        End Sub

    End Class
End Namespace
```

5-15. Work with Relative Paths

Problem

You want to set the current working directory so that you can use relative paths in your code.

Solution

Use the Shared GetCurrentDirectory and SetCurrentDirectory methods of the System.IO.Directory class.

How It Works

Relative paths are automatically interpreted in relation to the current working directory, which is the path of the current application by default. You can retrieve the current working directory by calling Directory.GetCurrentDirectory or change it using Directory.SetCurrentDirectory. In addition, you can use the Shared GetFullPath method of the System.IO.Path class to convert a relative path into an absolute path using the current working directory.

The Code

The following is a simple example that demonstrates working with relative paths.

```
Imports System
Imports System.IO

Namespace Apress.VisualBasicRecipes.Chapter05

    Public Class Recipe05_15
        Public Shared Sub Main()

            Console.WriteLine("Using: " & Directory.GetCurrentDirectory())
            Console.WriteLine("The relative path for 'file.txt' will " & ➥
"automatically become: '" & Path.GetFullPath("file.txt") & "'")
            Console.WriteLine()

            Console.WriteLine("Changing current directory to c:\")
            Directory.SetCurrentDirectory("C:\")

            Console.WriteLine("Now the relative path for 'file.txt' will " & ➥
"automatically become: '" & Path.GetFullPath("file.txt") & "'")

            ' Wait to continue.
            Console.WriteLine(Environment.NewLine)
            Console.WriteLine("Main method complete. Press Enter.")
            Console.ReadLine()

        End Sub

    End Class

End Namespace
```

Usage

The output for this example might be the following (if you run the application in the directory C:\temp).

```
Using: c:\temp
The relative path 'file.txt' will automatically become 'c:\temp\file.txt'

Changing current directory to c:\
The relative path 'file.txt' will automatically become 'c:\file.txt'
```

■**Caution** If you use relative paths, it's recommended that you set the working path at the start of each file inter-action. Otherwise, you could introduce unnoticed security vulnerabilities that could allow a malicious user to force your application into accessing or overwriting system files by tricking it into using a different working directory.

5-16. Create a Temporary File

Problem

You need to create a file that will be placed in the user-specific temporary directory and will have a unique name, so that it will not conflict with temporary files generated by other programs.

Solution

Use the Shared GetTempFileName method of the System.IO.Path class, which returns a path made up of the user's temporary directory and a randomly generated filename.

How It Works

You can use a number of approaches to generate temporary files. In simple cases, you might just create a file in the application directory, possibly using a GUID or a timestamp in conjunction with a random value as the filename. However, the Path class provides a helper method that can save you some work. It creates a file with a unique filename in the current user's temporary directory. On Windows XP, this is a folder similar to C:\Documents and Settings\[username]\Local Settings\temp by default.

The Code

The following example demonstrates creating a temporary file.

```
Imports System
Imports System.IO

Namespace Apress.VisualBasicRecipes.Chapter05

    Public Class Recipe05_16
        Public Shared Sub Main()
```

```
        Dim tempFile As String = Path.GetTempFileName

        Console.WriteLine("Using " & tempFile)

        Using fs As New FileStream(tempFile, FileMode.Open)
            ' Write some data
        End Using

        ' Now delete the file.
        File.Delete(tempFile)

        ' Wait to continue.
        Console.WriteLine(Environment.NewLine)
        Console.WriteLine("Main method complete. Press Enter.")
        Console.ReadLine()

    End Sub

    End Class
End Namespace
```

5-17. Get the Total Free Space on a Drive

Problem

You need to examine a drive and determine how many bytes of free space are available.

Solution

Use the DriveInfo.AvailableFreeSpace property.

How It Works

The DriveInfo class (new to .NET Framework 2.0) provides members that let you find out the drive type, free space, and many other details of a drive. In order to create a new DriveInfo object, you need to pass the drive letter or the drive root string to the constructor, such as 'C' or "C:\" for creating a DriveInfo instance representing the C drive of the computer. You could also retrieve the list of logical drives available by using the Shared Directory.GetLogicalDrives method, which returns an array of strings, each containing the root of the drive, such as "C:\". For more details on each drive, you create a DriveInfo instance, passing either the root or the letter corresponding to the logical drive. If you need a detailed description of each logical drive, call the DriveInfo.GetDrives method, which returns an array of DriveInfo objects, instead of using Directory.GetLogicalDrives.

■**Note** A System.IO.IOException exception is thrown if you try to access an unavailable network drive.

The Code

The following console application shows the available free space using the DriveInfo class for the given drive or for all logical drives if no argument is passed to the application.

```vb
Imports System
Imports System.IO

Namespace Apress.VisualBasicRecipes.Chapter05

    Public Class Recipe05_17

        Public Shared Sub Main(ByVal args As String())

            If args.Length = 1 Then
                Dim drive As New DriveInfo(args(0))

                Console.Write("Free space in {0}-drive (in kilobytes): ", args(0))
                Console.WriteLine(drive.AvailableFreeSpace / 1024)
            Else
                For Each drive As DriveInfo In DriveInfo.GetDrives

                    Try
                        Console.WriteLine("Free space in {0} - {1} KB: ", ➥
drive.RootDirectory, drive.AvailableFreeSpace / 1024)
                    Catch ex As IOException
                        Console.WriteLine(drive)
                    End Try

                Next
            End If

            ' Wait to continue.
            Console.WriteLine(Environment.NewLine)
            Console.WriteLine("Main method complete. Press Enter.")
            Console.ReadLine()

        End Sub

    End Class
End Namespace
```

Note In addition to the `AvailableFreeSpace` property, `DriveInfo` also defines a `TotalFreeSpace` property. The difference between these two properties is that `AvailableFreeSpace` takes into account disk quotas.

5-18. Show the Common File Dialog Boxes

Problem

You need to show the standard Windows dialog boxes for opening and saving files and for selecting a folder.

Solution

Use the OpenFileDialog, SaveFileDialog, and FolderBrowserDialog classes in the System.Windows. Forms namespace. Call the ShowDialog method to display the dialog box, examine the return value to determine whether the user clicked Open or Cancel, and retrieve the selection from the FileName or SelectedPath property.

How It Works

The .NET Framework provides objects that wrap many of the standard Windows dialog boxes, including those used for saving and selecting files and directories. These classes all inherit from System.Windows.Forms.CommonDialog and include the following:

- OpenFileDialog, which allows the user to select a file, as shown in Figure 5-2. The filename and path are provided to your code through the FileName property (or the FileNames collection, if you have enabled multiple file select by setting Multiselect to True). Additionally, you can use the Filter property to set the file format choices and set CheckFileExists. Filter lets you limit the file types that are displayed, and CheckFileExists ensures that only an existing file can be specified.

Figure 5-2. *OpenFileDialog shows the Open dialog box.*

- SaveFileDialog, which allows the user to specify a new file. The filename and path are provided to your code through the FileName property. You can also use the Filter property to set the file format choices, and set the CreatePrompt and OverwritePrompt Boolean properties to instruct .NET to display a confirmation if the user selects a new file or an existing file, respectively.

- FolderBrowserDialog, which allows the user to select (and optionally create) a directory, as shown in Figure 5-3. The selected path is provided through the SelectedPath property, and you can specify whether or not a Create New button should appear using the ShowNewFolderButton property.

Figure 5-3. *FolderBrowserDialog shows the Browse for Folder dialog box.*

When using OpenFileDialog or SaveFileDialog, you need to set the filter string, which specifies the allowed file extensions. If you do not set the filter string, the Type drop-down list will be empty, and all files will be shown in the dialog box.

The filter string is separated with the pipe character (|) in this format:

```
[Text label] | [Extension list separated by semicolons] | [Text label]
| [Extension list separated by semicolons] |  . . .
```

You can also set the Title (form caption) and the InitialDirectory.

The Code

The following code shows a Windows-based application that allows the user to load documents into a RichTextBox, edit the content, and then save the modified document. When opening and saving a document, the OpenFileDialog and SaveFileDialog classes are used.

```vb
' All designed code is stored in the autogenerated partial
' class called MainForm.Designer.vb. You can see this
' file by selecting Show All Files in Solution Explorer.
Partial Public Class MainForm

    Private Sub mnuOpen_Click(ByVal sender As Object, ByVal e As System.EventArgs) ➡
Handles mnuOpen.Click

        Dim dlg As New OpenFileDialog
```

```
        dlg.Filter = "Rich Text Files (*.rtf)|*.RTF|All Files (*.*)|*.*"
        dlg.CheckFileExists = True
        dlg.InitialDirectory = Application.StartupPath

        If dlg.ShowDialog = Windows.Forms.DialogResult.OK Then
            rtDoc.LoadFile(dlg.FileName)
            rtDoc.Enabled = True
        End If

    End Sub

    Private Sub mnuSave_Click(ByVal sender As Object, ByVal e As System.EventArgs) ➥
Handles mnuSave.Click

        Dim dlg As New SaveFileDialog

        dlg.Filter = "Rich Text Files (*.rtf)|*.RTF|Text Files (*.txt)|*.TXT|" & ➥
"All Files (*.*)|*.*"
        dlg.InitialDirectory = Application.StartupPath

        If dlg.ShowDialog = Windows.Forms.DialogResult.OK Then
            rtDoc.SaveFile(dlg.FileName)
        End If

    End Sub

    Private Sub mnuExit_Click(ByVal sender As Object, ByVal e As System.EventArgs) ➥
Handles mnuExit.Click

        Me.Close()

    End Sub
End Class
```

5-19. Use an Isolated Store

Problem

You need to store data in a file, but your application does not have the required FileIOPermission for the local hard drive.

Solution

Use the IsolatedStorageFile and IsolatedStorageFileStream classes from the System.IO. IsolatedStorage namespace. These classes allow your application to write data to a file in a user-specific directory without needing permission to access the local hard drive directly.

How It Works

The .NET Framework includes support for isolated storage, which allows you to read and write to a user-specific or machine-specific virtual file system that the common language runtime (CLR) manages.

When you create isolated storage files, the data is automatically serialized to a unique location in the user profile path. In Windows XP, the profile path is typically something like C:\Documents and Settings\[username]\Local Settings\Application Data\isolated storage\[guid_identifier]).

One reason you might use isolated storage is to give a partially trusted application limited ability to store data. For example, the default CLR security policy gives local code unrestricted FileIOPermission, which allows it to open or write to any file. Code that you run from a remote server on the local intranet is automatically assigned fewer permissions. It lacks the FileIOPermission, but it has the IsolatedStoragePermission, giving it the ability to use isolated stores. (The security policy also limits the maximum amount of space that can be used in an isolated store.) Another reason you might use an isolated store is to better secure data. For example, data in one user's isolated store will be restricted from another nonadministrative user.

By default, each isolated store is segregated by user and assembly. That means that when the same user runs the same application, the application will access the data in the same isolated store. However, you can choose to segregate it further by application domain, so that multiple AppDomain instances running in the same application receive different isolated stores.

The files are stored as part of a user's profile, so users can access their isolated storage files on any workstation they log on to if roaming profiles are configured on your local area network. (In this case, the store must be specifically designated as a roaming store by applying the IsolatedStorageFile.Roaming flag when it's created.) By letting the .NET Framework and the CLR provide these levels of isolation, you can relinquish responsibility for maintaining the separation between files, and you do not need to worry that programming oversights or misunderstandings will cause loss of critical data.

The Code

The following example shows how you can access isolated storage.

```
Imports System
Imports System.IO
Imports System.IO.IsolatedStorage

Namespace Apress.VisualBasicRecipes.Chapter05

    Public Class Recipe05_19
        Public Shared Sub Main(ByVal args As String())

            ' Create the store for the current user.
            Using store As IsolatedStorageFile = ➥
IsolatedStorageFile.GetUserStoreForAssembly
                ' Create a folder in the root of the isolated store.
                store.CreateDirectory("MyFolder")

                ' Create a file in the isolated store.
                Using fs As New IsolatedStorageFileStream("MyFile.txt", ➥
FileMode.Create, store)
                    Dim w As New StreamWriter(fs)

                    ' You can now write to the file as normal.
                    w.WriteLine("Test")
                    w.Flush()

                End Using
```

```
            Console.WriteLine("Current size: " & store.CurrentSize.ToString)
            Console.WriteLine("Scope: " & store.Scope.ToString)
            Console.WriteLine("Contained files include:")

            Dim files As String() = store.GetFileNames("*.*")
            For Each file As String In files
                Console.WriteLine(file)
            Next

        End Using


        '  Wait to continue.
        Console.WriteLine(Environment.NewLine)
        Console.WriteLine("Main method complete. Press Enter.")
        Console.ReadLine()

    End Sub

  End Class
End Namespace
```

The following demonstrates using multiple AppDomain instances running in the same application to receive different isolated stores.

```
'  Access isolated storage for the current user and assembly
'  (which is equivalent to the first example)."
store = IsolatedStorageFile.GetStore(IsolatedStorageScope.User Or ➥
IsolatedStorageScope.Assembly, Nothing, Nothing)

'  Access isolated storage for the current user, assembly,
'  and application domain.  In other words, this data is
'  accessible only by the current AppDomain instance.
store = IsolatedStorageFile.GetStore(IsolatedStorageScope.User Or ➥
IsolatedStorageScope.Assembly Or IsolatedStorageScope.Domain, Nothing, Nothing)
```

The preceding use of GetStore is equivalent to calling the GetUserStoreForDomain method of the IsolatedStorageFile class.

5-20. Monitor the File System for Changes

Problem

You need to react when a file system change is detected in a specific path (such as a file modification or creation).

Solution

Use the System.IO.FileSystemWatcher component, specify the path or file you want to monitor, and handle the Error, Created, Deleted, Renamed, and Changed events as needed.

How It Works

When linking together multiple applications and business processes, it's often necessary to create a program that waits idly and becomes active only when a new file is received or changed. You can create this type of program by scanning a directory periodically, but you face a key trade-off. The more often you scan, the more system resources you waste. The less often you scan, the longer it will take to detect a change. The solution is to use the FileSystemWatcher class to react directly to Windows file events.

To use FileSystemWatcher, you must create an instance and set the following properties:

- Path indicates the directory you want to monitor.

- Filter indicates the types of files you are monitoring.

- NotifyFilter indicates the type of changes you are monitoring.

FileSystemWatcher raises four key events: Created, Deleted, Renamed, and Changed. All of these events provide information through their FileSystemEventArgs parameter, including the name of the file (Name), the full path (FullPath), and the type of change (ChangeType). The Renamed event provides a RenamedEventArgs instance, which derives from FileSystemEventArgs, and adds information about the original filename (OldName and OldFullPath).

By default, the FileSystemWatcher is disabled. To start it, you must set the FileSystemWatcher.EnableRaisingEvents property to True. If you ever need to disable it, just set the property to False.

The Created, Deleted, and Renamed events require no configuration. However, if you want to use the Changed event, you need to use the NotifyFilter property to indicate the types of changes you want to watch. Otherwise, your program might be swamped by an unceasing series of events as files are modified.

The NotifyFilter property, which defaults to LastWrite, FileName, and DirectoryName, can be set using any combination of the following values from the System.IO.NotifyFilters enumeration:

- Attributes

- CreationTime

- DirectoryName

- FileName

- LastAccess

- LastWrite

- Security

- Size

The FileSystemWatcher is capable of detecting many file- or folder-related actions at once. It does this by creating and using threads from the ThreadPool to handle the appropriate events. As events occur, they are queued in an internal buffer. If this buffer overflows, some of the events may be lost. This overflow fires the Error event. You should handle this event to log or resolve this issue if it arises.

The Code

The following example shows a console application that handles Created and Deleted events, and tests these events by creating a test file.

```vb
Imports System
Imports System.IO
Imports System.Windows.Forms

Namespace Apress.VisualBasicRecipes.Chapter05

    Public Class Recipe05_20
        Public Shared Sub Main()

            Using watch As New FileSystemWatcher

                watch.Path = Application.StartupPath
                watch.Filter = "*.*"
                watch.IncludeSubdirectories = True

                ' Attach the event handlers.
                AddHandler watch.Created, AddressOf OnCreatedOrDeleted
                AddHandler watch.Deleted, AddressOf OnCreatedOrDeleted
                watch.EnableRaisingEvents = True

                Console.WriteLine("Press Enter to create a file.")
                Console.ReadLine()

                If File.Exists("test.bin") Then
                    File.Delete("test.bin")
                End If

                ' Create test.bin file.
                Using fs As New FileStream("test.bin", FileMode.Create)
                    ' Do something here...
                End Using

                Console.WriteLine("Press Enter to terminate the application.")
                Console.ReadLine()

            End Using

            ' Wait to continue.
            Console.WriteLine(Environment.NewLine)
            Console.WriteLine("Main method complete. Press Enter.")
            Console.ReadLine()

        End Sub

        ' Fires when a new file is created or deleted in the directory
        ' that is being monitored.
        Private Shared Sub OnCreatedOrDeleted(ByVal sender As Object, ➥
ByVal e As FileSystemEventArgs)

            ' Display the notification information.
            Console.WriteLine("{0}NOTIFICATION: {1} was {2}", ControlChars.Tab, ➥
e.FullPath, e.ChangeType.ToString)
            Console.WriteLine()
```

```
      End Sub

   End Class
End Namespace
```

5-21. Access a COM Port

Problem

You need to send data directly to a serial port.

Solution

Use the System.IO.Ports.SerialPort class. This class represents a serial port resource and defines methods that enable communication through it.

How It Works

.NET Framework 2.0 defines a System.IO.Ports namespace that contains several classes. The central class is SerialPort. A SerialPort instance represents a serial port resource and provides methods that let you communicate through it. The SerialPort class also exposes properties that let you specify the port, baud rate, parity, and other information. If you need a list of the available COM ports, the SerialPort class provides the GetPortNames method, which returns a string array containing the names of each port.

As an alternative, the My object contains the My.Computer.Ports class, which can be used to work with ports. This class contains the Shared SerialPortNames property and the Shared OpenSerialPort method. SerialPortNames is equivalent to the GetPortNames method, but it returns a read-only collection of strings. OpenSerialPort returns a SerialPort instance. This method has several overloads that let you correctly configure the returned instance.

The Code

The following example demonstrates a simple console application that lists all available COM ports and then writes a string to the first available one.

```
Imports System
Imports System.IO.Ports

Namespace Apress.VisualBasicRecipes.Chapter05

    Public Class Recipe05_21
        Public Shared Sub Main()

            ' Enumerate each of the available COM ports
            ' on the computer.
            Console.WriteLine("Available Ports on this computer:")
            For Each portName As String In SerialPort.GetPortNames
                Console.WriteLine("PORT: " & portName)
            Next
            Console.WriteLine()
```

```
        ' For this example, lets just grab the first item from
        ' the array returned by the GetPortNames method.
        Dim testPort As String = SerialPort.GetPortNames(0)
        Using port As New SerialPort(testPort)

            ' Set the properties.
            port.BaudRate = 9600
            port.Parity = Parity.None
            port.ReadTimeout = 10
            port.StopBits = StopBits.One

            ' Write a message into the port.
            port.Open()
            port.Write("Hello world!")
            port.Close()

            Console.WriteLine("Wrote to the {0} port.", testPort)

        End Using

        ' Wait to continue.
        Console.WriteLine(Environment.NewLine)
        Console.WriteLine("Main method complete. Press Enter.")
        Console.ReadLine()

    End Sub

    End Class
End Namespace
```

5-22. Get a Random Filename

Problem

You need to get a random name for creating a folder or a file.

Solution

Use the Path.GetRandomFileName method, which returns a random name.

How It Works

The System.IO.Path class includes a GetRandomFileName method, which is new to .NET Framework 2.0. This method generates a random string that can be used for creating a new file or folder.

The difference between GetRandomFileName and GetTempFileName (discussed in recipe 5-16) of the Path class is that GetRandomFileName just returns a random string and does not create a file, whereas GetTempFileName creates a new 0-byte temporary file and returns the path to the file.

5-23. Manipulate the Access Control Lists of a File or Directory

Problem

You want to modify the access control list (ACL) of a file or directory in the computer.

Solution

Use the `GetAccessControl` and `SetAccessControl` methods of the `File` or `Directory` class.

How It Works

.NET Framework 2.0 now includes support for ACLs for resources like I/O, registry, and threading classes. You can retrieve and apply the ACL for a resource by using the `GetAccessControl` and `SetAccessControl` methods defined in the corresponding resource classes. For example, the `File` and `Directory` classes define both these methods, which let you manipulate the ACLs for a file or directory.

To add or remove an ACL-associated right of a file or directory, you need to first retrieve the `FileSecurity` or `DirectorySecurity` object currently applied to the resource using the `GetAccessControl` method. Once you retrieve this object, you need to perform the required modification of the rights, and then apply the ACL back to the resource using the `SetAccessControl` method. Table 5-8 shows a list of the common methods used for adding and removing ACL permissions.

Table 5-8. *Key Methods for Adding and Removing ACLs*

Method	Description
AddAccessRule	Adds the permissions specified.
ResetAccessRule	Adds the permissions specified. If the specified permission already exists, it will be replaced.
RemoveAccessRule	Removes all of the permissions that match the specified rule.
RemoveAccessRuleAll	Removes all permissions for the user referenced in the specified rule.
RemoveAccessRuleSpecific	Removes the permissions specified.

The Code

The following example demonstrates the effect of denying Everyone Read access to a temporary file, using a console application. An attempt to read the file after a change in the ACL triggers a security exception.

```
Imports System
Imports System.IO
Imports System.Security.AccessControl
```

```vb
Namespace Apress.VisualBasicRecipes.Chapter05

    Public Class Recipe05_23
        Public Shared Sub Main()
            Dim fileName As String

            ' Create a new file and assign full control to 'Everyone'.
            Console.WriteLine("Press any key to write a new file...")
            Console.ReadKey(True)

            fileName = Path.GetRandomFileName
            Using testStream As New FileStream(fileName, FileMode.Create)
                ' Do something...
            End Using
            Console.WriteLine("Created a new file {0}.", fileName)
            Console.WriteLine()

            ' Deny 'Everyone' access to the file.
            Console.WriteLine("Press any key to deny 'Everyone' access " & ➥
"to the file.")
            Console.ReadKey(True)

            SetRule(fileName, "Everyone", FileSystemRights.Read, ➥
AccessControlType.Deny)

            Console.WriteLine("Removed access rights of 'Everyone'.")
            Console.WriteLine()

            ' Attempt to access the file.
            Console.WriteLine("Press any key to attempt to access the file...")
            Console.ReadKey(True)

            Dim stream As FileStream
            Try
                stream = New FileStream(fileName, FileMode.Create)
            Catch ex As Exception
                Console.WriteLine("Exception thrown : ")
                Console.WriteLine(ex.ToString)
            Finally
                If stream IsNot Nothing Then
                    stream.Close()
                    stream.Dispose()
                End If
            End Try

            ' Wait to contiue.
            Console.WriteLine(Environment.NewLine)
            Console.WriteLine("Main method complete. Press Enter.")
            Console.ReadLine()

        End Sub

        Private Shared Sub SetRule(ByVal filePath As String, ByVal account As ➥
```

```vb
String, ByVal rights As FileSystemRights, ByVal controlType As AccessControlType)

        ' Get a FileSecurity object that represents the
        ' current security settings.
        Dim fSecurity As FileSecurity = File.GetAccessControl(filePath)

        ' Update the FileSystemAccessRule with the new
        ' security settings.
        fSecurity.ResetAccessRule(New FileSystemAccessRule(account, rights, ➥
controlType))

        ' Set the new access settings.
        File.SetAccessControl(filePath, fSecurity)

    End Sub

  End Class
End Namespace
```

CHAPTER 6

■ ■ ■

XML Processing

One of the most remarkable aspects of the Microsoft .NET Framework is its deep integration with Extensible Markup Language (XML). In many .NET applications, you won't even be aware you're using XML technologies—they'll just be used behind the scenes when you serialize a Microsoft ADO.NET DataSet, call a web service, or read application settings from a Web.config configuration file. In other cases, you'll want to work directly with the System.Xml namespaces to manipulate XML data. Common XML tasks include parsing an XML file, validating it against a schema, applying an XSL transform to create a new document or Hypertext Markup Language (HTML) page, and searching intelligently with XPath. The recipes in this chapter describe how to do the following:

- Read, parse, and manipulate XML data (recipes 6-1, 6-2, 6-3, and 6-7)
- Search an XML document for specific nodes, by name (recipe 6-4), by namespace (recipe 6-5), or by using XPath (recipe 6-6)
- Validate an XML document with an XML schema (recipe 6-8)
- Serialize an object to XML (recipe 6-9), create an XML schema for a class (recipe 6-10), and generate the source code for a class based on an XML schema (recipe 6-11)
- Transform an XML document to another document using an XSL Transformations (XSLT) stylesheet (recipe 6-12)

6-1. Show the Structure of an XML Document in a TreeView

Problem

You need to display the structure and content of an XML document in a Windows-based application.

Solution

Load the XML document using the System.Xml.XmlDocument class. Create a re-entrant method that converts a single XmlNode into a System.Windows.Forms.TreeNode, and call it recursively to walk through the entire document.

How It Works

The .NET Framework provides several different ways to process XML documents. The one you use depends in part upon your programming task. One of the most fully featured classes is XmlDocument, which provides an in-memory representation of an XML document that conforms to the W3C Document Object Model (DOM). The XmlDocument class allows you to browse through the nodes in any direction, insert and remove nodes, and change the structure on the fly. For details of the DOM specification, go to http://www.w3c.org/DOM.

■Note The XmlDocument class is not scalable for very large XML documents, because it holds the entire XML content in memory at once. If you want a more memory-efficient alternative, and you can afford to read and process the XML piece by piece, consider the XmlReader and XmlWriter classes described in recipe 6-7.

To use the XmlDocument class, simply create a new instance of the class, and call the Load method with a filename, a Stream, a TextReader, or an XmlReader object. It is also possible to read the XML from a simple string with the LoadXML method. You can even supply a string with a URL that points to an XML document on the Web using the Load method. The XmlDocument instance will be populated with the tree of elements, or *nodes*, from the source document. The entry point for accessing these nodes is the root element. The XmlDocument.DocumentElement property provides an alternate method for directly accessing this root element. DocumentElement is an XmlElement object that can contain one or more nested XmlNode objects, which in turn can contain more XmlNode objects, and so on. An XmlNode is the basic ingredient of an XML file. Common XML nodes include elements, attributes, comments, and contained text.

When dealing with an XmlNode or a class that derives from it (such as XmlElement, XmlAttribute, or XmlDocument), you can use the following basic properties:

- ChildNodes is an XmlNodeList collection that contains the first level of nested nodes.
- Name is the name of the node.
- NodeType returns a member of the System.Xml.XmlNodeType enumeration that indicates the type of the node (element, attribute, text, and so on).
- Value is the content of the node, if it's a text, a CDATA, or an attribute node.
- Attributes provides a collection of node objects representing the attributes applied to the element.
- InnerText retrieves a string with the concatenated value of the node and all nested nodes.
- InnerXml retrieves a string with the concatenated XML markup for all nested nodes.
- OuterXml retrieves a string with the concatenated XML markup for the current node and all nested nodes.

The Code

The following example walks through every element of an XmlDocument using the ChildNodes property and a recursive method. Each node is displayed in a TreeView control, with descriptive text that either identifies it or shows its content.

```
Imports System
Imports System.Windows.Forms
Imports System.Xml
Imports System.IO
```

```vb
' All designed code is stored in the autogenerated partial
' class called XmlTreeDisplay.Designer.vb. You can see this
' file by selecting Show All Files in Solution Explorer.
Partial Public Class XmlTreeDisplay

    Private Sub cmdLoad_Click(ByVal sender As System.Object, ➥
ByVal e As System.EventArgs) Handles cmdLoad.Click

        ' Clear the tree.
        Dim doc As New XmlDocument

        Try
            doc.Load(txtXmlFile.Text)

            ' Populate the TreeView.
            ConvertXmlNodeToTreeNode(doc, treeXml.Nodes)

            ' Expand all nodes.
            treeXml.Nodes(0).ExpandAll()
        Catch ex As Exception
            MessageBox.Show(ex.Message)
        End Try

    End Sub

    Private Sub ConvertXmlNodeToTreeNode(ByVal thisXmlNode As XmlNode, ➥
ByVal treeNodes As TreeNodeCollection)

        ' Add a TreeNode node that represents this XmlNode.
        Dim newTreeNode As TreeNode = treeNodes.Add(thisXmlNode.Name)

        ' Customize the TreeNode text based on the XmlNode
        ' type and content.
        Select Case thisXmlNode.NodeType
            Case XmlNodeType.ProcessingInstruction
                newTreeNode.Text = thisXmlNode.Value
            Case XmlNodeType.XmlDeclaration
                newTreeNode.Text = "<?" & thisXmlNode.Name & " " & ➥
thisXmlNode.Value & "?>"
            Case XmlNodeType.Element
                newTreeNode.Text = "<" & thisXmlNode.Name & ">"
            Case XmlNodeType.Attribute
                newTreeNode.Text = "ATTRIBUTE: " & thisXmlNode.Name
            Case XmlNodeType.Text
                newTreeNode.Text = thisXmlNode.Value
            Case XmlNodeType.CDATA
                newTreeNode.Text = thisXmlNode.Value
            Case XmlNodeType.Comment
                newTreeNode.Text = "<!--" & thisXmlNode.Value & "-->"
        End Select
```

```
        ' Call this routine recursively for each attribute.
        ' (XmlAttribute is a subclass of XmlNode.)
        If Not thisXmlNode.Attributes Is Nothing Then
            For Each attribute As XmlAttribute In thisXmlNode.Attributes
                ConvertXmlNodeToTreeNode(attribute, newTreeNode.Nodes)
            Next
        End If

        ' Call this routine recursively for each child node.
        ' Typically, this child node represents a nested element
        ' or element content.
        For Each childNode As XmlNode In thisXmlNode.ChildNodes
            ConvertXmlNodeToTreeNode(childNode, newTreeNode.Nodes)
        Next

    End Sub

    Private Sub XmlTreeDisplay_Load(ByVal sender As Object, ➨
ByVal e As System.EventArgs) Handles Me.Load

        txtXmlFile.Text = Path.Combine(Application.StartupPath, ➨
"..\..\ProductCatalog.xml")

    End Sub

End Class
```

Usage

As an example, consider the following simple XML file (which is included with the sample code as the ProductCatalog.xml file).

```
<?xml version="1.0" ?>
<productCatalog>
    <catalogName>Jones and Jones Unique Catalog 2004</catalogName>
    <expiryDate>2005-01-01</expiryDate>

    <products>
        <product id="1001">
            <productName>Gourmet Coffee</productName>
            <description>The finest beans from rare Chilean
             plantations.</description>
            <productPrice>0.99</productPrice>
            <inStock>true</inStock>
        </product>
        <product id="1002">
            <productName>Blue China Tea Pot</productName>
            <description>A trendy update for tea drinkers.</description>
            <productPrice>102.99</productPrice>
            <inStock>true</inStock>
        </product>
    </products>
</productCatalog>
```

Figure 6-1 shows how this file will be rendered in the form.

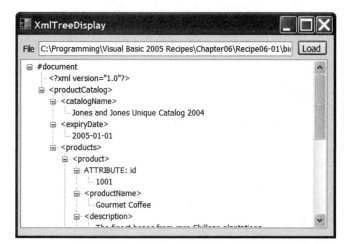

Figure 6-1. *The displayed structure of an XML document*

6-2. Insert Nodes in an XML Document

Problem

You need to modify an XML document by inserting new data, or you want to create an entirely new XML document in memory.

Solution

Create the node using the appropriate XmlDocument method (such as CreateElement, CreateAttribute, CreateNode, and so on). Then insert it using the appropriate XmlNode method (such as InsertAfter, InsertBefore, or AppendChild).

How It Works

Inserting a node into the XmlDocument class is a two-step process: create the node, and then insert it at the appropriate location. Optionally, you can then call XmlDocument.Save to persist changes.

To create a node, you use one of the XmlDocument methods starting with the word Create, depending on the type of node. This ensures the node will have the same namespace as the rest of the document. (Alternatively, you can supply a namespace as an additional string argument.) Next, you must find a suitable related node and use one of its insertion methods to add the new node to the tree.

The Code

The following example demonstrates this technique by programmatically creating a new XML document.

```vbnet
Imports System
Imports System.Xml

Namespace Apress.VisualBasicRecipes.Chapter06

    Public Class Recipe06_02
        Public Shared Sub Main()

            ' Create a new, empty document.
            Dim doc As New XmlDocument
            Dim docNode As XmlNode = doc.CreateXmlDeclaration("1.0", "UTF-8", ➥
Nothing)

            doc.AppendChild(docNode)

            ' Create and insert a new element.
            Dim productsNode As XmlNode = doc.CreateElement("Products")
            doc.AppendChild(productsNode)

            ' Create a nested element (with an attribute).
            Dim productNode As XmlNode = doc.CreateElement("Product")
            Dim productAttribute As XmlAttribute = doc.CreateAttribute("id")
            productAttribute.Value = "1001"
            productNode.Attributes.Append(productAttribute)
            productsNode.AppendChild(productNode)

            ' Create and add the subelements for this product node
            ' (with contained text data).
            Dim nameNode As XmlNode = doc.CreateElement("ProductName")
            nameNode.AppendChild(doc.CreateTextNode("Gourmet Coffee"))
            productNode.AppendChild(nameNode)
            Dim priceNode As XmlNode = doc.CreateElement("ProductPrice")
            priceNode.AppendChild(doc.CreateTextNode("0.99"))
            productNode.AppendChild(priceNode)

            ' Create and add another product node.
            productNode = doc.CreateElement("Product")
            productAttribute = doc.CreateAttribute("id")
            productAttribute.Value = "1002"
            productNode.Attributes.Append(productAttribute)
            productsNode.AppendChild(productNode)
            nameNode = doc.CreateElement("ProductName")
            nameNode.AppendChild(doc.CreateTextNode("Blue China Tea Pot"))
            productNode.AppendChild(nameNode)
            priceNode = doc.CreateElement("ProductPrice")
            priceNode.AppendChild(doc.CreateTextNode("102.99"))
            productNode.AppendChild(priceNode)

            ' Save the document (to the console window rather
            ' than a file).
            doc.Save(Console.Out)
            Console.ReadLine()
```

```
        End Sub

    End Class
End Namespace
```

When you run this code, the generated XML document looks like this:

```xml
<?xml version="1.0" encoding="UTF-8"?>
<Products>
  <Product id="1001">
    <ProductName>Gourmet Coffee</ProductName>
    <ProductPrice>0.99</ProductPrice>
  </Product>
  <Product id="1002">
    <ProductName>Blue China Tea Pot</ProductName>
    <ProductPrice>102.99</ProductPrice>
  </Product>
</Products>
```

6-3. Quickly Append Nodes in an XML Document

Problem

You need to add nodes to an XML document without requiring lengthy, verbose code.

Solution

Create a helper function that accepts an element name and content, and can generate the entire element at once. Alternatively, use the XmlDocument.CloneNode method to copy branches of an XmlDocument.

How It Works

Inserting a single element into an XmlDocument requires several lines of code. You can shorten this code in several ways. One approach is to create a dedicated helper class with higher-level methods for adding elements and attributes. For example, you could create an AddElement method that generates a new element, inserts it, and adds any contained text—the three operations needed to insert most elements.

The Code

The following is an example of a helper class for inserting elements.

```vbnet
Imports System
Imports System.Xml

Namespace Apress.VisualBasicRecipes.Chapter06

    Public Class XmlHelper
```

```
        Public Shared Function AddElement(ByVal elementName As String, ➥
ByVal textContent As String, ByVal parent As XmlNode) As XmlElement

            Dim element As XmlElement = ➥
parent.OwnerDocument.CreateElement(elementName)

            parent.AppendChild(element)

            If textContent IsNot Nothing Then
                Dim content As XmlNode
                content = parent.OwnerDocument.CreateTextNode(textContent)
                element.AppendChild(content)
            End If

            Return element

        End Function

        Public Shared Function AddAttribute(ByVal attributeName As String, ➥
ByVal textContent As String, ByVal parent As XmlNode) As XmlAttribute

            Dim attribute As XmlAttribute

            attribute = parent.OwnerDocument.CreateAttribute(attributeName)
            attribute.Value = textContent
            parent.Attributes.Append(attribute)

            Return attribute

        End Function

    End Class
End Namespace
```

You can now condense the XML-generating code from recipe 6-2 with the following simpler syntax.

```
Public Class Recipe06_03

    Public Shared Sub Main()

        ' Create the basic document.
        Dim doc As New XmlDocument
        Dim docNode As XmlNode = doc.CreateXmlDeclaration("1.0", "UTF-8", Nothing)
        doc.AppendChild(docNode)
        Dim products = doc.CreateElement("Products")
        doc.AppendChild(products)

        ' Add two products.
        Dim product As XmlNode = XmlHelper.AddElement("Product", Nothing, products)
        XmlHelper.AddAttribute("id", "1001", product)
        XmlHelper.AddElement("ProductName", "Gourmet Coffee", product)
        XmlHelper.AddElement("ProductPrice", "0.99", product)
```

```
    product = XmlHelper.AddElement("Product", Nothing, products)
    XmlHelper.AddAttribute("id", "1003", product)
    XmlHelper.AddElement("ProductName", "Blue China Tea Pot", product)
    XmlHelper.AddElement("ProductPrice", "102.99", product)

    ' Save the document (to the console window rather than a file)
    doc.Save(Console.Out)
    Console.ReadLine()

  End Sub
End Class
```

Alternatively, you might want to take the helper methods such as AddAttribute and AddElement and make them instance methods in a custom class you derive from XmlDocument.

Another approach to simplifying writing XML is to duplicate nodes using the XmlNode.CloneNode method. CloneNode accepts a Boolean deep parameter. If you set this parameter to True, CloneNode will duplicate the entire branch, with all nested nodes.

Here is an example that creates a new product node by copying the first node:

```
' (Add first product node).

' Create a new element based on an existing product.
product = product.CloneNode(True)

' Modify the node data.
product.Attributes(0).Value = "1002"
product.ChildNodes(0).ChildNodes(0).Value = "Blue China Tea Pot"
product.ChildNodes(1).ChildNodes(1).Value = "102.99"

' Add the new element.
products.AppendChild(product)
```

In this example, certain assumptions are being made about the existing nodes; for example, that the first child in the item node is always the name, and the second child is always the price. If such assumptions are not guaranteed to be true, you might need to examine the node name programmatically.

6-4. Find Specific Elements by Name

Problem

You need to retrieve a specific element or elements from an XmlDocument using only the element name.

Solution

Use the XmlDocument.GetElementsByTagName method, which searches an entire document and returns a System.Xml.XmlNodeList containing any matches.

How It Works

The XmlDocument class provides a convenient GetElementsByTagName method that searches an entire document for elements that have the indicated element name. It returns the results as a collection of XmlNode objects.

The Code

The following code demonstrates how you could use GetElementsByTagName to calculate the total price of items in a catalog by retrieving all elements with the name productPrice.

```
Imports System
Imports System.Xml

Namespace Apress.VisualBasicRecipes.Chapter06

    Public Class Recipe06_04
        Public Shared Sub Main()

            ' Load the document.
            Dim doc As New XmlDocument
            doc.Load("..\..\ProductCatalog.xml")

            ' Retrieve all prices.
            Dim totalPrice As Decimal = 0
            Dim prices As XmlNodeList = doc.GetElementsByTagName("productPrice")
            For Each price As XmlNode In prices
                ' Get the inner text of each matching element.
                totalPrice += Decimal.Parse(price.ChildNodes(0).Value)
            Next

            Console.WriteLine("Total catalog value: " & totalPrice.ToString)
            Console.ReadLine()

        End Sub

    End Class
End Namespace
```

Notes

You can also search portions of an XML document by using the XmlElement.GetElementsByTagName method. It searches all the descendant nodes looking for matches. To use this method, first retrieve an XmlNode that corresponds to an element. Then cast this object to an XmlElement. The following example demonstrates how to find the price node under the first product element.

```
' Retrieve a reference to the first product.
Dim product As XmlNode = doc.GetElementsByTagName("products")(0)

' Find the price under this product.
Dim price As XmlNode = DirectCast(product, ➡
XmlElement).GetElementsByTagName("productPrice")(0)
```

If your elements include an id attribute, you can also use a method called GetElementById to retrieve an element that has a matching id value.

6-5. Get XML Nodes in a Specific XML Namespace

Problem

You need to retrieve elements from a specific namespace using an `XmlDocument`.

Solution

Use the overload of the `XmlDocument.GetElementsByTagName` method that requires a namespace name as a string argument. Additionally, supply an asterisk (*) for the element name if you want to match all elements.

How It Works

Many XML documents contain nodes from more than one namespace. For example, an XML document that represents a scientific article might use a separate type of markup for denoting math equations and vector diagrams, or an XML document with information about a purchase order might aggregate client and order information with a shipping record. Similarly, an XML document that represents a business-to-business transaction might include portions from both companies, written in separate markup languages.

A common task in XML programming is to retrieve the elements found in a specific namespace. You can perform this task with the overloaded version of the `XmlDocument.GetElementsByTagName` method that requires a namespace name. You can use this method to find elements by name or to find all the elements in the specified namespace if you supply an asterisk for the element name.

The Code

As an example, consider the following compound XML document that includes order and client information, in two different namespaces (`http://mycompany/OrderML` and `http://mycompany/ClientML`).

```
<?xml version="1.0" ?>
<ord:order xmlns:ord="http://mycompany/OrderML"
 xmlns:cli="http://mycompany/ClientML">

    <cli:client>
       <cli:firstName>Vicky</cli:firstName>
       <cli:lastName>Kevin</cli:lastName>
    </cli:client>

    <ord:orderItem itemNumber="3211" />
    <ord:orderItem itemNumber="1155" />

</ord:order>
```

Here is a simple console application that selects all the elements in the `http://mycompany/OrderML` namespace:

```
Imports System
Imports System.Xml

Namespace Apress.VisualBasicRecipes.Chapter06
```

```
Public Class Recipe06_05
    Public Shared Sub Main()

        ' Load the document.
        Dim doc As New XmlDocument
        doc.Load("..\..\Order.xml")

        ' Retrieve all order elements.
        Dim matches As XmlNodeList = doc.GetElementsByTagName("*", ➥
"http://mycompany/OrderML")

        ' Display all the information.
        Console.WriteLine("Element {0}Attributes", ControlChars.Tab)
        Console.WriteLine("******* {0}**********", ControlChars.Tab)

        For Each node As XmlNode In matches
            Console.Write("{0}{1}", node.Name, ControlChars.Tab)
            For Each attribute As XmlAttribute In node.Attributes
                Console.Write(attribute.Value & " ")
            Next
            Console.WriteLine()
        Next
        Console.ReadLine()

    End Sub

End Class
End Namespace
```

The output of this program is as follows.

```
Element       Attributes
*******       **********
ord:order     http://mycompany/OrderML http://mycompany/ClientML
ord:orderItem 3211
ord:orderItem 1155
```

6-6. Find Elements with an XPath Search

Problem

You need to search an XML document for nodes using advanced search criteria. For example, you might want to search a particular branch of an XML document for nodes that have certain attributes or contain a specific number of nested child nodes.

Solution

Execute an XPath expression using the SelectNodes or SelectSingleNode method of the XmlDocument class.

How It Works

The XmlNode class defines two methods that perform XPath searches: SelectNodes and SelectSingleNode. These methods operate on all contained child nodes. Because the XmlDocument inherits from XmlNode, you can call XmlDocument.SelectNodes to search an entire document.

The Code

As an example, consider the following orders.xml document, which represents an order for two items. This document includes text and numeric data, nested elements, and attributes, so it provides a good way to test simple XPath expressions.

```
<?xml version="1.0"?>
<Order id="2004-01-30.195496">
  <Client id="ROS-930252034">
    <Name>Remarkable Office Supplies</Name>
  </Client>

  <Items>
    <Item id="1001">
      <Name>Electronic Protractor</Name>
      <Price>42.99</Price>
    </Item>
    <Item id="1002">
      <Name>Vorpal Stapler</Name>
      <Price>500.50</Price>
    </Item>
  </Items>
</Order>
```

Basic XPath syntax uses a pathlike notation. For example, the path /Order/Items/Item indicates an <Item> element that is nested inside an <Items> element, which, in turn, is nested in a root <Order> element. This is an absolute path. The following example uses an XPath absolute path to find the name of every item in an order:

```
Imports System
Imports System.Xml

Namespace Apress.VisualBasicRecipes.Chapter06

    Public Class Recipe06_06
        Public Shared Sub Main()

            ' Load the document.
            Dim doc As New XmlDocument
            doc.Load("..\..\Orders.xml")

            ' Retrieve the name of every item.
            ' This could not be accomplished as easily with the
            ' GetElementsByTagName method, because the Name elements are
            ' used in Item elements and Client elements, and so
            ' both types would be returned.
            Dim nodes As XmlNodeList = doc.SelectNodes("/Order/Items/Item/Name")
```

```
        For Each node As XmlNode In nodes
            Console.WriteLine(node.InnerText)
        Next
        Console.ReadLine()

    End Sub

  End Class
End Namespace
```

The output of this program is as follows.

```
Electronic Protractor
Vorpal Stapler
```

Notes

XPath provides a rich and powerful search syntax. Table 6-1 outlines some of the key ingredients in more advanced XPath expressions and includes examples that show how they would work with the order document. For a more detailed reference, refer to the W3C XPath recommendation at http://www.w3.org/TR/xpath.

Table 6-1. *XPath Expression Syntax*

Expression	Description	Example
/	Starts an absolute path that selects from the root node	/Order/Items/Item selects all Item elements that are children of an Items element, which is itself a child of the root Order element.
//	Starts a relative path that selects nodes anywhere	//Item/Name selects all the Name elements that are children of an Item element, regardless of where they appear in the document.
@	Selects an attribute of a node	/Order/@id selects the attribute named id from the root Order element.
*	Selects any element in the path	/Order/* selects both Items and Client nodes because both are contained by a root Order element.
|	Combines multiple paths	/Order/Items/Item/Name|Order/Client/Name selects the Name nodes used to describe a Client and the Name nodes used to describe an Item.
.	Indicates the current (default) node	If the current node is an Order, the expression ./Items refers to the related items for that order.
..	Indicates the parent node	//Name/.. selects any element that is parent to a Name, which includes the Client and Item elements.

Table 6-1. *XPath Expression Syntax*

Expression	Description	Example
[ ]	Defines selection criteria that can test a contained node or an attribute value	/Order[@id="2004-01-30.195496"] selects the Order elements with the indicated attribute value. /Order/Items/Item[Price > 50] selects products higher than $50 in price. /Order/Items/Item[Price > 50 and Name="Laser Printer"] selects products that match two criteria.
starts-with	Retrieves elements based on what text a contained element starts with	/Order/Items/Item[starts-with (Name, "C")] finds all Item elements that have a Name element that starts with the letter C.
position	Retrieves elements based on position	/Order/Items/Item[position()=2] selects the second Item element.
count	Counts elements. You specify the name of the child element to count or an asterisk (*) for all children.	/Order/Items/Item[count(Price) = 1] retrieves Item elements that have exactly one nested Price element.

■**Note** XPath expressions and all element and attribute names you use inside them are always case-sensitive, because XML itself is case-sensitive.

6-7. Read and Write XML Without Loading an Entire Document into Memory

Problem

You need to read XML from a stream or write it to a stream. However, you want to process the information one node at a time, rather than loading it all into memory with an XmlDocument.

Solution

To write XML, create an XmlWriter that wraps a stream and use Write methods (such as WriteStartElement and WriteEndElement). To read XML, create an XmlReader that wraps a stream, and call Read to move from node to node.

How It Works

The XmlWriter and XmlReader classes read or write XML directly from a stream one node at a time. These classes do not provide the same features for navigating and manipulating your XML as XmlDocument, but they do provide higher performance and a smaller memory footprint, particularly if you are dealing with large XML documents.

Both the XmlWriter and XmlReader are abstract classes, which means you cannot create an instance of them directly. Instead, you need to create an instance of a derived class, such as XmlTextWriter. In .NET Framework 2.0, the preferred convention is not to create a derived class directly. Instead, you should call the Create method of the XmlWriter or XmlReader and supply a URI string or a TextWriter or TextReader stream, respectively. The Create method will return the correct derived class based on the options you specify. This allows for a more flexible model. Because your code uses the base classes, it can work seamlessly with any derived class. For example, you could switch to a validating reader (as shown in recipe 6-8) without needing to modify your code.

To write XML to any stream, you can use the streamlined XmlWriter. It provides Write methods that write one node at a time. These include the following:

- WriteStartDocument, which writes the document prologue, and WriteEndDocument, which closes any open elements at the end of the document

- WriteStartElement, which writes an opening tag for the element you specify. You can then add more elements nested inside this element, or you can call WriteEndElement to write the closing tag

- WriteElementString, which writes an entire element, with an opening tag, a closing tag, and text content

- WriteAttributeString, which writes an entire attribute for the nearest open element, with a name and value

Using these methods usually requires less code than creating an XmlDocument by hand, as demonstrated in recipes 6-2 and 6-3.

To read the XML, you use the Read method of the XmlReader. This method advances the reader to the next node, excluding attributes, and returns true. If no more nodes can be found, it returns false. You can retrieve information about the current node through XmlReader properties, including its Name, Value, and NodeType.

To find out whether an element has attributes, you must explicitly test the HasAttributes property and then use the GetAttribute method to retrieve the attributes by name or index number. The XmlReader class can access only one node at a time, and it cannot move backward or jump to an arbitrary node, which gives much less flexibility than the XmlDocument class.

The Code

The following console application writes and reads a simple XML document using the XmlWriter and XmlReader classes. This is the same XML document created in recipes 6-2 and 6-3 using the XmlDocument class.

```
Imports System
Imports System.Xml
Imports System.IO
Imports System.Text

Namespace Apress.VisualBasicRecipes.Chapter06

    Public Class Recipe06_07
        Public Shared Sub Main()

            ' Create the file and writer.
            Dim fs As New FileStream("products.xml", FileMode.Create)
```

```vb
' If you want to configure additional details (like indenting,
' encoding, and new line handling), use the overload of the Create
' method that accepts an XmlWriterSettings object instead.
Dim w As XmlWriter = XmlWriter.Create(fs)

' Start the document and create the parent Products node.
w.WriteStartDocument()
w.WriteStartElement("Products")

' Write a product.
w.WriteStartElement("Product")
w.WriteAttributeString("id", "1001")
w.WriteElementString("ProductName", "Gourmet Coffee")
w.WriteElementString("ProductPrice", "0.99")
w.WriteEndElement()

' Write another product.
w.WriteStartElement("Product")
w.WriteAttributeString("id", "1002")
w.WriteElementString("ProductName", "Blue China Tea Pot")
w.WriteElementString("ProductPrice", "102.99")
w.WriteEndElement()

' End the Products node and document.
w.WriteEndElement()
w.WriteEndDocument()

' Flush and close the parent document.
w.Flush()
fs.Close()

Console.WriteLine("Document created. Press Enter to read it.")
Console.ReadLine()

fs = New FileStream("Products.xml", FileMode.Open)

' If you want to configure additional details (like comments,
' whitespace handling, or validation), use the overload of the
' Create method that accepts an XmlReaderSettings object instead.
Dim r As XmlReader = XmlReader.Create(fs)

' Read all nodes.
While r.Read

    If r.NodeType = XmlNodeType.Element Then
        Console.WriteLine()
        Console.WriteLine("<{0}>", r.Name)

        If r.HasAttributes Then
            For i As Integer = 0 To r.AttributeCount - 1
                Console.WriteLine("{0}ATTRIBUTE: {1}", ➥
ControlChars.Tab, r.GetAttribute(i))
            Next
        End If
```

```
            ElseIf r.NodeType = XmlNodeType.Text Then
                Console.WriteLine("{0}VALUE: {1}", ControlChars.Tab, r.Value)
            End If

        End While
        Console.ReadLine()
    End Sub

    End Class
End Namespace
```

Often, when using the XmlReader, you are searching for specific nodes, rather than processing every element as in this example. The approach used in this example does not work as well in this situation. It forces you to read element tags, text content, and CDATA sections separately, which means you need to explicitly keep track of where you are in the document. A better approach is to read the entire node and text content at once (for simple text-only nodes) by using the ReadElementString method. You can also use methods such as ReadToDescendant, ReadToFollowing, and ReadToNextSibling, which allow you to skip some nodes.

For example, you can use ReadToFollowing("Price") to skip straight to the next Price element, without worrying about whitespace, comments, or other elements before it. (If a Price element cannot be found, the XmlReader moves to the end of the document, and the ReadToFollowing method returns false.)

6-8. Validate an XML Document Against a Schema

Problem

You need to validate the content of an XML document by ensuring that it conforms to an XML schema.

Solution

When you call XmlReader.Create, supply an XmlReaderSettings object that indicates you want to perform validation. Then move through the document one node at a time by calling XmlReader.Read, catching any validation exceptions. To find all the errors in a document without catching exceptions, handle the ValidationEventHandler event on the XmlReaderSettings object given as a parameter to XmlReader.

How It Works

An XML schema defines the rules that a given type of XML document must follow. The schema includes rules that define the following:

- The elements and attributes that can appear in a document
- The data types for elements and attributes
- The structure of a document, including which elements are children of other elements
- The order and number of child elements that appear in a document
- Whether elements are empty, can include text, or require fixed values

At its most basic level, XML Schema Definition (XSD) defines the elements that can occur in an XML document. XSD documents are themselves written in XML, and you use a separate predefined element (named <element>) in the XSD document to indicate each element that is required in the target document. The type attribute indicates the data type. This recipe uses the product catalog first presented in recipe 6-1.

Here is an example for a product name:

```
<xsd:element name="productName" type="xsd:string" />
```

And here is an example for the product price:

```
<xsd:element name="productPrice" type="xsd:decimal" />
```

The basic schema data types are defined at http://www.w3.org/TR/xmlschema-2. They map closely to .NET data types and include String, Integer, Long, Decimal, Single, DateTime, Boolean, and Base64Binary—to name a few of the most frequently used types.

Both the productName and productPrice are *simple types* because they contain only character data. Elements that contain nested elements are called *complex types*. You can nest them together using a <sequence> tag, if order is important, or an <all> tag if it is not. Here is how you might model the <product> element in the product catalog. Notice that attributes are always declared after elements, and they are not grouped with a <sequence> or <all> tag because the order is not important:

```
<xsd:complexType name="product">
  <xsd:sequence>
    <xsd:element name="productName" type="xsd:string"/>
    <xsd:element name="productPrice" type="xsd:decimal"/>
    <xsd:element name="inStock" type="xsd:boolean"/>
  </xsd:sequence>
  <xsd:attribute name="id" type="xsd:integer"/>
</xsd:complexType>
```

By default, a listed element can occur exactly one time in a document. You can configure this behavior by specifying the maxOccurs and minOccurs attributes. Here is an example that allows an unlimited number of products in the catalog:

```
<xsd:element name="product" type="product" maxOccurs="unbounded" />
```

Here is the complete schema for the product catalog XML:

```
<?xml version="1.0"?>
<xsd:schema xmlns:xsd="http://www.w3.org/2001/XMLSchema">

    <!-- Define the complex type product. -->
    <xsd:complexType name="product">
        <xsd:sequence>
            <xsd:element name="productName" type="xsd:string"/>
            <xsd:element name="productPrice" type="xsd:decimal"/>
            <xsd:element name="inStock" type="xsd:boolean"/>
        </xsd:sequence>
        <xsd:attribute name="id" type="xsd:integer"/>
    </xsd:complexType>

    <!-- This is the structure the document must match.
        It begins with a productCatalog element that nests other elements. -->
    <xsd:element name="productCatalog">
        <xsd:complexType>
            <xsd:sequence>
                <xsd:element name="catalogName" type="xsd:string"/>
                <xsd:element name="expiryDate" type="xsd:date"/>
```

```
                <xsd:element name="products">
                    <xsd:complexType>
                        <xsd:sequence>
                            <xsd:element name="product" type="product"
                             maxOccurs="unbounded" />
                        </xsd:sequence>
                    </xsd:complexType>
                </xsd:element>
            </xsd:sequence>
        </xsd:complexType>
    </xsd:element>
```

`</xsd:schema>`

The XmlReader class can enforce these schema rules, providing you explicitly request a validating reader when you use the XmlReader.Create method. (Even if you do not use a validating reader, an exception will be thrown if the reader discovers XML that is not *well formed*, such as an illegal character, improperly nested tags, and so on.)

Once you have created your validating reader, the validation occurs automatically as you read through the document. As soon as an error is found, the XmlReader raises a ValidationEventHandler event with information about the error on the XmlReaderSettings object given at creation time. If you want, you can handle this event and continue processing the document to find more errors. If you do not handle this event, an XmlException will be raised when the first error is encountered and processing will be aborted.

The Code

The following example shows a utility class that displays all errors in an XML document when the ValidateXml method is called. Errors are displayed in a console window, and a final Boolean variable is returned to indicate the success or failure of the entire validation operation.

```
Imports System
Imports System.Xml
Imports system.Xml.Schema

Namespace Apress.VisualBasicRecipes.Chapter06

    Public Class ConsoleValidator

        ' Set to true if at least one error exists.
        Private m_Failed As Boolean
        Public ReadOnly Property Failed() As Boolean
            Get
                Return m_Failed
            End Get
        End Property

        Public Function ValidateXML(ByVal xmlFileName As String, ➥
ByVal schemaFileName As String) As Boolean

            ' Set the type of validation.
            Dim settings As New XmlReaderSettings
            settings.ValidationType = ValidationType.Schema
```

```
        ' Load the schema file.
        Dim schemas As New XmlSchemaSet
        settings.Schemas = schemas

        ' When loading the schema, specify the namespace it validates
        ' and the location of the file. Use Nothing to use the
        ' targetNamespace specified in the schema.
        schemas.Add(Nothing, schemaFileName)
        ' Specify an event handler for validation errors.
        AddHandler settings.ValidationEventHandler, AddressOf ➡
HandleValidationEvents

        ' Create the validating reader.
        Dim validator As XmlReader = XmlReader.Create(xmlFileName, settings)

        m_Failed = False
        Try
            ' Read all XML data.
            While validator.Read()
            End While
        Catch ex As Exception
            ' This happens if the XML document includes illegal characters
            ' or elements that aren't properly nested or closed.
            Console.WriteLine("A critical XML error has occurred.")
            Console.WriteLine(ex.Message)
            m_Failed = True
        Finally
            validator.Close()
        End Try
        Return Not m_Failed

    End Function

    Private Sub HandleValidationEvents(ByVal sender As Object, ➡
ByVal args As ValidationEventArgs)

        m_Failed = True

        ' Display the validation error.
        Console.WriteLine("Validation error: " & args.Message)
        Console.WriteLine()

    End Sub

    End Class
End Namespace
```

Here is how you would use the class to validate the product catalog:

```
Public Class Recipe06_08

    Public Shared Sub Main()

        Dim xmlValidator As New ConsoleValidator
        Console.WriteLine("Validating ProductCatalog.xml")
```

```
        Dim success As Boolean = xmlValidator.ValidateXML("..\..\" & ➥
"ProductCatalog.xml", "..\..\ProductCatalog.xsd")

        If Not success Then
            Console.WriteLine("Validation failed.")
        Else
            Console.WriteLine("Validation succeeded.")
        End If
        Console.ReadLine()

    End Sub

End Class
```

If the document is valid, no messages will appear, and the success variable will be set to true. But consider what happens if you use a document that breaks schema rules, such as the following ProductCatalog_Invalid.xml file.

```xml
<?xml version="1.0" ?>
<productCatalog>
    <catalogName>Acme Fall 2006 Catalog</catalogName>
    <expiryDate>Jan 1, 2007</expiryDate>

    <products>
        <product id="1001">
            <productName>Magic Ring</productName>
            <productPrice>$342.10</productPrice>
            <inStock>true</inStock>
        </product>
        <product id="1002">
            <productName>Flying Carpet</productName>
            <productPrice>982.99</productPrice>
            <inStock>Yes</inStock>
        </product>
    </products>
</productCatalog>
```

If you attempt to validate this document, the success variable will be set to false, and the output will indicate each error:

```
Validating ProductCatalog_Invalid.xml

Validation error: The 'expiryDate' element is invalid - The value 'Jan 1, 2007'
is invalid according to its datatype 'http://www.w3.org/2001/XMLSchema:date' -
The string 'Jan 1, 2007' is not a valid XsdDateTime value.

Validation error: The element 'product' has invalid child element 'productPrice'
List of possible elements expected: 'description'.

Validation error: The element 'product' has invalid child element 'productPrice'.
List of possible elements expected: 'description'.

Validation failed.
```

Finally, if you want to validate an XML document and load it into an in-memory XmlDocument, you need to take a slightly different approach. The XmlDocument provides its own Schemas property, along with a Validate method that checks the entire document in one step. When you call Validate, you supply a delegate that points to your validation event handler.

Here is how it works:

```
Dim doc As New XmlDocument
doc.Load("..\..\ProductCatalog.xml")

' Specify the schema information.
Dim schemas As New XmlSchemaSet
schemas.Add(Nothing, schemaFileName)
doc.Schemas = schemas

' Validate the document.
doc.Validate(AddressOf HandleValidationEvents)
```

■**Note** For more in-depth information regarding XML schemas, refer to http://www.w3.org/xml/schema.html.

6-9. Use XML Serialization with Custom Objects

Problem

You need to use XML as a serialization format. However, you don't want to process the XML directly in your code. Instead, you want to interact with the data using custom objects.

Solution

Use the System.Xml.Serialization.XmlSerializer class to transfer data from your object to XML, and vice versa. You can also mark up your class code with attributes to customize its XML representation.

How It Works

The XmlSerializer class allows you to convert objects to XML data, and vice versa. This process is used natively by web services and provides a customizable serialization mechanism that does not require a single line of custom code. The XmlSerializer class is even intelligent enough to correctly create arrays when it finds nested elements.

The only requirements for using XmlSerializer are as follows:

- The XmlSerializer serializes only properties and Public variables.

- The classes you want to serialize must include a default zero-argument constructor. The XmlSerializer uses this constructor when creating the new object during deserialization.

- All class properties must be readable *and* writable. This is because XmlSerializer uses the property Get accessor to retrieve information and the property Set accessor to restore the data after deserialization.

■**Note** You can also store your objects using .NET serialization and the `System.Runtime.Serialization.`
`Formatters.Soap.SoapFormatter` class. In this case, you simply need to make your class serializable; you do
not need to provide a default constructor or ensure all properties are writable. However, this gives you no control
over the format of the serialized XML.

To use XML serialization, you must first mark up your data objects with attributes that indicate
the desired XML mapping. You can find these attributes in the `System.Xml.Serialization` namespace.
The attributes are as follows:

- `XmlRoot` specifies the name of the root element of the XML file. By default, `XmlSerializer` will
  use the name of the class. You can apply this attribute to the class declaration.

- `XmlElement` indicates the element name to use for a property or `Public` variable. By default,
  `XmlSerializer` will serialize properties and `Public` variables using their names.

- `XmlAttribute` indicates that a property or `Public` variable should be serialized as an attribute,
  not an element, and specifies the attribute name.

- `XmlEnum` configures the text that should be used when serializing enumerated values. If you
  don't use `XmlEnum`, the name of the enumerated constant will be used.

- `XmlIgnore` indicates that a property or `Public` variable should not be serialized.

The Code

As an example, consider the product catalog first shown in recipe 6-1. You can represent this XML
document using `ProductCatalog` and `Product` objects. Here's the class code that you might use:

```
Imports System
Imports System.Xml
Imports System.Xml.Serialization
Imports System.IO

Namespace Apress.VisualBasicRecipes.Chapter06

    <XmlRoot("productCatalog")> _
    Public Class ProductCatalog

        <XmlElement("catalogName")> _
        Public CatalogName As String

        ' Use the date data type (and ignore the time portion
        ' in the serialized XML).
        <XmlElement(ElementName:="expiryDate", DataType:="date")> _
        Public ExpiryDate As DateTime

        ' Configure the name of the element that holds all products
        ' and the name of the product element itself.
        <XmlArray("products"), XmlArrayItem("product")> _
        Public Products As Product()

        Public Sub New()
        End Sub
```

```vbnet
    Public Sub New(ByVal catalogName As String, ByVal expiryDate As DateTime)

        Me.CatalogName = catalogName
        Me.ExpiryDate = expiryDate

    End Sub

End Class

Public Class Product

    <XmlElement("productName")> _
    Public ProductName As String = String.Empty

    <XmlElement("productPrice")> _
    Public ProductPrice As Decimal = 0

    <XmlElement("inStock")> _
    Public InStock As Boolean = False

    <XmlAttribute(AttributeName:="id", DataType:="integer")> _
    Public Id As String = String.Empty

    Public Sub New()
    End Sub

    Public Sub New(ByVal productName As String, ByVal productPrice As Decimal)

        Me.ProductName = productName
        Me.ProductPrice = productPrice

    End Sub

    End Class
End Namespace
```

Notice that these classes use the XML serialization attributes to rename element names (using Pascal casing in the class member names and camel casing in the XML tag names), indicate data types that are not obvious, and specify how <product> elements will be nested in the <productCatalog>.

Using these custom classes and the XmlSerializer object, you can translate XML into objects, and vice versa. The following is the code you would need to create a new ProductCatalog object, serialize the results to an XML document, deserialize the document back to an object, and then display the XML document.

```vbnet
Imports System
Imports System.Xml
Imports System.Xml.Serialization
Imports System.IO

Namespace Apress.VisualBasicRecipes.Chapter06

    Public Class Recipe06_09
        Public Shared Sub Main()
```

```vb
            ' Create the product catalog.
            Dim catalog = New ProductCatalog("New Catalog", ➥
DateTime.Now.AddYears(1))
            Dim products As Product() = New Product(1) {}

            products(0) = New Product("Product 1", CDec(42.99))
            products(1) = New Product("Product 2", CDec(202.99))

            catalog.Products = products

            ' Serialize the order to a file.
            Dim serializer As New XmlSerializer(GetType(ProductCatalog))
            Dim fs As New FileStream("ProductCatalog.xml", FileMode.Create)

            serializer.Serialize(fs, catalog)
            fs.Close()

            catalog = Nothing

            ' Deserialize the order from the file.
            fs = New FileStream("ProductCatalog.xml", FileMode.Open)
            catalog = DirectCast(serializer.Deserialize(fs), ProductCatalog)

            ' Serialize the order to the console window.
            serializer.Serialize(Console.Out, catalog)
            Console.ReadLine()

        End Sub

    End Class
End Namespace
```

The output of this program is as follows:

```xml
<?xml version="1.0" encoding="IBM437"?>
<productCatalog xmlns:xsi="http://www.w3.org/2001/XMLSchema-instance" xmlns:xsd=
"http://www.w3.org/2001/XMLSchema">
  <catalogName>New Catalog</catalogName>
  <expiryDate>2008-01-21</expiryDate>
  <products>
    <product id="">
      <productName>Product 1</productName>
      <productPrice>42.99</productPrice>
      <inStock>false</inStock>
    </product>
    <product id="">
      <productName>Product 2</productName>
      <productPrice>202.99</productPrice>
      <inStock>false</inStock>
    </product>
  </products>
</productCatalog>
```

6-10. Create a Schema for a .NET Class

Problem

You need to create an XML schema based on one or more VB .NET classes. This will allow you to validate XML documents before deserializing them with the XmlSerializer.

Solution

Use the XML Schema Definition Tool (xsd.exe) command-line utility included with the .NET Framework. Specify the name of your assembly as a command-line argument, and add the /t:[TypeName]
parameter to indicate the types for which you want to generate a schema.

How It Works

Recipe 6-9 demonstrated how to use the XmlSerializer to serialize .NET objects to XML and deserialize XML into .NET objects. But if you want to use XML as a way to interact with other applications,
business processes, or non–.NET Framework applications, you'll need an easy way to validate the
XML before you attempt to deserialize it. You will also need to define an XML schema document that
defines the structure and data types used in your XML format so that other applications can work
with it. One quick solution is to generate an XML schema using the xsd.exe command-line utility.

The xsd.exe utility is included with the .NET Framework. If you have installed Microsoft Visual
Studio 2005, you will find it in a directory like C:\Program Files\Microsoft Visual Studio 8\SDK\v2.0\Bin.
The xsd.exe utility can generate schema documents from compiled assemblies. You simply need to
supply the filename and indicate the class that represents the XML document with the / t:[TypeName]
parameter.

Usage

As an example, consider the ProductCatalog and Product classes shown in recipe 6-9. You could
create the XML schema for a product catalog with the following command line:

```
xsd Recipe6-09.exe /t:ProductCatalog
```

You need to specify only the ProductCatalog class on the command line because the Product
class is referenced by the ProductCatalog and will be included automatically. The generated schema
in this example will represent a complete product catalog, with contained product items. It will be
given the default filename schema0.xsd. You can now use the validation technique shown in recipe 6-8
to test whether the XML document can be successfully validated with the schema.

6-11. Generate a Class from a Schema

Problem

You need to create one or more VB .NET classes based on an XML schema. You can then create an
XML document in the appropriate format using these objects and the XmlSerializer.

Solution

Use the xsd.exe command-line utility included with the .NET Framework. Specify the name of your schema file as a command-line argument, and add the /c parameter to indicate you want to generate class code.

How It Works

Recipe 6-10 introduced the xsd.exe command-line utility, which you can use to generate schemas based on class definitions. The reverse operation—generating VB .NET source code based on an XML schema document—is also possible. This is primarily useful if you want to write a certain format of XML document but you do not want to manually create the document by writing individual nodes with the XmlDocument class or the XmlWriter class. Instead, by using xsd.exe, you can generate a set of full .NET objects. You can then serialize these objects to the required XML representation using the XmlSerializer, as described in recipe 6-9.

To generate source code from a schema, you simply need to supply the filename of the schema document and add the /c parameter to indicate you want to generate the required classes.

Usage

As an example, consider the schema shown in recipe 6-8. You can generate VB .NET code for this schema with the following command line:

```
xsd ProductCatalog.xsd /c
```

This will generate one file (ProductCatalog.cs) with two classes: Product and ProductCalalog. These classes are similar to the ones created in recipe 6-9, except that the class member names match the XML document exactly. Optionally, you can add the /f parameter. If you do, the generated classes will be composed of Public fields. If you do not, the generated classes will use Public properties instead (which simply wrap Private fields).

6-12. Perform an XSL Transform

Problem

You need to transform an XML document into another document using an XSLT stylesheet.

Solution

Use the System.Xml.Xsl.XslCompiledTransform class. Load the XSLT stylesheet using the XslCompiledTransform.Load method, and generate the output document by using the Transform method and supplying a source XML document.

How It Works

XSLT (or XSL transforms) is an XML-based language designed to transform one XML document into another document. You can use XSLT to create a new XML document with the same data but arranged in a different structure or to select a subset of the data in a document. You can also use it to create a different type of structured document. XSLT is commonly used in this manner to format an XML document into an HTML page.

The Code

This recipe transforms the orders.xml document shown in recipe 6-6 into an HTML document with a table and then displays the results. To perform this transformation, you'll need the following XSLT stylesheet:

```
<?xml version="1.0" encoding="UTF-8" ?>
<xsl:stylesheet xmlns:xsl="http://www.w3.org/1999/XSL/Transform"
    version="1.0" >

  <xsl:template match="Order">
    <html><body><p>
    Order <b><xsl:value-of select="Client/@id"/></b>
    for <xsl:value-of select="Client/Name"/></p>
    <table border="1">
    <td>ID</td><td>Name</td><td>Price</td>
    <xsl:apply-templates select="Items/Item"/>
    </table></body></html>
  </xsl:template>

  <xsl:template match="Items/Item">
    <tr>
    <td><xsl:value-of select="@id"/></td>
    <td><xsl:value-of select="Name"/></td>
    <td><xsl:value-of select="Price"/></td>
    </tr>
  </xsl:template>

</xsl:stylesheet>
```

Essentially, every XSLT stylesheet consists of a set of templates. Each template matches some set of elements in the source document, and then describes the contribution that the matched element will make to the resulting document. To match the template, the XSLT document uses XPath expressions, as described in recipe 6-6.

The orders.xslt stylesheet contains two template elements (as children of the root stylesheet element). The first template matches the root Order element. When the XSLT processor finds an Order element, it outputs the HTML elements necessary to start the HTML document and the text result of an XPath expression. In this case, the XPath expressions (Client/@id and Client/Name) match the id attribute and the Name element. It then starts a table with appropriate column headings and inserts some data about the client using the value-of command, which inserts the value of the specified element as text.

Next, the apply-templates command branches off and performs processing of any contained Item elements. This is required because there might be multiple Item elements. Each Item element is matched using the XPath expression Items/Item. The root Order node is not specified because Order is the current node. Finally, the initial template writes the HTML elements necessary to end the HTML document.

If you execute this transform on the sample orders.xml file shown in recipe 6-6, you will end up with an HTML document similar to the following.

```
<html>
  <body>
    <p>
    Order <b>ROS-930252034</b>
    for Remarkable Office Supplies</p>
    <table border="1">
      <td>ID</td>
      <td>Name</td>
      <td>Price</td>
      <tr>
        <td>1001</td>
        <td>Electronic Protractor</td>
        <td>42.99</td>
      </tr>
      <tr>
        <td>1002</td>
        <td>Vorpal Stapler</td>
        <td>500.50</td>
      </tr>
    </table>
  </body>
</html>
```

To apply an XSLT stylesheet in .NET, you use the XslCompiledTransform class. (Do not confuse this class with the similar XslTransform class—it still works but is deprecated in .NET Framework 2.0.)

The following code shows a Windows-based application that programmatically applies the transformation and then displays the transformed file in a window using the WebBrowser control:

```
Imports System
Imports System.Windows.Forms
Imports System.Xml.Xsl

'  All designed code is stored in the autogenerated partial
'  class called TransformXML.Designer.vb. You can see this
'  file by selecting Show All Files in Solution Explorer.
Partial Public Class TransformXml

    Private Sub TransformXml_Load(ByVal sender As Object, ➥
ByVal e As System.EventArgs) Handles Me.Load

        Dim transform As New XslCompiledTransform

        '  Load the XSLT stylesheet.
        transform.Load("..\..\orders.xslt")

        '  Transform orders.xml into orders.html using orders.xslt.
        transform.Transform("..\..\orders.xml", "orders.html")

        Browser.Navigate(Application.StartupPath & "\orders.html")

    End Sub
End Class
```

Figure 6-2 shows the application.

Figure 6-2. *The stylesheet output for orders.xml*

In this example, the code uses the overloaded version of the Transform method that saves the resulting document directly to disk, although you can receive it as a stream and process it inside your application instead. The following code shows an alternate approach that keeps the document content in memory at all times (with no external results file). The XslCompiledTransform writes the results to an XmlWriter that wraps a StringBuilder. The content is then copied from the StringBuilder into the WebBrowser through the handy WebBrowser.DocumentText property. The results are identical.

```
Dim htmlContent = New StringBuilder
Dim results As XmlWriter = XmlWriter.Create(htmlContent)

transform.Transform("..\..\orders.xml", results)
Browser.DocumentText = htmlContent.ToString
```

■**Note** For more in-depth information regarding XSLT, refer to http://www.w3.org/tr/xslt.

CHAPTER 7

■■■

Windows Forms

The Microsoft .NET Framework includes a rich set of classes for creating traditional Windows-based applications in the System.Windows.Forms namespace. These range from basic controls such as the TextBox, Button, and MainMenu classes to specialized controls such as TreeView, LinkLabel, and NotifyIcon. In addition, you will find all the tools you need to manage Multiple Document Interface (MDI) applications, integrate context-sensitive help, and even create multilingual user interfaces— all without needing to resort to the complexities of the Win32 API.

Most VB .NET developers quickly find themselves at home with the Windows Forms programming model. This chapter offers a number of tips and timesaving techniques that can make your Windows programming endeavors even more productive.

■Note Most of the recipes in this chapter use control classes, which are defined in the System.Windows. Forms namespace. When introducing these classes, the full namespace name is not indicated, and System. Windows.Forms is assumed.

The recipes in this chapter describe how to do the following:

- Add controls to a form programmatically at runtime so that you can build forms dynamically instead of only building static forms in the Visual Studio forms designer (recipe 7-1)

- Link arbitrary data objects to controls to provide an easy way to associate data with a control without the need to maintain additional data structures (recipe 7-2)

- Process all the controls on a form in a generic way (recipe 7-3)

- Track all the forms and MDI forms in an application (recipes 7-4 and 7-5)

- Save user-based and computer-based configuration information for Windows Forms applications using the mechanisms built into the .NET Framework and Windows (recipe 7-6)

- Force a list box to always display the most recently added item, so that users do not need to scroll up and down to find it (recipe 7-7)

- Assist input validation by restricting what data a user can enter into a textbox, and implement a component-based mechanism for validating user input and reporting errors (recipes 7-8 and 7-17)

- Implement a custom autocomplete combo box so that you can make suggests for completing words as users type data (recipe 7-9)

- Allow users to sort a list view based on the values in any column (recipe 7-10)

- Avoid the need to explicitly lay out controls on a form by using the Windows Forms layout controls (recipe 7-11)

- Use part of a main menu in a context menu (recipe 7-12)

- Provide multilingual support in your Windows Forms application (recipe 7-13)

- Create forms that cannot be moved and create borderless forms that can be moved (recipes 7-14 and 7-15)

- Create an animated system tray icon for your application (recipe 7-16)

- Support drag-and-drop functionality in your Windows Forms application (recipe 7-18)

- Provide context-sensitive help to the users of your Windows Forms application (recipe 7-19)

- Display Web-based information within your Windows application and allow users to browse the Web from within your application (recipe 7-20)

■**Note** Visual Studio, with its advanced design and editing capabilities, provides the easiest and most productive way to develop Windows Forms applications. Therefore, the recipes in this chapter—unlike those in most other chapters—rely heavily on the use of Visual Studio. Instead of focusing on the library classes that provide the required functionality, or looking at the code generated by Visual Studio, these recipes focus on how to achieve the recipe's goal using the Visual Studio user interface and the code that you must write manually to complete the required functionality. The separation of generated and manual code is particularly elegant in Visual Studio 2005 due to the extensive use it makes of partial types.

7-1. Add a Control Programmatically

Problem

You need to add a control to a form at runtime, not design time.

Solution

Create an instance of the appropriate control class. Then add the control object to a form or a container control by calling `Controls.Add` on the container. (The container's `Controls` property returns a `ControlCollection` instance.)

How It Works

In a .NET form-based application, there is really no difference between creating a control at design time and creating it at runtime. When you create controls at design time (using a tool like Microsoft Visual Studio), the necessary code is added to your form class. In .NET Framework 2.0, Visual Studio will also place this code in a separate source file using the partial type functionality. You can use the same code in your application to create controls on the fly. Just follow these steps:

1. Create an instance of the appropriate control class.

2. Configure the control properties accordingly (particularly the size and position coordinates).

3. Add the control to the form or another container. Every control implements a read-only
   `Controls` property that returns a `ControlCollection` containing references to all of its child
   controls. To add a child control, invoke the `Controls.Add` method.

4. If you need to handle the events for the new control, you can wire them up to existing methods.

If you need to add multiple controls to a form or container, you should call `SuspendLayout` on the
parent control before adding the dynamic controls, and then call `ResumeLayout` once you have finished.
This temporarily disables the layout logic used to position controls and will allow you to avoid significant performance overheads and weird flickering if many controls are being added.

The Code

The following example demonstrates the dynamic creation of a list of checkboxes. One checkbox is
added for each item in a `String` array. All the checkboxes are added to a panel that has its `AutoScroll`
property set to `True`, which gives basic scrolling support to the checkbox list.

```vb
Imports System
Imports System.Windows.Forms

' All designed code is stored in the autogenerated partial
' class called Recipe07-01.Designer.vb. You can see this
' file by selecting Show All Files in Solution Explorer.
Partial Public Class Recipe07_01

    Private Sub Recipe07_01_Load(ByVal sender As Object, ➥
ByVal e As System.EventArgs) Handles Me.Load

        ' Create an array of strings to use as the labels for
        ' the dynamic checkboxes.
        Dim foods As String() = {"Grain", "Bread", "Beans", "Eggs", "Chicken", ➥
"Milk", "Fruit", "Vegetables", "Pasta", "Rice", "Fish", "Beef"}

        ' Suspend the panel's layout logic while multiple controls
        ' are added.
        panel1.SuspendLayout()

        ' Specify the Y coordinate of the topmost checkbox in the list.
        Dim topPosition As Integer = 10

        ' Create one new checkbox for each name in the list of
        ' food types.
        For Each food As String In foods
            ' Create a new checkbox.
            Dim newCheckBox As New CheckBox

            ' Configure the new checkbox.
            newCheckBox.Top = topPosition
            newCheckBox.Left = 10
            newCheckBox.Text = food

            ' Set the Y coordinate of the next checkbox.
            topPosition += 30
```

```
          ' Add the checkbox to the panel contained by the form.
          panel1.Controls.Add(newCheckBox)
     Next

          ' Resume the form's layout logic now that all controls
          ' have been added.
          Me.ResumeLayout()

     End Sub
End Class
```

Usage

Figure 7-1 shows how the example will look when run.

Figure 7-1. *A dynamically generated checkbox list*

7-2. Link Data to a Control

Problem

You need to link an object to a specific control (perhaps to store some arbitrary information that relates to a given display item).

Solution

Store a reference to the object in the Tag property of the control.

How It Works

Every class that derives from Control inherits a Tag property. The Tag property is not used by the control or the .NET Framework. Instead, it's reserved as a convenient storage place for application-specific information. In addition, some other classes not derived from Control also provide a Tag property. Useful examples include the ListViewItem, TreeNode, and MenuItem classes.

Because the Tag property is defined as an Object type, you can use it to store any value type or reference type, from a simple number or string to a custom object you have defined. When retrieving data from the Tag property, you must cast the Object to the correct type before use.

The Code

The following example adds a list of filenames (as ListViewItem objects) to a ListView control. The corresponding System.IO.FileInfo object for each file is stored in the Tag property of its respective ListViewItem. When a user double-clicks one of the filenames, the code retrieves the FileInfo object from the Tag property and displays the filename and size using the MessageBox Shared method Show.

```
Imports System
Imports System.IO
Imports System.Windows.Forms

'  All designed code is stored in the autogenerated partial
'  class called Recipe07-02.Designer.vb. You can see this
'  file by selecting Show All Files in Solution Explorer.
Partial Public Class Recipe07_02

    Private Sub Recipe07_02_Load(ByVal sender As Object, ➡
ByVal e As System.EventArgs) Handles Me.Load

        ' Get all the files in the root directory/
        Dim rootDirectory As New DirectoryInfo("C:\")
        Dim files As FileInfo() = rootDirectory.GetFiles

        ' Display the name of each file in the ListView.
        For Each file As FileInfo In files
            Dim item As ListViewItem = listView1.Items.Add(file.Name)
            item.ImageIndex = 0

            ' Associate each FileInfo object with its ListViewItem.
            item.Tag = file
        Next

    End Sub

    Private Sub listView1_ItemActivate(ByVal sender As Object, ➡
ByVal e As System.EventArgs) Handles listView1.ItemActivate

        ' Get information from the linked FileInfo object and display
        ' it using a MessageBox.
        Dim item As ListViewItem = DirectCast(sender, ListView).SelectedItems(0)
        Dim file As FileInfo = DirectCast(item.Tag, FileInfo)
        Dim info As String = String.Format("{0} is {1} bytes.", file.FullName, ➡
file.Length)

        MessageBox.Show(info, "File Information")

    End Sub
End Class
```

Usage

Figure 7-2 shows how the example will look when run.

Figure 7-2. *Storing data in the Tag property*

7-3. Process All the Controls on a Form

Problem

You need to perform a generic task with all the controls on the form. For example, you may need to retrieve or clear their Text property, change their color, or resize them.

Solution

Iterate recursively through the collection of controls. Interact with each control using the properties and methods of the base Control class.

How It Works

You can iterate through the controls on a form using the ControlCollection object obtained from the Controls property. The ControlCollection includes all the controls that are placed directly on the form surface. However, if any of these controls are container controls (such as GroupBox, Panel, or TabPage), they might contain more controls. Thus, it's necessary to use recursive logic that searches the Controls collection of every control on the form.

The Code

The following example demonstrates the use of recursive logic to find every TextBox on a form and clears the text they contain. When a button is clicked, the code tests each control on the form to determine whether it is a TextBox by using the TypeOf keyword in conjunction with the Is operator.

```
Imports System
Imports System.IO
Imports System.Windows.Forms

'  All designed code is stored in the autogenerated partial
'  class called Recipe07-03.Designer.vb. You can see this
'  file by selecting Show All Files in Solution Explorer.
Partial Public Class Recipe07_03

    Private Sub cmdProcessAll_Click(ByVal sender As System.Object, ➡
ByVal e As System.EventArgs) Handles cmdProcessAll.Click

        ProcessControls(Me)

    End Sub

    Private Sub ProcessControls(ByVal ctrl As Control)

        '  Ignore the control unless it's a textbox.
        If TypeOf (ctrl) Is TextBox Then
            ctrl.Text = ""
        End If

        '  Process controls recursively. This is required
        '  if controls contain other controls (for
        '  example, if you use panels, group boxes, or other
        '  container controls).
        For Each ctrlChild As Control In ctrl.Controls
            ProcessControls(ctrlChild)
        Next

    End Sub
End Class
```

7-4. Track the Visible Forms in an Application

Problem

You need access to all of the open forms that are currently owned by an application.

Solution

Iterate through the FormCollection object that you get from the Shared property OpenForms of the Application object.

How It Works

In .NET Framework 2.0, Windows Forms applications automatically keep track of the open forms that they own. This information is accessed through the Application.OpenForms property, which returns a FormCollection object containing a Form object for each form the application owns. You can iterate through the FormCollection to access all Form objects or obtain a single Form object using its name (Form.Name) or its position in the FormCollection as an index.

The My object (see Chapter 5 for more information) provides an identical OpenForms property in the My.Application class. It also provides quick-and-easy design-time access to each form in the current project via the My.Forms class.

The Code

The following example demonstrates the use of the Application.OpenForms property and the FormCollection it returns to manage the active forms in an application. The example allows you to create new forms with specified names. A list of active forms is displayed when you click the Refresh List button. When you click the name of a form in the list, it is made the active form.

Because of the way the FormCollection works, more than one form may have the same name. If duplicate forms have the same name, the first one found will be activated. If you try to retrieve a Form using a name that does not exist, Nothing is returned. The following is the code for the application's main form.

```
Imports System
Imports System.Windows.Forms

'  All designed code is stored in the autogenerated partial
'  class called Recipe07-04.Designer.vb. You can see this
'  file by selecting Show All Files in Solution Explorer.
Public Class Recipe07_04

    Private Sub Recipe07_04_Load(ByVal sender As System.Object, ➡
ByVal e As System.EventArgs) Handles MyBase.Load

        '  Refresh the list to display the initial set of forms.
        RefreshForms()

    End Sub

    '  A button click event handler to create a new child form.
    Private Sub btnNewForm_Click(ByVal sender As System.Object, ➡
ByVal e As System.EventArgs) Handles btnNewForm.Click

        '  Create a new child form and set its name as specified.
        '  If no name is specified, use a default name.
        Dim child As New Recipe07_04Child

        If txtFormName.Text Is String.Empty Then
            child.Name = "Child Form"
        Else
            child.Name = txtFormName.Text
        End If

        '  Show the new child form.
        child.Show()

    End Sub

    '  List selection event handler to activate the selected form based on
    '  its name.
```

```vb
    Private Sub listForms_SelectedIndexChanged(ByVal sender As Object, ➡
ByVal e As System.EventArgs) Handles listForms.SelectedIndexChanged

        ' Activate the selected form using its name as the index into the
        ' collection of active forms. If there are duplicate forms with the
        ' same name, the first one found will be activated.
        Dim selectedForm As Form = Application.OpenForms(listForms.Text)

        ' If the form has been closed, using its name as an index into the
        ' FormCollection will return nothing. In this instance, update the
        ' list of forms.
        If selectedForm IsNot Nothing Then
            ' Activate the selected form.
            selectedForm.Activate()
        Else
            ' Display a message and refresh the form list.
            MessageBox.Show("Form closed; refreshing list...", "Form Closed")
            RefreshForms()
        End If

    End Sub

    ' A button click event handler to initiate a refresh of the list of
    ' active forms.
    Private Sub btnRefresh_Click(ByVal sender As System.Object, ➡
ByVal e As System.EventArgs) Handles btnRefresh.Click

        RefreshForms()

    End Sub

    ' A method to perform a refresh of the list of active forms.
    Private Sub RefreshForms()

        ' Clear the list and repopulate from the Application.OpenForms
        ' property.
        listForms.Items.Clear()

        For Each f As Form In Application.OpenForms
            listForms.Items.Add(f.Name)
        Next

    End Sub
End Class
```

The following is the code for the child forms you create by clicking the New Form button.

```vb
Imports System
Imports System.Windows.Forms

' All designed code is stored in the autogenerated partial
' class called Recipe07-04Child.Designer.vb. You can see this
' file by selecting Show All Files in Solution Explorer.
Partial Public Class Recipe07_04Child
```

```
' A button click event handler to close the child form.
Private Sub btnClose_Click(ByVal sender As System.Object, ➥
ByVal e As System.EventArgs) Handles btnClose.Click

    Close()

End Sub

' Display the name of the form when it is painted.
Private Sub Recipe07_04Child_Paint(ByVal sender As Object, ➥
ByVal e As System.Windows.Forms.PaintEventArgs) Handles Me.Paint

    ' Display the name of the form.
    lblFormName.Text = Name

End Sub
End Class
```

Notes

Versions 1.0 and 1.1 of the .NET Framework do not provide any way of determining which forms are currently owned by an application. (The one exception is MDI applications, as described in recipe 7-5.) If you want to determine which forms exist or which forms are displayed, or you want one form to call the methods or set the properties of another form, you will need to keep track of form instances on your own.

For tracking small numbers of forms, one useful approach is to create a Shared class consisting of Shared members. Each Shared member holds a reference to a specific Form. If you have many forms you need to track, such as in a document-based application where the user can create multiple instances of the same form, one per document, a generic collection such as a System.Collections. Generic.Dictionary(Of String,Form) is very useful. This lets you map a Form object to a name.

Whichever approach you take, each Form object should register itself with the tracker class when it is first created. A logical place to put this code is in the Form.Load event. Conversely, when the Form object is closed, it should deregister itself with the tracker class. Deregistration should occur in the Closing or Closed events of the Form class. This method would work very well as a base class from which each new form inherits.

Using either of these approaches, any code that requires access to a Form object can obtain a reference to it from the members of the tracker class, and even invoke operations on the Form instance directly through the tracker class if you are sure the Form object exists.

7-5. Find All MDI Child Forms

Problem

You need to find all the forms that are currently being displayed in an MDI application.

Solution

Iterate through the forms returned by the MdiChildren collection property of the MDI parent.

How It Works

The .NET Framework includes two convenient shortcuts for managing the forms open in MDI applications: the MdiParent and MdiChildren properties of the Form class. The MdiParent property of any MDI child returns a Form representing the containing parent window. The MdiChildren property returns an array containing all of the MDI child forms.

The Code

The following example presents an MDI parent window that allows you to create new MDI children by clicking the New item on the File menu. Each child window contains a label, which displays the date and time when the MDI child was created, and a button. When the button is clicked, the event handler walks through all the MDI child windows and displays the label text that each one contains. Notice that when the example enumerates the collection of MDI child forms, it converts the generic Form reference to the derived Recipe07_05Child form class so that it can use the LabelText property. The following is the Recipe07_05Parent class.

```
Imports System
Imports System.Windows.Forms

'  All designed code is stored in the autogenerated partial
'  class called Recipe07-05Parent.Designer.vb. You can see this
'  file by selecting Show All Files in Solution Explorer.
Partial Public Class Recipe07_05Parent

    '  When the New menu item is clicked, create a new MDI child.
    Private Sub mnuNew_Click(ByVal sender As System.Object, ➥
ByVal e As System.EventArgs) Handles mnuNew.Click

        Dim frm As New Recipe07_05Child

        frm.MdiParent = Me
        frm.Show()

    End Sub

End Class
```

The following is the Recipe07_05Child class.

```
Imports System
Imports System.Windows.Forms

'  All designed code is stored in the autogenerated partial
'  class called Recipe07-05Child.Designer.vb. You can see this
'  file by selecting Show All Files in Solution Explorer.
Partial Public Class Recipe07_05Child

    '  A property to provide easy access to the label data.
    Public ReadOnly Property LabelText() As String
        Get
            Return label.Text
        End Get
    End Property
```

```
' When a button on any of the MDI child forms is clicked, display the
' contents of each form by enumerating the MdiChildren collection.
Private Sub cmdShowAllWindows_Click(ByVal sender As System.Object, ➡
ByVal e As System.EventArgs) Handles cmdShowAllWindows.Click

    For Each frm As Form In Me.MdiParent.MdiChildren
        ' Cast the generic Form to the Recipe07_05Child derived class type.
        Dim child As Recipe07_05Child = DirectCast(frm, Recipe07_05Child)
        MessageBox.Show(child.LabelText, frm.Text)
    Next

End Sub

' Set the MDI child form's label to the current date/time.
Private Sub Recipe07_05Child_Load(ByVal sender As Object, ➡
ByVal e As System.EventArgs) Handles Me.Load

    label.Text = DateTime.Now.ToString

End Sub

End Class
```

Usage

Figure 7-3 shows how the example will look when run.

Figure 7-3. *Getting information from multiple MDI child windows*

7-6. Save Configuration Settings for a Form

Problem

You need to store configuration settings for a form so that they are remembered the next time that the form is shown.

Solution

Use the .NET Framework 2.0 Application Settings functionality, which is configurable at design time in Visual Studio.

How It Works

The Application Settings functionality in .NET Framework 2.0 provides an easy-to-use mechanism through which you can save application and user settings used to customize the appearance and operation of a Windows Forms application. You configure Application Settings through the Properties panel of each Windows control (including the main Windows Form) in your application. By expanding the ApplicationSettings property and clicking the ellipsis (three dots) to the right of (PropertyBinding), you can review and configure Application Settings for each property of the active control. See Figure 7-4 for an example.

When you configure a new Application Setting for a control's property, you must assign it a name, a default value, and a scope.

- The name allows you to both access the setting programmatically and reuse the Application Setting across multiple controls.

- The default value is used if the application cannot obtain a value from a configuration file at runtime.

- The scope is either User or Application.

Settings with an Application scope are stored in the application's configuration file (usually located in the same folder as the application assembly) and are read-only. The benefit of an Application scope is that you can change configuration settings by editing the configuration file without needing to recompile the application. Settings with a User scope are read-write by default and are stored in a file located in an *isolated store* (see recipe 5-18 for information about isolated stores).

When you configure your application to use Application Settings, Visual Studio actually autogenerates a wrapper class that provides access to the configuration file information, regardless of whether it is scoped as Application or User. This class, named MySettings, is in the Settings.Designer.vb file, which can be found in your project's My Project folder. This folder also contains the Settings.settings file. When you open this file in Visual Studio, it will display a dialog box that allows you to easily edit your application's settings. You will see these files only if you have turned on the Show All Files option in the Solution Explorer.

Figure 7-4. *Configuring Application Settings in Visual Studio*

The My.Settings class contains properties with names matching each of the Application Setting names you configured for your controls' properties. The controls will automatically read their configuration at startup, but you should store configuration changes prior to terminating your application by calling the My.Settings.Save method. You can also configure this to occur automatically by checking the Save My.Settings on Shutdown option in the Application section of your project's properties, as shown in Figure 7-5.

Figure 7-5. *Automatically saving settings on shutdown*

The Code

The following example shows how to update and save Application Settings, which are Size and Color in this case, at runtime.

```
Imports System
Imports System.ComponentModel
Imports System.Windows.Forms

'  All designed code is stored in the autogenerated partial
'  class called Recipe07-06.Designer.vb. You can see this
'  file by selecting Show All Files in Solution Explorer.
Partial Public Class Recipe07_06

    Private Sub Recipe07_06_Load(ByVal sender As Object, ➡
ByVal e As System.EventArgs) Handles Me.Load

        Me.Size = My.Settings.Size

    End Sub
```

```
    Private Sub Button_Click(ByVal sender As System.Object, ➡
ByVal e As System.EventArgs) Handles redButton.Click, blueButton.Click, ➡
greenButton.Click

        ' Change the color of the textbox depending on which button
        ' was pressed.
        Dim btn As Button = TryCast(sender, Button)

        If btn IsNot Nothing Then
            ' Set the BackColor of the textbox to the ForeColor of the button.
            textBox1.BackColor = btn.ForeColor

            ' Update the application settings with the new value.
            My.Settings.Color = textBox1.BackColor

        End If

    End Sub

    Private Sub Recipe07_06_FormClosing(ByVal sender As Object, ➡
ByVal e As System.Windows.Forms.FormClosingEventArgs) Handles Me.FormClosing

        ' Update the application settings for Form.
        My.Settings.Size = Me.Size

        ' Store all application settings.
        My.Settings.Save()

    End Sub

End Class
```

7-7. Force a List Box to Scroll to the Most Recently Added Item

Problem

You need to scroll a list box programmatically so that the most recently added items are visible.

Solution

Set the ListBox.TopIndex property, which sets the first visible list item.

How It Works

In some cases, you might have a list box that stores a significant amount of information or one that you add information to periodically. Often, the most recent information, which is added at the end of the list, is more important than the information at the top of the list. One solution is to scroll the list box so that recently added items are visible. The ListBox.TopIndex property enables you to do this by allowing you to specify which item is visible at the top of the list.

The Code

The following sample form includes a list box and a button. Each time the button is clicked, 20 items are added to the list box. Each time new items are added, the code sets the ListBox.TopIndex property and forces the list box to display the most recently added items. To provide better feedback, the same line is also selected.

```vb
Imports System
Imports System.Windows.Forms

' All designed code is stored in the autogenerated partial
' class called Recipe07-07.Designer.vb. You can see this
' file by selecting Show All Files in Solution Explorer.
Partial Public Class Recipe07_07

    Private counter As Integer = 1

    ' Button click event handler adds 20 new items to the ListBox.
    Private Sub cmdTest_Click(ByVal sender As Object, ➥
ByVal e As System.EventArgs) Handles cmdTest.Click

        ' Add 20 items.
        For i As Integer = 1 To 19
            counter += 1
            listBox1.Items.Add("Item " & counter.ToString())
        Next

        ' Set the TopIndex property of the ListBox to ensure the
        ' most recently added items are visible.
        listBox1.TopIndex = listBox1.Items.Count - 1
        listBox1.SelectedIndex = listBox1.Items.Count - 1

    End Sub
End Class
```

7-8. Restrict a Textbox to Accepting Only Specific Input

Problem

You need to create a textbox that will reject all nonnumeric keystrokes.

Solution

Use the MaskedTextBox control and set the Mask property to configure the input that is acceptable.

How It Works

One way to ensure user input is valid is to prevent invalid data from being entered in the first place. The MaskedTextBox control facilitates this approach. The MaskedTextBox.Mask property takes a string that specifies the input mask for the control. This mask determines what type of input a user can enter at each point in the control's text area. If the user enters an incorrect character, the control will beep if the BeepOnError property is True, and the MaskInputRejected event is raised so that you can customize the handling of incorrect input.

■**Note** The MaskedTextBox control will not solve all your user-input validation problems. While it does make some types of validation easy to implement, without customization, it will not ensure some common validation requirements are met. For example, you can specify that only numeric digits can be input, but you cannot specify that they must be less than a specific value, nor can you control the overall characteristics of the input value.

The Code

The following example demonstrates the use of the MaskedTextBox control. A series of buttons allows you to change the active mask on the MaskedTextBox control and experiment with the various masks. Notice that the control automatically tries to accommodate existing content with the new mask when the mask is changed. If the content is not allowed with the new mask, the control is cleared.

```vb
Imports System
Imports System.Windows.Forms

'  All designed code is stored in the autogenerated partial
'  class called Recipe07-08.Designer.vb. You can see this
'  file by selecting Show All Files in Solution Explorer.
Partial Public Class Recipe07_08

    Private Sub btnTime_Click(ByVal sender As System.Object, ➥
ByVal e As System.EventArgs) Handles btnTime.Click

        ' Set the input mask to that of a short time.
        Me.mskTextBox.UseSystemPasswordChar = False
        Me.mskTextBox.Mask = "00:00"
        Me.lblActiveMask.Text = Me.mskTextBox.Mask
        Me.mskTextBox.Focus()

    End Sub

    Private Sub btnDecimal_Click(ByVal sender As System.Object, ➥
ByVal e As System.EventArgs) Handles btnDecimal.Click

        ' Set the input mask to that of a decimal.
        Me.mskTextBox.UseSystemPasswordChar = False
        Me.mskTextBox.Mask = "999,999.00"
        Me.lblActiveMask.Text = Me.mskTextBox.Mask
        Me.mskTextBox.Focus()

    End Sub

    Private Sub btnDate_Click(ByVal sender As System.Object, ➥
ByVal e As System.EventArgs) Handles btnDate.Click

        ' Set the input mask to that of a short date.
        Me.mskTextBox.UseSystemPasswordChar = False
        Me.mskTextBox.Mask = "00/00/0000"
```

```
        Me.lblActiveMask.Text = Me.mskTextBox.Mask
        Me.mskTextBox.Focus()

    End Sub

    Private Sub btnUSZip_Click(ByVal sender As System.Object, ➡
ByVal e As System.EventArgs) Handles btnUSZip.Click

        ' Set the input mask to that of a US ZIP code.
        Me.mskTextBox.UseSystemPasswordChar = False
        Me.mskTextBox.Mask = "00000-9999"
        Me.lblActiveMask.Text = Me.mskTextBox.Mask
        Me.mskTextBox.Focus()

    End Sub

    Private Sub btnUKPost_Click(ByVal sender As System.Object, ➡
ByVal e As System.EventArgs) Handles btnUKPost.Click

        ' Set the input mask to that of a UK postcode.
        Me.mskTextBox.UseSystemPasswordChar = False
        Me.mskTextBox.Mask = ">LCCC 9LL"
        Me.lblActiveMask.Text = Me.mskTextBox.Mask
        Me.mskTextBox.Focus()

    End Sub

    Private Sub btnSecret_Click(ByVal sender As System.Object, ➡
ByVal e As System.EventArgs) Handles btnSecret.Click

        ' Set the input mask to that of a secret PIN.
        Me.mskTextBox.UseSystemPasswordChar = True
        Me.mskTextBox.Mask = "0000"
        Me.lblActiveMask.Text = Me.mskTextBox.Mask
        Me.mskTextBox.Focus()

    End Sub
End Class
```

Notes

The MaskedTextBox used in this recipe is new to .NET Framework 2.0. In previous versions of the .NET Framework, one approach was to use a standard TextBox control and handle the KeyPress events it raises. The KeyPress event is raised after each keystroke has been received but before it is displayed. You can use the KeyPressEventArgs event parameter to effectively cancel an invalid keystroke by setting its Handled property to True.

For example, to allow only numeric input, you must allow a keystroke only if it corresponds to a number (0 through 9) or a special control key (such as Delete or the arrow keys). The keystroke character is provided to the KeyPress event through the KeyPressEventArgs.KeyChar property. You can use two Shared methods of the System.Char class—IsDigit and IsControl—to quickly test the character.

7-9. Use an Autocomplete Combo Box

Problem

You want to create a combo box that automatically completes what the user is typing based on the item list.

Solution

You can implement a basic autocomplete combo box by creating a custom control that overrides the OnKeyPress and OnTextChanged methods of the ComboBox object.

■**Note** The ComboBox control in .NET Framework 2.0 provides autocomplete options. You can configure the behavior using the AutoCompleteMode property of the ComboBox class.

How It Works

An autocomplete control has many different variations. For example, the control may fill in values based on a list of recent selections (as Microsoft Excel does when you are entering cell values), or the control might display a drop-down list of near matches (as Microsoft Internet Explorer does when you are typing a URL). You can create a basic autocomplete combo box by handling the KeyPress and TextChanged events, or by creating a custom class that derives from ComboBox and overrides the OnKeyPress and OnTextChanged methods.

The Code

The following example contains an AutoCompleteComboBox control that derives from ComboBox. The AutoCompleteComboBox control supports autocompletion by overriding the OnKeyPress and OnTextChanged inherited methods. In the OnKeyPress method, the combo box determines whether or not an autocomplete replacement should be made. If the user pressed a character key (such as a letter), the replacement can be made, but if the user pressed a control key (such as the backspace key, the cursor keys, and so on), no action should be taken. The OnTextChanged method performs the actual replacement after the key processing is complete. This method looks up the first match for the current text in the list of items, and then adds the rest of the matching text. After the text is added, the combo box selects the characters between the current insertion point and the end of the text. This allows the user to continue typing and replace the autocomplete text if it is not what the user wants.

```
Imports System
Imports System.Windows.Forms

Public Class AutoCompleteCombobox
    Inherits ComboBox

        ' A private member to track if a special key is pressed, in
        ' which case, any text replacement operation will be skipped.
        Private controlKey As Boolean = False
```

```
    ' Determine whether a special key was pressed.
    Protected Overrides Sub OnKeyPress(ByVal e As ➡
System.Windows.Forms.KeyPressEventArgs)

        ' First call the overridden base class method.
        MyBase.OnKeyPress(e)

        ' Clear the text if the Escape key is pressed.
        If e.KeyChar = ChrW(Keys.Escape) Then
            ' Clear the text.
            Me.SelectedIndex = -1
            Me.Text = ""
            controlKey = True
        ElseIf Char.IsControl(e.KeyChar) Then
            ' Don't try to autocomplete when control key is pressed.
            controlKey = True
        Else
            ' Noncontrol keys should trigger autocomplete.
            controlKey = False
        End If

    End Sub

    ' Perform the text substitution.
    Protected Overrides Sub OnTextChanged(ByVal e As System.EventArgs)

        ' First call the overridden base class method.
        MyBase.OnTextChanged(e)

        If Not Me.Text = "" And Not controlKey Then
            ' Search the current contents of the combo box for a
            ' matching entry.
            Dim matchText As String = Me.Text
            Dim match As Integer = Me.FindString(matchText)

            ' If a matching entry is found, insert it now.
            If Not match = -1 Then
                Me.SelectedIndex = match

                ' Select the added text so it can be replaced
                ' if the user keeps trying.
                Me.SelectionStart = matchText.Length
                Me.SelectionLength = Me.Text.Length - Me.SelectionStart
            End If
        End If

    End Sub
End Class
```

Usage

The following code demonstrates the use of the AutoCompleteComboBox by adding it to a form and filling it with a list of words. In this example, the control is added to the form manually, and the list of words is retrieved from a text file named words.txt. As an alternative, you could compile the

AutoCompleteComboBox class to a separate class library assembly, and then add it to the Visual Studio Toolbox, so you could add it to forms at design time.

```
Imports System
Imports System.IO
Imports System.Drawing
Imports System.Windows.Forms

'  All designed code is stored in the autogenerated partial
'  class called Recipe07-09.Designer.vb. You can see this
'  file by selecting Show All Files in Solution Explorer.
Partial Public Class Recipe07_09

    Private Sub Recipe07_09_Load(ByVal sender As Object, ➥
ByVal e As System.EventArgs) Handles Me.Load
        '  Add the AutoCompleteComboBox to the form.
        Dim combo As New AutoCompleteComboBox

        combo.Location = New Point(10, 10)
        Me.Controls.Add(combo)

        '  Read the list of words from the file words.txt and add them
        '   to the AutoCompleteComboBox.
        Using fs As New FileStream("..\..\words.txt", FileMode.Open)
            Using r As New StreamReader(fs)
                While r.Peek > -1
                    Dim word As String = r.ReadLine
                    combo.Items.Add(word)
                End While
            End Using
        End Using

    End Sub
End Class
```

Figure 7-6 shows how the AutoCompleteComboBox will look when the example is run.

Figure 7-6. *An autocomplete combo box*

7-10. Sort a List View by Any Column

Problem

You need to sort a list view, but the built-in ListView.Sort method sorts based on only the first column.

Solution

Create a type that implements the System.Collections.IComparer interface and can sort ListViewItem objects. The IComparer type can sort based on any ListViewItem criteria you specify. Set the ListView.ListViewItemSorter property with an instance of the IComparer type before calling the ListView.Sort method.

How It Works

The ListView control provides a Sort method that orders items alphabetically based on the text in the first column. If you want to sort based on other column values or order items numerically, you need to create a custom implementation of the IComparer interface that can perform the work. The IComparer interface defines a single method named Compare, which takes two Object arguments and determines which one should be ordered first. Full details of how to implement the IComparer interface are available in recipe 13-3.

The Code

The following example demonstrates the creation of an IComparer implementation named ListViewItemComparer. This class relies on the Compare method of String and Decimal to perform appropriate comparisons. The ListViewItemComparer class also implements two additional properties: Column and Numeric. The Column property identifies the column that should be used for sorting. The Numeric property is a Boolean flag that can be set to True if you want to perform number-based comparisons instead of alphabetic comparisons. The numeric sorting is applied when the users clicks the first column.

When the user clicks a column heading, the example creates a ListViewItemComparer instance, configures the column to use for sorting, and assigns the ListViewItemComparer instance to the ListView.ListViewItemSorter property before calling the ListView.Sort method.

```
Imports System
Imports system.Collections
Imports System.Windows.forms

'  All designed code is stored in the autogenerated partial
'  class called Recipe07-10.Designer.vb. You can see this
'  file by selecting Show All Files in Solution Explorer.
Partial Public Class Recipe07_10

    Private Sub listView1_ColumnClick(ByVal sender As Object, ➥
ByVal e As System.Windows.Forms.ColumnClickEventArgs) Handles listView1.ColumnClick

        '  Create and/or configure the ListViewItemComparer to sort based on
        '  the column that was clicked.
        Dim sorter As ListViewItemComparer = TryCast(listView1.ListViewItemSorter, ➥
ListViewItemComparer)

        If sorter Is Nothing Then
            '  Create a new ListViewItemComparer.
            sorter = New ListViewItemComparer(e.Column)

            '  Use Decimal comparison for the first column.
            If e.Column = 0 Then
                sorter.Numeric = True
```

```vb
            Else
                sorter.Numeric = False
            End If

            listView1.ListViewItemSorter = sorter
        Else
            ' Use Decimal comparison for the first column.
            If e.Column = 0 Then
                sorter.Numeric = True
            Else
                sorter.Numeric = False
            End If

            ' Configure the existing ListViewItemComparer.
            If sorter.Column = e.Column Then
                sorter.Descending = Not sorter.Descending
            Else
                sorter.Column = e.Column
                sorter.Descending = False
            End If
        End If

        ' Sort the ListView.
        listView1.Sort()

    End Sub
End Class

Public Class ListViewItemComparer
    Implements IComparer

    ' Private members to configure comparer logic.
    Private m_Column As Integer
    Private m_Numeric As Boolean = False
    Private m_Descending As Boolean = False

    ' Property to get/set the column to use for comparison.
    Public Property Column() As Integer
        Get
            Return m_Column
        End Get
        Set(ByVal value As Integer)
            m_Column = value
        End Set
    End Property

    ' Property to get/set whether numeric comparison is required
    ' as opposed to the standard alphabetic comparison.
    Public Property Numeric() As Boolean
        Get
            Return m_Numeric
        End Get
```

```vb
            Set(ByVal value As Boolean)
                m_Numeric = value
            End Set
    End Property


    '   Property to get/set whether we are sorting in descending
    '   order or not.
    Public Property Descending() As Boolean
        Get
            Return m_Descending
        End Get
        Set(ByVal Value As Boolean)
            m_Descending = Value
        End Set
    End Property


    Public Sub New(ByVal columnIndex As Integer)
        Column = columnIndex
    End Sub


    Public Function Compare(ByVal x As Object, ByVal y As Object) ➥
As Integer Implements System.Collections.IComparer.Compare

        '   Convert the arguments to ListViewItem objects.
        Dim itemX As ListViewItem = TryCast(x, ListViewItem)
        Dim itemY As ListViewItem = TryCast(y, ListViewItem)

        '   Handle the logic for a Nothing reference as dictated by the
        '   IComparer interface. Nothing is considered less than
        '   any other value.
        If itemX Is Nothing And itemY Is Nothing Then
            Return 0
        ElseIf itemX Is Nothing Then
            Return -1
        ElseIf itemY Is Nothing Then
            Return 1
        End If

        '   Short-circuit condition where the items are references
        '   to the same object.
        If itemX Is itemY Then Return 0

        '   Determine if numeric comparison is required.
        If Numeric Then
            '   Convert column text to numbers before comparing.
            '   If the conversion fails, just use the value 0.
            Dim itemXVal, itemYVal As Decimal

            If Not Decimal.TryParse(itemX.SubItems(Column).Text, itemXVal) Then
                itemXVal = 0
            End If
            If Not Decimal.TryParse(itemY.SubItems(Column).Text, itemYVal) Then
                itemYVal = 0
            End If
```

```
            If Descending Then
                Return Decimal.Compare(itemYVal, itemXVal)
            Else
                Return Decimal.Compare(itemXVal, itemYVal)
            End If
        Else
            ' Keep the column text in its native string format
            ' and perform an alphabetic comparison.
            Dim itemXText As String = itemX.SubItems(Column).Text
            Dim itemYText As String = itemY.SubItems(Column).Text

            If Descending Then
                Return String.Compare(itemYText, itemXText)
            Else
                Return String.Compare(itemXText, itemYText)
            End If
        End If

    End Function
End Class
```

7-11. Lay Out Controls Automatically

Problem

You have a large set of controls on a form and you want them arranged automatically.

Solution

Use the FlowLayoutPanel container to dynamically arrange the controls using a horizontal or vertical flow, or use the TableLayoutPanel container to dynamically arrange the controls in a grid.

How It Works

The FlowLayoutPanel and TableLayoutPanel containers (both new to .NET Framework 2.0) simplify the design-time and runtime layout of the controls they contain. At both design time and runtime, as you add controls to one of these panels, the panel's logic determines where the control should be positioned, so you do not need to determine the exact location.

With the FlowLayoutPanel container, the FlowDirection and WrapContents properties determine where controls are positioned. FlowDirection controls the order and location of controls, and it can be set to LeftToRight (the default), TopDown, RightToLeft, or BottomUp. The WrapContents property controls whether controls run off the edge of the panel or wrap around to form a new line of controls. The default is to wrap controls.

With the TableLayoutPanel container, the RowCount and ColumnCount properties control how many rows and columns are currently in the panel's grid. The default for both of these properties is 0. The GrowStyle property determines how the grid grows to accommodate more controls once it is full, and it can be set to AddRows (the default), AddColumns, or FixedSize (which means the grid cannot grow).

Figure 7-7 shows the design-time appearance of both a TableLayoutPanel container and a FlowLayoutPanel container. The TableLayoutPanel panel is configured with three rows and three columns. The FlowLayoutPanel panel is configured to wrap contents and use left-to-right flow direction.

Figure 7-7. *Using a FlowLayoutPanel panel and a TableLayoutPanel panel*

7-12. Use Part of a Main Menu for a Context Menu

Problem

You need to create a context menu that shows the same menu items as those displayed as part of an application's main menu.

Solution

Use the CloneMenu method of the MenuItem class to duplicate the required portion of the main menu.

How It Works

In many applications, a control's context-sensitive menu duplicates a portion of the main menu. However, .NET does not allow you to create a MenuItem instance that is contained in more than one menu at a time.

The solution is to make a duplicate copy of a portion of the menu using the CloneMenu method, which returns a reference to the cloned item. The CloneMenu method not only copies the appropriate MenuItem items (and any contained submenus), but it also registers each MenuItem object with the same event handlers. Thus, when a user clicks a cloned menu item in a context menu, the event handler will be triggered as if the user had clicked the menu item in the main menu.

The Code

The following example uses the CloneMenu method to configure the context menu for a TextBox to be a duplicate of the File menu.

```
Imports system
Imports System.Drawing
Imports System.Windows.Forms
```

```vb
' All designed code is stored in the autogenerated partial
' class called Recipe07-12.Designer.vb. You can see this
' file by selecting Show All Files in Solution Explorer.
Partial Public Class Recipe07_12

    ' As the main form loads, clone the required section of the main
    ' menu and assign it to the ContextMenu propety of the TextBox.
    Private Sub Recipe07_12_Load(ByVal sender As Object, ➥
ByVal e As System.EventArgs) Handles Me.Load

        Dim mnuContext As New ContextMenu

        ' Copy the menu items from the File menu into a context menu.
        For Each mnuItem As MenuItem In mnuFile.MenuItems
            mnuContext.MenuItems.Add(mnuItem.CloneMenu)
        Next

        ' Attach the cloned menu to the TextBox.
        TextBox1.ContextMenu = mnuContext

    End Sub

    ' Event handler to display the ContextMenu for the TextBox.
    Private Sub TextBox1_MouseDown(ByVal sender As Object, ➥
ByVal e As System.Windows.Forms.MouseEventArgs) Handles TextBox1.MouseDown

        If e.Button = Windows.Forms.MouseButtons.Right Then
            TextBox1.ContextMenu.Show(TextBox1, New Point(e.X, e.Y))
        End If

    End Sub

    ' Event handler to process clicks on File/Open menu item.
    ' For the purpose of the example, simply show a message box.
    Private Sub mnuOpen_Click(ByVal sender As Object, ➥
ByVal e As System.EventArgs) Handles mnuOpen.Click
        MessageBox.Show("This is the event handler for Open.", "Recipe07-12")
    End Sub

    Private Sub mnuSave_Click(ByVal sender As Object, ➥
ByVal e As System.EventArgs) Handles mnuSave.Click
        MessageBox.Show("This is the event handler for Save.", "Recipe07-12")
    End Sub

    Private Sub mnuExit_Click(ByVal sender As Object, ➥
ByVal e As System.EventArgs) Handles mnuExit.Click
        MessageBox.Show("This is the event handler for Exit.", "Recipe07-12")
    End Sub

End Class
```

Usage

Figure 7-8 shows how the example will look when run.

Figure 7-8. *Copying part of a main menu to a context menu*

7-13. Make a Multilingual Form

Problem

You need to create a localizable form that can be deployed in more than one language.

Solution

Store all locale-specific information in resource files, which are compiled into satellite assemblies.

How It Works

The .NET Framework includes built-in support for localization through its use of resource files. The basic idea is to store information that is locale-specific (for example, button text) in a resource file. You can create resource files for each culture you need to support and compile them into satellite assemblies. When you run the application, .NET will automatically use the correct satellite assembly based on the locale settings of the current user/computer.

You can read to and write from resource files manually; they are XML files (see recipe 1-17 for more information about resource files). However, Visual Studio also includes extensive design-time support for localized forms. It works like this:

1. Set the `Localizable` property of a `Form` to `True` using the Properties window.

2. Set the `Language` property of the form to the locale for which you would like to enter information, as shown in Figure 7-9. Then configure the localizable properties of all the controls on the form. Instead of storing your changes in the designer-generated code for the form, Visual Studio will actually create a new resource file to hold your data.

Figure 7-9. *Selecting a language for localizing a form*

3. Repeat step 2 for each language that you want to support. Each time you enter a new locale for the form's `Language` property, a new resource file will be generated. If you select Project ➤ Show All Files from the Visual Studio menu, you will find these resource files under your form's folder, as shown in Figure 7-10. If you change the `Language` property to a locale you have already configured, your previous settings will reappear, and you will be able to modify them.

You can now compile and test your application on differently localized systems. Visual Studio will create a separate directory and satellite assembly for each resource file in the project. You can select Project ➤ Show All Files from the Visual Studio menu to see how these files are arranged, as shown in Figure 7-10.

Figure 7-10. *Satellite assembly and resource files structure*

The Code

Although you do not need to manually code any of the localization functionality, as a testing shortcut, you can force your application to adopt a specific culture by modifying the Thread.CurrentUICulture property of the application thread. However, you must modify this property before the form has loaded.

```
Imports System
Imports System.Threading
Imports System.Globalization
Imports System.Windows.Forms

'   All designed code is stored in the autogenerated partial
'   class called Recipe07-13.Designer.vb. You can see this
'   file by selecting Show All Files in Solution Explorer.
Partial Public Class Recipe07_13

    Public Shared Sub Main()

        Thread.CurrentThread.CurrentUICulture = New CultureInfo("fr")
        Application.Run(New Recipe07_13)

    End Sub

End Class
```

Usage

Figure 7-11 shows both the English and French versions of the example. As you can see, both the language and the layout of the form are different depending on the current locale.

Figure 7-11. *English and French localizations*

7-14. Create a Form That Cannot Be Moved

Problem

You want to create a form that occupies a fixed location on the screen and cannot be moved.

Solution

Make a borderless form by setting the FormBorderStyle property of the Form class to the value FormBorderStyle.None.

How It Works

You can create a borderless form by setting the FormBorderStyle property of a Form to None. Borderless forms cannot be moved. However, as their name implies, they also lack any kind of border. If you want a border, you will need to add it yourself, either with manual drawing code or by using a background image.

One other approach to creating an immovable form does provide a basic control-style border. First, set the ControlBox, MinimizeBox, and MaximizeBox properties of the form to False. Then set the Text property to an empty string. The form will have a raised gray border or black line (depending on the FormBorderStyle option you use), similar to a button. Figure 7-12 shows both types of immovable forms.

This form has no border at all

Exit

This form has a control-style border, but no maximize box, minimize box, control box, or text caption.

Exit

Figure 7-12. *Two types of forms that cannot be moved*

7-15. Make a Borderless Form Movable

Problem

You need to create a borderless form that can be moved. This might be the case if you are creating a custom window that has a unique look (for example, for a visually rich application such as a game or a media player).

Solution

Create another control that responds to the MouseDown, MouseUp, and MouseMove events and programmatically moves the form.

How It Works

Borderless forms omit a title bar, which makes it impossible for a user to move them. You can compensate for this shortcoming by adding a control to the form that serves the same purpose. For example, Figure 7-13 shows a form that includes a label to support dragging. The user can click this label, and then drag the form to a new location on the screen while holding down the mouse button. As the user moves the mouse, the form moves correspondingly, as though it were "attached" to the mouse pointer.

Figure 7-13. *A movable borderless form*

To implement this solution, take the following steps:

1. Create a form-level `Boolean` variable that tracks whether or not the form is currently being dragged.

2. When the label is clicked, the code sets the flag to indicate that the form is in drag mode. At the same time, the current mouse position is recorded. You add this logic to the event handler for the `Label.MouseDown` event.

3. When the user moves the mouse over the label, the form is moved correspondingly, so that the position of the mouse over the label is unchanged. You add this logic to the event handler for the `Label.MouseMove` event.

4. When the user releases the mouse button, the dragging mode is switched off. You add this logic to the event handler for the `Label.MouseUp` event.

The Code

The following example creates a borderless form that a user can move by clicking a form control and dragging the form.

```
Imports System
Imports System.Windows.Forms

'  All designed code is stored in the autogenerated partial
'  class called Recipe07-15.Designer.vb. You can see this
'  file by selecting Show All Files in Solution Explorer.
Partial Public Class Recipe07_15

    '  Boolean member tracks whether the form is in drag mode.
    '  If it is, mouse movements over the label will be translated
    '  into form movements.
    Private dragging As Boolean

    '  Stores the offset where the label is clicked.
    Private pointClicked As Point

    '  MouseDown event handler for the label initiates the dragging process.
    Private Sub lblDrag_MouseDown(ByVal sender As Object, ➥
ByVal e As System.Windows.Forms.MouseEventArgs) Handles lblDrag.MouseDown
```

```
            If e.Button = Windows.Forms.MouseButtons.Left Then
                ' Turn the drag mode on and store the point clicked.
                dragging = True
                pointClicked = New Point(e.X, e.Y)
            Else
                dragging = False
            End If

    End Sub

    ' MouseMove event handler for the label processes dragging movements if
    ' the form is in drag mode.
    Private Sub lblDrag_MouseMove(ByVal sender As Object, ➥
ByVal e As System.Windows.Forms.MouseEventArgs) Handles lblDrag.MouseMove

        If dragging Then

            Dim pointMoveTo As Point

            ' Find the current mouse position in screen coordinates.
            pointMoveTo = Me.PointToScreen(New Point(e.X, e.Y))

            ' Compensate for the position of the control clicked.
            pointMoveTo.Offset(-pointClicked.X, -pointClicked.Y)

            ' Move the form.
            Me.Location = pointMoveTo

        End If

    End Sub

    ' MouseUp event handler for the label switches off drag mode.
    Private Sub lblDrag_MouseUp(ByVal sender As Object, ➥
ByVal e As System.Windows.Forms.MouseEventArgs) Handles lblDrag.MouseUp
        dragging = False
    End Sub

    Private Sub cmdClose_Click(ByVal sender As System.Object, ➥
ByVal e As System.EventArgs) Handles cmdClose.Click
        Me.Close()
    End Sub

End Class
```

7-16. Create an Animated System Tray Icon

Problem

You need to create an animated system tray icon (perhaps to indicate the status of a long-running task).

Solution

Create and show a NotifyIcon control. Use a timer that fires periodically (every second or so) and updates the NotifyIcon.Icon property.

How It Works

The .NET Framework makes it easy to show a system tray icon with the NotifyIcon component. You simply need to add this component to a form and supply an icon by setting the Icon property. Optionally, you can add a linked context menu through the ContextMenu property. The NotifyIcon component automatically displays its context menu when it's right-clicked. You can animate a system tray icon by swapping the icon periodically.

The Code

The following example uses eight icons, each of which shows a moon graphic in a different stage of fullness. By moving from one image to another, the illusion of animation is created.

```
Imports System
Imports System.Windows.Forms

'  All designed code is stored in the autogenerated partial
'  class called Recipe07-16.Designer.vb. You can see this
'  file by selecting Show All Files in Solution Explorer.
Partial Public Class Recipe07_16

    '  An array to hold the set of Icons used to create the
    '  animation effect.
    Private images As Icon() = New Icon(8) {}

    '  An integer to identify the current icon to display.
    Dim offset As Integer = 0

    Private Sub Recipe07_16_Load(ByVal sender As Object, ➥
ByVal e As System.EventArgs) Handles Me.Load

        '  Load the basic set of eight icons.
        images(0) = New Icon("moon01.ico")
        images(1) = New Icon("moon02.ico")
        images(2) = New Icon("moon03.ico")
        images(3) = New Icon("moon04.ico")
        images(4) = New Icon("moon05.ico")
        images(5) = New Icon("moon06.ico")
        images(6) = New Icon("moon07.ico")
        images(7) = New Icon("moon08.ico")

    End Sub

    Private Sub timer_Elapsed(ByVal sender As Object, ➥
ByVal e As System.Timers.ElapsedEventArgs) Handles timer.Elapsed
```

```
    ' Change the icon. This event handler fires once every
    ' second (1000ms).
    notifyIcon.Icon = images(offset)
    offset += 1
    If offset > 7 Then offset = 0

    End Sub
End Class
```

7-17. Validate an Input Control

Problem

You need to alert the user of invalid input in a control, such as a TextBox.

Solution

Use the ErrorProvider component to display an error icon next to the offending control. Check for errors before allowing the user to continue.

How It Works

You can perform validation in a Windows-based application in a number of ways. One approach is to refuse any invalid character as the user presses a key, by using a MaskedTextBox control, as shown in recipe 7-8. Another approach is to respond to control validation events and prevent users from changing focus from one control to another if an error exists. A less invasive approach is to simply flag the offending control in some way, so that the user can review all the errors at once. You can use this approach by adding the ErrorProvider component to your form.

The ErrorProvider is a special property extender component that displays error icons next to invalid controls. You show the error icon next to a control by using the ErrorProvider.SetError method and specifying the appropriate control and a string error message. The ErrorProvider will then show a warning icon to the right of the control. When the user hovers the mouse above the warning icon, the detailed message appears. To clear an error, just pass an empty string to the SetError method.

You need to add only one ErrorProvider component to your form, and you can use it to display an error icon next to any control. To add the ErrorProvider, drag it on the form or into the component tray, or create it manually in code.

The Code

The following example checks the value that a user has entered into a textbox whenever the textbox loses focus. The code validates this textbox using a regular expression that checks to see if the value corresponds to the format of a valid e-mail address (see recipe 2-5 for more details on regular expressions). If validation fails, the ErrorProvider is used to display an error message. If the text is valid, any existing error message is cleared from the ErrorProvider. Finally, the Click event handler for the OK button steps through all the controls on the form and verifies that none of them have errors before allowing the example to continue. In this example, an empty textbox is allowed, although it would be a simple matter to perform additional checks when the OK button is clicked for situations where empty textboxes are not acceptable.

```vb
Imports System
Imports System.Windows.Forms
Imports System.Text.RegularExpressions

' All designed code is stored in the autogenerated partial
' class called Recipe07-17.Designer.vb. You can see this
' file by selecting Show All Files in Solution Explorer.
Partial Public Class Recipe07_17

    ' Button click event handler ensures the ErrorProvider is not
    ' reporting any error for each control before proceeding.
    Private Sub Button1_Click(ByVal sender As System.Object, ➡
ByVal e As System.EventArgs) Handles Button1.Click

        Dim errorText As String = String.Empty
        Dim invalidInput As Boolean = False

        For Each ctrl As Control In Me.Controls
            If Not errProvider.GetError(ctrl) = String.Empty Then
                errorText += " * " & errProvider.GetError(ctrl) & ➡
ControlChars.NewLine
                invalidInput = True
            End If
        Next

        If invalidInput Then
            MessageBox.Show(String.Format("This form contains the following " & ➡
"unresolved errors:{0}{0}{1}", ControlChars.NewLine, errorText, "Invalid Input", ➡
MessageBoxButtons.OK, MessageBoxIcon.Warning))
        Else
            Me.Close()
        End If

    End Sub

    ' When the TextBox loses focus, check that the contents are a valid
    ' email address.
    Private Sub txtEmail_Leave(ByVal sender As Object, ➡
ByVal e As System.EventArgs) Handles txtEmail.Leave

        ' Create a regular expression to check for valid email addresses.
        Dim emailRegEx As Regex

        emailRegEx = New Regex("^[\w-]+@([\w]+\.)+[\w]+$")

        ' Validate the text from the control that raised the event.
        Dim ctrl As Control = DirectCast(sender, Control)

        If emailRegEx.IsMatch(ctrl.Text) Or ctrl.Text = String.Empty Then
            errProvider.SetError(ctrl, String.Empty)
        Else
            errProvider.SetError(ctrl, "This is not a valid email address.")
        End If
```

```
    End Sub
End Class
```

Usage

Figure 7-14 shows how the ErrorProvider control indicates an input error for the TextBox control when the example is run.

Figure 7-14. *A validated form with the ErrorProvider*

7-18. Use a Drag-and-Drop Operation

Problem

You need to use the drag-and-drop feature to exchange information between two controls (possibly in separate windows or in separate applications).

Solution

Start a drag-and-drop operation using the DoDragDrop method of the Control class, and then respond to the DragEnter and DragDrop events.

How It Works

A drag-and-drop operation allows the user to transfer information from one place to another by clicking an item and dragging it to another location. A drag-and-drop operation consists of the following three basic steps:

1. The user clicks a control, holds down the mouse button, and begins dragging. If the control supports the drag-and-drop feature, it sets aside some information.

2. The user drags the mouse over another control. If this control accepts the dragged type of content, the mouse cursor changes to the special drag-and-drop icon (arrow and page). Otherwise, the mouse cursor becomes a circle with a line drawn through it.

3. When the user releases the mouse button, the data is sent to the control, which can then process it appropriately.

To support drag-and-drop functionality, you must handle the DragEnter, DragDrop, and (typically) MouseDown events. To start a drag-and-drop operation, you call the source control's DoDragDrop method. At this point, you submit the data and specify the type of operations that will be supported (copying, moving, and so on). Controls that can receive dragged data must have the AllowDrop property set to True. These controls will receive a DragEnter event when the mouse drags the data over them. At this point, you can examine the data that is being dragged, decide whether the control can accept the drop, and set the DragEventArgs.Effect property accordingly. The final step is to respond to the DragDrop event in the destination control, which occurs when the user releases the mouse button.

The DragEventArgs.Data property, which is an IDataObject, represents the data that is being dragged or dropped. IDataObject is an interface for transferring general data objects. You get the data by using the GetData method. The GetDataPresent method, which accepts a String or Type, is used to determine the type of data represented by the IDataObject.

The Code

The following example allows you to drag content between two textboxes, as well as to and from other applications that support drag-and-drop operations.

```
Imports System
Imports System.Windows.Forms

' All designed code is stored in the autogenerated partial
' class called Recipe07-18.Designer.vb. You can see this
' file by selecting Show All Files in Solution Explorer.
Partial Public Class Recipe07_18

    ' This event is fired when you drop the text on a TextBox.
    ' The text of the target TextBox will change to the drop
    ' text.
    Private Sub TextBox_DragDrop(ByVal sender As Object, ➥
ByVal e As System.Windows.Forms.DragEventArgs) Handles TextBox1.DragDrop, ➥
TextBox2.DragDrop

        Dim txt As TextBox = DirectCast(sender, TextBox)
        txt.Text = DirectCast(e.Data.GetData(DataFormats.Text), String)

    End Sub

    ' This event is fired when your cursor enters a TextBox while
    ' you are in a drag operation. It ensures you can only drop
    ' text.
    Private Sub TextBox_DragEnter(ByVal sender As Object, ➥
ByVal e As System.Windows.Forms.DragEventArgs) Handles TextBox1.DragEnter, ➥
TextBox2.DragEnter

        If e.Data.GetDataPresent(DataFormats.Text) Then
            e.Effect = DragDropEffects.Copy
        Else
            e.Effect = DragDropEffects.None
        End If

    End Sub

    ' This event is fired when you push down the mouse button
    ' while in a TextBox. This grabs the contents of the
    ' TextBox and starts the drag operation.
```

```
    Private Sub TextBox_MouseDown(ByVal sender As Object, ➡
ByVal e As System.Windows.Forms.MouseEventArgs) Handles TextBox1.MouseDown, ➡
TextBox2.MouseDown

        Dim txt As TextBox = DirectCast(sender, TextBox)
        txt.SelectAll()
        txt.DoDragDrop(txt.Text, DragDropEffects.Copy)

    End Sub
End Class
```

7-19. Use Context-Sensitive Help

Problem

You want to display a specific help file topic depending on the currently selected control.

Solution

Use the HelpProvider component, and set the HelpKeyword and HelpNavigator extended properties for each control.

How It Works

The .NET Framework provides support for context-sensitive help through the HelpProvider class. The HelpProvider class is a special extender control. You add it to the component tray of a form, and it extends all the controls on the form with a few additional properties, including HelpNavigator and HelpKeyword. For example, Figure 7-15 shows a form that has two controls and a HelpProvider named helpProvider1. The ListBox control, which is currently selected, has several help-specific properties that are provided through the HelpProvider.

To use context-sensitive help with HelpProvider, follow these three steps:

1. Set the HelpProvider.HelpNamespace property with the name of the help file (for example, myhelp.chm).

2. For every control that requires context-sensitive help, set the HelpNavigator extender property to HelpNavigator.Topic.

3. For every control that requires context-sensitive help, set the HelpKeyword extender property with the name of the topic that should be linked to this control. (The topic names are specific to the help file and can be configured in your help-authoring tools.)

If the user presses the F1 key while a control has focus, the help file will be launched automatically, and the linked topic will be displayed in the help window. If the user presses F1 while positioned on a control that does not have a linked help topic, the help settings for the containing control will be used (for example, a group box or a panel). If there are no containing controls or the containing control does not have any help settings, the form's help settings will be used. You can also use the HelpProvider methods to set or modify context-sensitive help mapping at runtime.

Figure 7-15. *The HelpProvider extender properties*

7-20. Display a Web Page in a Windows-Based Application

Problem

You want to display a web page and provide web-navigation capabilities within your Windows Forms application.

Solution

Use the WebBrowser control to display the web page and other standard controls like buttons and textboxes to allow the user to control the operation of the WebBrowser.

■**Caution**   The WebBrowser control is a managed wrapper around the WebBrowser ActiveX control, which is the same component used by Internet Explorer. This means that if you use a Main method, it must be annotated with the STAThread attribute. Furthermore, the component is very resource-intensive and should be disposed of correctly.

How It Works

The WebBrowser control (new to .NET Framework 2.0) makes it a trivial task to embed highly functional web browser capabilities into your Windows applications. The WebBrowser control is responsible for the display of web pages and maintaining page history, but it does not provide any controls for user interaction. Instead, the WebBrowser control exposes properties and events that you can manipulate programmatically to control the operation of the WebBrowser. This approach makes the WebBrowser control highly flexible and adaptable to almost any situation. Table 7-1 summarizes some of the commonly used WebBrowser members related to web navigation.

Table 7-1. *Commonly Used Members of the WebBrowser Control*

Member	Description
Property	
AllowNavigation	Controls whether the WebBrowser can navigate to another page after its initial page has been loaded
CanGoBack	Indicates whether the WebBrowser currently holds back page history, which would allow the GoBack method to succeed
CanGoForward	Indicates whether the WebBrowser currently holds forward page history, which would allow the GoForward method to succeed
IsBusy	Indicates whether the WebBrowser is currently busy downloading a page
Url	Holds the URL of the currently displayed/downloading page
Method	
GoBack	Displays the previous page in the page history, if there is one
GoForward	Displays the next page in the page history, if there is one
GoHome	Displays the home page of the current user as configured in Internet Explorer
Navigate	Displays the web page at the specified URL
Stop	Stops the current WebBrowser activity
Event	
DocumentCompleted	Signals that the active download has completed and the document is displayed in the WebBrowser

You can also use the WebBrowser.DocumentText property to set (or get) the currently displayed HTML contents of the WebBrowser. To manipulate the contents using the Document Object Model (DOM), get an HtmlDocument instance via the Document property.

The Code

The following example uses the WebBrowser control to allow users to navigate to a web page whose address is entered into a TextBox. Buttons also allow users to move forward and backward through page history and navigate directly to their personal home page.

```
Imports System
Imports System.Windows.Forms

' All designed code is stored in the autogenerated partial
' class called Recipe07-20.Designer.vb. You can see this
' file by selecting Show All Files in Solution Explorer.
Partial Public Class Recipe07_20

    Private Sub goButton_Click(ByVal sender As System.Object, ➡
ByVal e As System.EventArgs) Handles goButton.Click

        ' Navigate to the URL specified in the TextBox.
        webBrowser1.Navigate(textURL.Text)

    End Sub

    Private Sub backButton_Click(ByVal sender As System.Object, ➡
ByVal e As System.EventArgs) Handles backButton.Click

        ' Go to the previous page in the WebBrowser history.
        webBrowser1.GoBack()

    End Sub

    Private Sub homeButton_Click(ByVal sender As System.Object, ➡
ByVal e As System.EventArgs) Handles homeButton.Click

        ' Navigate to the current user's home page.
        webBrowser1.GoHome()

    End Sub

    Private Sub forwardButton_Click(ByVal sender As System.Object, ➡
ByVal e As System.EventArgs) Handles forwardButton.Click

        ' Go to the next page in the WebBrowser history.
        webBrowser1.GoForward()

    End Sub

    Private Sub Recipe07_20_Load(ByVal sender As Object, ➡
ByVal e As System.EventArgs) Handles Me.Load

        ' Navigate to the Apress home page when the application first
        ' loads.
        webBrowser1.Navigate("http://www.apress.com/")

    End Sub
```

```vb
' Event handler to perform general interface maintenance once a
' document has been loaded into the WebBrowser.
Private Sub webBrowser1_DocumentCompleted(ByVal sender As Object, ➥
ByVal e As System.Windows.Forms.WebBrowserDocumentCompletedEventArgs) Handles ➥
webBrowser1.DocumentCompleted

    ' Update the content of the TextBox to reflect the current URL.
    textURL.Text = webBrowser1.Url.ToString

    ' Enable or disable the Back button depending on whether the
    ' WebBrowser has back history
    If webBrowser1.CanGoBack Then
        backButton.Enabled = True
    Else
        backButton.Enabled = False
    End If

    ' Enable or disable the Forward button depending on whether the
    ' WebBrowser has forward history.
    If webBrowser1.CanGoForward Then
        forwardButton.Enabled = True
    Else
        forwardButton.Enabled = False
    End If

End Sub
End Class
```

CHAPTER 8

■■■

Multimedia

Multimedia is a very expansive subject that covers sound, video, graphics, and printing. The aim of this chapter is to briefly touch on each main topic. If you would like more detailed information, refer to books devoted to the subject, such as *Pro .NET 2.0 Graphics Programming* by Eric White (Apress, 2005) or *Pro .NET 2.0 Windows Forms and Custom Controls in VB 2005* by Matthew MacDonald (Apress, 2006).

The .NET Framework provides direct support for most multimedia functionality. The System. Drawing namespace provides support for manipulating two-dimensional drawings. Most of the classes in this namespace, such as Drawing2D and Graphics, wrap GDI32.dll and USER32.dll. These libraries provide the native Graphics Device Interface (GDI) functionality in the Windows application programming interface (API). They also make it easier to draw complex shapes, work with coordinates and transforms, and process images. The Printing namespace, which contains classes related to printing, is also part of the System.Drawing namespace. This namespace uses GDI support for drawing text or images to a Document object. While this class does provide support for enumerating and collecting information for installed printers, it is limited to local printers and it does not support all information, such as print jobs.

The System.Media namespace provides support for playing basic sounds, such as WAV files. If you want to show a video file or play more sophisticated audio files, such as MP3s, you will need to look beyond the .NET Framework.

This chapter presents recipes that show you how to use built-in .NET features and, where necessary, native Win32 libraries via P/Invoke or COM Interop. The recipes in this chapter describe how to do the following:

- Find the fonts installed in your system (recipe 8-1)

- Perform hit testing with shapes (recipe 8-2)

- Create an irregularly shaped form or control (recipe 8-3)

- Create a sprite that can be moved around (recipe 8-4)

- Display an image that can be made to scroll (recipe 8-5)

- Capture an image of the desktop (recipe 8-6)

- Enable double buffering to increase performance while redrawing (recipe 8-7)

- Create a thumbnail for an existing image (recipe 8-8)

- Play a beep or a system-defined sound (recipe 8-9), play a WAV file (recipe 8-10), play a non-WAV file such as an MP3 file (recipe 8-11), and play a video with DirectShow (recipe 8-12)

- Retrieve information about the printers installed in the machine (recipe 8-13), print a simple document (recipe 8-14), print a document that has multiple pages (recipe 8-15), print wrapped text (recipe 8-16), show a print preview (recipe 8-17), and manage print jobs (recipe 8-18)

8-1. Find All Installed Fonts

Problem

You need to retrieve a list of all the fonts installed on the current computer.

Solution

Create a new instance of the `System.Drawing.Text.InstalledFontCollection` class, which contains a collection of `FontFamily` objects representing all the installed fonts.

How It Works

The `InstalledFontCollection` class allows you to retrieve information about currently installed fonts. It derives from the `FontCollection` class, which allows you to get a list of font families as a collection in the `Families` property.

The Code

The following code shows a form that iterates through the font collection when it is first created. Every time it finds a font, it creates a new `Label` control that will display the font name in the given font face (at a size of 14 points). The `Label` is added to a `Panel` control named pnlFonts with `AutoScroll` set to `True`, allowing the user to scroll through the list of available fonts.

```
Imports System
Imports System.Drawing
Imports System.Windows.Forms
Imports System.Drawing.Text

'  All designed code is stored in the autogenerated partial
'  class called Recipe08-01.Designer.vb. You can see this
'  file by selecting Show All Files in Solution Explorer.
Partial Public Class Recipe08_01

    Private Sub Recipe08_01_Load(ByVal sender As Object, ➥
ByVal e As System.EventArgs) Handles Me.Load

        ' Create the font collection.
        Using fontFamilies As New InstalledFontCollection

            ' Iterate through all font families.
            Dim offset As Integer = 10

            For Each family As FontFamily In fontFamilies.Families

                Try
                    ' Create a label that will display text in this font.
                    Dim fontLabel As New Label

                    fontLabel.Text = family.Name
                    fontLabel.Font = New Font(family, 14)
                    fontLabel.Left = 10
```

```
                fontLabel.Width = pnlFonts.Width
                fontLabel.Top = offset

                ' Add the label to a scrollable Panel.
                pnlFonts.Controls.Add(fontLabel)
                offset += 30
            Catch ex As ArgumentException
                ' An ArgumentException will be thrown if the selected
                ' font does not support regular style (the default used
                ' when creating a font object). For this example, we
                ' will display an appropriate message in the list.
                Dim fontLabel As New Label

                fontLabel.Text = ex.Message
                fontLabel.Font = New Font("Arial", 10, FontStyle.Italic)
                fontLabel.ForeColor = Color.Red
                fontLabel.Left = 10
                fontLabel.Width = 500
                fontLabel.Top = offset

                ' Add the label to a scrollable Panel.
                pnlFonts.Controls.Add(fontLabel)
                offset += 30
            End Try

        Next

    End Using

    End Sub
End Class
```

Figure 8-1 shows the results of this simple test application.

Figure 8-1. *A list of installed fonts*

8-2. Perform Hit Testing with Shapes

Problem

You need to detect whether a user clicks inside a shape.

Solution

Test the point where the user clicked with methods such as `Rectangle.Contains` and `Region.IsVisible` (in the `System.Drawing` namespace) or `GraphicsPath.IsVisible` (in the System.Drawing.Drawing2D namespace), depending on the type of shape.

How It Works

Often, if you use GDI+ to draw shapes on a form, you need to be able to determine when a user clicks inside a given shape. This can be determined using a `Rectangle` and a `Point`. A `Rectangle` is defined by its height, width, and upper-left coordinates, which are reflected by the `Height`, `Width`, `X`, and `Y` properties. A `Point`, which is an X and Y coordinate, represents a specific location on the screen. The .NET Framework provides three methods to help with this task:

- The `Rectangle.Contains` method, which takes a point and returns true if the point is inside a given rectangle. In many cases, you can retrieve a rectangle for another type of object. For example, you can use `Image.GetBounds` to retrieve the invisible rectangle that represents the image boundaries. The `Rectangle` structure is a member of the `System.Drawing` namespace.

- The `GraphicsPath.IsVisible` method, which takes a point and returns true if the point is inside the area defined by a closed `GraphicsPath`. Because a `GraphicsPath` can contain multiple lines, shapes, and figures, this approach is useful if you want to test whether a point is contained inside a nonrectangular region. The `GraphicsPath` class is a member of the `System.Drawing.Drawing2D` namespace.

- The `Region.IsVisible` method, which takes a point and returns true if the point is inside the area defined by a `Region`. A `Region`, like the `GraphicsPath`, can represent a complex nonrectangular shape. `Region` is a member of the `System.Drawing` namespace.

The Code

The following example shows a form that creates a `Rectangle` and a `GraphicsPath`. By default, these two shapes are given light-blue backgrounds. However, an event handler responds to the `Form.MouseMove` event, checks to see whether the mouse pointer is in one of these shapes, and updates the shape's background to bright pink if the pointer is there.

Note that the highlighting operation takes place directly inside the `MouseMove` event handler. The painting is performed only if the current selection has changed. For simpler code, you could invalidate the entire form every time the mouse pointer moves in or out of a region and handle *all* the drawing in the `Form.Paint` event handler, but this would lead to more drawing and generate additional flicker as the entire form is repainted.

```
Imports System
Imports System.Drawing
Imports System.Windows.Forms
Imports System.Drawing.Drawing2D
```

```vb
' All designed code is stored in the autogenerated partial
' class called Recipe08-02.Designer.vb. You can see this
' file by selecting Show All Files in Solution Explorer.
Public Class Recipe08_02

    ' Define the shapes used on this form.
    Private path As GraphicsPath
    Private rect As Rectangle

    ' Define the flags that track where the mouse pointer is.
    Private inPath As Boolean = False
    Private inRectangle As Boolean = False

    ' Define the brushes used for painting the shapes.
    Private highlightBrush As Brush = Brushes.HotPink
    Private defaultBrush As Brush = Brushes.LightBlue

    Private Sub Recipe08_02_Load(ByVal sender As Object, ➡
ByVal e As System.EventArgs) Handles Me.Load

        ' Create the shapes that will be displayed.
        path = New GraphicsPath
        path.AddEllipse(10, 10, 100, 60)
        path.AddCurve(New Point() {New Point(50, 50), New Point(10, 33), ➡
New Point(80, 43)})
        path.AddLine(50, 120, 250, 80)
        path.AddLine(120, 40, 110, 50)
        path.CloseFigure()

        rect = New Rectangle(100, 170, 220, 170)

    End Sub

    Private Sub Recipe08_02_MouseMove(ByVal sender As Object, ➡
ByVal e As System.Windows.Forms.MouseEventArgs) Handles Me.MouseMove

        Using g As Graphics = Me.CreateGraphics
            ' Perform hit testing with rectangle.
            If rect.Contains(e.X, e.Y) Then
                If Not inRectangle Then
                    inRectangle = True

                    ' Highlight the rectangle.
                    g.FillRectangle(highlightBrush, rect)
                    g.DrawRectangle(Pens.Black, rect)
                End If
            ElseIf inRectangle Then
                inRectangle = False

                ' Restore the unhighlighted rectangle.
                g.FillRectangle(defaultBrush, rect)
                g.DrawRectangle(Pens.Black, rect)
            End If
```

```
                    ' Perform hit testing with path.
                If path.IsVisible(e.X, e.Y) Then
                    If Not inPath Then
                        inPath = True

                        ' Highlight the path.
                        g.FillPath(highlightBrush, path)
                        g.DrawPath(Pens.Black, path)
                    End If
                ElseIf inPath Then
                    inPath = False

                    ' Restore the unhighlighted path.
                    g.FillPath(defaultBrush, path)
                    g.DrawPath(Pens.Black, path)
                End If

        End Using

    End Sub

    Private Sub Recipe08_02_Paint(ByVal sender As Object, ➥
ByVal e As System.Windows.Forms.PaintEventArgs) Handles Me.Paint

        Dim g As Graphics = e.Graphics

        ' Paint the shapes according to the current selection.
        If inPath Then
            g.FillPath(highlightBrush, path)
            g.FillRectangle(defaultBrush, rect)
        ElseIf inRectangle Then
            g.FillRectangle(highlightBrush, rect)
            g.FillPath(defaultBrush, path)
        Else
            g.FillPath(defaultBrush, path)
            g.FillRectangle(defaultBrush, rect)
        End If

        g.DrawPath(Pens.Black, path)
        g.DrawRectangle(Pens.Black, rect)

    End Sub
End Class
```

Figure 8-2 shows the application in action.

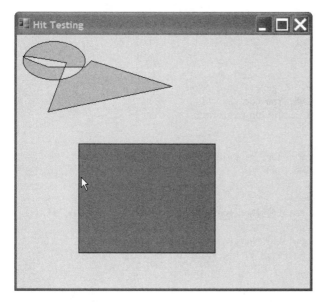

Figure 8-2. *Hit testing with a Rectangle object and a GraphicsPath object*

8-3. Create an Irregularly Shaped Control

Problem

You need to create a nonrectangular form or control.

Solution

Create a new `System.Drawing.Region` object that has the shape you want for the form, and assign it to the `Form.Region` or `Control.Region` property.

How It Works

To create a nonrectangular form or control, you first need to define the shape you want. The easiest approach is to use the `System.Drawing.Drawing2D.GraphicsPath` object, which can accommodate any combination of ellipses, rectangles, closed curves, and even strings. You can add shapes to a `GraphicsPath` instance using methods such as `AddEllipse`, `AddRectangle`, `AddClosedCurve`, and `AddString`. Once you are finished defining the shape you want, you can create a `Region` object from this `GraphicsPath`—just pass the `GraphicsPath` to the `Region` class constructor. Finally, you can assign the `Region` to the `Form.Region` property or the `Control.Region` property.

The Code

The following example creates an irregularly shaped form (shown in Figure 8-3) using two curves made of multiple points, which are converted into a closed figure using the `GraphicsPath.CloseAllFigures` method.

```vb
Imports System
Imports System.Drawing
Imports System.Windows.Forms
Imports System.Drawing.Drawing2D

'  All designed code is stored in the autogenerated partial
'  class called Recipe08-03.Designer.vb. You can see this
'  file by selecting Show All Files in Solution Explorer.
Partial Public Class Recipe08_03

    Private Sub Recipe08_03_Load(ByVal sender As Object, ➥
ByVal e As System.EventArgs) Handles Me.Load

        Dim path As New GraphicsPath
        Dim pointsA As Point() = New Point() {New Point(0, 0), New Point(40, 60), ➥
New Point(Me.Width - 100, 10)}
        Dim pointsB As Point() = New Point() {New Point(Me.Width - 40, ➥
Me.Height - 60), New Point(Me.Width, Me.Height), New Point(10, Me.Height)}

        path.AddCurve(pointsA)
        path.AddCurve(pointsB)

        path.CloseAllFigures()

        Me.Region = New Region(path)

    End Sub

    Private Sub cmdClose_Click(ByVal sender As System.Object, ➥
ByVal e As System.EventArgs) Handles cmdClose.Click

        Me.Close()

    End Sub

End Class
```

When you run the application, you will see results similar to Figure 8-3.

■**Note** Another method for creating nonrectangular forms (not controls) is using the BackgroundImage and TransparencyKey properties available in the Form class. However, this method could cause display problems when monitors are set to a color depth greater than 24-bit. For more information about this topic, refer to the Microsoft Knowledge Base article at http://support.microsoft.com/kb/822495.

For an example that demonstrates a nonrectangular control, refer to recipe 8-4.

Figure 8-3. *A nonrectangular form*

8-4. Create a Movable Sprite

Problem

You need to create a shape the user can manipulate on a form, perhaps by dragging it, resizing it, or otherwise interacting with it.

Solution

Create a custom control, and override the painting logic to draw a shape. Assign your shape to the Control.Region property. You can then use this Region to perform hit testing, which is demonstrated in recipe 8-2.

How It Works

If you need to create a complex user interface that incorporates many custom-drawn elements, you need a way to track these elements and allow the user to interact with them. The easiest approach in .NET is to create a dedicated control by deriving a class from System.Windows.Forms.Control. You can then customize the way this control appears and operates by adding the appropriate functionality to the appropriate events. For example, if the control needs to respond in a certain way when it is selected, you may want to add the needed functionality to the MouseEnter, MouseLeave, MouseUp, or MouseDown event.

The Code

The following example shows a control that represents a simple ellipse shape on a form. All controls are associated with a rectangular region on a form, so the EllipseShape control generates an ellipse that fills these boundaries (provided through the Control.ClientRectangle property). Once the shape has been generated, the Control.Region property is set according to the bounds on the ellipse.

This ensures events such as MouseMove, MouseDown, Click, and so on will occur only if the mouse is over the ellipse, not the entire client rectangle.

The following code shows the full EllipseShape code:

```vb
Imports System
Imports System.Drawing
Imports System.Windows.Forms
Imports System.Drawing.Drawing2D

' All designed code is stored in the autogenerated partial
' class called EllipseShape.Designer.vb. You can see this
' file by selecting Show All Files in Solution Explorer.
Public Class EllipseShape
    Inherits System.Windows.Forms.Control

    Dim path As GraphicsPath = Nothing

    Private Sub RefreshPath()

        ' Create the GraphicsPath for the shape (in this case
        ' an ellipse that fits inside the full control area)
        ' and apply it to the control by setting the Region
        ' property.
        path = New GraphicsPath
        path.AddEllipse(Me.ClientRectangle)
        Me.Region = New Region(path)

    End Sub

    Protected Overrides Sub OnPaint(ByVal e As System.Windows.Forms.PaintEventArgs)

        MyBase.OnPaint(e)

        If path IsNot Nothing Then
            e.Graphics.SmoothingMode = SmoothingMode.AntiAlias
            e.Graphics.FillPath(New SolidBrush(Me.BackColor), path)
            e.Graphics.DrawPath(New Pen(Me.ForeColor, 4), path)
        End If

    End Sub

    Private Sub EllipseShape_Resize(ByVal sender As Object, ➥
ByVal e As System.EventArgs) Handles Me.Resize

        RefreshPath()
        Me.Invalidate()

    End Sub

End Class
```

You could define the EllipseShape control in a separate class library assembly so you could add it to the Visual Studio .NET Toolbox and use it at design time. However, even without taking this step, it is easy to create a simple test application. The following Windows Forms application creates two ellipses and allows the user to drag both of them around the form, simply by holding the mouse down and moving the pointer.

```
Imports System
Imports System.Drawing
Imports System.Windows.Forms

' All designed code is stored in the autogenerated partial
' class called Recipe08-04.Designer.vb. You can see this
' file by selecting Show All Files in Solution Explorer.
Partial Public Class Recipe08_04

    ' Tracks when drag mode is on.
    Private isDraggingA As Boolean = False
    Private isDraggingB As Boolean = False

    ' The ellipse shape controls.
    Private ellipseA, ellipseB As EllipseShape

    Private Sub Recipe08_04_Load(ByVal sender As Object, ➥
ByVal e As System.EventArgs) Handles Me.Load

        ' Create and configure both ellipses.
        ellipseA = New EllipseShape
        ellipseA.Width = 100
        ellipseA.Height = 100
        ellipseA.Top = 30
        ellipseA.Left = 30
        ellipseA.BackColor = Color.Red
        Me.Controls.Add(ellipseA)

        ellipseB = New EllipseShape
        ellipseB.Width = 100
        ellipseB.Height = 100
        ellipseB.Top = 130
        ellipseB.Left = 130
        ellipseB.BackColor = Color.Azure
        Me.Controls.Add(ellipseB)

        ' Attach both ellipses to the same set of event handlers.
        AddHandler ellipseA.MouseDown, AddressOf Ellipse_MouseDown
        AddHandler ellipseA.MouseUp, AddressOf Ellipse_MouseUp
        AddHandler ellipseA.MouseMove, AddressOf Ellipse_MouseMove

        AddHandler ellipseB.MouseDown, AddressOf Ellipse_MouseDown
        AddHandler ellipseB.MouseUp, AddressOf Ellipse_MouseUp
        AddHandler ellipseB.MouseMove, AddressOf Ellipse_MouseMove

    End Sub
```

```
      Private Sub Ellipse_MouseDown(ByVal sender As Object, ByVal e As MouseEventArgs)

          If e.Button = Windows.Forms.MouseButtons.Left Then
              ' Get the control that triggered this event.
          Dim ctrl As Control = DirectCast(sender, Control)

              ctrl.Tag = New Point(e.X, e.Y)
              If ctrl Is ellipseA Then
                  isDraggingA = True
              Else
                  isDraggingB = True
              End If
          End If

      End Sub

      Private Sub Ellipse_MouseUp(ByVal sender As Object, ByVal e As MouseEventArgs)

          isDraggingA = False
          isDraggingB = False

      End Sub

      Private Sub Ellipse_MouseMove(ByVal sender As Object, ByVal e As MouseEventArgs)

          ' Get the control that triggered this event.
          Dim ctrl As Control = DirectCast(sender, Control)

          If (isDraggingA And (ctrl Is ellipseA)) Or (isDraggingB And ➡
(ctrl Is ellipseB)) Then

              ' Get the offset.
              Dim pnt As Point = DirectCast(ctrl.Tag, Point)

              ' Move the control.
              ctrl.Left = e.X + ctrl.Left - pnt.X
              ctrl.Top = e.Y + ctrl.Top - pnt.Y

          End If
      End Sub

End Class
```

Figure 8-4 shows the user about to drag an ellipse.

Figure 8-4. *Dragging custom shape controls on a form*

8-5. Create a Scrollable Image

Problem

You need to create a scrollable picture.

Solution

Leverage the automatic scroll capabilities of the System.Windows.Forms.Panel control by setting Panel.AutoScroll to True and placing a System.Windows.Forms.PictureBox control with the image content inside the Panel.

How It Works

The Panel control has built-in scrolling support, as shown in recipe 8-1. If you place any controls in it that extend beyond its bounds and you set Panel.AutoScroll to True, the panel will show scroll bars that allow the user to move through the content. This works particularly well with large images. You can load or create the image in memory, assign it to a picture box (which has no intrinsic support for scrolling), and then show the picture box inside the panel. The only consideration you need to remember is to make sure you set the picture box dimensions equal to the full size of the image you want to show.

The Code

The following example creates an image that represents a document. The image is generated as an in-memory bitmap, and several lines of text are added using the Graphics.DrawString method. The image is then bound to a picture box, which is shown in a scrollable panel.

```vb
Imports System
Imports System.Drawing
Imports System.Windows.Forms

'  All designed code is stored in the autogenerated partial
'  class called Recipe08-05.Designer.vb. You can see this
'  file by selecting Show All Files in Solution Explorer.
Public Class Recipe08_05

    Private Sub Recipe08_05_Load(ByVal sender As Object, ➡
ByVal e As System.EventArgs) Handles Me.Load

        Dim text As String = "The quick brown fox jumps over the lazy dog."

        Using fnt As New Font("Tahoma", 14)
            ' Create an in-memory bitmap.
            Dim bmp As New Bitmap(600, 600)

            Using g As Graphics = Graphics.FromImage(bmp)
                g.FillRectangle(Brushes.White, New Rectangle(0, 0, bmp.Width, ➡
bmp.Height))

                ' Draw several lines of text on the bitmap.
                For i As Integer = 1 To 10
                    g.DrawString(text, fnt, Brushes.Black, 50, 50 + i * 60)
                Next

            End Using

            ' Display the bitmap in the picture box.
            pictureBox1.BackgroundImage = bmp
            pictureBox1.Size = bmp.Size

        End Using

    End Sub

End Class
```

When you run the application, you will get results similar to those shown in Figure 8-5.

Figure 8-5. *Adding scrolling support to custom content*

8-6. Perform a Screen Capture

Problem

You need to take a snapshot of the current desktop.

Solution

Use the CopyFromScreen method of the Graphics class to copy screen contents.

How It Works

The Graphics class now includes CopyFromScreen methods that copy color data from the screen onto the drawing surface represented by a Graphics object. This method requires you to pass the source and destination points and the size of the image to be copied.

The Code

The following example captures the screen and displays it in a picture box. It first creates a new Bitmap object and then invokes CopyFromScreen to draw onto the Bitmap. After drawing, the image is assigned to the picture box.

```
Imports System
Imports System.Drawing
Imports System.Windows.Forms

'  All designed code is stored in the autogenerated partial
'  class called Recipe08-06.Designer.vb. You can see this
'  file by selecting Show All Files in Solution Explorer.
Partial Public Class Recipe08_06
```

```
    Private Sub cmdCapture_Click(ByVal sender As System.Object, ➥
ByVal e As System.EventArgs) Handles cmdCapture.Click

        Dim screenCapture As New Bitmap(Screen.PrimaryScreen.Bounds.Width, ➥
Screen.PrimaryScreen.Bounds.Height)

        Using g As Graphics = Graphics.FromImage(screenCapture)
            g.CopyFromScreen(0, 0, 0, 0, screenCapture.Size)
        End Using

        pictureBox1.Image = screenCapture

    End Sub

End Class
```

When you run the application and click the Capture button, you will get results similar to those shown in Figure 8-6.

Figure 8-6. *Capturing the screen contents*

8-7. Use Double Buffering to Increase Redraw Speed

Problem

You need to optimize drawing for a form or an authored control that is frequently refreshed, and you want to reduce flicker.

Solution

Set the `DoubleBuffered` property of the form to `True`.

How It Works

In some applications, you need to repaint a form or control frequently. This is commonly the case when creating animations. For example, you might use a timer to invalidate your form every second. Your painting code could then redraw an image at a new location, creating the illusion of motion. The problem with this approach is that every time you invalidate the form, Windows repaints the window background (clearing the form) and then runs your painting code, which draws the graphic element by element. This can cause substantial on-screen flicker.

Double buffering is a technique you can implement to reduce this flicker. With double buffering, your drawing logic writes to an in-memory bitmap, which is copied to the form at the end of the drawing operation in a single, seamless repaint operation. Flickering is reduced dramatically.

.NET Framework 2.0 provides a default double buffering mechanism for forms and controls. You can enable this by setting the `DoubleBuffered` property of your form or control to `True` or by using the `SetStyle` method.

The Code

The following example sets the `DoubleBuffered` property of the form to `True` and shows an animation of an image alternately growing and shrinking on the page. The drawing logic takes place in the `Form.Paint` event handler, and a timer invalidates the form in a preset interval so that the image can be redrawn. The user can choose whether to enable double buffering through a checkbox on the form. Without double buffering, the form flickers noticeably. When double buffering is enabled, however, the image grows and shrinks with smooth, flicker-free animation.

```vb
Imports System
Imports System.Drawing
Imports System.Windows.Forms
Imports System.Drawing.Drawing2D

' All designed code is stored in the autogenerated partial
' class called Recipe08-07.Designer.vb. You can see this
' file by selecting Show All Files in Solution Explorer.
Partial Public Class Recipe08_07

    ' Track the image size and the type of animation
    ' (expanding or shrinking).
    Private isShrinking As Boolean = False
    Private imageSize As Integer = 0

    ' Store the logo that will be painted on the form.
    Private img As Image

    Private Sub Recipe08_07_Load(ByVal sender As Object, ➥
ByVal e As System.EventArgs) Handles Me.Load

        ' Load the logo image from the file.
        img = Image.FromFile("test.jpg")
```

```vbnet
        ' Start the timer that invalidates the form.
        tmrRefresh.Start()

    End Sub

    Private Sub tmrRefresh_Tick(ByVal sender As Object, ➥
ByVal e As System.EventArgs) Handles tmrRefresh.Tick

        ' Change the desired image size according to the animation mode.
        If isShrinking Then
            imageSize -= 1
        Else
            imageSize += 1
        End If

        ' Change the sizing direction if it nears the form border.
        If imageSize > (Me.Width - 150) Then
            isShrinking = True
        ElseIf imageSize < 1 Then
            isShrinking = False
        End If

        Me.Invalidate()

    End Sub

    Private Sub Recipe08_07_Paint(ByVal sender As Object, ➥
ByVal e As System.Windows.Forms.PaintEventArgs) Handles Me.Paint

        Dim g As Graphics

        g = e.Graphics
        g.SmoothingMode = SmoothingMode.HighQuality

        ' Draw the background.
        g.FillRectangle(Brushes.Yellow, New Rectangle(New Point(0, 0), ➥
Me.ClientSize))

        ' Draw the logo image.
        g.DrawImage(img, 50, 50, 50 + imageSize, 50 + imageSize)

    End Sub

    Private Sub chkUseDoubleBuffering_CheckedChanged(ByVal sender As Object, ➥
ByVal e As System.EventArgs) Handles chkUseDoubleBuffering.CheckedChanged
        Me.DoubleBuffered = chkUseDoubleBuffering.Checked
    End Sub

End Class
```

■**Note** .NET Framework 3.0 offers options for handling double buffering manually. For more information about double buffering, refer to the MSDN documentation at `http://msdn2.microsoft.com/en-us/library/ms229622.aspx`.

8-8. Show a Thumbnail for an Image

Problem

You need to show thumbnails (small representations of pictures) for the images in a directory.

Solution

Read the image from the file using the `Shared FromFile` method of the `System.Drawing.Image` class. You can then retrieve a thumbnail using the `Image.GetThumbnailImage` method.

How It Works

The `Image` class provides the functionality for generating thumbnails through the `GetThumbnailImage` method. You simply need to pass the width and height of the thumbnail you want (in pixels), and the `Image` class will create a new `Image` object that fits these criteria. Antialiasing is used when reducing the image to ensure the best possible image quality, although some blurriness and loss of detail is inevitable. (*Antialiasing* is the process of removing jagged edges, often in resized graphics, by adding shading with an intermediate color.) In addition, you can supply a notification callback, allowing you to create thumbnails asynchronously.

When generating a thumbnail, it is important to ensure that the aspect ratio remains constant. For example, if you reduce a 200×100 picture to a 50×50 thumbnail, the width will be compressed to one quarter and the height will be compressed to one half, distorting the image. To ensure that the aspect ratio remains constant, you can change either the width or the height to a fixed size, and then adjust the other dimension proportionately.

■**Note** If you attempt to load a file that is not a supported image type, you will receive an `OutOfMemoryException`. This is important to know because it is not the error you might expect to receive in this situation.

The Code

The following example reads a bitmap file and generates a thumbnail that is not greater than 200×200 pixels while preserving the original aspect ratio:

```
Imports System
Imports System.Drawing
Imports System.Windows.Forms

'  All designed code is stored in the autogenerated partial
'  class called Recipe08-08.Designer.vb. You can see this
'  file by selecting Show All Files in Solution Explorer.
Partial Public Class Recipe08_08
```

```
    Private thumbNail As Image

    Private Sub Recipe08_08_Load(ByVal sender As Object, ➥
ByVal e As System.EventArgs) Handles Me.Load

        Using img As Image = Image.FromFile("test.jpg")

            Dim thumbnailWidth As Integer = 0
            Dim thumbnailHeight As Integer = 0

            ' Adjust the largest dimension to 200 pixels.
            ' This ensures that a thumbnail will not be larger than
            ' 200x200 pixel square for each one.
            If img.Width > img.Height Then
                thumbnailWidth = 200
                thumbnailHeight = Convert.ToInt32((CSng(200) / img.Width) * ➥
img.Height)
            Else
                thumbnailHeight = 200
                thumbnailWidth = Convert.ToInt32((CSng(200) / img.Height) * ➥
img.Width)
            End If

            thumbNail = img.GetThumbnailImage(thumbnailWidth, thumbnailHeight, ➥
Nothing, IntPtr.Zero)

        End Using

    End Sub

    Private Sub Recipe08_08_Paint(ByVal sender As Object, ➥
ByVal e As System.Windows.Forms.PaintEventArgs) Handles Me.Paint
        e.Graphics.DrawImage(thumbNail, 10, 10)
    End Sub

End Class
```

8-9. Play a Simple Beep or System Sound

Problem

You need to play a simple system-defined beep or sound.

Solution

Use the managed `Beep` method of the `Console` class or the `Play` method of the `SystemSound` class.

How It Works

.NET Framework 2.0 now has new additions such as the `Beep` method in the `Console` class and a new namespace `System.Media`, which provides classes for playing sound files.

Overloads of the Console.Beep method let you play a beep with the default frequency and duration or with a frequency and duration you specify. Frequency is represented in hertz (and must range from 37 to 32,767), and the duration is represented in milliseconds. Internally, these methods invoke the Beep Win32 function and use the computer's internal speaker. Thus, if the computer does not have an internal speaker, no sound will be produced.

The System.Media namespace contains the following classes:

- The SystemSound class represents a Windows sound event, such as an asterisk, beep, question, and so on. It also defines a Play method, which lets you play the sound associated with it.

- The SystemSounds class defines properties that let you obtain the SystemSound instance of a specific Windows sound event. For example, it defines an Asterisk property that returns a SystemSound instance associated with the asterisk Windows sound event.

- The SoundPlayer class lets you play WAV files. For more information about how to play a WAV file using this class, refer to recipe 8-10.

As an alternative for playing system sounds, you can also use the My namespace (refer to Chapter 5 for further details). My includes the My.Computer.Audio class, which contains the Shared PlaySystemSound method for playing system sounds. It takes a SystemSound object as its parameter.

The Code

The following example plays two different beeps and the asterisk sound in succession, using the Console and SystemSound classes:

```
Imports System
Imports System.Windows.Forms
Imports System.Media

'  All designed code is stored in the autogenerated partial
'  class called Recipe08-09.Designer.vb. You can see this
'  file by selecting Show All Files in Solution Explorer.
Partial Public Class Recipe08_09

    Private Sub Recipe08_09_Load(ByVal sender As Object, ➡
ByVal e As System.EventArgs) Handles Me.Load

        '  Play a beep with default frequency and
        '  duration (800 and 200, respectively)
        Console.Beep()

        '  Play a beep with frequency as 200 and duration as 300.
        Console.Beep(200, 300)

        '  Play the sound associated with the Asterisk event.
        SystemSounds.Asterisk.Play()

    End Sub

End Class
```

The following shows how to use the My namespace to play the system sound:

```
My.Computer.Audio.PlaySystemSound(SystemSounds.Asterisk)
```

8-10. Play a WAV File

Problem

You need to play a WAV file.

Solution

Create a new instance of the `System.Media.SoundPlayer` class, pass the location or stream of the WAV file, and invoke the `Play` method.

How It Works

.NET Framework 2.0 defines a new `System.Media` namespace that contains a `SoundPlayer` class. `SoundPlayer` contains constructors that let you specify the location of a WAV file or its stream. Once you have created an instance, you just need to invoke the `Play` method to play the file. The `Play` method creates a new thread to play the sound and is thus asynchronous (unless a stream is used). For playing the sound synchronously, use the `PlaySync` method. Note that `SoundPlayer` supports only the WAV format.

Before a file is played, it is loaded into memory. You can load a file in advance by invoking the `Load` or `LoadSync` method, depending on whether you want the operation to be asynchronous or synchronous.

The `My.Computer.Audio` class provides an alternative for playing WAV files. This class consists of the `Shared` methods `Play`, `PlaySystemSound` (refer to recipe 8-9), and `Stop`. The `Play` method, the equivalent of the `SoundPlayer.Play` method, uses the `PlayMode` parameter to configure how the sound is played. `PlayMode` is an `AudioPlayMode` enumerated type that can be set to `Background` (plays the sound asynchronously), `BackgroundLoop` (plays the sound asynchronously and loops until the `Stop` method is called), and `WaitToComplete` (plays the sound synchronously).

The Code

The following example shows a simple form that allows users to open any WAV file and play it:

```
Imports System
Imports System.Windows.Forms
Imports System.Media

'  All designed code is stored in the autogenerated partial
'  class called Recipe08-10.Designer.vb. You can see this
'  file by selecting Show All Files in Solution Explorer.
Partial Public Class Recipe08_10

    Private Sub cmdOpen_Click(ByVal sender As System.Object, ➥
ByVal e As System.EventArgs) Handles cmdOpen.Click

        ' Allow the user to choose a file.
        Dim openDialog As New OpenFileDialog

        openDialog.Filter = "WAV Files|*.wav|All Files|*.*"
```

```
If openDialog.ShowDialog = Windows.Forms.DialogResult.OK Then
    Dim player As New SoundPlayer(openDialog.FileName)

    Try
        player.Play()
    Catch ex As Exception
        MessageBox.Show("An error occurred while playing media.")
    Finally
        player.Dispose()
    End Try

End If

End Sub

End Class
```

To use the My namespace, remove references to the Player object and replace Player.Play() with this:

```
My.Computer.Audio.Play(openDialog.FileName)
```

8-11. Play a Sound File

Problem

You need to play a non-WAV format audio file such as an MP3 file.

Solution

Use the ActiveMovie COM component included with Windows Media Player, which supports WAV and MP3 audio.

How It Works

The ActiveMovie Quartz library provides a COM component that can play various types of audio files, including the WAV and MP3 formats. The Quartz type library is provided through quartz.dll and is included as a part of Microsoft DirectX with Media Player and the Windows operating system.

The first step for using the library is to generate an interop class that can manage the interaction between your .NET application and the unmanaged Quartz library. You can generate a C# class with this interop code using the Type Library Importer utility (Tlbimp.exe) and the following command line, where [WindowsDir] is the path for your installation of Windows:

```
tlbimp [WindowsDir]\system32\quartz.dll /out:QuartzTypeLib.dll
```

Alternatively, you can generate the interop class using Visual Studio by adding a reference. To do this, right-click your project in the Solution Explorer, choose Add Reference from the context menu, select the COM tab, and scroll down to select ActiveMovie Control Type Library, as shown in Figure 8-7.

Figure 8-7. *Adding the Quartz interop class*

Once the interop class is generated, you can work with the IMediaControl interface. You can specify the file you want to play using RenderFile, and you can control playback using methods such as Run, Stop, and Pause. The actual playback takes place on a separate thread, so it will not block your code.

While the .NET Framework will eventually release any references to a COM object and collect the memory it uses, it is best practice to do this yourself as soon as it is no longer needed. Managed code does not access COM objects directly, but instead uses a *runtime callable wrapper* (RCW). The RCW acts as a proxy between managed code and a referenced COM object. The Shared method ReleaseComObject, from the System.Runtime.InteropServices.Marshal class, properly destroys the RCW and the COM object it used.

The Code

The following example shows a simple form that allows you to open any audio file and play it. The COM object is destroyed using ReleaseComObject.

You can also use the Quartz library to show movie files, as demonstrated in recipe 8-12.

```
Imports System
Imports System.Windows.Forms
Imports QuartzTypeLib

' All designed code is stored in the autogenerated partial
' class called Recipe08-11.Designer.vb. You can see this
' file by selecting Show All Files in Solution Explorer.
Partial Public Class Recipe08_11

    Private Sub cmdOpen_Click(ByVal sender As System.Object, ➡
ByVal e As System.EventArgs) Handles cmdOpen.Click
```

```
    ' Allow the user to choose a file.
    Dim openDialog As New OpenFileDialog

    openDialog.Filter = "Media Files|*.wav;*.mp3;*.mp2;*.wma|All Files|*.*"

    If openDialog.ShowDialog = Windows.Forms.DialogResult.OK Then
        ' Access the IMediaControl interface.
        Dim graphManager As New QuartzTypeLib.FilgraphManager
        Dim mc As QuartzTypeLib.IMediaControl = DirectCast(graphManager, ➥
QuartzTypeLib.IMediaControl)

        ' Specify the file.
        mc.RenderFile(openDialog.FileName)

        Try
            mc.Run()
        Catch ex As Exception
            MessageBox.Show("An error occurred while playing media.")
        Finally
            ' Destroy the COM object (QuartzTypeLib) that we are using.
            System.Runtime.InteropServices.Marshal.ReleaseComObject(graphManager)
        End Try

    End If

    End Sub
End Class
```

8-12. Show a Video with DirectShow

Problem

You need to play a video file (such as an MPEG, an AVI, or a WMV file) in a Windows Forms application.

Solution

Use the ActiveMovie COM component included with Windows Media Player. Bind the video output to a picture box on your form by setting the IVideoWindow.Owner property to the PictureBox.Handle property.

How It Works

Although the .NET Framework does not include any managed classes for interacting with video files, you can leverage the functionality of DirectShow using the COM-based Quartz library included with Windows Media Player and the Windows operating system. For information about creating an interop assembly for the Quartz type library, refer to recipe 8-11.

Once you have created the interop assembly, you can use the IMediaControl interface to load and play a movie. This is essentially the same technique demonstrated in recipe 8-11 with audio files. However, if you want to show the video window inside your application interface (rather than in a separate stand-alone window), you must also use the IVideoWindow interface. The core FilgraphManager object can be cast to both the IMediaControl interface and the IVideoWindow interface (several other interfaces are also supported, such as IBasicAudio, which allows you to configure balance and volume settings). With the IVideoWindow interface, you can bind the video output to a control on your form, such as a Panel or a PictureBox. To do so, set the IVideoWindow.Owner property to the handle for the control, which you can retrieve using the Control.Handle property. Then call IVideoWindow.SetWindowPosition to set the window size and location. You can call this method to change the video size during playback (for example, if the form is resized).

The Code

The following example shows a simple form that allows users to open any video file and play it back in the provided picture box. The picture box is anchored to all sides of the form, so it changes size as the form resizes. The code responds to the PictureBox.SizeChanged event to change the size of the corresponding video window. Also, the reference to the QuartzTypeLib is destroyed using ReleaseComObject (discussed in recipe 8-11) when the form is closed.

```
Imports System
Imports System.Drawing
Imports System.Windows.Forms
Imports QuartzTypeLib

'  All designed code is stored in the autogenerated partial
'  class called Recipe08-12.Designer.vb. You can see this
'  file by selecting Show All Files in Solution Explorer.
Partial Public Class Recipe08_12

    '  Define the constants used for specifying the window style.
    Private Const WS_CHILD As Integer = &H40000000
    Private Const WS_CLIPCHILDREN As Integer = &H2000000

    '  Hold a form-level reference to the QuartzTypeLib.FilgraphManager
    '  object.
    Private graphManager As FilgraphManager

    '  Hold a form-level reference to the media control interface,
    '  so the code can control playback of the currently loaded
    '  movie.
    Private mc As IMediaControl = Nothing

    '  Hold a form-level reference to the video window in case it
    '  needs to be resized.
    Private videoWindow As IVideoWindow = Nothing

    Private Sub cmdOpen_Click(ByVal sender As System.Object, ➥
ByVal e As System.EventArgs) Handles cmdOpen.Click

        '  Allow the user to choose a file.
        Dim openDialog As New OpenFileDialog

        openDialog.Filter = "Media Files|*.mpg;*.avi;*.wma;*.mov;*.wav;*.mp2;*.mp3" & ➥
"|All Files|*.*"
```

```
        If openDialog.ShowDialog = Windows.Forms.DialogResult.OK Then

            ' Stop the playback for the current movie, if it exists.
            If mc IsNot Nothing Then mc.Stop()

            ' Load the movie file.
            graphmanager = New FilgraphManager
            graphManager.RenderFile(openDialog.FileName)

            ' Attach the view to a picture box on the form.
            Try
                videoWindow = DirectCast(graphmanager, IVideoWindow)
                videoWindow.Owner = pictureBox1.Handle.ToInt32
                videoWindow.WindowStyle = WS_CHILD Or WS_CLIPCHILDREN
                videoWindow.SetWindowPosition(pictureBox1.ClientRectangle.Left, ➥
pictureBox1.ClientRectangle.Top, pictureBox1.ClientRectangle.Width, ➥
pictureBox1.ClientRectangle.Height)
            Catch ex As Exception
                ' An error can occur if the file does not have a video
                ' source (for example, an MP3 file).
                ' You can ignore this error and still allow playback to
                ' continue (without any visualization).
            End Try

            ' Start the playback (asynchronously).
            mc = DirectCast(graphManager, IMediaControl)
            mc.Run()

        End If

    End Sub

    Private Sub pictureBox1_SizeChanged(ByVal sender As Object, ➥
ByVal e As System.EventArgs) Handles pictureBox1.SizeChanged

        If videoWindow IsNot Nothing Then

            Try
                videoWindow.SetWindowPosition(pictureBox1.ClientRectangle.Left, ➥
pictureBox1.ClientRectangle.Top, pictureBox1.ClientRectangle.Width, ➥
pictureBox1.ClientRectangle.Height)
            Catch ex As Exception
                ' Ignore the exception thrown when resizing the form
                ' when the file does not have a video source.
            End Try

        End If

    End Sub
```

```
        Private Sub Recipe08_12_FormClosed(ByVal sender As Object, ByVal e As ➡
    System.Windows.Forms.FormClosedEventArgs) Handles Me.FormClosed

            ' Destroy the COM object (QuartzTypeLib) that we are using.
            If mc IsNot Nothing Then
                System.Runtime.InteropServices.Marshal.ReleaseComObject(graphManager)
            End If

        End Sub

    End Class
```

Figure 8-8 shows an example of the output you will see.

Figure 8-8. *Playing a video file*

8-13. Retrieve Information About Installed Printers

Problem

You need to retrieve a list of available printers.

Solution

Read the names in the InstalledPrinters collection of the System.Drawing.Printing.PrinterSettings class.

How It Works

The PrinterSettings class encapsulates the settings for a printer and information about the printer. For example, you can use the PrinterSettings class to determine supported paper sizes, paper sources, and resolutions and check for the ability to print color or double-sided (*duplexed*) pages. In addition, you can retrieve default page settings for margins, page orientation, and so on.

The PrinterSettings class provides a Shared InstalledPrinters string collection, which includes the name of every printer installed on the computer. If you want to find out more information about the settings for a specific printer, create a PrinterSettings instance and set the PrinterName property accordingly.

The Code

The following code shows a console application that finds all the printers installed on a computer and displays information about the paper sizes and the resolutions supported by each one.

You do not need to take this approach when creating an application that provides printing features. As you will see in recipe 8-14, you can use the PrintDialog class to prompt the user to choose a printer and its settings. The PrintDialog class can automatically apply its settings to the appropriate PrintDocument without any additional code.

```vb
Imports System
Imports System.Drawing.Printing

Namespace Apress.VisualBasicRecipes.Chapter08
    Public Class Recipe08_13

        Public Shared Sub Main()

            For Each printerName As String In PrinterSettings.InstalledPrinters

                ' Display the printer name.
                Console.WriteLine("Printer: {0}", printerName)

                ' Retrieve the printer settings.
                Dim printer As New PrinterSettings
                printer.PrinterName = printerName

                ' Check that this is a valid printer.
                ' (This step might be requried if you read the printer name
                ' from a user-supplied value or a registry or configuration
                ' file setting.)
                If printer.IsValid Then
                    ' Display the list of valid resolutions.
                    Console.WriteLine("Supported Resolutions:")

                    For Each resolution As PrinterResolution In ➥
printer.PrinterResolutions
                        Console.WriteLine("  {0}", resolution)
                    Next
                    Console.WriteLine()

                    ' Display the list of valid paper sizes.
                    Console.WriteLine("Supported Paper Sizes:")

                    For Each size As PaperSize In printer.PaperSizes
                        If System.Enum.IsDefined(size.Kind.GetType, size.Kind) Then
                            Console.WriteLine("  {0}", size)
                        End If
```

```
                    Next
                    Console.WriteLine()
                End If
            Next
            Console.ReadLine()
        End Sub

    End Class
End Namespace
```

Usage

Here is the type of output this utility displays:

```
Printer: SnagIt 8
Supported Resolutions:
  [PrinterResolution High]
  [PrinterResolution Medium]
  [PrinterResolution Low]
  [PrinterResolution Draft]
  [PrinterResolution X=600 Y=600]
  [PrinterResolution X=300 Y=300]
  [PrinterResolution X=200 Y=200]
  [PrinterResolution X=100 Y=100]

Supported Paper Sizes:
  [PaperSize Letter Kind=Letter Height=1100 Width=850]
  [PaperSize Legal Kind=Legal Height=1400 Width=850]
  [PaperSize Executive Kind=Executive Height=1050 Width=725]
  [PaperSize A4 Kind=A4 Height=1169 Width=827]
  [PaperSize Envelope #10 Kind=Number10Envelope Height=950 Width=412]
  [PaperSize Envelope DL Kind=DLEnvelope Height=866 Width=433]
  [PaperSize Envelope C5 Kind=C5Envelope Height=902 Width=638]
  [PaperSize Envelope B5 Kind=B5Envelope Height=984 Width=693]
  [PaperSize Envelope Monarch Kind=MonarchEnvelope Height=750 Width=387]

Printer: Microsoft Office Document Image Writer
. . .
```

Note You can print a document in almost any type of application. However, your application must include a reference to the System.Drawing.dll assembly. If you are using a project type in Visual Studio that would not normally have this reference (such as a console application), you must add it.

8-14. Print a Simple Document

Problem

You need to print text or images.

Solution

Create a `PrintDocument` and write a handler for the `PrintDocument.PrintPage` event that uses the `DrawString` and `DrawImage` methods of the `Graphics` class to print data to the page.

How It Works

The .NET Framework uses an asynchronous event-based printing model. To print a document, you create a `System.Drawing.Printing.PrintDocument` instance, configure its properties, and then call its `Print` method, which schedules the print job. The common language runtime (CLR) will then fire the `BeginPrint`, `PrintPage`, and `EndPrint` events of the `PrintDocument` class on a new thread. You handle these events and use the provided `System.Drawing.Graphics` object to output data to the page. Graphics and text are written to a page in the same way as you draw to a window using GDI+. However, you might need to track your position on a page, because every `Graphics` class method requires explicit coordinates that indicate where to draw.

You configure printer settings through the `PrintDocument.PrinterSettings` and `PrintDocument.DefaultPageSettings` properties. The `PrinterSettings` property returns a full `PrinterSettings` object (as described in recipe 8-13), which identifies the printer that will be used. The `DefaultPageSettings` property provides a full `PageSettings` object that specifies printer resolution, margins, orientation, and so on. You can configure these properties in code, or you can use the `System.Windows.Forms.PrintDialog` class to let the user make the changes using the standard Windows Print dialog box, shown in Figure 8-9. In the Print dialog box, the user can select a printer and choose the number of copies. The user can also click the Properties button to configure advanced settings such as page layout and printer resolution. Finally, the user can either accept or cancel the print operation by clicking OK or Cancel.

Figure 8-9. *Using the PrintDialog class*

Before using the `PrintDialog` class, you must explicitly attach it to a `PrintDocument` object by setting the `PrintDialog.Document` property. Then any changes the user makes in the Print dialog box will be automatically applied to the `PrintDocument` object.

The Code

The following example provides a form with a single button. When the user clicks the button, the application creates a new `PrintDocument`, allows the user to configure print settings, and then starts an asynchronous print operation (provided the user clicks OK). An event handler responds to the `PrintPage` event and writes several lines of text and an image.

   This example has one limitation: it can print only a single page. To print more complex documents and span multiple pages, you will probably want to create a specialized class that encapsulates the document information, the current page, and so on, as described in recipe 8-15.

```
Imports System
Imports System.Drawing
Imports System.Windows.Forms
Imports System.Drawing.Printing
Imports System.IO


'  All designed code is stored in the autogenerated partial
'  class called Recipe08-14.Designer.vb. You can see this
'  file by selecting Show All Files in Solution Explorer.
Partial Public Class Recipe08_14

    Private Sub cmdPrint_Click(ByVal sender As System.Object, ➥
ByVal e As System.EventArgs) Handles cmdPrint.Click

        '  Create the document and attach an event handler.
        Dim doc As New PrintDocument

        AddHandler doc.PrintPage, AddressOf Doc_PrintPage

        '  Allow the user to choose a printer and specify other settings.
        Dim dlgSettings As New PrintDialog
        dlgSettings.Document = doc

        '  If the user clicked OK, print the document.
        If dlgSettings.ShowDialog = Windows.Forms.DialogResult.OK Then
            '  This method returns immediately, before the print job starts.
            '  The PrintPage event will fire asynchronously.
            doc.Print()
        End If

    End Sub

    Private Sub Doc_PrintPage(ByVal sender As Object, ByVal e As PrintPageEventArgs)

        '  Determine the font.
        Using fnt As New Font("Arial", 30)
            '  Determine the position on the page. In this case,
            '  we read the margin settings (although there is
            '  nothing that prevents your code from going outside
            '  the margin bounds).
            Dim x As Single = e.MarginBounds.Left
            Dim y As Single = e.MarginBounds.Top

            '  Determine the height of a line (based on the font used).
```

```
            Dim lineHeight As Single = Font.GetHeight(e.Graphics)

            ' Print five lines of text.
            For i As Integer = 1 To 5
                ' Draw the text with a black brush, using the
                ' font and coordinates we have determined.
                e.Graphics.DrawString("This is line " & i.ToString, Font, ➡
Brushes.Black, x, y)

                ' Move down the equivalent spacing of one line.
                y += lineheight
            Next
            y += lineHeight

            ' Draw an image.
            e.Graphics.DrawImage(Image.FromFile(Path.Combine( ➡
Application.StartupPath, "test.jpg")), x, y)

        End Using

    End Sub
End Class
```

8-15. Print a Multipage Document

Problem

You need to print complex documents with multiple pages and possibly print several different documents at once.

Solution

Place the information you want to print into a custom class that derives from `PrintDocument`, and in the `PrintPage` event handler, set the `PrintPageEventArgs.HasMorePages` property to `True` as long as pages are remaining.

How It Works

The `PrintDocument.PrintPage` event is triggered to let you to print only a single page. If you need to print more pages, you need to set the `PrintPageEventArgs.HasMorePages` property to `True` in the `PrintPage` event handler. As long as `HasMorePages` is set to `True`, the `PrintDocument` class will continue firing `PrintPage` events. However, it is up to you to track which page you are on, what data should be placed on each page, and what is the last page for which `HasMorePage` is not set to `True`. To facilitate this tracking, it is a good idea to create a custom class.

The Code

The following example shows a class called `TextDocument`. This class inherits from `PrintDocument` and adds three properties. `Text` stores an array of text lines, `PageNumber` reflects the last printed page, and `Offset` indicates the last line that was printed from the `Text` array.

```
Public Class TextDocument
    Inherits PrintDocument

    Private m_Text As String()
    Private m_PageNumber As Integer
    Private m_Offset As Integer

    Public Sub New(ByVal txt As String())

        Me.Text = txt

    End Sub

    Public Property Text() As String()
        Get
            Return m_Text
        End Get
        Set(ByVal value As String())
            m_Text = value
        End Set
    End Property

    Public Property PageNumber() As Integer
        Get
            Return m_PageNumber
        End Get
        Set(ByVal value As Integer)
            m_PageNumber = value
        End Set
    End Property

    Public Property Offset() As Integer
        Get
            Return m_Offset
        End Get
        Set(ByVal value As Integer)
            m_Offset = value
        End Set
    End Property

End Class
```

Depending on the type of material you are printing, you might want to modify this class. For example, you could store an array of image data, some content that should be used as a header or footer on each page, font information, or even the name of a file from which you want to read the information. Encapsulating the information in a single class makes it easier to print more than one document at the same time. This is especially important because the printing process runs in a new dedicated thread. As a consequence, the user is able to keep working in the application and therefore update your data while the pages are printing. So, this dedicated class should contain a copy of the data to print to avoid any concurrency problems.

The code that initiates printing is the same as in recipe 8-14, but now it creates a TextDocument instance instead of a PrintDocument instance. The PrintPage event handler keeps track of the current line and checks whether the page has space before attempting to print the next line. If a new page is needed, the HasMorePages property is set to True and the PrintPage event fires again for the next page.

If not, the print operation is deemed complete. This simple code sample also takes into account whether a line fits on the page, according to the height (see recipe 8-16).

The full form code is as follows:

```vb
Imports System
Imports System.Drawing
Imports System.Windows.Forms
Imports System.Drawing.Printing

'  All designed code is stored in the autogenerated partial
'  class called Recipe08-15.Designer.vb. You can see this
'  file by selecting Show All Files in Solution Explorer.
Partial Public Class Recipe08_15

    Private Sub cmdPrint_Click(ByVal sender As System.Object, ➡
ByVal e As System.EventArgs) Handles cmdPrint.Click

        '  Create a document with 100 lines.
        Dim printText As String() = New String(100) {}

        For i As Integer = 1 To 100
            printText(i) = i.ToString
            printText(i) += ": The quick brown fox jumps over the lazy dog."
        Next

        Dim doc As New TextDocument(printText)

        AddHandler doc.PrintPage, AddressOf Doc_PrintPage

        Dim dlgSettings As New PrintDialog
        dlgSettings.Document = doc

        '  If the user clicked OK, print the document.
        If dlgSettings.ShowDialog = Windows.Forms.DialogResult.OK Then
            '  This method returns immediately, before the print job starts.
            '  The PrintPage event will fire asynchronously.
            doc.Print()
        End If

    End Sub

    Private Sub Doc_PrintPage(ByVal sender As Object, ByVal e As PrintPageEventArgs)

        '  Retrieve the document that sent this event.
        Dim doc As TextDocument = DirectCast(sender, TextDocument)

        '  Determine the font and determine the line height.
        Using fnt As New Font("Arial", 10)
            Dim lineHeight As Single = Font.GetHeight(e.Graphics)

            '  Create variables to hold position on the page.
            Dim x As Single = e.MarginBounds.Left
            Dim y As Single = e.MarginBounds.Top
```

```
              ' Increment the page counter (to reflect the page that
              ' is about to be printed).
              doc.PageNumber += 1

              ' Print all the information that can fit on the page.
              ' This loop ends when the next line would go over the
              ' bottom margin or there are no more lines to print.
              While ((y + lineHeight) < e.MarginBounds.Bottom And doc.Offset <= ➥
doc.Text.GetUpperBound(0))
                      e.Graphics.DrawString(doc.Text(doc.Offset), Font, Brushes.Black, ➥
x, y)

                  ' Move to the next line of data.
                  doc.Offset += 1

                  ' Move the equivalent of one line down the page.
                  y += lineHeight
              End While

              If doc.Offset < doc.Text.GetUpperBound(0) Then
                  ' There is still at least one more page. Signal
                  ' this event to fire again.
                  e.HasMorePages = True
              Else
                  ' Printing is complete.
                  doc.Offset = 0
              End If

          End Using

      End Sub
End Class
```

8-16. Print Wrapped Text

Problem

You need to parse a large block of text into distinct lines that fit on one page.

Solution

Use the `Graphics.DrawString` method overload that accepts a bounding rectangle.

How It Works

Often, you will need to break a large block of text into separate lines that can be printed individually on a page. The .NET Framework can perform this task automatically, provided you use a version of the `Graphics.DrawString` method that accepts a bounding rectangle. You specify a rectangle that represents where you want the text to be displayed. The text is then wrapped automatically to fit within those confines.

The Code

The following code demonstrates this approach, using the bounding rectangle that represents the printable portion of the page. It prints a large block of text from a textbox on the form.

```vb
Imports System
Imports System.Drawing
Imports System.Windows.Forms
Imports System.Drawing.Printing

' All designed code is stored in the autogenerated partial
' class called Recipe08-16.Designer.vb. You can see this
' file by selecting Show All Files in Solution Explorer.
Partial Public Class Recipe08_16

    Private Sub cmdPrint_Click(ByVal sender As System.Object, ➥
ByVal e As System.EventArgs) Handles cmdPrint.Click

        ' Create the document and attach an event handler.
        Dim text As String = "Windows Server 2003 builds on the core strengths " & _
            "of the Windows family of operating systems--security, manageability, " & _
            "reliability, availability, and scalability. Windows Server 2003 " & _
            "provides an application environment to build, deploy, manage, and " & _
            "run XML web services. Additionally, advances in Windows Server 2003 " & _
            "provide many benefits for developing applications."

        Dim doc As New ParagraphDocument(text)
        AddHandler doc.PrintPage, AddressOf Doc_PrintPage

        ' Allow the user to choose a printer and specify other settings.
        Dim dlgsettings As New PrintDialog
        dlgsettings.Document = doc

        ' If the user clicked OK, print the document.
        If dlgsettings.ShowDialog = Windows.Forms.DialogResult.OK Then
            doc.Print()
        End If

    End Sub

    Private Sub Doc_PrintPage(ByVal sender As Object, ByVal e As PrintPageEventArgs)

        ' Retrieve the document that sent this event.
        Dim doc As ParagraphDocument = DirectCast(sender, ParagraphDocument)

        ' Define the font and text.
        Using fnt As New Font("Arial", 15)
            e.Graphics.DrawString(doc.Text, Font, Brushes.Black, ➥
e.MarginBounds, StringFormat.GenericDefault)
        End Using

    End Sub
End Class
```

```vbnet
Public Class ParagraphDocument
    Inherits PrintDocument

    Private m_Text As String

    Public Sub New(ByVal txt As String)
        Me.Text = txt
    End Sub

    Public Property Text() As String
        Get
            Return m_Text
        End Get
        Set(ByVal value As String)
            m_Text = value
        End Set
    End Property

End Class
```

Figure 8-10 shows the wrapped text.

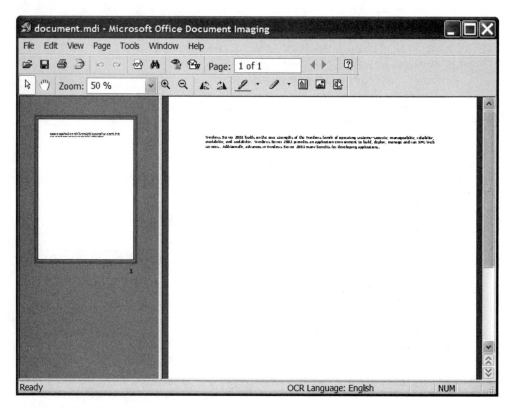

Figure 8-10. *The printed document with wrapping*

8-17. Show a Dynamic Print Preview

Problem

You need to use an on-screen preview that shows how a printed document will look.

Solution

Use `PrintPreviewDialog` or `PrintPreviewControl` (both of which are found in the `System.Windows.Forms` namespace).

How It Works

The .NET Framework provides two elements of user interface that can take a `PrintDocument` instance, run your printing code (such as the code demonstrated in recipe 8-15), and use it to generate a graphical on-screen preview:

- The `PrintPreviewDialog`, which shows a preview in a stand-alone form
- The `PrintPreviewControl`, which shows a preview in a control that can be embedded in one of your own custom forms

To use a stand-alone print preview form, create a `PrintPreviewDialog` object, assign its `Document` property, and call the `Show` method:

```
Dim dlgPreview As New PrintPreviewDialog
dlgPreview.Document = doc
dlgPreview.Show()
```

The Print Preview window (shown in Figure 8-11) provides all the controls the user needs to move from page to page, zoom in, and so on. The window even provides a print button that allows the user to send the document directly to the printer. You can tailor the window to some extent by modifying the `PrintPreviewDialog` properties.

You can also add a `PrintPreviewControl` control to any of your forms to show a preview along-side other information. In this case, you do not need to call the `Show` method. As soon as you set the `PrintPreviewControl.Document` property, the preview is generated. To clear the preview, set the `Document` property to `Nothing`. To refresh the preview, reassign the `Document` property. `PrintPreviewControl` shows only the preview pages, not any additional controls. However, you can add your own controls for zooming, tiling multiple pages, and so on. You simply need to adjust the `PrintPreviewControl` properties accordingly.

Figure 8-11. *Using the PrintPreviewDialog control*

The Code

As an example, consider the form shown in Figure 8-12. It incorporates a `PrintPreviewControl` and allows the user to select a zoom setting.

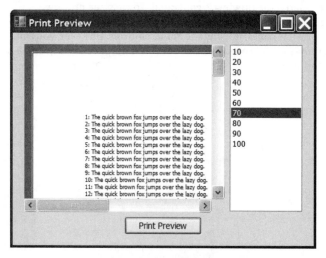

Figure 8-12. *Using the PrintPreviewControl in a custom window*

Here is the complete form code:

```vb
Imports System
Imports System.Drawing
Imports System.Windows.Forms
Imports System.Drawing.Printing

' All designed code is stored in the autogenerated partial
' class called Recipe08-17.Designer.vb. You can see this
' file by selecting Show All Files in Solution Explorer.
Partial Public Class Recipe08_17

    Private doc As PrintDocument

    Private Sub Recipe08_17_Load(ByVal sender As Object, ➥
ByVal e As System.EventArgs) Handles Me.Load

        ' Set the allowed zoom settings.
        For i As Integer = 1 To 10
            lstZoom.Items.Add((i * 10).ToString)
        Next

        ' Create a document with 100 lines.
        Dim printText As String() = New String(100) {}

        For i As Integer = 1 To 100
            printText(i) = i.ToString
            printText(i) += ": The quick brown fox jumps over the lazy dog."
        Next

        Dim doc As New TextDocument(printText)

        AddHandler doc.PrintPage, AddressOf Doc_PrintPage

        lstZoom.Text = "100"
        printPreviewControl.Zoom = 1
        printPreviewControl.Document = doc
        printPreviewControl.Rows = 2

    End Sub

    ' (PrintDocument.PrintPage event handler code omitted. See recipe 8-15.)

    Private Sub cmdPrint_Click(ByVal sender As System.Object, ➥
ByVal e As System.EventArgs) Handles cmdPrint.Click

        ' Set the zoom.
        printPreviewControl.Zoom = Single.Parse(lstZoom.Text) / 100

        ' Rebind the PrintDocument to refresh the preview.
        printPreviewControl.Document = doc

    End Sub
```

```
End Class
```

```
'  (TextDocument class code omitted. See recipe 8-15.)
```

8-18. Manage Print Jobs

Problem

You need to pause or resume a print job or a print queue.

Solution

Use Windows Management Instrumentation (WMI). You can retrieve information from the print queue using a query with the Win32_PrintJob class, and you can use the Pause and Resume methods of the WMI Win32_PrintJob and Win32_Printer classes to manage the queue.

How It Works

WMI allows you to retrieve a vast amount of system information using a querylike syntax. One of the tasks you can perform with WMI is to retrieve a list of outstanding print jobs, along with information about each one. You can also perform operations such as printing and resuming a job or all the jobs for a printer. To use WMI, you need to add a reference to the System.Management.dll assembly.

The Code

The following code shows a Windows application that interacts with the print queue. It performs a WMI query to get a list of all the outstanding print jobs on the computer and displays the job ID for each one in a list box. When the user selects the item, a more complete WMI query is performed, and additional details about the print job are displayed in a textbox. Finally, the user can click the Pause and Resume button after selecting a job to change its status.

Remember that Windows permissions might prevent you from pausing or resuming print jobs created by another user. In fact, permissions might even prevent you from retrieving status information and could cause a security exception to be thrown.

```
Imports System
Imports System.Drawing
Imports System.Windows.Forms
Imports System.Management
Imports System.Collections
Imports System.Text

'  All designed code is stored in the autogenerated partial
'  class called Recipe08-18.Designer.vb. You can see this
'  file by selecting Show All Files in Solution Explorer.
Partial Public Class Recipe08_18

    Private Sub cmdRefresh_Click(ByVal sender As System.Object, ➥
ByVal e As System.EventArgs) Handles cmdRefresh.Click
```

```vb
        ' Select all the outstanding print jobs.
        Dim query As String = "SELECT * FROM Win32_PrintJob"

        Using jobQuery As New ManagementObjectSearcher(query)
            Using jobs As ManagementObjectCollection = jobQuery.Get()
                ' Add the jobs in the queue to the list box.
                lstJobs.Items.Clear()
                txtJobInfo.Text = ""

                For Each job As ManagementObject In jobs
                    lstJobs.Items.Add(job("JobID"))
                Next
            End Using
        End Using

    End Sub

    Private Sub Recipe08_18_Load(ByVal sender As Object, ➡
ByVal e As System.EventArgs) Handles Me.Load

        cmdRefresh_Click(Nothing, Nothing)

    End Sub

    ' This helper method performs a WMI query and returns the
    ' WMI job for the currently selected list box item.
    Private Function GetSelectedJob(ByVal jobID As String) As ManagementObject

        Try
            ' Select the matching print job.
            Dim query As String = "SELECT * FROM Win32_PrintJob WHERE JobID='" & ➡
jobID & "'"

            Dim job As ManagementObject = Nothing

            Using jobQuery As New ManagementObjectSearcher(query)
                Dim jobs As ManagementObjectCollection = jobQuery.Get
                Dim enumerator As IEnumerator = jobs.GetEnumerator

                enumerator.MoveNext()
                job = DirectCast(enumerator.Current, ManagementObject)
            End Using

            Return job
        Catch ex As InvalidOperationException
            ' The current property of the enumerator is invalid.
            Return Nothing
        End Try

    End Function
```

```
    Private Sub lstJobs_SelectedIndexChanged(ByVal sender As Object, ➥
ByVal e As System.EventArgs) Handles lstJobs.SelectedIndexChanged

        Dim job As ManagementObject = GetSelectedJob(lstJobs.Text)

        If job Is Nothing Then
            txtJobInfo.Text = ""
            Exit Sub
        End If

        ' Display job information.
        Dim jobInfo As New StringBuilder

        jobInfo.AppendFormat("Document: {0}", job("Document").ToString)
        jobInfo.Append(Environment.NewLine)
        jobInfo.AppendFormat("DriverName: {0}", job("DriverName").ToString)
        jobInfo.Append(Environment.NewLine)
        jobInfo.AppendFormat("Status: {0}", job("Status").ToString)
        jobInfo.Append(Environment.NewLine)
        jobInfo.AppendFormat("Owner: {0}", job("Owner").ToString)
        jobInfo.Append(Environment.NewLine)
        jobInfo.AppendFormat("PagesPrinted: {0}", job("PagesPrinted").ToString)
        jobInfo.Append(Environment.NewLine)
        jobInfo.AppendFormat("TotalPages: {0}", job("TotalPages").ToString)

        If job("JobStatus") IsNot Nothing Then
            txtJobInfo.Text += Environment.NewLine
            txtJobInfo.Text += "JobStatus: " & job("JobStatus").ToString
        End If

        If job("StartTime") IsNot Nothing Then
            jobInfo.Append(Environment.NewLine)
            jobInfo.AppendFormat("StartTime: {0}", job("StartTime").ToString)
        End If
        txtJobInfo.Text = jobInfo.ToString

    End Sub

    Private Sub cmdPause_Click(ByVal sender As System.Object, ➥
ByVal e As System.EventArgs) Handles cmdPause.Click

        If lstJobs.SelectedIndex = -1 Then Exit Sub

        Dim job As ManagementObject = GetSelectedJob(lstJobs.Text)
```

```
        If job Is Nothing Then Exit Sub

        ' Attempt to pause the job.
        Dim returnValue As Integer = CType(job.InvokeMethod("Pause", Nothing), ➥
Integer)

        ' Display information about the return value.
        If returnValue = 0 Then
            MessageBox.Show("Successfully paused job.")
        Else
            MessageBox.Show("Unrecognized return value when pausing job.")
        End If

    End Sub

    Private Sub cmdResume_Click(ByVal sender As System.Object, ➥
ByVal e As System.EventArgs) Handles cmdResume.Click

        If lstJobs.SelectedIndex = -1 Then Exit Sub

        Dim job As ManagementObject = GetSelectedJob(lstJobs.Text)

        If job Is Nothing Then Exit Sub

        If (CInt(job("StatusMask") And 1)) = 1 Then
            ' Attempt to resume the job.
            Dim returnValue As Integer = CType(job.InvokeMethod("Resume", Nothing), ➥
Integer)

            ' Display information about the return value.
            If returnValue = 0 Then
                MessageBox.Show("Successfully resumed job.")
            ElseIf returnValue = 5 Then
                MessageBox.Show("Access denied.")
            Else
                MessageBox.Show("Unrecognized return value when resuming job.")
            End If

        End If

    End Sub

End Class
```

Figure 8-13 shows an example of running this application.

Figure 8-13. *Retrieving information from the print queue*

■**Note** Other WMI methods you might use in a printing scenario include `AddPrinterConnection`, `SetDefaultPrinter`, `CancelAllJobs`, and `PrintTestPage`, all of which work with the `Win32_Printer` class. For more information about WMI, refer to `http://www.microsoft.com/whdc/system/pnppwr/wmi/default.mspx`.

CHAPTER 9

■ ■ ■

Database Access

In the Microsoft .NET Framework, access to a wide variety of data sources is enabled through a group of classes collectively named Microsoft ADO.NET. Each type of data source is supported through the provision of a data provider. Each data provider contains a set of classes that not only implement a standard set of interfaces (defined in the System.Data namespace), but also provide functionality unique to the data source they support. These classes include representations of connections, commands, properties, data adapters, and data readers through which you interact with a data source.

■**Note** ADO.NET is an extensive subsection of the .NET Framework class library and includes a great deal of advanced functionality. For comprehensive coverage of ADO.NET, read David Sceppa's excellent book *Programming Microsoft ADO.NET 2.0 Core Reference* (Microsoft Press, 2006).

Table 9-1 lists the data providers included as standard with the .NET Framework.

Table 9-1. *.NET Framework Data Provider Implementations*

Data Provider	Description
.NET Framework Data Provider for ODBC	Provides connectivity (via COM Interop) to any data source that implements an ODBC interface. This includes Microsoft SQL Server, Oracle, and Microsoft Access databases. Data provider classes are contained in the System.Data.Odbc namespace and have the prefix Odbc.
.NET Framework Data Provider for OLE DB	Provides connectivity (via COM Interop) to any data source that implements an OLE DB interface. This includes Microsoft SQL Server, MSDE, Oracle, and Jet databases. Data provider classes are contained in the System.Data.OleDb namespace and have the prefix OleDb.
.NET Framework Data Provider for Oracle	Provides optimized connectivity to Oracle databases via Oracle client software version 8.1.7 or later. Data provider classes are contained in the System.Data.OracleClient namespace and have the prefix Oracle.
.NET Framework Data Provider for SQL Server	Provides optimized connectivity to Microsoft SQL Server version 7 and later (including MSDE) by communicating directly with the SQL Server data source, without the need to use ODBC or OLE DB. Data provider classes are contained in the System.Data.SqlClient namespace and have the prefix Sql.
.NET Compact Framework Data Provider for SQL Server CE	Provides connectivity to Microsoft SQL Server 2005 Compact Edition. Data provider classes are contained in the System.Data.SqlServerCe namespace and have the prefix SqlCe.

■**Tip** Where possible, the recipes in this chapter are programmed against the interfaces defined in the `System.`
`Data` namespace. This approach makes it easier to apply the solutions to any database. Adopting this approach in
your own code will make it more portable. However, the data provider classes that implement these interfaces often
implement additional functionality specific to their own database. Generally, you must trade off portability against
access to proprietary functionality when it comes to database code. Recipe 9-10 describes how you can use the
`System.Data.Common.DbProviderFactory` and associated classes (new to .NET Framework 2.0) to write
generic code that is not tied to a specific database implementation.

This chapter describes some of the most commonly used aspects of ADO.NET. The recipes in
this chapter describe how to do the following:

- Create, configure, open, and close database connections (recipe 9-1)

- Employ connection pooling to improve the performance and scalability of applications that
  use database connections (recipe 9-2)

- Create and securely store database connection strings (recipes 9-3 and 9-4)

- Execute SQL commands and stored procedures, and use parameters to improve their flexibility (recipes 9-5 and 9-6)

- Process the results returned by database queries as either a set of rows or as XML (recipes 9-7
  and 9-8)

- Execute database operations asynchronously, allowing your main code to continue with
  other tasks while the database operation executes in the background (recipe 9-9)

- Write generic ADO.NET code that can be configured to work against any relational database
  for which a data provider is available (recipe 9-10)

- Discover all instances of SQL Server 2000 and SQL Server 2005 available on a network
  (recipe 9-11)

■**Note** Unless otherwise stated, the recipes in this chapter have been written to use SQL Server 2005 Express
Edition running on the local machine and use the AdventureWorks sample database provided by Microsoft. To run
the examples against your own database, ensure the AdventureWorks sample is installed and update the recipe's
connection string to contain the name of your server instead of `.\sqlexpress`. You can obtain the script to set up
the AdventureWorks database from `http://www.microsoft.com/downloads/details.aspx?familyid=`
`E719ECF7-9F46-4312-AF89-6AD8702E4E6E&displaylang=en`. Download and run the AdventureWorksDB.msi
file. This site also contains the file SQLServerDatabasesAndSamplesOverview.htm, which contains instructions for
installing the AdventureWorks database.

9-1. Connect to a Database

Problem

You need to open a connection to a database.

Solution

Create a connection object appropriate to the type of database to which you need to connect. Configure the connection object by setting its ConnectionString property. Open the connection by calling the connection object's Open method.

How It Works

The first step in database access is to open a connection to the database. All connection objects inherit from the abstract (MustInherit) System.Data.Common.DbConnection class. This class implements the System.Data.IDbConnection interface. The DbConnection class represents a database connection, and each data provider includes a unique implementation. Here is the list of the implementations for the five standard data providers:

- System.Data.Odbc.OdbcConnection
- System.Data.OleDb.OleDbConnection
- System.Data.OracleClient.OracleConnection
- System.Data.SqlClient.SqlConnection
- System.Data.SqlServerCe.SqlCeConnection

You configure a connection object using a connection string. A connection string is a set of semicolon-separated name-value pairs. You can supply a connection string either as a constructor argument or by setting a connection object's ConnectionString property before opening the connection. Each connection class implementation requires that you provide different information in the connection string. Refer to the ConnectionString property documentation for each implementation to see the values you can specify. Possible settings include the following:

- The name of the target database server
- The name of the database to open initially
- Connection time-out values
- Connection-pooling behavior (see recipe 9-2)
- Authentication mechanisms to use when connecting to secured databases, including provision of a username and password if needed

Once configured, call the connection object's Open method to open the connection to the database. You can then use the connection object to execute commands against the data source (discussed in recipe 9-3). The properties of a connection object also allow you to retrieve information about the state of a connection and the settings used to open the connection. When you're finished with a connection, you should always call its Close method to free the underlying database connection and system resources. IDbConnection extends System.IDisposable, meaning that each connection class implements the Dispose method. Dispose automatically calls Close, making the Using statement a very clean and efficient way of using connection objects in your code.

You achieve optimum scalability by opening your database connection as late as possible and closing it as soon as you have finished. This ensures that you do not tie up database connections for long periods, so you give all code the maximum opportunity to obtain a connection. This is especially important if you are using connection pooling.

The Code

The following example demonstrates how to use both the SqlConnection and OleDbConnection classes to open a connection to a Microsoft SQL Server database running on the local machine that uses integrated Windows security.

```vb
Imports System
Imports System.Data
Imports System.Data.SqlClient
Imports System.Data.OleDb

Namespace Apress.VisualBasicRecipes.Chapter09

    Public Class Recipe09_01

        Public Shared Sub SqlConnectionExample()

            ' Configure an empty SqlConnection object.
            Using con As New SqlConnection

                ' Configure the SqlConnection object's connection string.
                con.ConnectionString = "Data Source=.\sqlexpress;Database=" & ➡
"AdventureWorks;Integrated Security=SSPI;"

                ' Open the database connection.
                con.Open()

                ' Display the information about the connection.
                If con.State = ConnectionState.Open Then
                    Console.WriteLine("SqlConnection Information:")
                    Console.WriteLine("  Connection State = " & con.State)
                    Console.WriteLine("  Connection String = " & ➡
con.ConnectionString)
                    Console.WriteLine("  Database Source = " & con.DataSource)
                    Console.WriteLine("  Database = " & con.Database)
                    Console.WriteLine("  Server Version = " & con.ServerVersion)
                    Console.WriteLine("  Workstation Id = " & con.WorkstationId)
                    Console.WriteLine("  Timeout = " & con.ConnectionTimeout)
                    Console.WriteLine("  Packet Size = " & con.PacketSize)
                Else
                    Console.WriteLine("SqlConenction failed to open.")
                    Console.WriteLine("  Connection State = " & con.State)
                End If

                ' Close the database connection.
                con.Close()

            End Using

        End Sub

        Public Shared Sub OleDbConnectionExample()
```

```vbnet
        ' Configure an empty SqlConnection object.
        Using con As New OleDbConnection

            ' Configure the SqlConnection object's connection string.
            con.ConnectionString = "Provider=SQLOLEDB;Data " & ➥
"Source=.\sqlexpress;Initial Cataglo=AdventureWorks;Integrated Security=SSPI;"

            ' Open the database connection.
            con.Open()

            ' Display the information about the connection.
            If con.State = ConnectionState.Open Then
                Console.WriteLine("OleDbConnection Information:")
                Console.WriteLine("  Connection State = " & con.State)
                Console.WriteLine("  Connection String = " & ➥
con.ConnectionString)
                Console.WriteLine("  Database Source = " & con.DataSource)
                Console.WriteLine("  Database = " & con.Database)
                Console.WriteLine("  Server Version = " & con.ServerVersion)
                Console.WriteLine("  Timeout = " & con.ConnectionTimeout)
            Else
                Console.WriteLine("OleDbConnection failed to open.")
                Console.WriteLine("  Connection State = " & con.State)
            End If

            ' Close the database connection.
            con.Close()

        End Using

    End Sub

    Public Shared Sub Main()

        ' Open connection using SqlConnection.
        SqlConnectionExample()
        Console.WriteLine(Environment.NewLine)

        ' Open connection using OleDbConnection.
        OleDbConnectionExample()
        Console.WriteLine(Environment.NewLine)

        ' Wait to continue.
        Console.WriteLine(Environment.NewLine)
        Console.WriteLine("Main method complete.  Press Enter.")
        Console.ReadLine()

    End Sub

End Class
End Namespace
```

9-2. Use Connection Pooling

Problem

You need to use a pool of database connections to improve application performance and scalability.

Solution

Configure the connection pool using settings in the connection string of a connection object.

How It Works

Connection pooling significantly reduces the overhead associated with creating and destroying database connections. Connection pooling also improves the scalability of solutions by reducing the number of concurrent connections a database must maintain. Many of these connections sit idle for a significant portion of their lifetimes.

With connection pooling, the first time you create a connection, the .NET Framework checks the pool to see if a connection is available. If the pool hasn't yet reached its limit, a new connection will be created and added to it. The next time you attempt to use a connection with the identical connection string, instead of a new connection being created and opened, the existing connection in the pool is used. When you close the connection, it is returned to the pool until it is needed again. Once created, a pool exists until your process terminates.

The SQL Server and Oracle data providers encapsulate connection-pooling functionality that they enable by default. One connection pool exists for each unique connection string you specify when you open a new connection. Each time you open a new connection with a connection string that you used previously, the connection is taken from the existing pool. Only if you specify a different connection string will the data provider create a new connection pool. You can control some characteristics of your pool using the connection string settings described in Table 9-2.

Table 9-2. *Connection String Settings That Control Connection Pooling*

Setting	Description
Connection Lifetime	Specifies the maximum time in seconds that a connection is allowed to live in the pool before it's closed. The age of a connection is tested only when the connection is returned to the pool. This setting is useful for minimizing pool size if the pool is not heavily used and also ensures optimal load balancing is achieved in clustered database environments. The default value is 0, which means connections exist for the life of the current process.
Connection Reset	Supported only by the SQL Server data provider. Specifies whether connections are reset as they are taken from the pool. A value of True (the default) ensures a connection's state is reset but requires an additional communication with the database.
Max Pool Size	Specifies the maximum number of connections that should be in the pool. Connections are created and added to the pool as required until this value is reached. If a request for a connection is made but there are no free connections, the calling code will block until a connection becomes available. The default value is 100.

Table 9-2. *Connection String Settings That Control Connection Pooling*

Setting	Description
Min Pool Size	Specifies the minimum number of connections that should be in the pool. On pool creation, this number of connections is created and added to the pool. During periodic maintenance, or when a connection is requested, connections are added to the pool to ensure the minimum number of connections is available. The default value is 0.
Pooling	Set to False to obtain a nonpooled connection. The default value is True.

The Code

The following example demonstrates the configuration of a connection pool that contains a minimum of 5 and a maximum of 15 connections. Connections expire after 10 minutes (600 seconds) and are reset each time a connection is obtained from the pool. The example also demonstrates how to use the Pooling setting to obtain a connection object that is not from a pool. This is useful if your application uses a single long-lived connection to a database.

```
Imports System
Imports System.Data.SqlClient

Namespace Apress.VisualBasicRecipes.Chapter09
    Public Class Recipe09_02

        Public Shared Sub Main()

            ' Obtain a pooled connection.
            Using con As New SqlConnection

                ' Configure the SqlConnection object's connection string.
                con.ConnectionString = "Data Source=.\sqlexpress;Database=" & _
"AdventureWorks;Integrated Security=SSPI;Min Pool Size=5;Max Pool Size=15;" & _
"Connection Reset=True;Connection Lifetime=600;"

                ' Open the database connection.
                con.Open()

                ' Access the database...

                ' Close the database connection.
                ' This returns the connection to the pool for reuse.
                con.Close()

            End Using

            ' Obtain a nonpooled connection.
            Using con As New SqlConnection

                ' Configure the SqlConnection object's connection string.
                con.ConnectionString = "Data Source=.\sqlexpress;Database=" & _
"AdventureWorks;Integrated Security=SSPI;Pooling=False;"

                ' Open the database connection.
```

```
                 con.Open()

                 '  Access the database...

                 '  Close the database connection.
                 con.Close()

             End Using

             '  Wait to continue.
             Console.WriteLine(Environment.NewLine)
             Console.WriteLine("Main method complete.  Press Enter.")
             Console.ReadLine()

         End Sub

     End Class
End Namespace
```

Notes

The ODBC and OLE DB data providers also support connection pooling, but they do not implement connection pooling within managed .NET classes, and you do not configure the pool in the same way as you do for the SQL Server and Oracle data providers. ODBC connection pooling is managed by the ODBC Driver Manager and configured using the ODBC Data Source Administrator tool in the Control Panel. OLE DB connection pooling is managed by the native OLE DB implementation. The most you can do is disable pooling by including the setting `OLE DB Services=-4;` in your connection string.

The SQL Server CE data provider does not support connection pooling, because SQL Server CE supports only a single concurrent connection.

9-3. Create a Database Connection String Programmatically

Problem

You need to programmatically create or modify a syntactically correct connection string by working with its component parts or by parsing a given connection string.

Solution

Use the `System.Data.Common.DbConnectionStringBuilder` class or one of its strongly typed subclasses that form part of an ADO.NET data provider.

How It Works

Connection strings are `String` objects that contain a set of configuration parameters in the form of name-value pairs separated by semicolons. These configuration parameters instruct the ADO.NET infrastructure how to open a connection to the data source you want to access and how to handle the life cycle of connections to that data source. As a developer, you will often simply define your connection string by hand and store it in a configuration file (see recipe 9-4). However, at times, you may want to build a connection string from component elements entered by a user, or you may want to parse an existing connection string into its component parts to allow you to manipulate it programmatically. The DbConnectionStringBuilder class (new to .NET Framework 2.0) and the classes derived from it provide both these capabilities.

DbConnectionStringBuilder is a class used to create connection strings from name-value pairs or to parse connection strings, but it does not enforce any logic on which configuration parameters are valid. Instead, each data provider (except the SQL Server CE data provider) includes a unique implementation derived from DbConnectionStringBuilder that accurately enforces the configuration rules for a connection string of that type. Here is the list of available DbConnectionStringBuilder implementations for standard data providers:

- System.Data.Odbc.OdbcConnectionStringBuilder

- System.Data.OleDb.OleDbConnectionStringBuilder

- System.Data.OracleClient.OracleConnectionStringBuilder

- System.Data.SqlClient.SqlConnectionStringBuilder

Each of these classes exposes properties for getting and setting the possible parameters for a connection string of that type. To parse an existing connection string, pass it as an argument when creating the DbConnectionStringBuilder derived class or set the ConnectionString property. If this string contains a keyword not supported by the type of connection, an ArgumentException exception is thrown.

The Code

The following example demonstrates the use of the SqlConnectionStringBuilder class to parse and construct SQL Server connection strings.

```vbnet
Imports System
Imports System.Data.SqlClient

Namespace Apress.VisualBasicRecipes.Chapter09
    Public Class Recipe09_03

        Public Shared Sub Main()

            ' Configure the SqlConnection object's connection string.
            Dim conString As String = "Data Source=.\sqlexpress;Database=" & ➥
"AdventureWorks;Integrated Security=SSPI;Min Pool Size=5;Max Pool Size=15;" & ➥
"Connection Reset=True;Connection Lifetime=600;"

            ' Parse the SQL Server connection string and display the component
            ' configuration parameters.
            Dim sb1 As New SqlConnectionStringBuilder(conString)

            Console.WriteLine("Parsed SQL Connection String Parameters:")
            Console.WriteLine("  Database Source = " & sb1.DataSource)
            Console.WriteLine("  Database = " & sb1.InitialCatalog)
            Console.WriteLine("  Use Integrated Security = " & ➥
sb1.IntegratedSecurity)
```

```
Console.WriteLine("  Min Pool Size = " & sb1.MinPoolSize)
Console.WriteLine("  Max Pool Size = " & sb1.MaxPoolSize)
Console.WriteLine("  Lifetime = " & sb1.LoadBalanceTimeout)
Console.WriteLine("  Connection Reset = " & sb1.ConnectionReset)

' Build a connection string from component parameters and display it.
Dim sb2 As New SqlConnectionStringBuilder(conString)

sb2.DataSource = ".\sqlexpress"
sb2.InitialCatalog = "AdventureWorks"
sb2.IntegratedSecurity = True
sb2.MinPoolSize = 5
sb2.MaxPoolSize = 15
sb2.LoadBalanceTimeout = 600
sb2.ConnectionReset = True

Console.WriteLine(Environment.NewLine)
Console.WriteLine("Constructed connection string:")
Console.WriteLine(" " & sb2.ConnectionString)

' Wait to continue.
Console.WriteLine(Environment.NewLine)
Console.WriteLine("Main method complete.  Press Enter.")
Console.ReadLine()

    End Sub

End Class
End Namespace
```

9-4. Store a Database Connection String Securely

Problem

You need to store a database connection string securely.

Solution

Store the connection string in an encrypted section of the application's configuration file.

■**Note** Protected configuration—the .NET Framework feature that lets you encrypt configuration information—relies on the key storage facilities of the Data Protection API (DPAPI) to store the secret key used to encrypt the configuration file. This solves the very difficult problem of code-based secret key management. Refer to recipe 11-19 for more information about the DPAPI.

How It Works

Database connection strings often contain secret information, or at the very least information that would be valuable to someone trying to attack your system. As such, you should not store connection strings in plaintext, nor is it sufficient to hard-code them into the application code. Strings embedded in an assembly can easily be retrieved using a disassembler. .NET Framework 2.0 adds a number of classes and capabilities that make storing and retrieving encrypted connection strings in your application's configuration trivial.

Unencrypted connection strings are stored in the machine or application configuration file in the `<connectionStrings>` section in the format shown here:

```
<configuration>
    <connectionStrings>
        <add name="ConnectionString1" connectionString="Data Source=➥
.\sqlexpress;Database=AdventureWorks;Integrated Security=SSPI;Min Pool Size=5; ➥
Max Pool Size=15;Connection Reset=True;Connection Lifetime=600;"
            providerName="System.Data.SqlClient" />
    </connectionStrings>
</configuration>
```

The easiest way to read this connection string is to use the indexed `ConnectionStrings` property of the `System.Configuration.ConfigurationManager` class. Specifying the name of the connection string you want as the property index will return a `System.Configuration.ConnectionStringSettings` object. The `ConnectionStringSettings.ConnectionString` property gets the connection string, and the `ConnectionStringSettings.ProviderName` property gets the provider name that you can use to create a data provider factory (see recipe 9-10). This process will work regardless of whether the connection string has been encrypted or written in plaintext.

To write a connection string to the application's configuration file, you must first obtain a `System.Configuration.Configuration` object, which represents the application's configuration file. The easiest way to do this is by calling the `System.Configuration.ConfigurationManager.OpenExeConfiguration` method. You should then create and configure a new `System.Configuration.ConnectionStringSettings` object to represent the stored connection string. You should provide a name, connection string, and data provider name for storage. Add the `ConnectionStringSettings` object to the `Configuration`'s `ConnectionStringsSection` collection available through the `Configuration.ConnectionStrings` property. Finally, save the updated file by calling the `Configuration.Save` method.

To encrypt the connection strings section of the configuration file, before saving the file, you must configure the `ConnectionStringsSection` collection. To do this, call the `ConnectionStringsSection.SectionInformation.ProtectSection` method and pass it a string containing the name of the protected configuration provider to use: either `RsaProtectedConfigurationProvider` or `DPAPIProtectedConfigurationProvider`. To disable encryption, call the `SectionInformation.Unprotect` method.

■**Note** To use the classes from the `System.Configuration` namespace discussed in this recipe, you must add a reference to the `System.Configuration.dll` assembly when you build your application.

The Code

The following example demonstrates the writing of an encrypted connection string to the application's configuration file and the subsequent reading and use of that connection string.

```vbnet
Imports System
Imports System.Configuration
Imports System.Data.SqlClient

Namespace Apress.VisualBasicRecipes.Chapter09
    Public Class Recipe09_04

        Private Shared Sub WriteEncryptedConnectionStringSection(ByVal name As ➥
String, ByVal constring As String, ByVal provider As String)

            ' Get the configuration file for the current application. Specify
            ' the ConfigurationUserLevel.None argument so that we get the
            ' configuration settings that apply to all users.
            Dim config As Configuration = ➥
ConfigurationManager.OpenExeConfiguration(ConfigurationUserLevel.None)

            ' Get the connectionStrings section from the configuration file.
            Dim section As ConnectionStringsSection = config.ConnectionStrings

            ' If the connectionString section does not exist, create it.
            If section Is Nothing Then
                section = New ConnectionStringsSection
                config.Sections.Add("connectionSettings", section)
            End If

            ' If it is not already encrypted, configure the connectionStrings
            ' section to be encrypted using the standard RSA Protected
            ' Configuration Provider.
            If Not section.SectionInformation.IsProtected Then
                '  Remove this statement to write the connection string in clear
                '  text for the purpose of testing.
                section.SectionInformation.ProtectSection ➥
("RsaProtectedConfigurationProvider")
            End If

            ' Create a new connection string element and add it to the
            ' connection string configuration section.
            Dim cs As New ConnectionStringSettings(name, constring, provider)
            section.ConnectionStrings.Add(cs)

            ' Force the connection string section to be saved.
            section.SectionInformation.ForceSave = True

            ' Save the updated configuration file.
            config.Save(ConfigurationSaveMode.Full)

        End Sub

        Public Shared Sub main()

            ' The connection string information to be written to the
            ' configuration file.
            Dim conName As String = "ConnectionString1"
            Dim conString As String = "Data Source=.\sqlexpress;Database=" & ➥
```

```
"AdventureWorks;Integrated Security=SSPI;Min Pool Size=5;Max Pool Size=5;" & ➡
"Connection Reset=True;Connection Lifetime=600;"
            Dim providerName As String = "System.Data.SqlClient"

            ' Write the new connection string to the application's
            ' configuration file.
            WriteEncryptedConnectionStringSection(conName, conString, providerName)

            ' Read the encrypted connection string settings from the
            ' application's configuration file.
            Dim cs2 As ConnectionStringSettings = ➡
ConfigurationManager.ConnectionStrings("ConnectionString1")

            ' Use the connection string to create a new SQL Server connection.
            Using con As New SqlConnection(cs2.ConnectionString)
                ' Issue database commands/queries...
            End Using

            ' Wait to continue.
            Console.WriteLine(Environment.NewLine)
            Console.WriteLine("Main method complete.  Press Enter.")
            Console.ReadLine()

        End Sub

    End Class
End Namespace
```

Notes

The example in this recipe uses the OpenExeConfiguration method to open the configuration file for the application. It accepts a ConfigurationUserLevel enumerator value, which is set to None to get the configuration settings for all users. If you need to access user-specific settings, you should use the PerUserRoaming or PerUserRoamingAndLocal value. PerUserRoaming refers to the current user's roaming configuration settings. PerUserRoamingAndLocal refers to the user's local settings.

9-5. Execute a SQL Command or Stored Procedure

Problem

You need to execute a SQL command or stored procedure on a database.

Solution

Create a command object appropriate to the type of database you intend to use. Configure the command object by setting its CommandType and CommandText properties. Execute the command using the ExecuteNonQuery, ExecuteReader, or ExecuteScalar method, depending on the type of command and its expected results.

How It Works

All command objects inherit the abstract (MustInherit) System.Data.Common.DbCommand class, which implements the System.Data.IDbCommand interface. The DbCommand class represents a database command, and each data provider includes a unique implementation. Here is the list of the implementations for the five standard data providers:

- System.Data.Odbc.OdbcCommand

- System.Data.OleDb.OleDbCommand

- System.Data.OracleClient.OracleCommand

- System.Data.SqlClient.SqlCommand

- System.Data.SqlServerCe.SqlCeCommand

To execute a command against a database, you must have an open connection (discussed in recipe 9-1) and a properly configured command object appropriate to the type of database you are accessing. You can create command objects directly using a constructor, but a simpler approach is to use the CreateCommand factory method of a connection object. The CreateCommand method returns a command object of the correct type for the data provider and configures it with the appropriate information (such as CommandTimeout and Connection) obtained from the connection you used to create the command. Before executing the command, you must configure the properties described in Table 9-3, which are common to all command implementations.

Table 9-3. *Common Command Object Properties*

Property	Description
CommandText	A String containing the text of the SQL command to execute or the name of a stored procedure. The content of the CommandText property must be compatible with the value you specify in the CommandType property.
CommandTimeout	An Integer that specifies the number of seconds to wait for the command to return before timing out and raising an exception. Defaults to 30 seconds.
CommandType	A value of the System.Data.CommandType enumeration that specifies the type of command represented by the command object. For most data providers, valid values are StoredProcedure, when you want to execute a stored procedure, and Text, when you want to execute a SQL text command. If you are using the OLE DB data provider, you can specify TableDirect when you want to return the entire contents of one or more tables. Refer to the .NET Framework SDK documentation for more details. Defaults to Text.
Connection	A DbConnection instance that provides the connection to the database on which you will execute the command. If you create the command using the IDbConnection.CreateCommand method, this property will be automatically set to the DbConnection instance from which you created the command.
Parameters	A System.Data.DbParameterCollection instance containing the set of parameters to substitute into the command. This property is optional. (See recipe 9-6 for details on how to use parameters.)
Transaction	A System.Data.DbTransaction instance representing the transaction into which to enlist the command. If the connection object used to create this method specified a transaction, this property will be automatically set to that instance. This property is optional. (See the .NET Framework SDK documentation for details about transactions.)

Once you have configured your command object, you can execute it in a number of ways, depending on the nature of the command, the type of data returned by the command, and the format in which you want to process the data.

- To execute a command that does not return database data (such as UPDATE, INSERT, DELETE, or CREATE TABLE), call ExecuteNonQuery. For the UPDATE, INSERT, and DELETE commands, the ExecuteNonQuery method returns an Integer that specifies the number of rows affected by the command. For commands that don't return rows, such as CREATE TABLE, ExecuteNonQuery returns the value −1.

- To execute a command that returns a result set, such as a SELECT statement or stored procedure, use the ExecuteReader method. ExecuteReader returns a DbDataReader instance (discussed in recipe 9-7) through which you have access to the result data. When the ExecuteReader command returns, the connection cannot be used for any other commands while the IDataReader is open. Most data providers also allow you to execute multiple SQL commands in a single call to the ExecuteReader method, as demonstrated in the example in this recipe, which also shows how to access each result set.

- If you want to execute a query but need only the value from the first column of the first row of result data, use the ExecuteScalar method. The value is returned as an Object reference that you must cast to the correct type.

■**Note** The IDbCommand implementations included in the Oracle and SQL data providers implement additional command execution methods. Recipe 9-8 describes how to use the ExecuteXmlReader method provided by the SqlCommand class. Refer to the .NET Framework's SDK documentation, at http://msdn2.microsoft.com/ en-us/library/system.data.oracleclient.oraclecommand(vs.80).aspx, for details on the additional ExecuteOracleNonQuery and ExecuteOracleScalar methods provided by the OracleCommand class.

The Code

The following example demonstrates the use of command objects to update a database record, return records from a query, and obtain a scalar value. Recipe 9-6 covers the use of stored procedures.

```
Imports System
Imports System.Data
Imports System.Data.SqlClient

Namespace Apress.VisualBasicRecipes.Chapter09
    Public Class Recipe09_05

        Public Shared Sub ExecuteNonQueryExample(ByVal con As IDbConnection)

            ' Create and configure a new command.
            Dim com As IDbCommand = con.CreateCommand
            com.CommandType = CommandType.Text
            com.CommandText = "UPDATE HumanResources.Employee SET Title = " & ➥
"'Production Supervisor' WHERE EmployeeID = 24;"

            ' Execute the command and process the result.
            Dim result As Integer = com.ExecuteNonQuery
```

```vb
            If result = 1 Then
                Console.WriteLine("Employee title updated.")
            ElseIf result > 1 Then
                Console.WriteLine("{0} employee titles updated.", result)
            Else
                Console.WriteLine("Employee title not updated.")
            End If

        End Sub

        Public Shared Sub ExecuteReaderExample(ByVal con As IDbConnection)

            ' Create and configure a new command.
            Dim com As IDbCommand = con.CreateCommand
            com.CommandType = CommandType.Text
            com.CommandText = "SET ROWCOUNT 10;SELECT Production.Product.Name," & ➥
"Production.Product.ListPrice FROM Production.Product " & ➥
"ORDER BY Production.Product.ListPrice DESC;SET ROWCOUNT 0;"

            ' Execute the command and process the results.
            Using reader As IDataReader = com.ExecuteReader

                While reader.Read
                    ' Display the product details.
                    Console.WriteLine("  {0} = {1}", ➥
reader("Name"), reader("ListPrice"))
                End While

            End Using

        End Sub

        Public Shared Sub ExecuteScalarExample(ByVal con As IDbConnection)

            ' Create and configure a new command.
            Dim com As IDbCommand = con.CreateCommand
            com.CommandType = CommandType.Text
            com.CommandText = "SELECT COUNT(*) FROM HumanResources.Employee;"

            ' Execute the command and cast the result.
            Dim result As Integer = CInt(com.ExecuteScalar)

            Console.WriteLine("Employee count = " & result)

        End Sub

        Public Shared Sub Main()

            ' Create a new SqlConnection object.
            Using con As New SqlConnection

                ' Configure the SqlConnection object's connection string.
                con.ConnectionString = "Data Source=.\sqlexpress;Database=" & ➥
"AdventureWorks;Integrated Security=SSPI;"
```

```
              ' Open the database connection and execute the example
              ' commands through the connection.
              con.Open()

              ExecuteNonQueryExample(con)
              Console.WriteLine(Environment.NewLine)

              ExecuteReaderExample(con)
              Console.WriteLine(Environment.NewLine)

              ExecuteScalarExample(con)
              Console.WriteLine(Environment.NewLine)

              ' Close the database connection.
              con.Close()

          End Using

          ' Wait to continue.
          Console.WriteLine(Environment.NewLine)
          Console.WriteLine("Main method complete.  Press Enter.")
          Console.ReadLine()

      End Sub

   End Class
End Namespace
```

9-6. Use Parameters in a SQL Command or Stored Procedure

Problem

You need to set the arguments of a stored procedure or use parameters in a SQL query to improve flexibility.

Solution

Create parameter objects appropriate to the type of command object you intend to execute. Configure the parameter objects' data types, values, and directions and add them to the command object's parameter collection using the `IDbCommand.Parameters.Add` method.

How It Works

All command objects support the use of parameters, so you can do the following:

- Set the arguments of stored procedures.
- Receive stored procedure return values.
- Substitute values into SQL queries at runtime.

All parameter objects inherit the abstract (MustInherit) System.Data.Common.DbParameter class, which implements the System.Data.IDataParameter interface. The DbParameter class represents a parameter, and each data provider includes a unique implementation. Here is the list of the implementations for the five standard data providers:

- System.Data.Odbc.OdbcParameter
- System.Data.OleDb.OleDbParameter
- System.Data.OracleClient.OracleParameter
- System.Data.SqlClient.SqlParameter
- System.Data.SqlServerCe.SqlCeParameter

To use parameters with a text command, you must identify where to substitute the parameter's value within the command. The ODBC, OLE DB, and SQL Server CE data providers support positional parameters; the location of each argument is identified by a question mark (?). For example, the following command identifies two locations to be substituted with parameter values.

```
UPDATE HumanResources.Employee SET Title = ? WHERE EmployeeId = ?
```

The SQL Server and Oracle data providers support named parameters, which allow you to identify each parameter location using a name preceded by the at symbol (@). Named parameters are very useful when you need to use the same parameter in multiple locations. Here is the equivalent command using named parameters:

```
UPDATE HumanResources.Employee SET Title = @title WHERE EmployeeId = @id
```

To specify the parameter values to substitute into a command, you must create parameter objects of the correct type and add them to the command object's parameter collection accessible through the Parameters property. You can add named parameters in any order, but you must add positional parameters in the same order they appear in the text command. When you execute your command, the value of each parameter is substituted into the command before it is executed against the data source. You can create parameter objects in the following ways:

- Use the CreateParameter method of the command object.
- Use the Parameters.Add method of the command object.
- Use System.Data.Common.DbProviderFactory.
- Directly create parameter objects using constructors and configure them using constructor arguments or through setting their properties. (This approach ties you to a specific database provider.)

A parameter object's properties describe everything about a parameter that the command object needs to use the parameter object when executing a command against a data source. Table 9-4 describes the properties that you will use most frequently when configuring parameters.

When using parameters to execute stored procedures, you must provide parameter objects to satisfy each argument required by the stored procedure, including both input and output arguments. If a stored procedure has a return value, the parameter to hold the return value (with a Direction property equal to ReturnValue) must be the first parameter added to the parameter collection.

Table 9-4. *Commonly Used Parameter Properties*

Property	Description
DbType	A value of the System.Data.DbType enumeration that specifies the type of data contained in the parameter. Commonly used values include String, Int32, DateTime, and Currency.
Direction	A value from the System.Data.ParameterDirection enumeration that indicates the direction in which the parameter is used to pass data. Valid values are Input, InputOutput, Output, and ReturnValue. The default is Input.
IsNullable	A Boolean that indicates whether the parameter accepts Nothing values. The default is False.
ParameterName	A String containing the name of the parameter.
Value	An Object containing the value of the parameter.

The Code

The following example demonstrates the use of parameters in SQL queries. The ParameterizedCommandExample method demonstrates the use of parameters in a SQL Server UPDATE statement. The ParameterizedCommandExample method's arguments include an open SqlConnection, an Integer, and a String. The values of the two strings are substituted into the UPDATE command using parameters. The StoredProcedureExample method demonstrates the use of parameters to call a stored procedure.

Since not all providers support named parameters, this example specifically uses SQL objects. Instead of using IDbConnection, IDbCommand, and IDataParameter, it uses the specific classes SqlConnection, SqlCommand, and SqlParameter, respectively.

```
Imports System
Imports System.Data
Imports System.Data.SqlClient

Namespace Apress.VisualBasicRecipes.Chapter09
    Public Class Recipe09_06

        Public Shared Sub ParameterizedCommandExample(ByVal con As SqlConnection, ➥
ByVal employeeID As Integer, ByVal title As String)

            ' Create and configure a new command containing 2 named parameters.
            Using com As SqlCommand = con.CreateCommand

                com.CommandType = CommandType.Text
                com.CommandText = "UPDATE HumanResources.Employee SET Title = " & ➥
"@title WHERE EmployeeID = @id;"

                ' Create a SqlParameter object for the title parameter.
                Dim p1 As SqlParameter = com.CreateParameter
                p1.ParameterName = "@title"
                p1.SqlDbType = SqlDbType.VarChar
                p1.Value = title
                com.Parameters.Add(p1)
```

```vb
            ' Use a shorthand syntax to add the id parameter.
            com.Parameters.Add("@id", SqlDbType.Int).Value = employeeID

            ' Execute the command and process the result.
            Dim result As Integer = com.ExecuteNonQuery

            If result = 1 Then
                Console.WriteLine("Employee {0} title updated to {1}", ➥
employeeID, title)
            ElseIf result > 1 Then
                ' Indicates multiple records were affected.
                Console.WriteLine("{0} records for employee {1} had the " & ➥
"title updated to {2}", result, employeeID, title)
            Else
                Console.WriteLine("Employee {0} title not updated.", employeeID)
            End If

        End Using

    End Sub

    Public Shared Sub StoredProcedureExample(ByVal con As SqlConnection, ➥
ByVal managerID As Integer)

        ' Create and configure a new command containing 2 named parameters.
        Using com As SqlCommand = con.CreateCommand

            com.CommandType = CommandType.StoredProcedure
            com.CommandText = "uspGetManagerEmployees"

            ' Create the required SqlParameter object.
            com.Parameters.Add("@ManagerID", SqlDbType.Int).Value = managerID

            ' Execute the command and process the result.
            Dim result As Integer = com.ExecuteNonQuery

            Using reader As IDataReader = com.ExecuteReader
                Console.WriteLine("Employees managed by manager #{0}.", ➥
managerID.ToString)

                While reader.Read
                    ' Display the product details.
                    Console.WriteLine("  {0}, {1} ({2})", reader("LastName"), ➥
reader("FirstName"), reader("employeeID"))
                End While

            End Using

        End Using

    End Sub

    Public Shared Sub Main()
```

```vbnet
    ' Create a new SqlConnection object.
    Using con As New SqlConnection

        ' Configure the SqlConnection object's connection string.
        con.ConnectionString = "Data Source=.\sqlexpress;Database=" & ➡
"AdventureWorks;Integrated Security=SSPI;"

        ' Open the database connection and execute the example
        ' commands through the connection.
        con.Open()

        ParameterizedCommandExample(con, 16, "Production Technician")
        Console.WriteLine(Environment.NewLine)

        StoredProcedureExample(con, 185)
        Console.WriteLine(Environment.NewLine)

        ' Close the database connection.
        con.Close()

    End Using

    ' Wait to continue.
    Console.WriteLine(Environment.NewLine)
    Console.WriteLine("Main method complete.  Press Enter.")
    Console.ReadLine()

End Sub

End Class
End Namespace
```

9-7. Process the Results of a SQL Query Using a Data Reader

Problem

You need to process the data contained in the System.Data.DbDataReader class instance returned when you execute the DbCommand.ExecuteReader method (see recipe 9-5).

Solution

Use the members of the DbDataReader class to move through the rows in the result set sequentially and access the individual data items contained in each row.

How It Works

The DbDataReader class represents a data reader, which is a forward-only, read-only mechanism for accessing the results of a SQL query. This is an abstract (MustInherit) class that implements the

System.Data.IDataReader interface. Each data provider includes a unique DbDataReader implementation. Here is the list of the implementations for the five standard data providers:

- System.Data.Odbc.OdbcDataReader
- System.Data.OleDb.OleDbDataReader
- System.Data.OracleClient.OracleDataReader
- System.Data.SqlClient.SqlDataReader
- System.Data.SqlServerCe.SqlCeDataReader

The IDataReader interface extends the System.Data.IDataRecord interface. Together, these interfaces declare the functionality that provides access to both the data and the structure of the data contained in the result set. Table 9-5 describes some of the commonly used members of the IDataReader and IDataRecord interfaces.

Table 9-5. *Commonly Used Members of Data Reader Classes*

Member	Description
Property	
FieldCount	Gets the number of columns in the current row.
IsClosed	Returns True if the IDataReader is closed; False if it's currently open.
Item	Returns an Object representing the value of the specified column in the current row. Columns can be specified using a zero-based integer index or a string containing the column name. You must cast the returned value to the appropriate type. This is the indexer for the IDataRecord interface.
Method	
GetDataTypeName	Gets the name of the data source data type as a String for a specified column.
GetFieldType	Gets a System.Type instance representing the data type of the value contained in the column specified using a zero-based integer index.
GetName	Gets the name of the column specified by using a zero-based integer index.
GetOrdinal	Gets the zero-based column ordinal for the column with the specified name.
GetSchemaTable	Returns a System.Data.DataTable instance that contains metadata describing the columns contained in the IDataReader.
IsDBNull	Returns True if the value in the specified column contains a data source null value; otherwise, it returns False.
NextResult	If the IDataReader includes multiple result sets because multiple statements were executed, NextResult moves to the next set of results. This method returns True or False, indicating whether or not there are more results. By default, the IDataReader is positioned on the first result set.
Read	Advances the reader to the next record. This method returns True or False, indicating whether or not there are more records. The reader always starts prior to the first record.

In addition to those members listed in Table 9-5, the data reader provides a set of methods for retrieving typed data from the current row. Each of the following methods takes an integer argument that identifies the zero-based index of the column from which the data should be returned: `GetBoolean`, `GetByte`, `GetBytes`, `GetChar`, `GetChars`, `GetDateTime`, `GetDecimal`, `GetDouble`, `GetFloat`, `GetGuid`, `GetInt16`, `GetInt32`, `GetInt64`, `GetString`.

The SQL Server and Oracle data readers also include methods for retrieving data as data source-specific data types. For example, the `SqlDataReader` includes methods such as `GetSqlByte`, `GetSqlDecimal`, and `GetSqlMoney`, and the `OracleDataReader` includes methods such as `GetOracleLob`, `GetOracleNumber`, and `GetOracleMonthSpan`. Refer to the .NET Framework SDK documentation for more details.

When you have finished with a data reader, you should always call its `Close` method so that you can use the database connection again. `IDataReader` extends `System.IDisposable`, meaning that each data reader class implements the `Dispose` method. `Dispose` automatically calls `Close`, making the `Using` statement a very clean and efficient way of using data readers.

The Code

The following example demonstrates the use of a data reader to process the contents of two result sets returned by executing a batch query containing two `SELECT` queries. The first result set is enumerated and displayed to the console. The second result set is inspected for metadata information, which is then displayed.

```vb
Imports System
Imports System.Data
Imports System.Data.SqlClient

Namespace Apress.VisualBasicRecipes.Chapter09
    Public Class Recipe09_07

        Public Shared Sub Main()

            ' Create a new SqlConnection object.
            Using con As New SqlConnection

                ' Configure the SqlConnection object's connection string.
                con.ConnectionString = "Data Source=.\sqlexpress;Database=" & _
"AdventureWorks;Integrated Security=SSPI;"

                ' Create and configure a new command.
                Using com As IDbCommand = con.CreateCommand

                    com.CommandType = CommandType.Text
                    com.CommandText = "SELECT BirthDate,FirstName,LastName " & _
"FROM HumanResources.Employee e INNER JOIN Person.Contact c ON " & _
"e.EmployeeID=c.ContactID ORDER BY BirthDate;SELECT * FROM HumanResources.Employee;"

                    ' Open the database connection and execute the example
                    ' commands through the connection.
                    con.Open()

                    ' Execute the command and obtain a data reader.
                    Using reader As IDataReader = com.ExecuteReader
```

```
                                ' Process the first set of results and display the
                                ' content of the result set.
                                Console.WriteLine("Employee Birthdays (By Age).")

                                While reader.Read
                                    Console.WriteLine("  {0,18:D} - {1} {2}", ➥
reader.GetDateTime(0), reader("FirstName"), reader(2))
                                End While
                                Console.WriteLine(Environment.NewLine)

                                ' Process the second set of results and display details
                                ' about the columns and data types in the result set.
                                reader.NextResult()
                                Console.WriteLine("Employee Table Metadata.")
                                For field As Integer = 0 To reader.FieldCount - 1
                                    Console.WriteLine("  Column Name:{0}  Type:{1}", ➥
reader.GetName(field), reader.GetDataTypeName(field))
                                Next

                    End Using

                        ' Close the database connection.
                        con.Close()

                End Using

            End Using

            ' Wait to continue.
            Console.WriteLine(Environment.NewLine)
            Console.WriteLine("Main method complete.  Press Enter.")
            Console.ReadLine()

        End Sub

    End Class
End Namespace
```

9-8. Obtain an XML Document from a SQL Server Query

Problem

You need to execute a query against a SQL Server 2000 (or later) database and retrieve the results as XML.

Solution

Specify the FOR XML clause in your SQL query to return the results as XML. Execute the command using the ExecuteXmlReader method of the System.Data.SqlClient.SqlCommand class, which returns a System.Xml.XmlReader object through which you can access the returned XML data.

How It Works

SQL Server 2000 (and later versions) provides direct support for XML. You simply need to add the clause FOR XML AUTO to the end of a SQL query to indicate that the results should be returned as XML. By default, the XML representation is not a full XML document. Instead, it simply returns the result of each record in a separate element, with all the fields as attributes. For example, this query:

```
SELECT DepartmentID, [Name] FROM HumanResources.Department FOR XML AUTO
```

returns XML with the following structure:

```
<HumanResources.Department DepartmentID="12" Name="Document Control" />
<HumanResources.Department DepartmentID="1" Name="Engineering" />
<HumanResources.Department DepartmentID="16" Name="Executive" />
```

Alternatively, you can add the ELEMENTS keyword to the end of a query to structure the results using nested elements rather than attributes. For example, this query:

```
SELECT DepartmentID, [Name] FROM HumanResources.Department FOR XML AUTO, ELEMENTS
```

returns XML with the following structure:

```
<HumanResources.Department>
  <DepartmentID>12</DepartmentID>
  <Name>Document Control</Name>
</HumanResources.Department>
<HumanResources.Department>
  <DepartmentID>1</DepartmentID>
  <Name>Engineering</Name>
</HumanResources.Department>
<HumanResources.Department>
  <DepartmentID>16</DepartmentID>
  <Name>Executive</Name>
</HumanResources.Department>
```

■**Tip** You can also fine-tune the format using the FOR XML EXPLICIT syntax. For example, this allows you to convert some fields to attributes and others to elements. Refer to SQL Server Books Online, http://msdn2.microsoft.com/en-us/library/ms189068.aspx, for more information.

When the ExecuteXmlReader command returns, the connection cannot be used for any other commands while the XmlReader is open. You should process the results as quickly as possible, and you must always close the XmlReader. Instead of working with the XmlReader and accessing the data sequentially, you can read the XML data into a System.Xml.XmlDocument. This way, all the data is retrieved into memory, and the database connection can be closed. You can then continue to interact with the XML document. (Chapter 6 contains numerous examples of how to use the XmlReader and XmlDocument classes.)

The Code

The following example demonstrates how to retrieve results as XML using the FOR XML clause and the ExecuteXmlReader method.

```
Imports System
Imports System.Xml
Imports System.Data
Imports System.Data.SqlClient

Namespace Apress.VisualBasicRecipes.Chapter09
    Public Class Recipe09_08

        Public Shared Sub ConnectedExample()

            ' Create a new SqlConnection object.
            Using con As New SqlConnection

                ' Configure the SqlConnection object's connection string.
                con.ConnectionString = "Data Source=.\sqlexpress;Database=" & ➡
"AdventureWorks;Integrated Security=SSPI;"

                ' Create and configure a new command that includes the
                ' FOR XML AUTO clause.
                Using com As SqlCommand = con.CreateCommand

                    com.CommandType = CommandType.Text
                    com.CommandText = "SELECT DepartmentID, [Name], GroupName " & ➡
"FROM HumanResources.Department FOR XML AUTO;"

                    ' Open the database connection.
                    con.Open()

                    ' Execute the command and retrieve an XmlReader to access
                    ' the results.
                    Using reader As XmlReader = com.ExecuteXmlReader
                        While reader.Read
                            Console.WriteLine("Element: " & reader.Name)

                            If reader.HasAttributes Then
                                For i As Integer = 0 To reader.AttributeCount - 1
                                    reader.MoveToAttribute(i)
                                    Console.Write(" {0}: {1}", reader.Name, ➡
reader.Value)
                                Next

                                ' Move the XmlReader back to the element node.
                                reader.MoveToElement()
                                Console.WriteLine(Environment.NewLine)
                            End If
                        End While
                    End Using

                    ' Close the database connection.
                    con.Close()
```

```vb
                End Using
            End Using

    End Sub

    Public Shared Sub DisconnectedExample()

        Dim doc As New XmlDocument

        ' Create a new SqlConnection object.
        Using con As New SqlConnection

            ' Configure the SqlConnection object's connection string.
            con.ConnectionString = "Data Source=.\sqlexpress;Database=" & ➥
"AdventureWorks;Integrated Security=SSPI;"

            ' Create and configure a new command that includes the
            ' FOR XML AUTO clause.
            Using com As SqlCommand = con.CreateCommand

                com.CommandType = CommandType.Text
                com.CommandText = "SELECT DepartmentID, [Name], GroupName " & ➥
"FROM HumanResources.Department FOR XML AUTO;"

                ' Open the database connection.
                con.Open()

                ' Load the XML data into the XmlDocument. Must first create a
                ' root element into which to place each result row element.
                Dim reader As XmlReader = com.ExecuteXmlReader
                doc.LoadXml("<results></results>")

                ' Create an XmlNode from the next XML element read from the
                ' reader.
                Dim newNode As XmlNode = doc.ReadNode(reader)

                While newNode IsNot Nothing
                    doc.DocumentElement.AppendChild(newNode)
                    newNode = doc.ReadNode(reader)
                End While

                ' Close the database connection.
                con.Close()

            End Using
        End Using

        ' Process the disconnected XmlDocument.
        Console.WriteLine(doc.OuterXml)

    End Sub

    Public Shared Sub Main()
```

```
        ConnectedExample()
        Console.WriteLine(Environment.NewLine)

        DisconnectedExample()
        Console.WriteLine(Environment.NewLine)

        ' Wait to continue.
        Console.WriteLine(Environment.NewLine)
        Console.WriteLine("Main method complete.  Press Enter.")
        Console.ReadLine()

    End Sub

  End Class
End Namespace
```

9-9. Perform Asynchronous Database Operations Against SQL Server

Problem

You need to execute a query or command against a SQL Server database as a background task while your application continues with other processing.

Solution

Use the BeginExecuteNonQuery, BeginExecuteReader, or BeginExecuteXmlReader method of the System.Data.SqlClient.SqlCommand class to start the database operation as a background task. These methods all return a System.IAsyncResult object that you can use to determine the operation's status or use thread synchronization to wait for completion. Use the IAsyncResult object and the corresponding EndExecuteNonQuery, EndExecuteReader, or EndExecuteXmlReader method to obtain the result of the operation.

■**Note** Only the SqlCommand class supports the asynchronous operations described in this recipe. The equivalent command classes for the Oracle, SQL Server CE, ODBC, and OLE DB data providers do not provide this functionality.

How It Works

You will usually execute operations against databases synchronously, meaning that the calling code blocks until the operation is complete. Synchronous calls are most common because your code will usually require the result of the operation before it can continue. However, sometimes it's useful to execute a database operation asynchronously, meaning that you start the method in a separate thread and then continue with other operations.

■Note To execute asynchronous operations over a `System.Data.SqlClient.SqlConnection` connection, you must specify the value `Asynchronous Processing=True` in its connection string.

As of .NET Framework 2.0, the `SqlCommand` class implements the asynchronous execution pattern similar to that discussed in recipe 4-2. As with the general asynchronous execution pattern described in recipe 4-2, the arguments of the asynchronous execution methods (`BeginExecuteNonQuery`, `BeginExecuteReader`, and `BeginExecuteXmlReader`) are the same as those of the synchronous variants (`ExecuteNonQuery`, `ExecuteReader`, and `ExecuteXmlReader`), but they take the following two additional arguments to support asynchronous completion:

- A `System.AsyncCallback` delegate instance that references a method that the runtime will call when the asynchronous operation completes. The method is executed in the context of a thread-pool thread. Passing `Nothing` means that no method is called and you must use another completion mechanism (discussed later in this recipe) to determine when the asynchronous operation is complete.

- An `Object` reference that the runtime associates with the asynchronous operation. The asynchronous operation does not use nor have access to this object, but it's available to your code when the operation completes, allowing you to associate useful state information with an asynchronous operation. For example, this object allows you to map results against initiated operations in situations where you initiate many asynchronous operations that use a common callback method to perform completion.

The `EndExecuteNonQuery`, `EndExecuteReader`, and `EndExecuteXmlReader` methods allow you to retrieve the return value of an operation that was executed asynchronously, but you must first determine when it has finished. Here are the four techniques for determining if an asynchronous method has finished:

- *Blocking*: This method stops the execution of the current thread until the asynchronous operation completes execution. In effect, this is much the same as synchronous execution. However, you do have the flexibility to decide exactly when your code enters the blocked state, giving you the opportunity to carry out some additional processing before blocking.

- *Polling*: This method involves repeatedly testing the state of an asynchronous operation to determine if it's complete. This is a very simple technique and is not particularly efficient from a processing perspective. You should avoid tight loops that consume processor time. It's best to put the polling thread to sleep for a period using `Thread.Sleep` between completion tests. Because polling involves maintaining a loop, the actions of the waiting thread are limited, but you can easily update some kind of progress indicator.

- *Waiting*: This method uses an object derived from the `System.Threading.WaitHandle` class to signal when the asynchronous method completes. Waiting is a more efficient version of polling and in addition allows you to wait for multiple asynchronous operations to complete. You can also specify time-out values to allow your waiting thread to fail if the asynchronous operation takes too long, or if you want to periodically update a status indicator.

- *Callback*: This is a method that the runtime calls when an asynchronous operation completes. The calling code does not need to take any steps to determine when the asynchronous operation is complete and is free to continue with other processing. Callbacks provide the greatest flexibility, but also introduce the greatest complexity, especially if you have many concurrently active asynchronous operations that all use the same callback. In such cases, you must use appropriate state objects to match completed methods against those you initiated.

■**Caution** When using the asynchronous capabilities of the SQL Server data provider, you must ensure that your code does not inadvertently dispose of objects that are still being used by other threads. Pay particular attention to SqlConnection and SqlCommand objects.

The Code

Recipe 4-2 provides examples of all of the completion techniques summarized in the preceding list. The following example demonstrates the use of an asynchronous call to execute a stored procedure on a SQL Server database. The code uses a callback to process the returned result set.

```
Imports System
Imports System.Data
Imports System.Threading
Imports System.Data.SqlClient

Namespace Apress.VisualBasicRecipes.Chapter09
    Public Class Recipe09_09

        ' A method to handle asynchronous completion using callbacks.
        Public Shared Sub CallBackHandler(ByVal result As IAsyncResult)

            ' Obtain a reference to the SqlCommand used to initiate the
            ' asynchronous operation.
            Using cmd As SqlCommand = TryCast(result.AsyncState, SqlCommand)
                ' Obtain the result of the stored procedure.
                Using reader As SqlDataReader = cmd.EndExecuteReader(result)

                    ' Display the results of the stored procedure to the console.
                    SyncLock Console.Out
                        Console.WriteLine("Bill of Materials:")
                        Console.WriteLine("ID      Description      Quantity    " & ➥
"ListPrice")

                        While reader.Read
                            ' Display the record details.
                            Console.WriteLine("{0}    {1}    {2}    {3}", ➥
reader("ComponentID"), reader("ComponentDesc"), reader("TotalQuantity"), ➥
reader("ListPrice"))
                        End While

                    End SyncLock

                End Using
            End Using

        End Sub
```

```vb
        Public Shared Sub Main()

            ' Create a new SqlConnection object.
            Using con As New SqlConnection

                ' Configure the SqlConnection object's connection string.
                ' You must specify Asynchronous Processing=True to support
                ' asynchronous operations over the connection.
                con.ConnectionString = "Data Source=.\sqlexpress;Database=" & ➥
"AdventureWorks;Integrated Security=SSPI;Asynchronous Processing=true;"

                ' Create and configure a new command to run a stored procedure.
                Using cmd As SqlCommand = con.CreateCommand

                    cmd.CommandType = CommandType.StoredProcedure
                    cmd.CommandText = "uspGetBillOfMaterials"

                    ' Create the required SqlParameter objects.
                    cmd.Parameters.Add("@StartProductID", SqlDbType.Int).Value = 771
                    cmd.Parameters.Add("@CheckDate", SqlDbType.DateTime).Value = ➥
DateTime.Parse("07/10/2000")

                    ' Open the database connection and execute the command
                    ' asynchronously. Pass the reference to the SqlCommand
                    ' used to initiate the asynchronous operation.
                    con.Open()
                    cmd.BeginExecuteReader(AddressOf CallBackHandler, cmd)
                End Using

                ' Continue with other processing.
                For count As Integer = 1 To 10
                    SyncLock Console.Out
                        Console.WriteLine("{0} : Continue processing...", ➥
DateTime.Now.ToString("HH:mm:ss.ffff"))
                    End SyncLock
                    Thread.Sleep(500)
                Next

                ' Close the database connection.
                con.Close()

                ' Wait to continue.
                Console.WriteLine(Environment.NewLine)
                Console.WriteLine("Main method complete.  Press Enter.")
                Console.ReadLine()

            End Using
        End Sub

    End Class
End Namespace
```

9-10. Write Database-Independent Code

Problem

You need to write code that can be configured to work against any relational database supported by an ADO.NET data provider.

Solution

Program to the ADO.NET data provider base classes that inherit the main interfaces, such as IDbConnection, in the System.Data namespace. Unlike the concrete implementations, such as SqlConnection, the base classes do not rely on features and data types that are unique to specific database implementations. Use factory classes and methods to instantiate the data provider objects you need to use.

How It Works

Using a specific data provider implementation (the SQL Server data provider, for example) simplifies your code and may be appropriate if you need to support only a single type of database or require access to specific features provided by that data provider, such as the asynchronous execution for SQL Server detailed in recipe 9-9. However, if you program your application against a specific data provider implementation, you will need to rewrite and test those sections of your code if you want to use a different data provider at some point in the future.

Table 9-6 contains a summary of the main interfaces you must program against when writing generic ADO.NET code that will work with any relational database's data provider. The table also explains how to create objects of the appropriate type that implement the interface. Many of the recipes in this chapter demonstrate the use of ADO.NET data provider interfaces over specific implementation, as highlighted in the table.

Table 9-6. *Data Provider Interfaces*

Interface	Description	Demonstrated In
IDbConnection	Represents a connection to a relational database. You must program the logic to create a connection object of the appropriate type based on your application's configuration information, or use the DbProviderFactory.CreateConnection factory method (discussed in this recipe).	Recipes 9-1 and 9-5
IDbCommand	Represents a SQL command that is issued to a relational database. You can create IDbCommand objects of the appropriate type using the IDbConnection. CreateCommand or DbProviderFactory. CreateCommand factory method.	Recipes 9-5 and 9-6
IDataParameter	Represents a parameter to an IDbCommand object. You can create IDataParameter objects of the correct type using the IDbCommand.CreateParameter, IDbCommand.Parameters.Add, or DbProviderFactory. CreateParameter factory method.	Recipe 9-6

Table 9-6. *Data Provider Interfaces*

Interface	Description	Demonstrated In
IDataReader	Represents the result set of a database query and provides access to the contained rows and columns. An object of the correct type will be returned when you call the IDbCommand.ExecuteReader method.	Recipes 9-5 and 9-7
IDataAdapter	Represents the set of commands used to fill a System.Data.DataSet from a relational database and to update the database based on changes to the DataSet. You must program the logic to create a data adapter object of the appropriate type based on your application's configuration information, or use the DbProviderFactory.CreateAdapter factory method (discussed in this recipe).	

The System.Data.Common.DbProviderFactory class is new to .NET Framework 2.0 and provides a set of factory methods for creating all types of data provider objects, making it very useful for implementing generic database code. Most important, DbProviderFactory provides a mechanism for obtaining an initial IDbConnection instance, which is the critical starting point to writing generic ADO.NET code. Each of the standard data provider implementations (except the SQL Server CE data provider) includes a unique factory class derived from DbProviderFactory. Here is the list of DbProviderFactory subclasses:

- System.Data.Odbc.OdbcFactory
- System.Data.OleDb.OleDbFactory
- System.Data.OracleClient.OracleClientFactory
- System.Data.SqlClient.SqlClientFactory

Note It's important to understand that there is no common data type for parameters. You are forced to use DbType, and you are responsible for understanding the mapping between your generic provider and your data source.

You can obtain an instance of the appropriate DbProviderFactory subclass using the DbProviderFactories class, which is effectively a factory of factories. Each data provider factory is described by configuration information in the machine.config file similar to that shown here for the SQL Server data adapter. This can be changed or overridden by application-specific configuration information if required.

```
<configuration>
 <system.data>
    <DbProviderFactories>
       <add name="SqlClient Data Provider" invariant="System.Data.SqlClient" ➥
description=".Net Framework Data Provider for SqlServer" type= ➥
"System.Data.SqlClient.SqlClientFactory, System.Data, Version=2.0.0.0, ➥
Culture=neutral, PublicKeyToken=b77a5c561934e089" />
       <add name="Odbc Data Provider" ... />
       <add name="OleDb Data Provider" ... />
       <add name="OracleClient Data Provider" ... />
```

```
            <add name="SQL Server CE Data ... />
          </DbProviderFactories>
       </system.data>
</configuration>
```

You can enumerate the available data provider factories by calling DbProviderFactories. GetFactoryClasses, which returns a System.Data.DataTable containing the following columns:

- Name, which contains a human-readable name for the provider factory. Taken from the name attribute in the configuration information.

- Description, which contains a human-readable description for the provider factory. Taken from the description attribute of the configuration information.

- InvariantName, which contains the unique name used to refer to the data provider factory programmatically. Taken from the invariant attribute of the configuration information.

- AssemblyQualifiedName, which contains the fully qualified name of the DbProviderFactory class for the data provider. Taken from the type attribute of the configuration information.

Normally, you would allow the provider to be selected at install time or the first time the application was run, and then store the settings as user or application configuration data. The most important piece of information is the InvariantName, which you pass to the DbProviderFactories.GetFactory method to obtain the DbProviderFactory implementation you will use to create your IDbConnection instances.

Note Prior to .NET Framework 2.0, it was difficult to write generic ADO.NET code because each data provider implemented its own exception class that did not extend a common base class. In .NET Framework 2.0, the System.Data.Common.DbException class has been added as the base class of all data provider-specific exceptions, making generic handling of database exceptions a reality.

The Code

The following example demonstrates the enumeration of all data providers configured for the local machine and application. It then uses the DbProviderFactories class to instantiate a DbProviderFactory object (actually a SqlClientFactory) from which it creates the appropriate IDbConnection. It then uses the factory methods of the data provider interfaces to create other required objects, resulting in code that is completely generic.

```vbnet
Imports System
Imports System.Data
Imports system.Data.Common

Namespace Apress.VisualBasicRecipes.Chapter09
    Public Class Recipe09_10

        Public Shared Sub Main()

            ' Obtain the list of ADO.NET data providers registered in the
            ' machine and application configuration file.
            Using providers As DataTable = DbProviderFactories.GetFactoryClasses
```

```vb
            ' Enumerate the set of data providers and display details.
            Console.WriteLine("Available ADO.NET Data Providers:")

            For Each prov As DataRow In providers.Rows
                Console.WriteLine(" Name:{0}", prov("Name"))
                Console.WriteLine("    Description:{0}", prov("Description"))
                Console.WriteLine("    Invariant Name:{0}", ➥
prov("InvariantName"))
            Next

        End Using

        ' Obtain the DbProviderFactory for SQL Server. The provider to use
        ' could be selected by the user or read from a configuration file.
        ' In this case, we simply pass the invariant name.
        Dim factory As DbProviderFactory = ➥
DbProviderFactories.GetFactory("System.Data.SqlClient")

        ' Use the DbProviderFactory to create the initial IDbConnection, and
        ' then the data provider interface factory methods for other objects.
        Using con As IDbConnection = factory.CreateConnection

            ' Normally, read the connection string from secure storage.
            ' See recipe 9-2. In this case, use a default value.
            con.ConnectionString = "Data Source=.\sqlexpress;Database=" & ➥
"AdventureWorks;Integrated Security=SSPI;"


            ' Create and configure a new command.
            Using com As IDbCommand = con.CreateCommand

                com.CommandType = CommandType.Text
                com.CommandText = "SET ROWCOUNT 10;SELECT prod.Name, " & ➥
"inv.Quantity FROM Production.Product prod INNER JOIN " & ➥
"Production.ProductInventory inv ON prod.ProductID = inv.ProductID ORDER BY " & ➥
"inv.Quantity DESC;"

                ' Open the connection.
                con.Open()

                ' Execute the command and process the results.
                Using reader As IDataReader = com.ExecuteReader

                    Console.WriteLine(Environment.NewLine)
                    Console.WriteLine("Quantity of the Ten Most Stocked " & ➥
"Products:")

                    While reader.Read
                        ' Display the product details.
                        Console.WriteLine("  {0} = {1}", reader("Name"), ➥
reader("Quantity"))
                    End While

                End Using
```

```
                    '  Close the database connection.
                    con.Close()

                End Using
            End Using

            '  Wait to continue.
            Console.WriteLine(Environment.NewLine)
            Console.WriteLine("Main method complete.  Press Enter.")
            Console.ReadLine()

        End Sub

    End Class
End Namespace
```

9-11. Discover All Instances of SQL Server on Your Network

Problem

You need to obtain a list of all instances of SQL Server 2000 or SQL Server 2005 that are accessible on the network.

Solution

Use the GetDataSources method of the System.Data.Sql.SqlDataSourceEnumerator class.

■Note Your code needs to be granted FullTrust to be able to execute the GetDataSources method.

How It Works

The addition of the new SqlDataSourceEnumerator class in .NET Framework 2.0 makes it easy to enumerate the SQL Server instances accessible on the network. In previous versions of the .NET Framework, you needed to create a COM Interop library to access the SQLDMO library to achieve this.

In .NET Framework 2.0, you simply obtain the singleton SqlDataSourceEnumerator instance via the Shared property SqlDataSourceEnumerator.Instance and call its GetDataSources method. The GetDataSources method returns a System.Data.DataTable that contains a set of System.Data.DataRow objects. Each DataRow represents a single SQL Server instance and contains the following columns:

- ServerName, which contains the name of the server where the SQL Server instance is hosted.
- InstanceName, which contains the name of the SQL Server instance or the empty string if the SQL Server is the default instance.
- IsClustered, which indicates whether the SQL Server instance is part of a cluster.
- Version, which contains the version of the SQL Server instance (8.00.x for SQL Server 2000 or 9.00.x for SQL Server 2005).

■**Caution** It is possible to configure SQL Server 2005 to be invisible to the GetDataSources method by disabling the SQL Server Browser. Therefore, you cannot assume that a SQL Server instance does not exist because you could not discover it.

The Code

The following example demonstrates the use of the SqlDataSourceEnumerator class to discover and display details of all SQL Server instances accessible (and visible) on the network.

```vbnet
Imports System
Imports System.Data
Imports system.Data.Sql

Namespace Apress.VisualBasicRecipes.Chapter09
    Public Class Recipe09_11

        Public Shared Sub Main()

            ' Obtain the DataTable of SQL Server instances.
            Using sqlSources As DataTable = ➡
SqlDataSourceEnumerator.Instance.GetDataSources()

                ' Enumerate the set of SQL Servers and display details.
                Console.WriteLine("Discover SQL Server Instances:")

                For Each source As DataRow In sqlSources.Rows
                    Console.WriteLine(" Server Name:{0}", source("ServerName"))
                    Console.WriteLine(" Instance Name:{0}", source("InstanceName"))
                    Console.WriteLine(" Is Clustered:{0}", source("IsClustered"))
                    Console.WriteLine(" Version:{0}", source("Version"))
                    Console.WriteLine(Environment.NewLine)
                Next

            End Using

            ' Wait to continue.
            Console.WriteLine(Environment.NewLine)
            Console.WriteLine("Main method complete.  Press Enter.")
            Console.ReadLine()

        End Sub

    End Class
End Namespace
```

CHAPTER 10

■■■

Networking and Remoting

The Microsoft .NET Framework includes a full set of classes for network programming. These classes support everything from socket-based programming with Transmission Control Protocol/Internet Protocol (TCP/IP) to downloading files and HTML pages from the Web over Hypertext Transfer Protocol (HTTP). Not only do these networking classes provide you with a rich set of tried-and-tested tools to use in your own distributed applications, they are also the foundation on which two high-level distributed programming models integral to the .NET Framework are built: Remoting and web services.

Although Remoting and web services share many similarities (for example, they both abstract cross-process and cross-machine calls as method invocations on remote objects), they also have fundamental differences. Web services are built using cross-platform standards and are based on the concept of XML messaging. Web services are executed by the ASP.NET runtime, which means they gain ASP.NET features such as output caching. This also means that web services are fundamentally stateless. Overall, web services are best suited when you need to cross platform boundaries (for example, with a Java client calling an ASP.NET web service) or trust boundaries (for example, in business-to-business transactions).

Remoting is a .NET-specific technology for distributed objects and is the successor to Distributed Component Object Model (DCOM). It's ideal for in-house systems in which all applications are built on the .NET platform, such as the backbone of an internal order-processing system. Remoting allows for different types of communication, including leaner binary messages and more efficient TCP/IP connections, which aren't supported by web services. In addition, Remoting is the only technology that supports stateful objects and bidirectional communication through callbacks. It's also the only technology that allows you to send custom .NET objects over the wire.

The recipes in this chapter describe how to do the following:

- Obtain configuration and network statistic information about the network interfaces on a computer, as well as detect when network configuration changes occur (recipes 10-1 and 10-2)

- Download files from File Transfer Protocol (FTP) and HTTP servers (recipes 10-3, 10-4, and 10-6)

- Respond to HTTP requests from within your application (recipe 10-5)

- Send e-mail messages with attachments using Simple Mail Transfer Protocol (SMTP) (recipe 10-7)

- Use the Domain Name System (DNS) to resolve a host name into an Internet Protocol (IP) address (recipe 10-8)

- Ping an IP address to determine whether it is accessible and calculate round-trip communication speeds by sending it an Internet Control Message Protocol (ICMP) Echo request (recipe 10-9)

- Communicate between programs through the direct use of TCP in both synchronous and asynchronous communication models (recipes 10-10 and 10-11)

- Communicate using User Datagram Protocol (UDP) datagrams where the connection-oriented and reliable TCP represents unnecessary overhead (recipe 10-12)

- Write web service proxy classes that read the web service uniform resource locator (URL) from a configuration file, thus avoiding the need to rebuild code if the URL changes (recipe 10-13)

- Provide credentials to allow a proxy class to authenticate against a secured web service (recipe 10-14)

- Call a web service method asynchronously to avoid the calling code blocking and waiting for the web service to respond (recipe 10-15)

- Create remotable objects and register them with the .NET Framework's Remoting infrastructure (recipes 10-16 and 10-17)

- Host a remote object in Internet Information Services (IIS) (recipe 10-18)

- Control the lifetime and versioning of remotable objects (recipes 10-19 and 10-20)

10-1. Obtain Information About the Local Network Interface

Problem

You need to obtain information about the network adapters and network configuration of the local machine.

Solution

Call the Shared method GetAllNetworkInterfaces of the System.Net.NetworkInformation.NetworkInterface class to get an array of objects derived from the abstract class NetworkInterface. Each object represents a network interface available on the local machine. Use the members of each NetworkInterface object to retrieve configuration information and network statistics for that interface.

How It Works

The addition of the System.Net.NetworkInformation namespace in .NET Framework 2.0 provides easy access to information about network configuration and statistics that was not readily available to .NET applications previously.

The primary means of retrieving network information are the properties and methods of the NetworkInterface class. You do not instantiate NetworkInterface objects directly. Instead, you call the Shared method NetworkInterface.GetAllNetworkInterfaces, which returns an array of NetworkInterface objects. Each object represents a single network interface on the local machine. You can then obtain network information and statistics about the interface using the NetworkInterface members described in Table 10-1.

Tip The System.Net.NetworkInformation.IPGlobalProperties class (new to .NET Framework 2.0) also provides access to useful information about the network configuration of the local computer.

Table 10-1. *Members of the NetworkInterface Class*

Member	Description
Properties	
Description	Gets a String that provides a general description of the interface.
Id	Gets a String that contains the unique identifier of the interface.
IsReceiveOnly	Gets a Boolean indicating whether the interface can only receive or can both send and receive data.
Name	Gets a String containing the name of the interface.
NetworkInterfaceType	Gets a value from the System.Net.NetworkInformation. NetworkInterfaceType enumeration that identifies the type of interface. Common values include Ethernet, FastEthernetT, and Loopback.
OperationalStatus	Gets a value from the System.Net.NetworkInformation. OperationalStatus enumeration that identifies the status of the interface. Common values include Down and Up.
Speed	Gets a Long that identifies the speed (in bits per second) of the interface as reported by the adapter, not based on dynamic calculation.
SupportsMulticast	Gets a Boolean indicating whether the interface is enabled to receive multicast packets.
Methods	
GetIPProperties	Returns a System.Net.NetworkInformation.IPInterfaceProperties object that provides access to the TCP/IP configuration information for the interface. Properties of the IPInterfaceProperties object provide access to WINS, DNS, gateway, and IP address configuration.
GetIPv4Statistics	Returns a System.Net.NetworkInformation.IPv4InterfaceStatistics object that provides access to the TCP/IP v4 statistics for the interface. The properties of the IPv4InterfaceStatistics object provide access to information about bytes sent and received, packets sent and received, discarded packets, and packets with errors.
GetPhysicalAddress	Returns a System.Net.NetworkInformation.PhysicalAddress object that provides access to the physical address of the interface. You can obtain the physical address as a Byte array using the method PhysicalAddress.GetAddressBytes or as a String using PhysicalAddress.ToString.
Supports	Returns a Boolean indicating whether the interface supports a specified protocol. You specify the protocol using a value from the System.Net.NetworkInformation.NetworkInterfaceComponent enumeration. Possible values include IPv4 and IPv6.

The NetworkInterface class also provides two other Shared members that you will find useful:

- The Shared property LoopbackInterfaceIndex returns an Integer identifying the index of the loopback interface within the NetworkInterface array returned by GetAllNetworkInterfaces.

- The Shared method GetIsNetworkAvailable returns a Boolean indicating whether any network connection is available; that is, has an OperationalStatus value of Up.

The Code

The following example uses the members of the NetworkInterface class to display information about all the network interfaces on the local machine.

```
Imports System
Imports System.Net.NetworkInformation

Namespace Apress.VisualBasicRecipes.Chapter10
    Public Class Recipe10_01

        Public Shared Sub Main()

            ' Only proceed if there is a network available.
            If NetworkInterface.GetIsNetworkAvailable Then
                ' Get the set of all NetworkInterface objects for the local
                ' machine.
                Dim interfaces As NetworkInterface() = ➥
NetworkInterface.GetAllNetworkInterfaces

                ' Iterate through the interfaces and display information.
                For Each ni As NetworkInterface In interfaces
                    ' Report basic interface information.
                    Console.WriteLine("Interface Name: {0}", ni.Name)
                    Console.WriteLine("    Description: {0}", ni.Description)
                    Console.WriteLine("    ID: {0}", ni.Id)
                    Console.WriteLine("    Type: {0}", ni.NetworkInterfaceType)
                    Console.WriteLine("    Speed: {0}", ni.Speed)
                    Console.WriteLine("    Status: {0}", ni.OperationalStatus)

                    ' Report physical address.
                    Console.WriteLine("    Physical Address: {0}", ➥
ni.GetPhysicalAddress().ToString)

                    ' Report network statistics for the interface.
                    Console.WriteLine("    Bytes Sent: {0}", ➥
ni.GetIPv4Statistics().BytesSent)
                    Console.WriteLine("    Bytes Received: {0}", ➥
ni.GetIPv4Statistics.BytesReceived)

                    ' Report IP configuration.
                    Console.WriteLine("    IP Addresses:")
                    For Each addr As UnicastIPAddressInformation In ➥
ni.GetIPProperties.UnicastAddresses
                        Console.WriteLine("      - {0} (lease expires {1})", ➥
addr.Address, DateTime.Now.AddSeconds(addr.DhcpLeaseLifetime))
                    Next
                    Console.WriteLine(Environment.NewLine)

                Next
            Else
                Console.WriteLine("No network available.")
            End If
```

```
    ' Wait to continue.
    Console.WriteLine(Environment.NewLine)
    Console.WriteLine("Main method complete.  Press Enter.")
    Console.ReadLine()

End Sub

End Class
End Namespace
```

10-2. Detect Changes in Network Connectivity

Problem

You need a mechanism to check whether changes to the network occur during the life of your application.

Solution

Add handlers to the Shared NetworkAddressChanged and NetworkAvailabilityChanged events implemented by the System.Net.NetworkInformation.NetworkChange class. The My object also offers a shared NetworkAvailabilityChanged event. This event is implemented by the My.Computer.Network class, which is part of the Microsoft.VisualBasic.Devices namespace. (See Chapter 5 for more information about the My object.)

How It Works

The NetworkChange class (new to .NET Framework 2.0) provides an easy-to-use mechanism that allows applications to be aware of changes to network addresses and general network availability. This allows your applications to adapt dynamically to the availability and configuration of the network.

The NetworkAvailabilityChanged event fires when a change occurs to general network availability. The NetworkAvailabilityChangedEventHandler delegate is used to handle this event and is passed a NetworkAvailabilityEventArgs object when the event fires. The NetworkAvailabilityEventArgs. IsAvailable property returns a Boolean value indicating whether the network is available or unavailable following the change.

The NetworkAvailabilityChanged event, of the My object, works in the same way as the matching event in the NetworkChange class. The only real difference is in naming. This version of the event uses the NetworkAvailableChangedEventHandler delegate to handle this event, but its event arguments parameter is a NetworkAvailableEventArgs object. Also, the property for retrieving network availability is named IsNetworkAvailable.

The NetworkAddressChanged event fires when the IP address of a network interface changes. An instance of the NetworkAddressChangedEventHandler delegate is required to handle these events. No event-specific arguments are passed to the event handler, which must call NetworkInterface. GetAllNetworkInterfaces (discussed in recipe 10-1) to determine what has changed and to take appropriate action. The My object does not offer an equivalent for this event.

The Code

The following example demonstrates how to use handlers that catch NetworkAddressChanged and NetworkAvailabilityChanged events and then displays status information to the console.

```vb
Imports System
Imports System.Net.NetworkInformation

Namespace Apress.VisualBasicRecipes.Chapter10
    Public Class Recipe10_02

        ' Declare a method to handle NetworkAvailabilityChanged events.
        Private Shared Sub NetworkAvailabilityChanged(ByVal sender As Object, ➥
ByVal e As NetworkAvailabilityEventArgs)

            '  Report whether the network is now available or unavailable.
            If e.IsAvailable Then
                Console.WriteLine("Network Available")
            Else
                Console.WriteLine("Network Unavailable")
            End If

        End Sub

        '  Declare a method to handle NetworkAddressChanged events.
        Private Shared Sub NetwordAddressChanged(ByVal sender As Object, ➥
ByVal e As EventArgs)

            Console.WriteLine("Current IP Addresses:")

            '  Iterate through the interfaces and display information.
            For Each ni As NetworkInterface In ➥
NetworkInterface.GetAllNetworkInterfaces
                For Each addr As UnicastIPAddressInformation In ➥
ni.GetIPProperties.UnicastAddresses
                    Console.WriteLine("        - {0} (lease expires {1})", ➥
addr.Address, DateTime.Now.AddSeconds(addr.DhcpLeaseLifetime))
                Next
            Next

        End Sub

        Public Shared Sub Main()

            '  Add the handlers to the NetworkChange events.
            AddHandler NetworkChange.NetworkAvailabilityChanged, ➥
AddressOf NetworkAvailabilityChanged
            AddHandler NetworkChange.NetworkAddressChanged, ➥
AddressOf NetworkAddressChanged
```

```vbnet
            ' Wait to continue.
            Console.WriteLine(Environment.NewLine)
            Console.WriteLine("Press Enter to stop waiting for network events.")
            Console.ReadLine()

        End Sub

    End Class
End Namespace
```

To use the My object equivalent of the NetworkAvailabilityChanged event, replace the NetworkAvailabilityChanged handler with the following:

```vbnet
' Declare a method to handle NetworkAvailabilityChanged events.
Private Shared Sub NetworkAvailabilityChanged(ByVal sender As Object, ➥
ByVal e As Microsoft.VisualBasic.Devices.NetworkAvailableEventArgs)

    ' Report whether the network is now available or unavailable.
    If e.IsNetworkAvailable Then
        Console.WriteLine("Network Available")
    Else
        Console.WriteLine("Network Unavailable")
    End If

End Sub
```

You also need to replace the current call to AddHandler with this:

```vbnet
AddHandler My.Computer.Network.NetworkAvailabilityChanged, AddressOf ➥
NetworkAvailabilityChanged
```

10-3. Download Data over HTTP or FTP

Problem

You need a quick, simple way to download data from the Internet using HTTP or FTP.

Solution

Use the methods of the System.Net.WebClient class or the DownloadFile method of the My.Computer. Network class. (Refer to Chapter 5 for more information about the My object.)

How It Works

The .NET Framework provides several mechanisms for transferring data over the Internet. One of the easiest approaches is to use the System.Net.WebClient class. WebClient provides many high-level methods that simplify the transfer of data by specifying the source as a uniform resource identifier (URI); Table 10-2 summarizes them. The URI can specify that a file (file://), FTP (ftp://), HTTP ((http://), or HTTPS (https://) scheme be used to download the resource.

Table 10-2. *Data Download Methods of the WebClient Class*

Method	Description
OpenRead	Returns a System.IO.Stream that provides access to the data from a specified URI.
OpenReadAsync	Same as OpenRead, but performs the data transfer using a thread-pool thread so that the calling thread does not block. Add an event handler to the OpenReadCompleted event to receive notification that the operation has completed.
DownloadData	Returns a Byte array that contains the data from a specified URI.
DownloadDataAsync	Same as DownloadData, but performs the data transfer using a thread-pool thread so that the calling thread does not block. Add an event handler to the DownloadDataCompleted event to receive notification that the operation has completed.
DownloadFile	Downloads data from a specified URI and saves it to a specified local file.
DownloadFileAsync	Same as DownloadFile, but performs the data transfer using a thread-pool thread so that the calling thread does not block. Add an event handler to the DownloadFileCompleted event to receive notification that the operation has completed.
DownloadString	Returns a String that contains the data from a specified URI. (This is new to .NET Framework 2.0.)
DownloadStringAsync	Same as DownloadString, but performs the data transfer using a thread-pool thread so that the calling thread does not block. Add an event handler to the DownloadStringCompleted event to receive notification that the operation has completed.

The asynchronous download methods were added in .NET Framework 2.0 and allow you to download data as a background task using a thread from the thread pool (discussed in recipe 4-1). When the download is finished or fails, the thread calls the appropriate OnXXX virtual methods that raise the corresponding event on the WebClient object, which you can handle using a method that matches the signature of the System.ComponentModel.AsyncCompletedEventHandler delegate if you don't want to derive a type from WebClient and override the virtual method. However, the WebClient object can handle only a single concurrent asynchronous download, making a WebClient object suitable for the background download of large single sets of data but not for the download of many files concurrently. (You could, of course, create multiple WebClient objects to handle multiple downloads.) You can cancel the outstanding asynchronous download using the method CancelAsync.

■**Tip** The WebClient class derives from System.ComponentModel.Component, so you can add it to the Visual Studio 2005 Form Designer Toolbox in order to allow you to easily set the properties or define the event handlers in a Windows Forms–based application.

If you need to download only a file, the My object also offers a DownloadFile method. As with the matching method in the WebClient class, you can specify a String or Uri for the address parameter. The My version of the method lets you specify a username and password or a System.Net.ICredential object, while the WebClient version requires you to use the Credentials property of the class, which accepts only an ICredential object. Unlike with the WebClient version, you can also specify a time-out using the connectionTimeout parameter or show a nonmodal progress dialog box (which includes a Cancel button) using the showUI parameter.

The Code

The following example downloads a specified resource from a URI as a string and, since it is an HTML page, parses it for any fully qualified URLs that refer to GIF files. It then downloads each of these files to the local hard drive.

```
Imports System
Imports System.IO
Imports System.Net
Imports System.Text.RegularExpressions

Namespace Apress.VisualBasicRecipes.Chapter10
    Public Class Recipe10_03

        Public Shared Sub Main()

            ' Specify the URI of the resource to parse.
            Dim remoteUri As String = "http://www.apress.com"

            ' Create a WebClient to perform the download.
            Dim client As New WebClient

            Console.WriteLine("Downloading {0}", remoteUri)

            ' Perform the download getting the resource as a string.
            Dim str As String = client.DownloadString(remoteUri)

            ' Use a regular expression to extract all fully qualified
            ' URIs that refer to GIF files.
            Dim matches As MatchCollection = Regex.Matches(str, ➥
"http\S+[^-,;:?]\.gif")

            ' Try to download each referenced GIF file.
            For Each expMatch As Match In matches
                For Each grp As Group In expMatch.Groups
                    ' Determine the local filename.
                    Dim downloadedFile As String = ➥
grp.Value.Substring(grp.Value.LastIndexOf("/") + 1)

                    Try
                        ' Download and store the file.
                        Console.WriteLine("Downloading {0} to file {1}", ➥
grp.Value, downloadedFile)

                        client.DownloadFile(New Uri(grp.Value), downloadedFile)
                    Catch ex As Exception
                        Console.WriteLine("Failed to download {0}", grp.Value)
                    End Try
                Next
            Next
```

```
'   Wait to continue.
Console.WriteLine(Environment.NewLine)
Console.WriteLine("Main method complete.  Press Enter.")
Console.ReadLine()

        End Sub

    End Class
End Namespace
```

Note The regular expression used in the example is simple and is not designed to cater to all possible URL structures. Recipes 2-5 and 2-6 discuss regular expressions.

Changing the code sample to use the `My` version of `DownloadFile` is as simple as replacing `client.DownloadFile` with `My.Computer.Network.DownloadFile`.

Notes

You may also want to upload data to resources specified as a URI, although this technique is not as commonly used as the other approaches discussed in this recipe. The `WebClient` class also provides the following methods for performing uploads that are equivalent to the download methods discussed previously:

- `OpenWrite`
- `OpenWriteAsync`
- `UploadData`
- `UploadDataAsync`
- `UploadFile`
- `UploadFileAsync`
- `UploadString`
- `UploadStringAsync`

Not to be outdone, `My` offers the `UploadFile` method, which is used in a similar fashion to the `DownloadFile` method.

10-4. Download a File and Process It Using a Stream

Problem

You need to retrieve a file from a web site, but you do not want to save it directly to the hard drive, or you do not have permission to do so. Instead, you need to process the data in your application directly in memory.

Solution

Use the `System.Net.WebRequest` class to create your request, the `System.Net.WebResponse` class to retrieve the response from the web server, and some form of reader (typically a `System.IO.StreamReader` for HTML or text data, or a `System.IO.BinaryReader` for a binary file) to parse the response data.

■**Note** You could also use the `OpenRead` method of the `System.Net.WebClient` class to open a stream. However, the additional capabilities of the `WebRequest` and `WebResponse` classes give you more control over the operation of the network request.

How It Works

Opening and downloading a stream of data from the Web using the `WebRequest` and `WebResponse` classes takes the following four basic steps:

1. Use the `Shared` method `Create` of the `WebRequest` class to specify the page you want. This method returns a `WebRequest`-derived object, depending on the type of URI you specify. For example, if you use an HTTP or HTTPS URI (with the scheme http:// or https://), you will create an `HttpWebRequest` instance. If you use a file system URI (with the scheme file://), you will create a `FileWebRequest` instance. In .NET Framework 2.0, you can also use an FTP URL (with the scheme ftp://), which will create an `FtpWebRequest`.

2. Use the `GetResponse` method of the `WebRequest` object to return a `WebResponse` object for the page. If the request times out, a `System.Net.WebException` will be thrown. You can configure the time-out for the network request through the `WebRequest.Timeout` property in milliseconds (the default value is 100000).

3. Create a `StreamReader` or a `BinaryReader` that wraps the stream returned by the `WebResponse.GetResponseStream` method.

4. Perform any steps you need to with the stream contents.

The Code

The following example retrieves and displays a graphic and the HTML content of a web page. Figure 10-1 shows the output.

```
Imports System
Imports System.Net
Imports System.IO
Imports System.Drawing
Imports System.Windows.Forms


'  All designed code is stored in the autogenerated partial
'  class called Recipe10-04.Designer.vb. You can see this
'  file by selecting Show All Files in Solution Explorer.
Public Class Recipe10_04

    Private Sub Recipe10_04_Load(ByVal sender As Object, ➥
ByVal e As System.EventArgs) Handles Me.Load

        Dim picUri As String = "http://www.apress.com/img/img05/Hex_RGB4.jpg"
        Dim htmlUri As String = "http://www.apress.com"
```

```
' Create the requests.
Dim requestPic As WebRequest = WebRequest.Create(picUri)
Dim requestHtml As WebRequest = WebRequest.Create(htmlUri)

' Get the responses. This takes the most significant amount of
' time, particularly if the file is large, because the whole
' response is retrieved.
Dim responsePic As WebResponse = requestPic.GetResponse
Dim responseHtml As WebResponse = requestHtml.GetResponse

' Read the image from the response stream.
picturebox1.image = Image.FromStream(responsePic.GetResponseStream)

' Read the text from the response stream.
Using r As New StreamReader(responseHtml.GetResponseStream)
    textbox1.text = r.ReadToEnd
End Using

    End Sub

End Class
```

Figure 10-1. *Downloading content from the Web using a stream*

10-5. Respond to HTTP Requests from Your Application

Problem

You want your application to be able to respond to HTTP requests programmatically.

Solution

Use the new `System.Net.HttpListener` class provided by .NET Framework 2.0.

■**Note** Your application must be running on Windows XP Service Pack 2 (or later) or Windows 2003 to use the `HttpListener` class; otherwise, a `System.PlatformNotSupportedException` will be thrown when you try to instantiate it. Check the `Boolean` returned by the `Shared` property `HttpListener.IsSupported` to see whether support is available.

How It Works

The `HttpListener` class provides an easy-to-use mechanism through which your programs can accept and respond to HTTP requests. To use the `HttpListener` class, follow these steps:

1. Instantiate an `HttpListener` object.

2. Configure the URI prefixes that the `HttpListener` object will handle using the `Prefixes` property. A URI prefix is a string that represents the starting portion of a URI, which consists of the schema type (such as http or https), a host, and optionally a path and port. The `Prefixes` property returns a `System.Net.HttpListenerPrefixCollection` collection to which you can add URI prefixes using the `Add` method. Each prefix must end with a forward slash (/), or a `System.ArgumentException` is thrown. If you specify a URL prefix that is already being handled, a `System.Net.HttpListenerException` is thrown. When a client makes a request, the request will be handled by the listener configured with the prefix that most closely matches the client's requested URL.

3. Start the `HttpListener` object by calling its `Start` method. You must call `Start` before the `HttpListener` object can accept and process HTTP requests.

4. Accept client requests using the `GetContext` method of the `HttpListener` object. The `GetContext` method will block the calling thread until a request is received and then returns a `System.Net.HttpListenerContext` object. Alternatively, you can use the `BeginGetContext` and `EndGetContext` methods to listen for requests on a thread-pool thread. When a request is received, the `System.AsynchCallback` delegate specified as the argument to the `BeginGetContext` method will be called and passed the `HttpListenerContext` object. Regardless of how it is obtained, the `HttpListenerContext` objects implements three read-only properties critical to the handling of a client request:

   - The `Request` property returns a `System.Net.HttpListenerRequest` through which you can access details of the client's request.

   - The `Response` property returns a `System.Net.HttpListenerResponse` through which you can configure the response to send to the client.

   - The `User` property returns an instance of a type implementing `System.Security.Principal.IPrincipal`, which you can use to obtain identity, authentication, and authorization information about the user associated with the request.

5. Configure the HTTP response through the members of the `HttpListenerResponse` object accessible through the `HttpListenerContext.Response` property.

6. Send the response by calling the `Close` method of the `HttpListenerResponse` object.

7. Once you have finished processing HTTP requests, call `Stop` on the `HttpListener` object to stop accepting more requests and pause the listener. Call `Close` to shut down the `HttpListener` object, which will wait until all outstanding requests have been processed, or call `Abort` to terminate the `HttpListener` object without waiting for requests to be complete.

The Code

The following example demonstrates how to use the HttpListener class to process HTTP requests. The example starts listening for five requests concurrently using the asynchronous BeginGetContext method and handles the response to each request by calling the RequestHandler method. Each time a request is handled, a new call is made to BeginGetContext so that you always have the capacity to handle up to five requests.

To open a connection to the example from your browser, enter the URL http://localhost:19080/ VisualBasicRecipes/ or http://localhost:20000/Recipe10-05/, and you will see the response from the appropriate request handler.

```
Imports System
Imports System.IO
Imports System.Net
Imports System.Text
Imports System.Threading

Namespace Apress.VisualBasicRecipes.Chapter10
    Public Class Recipe10_05

        Public Shared Sub Main()

            ' Quit gracefully if this feature is not supported.
            If Not HttpListener.IsSupported Then
                Console.WriteLine("You must be running this example on Windows" & ➡
" XP SP2, Windows Server 2003, or higher to create an HttpListener.")

                Exit Sub
            End If

            ' Create the HttpListener.
            listener = New HttpListener

            ' Configure the URI prefixes that will map to the HttpListener.
            listener.Prefixes.Add("http://localhost:19080/VisualBasicRecipes/")
            listener.Prefixes.Add("http://localhost:20000/Recipe10-05/")

            ' Start the HttpListener before listening for incoming requests.
            Console.WriteLine("Starting HTTP Server")
            listener.Start()
            Console.WriteLine("HTTP Server started")
            Console.WriteLine(Environment.NewLine)

            ' Create a number of asynchronous request handlers up to
            ' the configurable maximum. Give each a unique identifier.
            For count As Integer = 1 To maxRequestHandlers
                listener.BeginGetContext(AddressOf RequestHandler, ➡
"RequestHandler_" & Interlocked.Increment(requestHandlerID))
            Next

            ' Wait for the user to stop the HttpListener.
            Console.WriteLine("Press Enter to stop the HTTP Server.")
            Console.ReadLine()
```

```vb
    ' Stop accepting new requests.
    listener.Stop()

    ' Terminate the HttpListener without processing current requests.
    listener.Abort()

    ' Wait to continue.
    Console.WriteLine(Environment.NewLine)
    Console.WriteLine("Main method complete.  Press Enter.")
    Console.ReadLine()

End Sub

' Configure the maximum number of requests that can be
' handled concurrently.
Private Shared maxRequestHandlers As Integer = 5

' An integer used to assign each HTTP request handler a unique
' identifier.
Private Shared requestHandlerID As Integer = 0

' The HttpListener is the class that provides all the
' capabilities to receive and process HTTP requests.
Private Shared listener As HttpListener

' A method to asynchronously process individual requests
' and send responses.
Private Shared Sub RequestHandler(ByVal result As IAsyncResult)

    Console.WriteLine("{0}: Activated.", result.AsyncState)

    Try
        ' Obtain the HttpListenerContext for the new request.
        Dim context As HttpListenerContext = listener.EndGetContext(result)

        Console.WriteLine("{0}: Processing HTTP Request from {1} ({2}).", ➥
result.AsyncState, context.Request.UserHostName, context.Request.RemoteEndPoint)

        ' Build the response using a StreamWriter feeding the
        ' Response.OutputStream.
        Dim sw As New StreamWriter(context.Response.OutputStream, ➥
Encoding.UTF8)

        sw.WriteLine("<html>")
        sw.WriteLine("<head>")
        sw.WriteLine("<title>Visual Basic Recipes</title>")
        sw.WriteLine("</head>")
        sw.WriteLine("<body>")
        sw.WriteLine("Recipe 10-5: " & result.AsyncState)
        sw.WriteLine("</body>")
        sw.WriteLine("</html>")
        sw.Flush()
```

```
' Configure the response.
context.Response.ContentType = "text/html"
context.Response.ContentEncoding = Encoding.UTF8

' Close the response to send it to the client.
context.Response.Close()

Console.WriteLine("{0}: Sent HTTP response.", result.AsyncState)
Catch ex As ObjectDisposedException
Console.WriteLine("{0}: HttpListener disposed--shutting down.", ➥
result.AsyncState)
Finally
' Start another handler unless the HttpListener is closing.
If listener.IsListening Then
Console.WriteLine("{0}: Creating new request handler.", ➥
result.AsyncState)

listener.BeginGetContext(AddressOf RequestHandler, ➥
"RequestHandler_" & Interlocked.Increment(requestHandlerID))
End If
End Try

End Sub

End Class
End Namespace
```

10-6. Get an HTML Page from a Site That Requires Authentication

Problem

You need to retrieve a file from a web site, but the web site requires that you provide credentials for the purpose of authentication.

Solution

Use the System.Net.WebRequest and System.Net.WebResponse classes as described in recipe 10-4. Before making the request, configure the WebRequest.Credentials and WebRequest.Certificates properties with the necessary authentication information.

■**Tip** You could also use the System.Net.WebClient class (discussed in recipe 10-3). It also has Credentials and Certificates properties that allow you to associate user credentials with a web request.

How It Works

Some web sites require user authentication information. When connecting through a browser, this information might be submitted transparently (for example, on a local intranet site that uses Integrated

Windows authentication), or the browser might request this information with a login dialog box. When accessing a web page programmatically, your code needs to submit this information. The approach you use depends on the type of authentication implemented by the web site:

- If the web site is using basic or digest authentication, you can transmit a username and password combination by manually creating a new System.Net.NetworkCredential object, which implements the ICredentials and ICredentialsByHost interface, and assigning it to the WebRequest.Credentials property. With digest authentication, you may also supply a domain name.

- If the web site is using Integrated Windows authentication, you can take the same approach and manually create a new System.Net.NetworkCredential object. Alternatively, you can retrieve the current user login information from the System.Net.CredentialCache object using the DefaultCredentials property.

- If the web site requires a client certificate, you can load the certificate from a file using the System.Security.Cryptography.X509Certificates.X509Certificate2 class and add that to the HttpWebRequest.ClientCertificates collection.

- In .NET Framework 2.0, you can load an X.509 certificate from a certificate store using the class System.Security.Cryptography.X509Certificates.X509Store defined in the System.Security.dll assembly. You can either find a certificate in the store programmatically using the X509Store.Certificates.Find method or present users with a Windows dialog box and allow them to select the certificate. To present a dialog box, pass a collection of X.509 certificates contained in an X509Certificate2Collection object to the SelectFromCollection method of the System.Security.Cryptography.X509Certificates.X509Certificate2UI class.

The Code

The following example demonstrates all four of the basic approaches described previously. Note that you need to add a reference to the System.Security.dll assembly.

```
Imports System
Imports System.Net
Imports System.Security.Cryptography.X509Certificates

Namespace Apress.VisualBasicRecipes.Chapter10
    Public Class Recipe10_06

        Public Shared Sub Main()

            ' Create a WebRequest that authenticates the user with a
            ' username and password combination over basic authentication.
            Dim requestA As WebRequest = WebRequest.Create("http:" & _
"//www.somesite.com")
            requestA.Credentials = New NetworkCredential("username", "password")

            ' Create a WebRequest that authenticates the current user
            ' with Integrated Windows authentication.
            Dim requestB As WebRequest = WebRequest.Create("http:" & _
"//www.somesite.com")
            requestB.Credentials = CredentialCache.DefaultCredentials
```

```
            ' Create a WebRequest that authenticates the use with a client
            ' certificate loaded from a file.
            Dim requestC As HttpWebRequest = ➡
DirectCast(WebRequest.Create("http:"//www.somesite.com"), HttpWebRequest)
            Dim cert1 = X509Certificate.CreateFromCertFile("..\..\" & ➡
"TestCertificate.cer")
            requestC.ClientCertificates.Add(cert1)

            ' Create a WebRequest that authenticates the user with a client
            ' certificate loaded from a certificate store. Try to find a
            ' certificate with a specific subject, but if it is not found,
            ' present the user with a dialog so he can select the certificate
            ' to use from his personal store.
            Dim requestD As HttpWebRequest = ➡
DirectCast(WebRequest.Create("http://www.somesite.com"), HttpWebRequest)
            Dim store As New X509Store
            Dim certs As X509Certificate2Collection = ➡
store.Certificates.Find(X509FindType.FindBySubjectName, "Todd Herman", False)

            If certs.Count = 1 Then
                requestD.ClientCertificates.Add(certs(0))
            Else
                certs = X509Certificate2UI.SelectFromCollection( ➡
store.Certificates,"Select Certificate", "Select the certificate to use for " & ➡
"authentication.", X509SelectionFlag.SingleSelection)

                If Not certs.Count = 0 Then
                    requestD.ClientCertificates.Add(certs(0))
                End If
            End If

            ' Now issue the request and process the responses...

        End Sub

    End Class
End Namespace
```

10-7. Send E-mail Using SMTP

Problem

You need to send e-mail using an SMTP server.

Solution

Use the SmtpClient and MailMessage classes in the System.Net.Mail namespace.

Note In version 1.0 and 1.1 of the .NET Framework, you would send SMTP mail using the `SmtpMail` and `MailMessage` classes in the `System.Web.Mail` namespace from the `System.Web.dll` assembly. Both of these classes have been made obsolete. The `SmtpClient` and `MailMessage` classes discussed in this recipe are new to the `System.dll` assembly in .NET Framework 2.0, and both simplify and extend the functionality provided by earlier versions.

How It Works

An instance of the `SmtpClient` class provides the mechanism through which you communicate with the SMTP server. You configure the `SmtpClient` using the properties described in Table 10-3.

Table 10-3. *Properties of the SmtpClient Class*

Property	Description
ClientCertificates	Gets a System.Security.Cryptography.X509Certificates. X509CertificatesCollection to which you add the certificates to use for communicating with the SMTP server (if required).
Credentials	Gets or sets an implementation of the System.Net.ICredentialsByHost interface that represents the credentials to use to gain access to the SMTP server. The CredentialCache and NetworkCredential classes implement the ICredentialsByHost interface. Use NetworkCredential if you want to specify a single set of credentials and CredentialCache if you want to specify more than one.
EnableSsl	Gets or sets a Boolean value that indicates whether the SmtpClient should use Secure Sockets Layer (SSL) to communicate with the SMTP server.
Host	Gets or sets a String containing the host name or IP address of the SMTP server to use to send e-mail.
Port	Gets or sets an Integer value containing the port number to connect to on the SMTP server. The default value is 25.
Timeout	Gets or sets an Integer value containing the time-out in milliseconds when attempting to send e-mail. The default is 100 seconds.
UseDefaultCredentials	Gets or sets a Boolean value indicating whether the default user credentials are used when communicating with the SMTP server. If true, the credentials passed to the SMTP server are automatically obtained from the Shared property CredentialCache.DefaultCredentials.

Tip You can specify default settings for the `SmtpClient` in the `<mailSettings>` section of your machine or application configuration files. Configurable default values include the host, port, username, password, and whether or not the default credentials should be used.

Mail messages are represented by `MailMessage` objects, which you instantiate and then configure using the members summarized in Table 10-4.

■**Tip** For simple mail messages, the `MailMessage` class provides a constructor that allows you to specify the from, to, subject, and body information for the mail message as `String` arguments. This allows you to create a complete mail message in a single call.

Table 10-4. *Properties of the MailMessage Class*

Property	Description
Attachments	Gets or sets a System.Net.Mail.AttachmentCollection containing the set of attachments for the e-mail message. A System.Net.Mail.Attachment object represents each attachment. You can create Attachment objects from files or streams, and you can configure the encoding and content type for each attachment.
Bcc	Gets or sets a System.Net.Mail.MailAddressCollection containing the blind carbon copy addresses for the e-mail message. The MailAddressCollection contains one or more MailAddress objects.
Body	Gets or sets a String value that contains the body text of the e-mail message.
BodyEncoding	Gets or sets a System.Text.Encoding object that specifies the encoding for the body of the e-mail message. The default value is Nothing, resulting in a default encoding of us-ascii, which is equivalent to the Encoding object returned by the Shared property Encoding.ASCII.
CC	Gets or sets a System.Net.Mail.MailAddressCollection containing the carbon copy addresses for the e-mail message. The MailAddressCollection contains one or more MailAddress objects.
From	Gets or sets a System.Net.Mail.MailAddress containing the from address for the e-mail message.
IsBodyHtml	Gets or sets a Boolean value identifying whether the body of the e-mail message contains HTML.
ReplyTo	Gets or sets a System.Net.Mail.MailAddress containing the reply address for the e-mail message.
Subject	Gets or sets a String containing the subject for the e-mail message.
SubjectEncoding	Gets or sets a System.Text.Encoding object that specifies the encoding used to encode the subject of the e-mail subject. The default value is Nothing, resulting in a default encoding of us-ascii, which is equivalent to the Encoding object returned by the Shared property Encoding.ASCII.
To	Gets or sets a System.Net.Mail.MailAddressCollection containing the destination addresses for the e-mail message. The MailAddressCollection contains one or more MailAddress objects.

Once you have configured the `SmtpClient`, you can send your `MailMessage` objects using the `SmtpClient.Send` method, which will cause your code to block until the send operation is completed or fails. Alternatively, you can send mail using a thread from the thread pool by calling the `SendAsync` method. When you call `SendAsync`, your code will be free to continue other processing while the e-mail is sent. Add an event handler to the `SendCompleted` event to receive notification that the asynchronous send has completed.

■**Note** You cannot use SMTP to retrieve e-mail. For this task, you need the Post Office Protocol 3 (POP3) or the Internet Message Access Protocol (IMAP), neither of which is exposed natively in the .NET Framework.

The Code

The following example demonstrates how to use the `SmtpClient` class to send an e-mail message with multiple attachments to a set of recipients whose e-mail addresses are specified as command-line arguments.

```vb
Imports System
Imports System.Net
Imports System.Net.Mail

Namespace Apress.VisualBasicRecipes.Chapter10
    Public Class Recipe10_07

        Public Shared Sub Main(ByVal args As String())

            ' Create and configure the SmtpClient that will send the mail.
            ' Specify the host name of the SMTP server and the port used
            ' to send mail.
            Dim client As New SmtpClient("mail.somecompany.com", 25)

            ' Configure the SmtpClient with the credentials used to connect
            ' to the SMTP server.
            client.Credentials = New NetworkCredential("user@somecompany.com", ➡
"password")

            ' Create the MailMessage to represent the e-mail being sent.
            Using msg As New MailMessage

                ' Configure the e-mail sender and subject.
                msg.From = New MailAddress("author@visual-basic-recipes.com")
                msg.Subject = "Greetings from Visual Basic Recipes"

                ' Configure the e-mail body.
                msg.Body = "This is a message from Recipe 10-07 of Visual " & ➡
"Basic Recipes.  Attached is the source file and the binary for the recipe."

                ' Attach the files to the e-mail message and set their MIME type.
                msg.Attachments.Add(New Attachment("..\..\Recipe10-07.vb", ➡
"text/plain"))
                msg.Attachments.Add(New Attachment("Recipe10-07.exe", ➡
"application/octet-stream"))

                ' Iterate through the set of recipients specified on the
                ' command line. Add all addresses with the correct structure
                ' as recipients.
                For Each arg As String In args
                    ' Create a MailAdress from each value on the command line
                    ' and add it to the set of recipients.
```

```
            Try
                msg.To.Add(New MailAddress(arg))
            Catch ex As FormatException
                ' Proceed to the next specified recipient.
                Console.WriteLine("{0}: Error -- {1}", arg, ex.Message)
                Continue For
            End Try

            ' Send the message.
            client.Send(msg)
        Next

    End Using

    ' Wait to continue.
    Console.WriteLine(Environment.NewLine)
    Console.WriteLine("Main method complete.  Press Enter.")
    Console.ReadLine()

    End Sub

    End Class
End Namespace
```

10-8. Resolve a Host Name to an IP Address

Problem

You want to determine the IP address for a computer based on its fully qualified domain name by performing a DNS query.

Solution

In .NET Framework 2.0, use the method GetHostEntry of the System.Net.Dns class, and pass the computer's fully qualified domain name as a string parameter.

■**Note** In version 1.0 and 1.1 of the .NET Framework, you would use the method GetHostByName of the Dns class. This method is marked as obsolete in .NET Framework 2.0.

How It Works

On the Internet, the human-readable names that refer to computers are mapped to IP addresses, which is what TCP/IP requires in order to communicate between computers. For example, the name www.apress.com might be mapped to the IP address 65.19.150.100. To determine the IP address for a given name, the computer contacts a DNS server. The name or IP address of the DNS server contacted is configured as part of a computer's network configuration.

The entire process of name resolution is transparent if you use the System.Net.Dns class, which allows you to retrieve the IP address for a host name by calling GetHostEntry.

Tip The Dns class also provides the BeginGetHostEntry and EndGetHostEntry methods, which allow you to resolve IP addresses asynchronously. Also, the static method GetHostName returns the computer name of the local machine.

The Code

The following example retrieves the IP addresses of all computers whose fully qualified domain names are specified as command-line arguments.

```
Imports System
Imports System.Net

Namespace Apress.VisualBasicRecipes.Chapter10
    Public Class Recipe10_08

        Public Shared Sub Main(ByVal args As String())

            For Each comp As String In args

                Try
                    ' Retrieve the DNS entry for the specified computer.
                    Dim dnsEntry As IPHostEntry = Dns.GetHostEntry(comp)

                    ' The DNS entry may contain more than one IP address. Iterate
                    ' through them and display each one along with the type of
                    ' address (AddressFamily).
                    For Each address As IPAddress In dnsEntry.AddressList
                        Console.WriteLine("{0} = {1} ({2})", comp, address, ➥
address.AddressFamily)
                    Next
                Catch ex As Exception
                    Console.WriteLine("{0} = Error ({1})", comp, ex.Message)
                End Try
            Next

            ' Wait to continue.
            Console.WriteLine(Environment.NewLine)
            Console.WriteLine("Main method complete.  Press Enter.")
            Console.ReadLine()

        End Sub

    End Class
End Namespace
```

Usage

Running the example with the following command line:

```
recipe10-08 www.apress.com www.microsoft.com localhost somejunk
```

will produce the following output. Notice that multiple IP addresses are returned for some host names.

```
www.apress.com = 65.19.150.101 (InterNetwork)
www.microsoft.com = 207.46.20.60 (InterNetwork)
www.microsoft.com = 207.46.198.30 (InterNetwork)
www.microsoft.com = 207.46.198.60 (InterNetwork)
www.microsoft.com = 207.46.199.30 (InterNetwork)
www.microsoft.com = 207.46.225.60 (InterNetwork)
www.microsoft.com = 207.46.18.30 (InterNetwork)
www.microsoft.com = 207.46.19.30 (InterNetwork)
www.microsoft.com = 207.46.19.60 (InterNetwork)
localhost = 127.0.0.1 (InterNetwork)
somejunk = Error (No such host is known)
```

10-9. Ping an IP Address

Problem

You want to check to see whether a computer is online and accessible and gauge its response time.

Solution

Send a ping message. This message is sent using the ICMP, accessible through the Send method of the System.Net.NetworkInformation.Ping class.

■Note The Ping class is new to .NET Framework 2.0. To send a ping message in earlier versions of the .NET Framework, you had to undertake significant effort to manually create an ICMP request message using raw sockets and lengthy code.

How It Works

A ping message contacts a device at a specific IP address, passing it a test packet, and requests that the remote device respond by echoing back the packet. To gauge the connection latency between two computers, you can measure the time taken for a ping response to be received.

■Caution Many commercial web sites do not respond to ping requests because they represent an unnecessary processing overhead and are often used in denial of service attacks. The firewall that protects the site will usually filter out ping requests before they reach the specified destination. This will cause your ping request to time out.

The Ping class allows you to send ping messages using the Send method. The Send method provides a number of overloads, which allow you to specify the following:

- The IP address or host name of the target computer. You can specify this as a String or a System.Net.IPAddress object.

- The number of milliseconds to wait for a response before the request times out (specified as an Integer). The default is set to 5000.

- A Byte array of up to 65,500 data bytes that is sent with the ping request and that should be returned in the response.
- A System.Net.NetworkInformation.PingOptions object that specifies time-to-live and fragmentation options for the transmission of the ping message.

The Send method will return a System.Net.NetworkInformation.PingReply object. The Status property of the PingReply will contain a value from the System.Net.NetworkInformation.IPStatus enumeration from which you can determine the result of the ping request. The most common values will be Success and TimedOut. If the host name you pass to the Send method cannot be resolved, Send will throw an exception, but you must look at the InnerException to determine the cause of the problem.

The Ping class also provides a SendAsync method that performs the ping request using a thread-pool thread so that the calling thread does not block. When the ping is finished or fails because of a time-out, the thread raises the PingCompleted event on the Ping object, which you can handle using a method that matches the signature of the System.Net.NetworkInformation.PingCompletedEventHandler delegate. However, the Ping object can handle only a single concurrent request; otherwise, it will throw a System.InvalidOperationException.

■**Tip** The Ping class derives from System.ComponentModel.Component, so you can add it to the Visual Studio 2005 Form Designer Toolbox. This will allow you to easily set the properties or define the event handlers in a Windows Forms–based application.

The Code

The following example pings the computers whose domain names or IP addresses are specified as command-line arguments.

```
Imports System
Imports System.Net.NetworkInformation

Namespace Apress.VisualBasicRecipes.Chapter10
    Public Class Recipe10_09

        Public Shared Sub Main(ByVal args As String())

            ' Create an instance of the Ping class.
            Using png As New Ping
                Console.WriteLine("Pinging:")

                For Each comp As String In args

                    Try
                        Console.Write("    {0}...", comp)

                        ' Ping the specified computer with a time-out of 100ms.
                        Dim reply As PingReply = png.Send(comp, 100)
```

```
                        If reply.Status = IPStatus.Success Then
                            Console.WriteLine("Success - IP Address:{0} " & ➥
"Time:{1}ms", reply.Address, reply.RoundtripTime)
                        Else
                            Console.WriteLine(reply.Status.ToString)
                        End If

                    Catch ex As Exception
                        Console.WriteLine("Error ({0})", ex.InnerException.Message)
                    End Try

                Next

            End Using

            '  Wait to continue.
            Console.WriteLine(Environment.NewLine)
            Console.WriteLine("Main method complete.  Press Enter.")
            Console.ReadLine()

        End Sub

    End Class
End Namespace
```

Usage

Running the example with the following command line:

`recipe10-09 www.apress.com www.google.com localhost somejunk`

will produce the following output:

```
Pinging:
    www.apress.com...TimedOut
    www.google.com...Success - IP Address:216.239.59.104 Time:42ms
    localhost...Success - IP Address:127.0.0.1 Time:0ms
    somejunk...Error (No such host is known)
```

10-10. Communicate Using TCP

Problem

You need to send data between two computers on a network using a TCP/IP connection.

Solution

One computer (the server) must begin listening using the System.Net.Sockets.TcpListener class. Another computer (the client) connects to it using the System.Net.Sockets.TcpClient class. Once a connection is established, both computers can communicate using the System.Net.Sockets.NetworkStream class.

How It Works

TCP is a reliable, connection-oriented protocol that allows two computers to communicate over a network. It provides built-in flow control, sequencing, and error handling, which make it reliable and easy to program.

To create a TCP connection, one computer must act as the server and start listening on a specific endpoint. (An *endpoint* is a combination of an IP address and a port number.) The other computer must act as a client and send a connection request to the endpoint on which the first computer is listening. Once the connection is established, the two computers can take turns exchanging messages. The .NET Framework makes this process easy through its stream abstraction. Both computers simply write to and read from a `System.Net.Sockets.NetworkStream` to transmit data.

Note Even though a TCP connection always requires a server and a client, an individual application could be both. For example, in a peer-to-peer application, one thread is dedicated to listening for incoming requests (acting as a server), and another thread is dedicated to initiating outgoing connections (acting as a client). In the examples in this chapter, the client and server are provided as separate applications and are placed in separate subdirectories.

Once a TCP connection is established, the two computers can send any type of data by writing it to the `NetworkStream`. However, it's a good idea to begin designing a networked application by defining the application-level protocol that clients and servers will use to communicate. This protocol includes constants that represent the allowable commands, ensuring that your application code doesn't include hard-coded communication strings.

The Code

In this recipe's example, the defined protocol is basic. You would add more constants depending on the type of application. For example, in a file transfer application, you might include a client message for requesting a file. The server might then respond with an acknowledgment and return file details such as the file size. These constants should be compiled into a separate class library assembly, which must be referenced by both the client and server. Here is the code for the shared protocol:

```
Namespace Apress.VisualBasicRecipes.Chapter10

    Public Class Recipe10_10Shared

        Public Const AcknowledgeOK As String = "OK"
        Public Const AcknowledgeCancel = "Cancel"
        Public Const Disconnect As String = "Bye"
        Public Const RequestConnect As String = "Hello"

    End Class

End Namespace
```

The following code is a template for a basic TCP server. It listens on a fixed port, accepts the first incoming connection using the `TcpListener.AcceptTcpClient` method, and then waits for the client to request a disconnect. At this point, the server could call the `AcceptTcpClient` method again to wait for the next client, but instead it simply shuts down.

```vbnet
Imports System
Imports System.IO
Imports System.Net
Imports System.Net.Sockets

Namespace Apress.VisualBasicRecipes.Chapter10

    Public Class Recipe10_10Server

        Public Shared Sub Main()

            ' Create a new listener on port 8000.
            Dim listener As New TcpListener(IPAddress.Parse("127.0.0.1"), 8000)

            Console.WriteLine("About to initialize port.")
            listener.Start()
            Console.WriteLine("Listening for a connection...")

            Try
                ' Wait for a connection request, and return a TcpClient
                ' initialized for communication.
                Using client As TcpClient = listener.AcceptTcpClient
                    Console.WriteLine("Connection accepted.")

                    ' Retrieve the network stream.
                    Dim stream As NetworkStream = client.GetStream()

                    ' Create a BinaryWriter for writing to the stream.
                    Using w As New BinaryWriter(stream)
                        ' Create a BinaryReader for reading from the stream.
                        Using r As New BinaryReader(stream)

                            If r.ReadString = Recipe10_10Shared.RequestConnect Then
                                w.Write(Recipe10_10Shared.AcknowledgeOK)
                                Console.WriteLine("Connection completed.")

                                While Not r.ReadString = ➥
Recipe10_10Shared.Disconnect
                                End While

                                Console.WriteLine(Environment.NewLine)
                                Console.WriteLine("Disconnect request received.")
                            Else
                                Console.WriteLine("Can't complete connection.")
                            End If

                        End Using
                    End Using
                End Using

                Console.WriteLine("Connection closed.")

            Catch ex As Exception
                Console.WriteLine(ex.ToString)
```

```vbnet
            Finally
                ' Close the underlying socket (stop listening for
                ' new requests).
                listener.Stop()
                Console.WriteLine("Listener stopped.")
            End Try

            ' Wait to continue.
            Console.WriteLine(Environment.NewLine)
            Console.WriteLine("Main method complete.  Press Enter.")
            Console.ReadLine()

        End Sub

    End Class
End Namespace
```

The following code is a template for a basic TCP client. It contacts the server at the specified IP address and port. In this example, the loopback address (127.0.0.1) is used, which always points to the local computer. Keep in mind that a TCP connection requires two ports: one at the server end and one at the client end. However, only the server port to connect to needs to be specified. The outgoing client port can be chosen dynamically at runtime from the available ports, which is what the TcpClient class will do by default.

```vbnet
Imports System
Imports System.IO
Imports System.Net
Imports System.Net.Sockets

Namespace Apress.VisualBasicRecipes.Chapter10
    Public Class Recipe10_10Client

        Public Shared Sub Main()

            Dim client As New TcpClient

            Try

                Console.WriteLine("Attempting to connect to the server on " & ➥
"port 8000.")
                client.Connect(IPAddress.Parse("127.0.0.1"), 8000)
                Console.WriteLine("Connection established.")

                ' Retrieve the network stream.
                Dim stream As NetworkStream = client.GetStream()

                ' Create a BinaryWriter for writing to the stream.
                Using w As New BinaryWriter(stream)
                    ' Create a BinaryReader for reading from the stream.
                    Using r As New BinaryReader(stream)

                        ' Start a dialogue.
                        w.Write(Recipe10_10Shared.RequestConnect)
```

```
                        If r.ReadString = Recipe10_10Shared.AcknowledgeOK Then
                            Console.WriteLine("Connected.")
                            Console.WriteLine("Press Enter to disconnect.")
                            Console.ReadLine()
                            Console.WriteLine("Disconnecting...")
                            w.Write(Recipe10_10Shared.Disconnect)
                        Else
                            Console.WriteLine("Connection not completed.")
                        End If

                    End Using
                End Using

            Catch ex As Exception
                Console.WriteLine(ex.ToString)
            Finally
                '  Close the connection socket.
                client.Close()
                Console.WriteLine("Port closed.")
            End Try

            '  Wait to continue.
            Console.WriteLine(Environment.NewLine)
            Console.WriteLine("Main method complete.  Press Enter.")
            Console.ReadLine()

        End Sub

    End Class
End Namespace
```

Usage

Here's a sample connection transcript on the server side:

```
About to initialize port.
Listening for a connection...
Connection accepted.
Connection completed.

Disconnect request received.
Connection closed.
Listener stopped.
```

And here's a sample connection transcript on the client side:

```
Attempting to connect to the server on port 8000.
Connection established.
Connected.
Press Enter to disconnect.

Disconnecting...
Port closed.
```

10-11. Create a Multithreaded TCP Server That Supports Asynchronous Communications

Problem

You need to handle multiple network requests concurrently or perform a network data transfer as a background task while your program continues with other processing.

Solution

Use the `AcceptTcpClient` method of the `System.Net.Sockets.TcpListener` class to accept connections. Every time a new client connects, start a new thread to handle the connection. Alternatively, use the `TcpListener.BeginAcceptTcpClient` to accept a new client connection on a thread-pool thread using the asynchronous execution pattern (discussed in recipe 4-2).

To start a background task to handle the asynchronous sending of data, you can use the `BeginWrite` method of the `System.Net.Sockets.NetworkStream` class and supply a callback method—each time the callback is triggered, send more data.

How It Works

A single TCP endpoint (IP address and port) can serve multiple connections. In fact, the operating system takes care of most of the work for you. All you need to do is create a worker object on the server that will handle each connection on a separate thread. The `TcpListener.AcceptTcpClient` method returns a `TcpClient` when a connection is established. This should be passed off to a threaded worker object so that the worker can communicate with the remote client.

Alternatively, call the `TcpListener.BeginAcceptTcpClient` method to start an asynchronous operation using a thread-pool thread that waits in the background for a client to connect. `BeginAcceptTcpClient` follows the asynchronous execution pattern, allowing you to wait for the operation to complete or specify a callback that the .NET runtime will call when a client connects. (See recipe 4-2 for details on the options available.) Whichever mechanism you use, once `BeginAcceptTcpClient` has completed, call `EndAcceptTcpClient` to obtain the newly created `TcpClient` object.

To exchange network data asynchronously, you can use the `NetworkStream` class, which includes basic support for asynchronous communication through the `BeginRead` and `BeginWrite` methods. Using these methods, you can send or receive a block of data on one of the threads provided by the thread pool, without blocking your code. When sending data asynchronously, you must send raw binary data (an array of bytes). It's up to you to choose the amount you want to send or receive at a time.

One advantage of this approach when sending files is that the entire content of the file does not have to be held in memory at once. Instead, it is retrieved just before a new block is sent. Another advantage is that the server can abort the transfer operation easily at any time.

The Code

The following example demonstrates various techniques for handling network connections and communications asynchronously. The server (`Recipe10-11Server`) starts a thread-pool thread listening for new connections using the `TcpListener.BeginAcceptTcpClient` method and specifying a callback method to handle the new connections. Every time a client connects to the server, the callback method obtains the new TcpClient object and passes it to a new threaded ClientHandler object to handle client communications.

The ClientHandler object waits for the client to request data and then sends a large amount of data (read from a file) to the client. This data is sent asynchronously, which means ClientHandler could continue to perform other tasks. In this example, it simply monitors the network stream for messages sent from the client. The client reads only a third of the data before sending a disconnect message to the server, which terminates the remainder of the file transfer and drops the client connection.

Here is the code for the shared protocol:

```
Namespace Apress.VisualBasicRecipes.Chapter10

    Public Class Recipe10_11Shared

        Public Const AcknowledgeOK As String = "OK"
        Public Const AcknowledgeCancel = "Cancel"
        Public Const Disconnect As String = "Bye"
        Public Const RequestConnect As String = "Hello"
        Public Const RequestData = "Data"

    End Class

End Namespace
```

Here is the server code:

```
Imports System
Imports System.IO
Imports System.Net
Imports System.Threading
Imports System.Net.Sockets

Namespace Apress.VisualBasicRecipes.Chapter10
    Public Class Recipe10_11Server

        ' A flag used to indicate whether the server is shutting down.
        Private Shared m_Terminate As Boolean
        Public Shared ReadOnly Property Terminate() As Boolean
            Get
                Return m_Terminate
            End Get
        End Property

        ' A variable to track the identity of each client connection.
        Private Shared ClientNumber As Integer = 0

        ' A single TcpListener will accept all incoming client connections.
        Private Shared listener As TcpListener

        Public Shared Sub Main()
```

```
    ' Create a 100KB test file for use in the example. This file will
    ' be sent to clients that connect.
    Using fs As New FileStream("test.bin", FileMode.Create)
        fs.SetLength(100000)
    End Using

    Try
        ' Create a TcpListener that will accept incoming client
        ' connections on port 8000 of the local machine.
        listener = New TcpListener(IPAddress.Parse("127.0.0.1"), 8000)

        Console.WriteLine("Starting TcpListener...")

        ' Start the TcpListener accepting connections.
        m_Terminate = False
        listener.Start()

        ' Begin asynchronously listening for client connections. When a
        ' new connection is established, call the ConnectionHandler method
        ' to process the new connection.
        listener.BeginAcceptTcpClient(AddressOf ConnectionHandler, Nothing)

        ' Keep the server active until the user presses Enter.
        Console.WriteLine("Server awaiting connections.  Press Enter " & ➥
"to stop server.")
        Console.ReadLine()

    Finally
        ' Shut down the TcpListener. This will cause any outstanding
        ' asynchronous requests to stop and throw an exception in
        ' the ConnectionHandler when EndAcceptTcpClient is called.
        ' A more robust termination synchronization may be desired here,
        ' but for the purpose of this example, ClientHandler threads
        ' are all background threads and will terminate automatically when
        ' the main thread terminates. This is suitable for our needs.
        Console.WriteLine("Server stopping...")
        m_Terminate = True
        If listener IsNot Nothing Then listener.Stop()

    End Try

    ' Wait to continue.
    Console.WriteLine(Environment.NewLine)
    Console.WriteLine("Main method complete.  Press Enter.")
    Console.ReadLine()

End Sub

' A method to handle the callback when a connection is established
' from a client. This is a simple way to implement a dispatcher
' but lacks the control and scalability required when implementing
' full-blown asynchronous server applications.
Private Shared Sub ConnectionHandler(ByVal result As IAsyncResult)
```

```vb
                Dim client As TcpClient = Nothing

                ' Always end the asynchronous operation to avoid leaks.
                Try
                    ' Get the TcpClient that represents the new client connection.
                    client = listener.EndAcceptTcpClient(result)
                Catch ex As ObjectDisposedException
                    ' The server is shutting down and the outstanding asynchronous
                    ' request calls the completion method with this exception.
                    ' The exception is thrown when EndAcceptTcpClient is called.
                    ' Do nothing and return.
                    Exit Sub
                End Try

                Console.WriteLine("Dispatcher:  New connection accepted.")

                ' Begin asynchronously listening for the next client
                ' connection.
                listener.BeginAcceptTcpClient(AddressOf ConnectionHandler, Nothing)

                If client IsNot Nothing Then
                    ' Determine the identifier for the new client connection.
                    Interlocked.Increment(ClientNumber)

                    Dim clientName As String = "Client " & ClientNumber.ToString

                    Console.WriteLine("Dispatcher: Creating client handler ({0})", ➡
clientName)

                    ' Create a new ClientHandler to handle this connection.
                    Dim blah As New ClientHandler(client, clientName)

                End If

            End Sub

    End Class

    ' A class that encapsulates the logic to handle a client connection.
    Public Class ClientHandler

        ' The TcpClient that represents the connection to the client.
        Private client As TcpClient

        ' A name that uniquely identifies this ClientHandler.
        Private clientName As String

        ' The amount of data that will be written in one block (2KB).
        Private bufferSize As Integer = 2048

        ' The buffer that holds the data to write.
        Private buffer As Byte()

        ' Used to read data from the local file.
```

```vb
    Private testFile As FileStream

    '  A signal to stop sending data to the client.
    Private stopDataTransfer As Boolean

    Public Sub New(ByVal cli As TcpClient, ByVal cliID As String)

        Me.buffer = New Byte(bufferSize) {}
        Me.client = cli
        Me.clientName = cliID

        '  Create a new background thread to handle the client connection
        '  so that we do not consume a thread-pool thread for a long time
        '  and also so that it will be terminated when the main thread ends.
        Dim newThread As New Thread(AddressOf ProcessConnection)
        newThread.IsBackground = True
        newThread.Start()

    End Sub

    Private Sub ProcessConnection()

        Using client

            '  Create a BinaryReader to receive messages from the client. At
            '  the end of the using block, it will close both the BinaryReader
            '  and the underlying NetworkStream.
            Using reader As New BinaryReader(client.GetStream)

                If reader.ReadString = Recipe10_11Shared.RequestConnect Then

                    '  Create a BinaryWriter to send messages to the client.
                    '  At the end of the using block, it will close both the
                    '  BinaryWriter and the underlying NetworkStream.
                    Using writer As New BinaryWriter(client.GetStream)

                        writer.Write(Recipe10_11Shared.AcknowledgeOK)
                        Console.WriteLine(clientName & ": Connection " & ➥
"established.")

                        Dim message As String = ""

                        While Not message = Recipe10_11Shared.Disconnect

                            Try
                                '  Read the message from the client.
                                message = reader.ReadString
                            Catch ex As Exception
                                '  For the purpose of the example,
                                '  any exception should be taken
                                '  as a client disconnect.
                                message = Recipe10_11Shared.Disconnect
                            End Try
```

```vbnet
                                If message = Recipe10_11Shared.RequestData Then

                                    Console.WriteLine(clientName & ":" & ➡
"Requested data.", "Sending...")

                                    ' The filename could be supplied by the client,
                                    ' but in this example, a test file is
                                    ' hard-coded.
                                    testFile = New FileStream("test.bin", ➡
FileMode.Open, FileAccess.Read)

                                    ' Send the file size. This is how the client
                                    ' knows how much to read.
                                    writer.Write(testFile.Length.ToString)

                                    ' Start an asynchronous send operation.
                                    stopDataTransfer = False
                                    StreamData(Nothing)
                                ElseIf message = Recipe10_11Shared.Disconnect Then
                                    Console.WriteLine(clientName & ": Client " & ➡
"disconnecting...")

                                    stopDataTransfer = True
                                Else
                                    Console.WriteLine(clientName & ": Unknown " & ➡
"command.")

                            End If
                        End While
                    End Using
                Else
                    Console.WriteLine(clientName & ": Could not establish " & ➡
"connection.")
                End If
            End Using
        End Using
        Console.WriteLine(clientName & ": Client connection closed.")

    End Sub

    Private Sub StreamData(ByVal asyncResult As IAsyncResult)

        ' Always complete outstanding asynchronous operations to avoid
        ' leaks.
        If asyncResult IsNot Nothing Then

            Try
                client.GetStream.EndWrite(asyncResult)
            Catch ex As Exception
                ' For the purpose of the example, any exception obtaining
                ' or writing to the network should just terminate the
                ' download.
                testFile.Close()
                Exit Sub
            End Try

        End If
```

```vbnet
                    ' Check if the code has been triggerd to stop.
                    If Not stopDataTransfer And Not Recipe10_11Server.Terminate Then
                        ' Read the next block from the file.
                        Dim bytesRead As Integer = testFile.Read(buffer, 0, buffer.Length)

                        ' If no bytes are read, the stream is at the end of the file.
                        If bytesRead > 0 Then
                            Console.WriteLine(clientName & ": Streaming next block.")

                            ' Write the next block to the network stream.
                            client.GetStream.BeginWrite(buffer, 0, buffer.Length, ➥
AddressOf StreamData, Nothing)
                        Else
                            ' End the operation.
                            Console.WriteLine(clientName & ": File streaming complete.")
                            testFile.Close()
                        End If
                    Else
                        ' Client disconnected.
                        Console.WriteLine(clientName & ": Client disconnected.")
                        testFile.Close()
                    End If

            End Sub
        End Class

End Namespace
```

And here is the client code:

```vbnet
Imports System
Imports System.IO
Imports System.Net
Imports System.Net.Sockets

Namespace Apress.VisualBasicRecipes.Chapter10
    Public Class Recipe10_11Client

        Public Shared Sub Main()

            Using client As New TcpClient

                Console.WriteLine("Attempting to connect to the server on " & ➥
"port 8000.")

                ' Connect to the server.
                client.Connect(IPAddress.Parse("127.0.0.1"), 8000)

                ' Create a BinaryWriter for writing to the stream.
                Using writer As New BinaryWriter(client.GetStream)

                    ' Start a dialogue.
                    writer.Write(Recipe10_11Shared.RequestConnect)
```

```
                        '  Create a BinaryReader for reading from the stream.
                        Using reader As New BinaryReader(client.GetStream)

                            If reader.ReadString = Recipe10_11Shared.AcknowledgeOK Then
                                Console.WriteLine("Connection established.  Press " & ➥
"Enter to download data.")
                                Console.ReadLine()

                                '  Send message requesting data to server.
                                writer.Write(Recipe10_11Shared.RequestData)

                                '  The server should respond with the size of
                                '  the data it will send. Assume it does.
                                Dim fileSize As Integer = ➥
Integer.Parse(reader.ReadString())

                                '  Only get part of the data, then carry out a
                                '  premature disconnect.
                                For i As Integer = 1 To fileSize / 3
                                    Console.Write(client.GetStream.ReadByte)
                                Next

                                Console.WriteLine(Environment.NewLine)
                                Console.WriteLine("Press Enter to disconnect.")
                                Console.ReadLine()
                                Console.WriteLine("Disconnecting...")

                                writer.Write(Recipe10_11Shared.Disconnect)
                            Else
                                Console.WriteLine("Connection not completed.")
                            End If

                        End Using
                    End Using
                End Using

                '  Wait to continue.
                Console.WriteLine(Environment.NewLine)
                Console.WriteLine("Main method complete.  Press Enter.")
                Console.ReadLine()

            End Sub

        End Class
    End Namespace
```

10-12. Communicate Using UDP

Problem

You need to send data between two computers on a network using a UDP stream.

Solution

Use the `System.Net.Sockets.UdpClient` class, and use two threads: one to send data and the other to receive it.

How It Works

UDP is a connectionless protocol that doesn't include any flow control or error checking. Unlike TCP, UDP shouldn't be used where reliable communication is required. However, because of its lower overhead, UDP is often used for "chatty" applications where it is acceptable to lose some messages. For example, imagine you want to create a network in which individual clients send information about the current temperature at their locations to a server every few minutes. You might use UDP in this case because the communication frequency is high and the damage caused by losing a packet is trivial (because the server can just continue to use the last received temperature reading).

The Code

The application shown in the following code uses two threads: one to receive messages and one to send them. The application stops when the user presses the Enter key without any text to send. Notice that UDP applications cannot use the `NetworkStream` abstraction that TCP applications can. Instead, they must convert all data to a stream of bytes using an encoding class, as described in recipe 2-2.

```
Imports System
Imports System.Text
Imports System.Net
Imports System.Net.Sockets
Imports System.Threading

Namespace Apress.VisualBasicRecipes.Chapter10
    Public Class Recipe10_12

        Private Shared localPort As Integer

        Public Shared Sub Main()

            ' Define the endpoint where messages are sent.
            Console.Write("Connect to IP: ")
            Dim ip As String = Console.ReadLine
            Console.Write("Connect to port: ")
            Dim port As Integer = Int32.Parse(Console.ReadLine)

            Dim remoteEndPoint As New IPEndPoint(IPAddress.Parse(ip), port)

            ' Define the local endpoint (where messages are received).
            Console.Write("Local port for listening: ")
            localPort = Int32.Parse(Console.ReadLine)

            ' Create a new thread for receiving incoming messages.
            Dim receiveThread As New Thread(AddressOf ReceiveData)
            receiveThread.IsBackground = True
            receiveThread.Start()
```

```vbnet
Using client As New UdpClient
    Console.WriteLine("Type message and press Enter to send:")

    Try
        Dim txt As String

        Do
            txt = Console.ReadLine

            ' Send the text to the remote client.
            If Not txt.Length = 0 Then
                ' Encode the data to binary using UTF8 encoding.
                Dim data As Byte() = Encoding.UTF8.GetBytes(txt)

                ' Send the text to the remote client.
                client.Send(data, data.Length, remoteEndPoint)
            End If
        Loop While Not txt.Length = 0
    Catch ex As Exception
        Console.WriteLine(ex.ToString)
    Finally
        client.Close()
    End Try
End Using

' Wait to continue.
Console.WriteLine(Environment.NewLine)
Console.WriteLine("Main method complete.  Press Enter.")
Console.ReadLine()

End Sub

Private Shared Sub ReceiveData()

    Using client As New UdpClient(localPort)
        ' This is an endless loop, but since it is running in
        ' a background thread, it will be destroyed when the
        ' application (the main thread) ends.
        While True

            Try
                ' Receive bytes.
                Dim anyIP As New IPEndPoint(IPAddress.Any, 0)
                Dim data As Byte() = client.Receive(anyIP)

                ' Convert bytes to text using UTF8 encoding.
                Dim txt As String = Encoding.UTF8.GetString(data)

                ' Display the retrieved text.
                Console.WriteLine(">> " & txt)

            Catch ex As Exception
                Console.WriteLine(ex.ToString)
            End Try
```

```
                    End While
                End Using

            End Sub

        End Class
    End Namespace
```

Usage

To test this application, load two instances at the same time. On computer A, specify the IP address and port for computer B. On computer B, specify the IP address and port for computer A. You can then send text messages back and forth at will. You can test this application with clients on the local computer using the loopback alias 127.0.0.1, provided you use different listening ports. For example, imagine a situation with two UDP clients, client A and client B. Here's a sample transcript for client A:

```
Connect to IP: 127.0.0.1
Connect to port: 8001
Local port for listening: 8080
Type message and press Enter to send:
Hi there!
```

And here's the corresponding transcript for client B (with the received message):

```
Connect to IP: 127.0.0.1
Connect to port: 8080
Local port for listening: 8001
Type message and press Enter to send:
>> Hi there!
```

10-13. Avoid Hard-Coding the Web Service URL

Problem

You need to use a web service located at a URL that might change after you deploy the client application.

Solution

Use a dynamic URL, which will be retrieved automatically from the client application's configuration file. You can configure a dynamic URL in the URL Behavior section of a Web Reference's properties in Microsoft Visual Studio or by using the /urlkey parameter with the Web Services Description Language tool (wsdl.exe).

How It Works

When you create a web reference in Visual Studio 2005, the automatically generated proxy class is configured to use a dynamic URL as the address of the referenced web service. This allows you to specify an alternate URL without having to recompile your code, which contains the original URL to the service. This alternate URL, used to contact the web service at runtime, is read from your application's configuration file. The automatically generated configuration section looks something like the following, where the value element contains the URL of the web service:

```
<applicationSettings>
    <Recipe10_13.My.MySettings>
        <setting name="Recipe10_13_MyWebService_MyWebService" ➥
serializeAs="String">
            <value>http://localhost/TestWebService/MyWebService.asmx</value>
        </setting>
    </Recipe10_13.My.MySettings>
</applicationSettings>
```

■**Note** The name attribute in the configuration file, as shown in the preceding example, is automatically generated
based on the application name and the web service's namespace and class name, respectively.

In previous releases of Visual Studio, dynamic URLs were not the default behavior. In these
cases, you can configure the setting through the URL Behavior option in the Properties window for
the web reference, as shown in Figure 10-2.

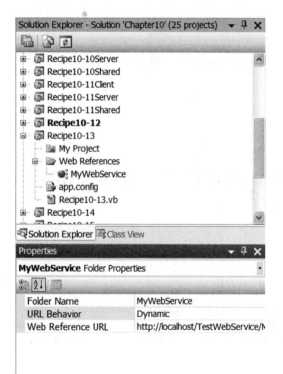

Figure 10-2. *Configuring a dynamic URL for a web service in Visual Studio*

If you use wsdl.exe from the command line to generate your web service proxy class, it uses a
static URL by default. To configure wsdl.exe to use a dynamic URL, you must use the /urlkey parameter
and specify the configuration setting name that the proxy class should read from the configuration file.
Here is an example:

```
wsdl http://localhost/TestWebService/MyWebService.asmx?WSDL /urlkey:MyWebService
```

Whether you're using Visual Studio or wsdl.exe, the automatically generated proxy class is coded in such a way that if the class doesn't find the configuration parameter containing a dynamic URL, it defaults to the static URL that was used during development.

■Tip You can always manually override the URL setting in your code by modifying the `Url` property of the proxy class after you instantiate it.

10-14. Set Authentication Credentials for a Web Service

Problem

You want a web service client to submit logon credentials for IIS authentication.

Solution

Configure the `Credentials` and `Certificates` properties of the web service's proxy class with the appropriate credentials prior to calling a web service method.

How It Works

You can configure web services, like web pages, to require users to authenticate using credentials such as usernames and passwords or X.509 certificates. Unlike web pages, web services have no built-in method for retrieving authentication information from the client, because web services are executed by other applications, not directly by the user. Thus, the application that's interacting with the web service bears the responsibility for submitting any required authentication information.

Similar to the `System.Net.WebRequest` discussed in recipe 10-4, the web service proxy classes automatically generated by Visual Studio and the Web Services Description Language tool (wsdl.exe) implement `Credentials` and `ClientCertificates` properties. Using these properties allows you to associate user credentials with web method calls. The approach you use depends on the type of authentication implemented by the web service:

- If the web service is using basic or digest authentication, you can transmit a username and password combination by manually creating a new `System.Net.NetworkCredential` object and assigning it to the proxy's `Credentials` property. With digest authentication, you may also supply a domain name.

- If the web service is using Integrated Windows authentication, you can take the same approach and manually create a new `NetworkCredential` object. Alternatively, you can configure the proxy to use the current user login information by setting the proxy's `UseDefaultCredentials` property to `True`.

- If the web service requires a client certificate, you can load the certificate from a file using the `System.Security.Cryptography.X509Certificates.X509Certificate2` class and add that to the proxy's `ClientCertificates` collection.

- In .NET Framework 2.0, you can load an X.509 certificate from a certificate store using the class System.Security.Cryptography.X509Certificates.X509Store. You can either find a certificate in the store programmatically using the X509Store.Certificates.Find method or present the users with a Windows dialog box using X509Store.Certificates.Select and allow them to select the certificate.

▓**Tip** To add more than one set of credentials to a proxy, create a CredentialCache object and add multiple NetworkCredential objects to the credential collection using the Add method. Add also allows you to specify the URI, port, and authentication mechanism for which each NetworkCredential object should be used. Then assign the CredentialCache object to the proxy's Credentials property.

The Code

The following web service provides a simple user authentication test. GetIISUser returns the user that was authenticated by IIS. If anonymous access is allowed, the result will be an empty string because no authentication will be performed. If anonymous access is denied, the result will be a string in the form [*DomainName*]\[*UserName*] or [*ComputerName*]\[*UserName*].

```
<WebMethod()> _
Public Function GetIISUser() As String
    Return User.Identity.Name
End Function
```

The following example shows how a client can access a web service that uses basic authentication, Integrated Windows authentication, and X.509 certificate–based authentication:

```
Imports System
Imports System.Net
Imports Recipe10_14.MyWebService
Imports System.Security.Cryptography.X509Certificates

Namespace Apress.VisualBasicRecipes.Chapter10
    Public Class Recipe10_14

        Public Shared Sub Main()

            ' Create a web service proxy. For the purpose of the example, set
            ' the ConnectionGroupName to a unique value to stop the
            ' ServicePointManager reusing the connection in future requests.
            Dim proxy1 As New MyWebService.MyWebService
            proxy1.ConnectionGroupName = "Test1"

            ' Configure the proxy with a set of credentials for use over basic
            ' authentication.
            Dim cache As New CredentialCache
            cache.Add(New Uri(proxy1.Url), "Basic", New NetworkCredential("user", ➥
"password"))
            proxy1.Credentials = cache

            ' Try to call the GetIISUser web method.
```

```
        Try
            Console.WriteLine("Authenticated user = {0}", proxy1.GetIISUser)
        Catch ex As WebException
            Console.WriteLine("Basic authentication failed")
        End Try

        ' Create a proxy that authenticates the current user
        ' with Integrated Windows authentication.
        Dim proxy2 As New MyWebService.MyWebService
        proxy2.ConnectionGroupName = "Test2"
        proxy2.Credentials = Nothing
        proxy2.UseDefaultCredentials = True

        Try
            Console.WriteLine("Authenticated user = {0}", proxy2.GetIISUser)
        Catch ex As WebException
            Console.WriteLine("Integrated Windows authentication failed")
        End Try

        ' Create a proxy that authenticates the user with a client
        ' certificate loaded from a file.
        Dim proxy3 As New MyWebService.MyWebService
        proxy3.ConnectionGroupName = "Test3"
        Dim cert1 As X509Certificate = ➡
X509Certificate.CreateFromCertFile("..\..\TestCertificate.cer")
        proxy3.ClientCertificates.Add(cert1)

        Try
            Console.WriteLine("Authenticated user = {0}", proxy3.GetIISUser)
        Catch ex As WebException
            Console.WriteLine("Certificate authentication failed")
        End Try

        ' Wait to continue.
        Console.WriteLine(Environment.NewLine)
        Console.WriteLine("Main method complete.  Press Enter")
        Console.ReadLine()

    End Sub

  End Class
End Namespace
```

Notes

When you want to use the credentials of the currently logged-on user, you should set the
UseDefaultCredentials property to True. This is demonstrated in the preceding example. However,
if you do this while Credentials is set to something other than DefaultCredentials or Nothing, an
InvalidOperationException will be thrown.

10-15. Call a Web Method Asynchronously

Problem

You need to invoke a web method on another thread so that your program can continue with other tasks (such as updating the user interface) while waiting for the response.

Solution

Use the proxy class's built-in asynchronous method and asynchronous completion event, which are automatically generated for every web method supported by the web service. The method is named XXXAsync, and the completion event is named XXXCompleted, where XXX is the name of the original, synchronous method.

How It Works

The automatically generated proxy class has the features you need to call any web method asynchronously. For example, consider the Wait web method shown in the following code, which pauses for a random number of seconds between a lower and an upper value:

```
'  Returns the specified string after a random delay
'  between a lower and upper bound.
<WebMethod()> _
Public Function Echo(ByVal str As String, ByVal lower As Integer, ➡
ByVal upper As Integer) As String

    '  Sleep for a random period of time between the specified
    '  lower and upper boundaries.
    Dim rand As New Random
    System.Threading.Thread.Sleep(rand.Next(lower, upper))

    '  Echo back the specified string.
    Return str

End Function
```

The proxy class generated for the web service that exposes the Echo method will also implement a method named EchoAsync, an event named EchoCompleted, an event argument data class named EchoCompletedEventArgs, and a delegate named EchoCompletedEventHandler. Together, these program elements allow you to call the Echo web method asynchronously and handle the result—regardless of whether the call fails or succeeds. All web methods follow the same model; only the names are changed. Each of these elements is described here:

- The EchoAsync method takes the same arguments as the Echo method, with the option of providing an additional Object argument that can be used for general state information. This extra state is passed to the EchoCompletedEventHandler (described next) when the asynchronous call completes and is often used to match completed events to original calls. When you call EchoAsync, the .NET Framework returns control immediately to the calling code so that it can continue processing, but executes the method on a thread from the thread pool.

- When the EchoAsync method completes, the proxy raises the EchoCompleted event using a thread from the thread pool. To handle these events, you must add an EchoCompletedEventHandler delegate to the event. The EchoCompletedEventHandler delegate declares two arguments. The first argument is an object that is a reference to the sender (or source) of the event, which is the proxy object. The second argument is an EchoCompletedEventArgs object, which is discussed next.

- The EchoCompletedEventArgs class provides access to the result of the asynchronous operation. The Cancelled property indicates whether the operation was canceled by a call to the CancelAsynch method, which was included in the proxy class. The Error property contains any exception that was raised that caused the asynchronous operation to fail, UserState contains the user state Object (if any) that was passed to the EchoAsync method, and Result is of the same type returned by Echo and contains the result of the asynchronous call if it succeeded.

Note The asynchronous model described in this recipe is new to the web service proxy code generated by Visual Studio 2005. In earlier versions of Visual Studio and in the code generated by the Web Services Description Language tool (wsdl.exe), a different asynchronous model is implemented. Instead of an XXXAsync method and the use of events, the proxy would have BeginXXX and EndXXX methods. This old approach had the benefit of providing you with System.Threading.WaitHandle objects for the asynchronous operations, which you could use for multithreaded synchronization.

The Code

The following example demonstrates how to call a web method named Echo asynchronously using the automatically generated EchoAsync method of the proxy. The EchoAsync method is called three times, and the second instance is canceled before it has a chance to complete. The EchoCompletedHandler method processes the results of the three asynchronous method calls.

```
Imports System
Imports System.Threading
Imports Recipe10_15.MyWebService

Namespace Apress.VisualBasicRecipes.Chapter10
    Public Class Recipe10_15

        Public Shared Sub Main()

            ' Create a proxy through which to execute the methods of
            ' the web service.
            Dim proxy As New MyWebService.MyWebService

            ' Add an event handler to the EchoCompleted event.
            AddHandler proxy.EchoCompleted, AddressOf EchoCompletedHandler

            ' Call the Echo three times asynchronously.
            proxy.EchoAsync("Echo String 1", 7000, 10000, "Test1")
            proxy.EchoAsync("Echo String 2", 5000, 10000, "Test2")
            proxy.EchoAsync("Echo String 3", 1000, 10000, "Test3")

            ' Quickly cancel the second asynchronous operation.
            proxy.CancelAsync("Test2")
```

```
                    '  Wait to continue.
                    Console.WriteLine(Environment.NewLine)
                    Console.WriteLine("Main method complete.  Press Enter.")
                    Console.ReadLine()

            End Sub

            '  A method to handle asynchronous Echo completion events.
            Private Shared Sub EchoCompletedHandler(ByVal sender As Object, ➥
        ByVal args As EchoCompletedEventArgs)

                If args.Error IsNot Nothing Then
                    Console.WriteLine("{0}: {1}", args.UserState, args.Error.Message)
                ElseIf args.Cancelled Then
                    Console.WriteLine("{0}: operation cancelled before completion.", ➥
        args.UserState)
                Else
                    Console.WriteLine("{0}: Succeeded, echoed string = {1}.", ➥
        args.UserState, args.Result)
                End If

            End Sub

        End Class
    End Namespace
```

10-16. Make an Object Remotable

Problem

You need to create a class that can be accessed from another application or another computer on the network. However, you don't need cross-platform compatibility, and you want optimum performance.

Solution

Make the class remotable by deriving from System.MarshalByRefObject, and create a component host that registers the class with the .NET Remoting infrastructure.

How It Works

Remoting allows you to make an object accessible across process and machine boundaries. While web services are ideal when you need to share functionality across platforms or trust boundaries, Remoting is the best-performing choice for a closed system in which all components are built on .NET and the Windows operating system. To use .NET Remoting, you need the following ingredients, each of which must reside in a separate assembly:

- *A remotable object*: This object can be accessed from other applications and computers and must derive from the System.MarshalByRefObject.

- *A component host*: This application registers the remotable type with the .NET Remoting infrastructure using the RemotingConfiguration class from the System.Runtime.Remoting namespace. You can use any type of long-running .NET Framework application for a component host (including Windows Forms–based applications, Windows services, console applications, and even IIS). As long as the component host is running, remote clients can create or connect to existing instances of the remotable object. The component host never interacts with the remotable objects directly. All it does is register the appropriate types with the .NET Remoting infrastructure. After this point, clients can create object instances, and the server application can continue with other tasks. However, when the component host is closed, any remotable objects will be destroyed, and no more hosted objects can be created.

- *A client application*: This application can create or connect to instances of the remotable class in the component host process and interact with them. The client uses the RemotingConfiguration class to register the types it wants to access remotely. The client application uses the RemotingConfiguration.Configure method to register the remote objects it wants to call. Once this step is taken, the client can create the object exactly as it would create a local object. However, the object will actually be created in the component host.

Figure 10-3 shows how these three parts interact. This example has only one client. However, it's also possible for multiple clients to create instances of the remotable class at the same time. In this case, you can configure the Remoting host, whether each client has its own remotable object instance or all clients share a single instance.

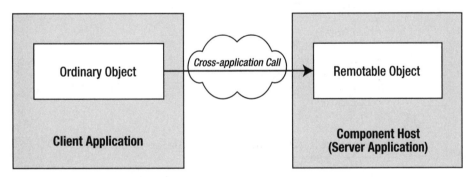

Figure 10-3. *Using a remotable class*

Note Ideally, the remote object won't retain any state. This characteristic allows you to use single-call activation, in which object instances are created at the beginning of each method call and released at the end, much like a web service. This ensures your objects consume the fewest possible server resources and saves you from the added complexity of implementing a lease policy to configure object lifetime.

The Code

The following example demonstrates the declaration of a remotable class that reads data from the Person.Contact table of the AdventureWorks database and returns a System.Data.DataTable. Notice that the only Remoting-specific code is the derivation of the class from the System.MarshalByRef class.

```vb
Imports System
Imports System.Data
Imports System.Data.SqlClient

Namespace Apress.VisualBasicRecipes.Chapter10

    ' Define a class that extends MarshalByRefObject, making it remotable.
    Public Class Recipe10_16
        Inherits MarshalByRefObject

        Private Shared connectionString As String = "Data Source=.\sqlexpress;" & ➥
"Initial Catalog=AdventureWorks;Integrated Security=SSPI;"

        ' The DataTable returned by this method is serializable, meaning that the
        ' data will be physically passed back to the caller across the network.
        Public Function GetContacts() As DataTable

            Dim SQL As String = "SELECT * FROM Person.Contact;"

            ' Create ADO.NET objects to execute the DB query.
            Using con As New SqlConnection(connectionString)
                Using com As New SqlCommand(SQL, con)
                    Dim adapter As New SqlDataAdapter(com)
                    Dim ds As New DataSet

                    ' Execute the command.
                    Try
                        con.Open()
                        adapter.Fill(ds, "Contacts")
                    Catch ex As Exception
                        Console.WriteLine(ex.ToString)
                    Finally
                        con.Close()
                    End Try

                    ' Return the first DataTable in the DataSet to the caller.
                    Return ds.Tables(0)

                End Using
            End Using

        End Function

        ' This method allows you to verify that the object is running remotely.
        Public Function GetHostLocation() As String
            Return AppDomain.CurrentDomain.FriendlyName
        End Function

    End Class
End Namespace
```

Usage

To use the `Recipe10_16` class remotely, you must host it and then create a client that uses the remote object. Here is the code for a simple console component host:

```vb
Imports System
Imports System.Runtime.Remoting

Namespace Apress.VisualBasicRecipes.Chapter10
    Public Class Recipe10_16Host

        Public Shared Sub Main()

            ' Register the remotable classes defined in the specified
            ' configuration file.
            RemotingConfiguration.Configure("Recipe10-16Host.exe.config", False)

            ' As long as this application is running, the registered remote
            ' objects will be accessible.
            Console.Clear()
            Console.WriteLine("Press Enter to shut down the host.")
            Console.ReadLine()

        End Sub

    End Class
End Namespace
```

The component host uses a new section in the standard configuration file (in this case Recipe10-16 Host.exe.config) to configure the classes it will support, the ports it will support for network communication, and the URI that the client will use to access the object. The host application must have a reference to the assembly, the Recipe10-16 assembly in this case, containing the implementation of the remote object class. The configuration file also configures the remote object to use single-call activation, meaning that a new object is created for each client call.

```xml
<?xml version="1.0" encoding="utf-8" ?>
<configuration>
  <system.runtime.remoting>
    <application>

      <!-- Define the remotable types. -->
      <service>
        <wellknown
            mode = "SingleCall"
            type = "Apress.VisualBasicRecipes.Chapter10.Recipe10_16, Recipe10-16"
            objectUri = "Recipe10-16.rem" />
      </service>

      <!-- Define the protocol used for network access.
          You can use tcp or http channels. -->
      <channels>
        <channel ref="tcp" port="19080" />
      </channels>
```

```
    </application>
  </system.runtime.remoting>
</configuration>
```

The following sample code shows a simple client that uses the remote object created earlier. Notice that in this example, the configuration of the Remoting infrastructure is performed program-matically instead of using the configuration file. You should avoid such an approach when using shared configuration values because using configuration files provides more flexibility. If you did use a configuration file for the client, it would look similar to this:

```
<?xml version="1.0" encoding="utf-8" ?>
<configuration>
  <system.runtime.remoting>
    <application>

      <client>
        <wellknown
            type="Apress.VisualBasicRecipes.Chapter10.Recipe10_16,Recipe10_16"
            url="tcp://localhost:19080/Recipe10-16.rem" />
      </client>

    </application>
  </system.runtime.remoting>
</configuration>
```

However, if you want to dynamically configure the Remoting infrastructure, you will need to be familiar with the approach demonstrated here. For detailed information, see *Advanced .NET Remoting, Second Edition* by Ingo Rammer and Mario Szpuszta (Apress, 2005). Note that as with the host, the assembly containing the declaration of the class that will be accessed remotely must still be explicitly referenced by the application.

```
Imports System
Imports System.Runtime.Remoting
Imports System.Runtime.Remoting.Channels
Imports System.Runtime.Remoting.Channels.Tcp
Imports System.Data

Namespace Apress.VisualBasicRecipes.Chapter10
    Public Class Recipe10_16Client

        Public Shared Sub Main()

            ' Register a new TCP Remoting channel to communicate with the
            ' remote object.
            ChannelServices.RegisterChannel(New TcpChannel, False)

            ' Register the classes that will be accessed remotely.
            RemotingConfiguration.RegisterWellKnownClientType( ➡
GetType(Recipe10_16), "tcp://localhost:19080/Recipe10-16.rem")

            ' Now any attempts to instantiate the Recipe10_16 class
            ' will actually create a proxy to a remote instance.
```

```
        '  Interact with the remote object through a proxy.
        Dim proxy As New Recipe10_16

        Try
            '  Display the name of the component host application domain
            '  where the object executes.
            Console.WriteLine("Object executing in: " & proxy.GetHostLocation)
        Catch ex As Exception
            Console.WriteLine(ex.ToString)
        End Try

        '  Get the DataTable from the remote object and display its contents.
        Dim dt As DataTable = proxy.GetContacts

        For Each row As DataRow In dt.Rows
            Console.WriteLine("{0}, {1}", row("LastName"), row("FirstName"))
        Next

        '  Wait to continue.
        Console.WriteLine(Environment.NewLine)
        Console.WriteLine("Main method complete.  Press Enter.")
        Console.ReadLine()

    End Sub

    End Class
End Namespace
```

10-17. Register All the Remotable Classes in an Assembly

Problem

You want to register all the remotable classes that are defined in an assembly without having to specify them in a configuration file.

Solution

Load the assembly with the remotable classes using reflection. Loop through all its `Public` types, and use the `RemotingConfiguration.RegisterWellKnownServiceType` method to register every remotable class.

How It Works

.NET makes it equally easy to register remotable classes through a configuration file or program-matically with code. The type being registered must extend `MarshalByRefObject`, and then you call `RemotingConfiguration.RegisterWellKnownServiceType`, passing on the type, the URI on which remote clients can connect to the type, and a value of the `System.Runtime.Remoting.WellKnownObjectMode` enumeration, which describes how the Remoting infrastructure should map client calls to object instances. The possible values are `SingleCall`, in which every incoming call is serviced by a new object, and Singleton, in which every incoming call is serviced by the same object. When using singleton objects, accurate state management and thread synchronization become critical.

The Code

The following server code searches for remotable classes in an assembly that is specified as a command-line argument. Each class derived from MarshalByRefObject is registered, and then the example displays the channel where the remotable object is available.

```
Imports System
Imports System.Reflection
Imports System.Runtime.Remoting
Imports System.Runtime.Remoting.Channels
Imports System.Runtime.Remoting.Channels.Tcp

Namespace Apress.VisualBasicRecipes.Chapter10
    Public Class Recipe10_17

        Public Shared Sub Main(ByVal args As String())

            ' Ensure there is an argument. We assume it is a valid
            ' filename.
            If Not args.Length = 1 Then Exit Sub

            ' Register a new TCP Remoting channel to communicate with
            ' the remote object.
            ChannelServices.RegisterChannel(New TcpChannel(19080), False)

            ' Get the registered Remoting channel.
            Dim channel As TcpChannel = ➡
DirectCast(ChannelServices.RegisteredChannels(0), TcpChannel)

            ' Create an Assembly object representing the assembly
            ' where remotable classes are defined.
            Dim remoteAssembly As Assembly = Assembly.LoadFrom(args(0))

            ' Process all the public types in the specified assembly.
            For Each remType As Type In remoteAssembly.GetExportedTypes()

                ' Check if type is remotable.
                If remType.IsSubclassOf(GetType(MarshalByRefObject)) Then
                    ' Register each type using the type name as the URI.
                    Console.WriteLine("Registering {0}", remType.Name)
                    RemotingConfiguration.RegisterWellKnownServiceType(remType, ➡
remType.Name, WellKnownObjectMode.SingleCall)

                    ' Determine the URL where this type is published.
                    Dim urls As String() = channel.GetUrlsForUri(remType.Name)
                    Console.WriteLine("Url:  {0}", urls(0))
                End If

            Next
```

```
        ' As long as this application is running, the registered remote
        ' objects will be accessible.
        Console.WriteLine(Environment.NewLine)
        Console.WriteLine("Press Enter to shut down the host.")
        Console.ReadLine()

    End Sub

End Class
End Namespace
```

Usage

Place the Recipe10-16.exe assembly in the directory where this recipe is and run the following command line:

```
recipe10-17 recipe10-16.exe
```

This will produce results similar to the following output:

```
Registering Recipe10_16
Url:  tcp://192.168.239.80:19080/Recipe10_16
```

Notes

The preceding code determines if a class is remotable by examining whether it derives from `MarshalByRefObject`. This approach always works, but it could lead you to expose some types that you don't want to make remotable. For example, the `System.Windows.Forms.Form` object derives indirectly from `MarshalByRefObject`. This means that if your remote object library contains any forms, they will be exposed remotely. To avoid this problem, don't include remotable types in your assembly unless you want to make them publicly available. Alternatively, identify the types you want to register with a custom attribute. You could then check for this attribute before registering a type.

10-18. Host a Remote Object in IIS

Problem

You want to create a remotable object in IIS (perhaps so that you can use SSL or IIS authentication) instead of a dedicated component host.

Solution

Place the configuration file and assembly in a directory (configured as an application within IIS), and modify the object URI so that it ends in .rem or .soap.

How It Works

Instead of creating a dedicated component host, you can host a remotable class in IIS. This allows you to ensure that the remotable classes will always be available, and it allows you to use IIS features such as SSL encryption and Integrated Windows authentication.

To host a remotable class in IIS, you must first create a virtual directory. The directory will contain two things: a configuration file named Web.config that registers the remotable classes and a Bin directory where you must place the corresponding class library assembly (or install the assembly in the GAC).

The configuration file for hosting in IIS is quite similar to the configuration file you use with a custom component host. However, you must follow several additional rules:

- You must use the HTTP channel (although you can use the binary formatter for smaller message sizes).

- You cannot specify a specific port number for listening. IIS listens on all the ports you have configured in IIS Manager. Typically, this will be ports 80 and 443 (for secure SSL communication).

- The object URI must end with .rem or .soap.

- When using IIS, you are stepping into ASP.NET territory. The configuration file you use here for Remoting must be named Web.config, which is the configuration file used by ASP.NET applications.

The Code

Here's an example Web.config file that registers the remote class shown in recipe 10-16:

```xml
<?xml version="1.0"?>
<configuration>
  <system.runtime.remoting>
    <application>
      <!-- Define the remotable types. -->
      <service>
        <wellknown mode="SingleCall" ➥
type="Apress.VisualBasicRecipes.Chapter10.Recipe10_16,Recipe10-16" ➥
objectUri="Recipe10-16.rem" />
      </service>

      <!-- Define the protocol used for network access.
      You can use only the http channel. -->
      <channels>
        <channel ref="http" />
      </channels>

      <!-- Uncomment the following section if you want to use the
      binary formatter rather than the default SOAP formatter.-->
      <!--
      <serverProviders>
        <formatter ref="binary" />
      </serverProviders>
      -->
    </application>
  </system.runtime.remoting>
</configuration>
```

Usage

A client can use an object hosted in IIS in the same way as an object hosted in a custom component host. However, the directory name will become part of the object URI. For example, if the Web.config file shown in the preceding code is hosted in the directory `http://localhost/RemoteObjects`, the full URL will be `http://localhost/RemoteObjects/Recipe10-16.rem`.

■**Note** When hosting an object with IIS, the account used to execute the object is the ASP.NET account defined in the Machine.config file. If this account doesn't have the rights to access the database (which is the default situation), you will receive an error when you try this example. Look at the .NET Framework for documentation on the `<processModel>` element.

10-19. Control the Lifetime of a Remote Object

Problem

You want to configure how long a singleton or client-activated object lives while not in use.

Solution

Configure a lease policy by using configuration file settings, override the `MarshalByRefObject.InitializeLifetimeService` method, or implement a custom lease provider.

How It Works

If a remotable object uses single-call activation, it will be destroyed automatically at the end of each method call. This behavior changes with client-activated and singleton objects, which are given a longer lifetime dictated by a *lifetime lease*. With the default settings, a remote object will be automatically destroyed if it's inactive for 2 minutes, provided it has been in existence for at least 5 minutes.

The component host, remote object, and client each have the opportunity to change lifetime settings, as described here:

- The component host can specify different lease lifetime defaults in the configuration file using the `<lifetime>` element, which is a child of the `<system.runtime.remoting>` element. The `leaseTime` attribute of the element specifies the default lifetime for all hosted objects. The `renewOnCallTime` attribute specifies the amount of time by which the lease is extended when a call is made against a hosted object. You can specify the values for both attributes as positive integers with a time unit suffix for days (D), hours (H), minutes (M), or seconds (S). For example, 10 hours is 10H, and 30 seconds is 30S.

- The remote class can override its `InitializeLifetimeService` method (inherited from `MarshalByRefObject`) to modify its initial lease settings by configuring and returning an object that implements the `System.Runtime.Remoting.Lifetime.ILease` interface. You obtain an `ILease` instance by calling the base class method `InitializeLifetimeService`. Then configure the returned `ILease` by setting the `InitialLeaseTime` and `RenewOnCallTime` properties to the desired values using `System.TimeSpan` objects. If you want the object to have an unlimited lifetime, simply return a `Nothing` reference instead of an `ILease` object. This is most commonly the case if you are creating a singleton object that needs to run independently (and permanently), even if clients aren't currently using it.

- The client can call the `MarshalByRefObject.GetLifetimeService` method on a specific remote object to retrieve an `ILease` instance. The client can then call the `ILease.Renew` method to specify a minimum amount of time the object should be kept alive.

The Code

The following example demonstrates how to use a component host's configuration file to control lifetime leases. The configuration gives each hosted object an initial lifetime of 10 minutes, and each time a member of the object is invoked, the lifetime is set to be at least 3 minutes.

```xml
<?xml version="1.0" encoding="utf-8" ?>
<configuration>
  <system.runtime.remoting>
    <application>

      <!-- Define the remotable types. -->
      <service>
        <wellknown
            mode = "SingleCall"
            type = "Apress.VisualBasicRecipes.Chapter10.Recipe10_19, Recipe10-19"
            objectUri = "Recipe10-19" />
      </service>

      <!-- Define the protocol used for network access.
           You can use tcp or http channels. -->
      <channels>
        <channel ref="tcp" port="19080" />
      </channels>

      <lifetime leaseTime="10M" renewOnCallTime="3M" />

    </application>
  </system.runtime.remoting>
</configuration>
```

The following example demonstrates how to use the second approach outlined where the remotable object overrides the InitializeLifetimeService method and takes control of its own lifetime. The example shows a remotable object that gives itself a default 10-minute lifetime and 3-minute renewal time.

```vb
Imports System
Imports System.Runtime.Remoting.Lifetime

Namespace Apress.VisualBasicRecipes.Chapter10

    ' Define a class that extends MarshalByRefObject, making it remotable.
    Public Class Recipe10_19
        Inherits MarshalByRefObject

        Public Overrides Function InitializeLifetimeService() As Object

            Dim lease As ILease = DirectCast(MyBase.InitializeLifetimeService(), ➡
ILease)
```

```
    '  Lease can only be configured if it is in an initial state.
    If lease.CurrentState = LeaseState.Initial Then
        lease.InitialLeaseTime = TimeSpan.FromMinutes(10)
        lease.RenewOnCallTime = TimeSpan.FromMinutes(3)
    End If

    Return lease

End Function

    ...

End Class
End Namespace
```

10-20. Control Versioning for Remote Objects

Problem

You want to create a component host that can host more than one version of the same object.

Solution

Install all versions of the remotable object into the global assembly cache (GAC), and explicitly register each version at a different URI endpoint. See recipe 1-14 for details on how to manage the assemblies in the GAC.

How It Works

.NET Remoting doesn't include any intrinsic support for versioning. When a client creates a remote object, the component host automatically uses the version in the local directory or, in the case of a shared assembly, the latest version from the GAC. To support multiple versions, you have three choices:

- *Create separate component host applications:* Each component host will host a different version of the remote object assembly and will register its version with a different URI. This approach forces you to run multiple component host applications at once and is most practical if you are using IIS hosting (as described in recipe 10-18).

- *Create an entirely new remote object assembly (instead of simply changing the version):* You can then register the classes from both assemblies at different URIs by using the same component host.

- *Install all versions of the remote object assembly in the GAC:* You can now create a component host that maps different URIs to specific versions of the remote object assembly.

The Code

Installing all versions of the remote object assembly in the GAC is the most flexible approach in cases where you need to support multiple versions. The following configuration file registers two versions of the RemoteObjects assembly at two different endpoints. Notice that you need to include the exact version number and public key token when using assemblies from the GAC. You can find this information by viewing the assembly in the Windows Explorer GAC plug-in (browse to C:\[*WindowsDir*]\Assembly). The client configuration file won't change at all (aside from updating the URI, if required). The client "chooses" the version it wants to use by using the corresponding URI.

```
<configuration>
  <system.runtime.remoting>
    <application>

      <service>

        <!-- The type information is split over two lines to accommodate the
             bounds of the page. In the configuration file, this information
             must all be placed on a single line. -->
        <wellknown mode="SingleCall"
          type="RemoteObjects.RemoteObject, RemoteObjects, Version 1.0.0.1,
              Culture=neutral, PublicKeyToken=8b5ed84fd25209e1"
          objectUri="RemoteObj_1.0" />

        <wellknown mode="SingleCall"
          type="RemoteObjects.RemoteObject, RemoteObjects, Version 2.0.0.1,
              Culture=neutral, PublicKeyToken=8b5ed84fd25209e1"
          objectUri="RemoteObj_2.0" />
      </service>

      <channels>
        <channel ref="tcp" port="19080" />
      </channels>

    </application>
  </system.runtime.remoting>
</configuration>
```

CHAPTER 11

■■■

Security and Cryptography

A principal goal of the Microsoft .NET Framework is to make computing more secure, especially with respect to the use of mobile code and distributed systems. Most modern operating systems (including Microsoft Windows) support user-based security, allowing you to control the actions and resources to which a user has access. However, in the highly connected world resulting from the proliferation of computer networks, particularly the Internet, it's insufficient to base security solely on the identity of a system's user. In the interest of security, code should not automatically receive the same level of trust that you assign to the person running the code.

The .NET Framework incorporates two complementary security models that address many of the issues associated with user and code security: code access security (CAS) and role-based security (RBS). CAS and RBS do not replace or duplicate the security facilities provided by the underlying operating system. They are platform-independent mechanisms that provide additional security capabilities to augment and enhance the overall security of your managed solutions. CAS uses information about the source and origin of an assembly (*evidence*) gathered at runtime to determine which actions and resources code from the assembly can access (*permissions*). The .NET Framework *security policy*—a hierarchical set of configurable rules—defines the mapping between evidence and permissions. The building blocks of security policy are *code groups*, which allow you to configure the mapping between evidence and permissions. The set of permissions granted to an assembly as a result of the security policy is known as the assembly's *grant set*.

The .NET Framework class library uses permission *demands* to protect its most important functionality from unauthorized access. A demand forces the common language runtime (CLR) to ensure that the whole stack of code calling a protected method has a specific permission. CAS ensures that the runtime capabilities of code depend on the level of trust you place in the creator and source of the code, not the level of trust you place in the user running the code.

Following a more traditional security model, RBS allows you to make runtime decisions based on the identity and roles of the user on whose behalf an application is running. On the Windows operating system, this equates to making decisions based on the Windows username and the Windows groups to which that user belongs. However, RBS provides a generic security mechanism that is independent of the underlying operating system, allowing you (with some development) to integrate with any user account system.

Another important aspect of the security features provided by the .NET Framework is *cryptography*. Cryptography is one of the most complex aspects of software development that any developer will use. The theory of modern cryptographic techniques is extremely difficult to understand and requires a level of mathematical knowledge that relatively few people have or need. Fortunately, the .NET Framework class library provides easy-to-use implementations of the most commonly used cryptographic techniques and support for the most popular and well-understood algorithms.

This chapter provides a wide variety of recipes that cover some of the more commonly used security capabilities provided by the .NET Framework. As you read the recipes in this chapter and think about how to apply the techniques to your own code, keep in mind that individual security features are rarely effective when implemented in isolation. In particular, cryptography does not equal security; the use of cryptography is merely one small element of creating a secure solution.

The recipes in this chapter describe how to do the following:

- Develop strong-named assemblies that can still be called by partially trusted code (recipe 11-1)

- Configure the .NET Framework security policy to turn off CAS completely or turn off only execution permission checks (recipes 11-2 and 11-3)

- Request specific code access permissions for your assemblies, determine at runtime what permissions the current assembly has, and inspect third-party assemblies to determine what permissions they need in order to run correctly (recipes 11-4, 11-5, 11-6, and 11-7)

- Control inheritance and member overrides using CAS (recipe 11-8)

- Inspect the evidence presented by an assembly to the runtime when the assembly is loaded (recipe 11-9)

- Integrate with Windows security to determine if a user is a member of a specific Windows group, restrict which users can execute your code, and impersonate other Windows users (recipes 11-10, 11-11, and 11-12)

- Generate random numbers that are nondeterministic and are suitable for use in security-sensitive applications (recipe 11-13)

- Use hash codes and keyed hash codes to store user passwords and determine if files have changed (recipes 11-14, 11-15, 11-16, and 11-17)

- Use encryption to protect sensitive data both in memory and when it is stored to disk (recipes 11-18 and 11-19)

■Note   For a broader explanation of secure programming and where cryptography fits in the overall security landscape, read *Writing Secure Code, Second Edition*, by Michael Howard and David LeBlanc (Microsoft Press, 2003), a modern classic of computer literature that contains a wealth of practical field-tested information. For more comprehensive coverage of the .NET security classes, see *Programming .NET Security* by Adam Freeman and Allen Jones (O'Reilly and Associates, 2003). Although not yet updated for .NET Framework 2.0, *Programming .NET Security* provides easily understood descriptions of security fundamentals, covers all the .NET security classes in detail, and demonstrates how to extend most aspects of the security framework.

11-1. Allow Partially Trusted Code to Use Your Strong-Named Assembly

Problem

You need to write a shared assembly that is accessible to code that is not fully trusted. By default, the runtime does not allow partially trusted code to access the types and members contained in a strong-named assembly.

Solution

Apply the assembly-level attribute `System.Security.AllowPartiallyTrustedCallersAttribute` to your shared assembly.

How It Works

To minimize the security risks posed by malicious code, the runtime does not allow assemblies granted only partial trust to access strong-named assemblies. This restriction dramatically reduces the opportunity for malicious code to attack your system, but the reasoning behind such a heavy-handed approach requires some explanation.

Assemblies that contain important functionality that is shared between multiple applications are usually strong-named and often installed in the global assembly cache (GAC). This is particularly true of the assemblies that constitute the .NET Framework class library. Other strong-named assemblies from well-known and widely distributed products will also be in the GAC and accessible to managed applications. The high chance that certain assemblies will be present in the GAC, their easy accessibility, and their importance to many different applications makes strong-named assemblies the most likely target for any type of subversive activity by malicious managed code.

Generally, the code most likely to be malicious is that which is loaded from remote locations, such as the Internet, over which you have little or no control. Under the default security policy in versions 1.*x* and 2.0 of the .NET Framework, all code run from the local machine has full trust, whereas code loaded from remote locations has only partial trust. Stopping partially trusted code from accessing strong-named assemblies means that partially trusted code has no opportunity to use the features of the assembly for malicious purposes, and cannot probe and explore the assembly to find exploitable holes. Of course, this theory hinges on the assumption that you correctly administer your security policy. If you simply assign all code full trust, not only will any assembly be able to access your strong-named assembly, but the code will also be able to access all of the functionality of the .NET Framework and even Win32 or any COM object through P/Invoke and COM Interop. That would be a security disaster!

■**Note** If you design, implement, and test your shared assembly correctly using CAS to restrict access to important members, you do not need to impose a blanket restriction to prevent partially trusted code from using your assembly. However, for an assembly of any significance, it's impossible to prove there are no security holes that malicious code can exploit. Therefore, you should carefully consider the need to allow partially trusted code to access your strong-named assembly before applying the AllowPartiallyTrustedCallers attribute. However, you might have no choice. If you are exposing public classes that provide events, you must apply this attribute. If you do not, an assembly that is not strong-named will be allowed to register a handler for one of your events, but when it is called, a security exception will be thrown. Code in an assembly that is not strong-named is not allowed to call code in a strong-named assembly.

The runtime stops partially trusted code from accessing strong-named assemblies by placing an implicit LinkDemand for the FullTrust permission set on every Public and Protected member of every publicly accessible type defined in the assembly. A LinkDemand verifies that the caller has the specified permissions, during just-in-time (JIT) compilation. This means that only assemblies granted the permissions equivalent to the FullTrust permission set are able to access the types and members from the strong-named assembly. Applying AllowPartiallyTrustedCallersAttribute to your strong-named assembly signals the runtime not to enforce the LinkDemand on the contained types and members.

■**Note** The runtime is responsible for enforcing the implicit LinkDemand security actions required to protect strong-named assemblies. The VB .NET assembler does not generate declarative LinkDemand statements at compile time.

The Code

The following code fragment shows the application of the attribute `AllowPartiallyTrustedCaller-sAttribute`. Notice that you must prefix the attribute with `Assembly:` to signal to the compiler that the target of the attribute is the assembly (also called a *global attribute*). Because you target the assembly, the attribute must be positioned after any top-level `Imports` statements, but before any namespace or type declarations.

```
Imports System.Security

<Assembly: AllowPartiallyTrustedCallers()>

Namespace Apress.VisualBasicRecipes.Chapter11

    Public Class Recipe11_01
        ' Implementation code...
    End Class

End Namespace
```

Tip It's common practice to contain all global attributes in a file separate from the rest of your application code. Microsoft Visual Studio uses this approach, creating a file named AssemblyInfo.vb (located in the My Projects folder, which is hidden by default) to contain all global attributes.

Notes

If, after applying `AllowPartiallyTrustedCallersAttribute` to your assembly, you want to restrict partially trusted code from calling only specific members, you should implement a `LinkDemand` for the `FullTrust` permission set on the necessary members, as shown in the following code fragment.

```
<System.Security.Permissions.PermissionSet(SecurityAction.LinkDemand, ➥
Name:="FullTrust")> _
Public Sub SomeMethod()
    ' Method code...
End Sub
```

11-2. Disable Code Access Security

Problem

You need to turn off all code access security (CAS) checks for the purpose of testing or debugging an application.

Solution

Use the Code Access Security Policy tool (Caspol.exe) and execute the command `caspol -s off` from the command line to temporarily disable code access security checks.

■**Note** You could permanently turn off CAS in .NET Framework 1.0 and 1.1 both programmatically and using Caspol.exe. In .NET Framework 2.0, you can turn off CAS only temporarily and only by using Caspol.exe.

How It Works

In some cases, code-level security might not be of interest to you. For example, when you are debugging code, you might want to exclude the possible interference caused by CAS. On rare occasions, the need for performance might outweigh the need for security. CAS is a key element of the .NET runtime's security model and one that sets it apart from many other computing platforms. Although CAS was implemented with performance in mind and has been used prudently throughout the .NET class library, some overhead is associated with each security demand and resulting stack walk that the runtime must execute to check every caller in the chain of execution.

■**Caution**   You should disable CAS only for performance reasons after you have exhausted all other possible measures to achieve the performance characteristics your application requires. Profiling your code will usually identify areas where you can improve performance significantly without the need to disable CAS. In addition, you should ensure that your system resources have appropriate protection using operating system security mechanisms, such as Windows access control lists (ACLs), before disabling CAS.

In these situations, you can temporarily disable CAS and remove the overhead and possible interference caused by code-level security checks. Turning off CAS has the effect of giving all code the ability to perform any action supported by the .NET Framework (equivalent to the `FullTrust` permission set). This includes the ability to load other code, call native libraries, and use pointers to access memory directly.

Caspol.exe is a utility provided with the .NET Framework that allows you to configure all aspects of your CAS policy from the command line. When you enter the command `caspol -s off` from the command line, you will see the following message indicating that CAS has been temporarily disabled.

```
Microsoft (r) .NET Framework CasPol 2.0.50727.42
Copyright (c) Microsoft Corporation. Al rights reserved.

CAS enforcement is being turned off temporarily. Press <enter> when you want to
restore the setting back on.
```

As the message states, CAS enforcement is off until you press Enter, or until the console in which Caspol.exe is running terminates.

Notes

In versions 1.0 and 1.1 of the .NET Framework, running the command `caspol -s off` turned off CAS enforcement permanently until you turned it on again using the command `caspol -s on`. In addition, it was possible to turn CAS on and off programmatically using the `System.Security.SecurityManager` class. The `SecurityManager` class contains a set of `Shared` methods and properties that provide access to critical security functionality and data. For example, the `SecurityEnabled` property turns CAS checks on and off.

To disable CAS, your code must run as a Windows Administrator and must have the `ControlPolicy` element of the permission `System.Security.Permissions.SecurityPermission`. You do not need any specific permissions to enable CAS.

Changing SecurityEnabled will not affect the enforcement of CAS in existing processes, nor will it affect new processes until you call the SavePolicy method, which saves the state of SecurityEnabled to the Windows registry. Unfortunately, the .NET Framework does not guarantee that changes to SecurityEnabled will correctly affect the operation of CAS in the current process, so you must change SecurityEnabled, and then launch a new process to achieve reliable and expected operation. The current on/off state of CAS is stored in the Windows registry in the key HKEY_LOCAL_MACHINE\ SOFTWARE\Microsoft\.NETFramework\Security\Policy as part of a set of flags contained in the Global Settings value. If the key does not exist, CAS defaults to on. Because CAS can no longer be permanently turned off in .NET Framework 2.0, this registry key is no longer used to control CAS.

The following example will work only on .NET Framework 1.0 and 1.1. It contains two methods (CasOn and CasOff) that demonstrate the code required to turn CAS on and off programmatically and persist the configuration change.

```
Imports System.Security

Namespace Apress.VisualBasicRecipes.Chapter11
    Public Class Recipe11_02

        ' A method to turn on CAS and persist the change.
        Public Sub CasOn()
            ' Turn on CAS checks.
            SecurityManager.SecurityEnabled = True

            ' Persist the configuration change.
            SecurityManager.SavePolicy()

        End Sub

        ' A method to turn off CAS and persist the change.
        Public Sub CasOff()
            ' Turn off CAS checks.
            SecurityManager.SecurityEnabled = False

            ' Persist the configuration change.
            SecurityManager.SavePolicy()

        End Sub

    End Class
End Namespace
```

11-3. Disable Execution Permission Checks

Problem

You need to load assemblies at runtime without the runtime checking them for execution permission.

Solution

In code, set the property `CheckExecutionRights` of the class `System.Security.SecurityManager` to `False` and persist the change by calling `SecurityManager.SavePolicy`. Alternatively, use the Code Access Security Policy tool (Caspol.exe), and execute the command `caspol -e off` from the command line.

How It Works

As the runtime loads each assembly, it ensures that the assembly's grant set (the permissions assigned to the assembly based on the security policy) includes the `Execution` element of `SecurityPermission`. The runtime implements a lazy policy resolution process, meaning that the grant set of an assembly is not calculated until the first time a security demand is made against the assembly. Not only does execution permission checking force the runtime to check that every assembly has the execution permission, but it also indirectly causes policy resolution for every assembly loaded, effectively negating the benefits of lazy policy resolution. These factors can introduce a noticeable delay as assemblies are loaded, especially when the runtime loads a number of assemblies together, as it does at application startup.

In many situations, simply allowing code to load and run is not a significant risk, as long as all other important operations and resources are correctly secured using CAS and operating system security. The `SecurityManager` class contains a set of `Shared` methods and properties that provide access to critical security functionality and data. For example, the `CheckExecutionRights` property turns on and off execution permission checks.

To modify the value of `CheckExecutionRights`, your code must have the `ControlPolicy` element of `SecurityPermission`. The change will affect the current process immediately, allowing you to load assemblies at runtime without the runtime checking them for execution permission. However, the change will not affect other existing processes. You must call the `SavePolicy` method to persist the change to the Windows registry for it to affect new processes.

The Code

The following example contains two methods (`ExecutionCheckOn` and `ExecutionCheckOff`) that demonstrate the code required to turn on and off execution permission checks and persist the configuration change.

```
Imports System.Security

Namespace Apress.VisualBasicRecipes.Chapter11
    Public Class Recipe11_03

        ' A method to turn on execution permission checking
        ' and persist the change.
        Public Sub ExecutionCheckOn()
            ' Turn on CAS checks.
            SecurityManager.CheckExecutionRights = True

            ' Persist the configuration change.
            SecurityManager.SavePolicy()

        End Sub
```

```
    '  A method to turn off execution permission checking
    '  and persist the change.
    Public Sub ExecutionCheckOff()
        ' Turn on CAS checks.
        SecurityManager.CheckExecutionRights = False

        ' Persist the configuration change.
        SecurityManager.SavePolicy()

    End Sub

  End Class
End Namespace
```

Notes

The .NET runtime allows you to turn off the automatic checks for execution permissions from within code or by using Caspol.exe. When you enter the command caspol -e off or its counterpart caspol -e on from the command line, the Caspol.exe utility actually sets the CheckExecutionRights property of the SecurityManager class before calling SecurityManager.SavePolicy.

11-4. Ensure the Runtime Grants Specific Permissions to Your Assembly

Problem

You need to ensure that the runtime grants your assembly those code access permissions that are critical to the successful operation of your application.

Solution

In your assembly, use permission requests to specify the code access permissions that your assembly must have. You declare permission requests using assembly-level code access permission attributes.

How It Works

The name *permission request* is a little misleading given that the runtime will never grant permissions to an assembly unless security policy dictates that the assembly should have those permissions. However, naming aside, permission requests serve an essential purpose, and although the way the runtime handles permission requests might initially seem strange, the nature of CAS does not allow for any obvious alternative.

Permission requests identify permissions that your code *must* have to function. For example, if you wrote a movie player that your customers could use to download and view movies from your web server, it would be disastrous if the user's security policy did not allow your player to open a network connection to your media server. Your player would load and run, but as soon as the user tried to connect to your server to play a movie, the application would crash with the exception System. Security.SecurityException. The solution is to include in your assembly a permission request for the code access permission required to open a network connection to your server (System.Net.

WebPermission or System.Net.SocketPermission, depending on the type of connection you need to open).

The runtime honors permission requests using the premise that it's better that your code never load than to load and fail sometime later when it tries to perform an action that it does not have permission to perform. Therefore, if after security policy resolution the runtime determines that the user does not have the appropriate permissions to satisfy the assembly's permission requests, the runtime will fail to load the assembly and will instead throw the exception System.Security.Policy. PolicyException. Since your own code failed to load, the runtime will handle this security exception during the assembly loading and transform it into a System.IO.FileLoadException exception that will terminate your program.

When you try to load an assembly from within code (either automatically or manually), and the loaded assembly contains permission requests that the security policy does not satisfy, the method you use to load the assembly will throw a PolicyException exception, which you must handle appropriately.

To declare a permission request, you must use the attribute counterpart of the code access permission that you need to request. All code access permissions have an attribute counterpart that you use to construct declarative security statements, including permission requests. For example, the attribute counterpart of SocketPermission is SocketPermissionAttribute, and the attribute counterpart of WebPermission is WebPermissionAttribute. All permissions and their attribute counterparts follow the same naming convention and are members of the same namespace.

When making a permission request, it's important to remember the following:

- You must declare the permission request after any top-level Imports statements but before any namespace or type declarations.

- The attribute must target the assembly, so you must prefix the attribute name with Assembly.

- You do not need to include the Attribute portion of an attribute's name, although you can.

- You must specify SecurityAction.RequestMinimum as the first positional argument of the attribute. This value identifies the statement as a permission request.

- You must configure the attribute to represent the code access permission you want to request using the attribute's properties. Refer to the .NET Framework SDK documentation for details of the properties implemented by each code access security attribute.

- To make more than one permission request, simply include multiple permission request statements.

The Code

The following example is a console application that includes two permission requests: one for SocketPermission and the other for SecurityPermission. If you try to execute the PermissionRequestExample application and your security policy does not grant the assembly the requested permissions, you will get a FileLoadException exception, and the application will not execute. Using the default security policy, this will happen if you run the assembly from a network share, because assemblies loaded from the intranet zone are not granted SocketPermission.

```
Imports System
Imports System.Net
Imports System.Security.Permissions

' Permission request for SocketPermission that allows the code to
' open a TCP connection to the specified host and port.
<Assembly: SocketPermission(SecurityAction.RequestMinimum, Access:="Connect", ➥
Host:="www.fabrikam.com", Port:="3538", Transport:="Tcp")>
```

```
' Permission request for the UnmanagedCode element of SecurityPermission,
' which controls the code's ability to execute unmanaged code.
<Assembly: SecurityPermission(SecurityAction.RequestMinimum, UnmanagedCode:=True)>

Namespace Apress.VisualBasicRecipes.Chapter11
    Public Class Recipe11_04

        Public Shared Sub Main()

            ' Do something

            ' Wait to continue.
            Console.Write("Main method complete.  Press Enter.")
            Console.ReadLine()

        End Sub

    End Class
End Namespace
```

11-5. Limit the Permissions Granted to Your Assembly

Problem

You need to restrict the code access permissions granted to your assembly, ensuring that people and other software can never use your code as a mechanism through which to perform undesirable or malicious actions.

Solution

Use declarative security statements to specify optional permission requests and permission refusal requests in your assembly. Optional permission requests define the maximum set of permissions that the runtime will grant to your assembly. Permission refusal requests specify particular permissions that the runtime should not grant to your assembly.

How It Works

In the interest of security, it's ideal if your code has only those code access permissions required to perform its function. This minimizes the opportunities for people and other code to use your code to carry out malicious or undesirable actions. The problem is that the runtime resolves an assembly's permissions using security policy, which a user or an administrator configures. Security policy could be different in every location where your application is run, and you have no control over what permissions the security policy assigns to your code.

Although you cannot control security policy in all locations where your code runs, the .NET Framework provides two mechanisms through which you can reject permissions granted to your assembly:

- *Refuse request*: This allows you to identify specific permissions that you do not want the runtime to grant to your assembly. After policy resolution, if the final grant set of an assembly contains any permission specified in a refuse request, the runtime removes that permission.

- *Optional permission request*: This defines the maximum set of permissions that the runtime can grant to your assembly. If the final grant set of an assembly contains any permissions other than those specified in the optional permission request, the runtime removes those permissions. Unlike as with a minimum permission request (discussed in recipe 11-4), the runtime will not refuse to load your assembly if it cannot grant all of the permissions specified in the optional request.

The approach you use depends on how many permissions you want to reject. If you want to reject only a handful of permissions, a refuse request is easier to code. You just specify the permissions that you do not want to grant to your assembly. However, if you want to reject a large number of permissions, it's easier to code an optional request for the few permissions that you do want; all others not specified will be refused by the assembly.

You include optional and refuse requests in your code using declarative security statements with the same syntax as the minimum permission requests discussed in recipe 11-4. The only difference is the value of the `System.Security.Permissions.SecurityAction` that you pass to the permission attribute's constructor. Use `SecurityAction.RequestOptional` to declare an optional permission request and `SecurityAction.RequestRefuse` to declare a refuse request. As with minimal permission requests, you must declare optional and refuse requests as global attributes by beginning the permission attribute name with the prefix `Assembly`. In addition, all requests must appear after any top-level `Imports` statements but before any namespace or type declarations.

The Code

The code shown here demonstrates an optional permission request for the Internet permission set. The Internet permission set is a named permission set defined by the default security policy. When the runtime loads the example, it will not grant the assembly any permission that is not included within the Internet permission set. (Consult the .NET Framework SDK documentation for details of the permissions contained in the Internet permission set.)

```
Imports System.Security.Permissions

<Assembly: PermissionSet(SecurityAction.RequestOptional, Name:="Internet")>

Namespace Apress.VisualBasicRecipes.Chapter11

    Public Class Recipe11_05_OptionalRequest
        ' Class implementation...
    End Class

End Namespace
```

In contrast to the preceding example, the following example uses a refuse request to single out the permission `System.Security.Permissions.FileIOPermission`—representing write access to the C: drive—for refusal.

```
Imports System.Security.Permissions

<Assembly: FileIOPermission(SecurityAction.RequestRefuse, Write:="C:\")>

Namespace Apress.VisualBasicRecipes.Chapter11
```

```
Public Class Recipe11_05_RefuseRequest
    ' Class implementation...
End Class

End Namespace
```

11-6. View the Permissions Required by an Assembly

Problem

You need to view the permissions that an assembly must be granted in order to run correctly.

Solution

Use the Permissions Calculator (Permcalc.exe) supplied with the .NET Framework SDK version 2.0 or the Permissions View tool (Permview.exe) supplied with the .NET Framework SDK versions 1.0 and 1.1.

How It Works

To configure security policy correctly, you need to know the code access permission requirements of the assemblies you intend to run. This is true of both executable assemblies and libraries that you access from your own applications. With libraries, it's also important to know which permissions the assembly refuses so that you do not try to use the library to perform a restricted action, which would result in a System.Security.SecurityException exception.

The Permissions View tool (Permview.exe), supplied with the .NET Framework SDK versions 1.0 and 1.1, allows you to view the minimal, optional, and refuse permission requests made by an assembly. By specifying the /decl switch, you can view all of the declarative security statements contained in an assembly, including declarative demands and asserts. This can give you a good insight into what the assembly is trying to do and allow you to configure security policy appropriately. However, Permview.exe does not show the imperative security operations contained within the assembly. Imperative security refers to statements in code that create and use an instance of the required permissions object.

The Permissions Calculator (Permcalc.exe) supplied with the .NET Framework SDK version 2.0 overcomes this limitation. Permcalc.exe walks through an assembly and provides an estimate of the permissions the assembly requires to run, regardless of whether they are declarative or imperative.

■**Note** The Permissions View tool (Permview.exe) is not supplied with the .NET Framework SDK version 2.0. Permview.exe from previous versions of the .NET Framework does not work correctly with .NET 2.0 assemblies. This is unfortunate, as Permcalc.exe does not provide a direct replacement for some of the useful functionality provided by Permview.exe. Although Permcalc.exe can determine both the imperative and declarative demands an assembly makes, it does not report the minimal, optional, and refusal requests made within an assembly.

The Code

The following example shows a class that declares a minimum, optional, and refusal request, as well as a number of imperative security demands.

```
Imports System
Imports System.Net
Imports System.Security.Permissions

' Minimum permission request for SocketPermission.
<Assembly: SocketPermission(SecurityAction.RequestMinimum, Unrestricted:=True)>

' Optional permission request for IsolatedStorageFilePermission.
<Assembly: IsolatedStorageFilePermission(SecurityAction.RequestOptional, ➥
Unrestricted:=True)>

' Refuse request for ReflectionPermission.
<Assembly: ReflectionPermission(SecurityAction.RequestRefuse, Unrestricted:=True)>

Namespace Apress.VisualBasicRecipes.Chapter11
    Public Class Receipe11_06

        Public Shared Sub Main()

            ' Create and configure a FileIOPermission object that represents
            ' write access to the C:\Data folder.
            Dim fileIOPerm As New FileIOPermission(FileIOPermissionAccess.Write, ➥
"C:\Data")

            ' Make the demand.
            fileIOPerm.Demand()

            ' Do something...

            ' Wait to continue.
            Console.Write("Main method complete.  Press Enter.")
            Console.ReadLine()

        End Sub

    End Class
End Namespace
```

Usage

Executing the command `permcalc -sandbox Recipe11-06.exe` will generate a file named sandbox. PermCalc.xml that contains XML representations of the permissions required by the assembly. The sandbox parameter creates a private area (sandbox) for an application, with the minimum permissions in which the application requires to run. Where the exact requirements of a permission cannot be determined (because it is based on runtime data), Permcalc.exe reports that unrestricted permissions of that type are required. You can instead default to the Internet zone permissions using the `-Internet` flag. Here are the contents of sandbox.PermCalc.xml when run against the sample code.

```
<?xml version="1.0"?>
<Sandbox>
  <PermissionSet version="1" class="System.Security.PermissionSet">
    <IPermission Write="C:\Data" version="1"
        class="System.Security.Permissions.FileIOPermission, mscorlib,
        Version=2.0.0.0, Culture=neutral,
        PublicKeyToken=b77a5c561934e089" />
    <IPermission version="1"
        class="System.Security.Permissions.SecurityPermission,
        mscorlib, Version=2.0.0.0, Culture=neutral,
        PublicKeyToken=b77a5c561934e089" Flags="Execution" />
    <IPermission version="1" class="System.Security.Permissions.UIPermission,
        mscorlib, Version=2.0.0.0, Culture=neutral,
        PublicKeyToken=b77a5c561934e089" Unrestricted="true" />
    <IPermission version="1" class="System.Net.SocketPermission, System,
        Version=2.0.0.0, Culture=neutral, PublicKeyToken=b77a5c561934e089"
        Unrestricted="true" />
  </PermissionSet>
</Sandbox>
```

11-7. Determine at Runtime If Your Code Has a Specific Permission

Problem

You need to determine at runtime if your assembly has a specific permission, such as write access to files.

Solution

Instantiate and configure the permission you want to test for, and then pass it as an argument to the Shared method IsGranted of the class System.Security.SecurityManager.

How It Works

Using minimum permission requests, you can ensure that the runtime grants your assembly a specified set of permissions. As a result, when your code is running, you can safely assume that it has the requested minimum permissions. However, you might want to implement opportunistic functionality that your application offers only if the runtime grants your assembly appropriate permissions. This approach is partially formalized using optional permission requests, which allow you to define a set of permissions that your code could use if the security policy granted them, but are not essential for the successful operation of your code. (Recipe 11-5 provides more details on using optional permission requests.)

The problem with optional permission requests is that the runtime has no ability to communicate to your assembly which of the requested optional permissions it has granted. You can try to use a protected operation and fail gracefully if the call results in the exception System.Security.SecurityException. However, it's more efficient to determine in advance if you have the necessary permissions. You can then build logic into your code to avoid invoking secured members that will cause stack walks and raise security exceptions.

■**Note** IsGranted checks the grant set of only the calling assembly. It does not do a full stack walk to evaluate the grant set of other assemblies on the call stack.

The Code

The following example demonstrates how to use the IsGranted method to determine if the assembly has write permission to the directory C:\Data. You could make such a call each time you needed to test for the permission, but it's more efficient to use the returned Boolean value to set a configuration flag indicating whether to allow users to save files.

```
Imports System.Security
Imports System.Security.Permissions

Namespace Apress.VisualBasicRecipes.Chapter11
    Public Class Recipe11_07
        ' Define a variable to indicate whether the assembly has write
        ' access to the C:\Data folder.
        Private canWrite As Boolean = False

        Public Sub New()
            ' Create and configure a FileIOPermission object that
            ' represents write access the the C:\Data folder.
            Dim fileIOPerm As New FileIOPermission(FileIOPermissionAccess.Write, ➡
"C:\Data")

            ' Test if the current assembly has the specified permission.
            canWrite = SecurityManager.IsGranted(fileIOPerm)

        End Sub

    End Class
End Namespace
```

11-8. Restrict Who Can Extend Your Classes and Override Class Members

Problem

You need to control what code can extend your classes through inheritance and which class members a derived class can override.

Solution

Use declarative security statements to apply the SecurityAction.InheritanceDemand to the declarations of the classes and members that you need to protect.

■**Note** In .NET Framework 2.0, assemblies granted `FullTrust` can extend a class regardless of the security demands implemented on the class. This means that the `InheritanceDemand` is useful in environments where assembly permissions are closely managed, because you can still ensure that malicious or unauthorized code cannot extend your critical business classes. However, the `InheritanceDemand` does not allow you to protect classes that you develop and distribute to other environments, as part of a packaged product, for example. Although this may seem like a useful feature has been lost, there were always ways for a determined programmer to write and run fully trusted assemblies to overcome the `InheritanceDemand`. The approach taken in .NET 2.0 is simply to avoid people placing too much confidence in a security feature that was at best an inconvenience to the determined hacker.

How It Works

Language modifiers such as `NotOverridable`, `NotInheritable`, `Public`, `Private`, and `Overridable` give you a level of control over the ability of classes to inherit from your class and override its members. However, these modifiers are inflexible, providing no selectivity in restricting which code can extend a class or override its members. For example, you might want to allow only code written by your company or department to extend business-critical classes. By applying an `InheritanceDemand` to your class or member declaration, you can specify runtime permissions that a class must have to extend your class or override particular members. Remember that the permissions of a class are the permissions of the assembly in which the class is declared.

Although you can demand any permission or permission set in your `InheritanceDemand`, it's more common to demand identity permissions. Identity permissions represent evidence presented to the runtime by an assembly. If an assembly presents certain types of evidence at load time, the runtime will automatically assign the assembly the appropriate identity permission. Identity permissions allow you to use regular imperative and declarative security statements to base security decisions directly on code identity, without the need to evaluate evidence objects directly. Table 11-1 lists the type of identity permission generated for each type of evidence. (Evidence types are members of the `System.Security.Policy` namespace, and identity permission types are members of the `System.Security.Permissions` namespace.)

Table 11-1. *Evidence Classes That Generate Identity Permissions*

Evidence Class	Identity Permission
Publisher	PublisherIdentityPermission
Site	SiteIdentityPermission
StrongName	StrongNameIdentityPermission
Url	UrlIdentityPermission
Zone	ZoneIdentityPermission

■**Note** The runtime assigns identity permissions to an assembly based on the evidence presented by the assembly. You cannot assign additional identity permissions to an assembly through the configuration of security policy.

You must use declarative security syntax to implement an InheritanceDemand, and so you must use the attribute counterpart of the permission class that you want to demand. All permission classes, including InheritanceDemand, have an attribute counterpart that you use to construct declarative security statements. For example, the attribute counterpart of PublisherIdentityPermission is PublisherIdentityPermissionAttribute, and the attribute counterpart of StrongNameIdentityPermission is StrongNameIdentityPermissionAttribute. All permissions and their attribute counterparts follow the same naming convention and are members of the same namespace.

To control which code can extend your class, apply the InheritanceDemand to the class declaration using one of the permissions listed in Table 11-1. To control which code can override specific members of a class, apply the InheritanceDemand to the member declaration.

The Code

The following example demonstrates the use of an InheritanceDemand on both a class and a method. Applying a PublisherIdentityPermissionAttribute to the Recipe11_08 class means only classes in assemblies signed by the publisher certificate contained in the pubcert.cer file (or assemblies granted FullTrust) can extend the class. The contents of the pubcert.cer file are read at compile time, and the necessary certificate information is built into the assembly metadata. To demonstrate that other permissions can also be used with an InheritanceDemand, the PermissionSetAttribute is used to allow only classes granted the FullTrust permission set to override the method SomeProtectedMethod.

```
Imports System.Security.Permissions
Namespace Apress.VisualBasicRecipes.Chapter11

    <PublisherIdentityPermission(SecurityAction.InheritanceDemand, ➡
CertFile:="pubcert.cer")> _
    Public Class Recipe11_08

        <PermissionSet(SecurityAction.InheritanceDemand, Name:="FullTrust")> _
        Public Sub SomeProtectedMethod()
            '  Method implementation...
        End Sub

    End Class
End Namespace
```

11-9. Inspect an Assembly's Evidence

Problem

You need to inspect the evidence that the runtime assigned to an assembly.

Solution

Obtain a System.Reflection.Assembly object that represents the assembly in which you are interested. Get the System.Security.Policy.Evidence collection from the Evidence property of the Assembly object, and access the contained evidence objects using the GetEnumerator, GetHostEnumerator, or GetAssemblyEnumerator method of the Evidence class.

How It Works

The Evidence class represents a collection of evidence objects. The read-only Evidence property of the Assembly class returns an Evidence collection object that contains all of the evidence objects that the runtime assigned to the assembly as the assembly was loaded.

The Evidence class actually contains two collections, representing different types of evidence:

- *Host evidence* includes those evidence objects assigned to the assembly by the runtime or the trusted code that loaded the assembly.

- *Assembly evidence* represents custom evidence objects embedded into the assembly at build time.

The Evidence class implements three methods for enumerating the evidence objects it contains: GetEnumerator, GetHostEnumerator, and GetAssemblyEnumerator. The GetHostEnumerator and GetAssemblyEnumerator methods return a System.Collections.IEnumerator instance that enumerates only those evidence objects from the appropriate collection. The GetEnumerator method returns an IEnumerator instance that enumerates *all* of the evidence objects contained in the Evidence collection.

■**Note** Evidence classes do not extend a standard base class or implement a standard interface. Therefore, when working with evidence programmatically, you need to test the type of each object and know what particular types you are seeking. (See recipe 3-11 for details on how to test the type of an object at runtime.)

The Code

The following example demonstrates how to display the host and assembly evidence of an assembly on the console. The example relies on the fact that all standard evidence classes override the Object.ToString method to display a useful representation of the evidence object's state. Although interesting, this example does not always show the evidence that an assembly would have when loaded from within your program. The runtime host (such as the Microsoft ASP.NET or Internet Explorer runtime host) is free to assign additional host evidence as it loads an assembly.

```
Imports System
Imports System.Reflection
Imports System.Collections
Imports System.Security.Policy

Namespace Apress.VisualBasicRecipes.Chapter11
    Public Class Recipe11_09

        Public Shared Sub Main(ByVal args As String())

            ' Load the specified assembly.
            Dim a As Assembly = Assembly.LoadFrom(args(0))

            ' Get the evidence collection from the
            ' loaded assembly.
            Dim e As Evidence = a.Evidence

            ' Display the host evidence.
            Dim x As IEnumerator = e.GetHostEnumerator
```

```
            Console.Write("HOST EVIDENCE COLLECTION:")

            While x.MoveNext
                Console.Write(x.Current.ToString)
                Console.Write("Press Enter to see next evidence.")
                Console.ReadLine()
            End While

            ' Display the assembly evidence.
            x = e.GetAssemblyEnumerator()

            Console.Write("ASSEMBLY EVIDENCE COLLECTION:")

            While x.MoveNext
                Console.Write(x.Current.ToString)
                Console.Write("Press Enter to see next evidence.")
                Console.ReadLine()
            End While

            ' Wait to continue.
            Console.Write("Main method complete.  Press Enter.")
            Console.ReadLine()

        End Sub

    End Class
End Namespace
```

Note All of the standard evidence classes provided by the .NET Framework are immutable, ensuring that you cannot change their values after the runtime has created them and assigned them to the assembly. In addition, you cannot add or remove items while you are enumerating across the contents of a collection using an IEnumerator; otherwise, the MoveNext method throws a System.InvalidOperationException exception.

11-10. Determine If the Current User Is a Member of a Specific Windows Group

Problem

You need to determine if the current user of your application is a member of a specific Windows user group.

Solution

Obtain a System.Security.Principal.WindowsIdentity object representing the current Windows user by calling the Shared method WindowsIdentity.GetCurrent. Create a System.Security.Principal. WindowsPrincipal class using the WindowsIdentity class, and then call the method IsInRole of the WindowsPrincipal object.

How It Works

The role-based security (RBS) mechanism of the .NET Framework abstracts the user-based security features of the underlying operating system through the following two key interfaces:

- The System.Security.Principal.IIdentity interface, which represents the entity on whose behalf code is running; for example, a user or service account.

- The System.Security.Principal.IPrincipal interface, which represents the entity's IIdentity and the set of roles to which the entity belongs. A *role* is simply a categorization used to group entities with similar security capabilities, such as a Windows user group.

To integrate RBS with Windows user security, the .NET Framework provides the following two Windows-specific classes that implement the IIdentity and IPrincipal interfaces:

- System.Security.Principal.WindowsIdentity, which implements the IIdentity interface and represents a Windows user.

- System.Security.Principal.WindowsPrincipal, which implements IPrincipal and represents the set of Windows groups to which the user belongs.

Because .NET RBS is a generic solution designed to be platform-independent, you have no access to the features and capabilities of the Windows user account through the IIdentity and IPrincipal interfaces, and you must frequently use the WindowsIdentity and WindowsPrincipal objects directly.

To determine if the current user is a member of a specific Windows group, you must first call the Shared method WindowsIdentity.GetCurrent. The GetCurrent method returns a WindowsIdentity object that represents the Windows user on whose behalf the current thread is running. An overload of the GetCurrent method new to .NET Framework 2.0 takes a Boolean argument and allows you to control what is returned by GetCurrent if the current thread is impersonating a user different from the one associated with the process. If the argument is True, GetCurrent returns a WindowsIdentity representing the impersonated user, or it returns Nothing if the thread is not impersonating a user. If the argument is False, GetCurrent returns the WindowsIdentity of the thread if it is not impersonating a user, or it returns the WindowsIdentity of the process if the thread is currently impersonating a user.

■**Note** The WindowsIdentity class provides overloaded constructors that, when running on Microsoft Windows Server 2003 or later platforms, allow you to obtain a WindowsIdentity object representing a named user. You can use this WindowsIdentity object and the process described in this recipe to determine if that user is a member of a specific Windows group. If you try to use one of these constructors when running on an earlier version of Windows, the WindowsIdentity constructor will throw an exception. On Windows platforms preceding Windows Server 2003, you must use native code to obtain a Windows access token representing the desired user. You can then use this access token to instantiate a WindowsIdentity object. Recipe 11-12 explains how to obtain Windows access tokens for specific users.

Once you have a WindowsIdentity, instantiate a new WindowsPrincipal object, passing the WindowsIdentity object as an argument to the constructor. Finally, call the IsInRole method of the WindowsPrincipal object to test if the user is in a specific group (role). IsInRole returns True if the user is a member of the specified group; otherwise, it returns False. The IsInRole method provides four overloads:

- The first overload takes a String containing the name of the group for which you want to test. The group name must be of the form [*DomainName*]\[*GroupName*] for domain-based groups and [*MachineName*]\[*GroupName*] for locally defined groups. If you want to test for membership of a standard Windows group, use the form BUILTIN\[*GroupName*] or the other overload that takes a value from the System.Security.Principal.WindowsBuiltInRole enumeration. IsInRole performs a case-insensitive test for the specified group name.

- The second IsInRole overload accepts an Integer, which specifies a Windows role identifier (RID). RIDs provide a mechanism to identify groups that is independent of language and localization.

- The third IsInRole overload accepts a member of the System.Security.Principal.Windows-BuiltInRole enumeration. The WindowsBuiltInRole enumeration defines a set of members that represent each of the built-in Windows groups. As with RIDs, these groups are independent of language and localization.

- The fourth IsInRole overload (new to .NET Framework 2.0) accepts a System.Security.Principal.SecurityIdentifier object that represents the security identifier (SID) of the group for which you want to test.

Table 11-2 lists the name, RID, and WindowsBuiltInRole value for each of the standard Windows groups.

Table 11-2. *Windows Built-In Account Names and Identifiers*

Account Name	RID (Hex)	WindowsBuiltInRole Value
BUILTIN\Account Operators	0x224	AccountOperator
BUILTIN\Administrators	0x220	Administrator
BUILTIN\Backup Operators	0x227	BackupOperator
BUILTIN\Guests	0x222	Guest
BUILTIN\Power Users	0x223	PowerUser
BUILTIN\Print Operators	0x226	PrintOperator
BUILTIN\Replicators	0x228	Replicator
BUILTIN\Server Operators	0x225	SystemOperator
BUILTIN\Users	0x221	User

The Code

The following example demonstrates how to test whether the current user is a member of a set of named Windows groups. You specify the groups that you want to test for as command-line arguments. Remember to prefix the group name with the machine or domain name, or BUILTIN for standard Windows groups.

```
Imports System
Imports System.Security.Principal

Namespace Apress.VisualBasicRecipes.Chapter11
    Public Class Recipe11_10

        Public Shared Sub Main(ByVal args As String())

            ' Obtain a WindowsIdentity object representing the currently
            ' logged on Windows user.
            Dim identity As WindowsIdentity = WindowsIdentity.GetCurrent

            ' Create a Windows Principal object that represents the security
            ' capabilities of the specified WindowsIdentity; in this case,
            ' the Windows groups to which the current user belongs.
            Dim principal As New WindowsPrincipal(identity)

            ' Iterate through the group names specified as command-line
            ' arguments and test to see if the current user is a member of
            ' each one.
            For Each role As String In args
                Console.WriteLine("Is {0} a member of {1}? = {2}", identity.Name, ➥
role, principal.IsInRole(role))
            Next

            ' Wait to continue.
            Console.WriteLine(Environment.NewLine)
            Console.Write("Main method complete.  Press Enter.")
            Console.ReadLine()

        End Sub

    End Class
End Namespace
```

Usage

If you run this example as a user named Robb on a computer named MACHINE using this command:

Recipe11-10 BUILTIN\Administrators BUILTIN\Users MACHINE\Accountants

you will see console output similar to the following:

```
Is MACHINE\Robb a member of BUILTIN\Administrators? = False
Is MACHINE\Robb a member of BUILTIN\Users? = True
Is MACHINE\Robb a member of MACHINE\Accountants? = True
```

11-11. Restrict Which Users Can Execute Your Code

Problem

You need to restrict which users can execute elements of your code based on the user's name or the roles of which the user is a member.

Solution

Use the permission class `System.Security.Permissions.PrincipalPermission` and its attribute counterpart `System.Security.Permissions.PrincipalPermissionAttribute` to protect your program elements with RBS demands.

How It Works

The .NET Framework supports both imperative and declarative RBS (refer to recipe 11-10) demands. The class `PrincipalPermission` provides support for imperative security statements, and its attribute counterpart `PrincipalPermissionAttribute` provides support for declarative security statements. RBS demands use the same syntax as CAS demands, but RBS demands specify the name the current user must have, or more commonly, the roles of which the user must be a member. An RBS demand instructs the runtime to look at the name and roles of the current user, and if that user does not meet the requirements of the demand, the runtime throws a `System.Security.SecurityException` exception.

To make an imperative security demand, you must first create a `PrincipalPermission` object specifying the username or role name you want to demand, and then you must call its `Demand` method. You can specify only a single username and role name per demand. If either the username or the role name is `Nothing`, any value will satisfy the demand. Unlike with code access permissions, an RBS demand does not result in a stack walk; the runtime evaluates only the username and roles of the current user.

To make a declarative security demand, you must annotate the class or member you want to protect with a correctly configured `PrincipalPermissionAttribute` attribute. Class-level demands apply to all members of the class, unless a member-specific demand overrides the class demand.

Generally, you are free to choose whether to implement imperative or declarative demands. However, imperative security demands allow you to integrate RBS demands with code logic to achieve more sophisticated demand behavior. In addition, if you do not know the role or usernames to demand at compile time, you must use imperative demands. Declarative demands have the advantage that they are separate from code logic and easier to identify. In addition, you can view declarative demands using the Permview.exe tool (discussed in recipe 11-6). Whether you implement imperative or declarative demands, you must ensure that the runtime has access to the name and roles for the current user to evaluate the demand correctly.

The `System.Threading.Thread` class represents an operating system thread running managed code. The `Shared` property `CurrentPrincipal` of the `Thread` class contains an `IPrincipal` instance representing the roles on whose behalf the managed thread is running.

At the operating system level, each thread also has an associated Windows access token (represented by the `WindowsIdentity` class), which represents the Windows account on whose behalf the thread is running. The `IPrincipal` instance and the Windows access token are two separate entities. Windows uses its access token to enforce operating system security, whereas the .NET runtime uses its `IPrincipal` instance to evaluate application-level RBS demands. The identity and principal are separate entities, and they may represent different user accounts, as noted in recipe 11-12.

The benefit of this approach is that you can implement a user and an RBS model within your application using a proprietary user accounts database, without the need for all users to have Windows user accounts. This is a particularly useful approach in large-scale, publicly accessible Internet applications.

By default, the Thread.CurrentPrincipal property is undefined. Because obtaining user-related information can be time-consuming, and only a minority of applications use this information, the .NET designers opted for lazy initialization of the CurrentPrincipal property. The first time code gets the Thread.CurrentPrincipal property, the runtime assigns an IPrincipal instance to the property using the following logic:

- If the application domain in which the current thread is executing has a default principal, the runtime assigns this principal to the Thread.CurrentPrincipal property. By default, application domains do not have default principals. You can set the default principal of an application domain by calling the method SetThreadPrincipal on a System.AppDomain object that represents the application domain you want to configure. Code must have the ControlPrincipal element of SecurityPermission to call SetThreadPrincipal. You can set the default principal only once for each application domain; a second call to SetThreadPrincipal results in the exception System.Security.Policy.PolicyException.

- If the application domain does not have a default principal, the application domain's principal policy determines which IPrincipal implementation to create and assign to Thread.CurrentPrincipal. To configure principal policy for an application domain, obtain an AppDomain object that represents the application domain and call the object's SetPrincipalPolicy method. The SetPrincipalPolicy method accepts a member of the enumeration System.Security.Principal.PrincipalPolicy, which specifies the type of IPrincipal object to assign to Thread.CurrentPrincipal. Code must have the ControlPrincipal element of SecurityPermission to call SetPrincipalPolicy. Table 11-3 lists the available PrincipalPolicy values; the default value is UnauthenticatedPrincipal.

- If your code has the ControlPrincipal element of SecurityPermission, you can instantiate your own IPrincipal object and assign it to the Thread.CurrentPrincipal property directly. This will prevent the runtime from assigning default IPrincipal objects or creating new ones based on principal policy.

Table 11-3. *Members of the PrincipalPolicy Enumeration*

Member Name	Description
NoPrincipal	No IPrincipal object is created. Thread.CurrentPrincipal returns Nothing.
UnauthenticatedPrincipal	An empty System.Security.Principal.GenericPrincipal object is created and assigned to Thread.CurrentPrincipal.
WindowsPrincipal	A WindowsPrincipal object representing the currently logged-on Windows user is created and assigned to Thread.CurrentPrincipal.

Whatever method you use to establish the IPrincipal for the current thread, you must do so before you use RBS demands, or the correct user (IPrincipal) information will not be available for the runtime to process the demand. Normally, when running on the Windows platform, you would set the principal policy of an application domain to PrincipalPolicy.WindowsPrincipal (as shown here) to obtain Windows user information.

```
'  Obtain a reference to the current application domain.
Dim currentAppDomain As AppDomain = System.AppDomain.CurrentDomain

'  Configure the current application domain to use Windows-based principals.
currentAppDomain.SetPrincipalPolicy(➡
Security.Principal.PrincipalPolicy.WindowsPrincipal)
```

The Code

The following example demonstrates the use of imperative and declarative RBS demands. The example shows three methods protected using imperative RBS demands (Method1, Method2, and Method3), and then three other methods protected using the equivalent declarative RBS demands (Method4, Method5, and Method6).

```
Imports System
Imports System.Security.Permissions

Namespace Apress.VisualBasicRecipes.Chapter11
    Public Class Recipe11_11

        Public Shared Sub Method1()

            '  An imperative role-based security demand for the current
            '  principal to represent an identity with the name Amy. The
            '  roles of the principal are irrelevant.
            Dim perm As New PrincipalPermission("MACHINE\Amy", Nothing)

            '  Make the demand.
            perm.Demand()

        End Sub

        Public Shared Sub Method2()

            '  An imperative role-based security demand for the current
            '  principal to be a member of the roles Managers or Developers.
            '  If the principal is a member of either role, access is granted.
            '  Using the PrincipalPermission, you can express only an OR type
            '  relationship. This is because the PrincipalPolicy.Intersect method
            '  always returns an empty permission unless the two inputs are the
            '  same. However, you can use code logic to implement more complex
            '  conditions. In this case, the name of the identity is irrelevant.
            Dim perm1 As New PrincipalPermission(Nothing, "MACHINE\Managers")
            Dim perm2 As New PrincipalPermission(Nothing, "MACHINE\Developers")

            '  Make the demand.
            perm1.Union(perm2).Demand()

        End Sub

        Public Shared Sub Method3()
```

```
        ' An imperative role-based security demand for the current principal
        ' to represent an identity with the name Amy AND be a member of the
        ' Managers role.
        Dim perm As New PrincipalPermission("MACHINE\Amy", "MACHINE\Managers")

        ' Make the demand.
        perm.Demand()

    End Sub

    ' A declarative role-based security demand for the current principal
    ' to represent an identity with the name Amy.
    <PrincipalPermission(SecurityAction.Demand, Name:="MACHINE\Amy")> _
    Public Shared Sub Method4()

        ' Method implementation...

    End Sub

    ' A declarative role-based security demand for the current principal
    ' to be a member of the roles Managers OR Developers. If the principal
    ' is a member of either role, access is granted. You can express only
    ' an OR type relationship, not an AND relationship.
    <PrincipalPermission(SecurityAction.Demand, Role:="MACHINE\Managers"), ➥
PrincipalPermission(SecurityAction.Demand, Role:="MACHINE\Developers")> _
    Public Shared Sub Method5()

        ' Method implementation...

    End Sub

    ' A declarative role-based security demand for the current principal
    ' to represent an identity with the name Amy and be a member of the
    ' Managers role.
    <PrincipalPermission(SecurityAction.Demand, Name:="MACHINE\Amy", ➥
Role:="MACHINE\Managers")> _
    Public Shared Sub Method6()

        ' Method implementation...

    End Sub

    End Class
End Namespace
```

11-12. Impersonate a Windows User

Problem

You need your code to run in the context of a Windows user other than the currently active user account.

Solution

Obtain a System.Security.Principal.WindowsIdentity object representing the Windows user you need to impersonate, and then call the Impersonate method of the WindowsIdentity object.

How It Works

Every Windows thread has an associated *access token*, which represents the Windows account on whose behalf the thread is running. The Windows operating system uses the access token to determine whether a thread has the appropriate permissions to perform protected operations on behalf of the account, such as read and write files, reboot the system, and change the system time.

By default, a managed application runs in the context of the Windows account that executed the application. This is normally desirable behavior, but sometimes you will want to run an application in the context of a different Windows account. This is particularly true in the case of server-side applications that process transactions on behalf of the users remotely connected to the server.

It's common for a server application to run in the context of a Windows account created specifically for the application—a service account. This service account will have minimal permissions to access system resources. Enabling the application to operate as though it were the connected user permits the application to access the operations and resources appropriate to that user's security clearance. When an application assumes the identity of another user, it's known as *impersonation*. Correctly implemented, impersonation simplifies security administration and application design, while maintaining user accountability.

■**Note** As discussed in recipe 11-11, a thread's Windows access token and its .NET principal are separate entities and can represent different users. The impersonation technique described in this recipe changes only the Windows access token of the current thread; it does not change the thread's principal. To change the thread's principal, code must have the ControlPrincipal element of SecurityPermission and assign a new System.Security. Principal.IPrincipal object to the CurrentPrincipal property of the current System.Threading.Thread.

The System.Security.Principal.WindowsIdentity class provides the functionality through which you invoke impersonation. However, the exact process depends on which version of Windows your application is running. If it's running on Windows Server 2003 or later, the WindowsIdentity class supports constructor overloads that create WindowsIdentity objects based on the account name of the user you want to impersonate. On all previous versions of Windows, you must first obtain a System.IntPtr containing a reference to a Windows access token that represents the user to impersonate. To obtain the access token reference, you must use a native method such as the LogonUser function from the Win32 API.

■**Caution** A major issue with performing impersonation on Microsoft Windows 2000 and Windows NT is that an account must have the Windows privilege SE_TCB_NAME to execute LogonUser. This requires you to configure Windows security policy and grant the account the right to "act as part of operating system." This grants the account a very high level of trust. You should never grant the privilege SE_TCB_NAME directly to user accounts. The requirement for an account to have the SE_TCB_NAME privilege no longer exists for Windows 2003, Windows XP, and Windows Vista.

Once you have a WindowsIdentity object representing the user you want to impersonate, call its Impersonate method. From that point on, all actions your code performs occur in the context of the impersonated Windows account. The Impersonate method returns a System.Security.Principal.

WindowsSecurityContext object, which represents the active account prior to impersonation. To revert to the original account, call the Undo method of this WindowsSecurityContext object.

The Code

The following example demonstrates impersonation of a Windows user. The example uses the LogonUser function of the Win32 API to obtain a Windows access token for the specified user, impersonates the user, and then reverts to the original user context.

```
Imports System
Imports System.IO
Imports System.Security.Principal
Imports System.Security.Permissions
Imports System.Runtime.InteropServices

' Ensure the assembly has permission to execute unmanaged code
' and control the thread principal.
<Assembly: SecurityPermission(SecurityAction.RequestMinimum, UnmanagedCode:=True, ➥
ControlPrincipal:=True)>
Namespace Apress.VisualBasicRecipes.Chapter11
    Public Class Recipe11_12

        ' Define some constants for use with the LogonUser function.
        Const LOGON32_PROVIDER_DEFAULT As Integer = 0
        Const LOGON32_LOGON_INTERACTIVE As Integer = 2

        ' Import the Win32 LogonUser function from advapi32.dll. Specify
        ' "SetLastError = True" to correctly support access to Win32 error
        ' codes.
        <DllImport("advapi32.dll", SetLastError:=True, CharSet:=CharSet.Unicode)> _
        Private Shared Function LogonUser(ByVal userName As String, ➥
ByVal domain As String, ByVal password As String, ByVal logonType As Integer, ➥
ByVal logonProvider As Integer, ByRef accessToken As IntPtr) As Boolean
        End Function

        Public Shared Sub Main(ByVal args As String())

            ' Create a new IntPtr to hold the access token returned by the
            ' LogonUser function.
            Dim accessToken As IntPtr = IntPtr.Zero

            ' Call the LogonUser function to obtain an access token for the
            ' specified user. The accessToken variable is passed to LogonUser
            ' by reference and will contain a reference to the Windows access
            ' token if LogonUser is successful.
            Dim success As Boolean = LogonUser(args(0), ".", args(1), ➥
LOGON32_LOGON_INTERACTIVE, LOGON32_PROVIDER_DEFAULT, accessToken)

            ' If LogonUser returns false, an error has occurred.
            ' Display the error and exit.
```

```
            If Not success Then
                  Console.WriteLine("LogonUser returned error {0}", ➥
Marshal.GetLastWin32Error())
            Else
                  ' Display the active identity.
                  Console.WriteLine("Identity before impersonation = {0}", ➥
WindowsIdentity.GetCurrent.Name)
                  ' Create a new WindowsIdentity from the Windows access token.
                  Dim identity As New WindowsIdentity(accessToken)

                  ' Impersonate the specified user, saving a reference to the
                  ' returned WindowsImpersonationContext, which contains the
                  ' information necessary to revert to the original user context.
                  Dim impContext As WindowsImpersonationContext = ➥
identity.Impersonate

                  ' Display the active identity.
                  Console.WriteLine("Identity during impersonation = {0}", ➥
WindowsIdentity.GetCurrent.Name)

                  ' Perform actions as the impersonated user...

                  ' Revert to the original Windows user using the
                  ' WindowsImpersonationContext object.
                  impContext.Undo()

                  ' Display the active identity.
                  Console.WriteLine("Identity after impersonation = {0}", ➥
WindowsIdentity.GetCurrent.Name)

                  ' Wait to continue.
                  Console.WriteLine(Environment.NewLine)
                  Console.WriteLine("Main method complete.  Press Enter.")
                  Console.ReadLine()

            End If

        End Sub

    End Class
End Namespace
```

Usage

The example expects two command-line arguments: the account name of the user on the local machine to impersonate and the account's password. For example, the command Recipe11-12 Administrator password impersonates the user Administrator, as long as that user exists in the local accounts database and has the password "password."

11-13. Create a Cryptographically Random Number

Problem

You need to create a random number that is suitable for use in cryptographic and security applications.

Solution

Use a cryptographic random number generator, derived from `System.Security.Cryptography.RandomNumberGenerator` such as the `System.Security.Cryptography.RNGCryptoServiceProvider` class.

How It Works

The `System.Random` class is a pseudo-random number generator that uses a mathematical algorithm to simulate the generation of random numbers. In fact, the algorithm it uses is deterministic, meaning that you can always calculate what the next number will be based on the previously generated number. This means that numbers generated by the `Random` class are unsuitable for use in situations in which security is a priority, such as generating encryption keys and passwords.

When you need a nondeterministic random number for use in cryptographic or security-related applications, you must use a random number generator derived from the class `RandomNumberGenerator`. The `RandomNumberGenerator` class is an abstract (`MustInherit`) class from which all concrete .NET random number generator classes should inherit. Currently, the `RNGCryptoServiceProvider` class is the only concrete implementation provided. The `RNGCryptoServiceProvider` class provides a managed wrapper around the `CryptGenRandom` function of the Win32 CryptoAPI, and you can use it to fill `Byte` arrays with cryptographically random `Byte` values.

■Note The numbers produced by the `RNGCryptoServiceProvider` class are not truly random. However, they are sufficiently random to meet the requirements of cryptography and security applications in most commercial and government environments.

As is the case with many of the .NET cryptography classes, the `RandomNumberGenerator` base class is a factory for the concrete implementation classes that derive from it. Calling `RandomNumberGenerator.Create("System.Security.Cryptography.RNGCryptoServiceProvider")` will return an instance of `RNGCryptoServiceProvider` that you can use to generate random numbers. In addition, because `RNGCryptoServiceProvider` is the only concrete implementation provided, it's the default class created if you call the `Create` method without arguments, as in `RandomNumberGenerator.Create()`.

Once you have a `RandomNumberGenerator` instance, the method `GetBytes` fills a `Byte` array with random `Byte` values. As an alternative, you can use the `GetNonZeroBytes` method if you need random data that contains no zero values.

The Code

The following example instantiates an `RNGCryptoServiceProvider` object and uses it to generate random values.

```vbnet
Imports System
Imports System.Security.Cryptography

Namespace Apress.VisualBasicRecipes.Chapter11
    Public Class Recipe11_13

        Public Shared Sub Main()

            ' Create a byte array to hold the random data.
            Dim number As Byte() = New Byte(32) {}

            ' Instantiate the default random number generator.
            Dim rng As RandomNumberGenerator = RandomNumberGenerator.Create

            ' Generate 32 bytes of random data.
            rng.GetBytes(number)

            ' Display the random number.
            Console.WriteLine(BitConverter.ToString(number))

            ' Wait to continue.
            Console.WriteLine(Environment.NewLine)
            Console.WriteLine("Main method compelte.  Press Enter.")
            Console.ReadLine()

        End Sub

    End Class
End Namespace
```

■**Note** The computational effort required to generate a random number with `RNGCryptoServiceProvider` is significantly greater than that required by `Random`. For everyday purposes, the use of `RNGCryptoServiceProvider` is overkill. You should consider the quantity of random numbers you need to generate and the purpose of the numbers before deciding to use `RNGCryptoServiceProvider`. Excessive and unnecessary use of the `RNGCryptoServiceProvider` class could have a noticeable effect on application performance if many random numbers are generated.

11-14. Calculate the Hash Code of a Password

Problem

You need to store a user's password securely so that you can use it to authenticate the user in the future.

Solution

Create and store a cryptographic hash code of the password using a hashing algorithm class derived from the `System.Security.Cryptography.HashAlgorithm` class. On future authentication attempts, generate the hash of the password entered by the user and compare it to the stored hash code.

■**Caution** You should never store a user's plaintext password, because it is a major security risk and one that most users would not appreciate, given that many of them will use the same password to access multiple systems.

How It Works

Hashing algorithms are one-way cryptographic functions that take plaintext of variable length and generate a fixed-size numeric value. They are *one-way* because it's nearly impossible to derive the original plaintext from the hash code. Hashing algorithms are deterministic; applying the same hashing algorithm to a specific piece of plaintext always generates the same hash code. This makes hash codes useful for determining if two blocks of plaintext (passwords in this case) are the same. The design of hashing algorithms ensures that the chance of two different pieces of plaintext generating the same hash code is extremely small (although not impossible). In addition, there is no correlation between the similarity of two pieces of plaintext and their hash codes; minor differences in the plaintext cause significant differences in the resulting hash codes.

When using passwords to authenticate a user, you are not concerned with the content of the password that the user enters. You need to know only that the entered password matches the password that you have recorded for that user in your accounts database.

The nature of hashing algorithms makes them ideal for storing passwords securely. When the user provides a new password, you must create the hash code of the password and store it, and then discard the plaintext password. Each time the user tries to authenticate with your application, calculate the hash code of the password that user provides and compare it with the hash code you have stored.

■**Note** People regularly ask how to obtain a password from a hash code. The simple answer is that you cannot. The whole purpose of a hash code is to act as a token that you can freely store without creating security holes. If a user forgets a password, you cannot derive it from the stored hash code. Rather, you must either reset the account to some default value or generate a new password for the user.

Generating hash codes is simple in the .NET Framework. The MustInherit class HashAlgorithm provides a base from which all concrete hashing algorithm implementations derive. The .NET Framework class library includes the seven hashing algorithm implementations listed in Table 11-4; each implementation class is a member of the System.Security.Cryptography namespace. The classes with names ending in CryptoServiceProvider wrap functionality provided by the native Win32 CryptoAPI, whereas those with names ending in Managed are fully implemented in managed code. In the case of sha1, SHA1CryptoServiceProvider and SHA1Managed both implement the same algorithm, but the SHA1Managed class uses the *managed* library rather than wrapping the CryptoAPI (CAPI).

Table 11-4. *Hashing Algorithm Implementations*

Algorithm Name	Class Name	Hash Code Size (in Bits)
MD5	MD5CryptoServiceProvider	128
RIPEMD160 or RIPEMD-160	RIPEMD160Managed	160
SHA or SHA1	SHA1CryptoServiceProvider	160
SHA1Managed	SHA1Managed	160
SHA256 or SHA-256	SHA256Managed	256

Table 11-4. *Hashing Algorithm Implementations*

Algorithm Name	Class Name	Hash Code Size (in Bits)
SHA384 or SHA-384	SHA384Managed	384
SHA512 or SHA-512	SHA512Managed	512

Although you can create instances of the hashing algorithm classes directly, the HashAlgorithm base class is a factory for the concrete implementation classes that derive from it. Calling the Shared method HashAlgorithm.Create will return an object of the specified type. Using the factory approach allows you to write generic code that can work with any hashing algorithm implementation. Note that unlike in recipe 11-13, you do not pass the class name as parameter to the factory; instead, you pass the algorithm name. If you do not specify an algorithm name, the default, SHA1Managed, is used.

Once you have a HashAlgorithm object, its ComputeHash method accepts a Byte array argument containing plaintext and returns a new Byte array containing the generated hash code. Table 11-4 shows the size of hash code (in bits) generated by each hashing algorithm class.

■**Note** The SHA1Managed algorithm cannot be implemented using the factory approach. It must be instantiated directly.

The Code

The example shown here demonstrates the creation of a hash code from a string, such as a password. The application expects two command-line arguments: the name of the hashing algorithm to use and the string from which to generate the hash. Because the HashAlgorithm.ComputeHash method requires a Byte array, you must first byte-encode the input string using the class System.Text. Encoding, which provides mechanisms for converting strings to and from various character-encoding formats.

```
Imports System
imports System.Text
imports System.Security.Cryptography

Namespace Apress.VisualBasicRecipes.Chapter11
    Public Class Recipe11_14

        Public Shared Sub Main(ByVal args As String())

            ' Create a HashAlgorithm of the type specified by the first
            ' command-line argument.
            Dim hashAlg As HashAlgorithm = Nothing

            ' The SHA1Managed algorithm cannot be implemented using the
            ' factory approach. It must be instantiated directly.
            If args(0).CompareTo("SHA1Managed") = 0 The
                hashAlg = New SHA1Managed
            Else
                hashAlg = HashAlgorithm.Create(args(0))
            End If
```

```
    Using hashAlg

        ' Convert the password string, provided as the second
        ' command-line argument, to an array of bytes.
        Dim pwordData As Byte() = Encoding.Default.GetBytes(args(1))

        ' Generate the hash code of the password.
        Dim hash As Byte() = hashAlg.ComputeHash(pwordData)

        ' Display the hash code of the password to the console.
        Console.WriteLine(BitConverter.ToString(hash))

        ' Wait to continue.
        Console.WriteLine(Environment.NewLine)
        Console.WriteLine("Main method complete.  Press Enter.")
        Console.ReadLine()

    End Using

    End Sub

  End Class
End Namespace
```

Usage

Running the following command:

```
Recipe11-14 SHA1 ThisIsMyPassword
```

will display the following hash code to the console:

```
30-B8-BD-58-29-88-89-00-D1-5D-2B-BE-62-70-D9-BC-65-B0-70-2F
```

In contrast, executing this command:

```
Recipe11-14 RIPEMD-160 ThisIsMyPassword
```

will display the following hash code:

```
0C-39-3B-2E-8A-4E-D3-DD-FB-E3-C8-05-E4-62-6F-6B-76-7C-7A-49
```

11-15. Calculate the Hash Code of a File

Problem

You need to determine if the contents of a file have changed over time.

Solution

Create a cryptographic hash code of the file's contents using the ComputeHash method of the System. Security.Cryptography.HashAlgorithm class. Store the hash code for future comparison against newly generated hash codes.

How It Works

As well as allowing you to store passwords securely (discussed in recipe 11-14), hash codes provide an excellent means of determining if a file has changed. By calculating and storing the cryptographic hash of a file, you can later recalculate the hash of the file to determine if the file has changed in the interim. A hashing algorithm will produce a very different hash code even if the file has been changed only slightly, and the chances of two different files resulting in the same hash code are extremely small.

■**Caution** Standard hash codes are not suitable for sending with a file to ensure the integrity of the file's contents. If someone intercepts the file in transit, that person can easily change the file and recalculate the hash code, leaving the recipient none the wiser. Recipe 11-17 discusses a variant of the hash code—a keyed hash code—that is suitable for ensuring the integrity of a file in transit.

The HashAlgorithm class makes it easy to generate the hash code of a file. First, instantiate one of the concrete hashing algorithm implementations derived from the HashAlgorithm class. To instantiate the desired hashing algorithm class, pass the name of the hashing algorithm to the HashAlgorithm. Create method, as described in recipe 11-14. See Table 11-4 for a list of valid hashing algorithm names. Then, instead of passing a Byte array to the ComputeHash method, you pass a System.IO. Stream object representing the file from which you want to generate the hash code. The HashAlgorithm object handles the process of reading data from the Stream and returns a Byte array containing the hash code for the file.

■**Note** The SHA1Managed algorithm cannot be implemented using the factory approach. It must be instantiated directly.

The Code

The example shown here demonstrates the generation of a hash code from a file. The application expects two command-line arguments: the name of the hashing algorithm to use and the name of the file from which the hash is calculated.

```
Imports System
Imports System.IO
Imports System.Security.Cryptography

Namespace Apress.VisualBasicRecipes.Chapter11
    Public Class Recipe11_15

        Public Shared Sub Main(ByVal args As String())
```

```vb
' Create a HashAlgorithm of the type specified by the first
' command-line argument.
Dim hashAlg As HashAlgorithm = Nothing

' The SHA1Managed algorithm cannot be implemented using the
' factory approach. It must be instantiated directly.
If args(0).CompareTo("SHA1Managed") = 0 Then
    hashAlg = New SHA1Managed
Else
    hashAlg = HashAlgorithm.Create(args(0))
End If

' Open a FileStream to the file specified by the second
' command-line argument.
Using fileArg As New FileStream(args(1), FileMode.Open, FileAccess.Read)

    ' Generate the hash code of the password.
    Dim hash As Byte() = hashAlg.ComputeHash(fileArg)

    ' Display the hash code of the password to the console.
    Console.WriteLine(BitConverter.ToString(hash))

    ' Wait to continue.
    Console.WriteLine(Environment.NewLine)
    Console.WriteLine("Main method complete.  Press Enter.")
    Console.ReadLine()

End Using

End Sub

End Class
End Namespace
```

Usage

Running this command:

```
Recipe11-15 SHA1 Recipe11-15.exe
```

will display the following hash code to the console:

```
F9-0E-31-C7-57-82-11-A3-9B-9F-0C-A3-CB-54-4C-34-68-30-19-58
```

In contrast, executing this command:

```
Recipe11-15 RIPEMD-160 Recipe11-15.exe
```

will display the following hash code:

```
FB-21-82-E7-0F-BA-71-C4-0B-A0-9A-EB-BC-9D-D3-44-6E-D7-5A-CA
```

11-16. Verify a Hash Code

Problem

You need to verify a password or confirm that a file remains unchanged by comparing two hash codes.

Solution

Convert both the old and the new hash codes to hexadecimal code strings, Base64 strings, or Byte arrays and compare them.

How It Works

You can use hash codes to determine if two pieces of data (such as passwords or files) are the same, without the need to store, or even maintain access to, the original data. To determine if data changes over time, you must generate and store the original data's hash code. Later, you can generate another hash code for the data and compare the old and new hash codes, which will show if any change has occurred. The format in which you store the original hash code will determine the most appropriate way to verify a newly generated hash code against the stored one.

Note The recipes in this chapter use the ToString method of the class System.BitConverter to convert Byte arrays to hexadecimal string values for display. Although easy to use and appropriate for display purposes, this approach may be inappropriate for use when storing hash codes, because it places a hyphen (-) between each byte value (for example, 4D-79-3A-C9-. . .). In addition, the BitConverter class does not provide a method to parse such a string representation back into a Byte array.

Hash codes are often stored in text files, either as hexadecimal strings (for example, *89D22213170A9CFF09A392F00E2C6C4EDC1B0EF9*), or as Base64-encoded strings (for example, *idIiExcKnP8Jo5LwDixsTtwbDvk=*). Alternatively, hash codes may be stored in databases as raw byte values. Regardless of how you store your hash code, the first step in comparing old and new hash codes is to get them both into a common form.

The Code

This following example contains three methods that use different approaches to compare hash codes:

- VerifyHexHash: This method converts a new hash code (a Byte array) to a hexadecimal string for comparison to an old hash code. Other than the BitConverter.ToString method, the .NET Framework class library does not provide an easy method to convert a Byte array to a hexadecimal string. You must program a loop to step through the elements of the byte array, convert each individual byte to a string, and append the string to the hexadecimal string representation of the hash code. The use of a System.Text.StringBuilder avoids the unnecessary creation of new strings each time the loop appends the next byte value to the result string. (See recipe 2-1 for more details.)

- VerifyB64Hash: This method takes a new hash code as a Byte array and the old hash code as a Base64-encoded string. The method encodes the new hash code as a Base64 string and performs a straightforward string comparison of the two values.

- VerifyByteHash: This method compares two hash codes represented as Byte arrays. The .NET Framework class library does not include a method that performs this type of comparison, and so you must program a loop to compare the elements of the two arrays. This code uses a few timesaving techniques, namely ensuring that the Byte arrays are the same length before starting to compare them and returning False on the first difference found.

```vb
Imports System
Imports System.Text
Imports System.Security.Cryptography

Namespace Apress.VisualBasicRecipes.Chapter11
    Public Class Recipe11_16

        ' A method to compare a newly generated hash code with an
        ' existing hash code that's represented by a hex code string.
        Private Shared Function VerifyHexHash(ByVal hash As Byte(), ➥
ByVal oldHashString As String)

            ' Create a string representation of the hash code bytes.
            Dim newHashString As New StringBuilder(hash.Length)

            ' Append each byte as a two-character uppercase hex string.
            For Each b As Byte In hash
                newHashString.AppendFormat("{0:X2}", b)
            Next

            ' Compare the string representation of the old and new hash
            ' codes and return the result.
            Return oldHashString.Replace("-", "") = newHashString.ToString

        End Function

        ' A method to compare a newly generated hash code with an
        ' existing hash code that's represented by a Base64-encoded
        ' string.
        Private Shared Function VerifyB64Hash(ByVal hash As Byte(), ➥
ByVal oldHashString As String) As Boolean

            ' Create a Base64 representation of the hash code bytes.
            Dim newHashString As String = Convert.ToBase64String(hash)

            ' Compare the string representations of the old and new hash
            ' codes and return the result.
            Return oldHashString = newHashString

        End Function

        ' A method to compare a newly generated hash code with an
        ' existing hash code represented by a byte array.
        Private Shared Function VerifyByteHash(ByVal hash As Byte(), ➥
ByVal oldHash As Byte()) As Boolean
```

```vbnet
            ' If either array is nothing or the arrays are different lengths,
            ' then they are not equal.
            If hash Is Nothing Or oldHash Is Nothing Or Not (hash.Length = ➡
        oldHash.Length) Then
                Return False
            End If

            ' Step through the byte arrays and compare each byte value.
            For count As Integer = 0 To hash.Length - 1
                If Not hash(count) = oldHash(count) Then Return False
            Next

            ' Hash codes are equal.
            Return True

        End Function

    End Class
End Namespace
```

11-17. Ensure Data Integrity Using a Keyed Hash Code

Problem

You need to transmit a file to someone and provide the recipient with a means to verify the integrity of the file and its source.

Solution

Share a secret key with the intended recipient. This key would ideally be a randomly generated number, but it could also be a phrase that you and the recipient agree to use. Use the key with one of the keyed hashing algorithm classes derived from the System.Security.Cryptography. KeyedHashAlgorithm class to create a keyed hash code. Send the hash code with the file. On receipt of the file, the recipient will generate the keyed hash code of the file using the shared secret key. If the hash codes are equal, the recipient knows that the file is from you and that it has not changed in transit.

How It Works

Hash codes are useful for comparing two pieces of data to determine if they are the same, even if you no longer have access to the original data. However, you cannot use a hash code to reassure the recipient of data as to the data's integrity. If someone could intercept the data, that person could replace the data and generate a new hash code. When the recipient verifies the hash code, it will seem correct, even though the data is actually nothing like what you sent originally.

A simple and efficient solution to the problem of data integrity is a *keyed hash code*. A keyed hash code is similar to a normal hash code (discussed in recipes 11-14 and 11-15); however, the keyed hash code incorporates an element of secret data—a *key*—known only to the sender and the receiver. Without the key, a person cannot generate the correct hash code from a given set of data. When you successfully verify a keyed hash code, you can be certain that only someone who knows the secret key could generate the hash code.

■**Caution** The secret key must remain secret. Anyone who knows the secret key can generate valid keyed hash codes, meaning that you would be unable to determine if someone else who knew the key had changed the content of a document. For this reason, you should not transmit or store the secret key with the document whose integrity you are trying to protect.

Generating keyed hash codes is similar to generating normal hash codes. All HMAC algorithm classes, excluding MACTripleDES, derive themselves from the HMAC base class, which inherits the KeyedHashAlgorithm class, which inherits the HashAlgorithm class. MACTripleDES inherits the KeyedHashAlgorithm base class directly. The .NET Framework class library includes the seven keyed hashing algorithm implementations listed in Table 11-5. Each implementation is a member of the namespace System.Security.Cryptography.

Table 11-5. *Keyed Hashing Algorithm Implementations*

Algorithm/Class Name	Key Size (in Bits)	Hash Code Size (in Bits)
HMACMD5 (new in .NET 2.0)	Any	128
HMACRIPEMD160 (new in .NET 2.0)	Any	160
HMACSHA1	Any	160
HMACSHA256 (new in .NET 2.0)	Any	256
HMACSHA384 (new in .NET 2.0)	Any	384
HMACSHA512 (new in .NET 2.0)	Any	512
MACTripleDES	128, 192	64

As with the standard hashing algorithms, you can either create keyed hashing algorithm objects directly or use the Shared factory method KeyedHashAlgorithm.Create and pass the algorithm name as an argument. Using the factory approach allows you to write generic code that can work with any keyed hashing algorithm implementation, but as shown in Table 11-5, MACTripleDES supports fixed key lengths that you must accommodate in generic code.

If you use constructors to instantiate a keyed hashing object, you can pass the secret key to the constructor. Using the factory approach, you must set the key using the Key property inherited from the KeyedHashAlgorithm class. Then call the ComputeHash method and pass either a Byte array or a System.IO.Stream object. The keyed hashing algorithm will process the input data and return a Byte array containing the keyed hash code. Table 11-5 shows the size of hash code generated by each keyed hashing algorithm.

The Code

The following example demonstrates the generation of a keyed hash code from a file. The example uses the given class to generate the keyed hash code, and then displays it to the console. The example requires three command-line arguments: the name of the file from which the hash is calculated, the name of the algorithm to instantiate, and the key to use when calculating the hash.

```vbnet
Imports System
Imports System.IO
Imports System.Text
Imports System.Security.Cryptography

Namespace Apress.VisualBasicRecipes.Chapter11
    Public Class Recipe11_17

        Public Shared Sub Main(ByVal args As String())

            ' Create a byte array from the key string, which is the
            ' third command-line argument.
            Dim key As Byte() = Encoding.Default.GetBytes(args(2))

            ' Create a KeyedHashAlgorithm derived object to generate the keyed
            ' hash code for the input file. Pass the byte array representing
            ' the key to the constructor.
            Using hashAlg As KeyedHashAlgorithm = KeyedHashAlgorithm.Create(args(1))

                ' Assign the key.
                hashAlg.Key = key

                ' Open a FileStream to read the input file. The filename is
                ' specified by the first command-line argument.
                Using argFile As New FileStream(args(0), FileMode.Open, ➡
FileAccess.Read)

                    ' Generate the keyed hash code of the file's contents.
                    Dim hash As Byte() = hashAlg.ComputeHash(argFile)

                    ' Display the keyed hash code to the console.
                    Console.WriteLine(BitConverter.ToString(hash))

                End Using
            End Using

            ' Wait to continue.
            Console.WriteLine(Environment.NewLine)
            Console.WriteLine("Main method compelte.  Press Enter.")
            Console.ReadLine()

        End Sub

    End Class
End Namespace
```

Usage

Executing the following command:

Recipe11-17 Recipe11-17.exe HMACSHA1 secretKey

will display the following hash code to the console:

```
53-E6-03-59-C8-BB-F6-74-51-BF-B6-C3-75-B2-78-0B-43-01-3A-E0
```

In contrast, executing this command:

```
Recipe11-17 Recipe11-17.exe HMACSHA1 anotherKey
```

will display the following hash code to the console:

```
70-2C-77-88-86-87-F4-89-0D-E2-DD-0A-B3-85-B7-4E-E6-7D-67-F6
```

11-18. Work with Security-Sensitive Strings in Memory

Problem

You need to work with sensitive string data, such as passwords or credit card numbers, in memory and need to minimize the risk of other people or processes accessing that data.

Solution

Use the class `System.Security.SecureString` to hold the sensitive data values in memory.

How It Works

Storing sensitive data such as passwords, personal details, and banking information in memory as `String` objects is insecure for many reasons, including the following:

- `String` objects are not encrypted.

- The immutability of `String` objects means that whenever you change the `String`, the old `String` value is left in memory until it is dereferenced by the garbage collector and eventually overwritten.

- Because the garbage collector is free to reorganize the contents of the managed heap, multiple copies of your sensitive data may be present on the heap.

- If part of your process address space is swapped to disk or a memory dump is written to disk, a copy of your data may be stored on the disk.

Each of these factors increases the opportunities for others to access your sensitive data. In .NET Framework versions 1.0 and 1.1, one solution to these problems is to use `Byte` arrays to hold an encrypted version of the sensitive data. You have much better control over a `Byte` array than you do with a `String`; principally, you can wipe the array any time you like. .NET Framework 2.0 introduces the `SecureString` class to simplify the task of working with sensitive `String` data in memory.

You create a `SecureString` as either initially empty or from a pointer to a character (`Char`) array. Then you manipulate the contents of the `SecureString` one character at a time using the methods `AppendChar`, `InsertAt`, `RemoveAt`, and `SetAt`. As you add characters to the `SecureString`, they are encrypted using the capabilities of the Data Protection API (DPAPI).

> **■Note** The SecureString class uses features of the DPAPI and is available only on Windows 2000 SP3 and later operating system versions.

The SecureString class also provides a method named MakeReadOnly. As the name suggests, calling MakeReadOnly configures the SecureString to no longer allow its value to be changed. Attempting to modify a SecureString marked as read-only results in the exception System.InvalidOperationException being thrown. Once you have set the SecureString to read-only, it cannot be undone.

The SecureString class has a ToString method, but rather than retrieving a string representation of the contained data, it returns only a representation of the type (System.Security.SecureString). Instead, the class System.Runtime.InteropServices.Marshal implements a number of Shared methods that take a SecureString object; decrypts it; converts it to a binary string, a block of ANSI, or a block of Unicode data; and returns a System.IntPtr object that points to the converted data. The Marshal class also offers Shared methods for displaying the contents referenced by an IntPtr. Here is a code snippet to demonstrate this:

```
' Retrieve a pointer to the data contained in a
' SecureString.
Dim secureStringPtr As IntPtr = ➥
Marshal.SecureStringToGlobalAllocUnicode(mySecureString)

' Retrieve a string representation of the data
' referenced by a pointer.
Dim clearText As String = Marshal.PtrToStringAuto(secureStringPtr)

' Display the secure string contents in clear text.
Console.WriteLine(clearText))
```

At any time, you can call the SecureString.Clear method to clear the sensitive data, and when you have finished with the SecureString object, call its Dispose method to clear the data and free the memory. SecureString implements System.IDisposable.

> **■Note** Although it might seem that the benefits of the SecureString class are limited, because there is no way in Windows Forms applications to get such a secured string from the GUI without first retrieving a nonsecured String through a TextBox or another control, it is likely that third parties and future additions to the .NET Framework will use the SecureString class to handle sensitive data. This is already the case in System.Diagnostics. ProcessStartInfo, where using a SecureString, you can set the Password property to the password of the user context in which the new process should be run.

The Code

The following example reads a username and password from the console and starts Notepad.exe as the specified user. The password is masked on input and stored in a SecureString in memory, maximizing the chances of the password remaining secret.

```
Imports System
Imports System.Security
Imports System.Diagnostics

Namespace Apress.VisualBasicRecipes.Chapter11
    Public Class Recipe11_18
```

```vb
Public Shared Function ReadString() As SecureString

    ' Create a new empty SecureString.
    Dim str As New SecureString

    ' Read the string from the console one
    ' character at a time without displaying it.
    Dim nextChar As ConsoleKeyInfo = Console.ReadKey(True)

    ' Read characters until Enter is pressed.
    While Not nextChar.Key = ConsoleKey.Enter

        If nextChar.Key = ConsoleKey.Backspace Then
            If str.Length > 0 Then
                ' Backspace pressed. Remove the last character.
                str.RemoveAt(str.Length - 1)

                Console.Write(nextChar.KeyChar)
                Console.Write(" ")
                Console.Write(nextChar.KeyChar)
            Else
                Console.Beep()
            End If
        Else
            ' Append the character to the SecureString and
            ' display a masked character.
            str.AppendChar(nextChar.KeyChar)
            Console.Write("*")
        End If

        ' Read the next character.
        nextChar = Console.ReadKey(True)

    End While

    ' String entry finished.  Make it read-only.
    str.MakeReadOnly()

    Return str

End Function

Public Shared Sub Main()

    Dim user As String = ""

    ' Get the username under which Notepad.exe will be run.
    Console.Write("Enter the user name: ")
    user = Console.ReadLine
```

```
' Get the user's password as a SecureString.
Console.Write("Enter the user's password: ")
Using pword As SecureString = ReadString()

    ' Start Notepad as the specified user.
    Dim startInfo As New ProcessStartInfo

    startInfo.FileName = "Notepad.exe"
    startInfo.UserName = user
    startInfo.Password = pword
    startInfo.UseShellExecute = False

    ' Create a new Process object.
    Using proc As New Process

        ' Assign the ProcessStartInfo to the Process object.
        proc.StartInfo = startInfo

        Try
            ' Start the new process.
            proc.Start()
        Catch ex As Exception
            Console.WriteLine(Environment.NewLine)
            Console.WriteLine(Environment.NewLine)
            Console.WriteLine("Could not start Notepad process.")
            Console.WriteLine(ex.ToString)
        End Try

    End Using

End Using

' Wait to continue.
Console.WriteLine(Environment.NewLine)
Console.WriteLine("Main method complete.  Press Enter")
Console.ReadLine()

    End Sub

End Class
End Namespace
```

11-19. Encrypt and Decrypt Data Using the Data Protection API

Problem

You need a convenient way to securely encrypt data without the headache associated with key management.

Solution

Use the `ProtectedData` and `ProtectedMemory` classes of the `System.Security.Cryptography` namespace in .NET Framework 2.0 to access the encryption and key management capabilities provided by the DPAPI.

How It Works

Given that the .NET Framework provides you with well-tested implementations of the most widely used and trusted encryption algorithms, the biggest challenge you face when using cryptography is key management—namely the effective generation, storage, and sharing of keys to facilitate the use of cryptography. In fact, key management is the biggest problem facing most people when they want to securely store or transmit data using cryptographic techniques. If implemented incorrectly, key management can easily render useless all of your efforts to encrypt your data.

DPAPI provides encryption and decryption services without the need for you to worry about key management. DPAPI automatically generates keys based on Windows user credentials, stores keys securely as part of your profile, and even provides automated key expiry without losing access to previously encrypted data.

■**Note** DPAPI is suitable for many common uses of cryptography in Windows applications, but will not help you in situations that require you to distribute or share secret or public keys with other users.

In versions 1.0 and 1.1 of the .NET Framework, you needed to use P/Invoke to work with DPAPI. .NET Framework 2.0 introduces in `System.Security` two managed classes that provide easy access to the encryption and decryption capabilities of DPAPI: `ProtectedData` and `ProtectedMemory`. Both classes allow you to encrypt a `Byte` array by passing it to the `Shared` method `Protect`, and decrypt a `Byte` array of encrypted data by passing it the `Shared` method `Unprotect`. The difference in the classes is in the scope that they allow you to specify when you encrypt and decrypt data.

■**Caution** You must use `ProtectedData` if you intend to store encrypted data and reboot your machine before decrypting it. `ProtectedMemory` will be unable to decrypt data that was encrypted before a reboot.

When you call `ProtectedData.Protect`, you specify a value from the enumeration `System.Security.Cryptography.DataProtectionScope`. The following are the possible values:

- `CurrentUser`, which means that only code running in the context of the current user can decrypt the data
- `LocalMachine`, which means that any code running on the same computer can decrypt the data

When you call `ProtectedMemory.Protect`, you specify a value from the enumeration `System.Security.Cryptography.MemoryProtectionScope`. The possible values are as follows:

- `CrossProcess`, which means that any code in any process can decrypt the encrypted data
- `SameLogon`, which means that only code running in the same user context can decrypt the data
- `SameProcess`, which means that only code running in the same process can decrypt the data

Both classes allow you to specify additional data (*entropy*) when you encrypt your data. This entropy is used to further encrypt the data, making certain types of cryptographic attacks less likely to succeed. If you choose to use entropy when you protect data, you must use the same entropy value when you unprotect the data. It is not essential that you keep the entropy data secret, so it can be stored freely without encryption.

The Code

The following example demonstrates the use of the `ProtectedData` class to encrypt a string entered at the console by the user. Note that you need to reference the `System.Security` assembly.

```
Imports System
Imports System.Text
Imports System.Security.Cryptography

Namespace Apress.VisualBasicRecipes.Chapter11
    Public Class Recipe11_19

        Public Shared Sub Main()

            ' Read the string from the console.
            Console.Write("Enter the string to encrypt: ")
            Dim str As String = Console.ReadLine

            ' Create a byte array of entropy to use in the encryption process.
            Dim entropy As Byte() = {0, 1, 2, 3, 4, 5, 6, 7, 8}

            ' Encrypt the entered string after converting it to a
            ' byte array. Use CurrentUser scope so that only the
            ' current user can decrypt the data.
            Dim enc As Byte() = ProtectedData.Protect( ➡
Encoding.Default.GetBytes(str), entropy, DataProtectionScope.CurrentUser)

            ' Display the encrypted data to the console.
            Console.WriteLine(Environment.NewLine)
            Console.WriteLine("Encrypted string = {0}", BitConverter.ToString(enc))

            ' Attempt to decrypt the data using CurrentUser scope.
            Dim dec As Byte() = ProtectedData.Unprotect(enc, entropy, ➡
DataProtectionScope.CurrentUser)

            ' Display the data decrypted using CurrentUser scope.
            Console.WriteLine(Environment.NewLine)
            Console.WriteLine("Decrypted data using CurrentUser scope = {0}", ➡
Encoding.Default.GetString(dec))

            ' Wait to continue.
            Console.WriteLine(Environment.NewLine)
            Console.WriteLine("Main method complete.  Press Enter.")
            Console.ReadLine()

        End Sub

    End Class
End Namespace
```

CHAPTER 12

■ ■ ■

Unmanaged Code Interoperability

The Microsoft .NET Framework is an extremely ambitious platform, combining a managed runtime (the common language runtime, or CLR), a platform for hosting web applications (Microsoft ASP.NET), and an extensive class library for building all types of applications. However, as expansive as the .NET Framework is, it does not duplicate all the features that are available in unmanaged code. Currently, the .NET Framework does not include every function that is available in the Win32 API, and many businesses are using complex proprietary solutions that they have built with COM-based languages such as Microsoft Visual Basic 6 (VB6) and Visual C++ 6.

Fortunately, Microsoft does not intend for businesses to abandon the code base they have built up when they move to the .NET platform. Instead, the .NET Framework is equipped with interoperability features that allow you to use legacy code from .NET Framework applications and even access .NET assemblies as though they were COM components. The recipes in this chapter describe how to do the following:

- Call functions defined in an unmanaged DLL, get the handles for a control or window, invoke an unmanaged function that uses a structure, invoke unmanaged callback functions, and retrieve unmanaged error information (recipes 12-1 through 12-5)

- Use COM components from .NET Framework applications, release COM components, and use optional parameters (recipes 12-6 through 12-8)

- Use ActiveX controls from .NET Framework applications (recipe 12-9)

- Expose the functionality of a .NET assembly as a COM component (recipe 12-10)

■**Note** *Managed* code refers to code developed in a .NET language (such as VB .NET and C#). This code is compiled to Microsoft Intermediary Language (MSIL) and runs within the CLR. When the code is executed, it is compiled to machine language using the just-in-time (JIT) compiler. *Unmanaged* code refers to code developed in a non-.NET language (such as C++ or VB6). This code is compiled directly to machine language. If you use Visual C++ .NET, you can create managed or unmanaged code, depending on the project type you select.

12-1. Call a Function in an Unmanaged DLL

Problem

You need to call a function in a DLL. This function might be a part of the Win32 API or your own legacy code.

Solution

Declare a method in your VB .NET code that you will use to access the unmanaged function. Declare this method as `Shared` and apply the attribute `System.Runtime.InteropServices.` `DllImportAttribute` to specify the DLL file and the name of the unmanaged function.

How It Works

To use a C function from an external library, all you need to do is declare it appropriately. The CLR automatically handles the rest, including loading the DLL into memory when the function is called and marshaling the parameters from .NET data types to C data types. The .NET service that supports this cross-platform execution is named PInvoke (Platform Invoke), and the process is usually seamless. Occasionally, you will need to do a little more work, such as when you need to support in-memory structures, callbacks, or mutable strings.

PInvoke is often used to access functionality in the Win32 API, particularly Win32 features that are not present in the set of managed classes that make up the .NET Framework. Three core libraries make up the Win32 API:

- Kernel32.dll includes operating system-specific functionality such as process loading, context switching, and file and memory I/O.

- User32.dll includes functionality for manipulating windows, menus, dialog boxes, icons, and so on.

- GDI32.dll includes graphical capabilities for drawing directly on windows, menus, and control surfaces, as well as for printing.

As an example, consider the Win32 API functions used for writing and reading INI files, such as `GetPrivateProfileString` and `WritePrivateProfileString`, in Kernel32.dll. The .NET Framework does not include any classes that wrap this functionality. However, you can import these functions using the attribute `DllImportAttribute`, like this:

```
<DllImport("kernel32.dll", EntryPoint:="WritePrivateProfileString")> _
Private Shared Function WritePrivateProfileString(ByVal lpAppName As String, ➥
    ByVal lpKeyName As String, ByVal lpString As String, ➥
    ByVal lpFileName As String) As Boolean
End Function
```

The arguments specified in the signature of the `WritePrivateProfileString` method must match the DLL method, or a runtime error will occur when you attempt to invoke it. Remember that you do not define any method body, because the declaration refers to a method in the DLL. The `EntryPoint` portion of the attribute `DllImportAttribute` is optional in this example. You do not need to specify the `EntryPoint` when the declared function name matches the function name in the external library.

The Code

The following is an example of using some Win32 API functions to get INI file information. It declares the unmanaged functions used and exposes `Public` methods to call them. The code first displays the current value of a key in the INI file, modifies it, retrieves the new value, and then writes the default value.

```
Imports System
Imports System.Runtime.InteropServices
Imports System.Text
```

```
Namespace Apress.VisualBasicRecipes.Chapter12
    Public Class Recipe12_01

        ' Declare the unmanaged functions
        <DllImport("kernel32.dll", EntryPoint:="GetPrivateProfileString")> _
        Private Shared Function GetPrivateProfileString(ByVal lpAppName As ➡
String, ByVal lpKeyName As String, ByVal lpDefault As String, ByVal ➡
lpReturnedString As StringBuilder, ByVal nSize As Integer, ByVal lpFileName As ➡
String) As Integer
        End Function

        <DllImport("kernel32.dll", EntryPoint:="WritePrivateProfileString")> _
        Private Shared Function WritePrivateProfileString(ByVal lpAppName As ➡
String, ByVal lpKeyName As String, ByVal lpString As String, ByVal lpFileName As ➡
String) As Boolean
        End Function

        Public Shared Sub main()

            Dim val As String

            ' Obtain current value.
            val = GetIniValue("SampleSection", "Key1", "initest.ini")
            Console.WriteLine("Value of Key1 in [SampleSection] is: {0}", val)

            ' Write a new value.
            WriteIniValue("SampleSection", "Key1", "New Value", "initest.ini")

            ' Obtain the new value.
            val = GetIniValue("SampleSection", "Key1", "initest.ini")
            Console.WriteLine("Value of Key1 in [SampleSection] is now: {0}", val)

            ' Write original value.
            WriteIniValue("SampleSection", "Key1", "Value1", "initest.ini")

            ' Wait to continue.
            Console.WriteLine(Environment.NewLine)
            Console.WriteLine("Main method complete.  Press Enter.")
            Console.ReadLine()

        End Sub

        Public Shared Function GetIniValue(ByVal section As String, ➡
ByVal key As String, ByVal fileName As String) As String

            Dim chars As Integer = 256
            Dim buffer As New StringBuilder(chars)

            If Not GetPrivateProfileString(section, key, "", buffer, chars, ➡
fileName) = 0 Then
                Return buffer.ToString
            Else
                Return Nothing
            End If
```

```
    End Function

    Public Shared Function WriteIniValue(ByVal section As String, ➥
ByVal key As String, ByVal value As String, ByVal fileName As String) As String
        Return WritePrivateProfileString(section, key, value, fileName)
    End Function

  End Class
End Namespace
```

■**Note** The GetPrivateProfileString method is declared with one StringBuilder parameter (lpReturnedString). This is because this string must be mutable; when the call completes, it will contain the returned INI file information. Whenever you need a mutable string, you must substitute StringBuilder in place of the String class. Often, you will need to create the StringBuilder object with a character buffer of a set size, and then pass the size of the buffer to the function as another parameter. You can specify the number of characters in the StringBuilder constructor. See recipe 2-1 for more information about using the StringBuilder class.

Usage

You can test this program quite easily. First, in the application folder, create the inittest.ini file shown here:

```
[SampleSection]
Key1=Value1
```

Now, execute Recipe12-01.exe. You will get an output such as this:

```
Value of Key1 in [SampleSection] is: Value1
Value of Key1 in [SampleSection] is now: New Value


Main method complete. Press Enter.
```

12-2. Get the Handle for a Control, Window, or File

Problem

You need to call an unmanaged function, such as GetWindowText, that requires the handle for a control, a window, or a file.

Solution

Many classes, including all Control-derived classes and the FileStream class, return the handle of the unmanaged Windows object they are wrapping as an IntPtr through a property named Handle. Other classes also provide similar information; for example, the System.Diagnostics.Process class provides a Process.MainWindowHandle property in addition to the Handle property.

How It Works

The .NET Framework does not hide underlying details such as the operating system handles used for controls and windows. Although you usually will not use this information, you can retrieve it if you need to call an unmanaged function that requires it. Many Microsoft Win32 API functions, for example, require control or window handles.

The Code

As an example, consider the Windows-based application shown in Figure 12-1. It consists of a single window that always stays on top of all other windows regardless of focus. (This behavior is enforced by setting the Form.TopMost property to True.) The form also includes a timer that periodically calls the unmanaged GetForegroundWindow and GetWindowText Win32 API functions to determine which window is currently active and its caption, respectively.

Figure 12-1. *Retrieving information about the active window*

One additional detail in this example is that the code also uses the Form.Handle property to get the handle of the main application form. It then compares it with the handle of the active form to test if the current application has focus. The following is the complete code for this form.

```vb
Imports System
Imports System.Windows.Forms
Imports System.Runtime.InteropServices
Imports System.Text

' All designed code is stored in the autogenerated partial
' class called ActiveWindowInfo.Designer.vb. You can see this
' file by selecting Show All Files in Solution Explorer.
Partial Public Class ActiveWindowInfo

    ' Declare external functions.
    <DllImport("user32.dll")> _
    Private Shared Function GetForegroundWindow() As IntPtr
    End Function

    <DllImport("user32.dll")> _
    Private Shared Function GetWindowText(ByVal hWnd As IntPtr, ➥
ByVal text As StringBuilder, ByVal count As Integer) As Integer
    End Function
```

```
    Private Sub tmrRefresh_Tick(ByVal sender As System.Object, ➥
ByVal e As System.EventArgs) Handles tmrRefresh.Tick

        Dim chars As Integer = 256
        Dim buff As New StringBuilder(chars)

        ' Obtain the handle of the active window.
        Dim handle As IntPtr = GetForeGroundWindow()

        ' Update the controls.
        If GetWindowText(handle, buff, chars) > 0 Then
            lblCaption.Text = buff.ToString
            lblHandle.Text = handle.ToString

            If handle = Me.Handle Then
                lblCurrent.Text = "True"
            Else
                lblCurrent.Text = "False"
            End If

        End If

    End Sub
End Class
```

■**Caution** The Windows Forms infrastructure manages window handles for forms and controls transparently.
Changing some of their properties can force the CLR to create a new native window behind the scenes, and a new
handle gets wrapped with a different handle. For that reason, you should always retrieve the handle before you use
it (rather than storing it in a member variable for a long period of time).

12-3. Call an Unmanaged Function That Uses a Structure

Problem

You need to call an unmanaged function, such as GetVersionEx, that accepts a structure as a parameter.

Solution

Define the structure in your VB .NET code. Use the attribute System.Runtime.InteropServices.
StructLayoutAttribute to configure how the structure fields are laid out in memory. Use the Shared
SizeOf method of the System.Runtime.InteropServices.Marshal class if you need to determine the
size of the unmanaged structure in bytes.

How It Works

In VB .NET code, you are not able to directly control how type fields are laid out once the memory is
allocated. Instead, the CLR is free to arrange fields to optimize performance, especially in the context of

moving memory around during garbage collection. This can cause problems when interacting with legacy functions, such as those written in C, that expect structures to be laid out sequentially in memory to follow their definition in include files. Fortunately, the .NET Framework allows you to solve this problem by using the attribute StructLayoutAttribute, which lets you specify how the members of a given class or structure should be arranged in memory.

The Code

As an example, consider the unmanaged GetVersionEx function provided in the Kernel32.dll file. This function accepts a pointer to an OSVERSIONINFO structure and uses it to return information about the current operating system version. To use the OSVERSIONINFO structure in VB .NET code, you must define it with the attribute StructLayoutAttribute, as shown here:

```
<StructLayout(LayoutKind.Sequential)> _
Public Structure OSVersionInfo

    Public dwOSVersionInfoSize As Integer
    Public dwMajorVersion As Integer
    Public dwMinorVersion As Integer
    Public dwBuildNumber As Integer
    Public dwPlatformId As Integer
    <MarshalAs(UnmanagedType.ByValTStr, SizeConst:=128)> _
    Public szCSDVersion As String

End Structure
```

Note that this structure also uses the attribute System.Runtime.InteropServices. MarshalAsAttribute, which is required for fixed-length strings. In this example, MarshalAsAttribute specifies the string will be passed by value and will contain a buffer of exactly 128 characters, as specified in the OSVERSIONINFO structure. This example uses sequential layout, which means the data types in the structure are laid out in the order they are listed in the class or structure.

Instead of using sequential layout, you could use LayoutKind.Explicit; in which case, you must define the byte offset of each field using FieldOffsetAttribute. This layout is useful when dealing with an irregularly packed structure or one where you want to omit some of the fields that you do not want to use. Here is an example that defines the OSVersionInfo class with an explicit layout:

```
<StructLayout(LayoutKind.Explicit)> _
Public Structure OSVersionInfo2

    <FieldOffset(0)> Public dwOSVersionInfoSize As Integer
    <FieldOffset(4)> Public dwMajorVersion As Integer
    <FieldOffset(8)> Public dwMinorVersion As Integer
    <FieldOffset(12)> Public dwBuildNumber As Integer
    <FieldOffset(16)> Public dwPlatformId As Integer
    <MarshalAs(UnmanagedType.ByValTStr, SizeConst:=128)> _
    <FieldOffset(20)> Public szCSDVersion As String

End Structure
```

Now that you've defined the structure used by the GetVersionEx function, you can declare the function and then use it. The following console application shows all the code you will need. A parameter marked with the InAttribute (<[In]()>) is marshaled from the calling assembly to the unmanaged function, while one marked with the OutAttribute (<Out()>) is marshaled in the opposite direction. If neither of these attributes is used, then marshaling is decided based on how the parameter is passed

(ByRef or ByVal). In this example, you need to make sure that OSVersionInfo is marshaled in both directions, so both attributes are applied. In addition, the code uses the Marshal.SizeOf method to calculate the size the marshaled structure will occupy in memory.

```vb
Imports System
Imports System.Runtime.InteropServices

Namespace Apress.VisualBasicRecipes.Chapter12

    <StructLayout(LayoutKind.Sequential)> _
    Public Structure OSVersionInfo

        Public dwOSVersionInfoSize As Integer
        Public dwMajorVersion As Integer
        Public dwMinorVersion As Integer
        Public dwBuildNumber As Integer
        Public dwPlatformId As Integer
        <MarshalAs(UnmanagedType.ByValTStr, SizeConst:=128)> _
        Public szCSDVersion As String

    End Structure

    Public Class Recipe12_03

        ' Declare the external function.
        <DllImport("kernel32.dll")> _
        Public Shared Function GetVersionEx(<[In](), Out()> ByRef osvi As ➡
OSVersionInfo) As Boolean
        End Function

        Public Shared Sub Main()

            Dim osvi As New OSVersionInfo

            osvi.dwOSVersionInfoSize = Marshal.SizeOf(osvi)

            ' Obtain the OS version information.
            GetVersionEx(osvi)

            ' Display the version information.
            Console.WriteLine("Class Size: " & osvi.dwOSVersionInfoSize.ToString)
            Console.WriteLine("Major Version: " & osvi.dwMajorVersion.ToString)
            Console.WriteLine("Minor Version: " & osvi.dwMinorVersion.ToString)
            Console.WriteLine("Build Number: " & osvi.dwBuildNumber.ToString)
            Console.WriteLine("Platform Id: " & osvi.dwPlatformId.ToString)
            Console.WriteLine("CSD Version: " & osvi.szCSDVersion.ToString)
            Console.WriteLine("Platform: " & ➡
Environment.OSVersion.Platform.ToString)
            Console.WriteLine("Version: " & Environment.OSVersion.Version.ToString)

            ' Wait to continue.
            Console.WriteLine(Environment.NewLine)
            Console.WriteLine("Main method complete.  Press Enter.")
            Console.ReadLine()
```

```
      End Sub

    End Class
End Namespace
```

Usage

If you run this application on a Windows XP system, you will see information such as this:

```
Class Size: 148
Major Version: 5
Minor Version: 1
Build Number: 2600
Platform Id: 2
CSD Version: Service Pack 2
Platform: Win32NT
Version: 5.1.2600.131072
```

12-4. Call an Unmanaged Function That Uses a Callback

Problem

You need to call an asynchronous unmanaged function, such as EnumWindows, and allow it to call a method, or make a *callback*, in your code.

Solution

Create a delegate that has the required signature for the callback. Use this delegate when defining and using the unmanaged function.

How It Works

Many of the Win32 API functions use callbacks. For example, if you want to retrieve the name of all the top-level windows that are currently open, you can call the unmanaged EnumWindows function in the User32.dll file. When calling EnumWindows, you need to supply a pointer to a function in your code. The Windows operating system will then call this function repeatedly, once for each top-level window that it finds, and pass the window handle to your code.

The .NET Framework allows you to handle callback scenarios like this without resorting to pointers and unsafe code blocks. Instead, you can define and use a delegate that points to your callback function. When you pass the delegate to the EnumWindows function, for example, the CLR will automatically marshal the delegate to the expected unmanaged function pointer.

The Code

Following is a console application that uses EnumWindows with a callback to display the name of every open window.

```vb
Imports System
Imports System.Text
Imports System.Runtime.InteropServices

Namespace Apress.VisualBasicRecipes.Chapter12
    Public Class Recipe12_04

        ' The signature for the callback method.
        Public Delegate Function CallBack(ByVal hwnd As IntPtr, ➥
ByVal lParam As Integer) As Boolean

        ' The unmanaged function that will trigger the callback
        ' as it enumerates the open windows.
        <DllImport("user32.dll")> _
        Public Shared Function EnumWindows(ByVal windowCallback As CallBack, ➥
ByVal param As Integer) As Integer
        End Function

        <DllImport("user32.dll")> _
        Public Shared Function GetWindowText(ByVal hWnd As IntPtr, ➥
ByVal text As StringBuilder, ByVal count As Integer) As Integer
        End Function

        Public Shared Sub Main()

            ' Request that the operating system enumerate all windows,
            ' and trigger your callback with the handle of each one.
            EnumWindows(AddressOf DisplayWindowInfo, 0)

            ' Wait to continue.
            Console.WriteLine(Environment.NewLine)
            Console.WriteLine("Main method complete.  Press Enter.")
            Console.ReadLine()

        End Sub

        ' The method that will receive the callback. The second
        ' parameter is not used, but is needed to match the
        ' callback's signature.
        Public Shared Function DisplayWindowInfo(ByVal hWnd As IntPtr, ➥
ByVal lParam As Integer) As Boolean

            Dim chars As Integer = 100
            Dim buf As New StringBuilder(chars)

            If Not GetWindowText(hWnd, buf, chars) = 0 Then
                Console.WriteLine(buf)
            End If
            Return True

        End Function

    End Class
End Namespace
```

12-5. Retrieve Unmanaged Error Information

Problem

You need to retrieve error information (either an error code or a text message) explaining why a Win32 API call failed.

Solution

On the declaration of the unmanaged method, set the `SetLastError` field of the `DllImportAttribute` to `True`. If an error occurs when you execute the method, call the `Shared Marshal.GetLastWin32Error` method to retrieve the error code. To get a text description for a specific error code, use the unmanaged `FormatMessage` function.

How It Works

You cannot retrieve error information directly using the unmanaged `GetLastError` function. The problem is that the error code returned by `GetLastError` might not reflect the error caused by the unmanaged function you are using. Instead, it might be set by other .NET Framework classes or the CLR. You can retrieve the error information safely using the `Shared Marshal.GetLastWin32Error` method. This method should be called immediately after the unmanaged call, and it will return the error information only once. (Subsequent calls to `GetLastWin32Error` will simply return the error code 127.) In addition, you must specifically set the `SetLastError` field of the `DllImportAttribute` to `True` to indicate that errors from this function should be cached.

```
<DllImport("user32.dll", SetLastError:=True)>
```

You can extract additional information from the Win32 error code using the unmanaged `FormatMessage` function from the Kernel32.dll file.

The Code

The following console application attempts to show a message box, but submits an invalid window handle. The error information is retrieved with `Marshal.GetLastWin32Error`, and the corresponding text information is retrieved using `FormatMessage`.

```vb
Imports System
Imports System.Runtime.InteropServices

Namespace Apress.VisualBasicRecipes.Chapter12
    Public Class Recipe12_05

        ' Declare the unmanaged functions.
        <DllImport("kernel32.dll")> _
        Private Shared Function FormatMessage(ByVal dwFlags As Integer, ➡
ByVal lpSource As Integer, ByVal dwMessage As Integer, ➡
ByVal dwLanguageId As Integer, ByRef lpBuffer As String, ByVal nSize As Integer, ➡
ByVal Arguments As Integer) As Integer
        End Function
```

```vbnet
        <DllImport("user32.dll", SetLastError:=True)> _
        Public Shared Function MessageBox(ByVal hWnd As IntPtr, ➡
ByVal pText As String, ByVal pCaption As String, ByVal uType As Integer) As Integer
        End Function

        Public Shared Sub Main()

            ' Invoke the MessageBox function passing an invalid
            ' window handle and thus forcing an error.
            Dim badWindowHandle As IntPtr = New IntPtr(-1)

            MessageBox(badWindowHandle, "Message", "Caption", 0)

            ' Obtain the error information.
            Dim errorCode As Integer = Marshal.GetLastWin32Error

            If Not errorCode = 0 Then
                Console.WriteLine(errorCode)
                Console.WriteLine(GetErrorMessage(errorCode))
            End If

            ' Wait to continue.
            Console.WriteLine(Environment.NewLine)
            Console.WriteLine("Main method complete.  Press Enter.")
            Console.ReadLine()

        End Sub

        ' GetErrorMessage formats and returns an error message
        ' corresponding to the input error code.
        Public Shared Function GetErrorMessage(ByVal errorCode As Integer) As String

            Dim FORMAT_MESSAGE_ALLOCATE_BUFFER As Integer = &H100
            Dim FORMAT_MESSAGE_IGNORE_INSERTS As Integer = &H200
            Dim FORMAT_MESSAGE_FROM_SYSTEM As Integer = &H1000

            Dim messageSize As Integer = 255
            Dim lpMsgBuf As String = ""
            Dim dwFlags As Integer = FORMAT_MESSAGE_ALLOCATE_BUFFER Or ➡
FORMAT_MESSAGE_FROM_SYSTEM Or FORMAT_MESSAGE_IGNORE_INSERTS

            Dim retVal As Integer = FormatMessage(dwFlags, 0, errorCode, 0, ➡
lpMsgBuf, messageSize, 0)
            If retVal = 0 Then
                Return Nothing
            Else
                Return lpMsgBuf
            End If

        End Function

    End Class
End Namespace
```

Usage

Here is the output generated by the preceding program:

```
1400
Invalid window handle.
```

12-6. Use a COM Component in a .NET Client

Problem

You need to use a COM component, such as the older ADODB components, in a .NET client.

Solution

Use a primary interop assembly (PIA), if one is available. Otherwise, generate a runtime callable wrapper (RCW) using the Type Library Importer (Tlbimp.exe) or the Add Reference feature in Visual Studio .NET.

How It Works

The .NET Framework includes extensive support for COM interoperability. To allow .NET clients to interact with a COM component, .NET uses an RCW—a special .NET proxy class that sits between your .NET code and the COM component. The RCW handles all the details, including marshaling data types, using the traditional COM interfaces, and handling COM events.

You have the following three options for using an RCW:

- Obtain an RCW from the author of the original COM component. In this case, the RCW is created from a PIA provided by the publisher, as Microsoft does for Microsoft Office.

- Generate an RCW using the Tlbimp.exe command-line utility or Visual Studio .NET.

- Create your own RCW using the types in the System.Runtime.InteropServices namespace. (This can be an extremely tedious and complicated process.)

If you want to use Visual Studio .NET to generate an RCW, you simply need to select Add Reference from the Project menu, and then select the appropriate component from the COM tab. When you click OK, the PIA will be generated and added to your project references. After that, you can use the Object Browser to inspect the namespaces and classes that are available.

If possible, you should always use a PIA instead of generating your own RCW. PIAs are more likely to work as expected, because they are created and digitally signed by the original component publisher. They might also include additional .NET refinements or enhancements. If a PIA is registered on your system for a COM component, Visual Studio .NET will automatically use that PIA when you add a reference to the COM component. For example, the .NET Framework includes an adodb.dll assembly that allows you to use the ADO classic COM objects. If you add a reference to the Microsoft ActiveX Data Objects component, this PIA will be used automatically; no new RCW will be generated. Similarly, Microsoft Office 2003 provides a PIA that improves .NET support for Office Automation. However, you must download this assembly from the MSDN web site (at http://msdn.microsoft.com/downloads/list/office.asp).

If you are not using Visual Studio .NET, you can create a wrapper assembly using the Tlbimp.exe command-line utility that is included with the .NET Framework. The only mandatory piece of information is the filename that contains the COM component. For example, the following statement creates an RCW with the default filename and namespace, assuming that the MyCOMComponent.dll file is in the current directory.

```
tlbimp MyCOMComponent.dll
```

Assuming that MyCOMComponent.dll has a type named MyClasses, the generated RCW file will have the name MyClasses.dll and will expose its classes through a namespace named MyClasses. You can also configure these options with command-line parameters, as described in the MSDN reference. For example, you can use /out:[Filename] to specify a different assembly filename and /namespace:[Namespace] to set a different namespace for the generated classes. You can also specify a key file using /keyfile[keyfilename] so that the component will be signed and given a strong name, allowing it to be placed in the global assembly cache (GAC). Use the /primary parameter to create a PIA.

The Code

The following example shows how you can use COM Interop to access the classic ADO objects from a .NET Framework application.

```
Imports System

Namespace Apress.VisualBasicRecipes.Chapter12
    Public Class Recipe12_06

        ' Be sure to add a reference to ADODB (runtime version 1.1.4322)
        ' to the project.
        Public Shared Sub Main()

            ' This example assumes that you have the AdventureWorks
            ' sample database installed. If you don't, you will need
            ' to change the connectionString accordingly.

            ' Create a new ADODB connection.
            Dim con As New ADODB.Connection
            Dim connectionString As String = "Provider=SQLOLEDB.1;Data " & ➥
Source=.\sqlexpress;Initial Catalog=AdventureWorks;Integrated Security=SSPI;"

            con.Open(connectionString, Nothing, Nothing, 0)

            ' Execute a SELECT query.
            Dim recordsAffected As Object = Nothing
            Dim rs As ADODB.Recordset = con.Execute("SELECT * FROM " & ➥
HumanResources.Employee;", recordsAffected, 0)

            ' Print out the results.
            While Not rs.EOF = True

                Console.WriteLine(rs.Fields("EmployeeID").Value)
                rs.MoveNext()

            End While
```

```
    ' Wait to continue.
    Console.WriteLine(Environment.NewLine)
    Console.WriteLine("Main method complete.  Press Enter.")
    Console.ReadLine()

End Sub

    End Class
End Namespace
```

12-7. Release a COM Component Quickly

Problem

You need to ensure that a COM component is removed from memory immediately, without waiting for garbage collection to take place, or you need to make sure that COM objects are released in a specific order.

Solution

Release the reference to the underlying COM object using the Shared Marshal.FinalReleaseComObject method and passing the appropriate RCW reference.

How It Works

COM uses reference counting to determine when objects should be released. When you use an RCW, the reference will be held to the underlying COM object, even when the object variable goes out of scope. The reference will be released only when the garbage collector disposes of the RCW object. As a result, you cannot control when or in what order COM objects will be released from memory.

To get around this limitation, you usually use the Marshal.ReleaseComObject method. However, if the COM object's pointer is marshaled several times, you need to repeatedly call this method to decrease the count to zero. However, the FinalReleaseComObject method allows you to release all references in one go, by setting the reference count of the supplied RCW to zero. This means that you do not need to loop and invoke ReleaseComObject to completely release an RCW. Once an object is released in this manner, it can no longer be used unless it's re-created.

For example, in the ADO example in recipe 12-6, you could release the underlying ADO Recordset and Connection objects by adding these two lines to the end of your code:

```
System.Runtime.InteropServices.Marshal.FinalReleaseComObject(rs)
System.Runtime.InteropServices.Marshal.FinalReleaseComObject(con)
```

■**Note** The ReleaseComObject method does not actually release the COM object; it just decrements the reference count. If the reference count reaches zero, the COM object will be released. FinalReleaseComObject works by setting the reference count of an RCW to zero. It thus bypasses the internal count logic and releases all references.

12-8. Use Optional Parameters

Problem

You need to call a method in a COM component without supplying all the required parameters.

Solution

Use the `Type.Missing` field.

How It Works

The .NET Framework is designed with a heavy use of method overloading. Most methods are overloaded several times so that you can call the version that requires only the parameters you choose to supply. COM, on the other hand, does not support method overloading. Instead, COM components usually use methods with a long list of optional parameters. You do not need to specify values for the optional parameters. For example, if a method includes three optional parameters, you can assign a value to the first and third one, skipping the second one. Passing `Nothing` to the second optional parameter would have the same effect. However, COM parameters are often passed by reference, which means your code cannot simply pass a `Nothing` reference. Instead, it must declare an object variable and then pass that variable.

You can mitigate the problem to some extent by supplying the `Type.Missing` field whenever you wish to omit an optional parameter. If you need to pass a parameter by reference, you can simply declare a single object variable, set it equal to `Type.Missing`, and use it in all cases, like this:

```
Private Shared n As Object = Type.Missing
```

The Code

The following example uses the Microsoft Word COM objects to programmatically create and show a document. Many of the methods the example uses require optional parameters passed by reference. You will notice that the use of the `Type.Missing` field simplifies this code greatly. Each use is emphasized in the code listing.

```
Imports System
Imports Microsoft.Office.Interop

Namespace Apress.VisualBasicRecipes.Chapter12

    ' This recipe requires a reference to Word and
    ' Microsoft.Office.Core.
    Public Class Recipe12_08

        Private Shared n As Object = Type.Missing

        Public Shared Sub Main()

            ' Start Word in the background.
            Dim app As New Word.Application
            app.DisplayAlerts = Word.WdAlertLevel.wdAlertsNone
```

```vbnet
' Create a new document (this is not visible to the user).
Dim doc As Word.Document = app.Documents.Add(n, n, n, n)

Console.WriteLine()
Console.WriteLine("Creating new document.")
Console.WriteLine()

' Add a heading and two lines of text.
Dim range As Word.Range = doc.Paragraphs.Add(n).Range

range.InsertBefore("Test Document")
range.Style = "Heading 1"

range = doc.Paragraphs.Add(n).Range
range.InsertBefore("Line one." & ControlChars.CrLf & "Line two.")
range.Font.Bold = 1

' Show a print preview, and make Word visible.
doc.PrintPreview()
app.Visible = True

' Wait to continue.
Console.WriteLine(Environment.NewLine)
Console.WriteLine("Main method complete.  Press Enter.")
Console.ReadLine()

    End Sub

    End Class
End Namespace
```

12-9. Use an ActiveX Control in a .NET Client

Problem

You need to place an ActiveX control on a form or a user control in a .NET Framework application.

Solution

Use an RCW exactly as you would with an ordinary COM component (see recipe 12-6). To work with the ActiveX control at design time, add it to the Visual Studio .NET Toolbox.

How It Works

As with COM components, the .NET Framework fully supports the use of ActiveX controls. When working with COM (detailed in recipe 12-6), an RCW is required to allow communication between your code and the COM object. An ActiveX control differs in that it requires two RCWs. The first RCW provides communication between the COM object and the second RCW. The second RCW is required to communicate between the first COM object and your Windows form.

This extra wrapper is required because any control you use on your form *must* derive from System.Windows.Forms.Control. The second wrapper derives from the System.Windows.Forms.AxHost class, which derives from System.Windows.Forms.Control. This provides the standard .NET control properties, methods, and events (such as Location, Size, Anchor, and so on).

Several methods are available for creating the necessary RCWs. One method is to use the Aximp.exe command-line utility. This tool is the equivalent to Tlbimp.exe, which is used to generate an RCW for COM components. You just run aximp and supply the path to the ActiveX component. The following is an example of using this tool on the Microsoft Masked Edit control.

```
aximp c:\windows\system32\msmask32.ocx
```

This will generate MSMask.dll, the *first* wrapper, and AxMSMask.dll, the *second* wrapper. The MSMask.dll file is identical to the RCW that Tlbimp.exe would have produced for a COM component. The main component of the AxMSMask.dll file is the AxMaskEdBox class, which is part of the AxMSMask namespace. The Ax prefix represents the word *ActiveX* and indicates which wrapper derives from the AxHost class. To use the control in your project, you just need to add a reference to both these assemblies, and then create an instance of the control. The following code snippet demonstrates creating an instance of the control and adding it to a form:

```
' Create a new instance of the ActiveX control.
Dim AxMaskEdBox1 As New AxMSMask.AxMaskEdBox

' Set some properties.
AxMaskEdBox1.Location = New Point(0, 0)
AxMaskEdBox1.Size = New Size(200, 50)

' Add the control to the form.
Me.Controls.Add(AxMaskEdBox1)
```

The .NET Framework also offers the AxImporter class, found in the System.Windows.Forms.Design namespace. This class lets you generate the appropriate wrapper assemblies by using the GenerateFromFile or GenerateFromTypeLibrary method. Both methods return the assembly qualified name for the ActiveX control defined by the newly created assemblies. The AxImporter constructor takes an AxImporter.Option class instance. This class contains several properties that represent options the importer will use, but only the OutputDirectory property is required. You then use one of the methods, such as GenerateFromFile, to create the necessary wrappers. Once the assemblies have been generated, you can reference them at design time, as you would any other component, or you can reference them at runtime using reflection (described in Chapter 3). The following sample code demonstrates using AxImporter to create and use an instance of the Masked Edit control at runtime.

```
' Create the AxImporter options and set the output
' directory.
Dim axOptions As New AxImporter.Options
axOptions.outputDirectory = "C:\"

' Create the AxImporter object and generate the wrappers
' for the c:\windows\system32\msmask32.ocx file.
Dim aximp As New AxImporter(axOptions)
Dim fi As New FileInfo("C:\windows\system32\msmask32.ocx")
Dim assemblyName As String = aximp.GenerateFromFile(fi)

' Load the ActiveX RCW and create an instance of the control
' type named in assemblyName (which is "AxMSMask.AxMaskEdBox,AxMSMask").
Dim MSMaskAssembly As Assembly = Assembly.LoadFrom("C:\AxMSMask.dll")
Dim AxMaskEdBox1 As Object = ➡
MSMaskAssembly.CreateInstance(assemblyName.Substring(0, ➡
```

```
assemblyName.IndexOf(",")))

' Set some properties.
AxMaskEdBox1.Location = New Point(0, 0)
AxMaskEdBox1.Size = New Size(200, 50)

' Add the control to the form.
Me.Controls.Add(AxMaskEdBox1)
```

The simplest method, if you are using Visual Studio, is to add the ActiveX control to the Toolbox. You do this by selecting Choose Toolbox Items from the Tools menu. This will add an icon representing the ActiveX control to the Toolbox. Once you place the control on your form, the required RCWs will be created, and the appropriate references will be added to your project. The only difference between these generated files and those created by the two previous methods are the names. This method will name the files AxInterop.MSMask.dll and Interop.MSMask.dll.

Adding the control in this manner will automatically generate code in the hidden designer region of your form. That code will look similar to this:

```
Me.AxMaskEdBox1 = New AxMSMask.AxMaskEdBox
CType(Me.AxMaskEdBox1, System.ComponentModel.ISupportInitialize).BeginInit()
'
'AxMaskEdBox1
'
Me.AxMaskEdBox1.Location = New System.Drawing.Point(10, 15)
Me.AxMaskEdBox1.Name = "AxMaskEdBox1"
Me.AxMaskEdBox1.OcxState = CType(resources.GetObject("AxMaskEdBox1.OcxState"), ➥
System.Windows.Forms.AxHost.State)
Me.AxMaskEdBox1.Size = New System.Drawing.Size(247, 43)
Me.AxMaskEdBox1.TabIndex = 0
Me.Controls.Add(Me.AxMaskEdBox1)
```

12-10. Expose a .NET Component to COM

Problem

You need to create a .NET component that can be called by a COM client.

Solution

Create an assembly that follows certain restrictions identified in this recipe. Export a type library for this assembly using the Type Library Exporter (Tlbexp.exe) command-line utility.

How It Works

The .NET Framework includes support for COM clients to use .NET components. When a COM client needs to create a .NET object, the CLR creates the managed object and a COM callable wrapper (CCW) that wraps the object. The COM client interacts with the managed object through the CCW. No matter how many COM clients are attempting to access a managed object, only one CCW is created for it.

Types that need to be accessed by COM clients must meet certain requirements:

- The managed type (class, interface, struct, or enum) must be `Public`.

- If the COM client needs to create the object, it must have a `Public` default constructor. COM does not support parameterized constructors.

- The members of the type that are being accessed must be `Public` instance members. `Private`, `Protected`, `Friend`, and `Shared` members are not accessible to COM clients.

In addition, you should consider the following recommendations:

- You should not create inheritance relationships between classes, because these relationships will not be visible to COM clients (although .NET will attempt to simulate this by declaring a shared base class interface).

- The classes you are exposing should implement an interface. If they don't implement an interface, one will be generated automatically. Changing the class in the future may cause versioning issues, so implementing your own interface is highly suggested. You use the `ClassInterfaceAttribute` to turn off the automatic generation of the interface and specify your own. For added versioning control, you can use the attribute `System.Runtime.InteropServices.GuidAttribute` to specify the GUID that should be assigned to an interface.

- Ideally, you should give the managed assembly a strong name so that it can be installed into the GAC and shared among multiple clients.

In order for a COM client to create the .NET object, it requires a type library (a .tlb file). The type library can be generated from an assembly using the Tlbexp.exe command-line utility. Here is an example of the syntax you use:

```
tlbexp ManagedLibrary.dll
```

Tlbexp.exe includes several options that affect how the tool runs and the output is produced. For example, you can use `/out` to specify the path and/or name produced by the utility. If you don't use this option, the file is created in the current directory with a name based on the assembly name and ending with .tlb. For automation purposes, you could use the `/silent` option to suppress all messages.

Once you generate the type library, you can reference it from the unmanaged development tool. With Visual Basic 6, you reference the .tlb file from the Project➤References dialog box. In Visual C++ 6, you can use the `#import` statement to import the type definitions from the type library.

CHAPTER 13

Commonly Used Interfaces and Patterns

The recipes in this chapter show you how to implement patterns you will use frequently during the development of Microsoft .NET Framework applications. Some of these patterns are formalized using interfaces defined in the .NET Framework class library. Others are less rigid, but still require you to take specific approaches to their design and implementation of your types. The recipes in this chapter describe how to do the following:

- Create serializable types that you can easily store to disk, send across the network, or pass by value across application domain boundaries (recipe 13-1)

- Provide a mechanism that creates accurate and complete copies (clones) of objects (recipe 13-2)

- Implement types that are easy to compare and sort (recipe 13-3)

- Support the enumeration of the elements contained in custom collections by creating a custom iterator (recipe 13-4)

- Ensure that a type that uses unmanaged resources correctly releases those resources when they are no longer needed (recipe 13-5)

- Display string representations of objects that vary based on format specifiers (recipe 13-6)

- Correctly implement custom exception and event argument types, which you will use frequently in the development of your applications (recipes 13-7 and 13-8)

- Implement the commonly used Singleton and Observer design patterns using the built-in features of VB .NET and the .NET Framework class library (recipes 13-9 and 13-10)

13-1. Implement a Serializable Type

Problem

You need to implement a custom type that is serializable, allowing you to do the following:

- Store instances of the type to persistent storage (for example, a file or a database).

- Transmit instances of the type across a network.

- Pass instances of the type "by value" across application domain boundaries.

Solution

For serialization of simple types, apply the attribute System.SerializableAttribute to the type declaration. For types that are more complex, or to control the content and structure of the serialized data, implement the interface System.Runtime.Serialization.ISerializable.

How It Works

Recipe 2-13 showed how to serialize and deserialize an object using the formatter classes provided with the .NET Framework class library. However, types are not serializable by default. To implement a custom type that is serializable, you must apply the attribute SerializableAttribute to your type declaration. As long as all of the data fields in your type are serializable types, applying SerializableAttribute is all you need to do to make your custom type serializable. If you are implementing a custom class that derives from a base class, the base class must also be serializable.

■**Caution** Classes that derive from a serializable type don't inherit the attribute SerializableAttribute. To make derived types serializable, you must explicitly declare them as serializable by applying the SerializableAttribute attribute.

Each formatter class contains the logic necessary to serialize types decorated with SerializableAttribute and will correctly serialize all Public, Protected, and Private fields. You can exclude specific fields from serialization by applying the attribute System.NonSerializedAttribute to those fields. As a rule, you should exclude the following fields from serialization:

- Fields that contain nonserializable data types

- Fields that contain values that might be invalid when the object is deserialized, such as memory addresses, thread IDs, and unmanaged resource handles

- Fields that contain sensitive or secret information, such as passwords, encryption keys, and the personal details of people and organizations

- Fields that contain data that is easily re-creatable or retrievable from other sources, especially if the data is large

If you exclude fields from serialization, you must implement your type to compensate for the fact that some data will not be present when an object is deserialized. Unfortunately, you cannot create or retrieve the missing data fields in an instance constructor, because formatters do not call constructors during the process of deserializing objects. The best approach for achieving fine-grained control of the serialization of your custom types is to use the attributes from the System.Runtime. Serialization namespace described in Table 13-1. These attributes allow you to identify methods of the serializable type that the serialization process should execute before and after serialization and deserialization. Any method annotated with one of these attributes must take a single System. Runtime.Serialization.StreamingContext argument, which contains details about the source or intended destination of the serialized object so that you can determine what to serialize. For example, you might be happy to serialize secret data if it's destined for another application domain in the same process, but not if the data will be written to a file.

Table 13-1. *Attributes to Customize the Serialization and Deserialization Processs*

Attribute	Description
OnSerializingAttribute	Apply this attribute to a method to have it executed before the object is serialized. This is useful if you need to modify object state before it is serialized. For example, you may need to convert a DateTime field to UTC time for storage.
OnSerializedAttribute	Apply this attribute to a method to have it executed after the object is serialized. This is useful in case you need to revert the object state to what it was before the method annotated with OnSerializingAttribute was run.
OnDeserializingAttribute	Apply this attribute to a method to have it executed before the object is deserialized. This is useful if you need to modify the object state prior to deserialization.
OnDeserializedAttribute	Apply this attribute to a method to have it executed after the object is deserialized. This is useful if you need to re-create additional object state that depends on the data that was deserialized with the object or modify the deserialized state before the object is used.

As types evolve, you often add new member variables to support new features. This new state causes a problem when deserializing old objects because the new member variables are not part of the serialized object. .NET Framework 2.0 introduces the attribute System.Runtime.Serialization. OptionalFieldAttribute. When you create a new version of a type and add data members, annotate them with OptionalFieldAttribute, and the deserialization process will not fail if they are not present. You can then annotate new methods with OnDeserializedAttribute (see Table 13-1) to configure the new member variables appropriately.

For the majority of custom types, the mechanisms described will be sufficient to meet your serialization needs. If you require more control over the serialization process, you can implement the interface ISerializable. The formatter classes use different logic when serializing and deserializing instances of types that implement ISerializable. To implement ISerializable correctly you must do the following:

- Declare that your type implements ISerializable.

- Apply the attribute SerializableAttribute to your type declaration as just described. What gets serialized is determined by the GetObjectData method, rather than relying on automatic serialization. For this reason, you shouldn't use NonSerializedAttribute because it will have no effect.

- Implement the ISerializable.GetObjectData method (used during serialization), which takes the argument types System.Runtime.Serialization.SerializationInfo and System. Runtime.Serialization.StreamingContext.

- Implement a nonpublic constructor (used during deserialization) that accepts the same arguments as the GetObjectData method. Remember that if you plan to derive classes from your serializable class, you should make the constructor Protected.

- If you are creating a serializable class from a base class that also implements ISerializable, your type's GetObjectData method and deserialization constructor must call the equivalent method and constructor in the base class.

During serialization, the formatter calls the GetObjectData method and passes it
SerializationInfo and StreamingContext references as arguments. Your type must populate
the SerializationInfo object with the data you want to serialize. The SerializationInfo class acts
as a list of field/value pairs and provides the AddValue method to let you store a field with its value.
In each call to AddValue, you must specify a name for the field/value pair; you use this name during
deserialization to retrieve the value of each field. The AddValue method has 16 overloads that allow
you to add values of different data types to the SerializationInfo object.

When a formatter deserializes an instance of your type, it calls the deserialization constructor,
again passing a SerializationInfo and a StreamingContext reference as arguments. Your type must
extract the serialized data from the SerializationInfo object using one of the SerializationInfo.
Get* methods; for example, using GetString, GetInt32, or GetBoolean. The StreamingContext object
provides information about the purpose and destination of the serialized data, allowing you to
choose which data to serialize. During deserialization, the StreamingContext object provides information about the source of the serialized data, allowing you to mirror the logic you implemented for
serialization.

■**Note** During standard serialization operations, the formatters do not use the capabilities of the StreamingContext
object to provide specifics about the source, destination, and purpose of serialized data. However, if you wish to
perform customized serialization, your code can configure the formatter's StreamingContext object prior to initiating
serialization and deserialization. Consult the .NET Framework SDK documentation for details of the StreamingContext
class.

The Code

The following example demonstrates a serializable Employee class that implements the ISerializable
interface. In this example, the Employee class does not serialize the Address property if the provided
StreamingContext object specifies that the destination of the serialized data is a file. The Main method
demonstrates the serialization and deserialization of an Employee object.

```
Imports System
Imports System.IO
Imports System.Text
Imports System.Runtime.Serialization
Imports System.Runtime.Serialization.Formatters.Binary

Namespace Apress.VisualBasicRecipes.Chapter13

    <Serializable()> _
    Public Class Employee
        Implements ISerializable

        Private m_Name As String
        Private m_Age As Integer
        Private m_Address As String

        ' Simple Employee constructor.
        Public Sub New(ByVal name As String, ByVal age As Integer, ➡
ByVal address As String)
```

```vbnet
            m_Name = name
            m_Age = age
            m_Address = address

        End Sub

        ' Constructor required to enable a formatter to deserialize an
        ' Employee object. You should declare the constructor protected
        ' to help ensure it is not called unnecessarily.
        Private Sub New(ByVal info As SerializationInfo, ➡
ByVal context As StreamingContext)

            ' Extract the name and age of the employee, which will always be
            ' present in the serialized data regardless of the value of the
            ' StreamingContext.
            m_Name = info.GetString("Name")
            m_Age = info.GetInt32("Age")

            ' Attempt to extract the employee's address and fail gracefully
            ' if it is not available.
            Try
                m_Address = info.GetString("Address")
            Catch ex As SerializationException
                m_Address = Nothing
            End Try

        End Sub

        ' Public property to provide access to the employee's name.
        Public Property Name() As String
            Get
                Return m_Name
            End Get
            Set(ByVal Value As String)
                m_Name = Value
            End Set
        End Property

        ' Public property to provide access to the employee's age.
        Public Property Age() As Integer
            Get
                Return m_Age
            End Get
            Set(ByVal value As Integer)
                m_Age = value
            End Set
        End Property

        ' Public property to provide access to the employee's address.
        ' Uses lazy initialization to establish address because a
        ' deserialized object will not have an address value.
```

```vb
        Public Property Address() As String
            Get
                If m_Address Is Nothing Then
                    ' Load the address from persistent storage.
                    ' In this case, set it to an empty string.
                    m_Address = String.Empty
                End If

                Return m_Address
            End Get
            Set(ByVal value As String)
                m_Address = value
            End Set
        End Property

        ' Declared by the ISerializable interface, the GetObjectData method
        ' provides the mechanism with which a formatter obtains the object
        ' data that it should serialize.
        Public Sub GetObjectData(ByVal info As SerializationInfo, ➥
ByVal context As StreamingContext) Implements.ISerializable.GetObjectData

            ' Always serialize the employee's name and age.
            info.AddValue("Name", Name)
            info.AddValue("Age", Age)

            ' Don't serialize the employee's address if the StreamingContext
            ' indicates that the serialized data is to be written to a file.
            If (context.State And StreamingContextStates.File) = 0 Then
                info.AddValue("Address", Address)
            End If

        End Sub

        ' Override Object.ToString to return a string representation of the
        ' Employee state.
        Public Overrides Function ToString() As String

            Dim str As New StringBuilder

            str.AppendFormat("Name: {0}{1}", Name, ControlChars.CrLf)
            str.AppendFormat("Age: {0}{1}", Age, ControlChars.CrLf)
            str.AppendFormat("Address: {0}{1}", Address, ControlChars.CrLf)

            Return str.ToString

        End Function

    End Class

    ' A class to demonstrate the use of Employee.
    Public Class Recipe13_01
```

```vb
Public Shared Sub Main()

    ' Create an Employee object representing an employee named Alex.
    Dim emp As New Employee("Alex", 35, "Retroville")

    ' Display Employee object.
    Console.WriteLine(emp.ToString())

    ' Serialize the Employee object specifying another application domain
    ' as the destination of the serialized data. All data including the
    ' employee's address is serialized.
    Dim str As Stream = File.Create("Alex.bin")
    Dim bf As New BinaryFormatter
    bf.Context = New StreamingContext(StreamingContextStates.CrossAppDomain)
    bf.Serialize(str, emp)
    str.Close()

    ' Deserialize and display the Employee object.
    str = File.OpenRead("Alex.bin")
    bf = New BinaryFormatter
    emp = DirectCast(bf.Deserialize(str), Employee)
    str.Close()
    Console.WriteLine(emp.ToString())

    ' Serialize the Employee object specifying a file as the destination
    ' of the serialized data. In this case, the employee's address is not
    ' included in the serialized data.
    str = File.Create("Alex.bin")
    bf = New BinaryFormatter
    bf.Context = New StreamingContext(StreamingContextStates.File)
    bf.Serialize(str, emp)
    str.Close()

    ' Deserialize and display the Employee.
    str = File.OpenRead("Alex.bin")
    bf = New BinaryFormatter
    emp = DirectCast(bf.Deserialize(str), Employee)
    str.Close()
    Console.WriteLine(emp.ToString())

    ' Wait to continue.
    Console.WriteLine(Environment.NewLine)
    Console.WriteLine("Main method complete.  Press Enter.")
    Console.ReadLine()

End Sub

End Class
End Namespace
```

13-2. Implement a Cloneable Type

Problem

You need to create a custom type that provides a simple mechanism for programmers to create copies of type instances.

Solution

Implement the System.ICloneable interface.

How It Works

When you assign one value type to another, you create a copy of the value. No link exists between the two values—a change to one will not affect the other. However, when you assign one reference type to another (excluding strings, which receive special treatment by the runtime), you do not create a new copy of the reference type. Instead, both reference types refer to the same object, and changes to the value of the object are reflected in both references. To create a true copy of a reference type, you must *clone* the object to which it refers.

The ICloneable interface identifies a type as cloneable and declares the Clone method as the mechanism through which you obtain a clone of an object. The Clone method takes no arguments and returns a System.Object, regardless of the implementing type. This means that once you clone an object, you must explicitly cast the clone to the correct type.

The approach you take to implementing the Clone method for a custom type depends on the data members declared within the type. If the custom type contains only value-type (Integer, Byte, and so on) and System.String data members, you can implement the Clone method by instantiating a new object and setting its data members to the same values as the current object. The Object class (from which all types derive) includes the Protected method MemberwiseClone, which automates this process.

If your custom type contains reference-type data members, you must decide whether your Clone method will perform a *shallow copy* or a *deep copy*. A shallow copy means that any reference-type data members in the clone will refer to the same objects as the equivalent reference-type data members in the original object. A deep copy means that you must create clones of the entire object graph so that the reference-type data members of the clone refer to physically independent copies (clones) of the objects referenced by the original object.

A shallow copy is easy to implement by calling the MemberwiseClone method from within your Clone method. However, a deep copy is often what programmers expect when they first clone an object, but it's rarely what they get. This is especially true of the collection classes in the System.Collections namespace, which all implement shallow copies in their Clone methods. Although it would often be useful if these collections implemented a deep copy, there are two key reasons why types (especially generic collection classes) do not implement deep copies:

- Creating a clone of a large object graph is processor-intensive and memory-intensive.

- General-purpose collections can contain wide and deep object graphs consisting of any type of object. Creating a deep-copy implementation to cater to such variety is not feasible because some objects in the collection might not be cloneable, and others might contain circular references, which would send the cloning process into an infinite loop.

For strongly typed collections in which the nature of the contained elements are understood and controlled, a deep copy can be a very useful feature; for example, the `System.Xml.XmlNode` implements a deep copy in its `Clone` method. This allows you to create true copies of entire XML object hierarchies with a single statement.

■**Tip** If you need to clone an object that does not implement `ICloneable` but is serializable, you can often serialize and then deserialize the object to achieve the same result as cloning. However, be aware that the serialization process might not serialize all data members (as discussed in recipe 13-1). Likewise, if you create a custom serializable type, you can potentially use the serialization process just described to perform a deep copy within your `ICloneable.Clone` method implementation. To clone a serializable object, use the class `System.Runtime.Serialization.Formatters.Binary.BinaryFormatter` to serialize the object to, and then deserialize the object from a `System.IO.MemoryStream` object.

The Code

The following example demonstrates various approaches to cloning. The simple class named `Employee` contains only `String` and `Integer` members, and so relies on the inherited `MemberwiseClone` method to create a clone. The `Team` class contains an implementation of the `Clone` method that performs a deep copy. The `Team` class contains a collection of `Employee` objects, representing a team of people. When you call the `Clone` method of a `Team` object, the method creates a clone of every contained `Employee` object and adds it to the cloned `Team` object. The `Team` class provides a `Private` constructor to simplify the code in the `Clone` method. The use of constructors is a common approach to simplify the cloning process.

```
Imports System
Imports System.Text
Imports System.Collections.Generic

Namespace Apress.VisualBasicRecipes.Chapter13

    Public Class Employee
        Implements ICloneable

        Public Name As String
        Public Title As String
        Public Age As Integer

        ' Simple Employee constructor.
        Public Sub New(ByVal _name As String, ByVal _title As String, ➡
ByVal _age As Integer)

            Name = _name
            Title = _title
            Age = _age

        End Sub

        ' Create a clone using the Object.MemberwiseClone method because
        ' the Employee class contains only string and value types.
        Public Function Clone() As Object Implements System.ICloneable.Clone
            Return Me.MemberwiseClone
        End Function
```

```vbnet
    '  Returns a string representation of the Employee object.
    Public Overrides Function ToString() As String
        Return String.Format("{0} ({1}) - Age {2}", Name, Title, Age)
    End Function

End Class

Public Class Team
    Implements ICloneable

    '  A List to hold the Employee team members.
    Public TeamMembers As New List(Of Employee)

    Public Sub New()
    End Sub

    '  Adds an Employee object to the team.
    Public Sub AddMember(ByVal member As Employee)
        TeamMembers.Add(member)
    End Sub

    '  Override Object.ToString to return a string representation
    '  of the entire team.
    Public Overrides Function ToString() As String

        Dim str As New StringBuilder

        For Each e As Employee In TeamMembers
            str.AppendFormat("  {0}{1}", e, ControlChars.CrLf)
        Next

        Return str.ToString

    End Function

    '  Implementation of ICloneable.Clone.
    Public Function Clone() As Object Implements System.ICloneable.Clone

        '  Create a deep copy of the team.
        Dim newTeam As New Team

        For Each e As Employee In Me.TeamMembers
            '  Clone the individual Employee objects and
            '  add them to the List.
            newTeam.AddMember(DirectCast(e.Clone; Employee))
        Next

        Return newTeam

    End Function

End Class
```

```vbnet
' A class to demonstrate the use of Employee.
Public Class Recipe13_02

    Public Shared Sub Main()

        ' Create the original team.
        Dim newTeam As New Team
        newTeam.AddMember(New Employee("Dave", "Architect", 34))
        newTeam.AddMember(New Employee("Alex", "Designer", 35))
        newTeam.AddMember(New Employee("Robb", "Developer", 25))

        ' Clone the original team.
        Dim clonedTeam As Team = DirectCast(newTeam.Clone, Team)

        ' Display the original team.
        Console.WriteLine("Original Team:")
        Console.WriteLine(newTeam)

        ' Display the cloned team.
        Console.WriteLine("Cloned Team:")
        Console.WriteLine(clonedTeam)

        ' Make change.
        Console.WriteLine("*** Make a change to original team ***")
        Console.WriteLine(Environment.NewLine)

        newTeam.TeamMembers(0).Name = "Jason"
        newTeam.TeamMembers(0).Title = "Supervisor"
        newTeam.TeamMembers(0).Age = 30

        ' Display the original team.
        Console.WriteLine("Original Team:")
        Console.WriteLine(newTeam)

        ' Display the cloned team.
        Console.WriteLine("Cloned Team:")
        Console.WriteLine(clonedTeam)

        ' Wait to continue.
        Console.WriteLine(Environment.NewLine)
        Console.WriteLine("Main method complete.  Press Enter.")
        Console.Read()

    End Sub

End Class
End Namespace
```

13-3. Implement a Comparable Type

Problem

You need to provide a mechanism that allows you to compare custom types, enabling you to easily sort collections containing instances of those types.

Solution

To provide a standard comparison mechanism for a type, implement the generic System.IComparable<T> interface. To support the comparison of a type based on more than one characteristic, create separate types that implement the generic System.Collections.Generic.IComparer<T> interface.

■**Caution** The System.IComparable and System.Collections.IComparer interfaces available prior to .NET Framework 2.0 do not use generics to ensure type safety. When working with .NET Framework 1.0 or 1.1, you must take extra precautions to ensure the objects passed to the methods of these interfaces are of the appropriate type.

How It Works

If you need to sort your type into only a single order, such as ascending ID number or alphabetically based on surname, you should implement the IComparable(Of T) interface. IComparable(Of T) defines a single method named CompareTo, shown here:

```
Public Function CompareTo(ByVal other As T) As Integer
End Function
```

According to the specification of the CompareTo method, the object (other) passed to the method must be an object of the same type as that being called, or CompareTo must throw a System. ArgumentException exception. This is less important in .NET Framework 2.0, given that the implementation of IComparable uses generics and is type-safe, ensuring that the argument is of the correct type. The value returned by CompareTo should be calculated as follows:

- If the current object is less than other, return less than zero (for example, –1).
- If the current object has the same value as other, return zero.
- If the current object is greater than other, return greater than zero (for example, 1).

What these comparisons mean depends on the type implementing the IComparable interface. For example, if you were sorting people based on their surname, you would do a String comparison on this field. However, if you wanted to sort by birthday, you would need to perform a comparison of the corresponding System.DateTime fields.

To support a variety of sort orders for a particular type, you must implement separate helper types that implement the IComparer(Of T) interface, which defines the Compare method shown here:

```
Public Function CompareTo(ByVal x As T, ByVal y As T) As Integer
End Function
```

These helper types must encapsulate the necessary logic to compare two objects and return a value based on the following logic:

- If x is less than y, return less than zero (for example, –1).

- If x has the same value as y, return zero.

- If x is greater than y, return greater than zero (for example, 1).

The Code

The Newspaper class listed here demonstrates the implementation of both the IComparable and IComparer interfaces. The Newspaper.CompareTo method performs a case-insensitive comparison of two Newspaper objects based on their Name properties. A Private nested class named AscendingCirculationComparer implements IComparer and compares two Newspaper objects based on their Circulation properties. An AscendingCirculationComparer object is obtained using the Shared Newspaper.CirculationSorter property.

The Main method shown here demonstrates the comparison and sorting capabilities provided by implementing the IComparable and IComparer interfaces. The method creates a System.Collections. ArrayList collection containing five Newspaper objects. Main then sorts the ArrayList twice using the ArrayList.Sort method. The first Sort operation uses the default Newspaper comparison mechanism provided by the IComparable.CompareTo method. The second Sort operation uses an AscendingCirculationComparer object to perform comparisons through its implementation of the IComparer.Compare method.

```
Imports System
Imports System.Collections.Generic

Namespace Apress.VisualBasicRecipes.Chapter13
    Public Class Newspaper
        Implements IComparable(Of Newspaper)

        Private _name As String
        Private _circulation As Integer

        ' Simple Newspaper constructor.
        Public Sub New(ByVal name As String, ByVal circulation As Integer)

            _name = name
            _circulation = circulation

        End Sub

        ' Declare a read-only property that returns an instance of the
        ' AscendingCirculationComparer.
        Public Shared ReadOnly Property CirculationSorter() As ➥
IComparer(Of Newspaper)
            Get
                Return New AscendingCirculationComparer
            End Get
        End Property

        ' Declare a read-only property to access _name field.
        Public ReadOnly Property Name() As String
            Get
                Return _name
            End Get
        End Property
```

```vb
    ' Declare a read-only property to access _circulation field.
    Public ReadOnly Property Circulation() As String
        Get
            Return _circulation
        End Get
    End Property

    ' Override Object.ToString.
    Public Overrides Function ToString() As String
        Return String.Format("{0}: Circulation = {1}", _name, _circulation)
    End Function

    ' Implementation of IComparable.CompareTo. The generic definition
    ' of IComparable allows us to ensure that the argument provided
    ' must be a Newspaper object. Comparison is based on a case-
    ' insensitive comparison of the Newspaper names.
    Public Function CompareTo(ByVal other As Newspaper) As Integer ➥
Implements System.IComparable(Of Newspaper).CompareTo

        ' IComparable dictates that an object is always considered
        ' greater than nothing.
        If other Is Nothing Then Return 1

        ' Short-circuit the case where the other Newspaper object is a
        ' reference to this one.
        If other Is Me Then Return 0

        ' Calculate return value by performing a case-insensitive
        ' comparison of the Newspaper names.

        ' Because the Newspaper name is a string, the easiest approach
        ' is to reply on the comparison capabilities of the string
        ' class, which perform culture-sensitive string comparisons.
        Return String.Compare(Me.Name, other.Name, True)

    End Function

    Private Class AscendingCirculationComparer
        Implements IComparer(Of Newspaper)

        ' Implementation of IComparer.Compare. The generic definition of
        ' IComparer allows us to ensure both arguments are Newspaper
        ' objects.
        Public Function Compare(ByVal x As Newspaper, ➥
ByVal y As Newspaper) As Integer Implements ➥
System.Collections.Generic.IComparer(Of Newspaper).Compare

            ' Handle logic for nothing reference as dictated by the
            ' IComparer interface. Nothing is considered less than
            ' any other value.
            If x Is Nothing And y Is Nothing Then
                Return 0
```

```vbnet
            ElseIf x Is Nothing Then
                Return -1
            ElseIf y Is Nothing Then
                Return 1
            End If

            '  Short-circuit condition where x and y are references.
            '  to the same object.
            If x Is y Then
                Return 0
            End If

            '  Compare the circulation figures. IComparer dictates that:
            '       return less than zero if x < y
            '       return zero if x = y
            '       return greater than zero if x > y
            '  This logic is easily implemented using integer arithmetic.
            Return x.Circulation - y.Circulation

        End Function

    End Class
End Class

'  A class to demonstrate the use of Newspaper.
Public Class Recipe13_03

    Public Shared Sub Main()

        Dim newspapers As New List(Of Newspaper)

        newspapers.Add(New Newspaper("The Washington Post", 125780))
        newspapers.Add(New Newspaper("The Times", 55230))
        newspapers.Add(New Newspaper("The Sun", 88760))
        newspapers.Add(New Newspaper("The Herald", 5670))
        newspapers.Add(New Newspaper("The Gazette", 235950))

        Console.Clear()
        Console.WriteLine("Unsorted newspaper list:")

        For Each n As Newspaper In newspapers
            Console.WriteLine("  {0}", n)
        Next

        '  Sort the newspaper list using the object's implementation
        '  of IComparable.CompareTo.
        Console.WriteLine(Environment.NewLine)
        Console.WriteLine("Newspaper list sorted by name (default order):")
        newspapers.Sort()

        For Each n As Newspaper In newspapers
            Console.WriteLine("  {0}", n)
        Next
```

```
                  ' Sort the newspaper list using the supplied IComparer object.
                  Console.WriteLine(Environment.NewLine)
                  Console.WriteLine("Newspaper list sorted by circulation:")
                  newspapers.Sort(Newspaper.CirculationSorter)

                  For Each n As Newspaper In newspapers
                      Console.WriteLine("  {0}", n)
                  Next

                  ' Wait to continue.
                  Console.WriteLine(Environment.NewLine)
                  Console.WriteLine("Main method complete.  Press Enter.")
                  Console.ReadLine()

          End Sub

      End Class
End Namespace
```

Usage

Running the example will produce the results shown here. The first list of newspapers is unsorted, the second is sorted using the IComparable interface, and the third is sorted using a comparer class that implements IComparer.

```
Unsorted newspaper list:
  The Washington Post: Circulation = 125780
  The Times: Circulation = 55230
  The Sun: Circulation = 88760
  The Herald: Circulation = 5670
  The Gazette: Circulation = 235950

Newspaper list sorted by name (default order):
  The Gazette: Circulation = 235950
  The Herald: Circulation = 5670
  The Sun: Circulation = 88760
  The Times: Circulation = 55230
  The Washington Post: Circulation = 125780

Newspaper list sorted by circulation:
  The Herald: Circulation = 5670
  The Times: Circulation = 55230
  The Sun: Circulation = 88760
  The Washington Post: Circulation = 125780
  The Gazette: Circulation = 235950
```

13-4. Implement an Enumerable Type Using a Custom Iterator

Problem

You need to create a collection type whose contents you can enumerate using a For Each statement.

Solution

Implement the interface System.Collections.IEnumerable or System.Collections.Generic.
IEnumerable(Of T) on your collection type. The GetEnumerator method of the IEnumerable interface
returns an *enumerator*, which is an object that implements either the System.Collections.IEnumerator
or System.Collections.Generic.IEnumerator(Of T) *interface, respectively*. The IEnumerator interface
defines the methods used by the For Each statement to enumerate the collection.

Implement a private inner class within the enumerable type that implements the interface
IEnumerator and can iterate over the enumerable type while maintaining appropriate state information. In the GetEnumerator method of the enumerable type, create and return an instance of the
iterator class.

Caution The IEnumerable and IEnumerator interfaces from the System.Collections.Generic
namespace mentioned in this recipe are new to .NET Framework 2.0. The interfaces from which these two interfaces inherit are also named IEnumerable and IEnumerator but are located in the System.Collections
namespace. This recipe will work using .NET Framework 1.0 or 1.1, but generic collections are not supported.

How It Works

A numeric indexer allows you to iterate through the elements of most standard collections using a
For loop. However, this technique does not always provide an appropriate abstraction for nonlinear
data structures, such as trees and multidimensional collections. The For Each statement provides
an easy-to-use and syntactically elegant mechanism for iterating through a collection of objects,
regardless of their internal structures.

In order to support For Each semantics, the type containing the collection of objects should
implement the IEnumerable interface. The IEnumerable interface declares a single method named
GetEnumerator, which does not take any arguments and returns an object that implements
IEnumerator.

The next step is to implement a separate class that implements the IEnumerator interface.
The IEnumerator interface provides a read-only, forward-only cursor for accessing the members
of the underlying collection. Table 13-2 describes the members of the IEnumerator interface. The
IEnumerator instance returned by GetEnumerator is your custom iterator—the object that actually
supports enumeration of the collection's data elements.

If your collection class contains different types of data that you want to enumerate separately,
implementing the IEnumerable interface on the collection class is insufficient. In this case, you would
implement a number of properties that returned different IEnumerator instances that handle each
specific data type. For example, you might have a class that includes a collection of employees and a
collection of tasks. You would create the Employees property, which would return an IEnumerator for
the employee collection and the Tasks property, which would return an IEnumerator for the task
collection.

Table 13-2. *Members of the IEnumerator Interface*

Member	Description
Current	Property that returns the current data element. When the enumerator is created, Current refers to a position preceding the first data element. This means you must call MoveNext before using Current. If Current is called and the enumerator is positioned before the first element or after the last element in the data collection, Current must throw a System.InvalidOperationException.
MoveNext	Method that moves the enumerator to the next data element in the collection. Returns True if there are more elements; otherwise, it returns False. If the underlying source of data changes during the life of the enumerator, MoveNext must throw an InvalidOperationException.
Reset	Method that moves the enumerator to a position preceding the first element in the data collection. If the underlying source of data changes during the life of the enumerator, Reset must throw an InvalidOperationException.

The Code

The TeamMember, Team, and TeamMemberEnumerator classes in the following example demonstrate the implementation of a custom iterator using the IEnumerable and IEnumerator interfaces. The TeamMember class represents a member of a team. The Team class, which represents a team of people, is a collection of TeamMember objects. Team implements the IEnumerable interface and declares a separate class, named TeamMemberEnumerator, to provide enumeration functionality. Team implements the *Observer pattern* using delegate and event members to notify all TeamMemberEnumerator objects if their underlying Team changes. (See recipe 13-10 for a detailed description of the Observer pattern.) The TeamMemberEnumerator class is a Private nested class, so you cannot create instances of it other than through the Team.GetEnumerator method.

This example also demonstrates what happens when you attempt to change the collection you are enumerating through. In this case, an InvalidOperationException is thrown.

```
Imports System
Imports System.Collections.Generic
Imports System.Text.RegularExpressions

Namespace Apress.VisualBasicRecipes.Chapter13

    ' The TeamMember class represents an individual team member.
    Public Class TeamMember

        Public Name As String
        Public Title As String

        ' Simple TeamMember constructor.
        Public Sub New(ByVal _name As String, ByVal _title As String)

            Me.Name = _name
            Me.Title = _title

        End Sub
```

```vbnet
    ' Returns a string representation of the TeamMember.
    Public Overrides Function ToString() As String
        Return String.Format("{0} ({1})", Name, Title)
    End Function

End Class

' Team class represents a collection of TeamMember objects.
' It implements the IEnumerable interface to support enumerating
' TeamMember objects.
Public Class Team
    Implements IEnumerable

    ' A delegate that specifies the signature that all team change
    ' event handler methods must implement.
    Public Delegate Sub TeamChangedEventHandler(ByVal source As Team, ➥
ByVal e As EventArgs)

    ' A List to contain the TeamMember objects.
    Private teamMembers As List(Of TeamMember)

    ' The event used to notify that the Team  has changed.
    Public Event TeamChange As TeamChangedEventHandler

    ' Team constructor.
    Public Sub New()
        teamMembers = New List(Of TeamMember)
    End Sub

    ' Implement the IEnumerable.GetEnumerator method.
    Public Function GetEnumerator() As System.Collections.IEnumerator ➥
Implements System.Collections.IEnumerable.GetEnumerator
        Return New TeamMemberEnumerator(Me)
    End Function

    ' Adds a TeamMember object to the Team.
    Public Sub AddMember(ByVal member As TeamMember)

        teamMembers.Add(member)

        ' Notify listeners that the list has changed.
        RaiseEvent TeamChange(Me, EventArgs.Empty)

    End Sub

    ' TeamMemberEnumerator is a private nested class that provides
    ' the functionality to enumerate the TeamMembers contained in
    ' a Team collection. As a nested class, TeamMemberEnumerator
    ' has access to the private members of the Team class.
    Private Class TeamMemberEnumerator
        Implements IEnumerator
```

```vbnet
        ' The Team that this object is enumerating.
        Private sourceTeam As Team

        ' Boolean to indicate whether underlying Team has changed
        ' and so is invalid for further enumeration.
        Private teamInvalid As Boolean = False

        ' Integer to identify the current TeamMember. Provides
        ' the index of the TeamMember in the underlying List
        ' used by the Team collection. Initialize to -1, which is
        ' the index prior to the first element.
        Private currentMember As Integer = -1

        ' The constructor takes a reference to the Team that is
        ' the source of the enumerated data.
        Friend Sub New(ByVal _team As Team)

            Me.sourceTeam = _team

            ' Register with sourceTeam for change notifications.
            AddHandler Me.sourceTeam.TeamChange, AddressOf Me.TeamChange

        End Sub

        ' Implement the IEnumerator.Current property.
        Public ReadOnly Property Current() As Object Implements ➥
System.Collections.IEnumerator.Current
            Get
                ' If the TeamMemberEnumerator is positioned before
                ' the first element or after the last element, then
                ' throw an exception.
                If currentMember = -1 Or currentMember > ➥
(sourceTeam.teamMembers.Count - 1) Then
                    Throw New InvalidOperationException
                End If

                ' Otherwise, return the current TeamMember.
                Return sourceTeam.teamMembers(currentMember)

            End Get
        End Property

        ' Implement the IEnumerator.MoveNext method.
        Public Function MoveNext() As Boolean Implements ➥
System.Collections.IEnumerator.MoveNext

            ' If underlying Team is invalid, throw exception.
            If teamInvalid Then
                Throw New InvalidOperationException("Team modified")
            End If

            ' Otherwise, progress to the next TeamMember.
            currentMember += 1
```

```vb
        ' Return false if we have moved past the last TeamMember.
        If currentMember > (sourceTeam.teamMembers.Count - 1) Then
            Return False
        Else
            Return True
        End If

    End Function

    ' Implement the IEnumerator.Reset method. This method
    ' resets the position of the TeamMemberEnumerator to
    ' the beginning of the TeamMembers collection.
    Public Sub Reset() Implements System.Collections.IEnumerator.Reset

        ' If underlying Team is invalid, throw exception.
        If teamInvalid Then
            Throw New InvalidOperationException("Team modified")
        End If

        ' Move the currentMember pointer back to the index
        ' preceding the first element.
        currentMember = -1

    End Sub

    ' An event handler to handle notification that the underlying
    ' Team collection has changed.
    Friend Sub TeamChange(ByVal source As Team, ByVal e As EventArgs)

        ' Signal that the underlying Team is now invalid.
        teamInvalid = True

    End Sub

    End Class
End Class

' A class to demonstrate the use of Team.
Public Class Recipe13_04

    Public Shared Sub Main()

        ' Create a new Team.
        Dim newTeam As New Team

        newTeam.AddMember(New TeamMember("Kevin", "Ninja"))
        newTeam.AddMember(New TeamMember("Vicky", "Magician"))
        newTeam.AddMember(New TeamMember("Richard", "Paladin"))

        ' Enumerate the Team.
        Console.Clear()
        Console.WriteLine("Enumerate with a for each loop:")
```

```vbnet
        For Each member As TeamMember In newTeam
            Console.WriteLine(member.ToString)
        Next

        ' Enumerate using a while loop.
        Console.WriteLine(Environment.NewLine)
        Console.WriteLine("Enumerate with while loop:")

        Dim e As IEnumerator = newTeam.GetEnumerator

        While e.MoveNext
            Console.WriteLine(e.Current)
        End While

        ' Enumerate the Team and try to add a Team Member.
        ' (This will cause an exception to be thrown.)
        Console.WriteLine(Environment.NewLine)
        Console.WriteLine("Modify while enumerating:")

        For Each member As TeamMember In newTeam
            Console.WriteLine(member.ToString)
            newTeam.AddMember(New TeamMember("Harry", "Wizard"))
        Next

        ' Wait to continue.
        Console.WriteLine(Environment.NewLine)
        Console.WriteLine("Main method complete.  Press Enter.")
        Console.ReadLine()

    End Sub

End Class
End Namespace
```

Notes

The preceding example demonstrates creating your own iterator for a custom collection. You could have simply created a new collection that inherits from one of the base generic classes, such as List(Of T). Since the base class is already enumerable, your class would automatically have this ability. You would not need to create your own enumerator class as required in the previous example. If you wanted to try this, you would replace the entire Team class with this version:

```vbnet
' Team class represents a generic collection of TeamMember objects.
' It inherits the List(Of TeamMember) class so it automatically
' supports enumerating TeamMember objects.
Public Class Team
    Inherits List(Of TeamMember)

    ' A delegate that specifies the signature that all Team change
    ' event handler methods must implement.
    Public Delegate Sub TeamChangedEventHandler(ByVal source As Team, ➥
ByVal e As EventArgs)

    ' The event used to notify that the Team has changed.
```

```
Public Event TeamChange As TeamChangedEventHandler

' Team constructor.
Public Sub New()
End Sub

' Adds a TeamMember object to the Team.
Public Overloads Sub Add(ByVal member As TeamMember)

    MyBase.Add(member)

    ' Notify listeners that the list has changed.
    RaiseEvent TeamChange(Me, EventArgs.Empty)

End Sub

End Class
```

Here, to mimic the main example, you override the base Add method so you can raise the TeamChange event. This means you need to replace calls to the AddMembers method with calls to the Add method.

13-5. Implement a Disposable Class

Problem

You need to create a class that references unmanaged resources and provide a mechanism for users of the class to free those unmanaged resources deterministically.

Solution

Implement the System.IDisposable interface, and release the unmanaged resources when client code calls the IDisposable.Dispose method.

How It Works

An unreferenced object continues to exist on the managed heap and consume resources until the garbage collector releases the object and reclaims the resources. The garbage collector will automatically free managed resources (such as memory), but it will not free unmanaged resources (such as file handles and database connections) referenced by managed objects. If an object contains data members that reference unmanaged resources, the object must free those resources explicitly or they will remain in memory for an unknown length of time.

One solution is to declare a destructor—or finalizer—for the class (*destructor* is a C++ term equivalent to the more general .NET term *finalizer*). Prior to reclaiming the memory consumed by an instance of the class, the garbage collector calls the object's finalizer. The finalizer can take the necessary steps to release any unmanaged resources. Unfortunately, because the garbage collector uses a single thread to execute all finalizers, use of finalizers can have a detrimental effect on the efficiency of the garbage collection process, which will affect the performance of your application. In addition, you cannot control when the runtime frees unmanaged resources because you cannot call an object's finalizer directly, and you have only limited control over the activities of the garbage collector using the System.GC class.

As a complementary mechanism to using finalizers, the .NET Framework defines the *Dispose pattern* as a means to provide deterministic control over when to free unmanaged resources. To implement the Dispose pattern, a class must implement the IDisposable interface, which declares a single method named Dispose. In the Dispose method, you must implement the code necessary to release any unmanaged resources and remove the object from the list of objects eligible for finalization if a finalizer has been defined.

Instances of classes that implement the Dispose pattern are called *disposable objects*. When code has finished with a disposable object, it calls the object's Dispose method to free all resources and make it unusable, but still relies on the garbage collector to eventually release the object memory. It's important to understand that the runtime does not enforce disposal of objects; it's the responsibility of the client to call the Dispose method. However, because the .NET Framework class library uses the Dispose pattern extensively, VB .NET provides the Using statement to simplify the correct use of disposable objects. The following code shows the structure of a Using statement:

```
Using fs As New FileStream("SomeFile.txt", FileMode.Open)
End Using
```

When the code reaches the end of the block in which the disposable object was declared, the object's Dispose method is automatically called, even if an exception is raised. Furthermore, once you leave the Using block, the object is out of scope and can no longer be accessed, so you cannot use a disposed object accidentally.

Here are some points to consider when implementing the Dispose pattern:

- Client code should be able to call the Dispose method repeatedly with no adverse effects.

- In multithreaded applications, it's important that only one thread execute the Dispose method concurrently. It's normally the responsibility of the client code to ensure thread synchronization, although you could decide to implement synchronization within the Dispose method.

- The Dispose method should not throw exceptions.

- Because the Dispose method does all necessary cleaning up, you do not need to call the object's finalizer. Your Dispose method should call the GC.SuppressFinalize method to ensure the finalizer is not called during garbage collection.

- Implement a finalizer that calls the unmanaged cleanup part of your Dispose method as a safety mechanism in case client code does not call Dispose correctly. However, avoid referencing managed objects in finalizers, because you cannot be certain of the object's state.

- If a disposable class extends another disposable class, the Dispose method of the child must call the Dispose method of its base class. Wrap the child's code in a Try block and call the parent's Dispose method in a Finally clause to ensure execution.

- Other instance methods and properties of the class should throw a System.ObjectDisposedException exception if client code attempts to execute a method on an already disposed object.

The Code

The following example demonstrates a common implementation of the Dispose pattern.

```vbnet
Imports System
Namespace Apress.VisualBasicRecipes.Chapter13

    ' Implement the IDisposable interface in an
    ' example class.
    Public Class DisposeExample
        Implements IDisposable

        ' Private data member to signal if the object has already
        ' been disposed.
        Private isDisposed As Boolean = False

        ' Private data member that holds the handle to an unmanaged
        ' resource.
        Private resourceHandle As IntPtr

        ' Constructor.
        Public Sub New()

            ' Constructor code obtains reference to an unmanaged
            ' resource.
            resourceHandle = IntPtr.Zero

        End Sub

        ' Protected overload of the Dispose method. The disposing argument
        ' signals whether the method is called by consumer code (true), or by
        ' the garbage collector (false). Note that this method is not part
        ' of the IDisposable interface because it has a different signature to
        ' the parameterless Dispose method.
        Protected Overridable Sub Dispose(ByVal disposing As Boolean)

            ' Don't try to dispose of the object twice.
            If Not Me.isDisposed Then

                ' Determine if consumer code or the garbage collector is
                ' calling. Avoid referencing other managed objects during
                ' finalization.
                If disposing Then
                    ' Method called by consumer code. Call the Dispose method
                    ' of any managed data members that implement the IDisposable
                    ' interface.
                    ' ...
                End If

                ' Whether called by consumer code or the garbage collector,
                ' free all unmanaged resources and set the value of managed
                ' data members to nothing. In the case of an inherited type,
                ' call base.Dispose(disposing).
            End If

            ' Signal that this object has been disposed.
            Me.isDisposed = True
        End Sub
```

```
    ' Public implementation of the IDisposable.Dispose method, called
    ' by the consumer of the object in order to free unmanaged resources.
    Public Sub Dispose() Implements IDisposable.Dispose

        ' Call the protected Dispose overload and pass a value of "True"
        ' to indicate that Dispose is being called by consumer code, not
        ' by the garbage collector.
        Dispose(True)

        ' Because the Dispose method performs all necessary cleanup,
        ' ensure the garbage collector does not call the class destructor.
        GC.SuppressFinalize(Me)

    End Sub

    ' Destructor / Finalizer. Because Dispose calls GC.SuppressFinalize,
    ' this method is called by the garbage collection process only if
    ' the consumer of the object does not call Dispose as it should.
    Protected Overrides Sub Finalize()

        ' Call the Dispose method as opposed to duplicating the code to
        ' clean up any unmanaged resources. Use the protected Dispose
        ' overload and pass a value of "False" to indicate that Dispose is
        ' being called during the garbage collection process, not by the
        ' consumer code.
        Dispose(False)

    End Sub

    ' Before executing any functionality, ensure that Dispose had not
    ' already been executed on the object.
    Public Sub SomeMethod()

        ' Throw an exception if the object has already been disposed.
        If isDisposed Then
            Throw New ObjectDisposedException("DisposeExample")
        End If

        ' Execute method functionality.
        ' ...

    End Sub

End Class

' A class to demonstrate the use of DisposeExample.
Public Class Recipe13_05

    Public Shared Sub Main()
```

```
'   The Using statement ensures the Dispose method is called
'   even if an exception occurs.
Using d As New DisposeExample
    '   Do something with d.
End Using

'   Wait to continue.
Console.WriteLine(Environment.NewLine)
Console.WriteLine("Main method complete.  Press Enter.")
Console.ReadLine()

        End Sub

    End Class
End Namespace
```

13-6. Implement a Formattable Type

Problem

You need to implement a type that can create different string representations of its content based on the use of format specifiers, for use in formatted strings.

Solution

Implement the System.IFormattable interface.

How It Works

The following code fragment demonstrates the use of format specifiers in the WriteLine method of the System.Console class. The codes in the braces (emphasized in the example) are the format specifiers.

```
Dim a As Double = 345678.5678
Dim b As UInteger = 12000
Dim c As Byte = 254

Console.WriteLine("a = {0}, b = {1}, and c = {2}", a, b, c)
Console.WriteLine("a = {0:c0}, b = {1:n4}, and c = {2,10:x5}", a, b, c)
```

When run on a machine configured with English (United States) regional settings, this code will result in the output shown here:

```
a = 345678.5678, b = 12000, and c = 254
a = $345,679, b = 12,000.0000, and c =      000fe
```

As you can see, changing the contents of the format specifiers changes the format of the output significantly, even though the data has not changed. To enable support for format specifiers in your own types, you must implement the IFormattable interface. IFormattable declares a single method named ToString with the following signature:

```
Public Function ToString(ByVal format As String, ByVal formatProvider As ➡
IFormatProvider) As String
End Function
```

The format argument is a System.String containing a *format string*. The format string is the portion of the format specifier that follows the colon. For example, in the format specifier {2,10:x5} used in the previous example, x5 is the format string. The format string contains the instructions the IFormattable instance should use when it's generating the string representation of its content. The .NET Framework documentation for IFormattable states that types that implement IFormattable must support the G (general) format string, but that the other supported format strings depend on the implementation. The format argument will be Nothing if the format specifier does not include a format string component; for example, {0} or {1,20}.

The formatProvider argument is a reference to an instance of a type that implements System.IFormatProvider and that provides access to information about the cultural and regional preferences to use when generating the string representation of the IFormattable object. This information includes data such as the appropriate currency symbol or number of decimal places to use. By default, formatProvider is Nothing, which means you should use the current thread's regional and cultural settings, available through the Shared method CurrentCulture of the System.Globalization.CultureInfo class. Some methods that generate formatted strings, such as String.Format, allow you to specify an alternative IFormatProvider to use, such as CultureInfo, DateTimeFormatInfo or NumberFormatInfo.

The .NET Framework uses IFormattable primarily to support the formatting of value types, but it can be used to good effect with any type.

The Code

The following example contains a class named Person that implements the IFormattable interface. The Person class contains the title and names of a person and will render the person's name in different formats depending on the format strings provided. The Person class does not make use of regional and cultural settings provided by the formatProvider argument. The Main method demonstrates how to use the formatting capabilities of the Person class.

```
Imports System

Namespace Apress.VisualBasicRecipes.Chapter13
    Public Class Person
        Implements IFormattable

        ' Private members to hold the person's title and name details.
        Private title As String
        Private names As String()

        ' Constructor used to set the person's title and names.
        Public Sub New(ByVal _title As String, ByVal ParamArray _names As String())

            Me.title = _title
            Me.names = _names

        End Sub
```

```vbnet
        ' Override the Object.ToString method to return the person's
        ' name using the general format.
        Public Overrides Function ToString() As String
            Return ToString("G", Nothing)
        End Function

        ' Implementation of the IFormattable.ToString method to return the
        ' person's name in different forms based on the format string
        ' provided.
        Public Overloads Function ToString(ByVal format As String, ➥
ByVal formatProvider As System.IFormatProvider) As String ➥
Implements System.IFormattable.ToString

            Dim result As String = Nothing

            ' Use the general format if none is specified.
            If format Is Nothing Then format = "G"

            ' The contents of the format string determine the format of the
            ' name returned.
            Select Case format.ToUpper()(0)
                Case "S"
                    ' Use short form - first initial and surname if a surname
                    ' was supplied.
                    If names.Length > 1 Then
                        result = names(0)(0) & ". " & names(names.Length - 1)
                    Else
                        result = names(0)
                    End If
                Case "P"
                    ' Use polite form - title, initials, and surname.
                    ' Add the person's title to the result.
                    If title IsNot Nothing And Not title.Length = 0 Then
                        result = title & ". "
                    End If

                    ' Add the person's initials and surname.
                    For count As Integer = 0 To names.Length - 1

                        If Not count = (names.Length - 1) Then
                            result += names(count)(0) & ". "
                        Else
                            result += names(count)
                        End If

                    Next
                Case "I"
                    ' Use informal form - first name only.
                    result = names(0)
```

```vbnet
                    Case Else
                        ' Use general.default form - first name and surname (if
                        ' a surname is supplied).
                        If names.Length > 1 Then
                            result = names(0) & " " & names(names.Length - 1)
                        Else
                            result = names(0)
                        End If
                End Select

                Return result

            End Function

            ' A class to demonstrate the use of Person.
            Public Class Recipe13_06

                Public Shared Sub Main()
                    ' Create a Person object representing a man with the name
                    ' Dr. Gaius Baltar.
                    Dim newPerson As New Person("Dr", "Gaius", "Baltar")

                    ' Display the person's name using a variety of format strings.
                    Console.WriteLine("Dear {0:G}", newPerson)
                    Console.WriteLine("Dear {0:P}", newPerson)
                    Console.WriteLine("Dear {0:I},", newPerson)
                    Console.WriteLine("Dear {0}", newPerson)
                    Console.WriteLine("Dear {0:S},", newPerson)

                    ' Wait to continue.
                    Console.WriteLine(Environment.NewLine)
                    Console.WriteLine("Main method complete.  Press Enter.")
                    Console.ReadLine()

                End Sub

            End Class

        End Class
End Namespace
```

Usage

When executed, the preceding example produces the following output:

```
Dear Gaius Baltar
Dear Dr. G. Baltar
Dear Gaius,
Dear Gaius Baltar
Dear G. Baltar,
```

13-7. Implement a Custom Exception Class

Problem

You need to create a custom exception class so that you can use the runtime's exception-handling mechanism to handle application-specific exceptions.

Solution

Create a serializable class that extends the `System.Exception` class or inherits from it. Add support for any custom data members required by the exception, including constructors and properties required to manipulate the data members.

■Tip If you need to define a number of custom exceptions for use in a single application or library, you should define a single custom exception that extends `System.Exception` and use this as a common base class for all of your other custom exceptions. There is very little point in extending `System.ApplicationException`, as is often recommended. Doing so simply introduces another level in your exception hierarchy and provides little if any benefit when handling your exception classes—after all, catching a nonspecific exception like `ApplicationException` is just as bad a practice as catching `Exception`.

How It Works

Exception classes are unique in the fact that you do not declare new classes solely to implement new or extended functionality. The runtime's exception-handling mechanism—exposed by the VB .NET statements `Try`, `Catch`, and `Finally`—works based on the *type* of exception thrown, not the functional or data members implemented by the thrown exception.

If you need to throw an exception, you should use an existing exception class from the .NET Framework class library, if a suitable one exists. For example, some useful exceptions include the following:

- `System.ArgumentNullException`, thrown when code passes a `Nothing` argument value to your method that does not support `Nothing` arguments

- `System.ArgumentOutOfRangeException`, thrown when code passes an inappropriately large or small argument value to your method

- `System.FormatException`, thrown when code attempts to pass your method a `String` argument containing incorrectly formatted data

If none of the existing exception classes meets your needs, or you feel your application would benefit from using application-specific exceptions, it's a simple matter to create your own exception class. In order to integrate your custom exception with the runtime's exception-handling mechanism and remain consistent with the pattern implemented by .NET Framework–defined exception classes, you should do the following:

- Give your exception class a meaningful name ending in the word `Exception`, such as `TypeMismatchException` or `RecordNotFoundException`.

- Mark your exception class as `NotInheritable` if you do not intend other exception classes to extend it.

- Implement additional data members and properties to support custom information that the exception class should provide.

- Implement at least one of the Public constructors with the signatures shown here and ensure they call the base class constructor. Best practices dictate that you should implement the first three constructors. The last constructor is used if your type is serializable.

```
Public Sub New
    MyBase.New
End Sub

Public Sub New(ByVal msg As String)
    MyBase.New(msg)
End Sub

Public Sub New(ByVal msg As String, ByVal inner As Exception)
    MyBase.New(msg, inner)
End Sub
Public Sub New(ByVal info As SerializationInfo, ➡
ByVal context As StreamingContext)
    MyBase.New(info, context)
End Sub
```

- Make your exception class serializable so that the runtime can marshal instances of your exception across application domain and machine boundaries. Applying the attribute System.SerializableAttribute is sufficient for exception classes that do not implement custom data members. However, because Exception implements the interface System. Runtime.Serialization.ISerializable, if your exception declares custom data members, you must override the ISerializable.GetObjectData method of the Exception class as well as implement a deserialization constructor with this signature. If your exception class is NotInheritable, mark the deserialization constructor as Private; otherwise, mark it as Protected. The GetObjectData method and deserialization constructor must call the equivalent base class method to allow the base class to serialize and deserialize its data correctly. (See recipe 13-1 for details on making classes serializable.)

■**Tip** In large applications, you will usually implement quite a few custom exception classes. It pays to put significant thought into how you organize your custom exceptions and how code will use them. Generally, avoid creating new exception classes unless code will make specific efforts to catch that exception; use data members, not additional exception classes, to achieve informational granularity.

The Code

The following example is a custom exception named CustomException that extends Exception and declares two custom data members: a String named stringInfo and a Boolean named booleanInfo.

```
Imports System
Imports System.Runtime.Serialization

Namespace Apress.VisualBasicRecipes.Chapter13

    ' Mark CustomException as Serializable.
```

```vb
<Serializable()> _
Public NotInheritable Class CustomException
    Inherits Exception

    ' Custom data members for CustomException.
    Private m_StringInfo As String
    Private m_BooleanInfo As Boolean

    ' Three standard constructors that simply call the base
    ' class constructor or System.Exception.
    Public Sub New()
        MyBase.New()
    End Sub

    Public Sub New(ByVal message As String)
        MyBase.New(message)
    End Sub

    Public Sub New(ByVal message As String, ByVal inner As Exception)
        MyBase.New(message, inner)
    End Sub

    ' The deserialization constructor required by the ISerialization
    ' interface. Because CustomException is NotInheritable, this constructor
    ' is private. If CustomException were not NotInheritable, this constructor
    ' should be declared as protected so that derived classes can call
    ' it during deserialization.
    Private Sub New(ByVal info As SerializationInfo, ➥
ByVal context As StreamingContext)
        MyBase.New(info, context)

        ' Deserialize each custom data member.
        m_StringInfo = info.GetString("StringInfo")
        m_BooleanInfo = info.GetBoolean("BooleanInfo")

    End Sub

    ' Additional constructors to allow code to set the custom data
    ' members.
    Public Sub New(ByVal _message As String, ByVal _StringInfo As String, ➥
ByVal _BooleanInfo As Boolean)
        MyBase.New(_message)

        m_StringInfo = _StringInfo
        m_BooleanInfo = _BooleanInfo

    End Sub

    Public Sub New(ByVal _message As String, ByVal inner As Exception, ➥
ByVal _stringinfo As String, ByVal _booleanInfo As Boolean)
        MyBase.New(_message, inner)
```

```vbnet
            m_StringInfo = _stringinfo
            m_BooleanInfo = _booleanInfo

        End Sub

        ' Read-only properties that provide access to the custom data members.
        Public ReadOnly Property StringInfo() As String
            Get
                Return m_StringInfo
            End Get
        End Property

        Public ReadOnly Property BooleanInfo() As Boolean
            Get
                Return m_BooleanInfo
            End Get
        End Property

        ' The GetObjectData method (declared in the ISerializable interface)
        ' is used during serialization of CustomException. Because
        ' CustomException declares custom data members, it must override
        ' the base class implementation of GetObjectData.
        Public Overrides Sub GetObjectData(ByVal info As SerializationInfo, ➥
ByVal context As StreamingContext)

            ' Serialize the custom data members.
            info.AddValue("StringInfo", m_StringInfo)
            info.AddValue("BooleanInfo", m_BooleanInfo)

            ' Call the base class to serialize its members.
            MyBase.GetObjectData(info, context)

        End Sub

        ' Override the base class Message property to include the custom data
        ' members.
        Public Overrides ReadOnly Property Message() As String
            Get
                Dim msg As String = MyBase.Message

                If StringInfo IsNot Nothing Then
                    msg += Environment.NewLine & StringInfo & " = " & BooleanInfo
                End If

                Return msg
            End Get
        End Property

    End Class

    ' A class to demonstrate the use of CustomException.
    Public Class Recipe13_07
```

```vbnet
    Public Shared Sub Main()

        Try
            '  Create and throw a CustomException object.
            Throw New CustomException("Some error", "SomeCustomMessage", True)
        Catch ex As CustomException
            Console.WriteLine(ex.Message)
        End Try

        '  Wait to continue.
        Console.WriteLine(Environment.NewLine)
        Console.WriteLine("Main method complete.  Press Enter.")
        Console.ReadLine()

    End Sub

End Class
End Namespace
```

13-8. Implement a Custom Event Argument

Problem

When you raise an event, you need to pass an object that contains data related to the event that would be useful when handling it. For example, the MouseEventArgs class (used by the MouseDown event) includes the Button property, which indicates which mouse button was pressed.

Solution

Create a custom event argument class derived from the System.EventArg class. When you raise the event, create an instance of your event argument class and pass it to the event handlers.

How It Works

When you declare your own event types, you will often want to pass event-specific state to any listening event handlers. To create a custom event argument class that complies with the *Event pattern* defined by the .NET Framework, you should do the following:

- Derive your custom event argument class from the EventArgs class. The EventArgs class contains no data and is used with events that do not need to pass event state.

- Give your event argument class a meaningful name ending in EventArgs, such as DiskFullEventArgs or MailReceivedEventArgs.

- Mark your argument class as NotInheritable if you do not intend other event argument classes to extend it.

- Implement additional data members and properties to support event state that you need to pass to event handlers. It's best to make event state immutable, so you should use Private ReadOnly data members and use Public properties to provide read-only access to the data members.

- Implement a Public constructor that allows you to set the initial configuration of the event state.

- Make your event argument class serializable so that the runtime can marshal instances of it across application domain and machine boundaries. Applying the attribute System. SerializableAttribute is usually sufficient for event argument classes. However, if your class has special serialization requirements, you must also implement the interface System. Runtime.Serialization.ISerializable. (See recipe 13-1 for details on making classes serializable.)

The Code

The following example demonstrates the implementation of an event argument class named MailReceivedEventArgs. Theoretically, an e-mail server passes instances of the MailReceivedEventArgs class to event handlers in response to the receipt of an e-mail message. The MailReceivedEventArgs class contains information about the sender and subject of the received e-mail message.

```
Imports System

Namespace Apress.VisualBasicRecipes.Chapter13

    <Serializable()> _
    Public NotInheritable Class MailReceivedEventArgs
        Inherits EventArgs

        ' Private read-only members that hold the event state that is to be
        ' distributed to all event handlers. The MailReceivedEventArgs class
        ' will specify who sent the received mail and what the subject is.
        Private ReadOnly m_From As String
        Private ReadOnly m_Subject As String

        ' Constuctor, initializes event state.
        Public Sub New(ByVal _from As String, ByVal _subject As String)

            Me.m_From = _from
            Me.m_Subject = _subject

        End Sub

        ' Read-only properties to provide access to event state.
        Public ReadOnly Property From() As String
            Get
                Return m_From
            End Get
        End Property

        Public ReadOnly Property Subject() As String
            Get
                Return m_Subject
            End Get
        End Property

    End Class

    ' A class to demonstrate the use of MailReceivedEventArgs.
```

```vb
Public Class Recipe13_08

    Public Shared Sub Main()

        Dim args As New MailReceivedEventArgs("Mike", "Work Plan")

        Console.WriteLine("From: {0}, Subject: {1}", args.From, args.Subject)

        ' Wait to continue.
        Console.WriteLine(Environment.NewLine)
        Console.WriteLine("Main method complete.  Press Enter.")
        Console.ReadLine()

    End Sub

End Class
End Namespace
```

Notes

The preceding example mainly deals with creating a custom EventArgs class. If the example were part of a full application, you would most likely have an event (such as MailReceived) that would accept an instance of MailReceivedEventArgs as the second parameter. Your Mail class would appropriately raise this event, passing an instance of MailReceivedEventArgs. Recipe 13-10 goes into more detail on handling custom events and even arguments this way.

13-9. Implement the Singleton Pattern

Problem

You need to ensure that only a single instance of a type exists at any given time and that the single instance is accessible to all elements of your application.

Solution

Implement the type using the *Singleton pattern*.

How It Works

Of all the identified patterns, the Singleton pattern is perhaps the most widely known and commonly used. The purpose of the Singleton pattern is to ensure that only one instance of a type exists at a given time and to provide global access to the functionality of that single instance. You can implement the type using the Singleton pattern by doing the following:

- Implement a Private Shared member within the type to hold a reference to the single instance of the type.

- Implement a publicly accessible Shared property in the type to provide read-only access to the singleton instance.

- Implement only a Private constructor so that code cannot create additional instances of the type.

The Code

The following example demonstrates an implementation of the Singleton pattern for a class named SingletonExample.

```
Imports System

Namespace Apress.VisualBasicRecipes.Chapter13
    Public Class SingletonExample

        ' A shared member to hold a reference to the singleton instance.
        Private Shared m_Instance As SingletonExample

        ' A shared constructor to create the singleton instance. Another
        ' alternative is to use lazy initialization in the Instance property.
        Shared Sub New()
            m_Instance = New SingletonExample
        End Sub

        ' A private constructor to stop code from creating additional
        ' instances of the singleton type.
        Private Sub New()
        End Sub

        ' A public property to provide access to the singleton instance.
        Public Shared ReadOnly Property Instance() As SingletonExample
            Get
                Return m_Instance
            End Get
        End Property

        ' Public methods that provide singleton functionality.
        Public Sub TestMethod1()
            Console.WriteLine("Test Method 1 ran.")
        End Sub

        Public Sub TestMethod2()
            Console.WriteLine("Test Method 2 ran.")
        End Sub

    End Class
End Namespace
```

Usage

To invoke the functionality of the SingletonExample class, you can obtain a reference to the singleton using the Instance property and then call its methods. Alternatively, you can execute members of the singleton directly through the Instance property. The following code shows both approaches.

```
Public Class Recipe13_09
    Public Shared Sub Main()

        ' Obtain reference to a singleton and invoke methods.
        Dim s As SingletonExample = SingletonExample.Instance
        s.TestMethod1()
```

```
      ' Execute singleton functionality without a reference.
      SingletonExample.Instance.TestMethod2()

      ' Wait to continue.
      Console.WriteLine(Environment.NewLine)
      Console.WriteLine("Main method complete.  Press Enter.")
      Console.ReadLine()

    End Sub
End Class
```

13-10. Implement the Observer Pattern

Problem

You need to implement an efficient mechanism for an object (the *subject*) to notify other objects (the *observers*) about changes to its state.

Solution

Implement the *Observer pattern* using delegate types as type-safe function pointers and event types to manage and notify the set of observers.

How It Works

The traditional approach to implementing the Observer pattern is to implement two interfaces: one to represent an observer (IObserver) and the other to represent the subject (ISubject). Objects that implement IObserver register with the subject, indicating that they want to be notified of important events (such as state changes) affecting the subject. The subject is responsible for managing the list of registered observers and notifying them in response to events affecting the subject. The subject usually notifies observers by calling a Notify method declared in the IObserver interface. The subject might pass data to the observer as part of the Notify method, or the observer might need to call a method declared in the ISubject interface to obtain additional details about the event.

Although you are free to implement the Observer pattern in VB .NET using the approach just described, the Observer pattern is so pervasive in modern software solutions that VB .NET and the .NET Framework include event and delegate types to simplify its implementation. The use of events and delegates means that you do not need to declare IObserver and ISubject interfaces. In addition, you do not need to implement the logic necessary to manage and notify the set of registered observers—the area where most coding errors occur.

The .NET Framework uses one particular implementation of the event-based and delegate-based Observer pattern so frequently that it has been given its own name: the *Event pattern*. (Pattern purists might prefer the name *Event idiom*, but Event pattern is the name most commonly used in Microsoft documentation.)

The Code

The example for this recipe contains a complete implementation of the Event pattern, which includes the following types:

- Thermostat class (the subject of the example), which keeps track of the current temperature and notifies observers when a temperature change occurs

- TemperatureChangedEventArgs class, which is a custom implementation of the System. EventArgs class used to encapsulate temperature change data for distribution during the notification of observers

- TemperatureChangedEventHandler delegate, which defines the signature of the method that all observers of a Thermostat object should implement if they want to be notified in the event of temperature changes

- TemperatureChangeObserver and TemperatureAverageObserver classes, which are observers of the Thermostat class

The TemperatureChangedEventArgs class (in the following listing) derives from the class System. EventArgs. The custom event argument class should contain all of the data that the subject needs to pass to its observers when it notifies them of an event. If you do not need to pass data with your event notifications, you do not need to define a new argument class; simply pass EventArgs.Empty or Nothing as the argument when you raise the event. (See recipe 13-8 for details on implementing custom event argument classes.)

Namespace Apress.VisualBasicRecipes.Chapter13

```
    ' An event argument class that contains information about a temperature
    ' change event. An instance of this class is passed with every event.
    <Serializable()> _
    Public Class TemperatureChangedEventArgs
        Inherits EventArgs

        ' Private data members contain the old and new temperature readings.
        Private ReadOnly m_OldTemperature As Integer
        Private ReadOnly m_NewTemperature As Integer

        ' Constructor that takes the old and new temperature values.
        Public Sub New(ByVal oldTemp As Integer, ByVal newTemp As Integer)

            m_OldTemperature = oldTemp
            m_NewTemperature = newTemp

        End Sub

        ' Read-only properties provide access to the temperature values.
        Public ReadOnly Property OldTemperature()
            Get
                Return m_OldTemperature
            End Get
        End Property

        Public ReadOnly Property NewTemperature()
            Get
                Return m_NewTemperature
            End Get
        End Property

    End Class
End NameSpace
```

The following code shows the declaration of the `TemperatureChangedEventHandler` delegate. Based on this declaration, all observers must implement a subroutine (the name is unimportant), which takes two arguments: an `Object` instance as the first argument and a `TemperatureChangedEventArgs` object as the second. During notification, the `Object` argument is a reference to the `Thermostat` object that raises the event, and the `TemperatureChangedEventArgs` argument contains data about the old and new temperature values.

```
Namespace Apress.VisualBasicRecipes.Chapter13

    ' A delegate that specifies the signature that all temperature event
    ' handler methods must implement.
    Public Delegate Sub TemperatureChangedEventHandler(ByVal sender As Object, ➥
ByVal args As TemperatureChangedEventArgs)


End NameSpace
```

For the purpose of demonstrating the Observer pattern, the example contains two different observer types: `TemperatureAverageObserver` and `TemperatureChangeObserver`. Both classes have the same basic implementation. `TemperatureAverageObserver` keeps a count of the number of temperature change events and the sum of the temperature values, and displays an average temperature when each event occurs. `TemperatureChangeObserver` displays information about the change in temperature each time a temperature change event occurs.

The following listing shows the `TemperatureChangeObserver` and `TemperatureAverageObserver` classes. Notice that the constructors take references to the `Thermostat` object that the `TemperatureChangeObserver` or `TemperatureAverageObserver` object should observe. When you instantiate an observer, pass it a reference to the subject. The observer's constructor must handle the observer's event by using `AddHandler` and specifying the delegate method preceded by the `AddressOf` keyword.

Once the `TemperatureChangeObserver` or `TemperatureAverageObserver` object has registered its delegate instance with the `Thermostat` object, you need to maintain a reference to this `Thermostat` object only if you want to stop observing it later on. In addition, you do not need to maintain a reference to the subject, because a reference to the event source is included as the first argument each time the `Thermostat` object raises an event through the `TemperatureChange` method.

```
Namespace Apress.VisualBasicRecipes.Chapter13

    ' A thermostat observer that displays information about the change in
    ' temperature when a temperature change event occurs.
    Public Class TemperatureChangeObserver

        ' A constructor that takes a reference to the Thermostat object that
        ' the TemperatureChangeObserver object should observe.
        Public Sub New(ByVal t As Thermostat)

            ' Add a handler for the TemperatureChanged event.
            AddHandler t.TemperatureChanged, AddressOf Me.TemperatureChange

        End Sub

        ' The method to handle temperature change events.
        Public Sub TemperatureChange(ByVal sender As Object, ➥
ByVal args As TemperatureChangedEventArgs)
            Console.WriteLine("ChangeObserver: Old={0}, New={1}, Change={2}", ➥
```

```vbnet
                args.OldTemperature, args.NewTemperature, args.NewTemperature - args.OldTemperature)
            End Sub

    End Class

    ' A Thermostat observer that displays information about the average
    ' temperature when a temperature change event occurs.
    Public Class TemperatureAverageObserver

        ' Sum contains the running total of temperature readings.
        ' Count contains the number of temperature events received.
        Private sum As Integer = 0
        Private count As Integer = 0

        ' A constructor that takes a reference to the Thermostat object that
        ' the TemperatureAverageObserver object should observe.
        Public Sub New(ByVal T As Thermostat)
            ' Add a handler for the TemperatureChanged event.
            AddHandler T.TemperatureChanged, AddressOf Me.TemperatureChange
        End Sub

        ' The method to handle temperature change events.
        Public Sub TemperatureChange(ByVal sender As Object, ➥
ByVal args As TemperatureChangedEventArgs)

            count += 1
            sum += args.NewTemperature

            Console.WriteLine("AverageObserver: Average={0:F}", ➥
CDbl(sum) / CDbl(count))

        End Sub

    End Class
End NameSpace
```

Finally, the Thermostat class is the observed object in this Observer (Event) pattern. In theory, a monitoring device sets the current temperature by calling the Temperature property on a Thermostat object. This causes the Thermostat object to raise its TemperatureChange event and send a TemperatureChangedEventArgs object to each observer.

The example contains a Recipe13_10 class that defines a Main method to drive the example. After creating a Thermostat object and two different observer objects, the Main method repeatedly prompts you to enter a temperature. Each time you enter a new temperature, the Thermostat object notifies the listeners, which display information to the console. The following is the code for the Thermostat class.

```vbnet
Namespace Apress.VisualBasicRecipes.Chapter13

    ' A class that represents a Thermostat, which is the source of temperature
    ' change events. In the Observer pattern, a Thermostat object is the
    ' subject that observers listen to for change notifications.
    Public Class Thermostat

        ' Private field to hold current temperature.
        Private m_Temperature As Integer = 0
```

```vbnet
    ' The event used to maintain a list of observer delegates and raise
    ' a temperature change event when a temperature change occurs.
    Public Event TemperatureChanged As TemperatureChangedEventHandler

    ' A protected method used to raise the TemperatureChanged event.
    ' Because events can be triggered only from within the containing
    ' type, using a protected method to raise the event allows derived
    ' classes to provide customized behavior and still be able to raise
    ' the base class event.
    Protected Overridable Sub OnTemperatureChanged(ByVal args As➥
TemperatureChangedEventArgs)

        ' Notify all observers.
        RaiseEvent TemperatureChanged(Me, args)

    End Sub

    ' Public property to get and set the current temperature. The "set"
    ' side of the property is responsible for raising the temperature
    ' change event to notify all observers of a change in temperature.
    Public Property Temperature() As Integer
        Get
            Return m_Temperature
        End Get
        Set(ByVal value As Integer)
            ' Create a new event argument object containing the old and
            ' new temperatures.
            Dim args As New TemperatureChangedEventArgs(m_Temperature, value)

            ' Update the current temperature.
            m_Temperature = value

            ' Raise the temperature change event.
            OnTemperatureChanged(args)

        End Set
    End Property

End Class

' A class to demonstrate the use of the Observer pattern.
Public Class Recipe13_10

    Public Shared Sub Main()

        ' Create a Thermostat instance.
        Dim myThemoStat As New Thermostat

        ' Create the Thermostat observers.
        Dim changeObserver As New TemperatureChangeObserver(myThemoStat)
        Dim averageObserver As New TemperatureAverageObserver(myThemoStat)
```

```
        '  Loop, getting temperature readings from the user.
        '  Any non-integer value will terminate the loop.
        Do
            Console.WriteLine(Environment.NewLine)
            Console.Write("Enter current temperature: ")

            Try
                '  Convert the user's input to an integer and use it to set
                '  the current temperature of the Thermostat.
                myThemoStat.Temperature = Int32.Parse(Console.ReadLine)
            Catch ex As Exception
                '  Use the exception condition to trigger termination.
                Console.WriteLine("Terminating Observer Pattern Example.")

                '  Wait to continue.
                Console.WriteLine(Environment.NewLine)
                Console.WriteLine("Main method complete.  Press Enter.")
                Console.ReadLine()
                Return

            End Try
        Loop While True

    End Sub

    End Class
End Namespace
```

Usage

The following listing shows the kind of output you should expect if you build and run the previous example. The bold values show your input.

```
Enter current temperature: 35
ChangeObserver: Old=0, New=35, Change=35
AverageObserver: Average=35.00

Enter current temperature: 37
ChangeObserver: Old=35, New=37, Change=2
AverageObserver: Average=36.00

Enter current temperature: 40
ChangeObserver: Old=37, New=40, Change=3
AverageObserver: Average=37.33
```

CHAPTER 14

Windows Integration

The intention of the Microsoft .NET Framework is to run on a wide variety of operating systems to improve code mobility and simplify cross-platform integration. At the time this book was written, versions of the .NET Framework were available for various operating systems, including Microsoft Windows, FreeBSD, Linux, and Mac OS X. However, many of these implementations are yet to be widely adopted. Microsoft Windows is currently the operating system on which the .NET Framework is most commonly installed.

The .NET Framework includes functionality for working with several components (such as the registry and event log) that are integrated with the Windows operating system. While other platforms may provide equivalent functionality, the recipes in this chapter focus specifically on the Windows implementations and cover the following topics:

- Retrieve runtime environment information (recipes 14-1 and 14-2)
- Write to the Windows event log (recipe 14-3)
- Read, write, and search the Windows registry (recipe 14-4 and 14-5)
- Create and install Windows services (recipes 14-6 and 14-7)
- Create a shortcut on the Windows Start menu or desktop (recipe 14-8)

■Note The majority of functionality discussed in this chapter is protected by code access security permissions enforced by the common language runtime (CLR). See the .NET Framework software development kit (SDK) documentation for the specific permissions required to execute each member.

14-1. Access Runtime Environment Information

Problem

You need to access information about the runtime environment and platform in which your application is running.

Solution

Use the members of the System.Environment class.

How It Works

The Environment class provides a set of Shared members that you can use to obtain (and in some cases modify) information about the environment in which an application is running. Table 14-1 describes some of the most commonly used Environment members.

Table 14-1. *Commonly Used Members of the Environment Class*

Member	Description
Properties	
CommandLine	Gets a String containing the command line used to execute the current application, including the application name. (See recipe 1-5 for details.)
CurrentDirectory	Gets and sets a String containing the current application directory. Initially, this property will contain the name of the directory in which the application was started.
HasShutdownStarted	Gets a Boolean that indicates whether the CLR has started to shut down or the current application domain has started unloading.
MachineName	Gets a String containing the name of the machine.
OSVersion	Gets a System.OperatingSystem object that contains information about the platform and version of the underlying operating system. See the paragraph following this table for more details.
ProcessorCount	Gets the number of processors on the machine.
SystemDirectory	Gets a String containing the fully qualified path of the system directory; that is, the system32 subdirectory of the Windows installation folder.
TickCount	Gets an Integer representing the number of milliseconds that have elapsed since the system was started.
UserDomainName	Gets a String containing the Windows domain name to which the current user belongs. This will be the same as MachineName if the user has logged in on a machine account instead of a domain account.
UserInteractive	Gets a Boolean indicating whether the application is running in user interactive mode; in other words, its forms and message boxes will be visible to the logged-on user. UserInteractive will return False when the application is running as a service or is a web application.
UserName	Gets a String containing the name of the user that started the current thread, which can be different from the logged-on user in case of impersonation.
Version	Gets a System.Version object that contains information about the version of the CLR.

Table 14-1. *Commonly Used Members of the Environment Class*

Member	Description
Methods	
ExpandEnvironmentVariables	Replaces the names of environment variables in a String with the value of the variable. (See recipe 14-2 for details.)
GetCommandLineArgs	Returns a String array containing all elements of the command line used to execute the current application, including the application name. (See recipe 1-5 for details.)
GetEnvironmentVariable	Returns a String containing the value of a specified environment variable. (See recipe 14-2 for details.)
GetEnvironmentVariables	Returns an object implementing System.Collections. IDictionary, which contains all environment variables and their values. (See recipe 14-2 for details.)
GetFolderPath	Returns a String containing the path to a special system folder specified using the System.Environment.SpecialFolder enumeration. This includes folders for the Internet cache, cookies, history, desktop, and favorites. (See the .NET Framework SDK documentation for a complete list of values.)
GetLogicalDrives	Returns a String array containing the names of all logical drives, including network mapped drives. Note that each drive has the following syntax: <*drive letter*>:\.

The System.OperatingSystem object returned by OSVersion contains four properties:

- The Platform property returns a value of the System.PlatformID enumeration identifying the current operating system; valid values are Unix, Win32NT, Win32S, Win32Windows, and WinCE.

- The ServicePack property returns a String identifying the service pack level installed on the computer. If no service packs are installed, or service packs are not supported, an empty String is returned.

- The Version property returns a System.Version object that identifies the specific operating system version. This class includes the Build, Major, MajorRevision, Minor, MinorRevision, and Revision properties, which allow you to get each specific part of the complete version number.

- The VersionString property returns a concatenated string summary of the Platform, ServicePack, and Version properties.

To determine the operating system on which you are running, you must use both the platform and the version information, as detailed in Table 14-2.

Table 14-2. *Determining the Current Operating System*

PlatformID	Major Version	Minor Version	Operating System
Win32Windows	4	10	Windows 98
Win32Windows	4	90	Windows ME
Win32NT	4	0	Windows NT 4
Win32NT	5	0	Windows 2000
Win32NT	5	1	Windows XP
Win32NT	5	2	Windows Server 2003
Win32NT	6	0	Windows Vista

The Code

The following example uses the `Environment` class to display information about the current environment to the console.

```
Imports System

Namespace Apress.VisualBasicRecipes.Chapter14
    Public Class Recipe14_01

        Public Shared Sub Main()

            ' Command line.
            Console.WriteLine("Command line : " & Environment.CommandLine)

            ' OS and CLR version information.
            Console.WriteLine(Environment.NewLine)
            Console.WriteLine("OS PlatformID : " & Environment.OSVersion.Platform)
            Console.WriteLine("OS Major Version : " & ➥
Environment.OSVersion.Version.Major)
            Console.WriteLine("OS Minor Version : " & ➥
Environment.OSVersion.Version.Minor)
            Console.WriteLine("CLR Version : " & Environment.Version.ToString)

            ' User, machine and domain name information.
            Console.WriteLine(Environment.NewLine)
            Console.WriteLine("User Name : " & Environment.UserName)
            Console.WriteLine("Domain Name : " & Environment.UserDomainName)
            Console.WriteLine("Machine Name : " & Environment.MachineName)

            ' Other environment information.
            Console.WriteLine(Environment.NewLine)
            Console.WriteLine("Is interactive? : " & Environment.UserInteractive)
            Console.WriteLine("Shutting down? : " & Environment.HasShutdownStarted)
            Console.WriteLine("Ticks since startup : " & Environment.TickCount)

            ' Display the names of all logical drives.
            Console.WriteLine(Environment.NewLine)
```

```
        For Each s As String In Environment.GetLogicalDrives
            Console.WriteLine("Logical drive : " & s)
        Next

        ' Standard folder information.
        Console.WriteLine(Environment.NewLine)
        Console.WriteLine("Current folder : " & Environment.CurrentDirectory)
        Console.WriteLine("System folder : " & Environment.SystemDirectory)

        ' Enumerate all special folders and display them.
        Console.WriteLine(Environment.NewLine)
        For Each s As Environment.SpecialFolder In ➡
[Enum].GetValues(GetType(Environment.SpecialFolder))
            Console.WriteLine("{0} folder : {1}", s, ➡
Environment.GetFolderPath(s))
        Next

        ' Wait to continue.
        Console.WriteLine(Environment.NewLine)
        Console.WriteLine("Main method complete.  Press Enter.")
        Console.ReadLine()

    End Sub

  End Class
End Namespace
```

14-2. Retrieve the Value of an Environment Variable

Problem

You need to retrieve the value of an environment variable for use in your application.

Solution

Use the GetEnvironmentVariable, GetEnvironmentVariables, and ExpandEnvironmentVariables methods of the Environment class.

How It Works

The GetEnvironmentVariable method allows you to retrieve a string containing the value of a single named environment variable, whereas the GetEnvironmentVariables method returns an object implementing IDictionary that contains the names and values of all environment variables as strings. .NET Framework 2.0 introduces additional overloads of the GetEnvironmentVariable and GetEnvironmentVariables methods, which take a System.EnvironmentVariableTarget argument, allowing you to specify a subset of environment variables to return based on the target of the variable: Machine, Process, or User.

The ExpandEnvironmentVariables method provides a simple mechanism for substituting the value of an environment variable into a string by including the variable name enclosed in percent signs (%) within the string.

The Code

Here is an example that demonstrates how to use all three methods:

```
Imports System
Imports System.Collections

Namespace Apress.VisualBasicRecipes.Chapter14
    Public Class Recipe14_02

        Public Shared Sub Main()

            ' Retrieve a named environment variable.
            Console.WriteLine("Path = " & GetEnvironmentVariable("Path"))
            Console.WriteLine(Environment.NewLine)

            ' Substitute the value of named environment variables.
            Console.WriteLine(ExpandEnvironmentVariables("The Path on " & ➡
"%computername% is %path%"))

            ' Retrieve all environment variables targeted at the process and
            ' display the values of all that begin with the letter U.
            Dim vars As IDictionary = ➡
GetEnvironmentVariables(EnvironmentVariableTarget.Process)

            For Each s As String In vars.Keys
                If s.ToUpper.StartsWith("U") Then
                    Console.WriteLine(s & " = " & vars(s))
                End If
            Next

            ' Wait to continue.
            Console.WriteLine(Environment.NewLine)
            Console.WriteLine("Main method complete.  Press Enter.")
            Console.ReadLine()

        End Sub

    End Class
End Namespace
```

14-3. Write an Event to the Windows Event Log

Problem

You need to write an event to the Windows event log.

Solution

Use the members of the System.Diagnostics.EventLog class to create a log (if required), register an event source, and write events.

How It Works

You can write to the Windows event log using the Shared methods of the EventLog class, or you can create an EventLog object and use its members. Whichever approach you choose, before writing to the event log, you must decide which log you will use and register an event source against that log. The event source is simply a string that uniquely identifies your application. An event source may be registered against only one log at a time.

By default, the event log contains three separate logs: Application, System, and Security. Usually, you will write to the Application log, but you might decide your application warrants a custom log in which to write events. You do not need to explicitly create a custom log; when you register an event source against a log, if the specified log doesn't exist, it's created automatically.

Once you have decided on the destination log and registered an event source, you can start to write event log entries using the WriteEntry method. WriteEntry provides a variety of overloads that allow you to specify some or all of the following values:

- A String containing the event source for the log entry (Shared versions of WriteEntry only).

- A String containing the message for the log entry.

- A value from the System.Diagnostics.EventLogEntryType enumeration, which identifies the type of log entry. Valid values are Error, FailureAudit, Information, SuccessAudit, and Warning.

- An Integer that specifies an application-specific event ID for the log entry.

- A Short that specifies an application-specific subcategory for the log entry.

- A Byte array containing any raw data to associate with the log entry.

■Note The methods of the EventLog class also provide overloads that support the writing of events to the event log of remote machines. See the .NET Framework SDK documentation for more information.

The Code

The following example demonstrates how to use the Shared members of EventLog class to write an entry to the event log of the local machine.

```
Imports System
Imports System.Diagnostics

Namespace Apress.VisualBasicRecipes.Chapter14
    Public Class Recipe14_03

        Public Shared Sub Main()

            ' If it does not exist, register an event source for this
            ' application against the Application log of the local machine.
            ' Trying to register an event source that already exists on the
            ' specified machine will throw a System.ArgumentException.
            If Not EventLog.SourceExists("Visual Basic 2005 Recipes") Then
```

```
                EventLog.CreateEventSource("Visual Basic 2005 Recipes", ➥
"Application")
            End If

            ' Write an event to the event log.
            EventLog.WriteEntry("Visual Basic 2005 Recipes", ➥
"A simple test event.", EventLogEntryType.Information, 1, 0, ➥
New Byte() {10, 55, 200})

            ' Wait to continue.
            Console.WriteLine(Environment.NewLine)
            Console.WriteLine("Main method complete.  Press Enter.")
            Console.ReadLine()

            ' Remove the event source.
            EventLog.DeleteEventSource("Visual Basic 2005 Recipes")

        End Sub

    End Class
End Namespace
```

Usage

After you run the sample code, launch the Event Viewer (EventVwr.exe) and find the last entry with a source of "Visual Basic 2005 Recipes." Figure 14-1 shows how the log entry will look.

Figure 14-1. *Custom message written to the event log*

14-4. Read and Write to the Windows Registry

Problem

You need to read information from, or write information to, the Windows registry.

Solution

Use the methods `GetValue` and `SetValue` of the `Microsoft.Win32.Registry` class.

■Tip The `GetValue` and `SetValue` methods open a registry key, get or set its value, and close the key each time they are called. This means they are inefficient when used to perform many read or write operations. The `GetValue` and `SetValue` methods of the `Microsoft.Win32.RegistryKey` class, discussed in recipe 14-5, will provide better performance if you need to perform many read or write operations on the registry.

How It Works

The `GetValue` and `SetValue` methods (new to .NET 2.0) allow you to read and write named values in named registry keys. `GetValue` takes three arguments:

- A `String` containing the fully qualified name of the key you want to read. The key name must start with one of the following root key names:
  - HKEY_CLASSES_ROOT
  - HKEY_CURRENT_CONFIG
  - HKEY_CURRENT_USER
  - HKEY_DYN_DATA
  - HKEY_LOCAL_MACHINE
  - HKEY_PERFORMANCE_DATA
  - HKEY_USERS
- A `String` containing the name of the value in the key you want to read.
- An `Object` containing the default value to return if the named value is not present in the key.

`GetValue` returns an `Object` containing either the data read from the registry or the default value specified as the third argument if the named value is not found. If the specified key does not exist, `GetValue` returns `Nothing`.

`SetValue` offers two overloads. The most functional expects the following arguments:

- A `String` containing the fully qualified name of the key you want to write. The key must start with one of the root key names specified previously. If the registry key does not exist, it is created automatically.
- A `String` containing the name of the value in the key you want to write.
- An `Object` containing the value to write.
- An element of the `Microsoft.Win32.RegistyValueKind` enumeration that specifies the registry data type that should be used to hold the data.

The second overload allows you to call the SetValue method without specifying the RegistryValueKind argument. In this case, SetValue attempts to automatically determine what the data type should be, based on the data type of the Object argument. A 32-bit integer type will be inferred as a Dword value, and any other numeric type will be inferred as a String. Environment variables, such as %PATH%, will be ignored by this overload and inferred as a normal String. Use the previously mentioned overload if you need to ensure the correct data type is used.

The My object offers the My.Computer.Registry class as an alternative. This class includes only two methods: SetValue and GetValue, which are identical to the SetValue and GetValue methods from the Microsoft.Win32.Registry class. (Refer to Chapter 5 for more information about the My object.)

The Code

The following example demonstrates how to use GetValue and SetValue to read from and write to the registry. Every time the example is run, it reads usage information from the registry and displays it to the screen. The example also updates the stored usage information, which you can see the next time you run the example.

```vbnet
Imports System
Imports Microsoft.Win32

Namespace Apress.VisualBasicRecipes.Chapter14
    Public Class Recipe14_04

        Public Shared Sub Main()

            ' Variables to hold usage information read from registry.
            Dim lastUser As String
            Dim lastRun As String
            Dim runCount As Integer

            ' Read the name of the last user to run the application from the
            ' registry. This is stored as the default value of the key and is
            ' accessed by not specifying a value name. Cast the returned object
            ' to a string.
            lastUser = DirectCast(Registry.GetValue("HKEY_CURRENT_USER\" & _
"Software\Apress\Visual Basic 2005 Recipes", "", "Nobody"), String)

            ' If lastUser is Nothing, it means that the specified registry key
            ' does not exist.
            If lastUser Is Nothing Then
                lastUser = "Nobody"
                lastRun = "Never"
                runCount = 0
            Else
                ' Read the last run date and specify a default value of
                ' Never. Cast the returned Object to a String.
                lastRun = DirectCast(Registry.GetValue("HKEY_CURRENT_USER\" & _
"Software\Apress\Visual Basic 2005 Recipes", "LastRun", "Never"), String)

                ' Read the run count value and specify a default value of
                ' 0 (zero). Cast the returned Object to an Integer.
                runCount = DirectCast(Registry.GetValue("HKEY_CURRENT_USER\" & _
```

```
"Software\Apress\Visual Basic 2005 Recipes", "RunCount", 0), Integer)
            End If

            ' Display the usage information.
            Console.WriteLine("Last user name: " & lastUser)
            Console.WriteLine("Last run date/time: " & lastRun)
            Console.WriteLine("Previous executions: " & runCount)

            ' Update the usage information. It doesn't matter if the registry
            ' key exists or not; SetValue will automatically create it.

            ' Update the last user information with the current username.
            ' Specifiy that this should be stored as the default value
            ' for the key by using an empty string as the value name.
            Registry.SetValue("HKEY_CURRENT_USER\Software\Apress\Visual Basic " & ➥
"2005 Recipes", "", Environment.UserName, RegistryValueKind.String)

            ' Update the last run information with the current date and time.
            ' Specify that this should be stored as a String value in the
            ' registry.
            Registry.SetValue("HKEY_CURRENT_USER\Software\Apress\Visual Basic " & ➥
"2005 Recipes", "LastRun", DateTime.Now.ToString, RegistryValueKind.String)

            ' Update the usage count information. Specify that this should
            ' be stored as an Integer value in the registry.
            runCount += 1
            Registry.SetValue("HKEY_CURRENT_USER\Software\Apress\Visual Basic " & ➥
"2005 Recipes", "RunCount", runCount, RegistryValueKind.DWord)

            ' Wait to continue.
            Console.WriteLine(Environment.NewLine)
            Console.WriteLine("Main method complete.  Press Enter.")
            Console.ReadLine()

        End Sub

    End Class
End Namespace
```

Usage

When you execute Recipe14-04.exe for the first time, you will get output such as this:

```
Last user name: Nobody
Last run date/time: Never
Previous executions: 0
```

Subsequent executions will result in output such as this:

```
Last user name: Administrator
Last run date/time: 5/10/2007 9:42:38 PM
Previous executions: 1
```

14-5. Search the Windows Registry

Problem

You need to search the Windows registry for a key that contains a specific value or content.

Solution

Use the Microsoft.Win32.Registry class to obtain a Microsoft.Win32.RegistryKey object that represents the root key of a registry hive you want to search. Use the members of this RegistryKey object to navigate through and enumerate the registry key hierarchy, as well as to read the names and content of values held in the keys.

How It Works

You must first obtain a RegistryKey object that represents a base-level key and navigate through the hierarchy of RegistryKey objects as required. The Registry class implements a set of seven Shared properties that return RegistryKey objects representing base-level registry keys; Table 14-3 describes the registry location to where each of these fields maps. The My object offers the My.Computer.Registry class, which includes an identical set of properties that provide the same functionality as their Microsoft.Win32.Registry counterparts. (Refer to Chapter 5 for more information about the My object.)

Table 14-3. *Shared Fields of the Registry Class*

Field	Registry Mapping
ClassesRoot	HKEY_CLASSES_ROOT
CurrentConfig	HKEY_CURRENT_CONFIG
CurrentUser	HKEY_CURRENT_USER
DynData	HKEY_DYN_DATA
LocalMachine	HKEY_LOCAL_MACHINE
PerformanceData	HKEY_PERFORMANCE_DATA
Users	HKEY_USERS

■**Tip** The Shared method RegistryKey.OpenRemoteBaseKey allows you to open a registry base key on a remote machine. See the .NET Framework SDK documentation for details of its use.

Once you have the base-level RegistryKey object, you must navigate through its child subkeys recursively. To support navigation, the RegistryKey class allows you to do the following:

- Get the number of immediate subkeys using the `SubKeyCount` property.

- Get a `String` array containing the names of all subkeys using the `GetSubKeyNames` method.

- Get a `RegistryKey` reference to a subkey using the `OpenSubKey` method. The `OpenSubKey` method provides two overloads: the first opens the named key as read-only, and the second accepts a `Boolean` argument that, if true, will open a writable `RegistryKey` object.

Once you obtain a `RegistryKey`, you can create, read, update, and delete subkeys and values using the methods listed in Table 14-4. Methods that modify the contents of the key require you to have a writable `RegistryKey` object.

Table 14-4. *RegistryKey Methods to Create, Read, Update, and Delete Registry Keys and Values*

Method	Description
CreateSubKey	Creates a new subkey with the specified name and returns a writable `RegistryKey` object. If the specified subkey already exists, `CreateSubKey` returns a writable reference to the existing subkey.
DeleteSubKey	Deletes the subkey with the specified name, which must be empty of subkeys (but not values); otherwise, a `System.InvalidOperationException` is thrown.
DeleteSubKeyTree	Deletes the subkey with the specified name along with all of its subkeys.
DeleteValue	Deletes the value with the specified name from the current key.
GetValue	Returns the value with the specified name from the current key. The value is returned as an `Object`, which you must cast to the appropriate type. The simplest form of `GetValue` returns `Nothing` if the specified value doesn't exist. An overload allows you to specify a default value to return (instead of `Nothing`) if the named value doesn't exist.
GetValueKind	Returns the registry data type of the value with the specified name in the current key. The value is returned as a member of the `Microsoft.Win32.RegistryValueKind` enumeration.
GetValueNames	Returns a `String` array containing the names of all values in the current registry key. If the key includes a default value, represented by an empty string, the empty string will be included in the array of names returned by this method.
SetValue	Creates (or updates) the value with the specified name. In .NET 2.0, you can specify the data type used to store the value with the overload that takes a `RegistryValueKind` as the last parameter. If you don't provide such a value, one will be calculated automatically, based on the managed type of the object you pass as the value to set.

The `RegistryKey` class implements `IDisposable`. You should call the `IDisposable.Dispose` method to free operating system resources when you have finished with the `RegistryKey` object.

The Code

The following example takes a single command-line argument and recursively searches the `CurrentUser` hive of the registry looking for keys with names matching the supplied argument. When the example finds a match, it displays all `String` type values contained in the key to the console.

```vbnet
Imports System
Imports Microsoft.Win32

Namespace Apress.VisualBasicRecipes.Chapter14
    Public Class Recipe14_05

        Public Shared Sub SearchSubKeys(ByVal root As RegistryKey, ➥
ByVal searchKey As String)

            ' Loop through all subkeys contained in the current key.
            For Each keyName As String In root.GetSubKeyNames

                Try
                    Using key As RegistryKey = root.OpenSubKey(keyName)
                        If keyName = searchKey Then printkeyvalues(key)
                        SearchSubKeys(key, searchKey)
                    End Using
                Catch ex As Security.SecurityException
                    ' Ignore SecurityException for the purpose of this example.
                    ' Some subkeys of HKEY_CURRENT_USER are secured and will
                    ' throw a SecurityException when opened.
                End Try
            Next

        End Sub

        Public Shared Sub PrintKeyValues(ByVal key As RegistryKey)

            ' Display the name of the matching subkey and the number of
            ' values it contains.
            Console.WriteLine("Registry key found : {0} contains {1} values", ➥
key.Name, key.ValueCount)

            ' Loop through the values and display.
            For Each valueName As String In key.GetValueNames

                If TypeOf key.GetValue(valueName) Is String Then
                    Console.WriteLine("  Value : {0} = {1}", valueName, ➥
key.GetValue(valueName))
                End If

            Next

        End Sub

        Public Shared Sub Main(ByVal args As String())

            If args.Length > 0 Then
                ' Open the CurrentUser base key.
                Using root As RegistryKey = Registry.CurrentUser
                    ' Search recursively through the registry for any keys
                    ' with the specified name.
                    SearchSubKeys(root, args(0))
                End Using
            End If
```

```
          ' Wait to continue.
          Console.WriteLine(Environment.NewLine)
          Console.WriteLine("Main method complete.  Press Enter.")
          Console.ReadLine()

      End Sub

  End Class
End Namespace
```

Usage

Running the example using the command `Recipe14-05 Environment` will display output similar to the following when executed using the command on a machine running Windows XP:

```
Registry key found : HKEY_CURRENT_USER\Environment contains 2 values
  Value : TEMP = C:\Documents and Settings\Allen\Local Settings\Temp
  Value : TMP = C:\Documents and Settings\Allen\Local Settings\Temp
```

14-6. Create a Windows Service

Problem

You need to create an application that will run as a Windows service.

Solution

Create a class that extends `System.ServiceProcess.ServiceBase`. Use the inherited properties to control the behavior of your service, and override inherited methods to implement the functionality required. Implement a `Main` method that creates an instance of your service class and passes it to the `Shared ServiceBase.Run` method.

> ■**Note** The ServiceBase class is defined in the `System.ServiceProcess` assembly, so you must include a reference to this assembly when you build your service class.

How It Works

To create a Windows service manually, you must implement a class derived from the `ServiceBase` class. The `ServiceBase` class provides the base functionality that allows the Windows Service Control Manager (SCM) to configure the service, operate the service as a background task, and control the life cycle of the service. The SCM also controls how other applications can manage the service programmatically.

> ■**Tip** If you are using Microsoft Visual Studio, you can use the Windows Service project template to create a Windows service. The template provides the basic code infrastructure required by a Windows service class, which you can extend with your custom functionality.

To control your service, the SCM uses the eight Protected methods inherited from ServiceBase class described in Table 14-5. You should override these virtual methods to implement the functionality and behavior required by your service. Not all services must support all control messages. The CanXXX properties inherited from the ServiceBase class declare to the SCM which control messages your service supports. Table 14-5 specifies the property that controls each operation.

Table 14-5. *Methods That Control the Operation of a Service*

Method	Description
OnStart	All services must support the OnStart method, which the SCM calls to start the service. The SCM passes a String array containing arguments specified for the service. These arguments can be specified when the ServiceController.Start method is called and are usually configured in the service's property window in Windows Control Panel. However, they are rarely used because it is better for the service to retrieve its configuration information directly from a configuration file or the Windows registry. The OnStart method must normally return within 30 seconds, or the SCM will abort the service. Your service must call the RequestAdditionalTime method of the ServiceBase class if it requires more time; specify the additional milliseconds required as an Integer.
OnStop	Called by the SCM to stop a service. The SCM will call OnStop only if the CanStop property is set to True, which it is by default.
OnPause	Called by the SCM to pause a service. The SCM will call OnPause only if the CanPauseAndContinue property, which is False by default, is set to True.
OnContinue	Called by the SCM to continue a paused service. The SCM will call OnContinue only if the CanPauseAndContinue property, which is False by default, is set to True.
OnShutdown	Called by the SCM when the system is shutting down. The SCM will call OnShutdown only if the CanShutdown property, which is False by default, is set to True.
OnPowerEvent	Called by the SCM when a system-level power status change occurs, such as a laptop going into suspend mode. The SCM will call OnPowerEvent only if the CanHandlePowerEvent property, which is False by default, is set to True.
OnCustomCommand	Allows you to extend the service control mechanism with custom control messages. See the .NET Framework SDK documentation for more details.
OnSessionChange	Called by the SCM when a change event is received from the Terminal Services session or when users log on and off the local machine. A System.ServiceProcess.SessionChangeDescription object passed as an argument by the SCM contains details of what type of session change occurred. The SCM will call OnSessionChange only if the CanHandleSessionChangeEvent property, which is False by default, is set to True. This method is new in .NET Framework 2.0.

As mentioned in Table 14-5, the OnStart method is expected to return within 30 seconds, so you should not use OnStart to perform lengthy initialization tasks when you can avoid it. A service class should implement a constructor that performs initialization, including configuring the inherited properties of the ServiceBase class. In addition to the properties that declare the control messages supported by a service, the ServiceBase class implements three other important properties:

- `ServiceName` is the name used internally by the SCM to identify the service and must be set before the service is run.

- `AutoLog` controls whether the service automatically writes entries to the event log when it receives any of the `OnStart`, `OnStop`, `OnPause`, and `OnContinue` control messages (see Table 14-5).

- `EventLog` provides access to an `EventLog` object that's preconfigured with an event source name that's the same as the `ServiceName` property registered against the Application log. (See recipe 14-3 for more information about the `EventLog` class.)

The final step in creating a service is to implement a `Shared Main` method. The `Main` method must create an instance of your service class and pass it as an argument to the `Shared` method `ServiceBase.Run`.

The Code

The following Windows service example uses a configurable `System.Timers.Timer` to write an entry to the Windows event log periodically. You can start, pause, and stop the service using the Services application in the Control Panel.

```vb
Imports System
Imports System.Timers
Imports System.ServiceProcess

Namespace Apress.VisualBasicRecipes.Chapter14

    Class Recipe14_06
        Inherits ServiceBase

        ' A timer that controls how frequenty the example writes to the
        ' event log.
        Private serviceTimer As Timer

        Public Sub New()

            ' Set the ServiceBase.ServiceName property.
            ServiceName = "Recipe 14_06 Service"

            ' Configure the level of control available on the service.
            CanStop = True
            CanPauseAndContinue = True
            CanHandleSessionChangeEvent = True

            ' Configure the service to log important events to the
            ' Application event log automatically.
            AutoLog = True

        End Sub

        ' The method executed when the timer expires and writes an
        ' entry to the Application event log.
        Private Sub WriteLogEntry(ByVal sender As Object, ➥
ByVal e As ElapsedEventArgs)
```

```vb
        ' In case this is a long-running process, stop the timer
        ' so it won't attempt to execute multiple times.
        serviceTimer.Stop()

        ' Use the EventLog object automatically configured by the
        ' ServiceBase class to write to the event log.
        EventLog.WriteEntry("Recipe14_06 Service active : " & e.SignalTime)

        ' Restart the timer.
        serviceTimer.Start()

    End Sub

    Protected Overrides Sub OnStart(ByVal args() As String)

        ' Obtain the interval between log entry writes from the first
        ' argument. Use 5000 milliseconds by default and enforce a 1000
        ' millisecond minimum.
        Dim interval As Double

        Try
            interval = Double.Parse(args(0))
            interval = Math.Max(1000, interval)
        Catch ex As Exception
            interval = 5000
        End Try

        EventLog.WriteEntry(String.Format("Recipe14_06 Service starting.  " & ➡
"Writing log entries every {0} milliseconds...", interval))

        ' Create, configure and start a System.Timers.Timer to
        ' periodically call the WriteLogEntry method. The Start
        ' and Stop methods of the System.Timers.Timer class
        ' make starting, pausing, resuming and stopping the
        ' service straightforward.
        serviceTimer = New Timer
        serviceTimer.Interval = interval
        serviceTimer.AutoReset = True
        AddHandler serviceTimer.Elapsed, AddressOf WriteLogEntry
        serviceTimer.Start()

    End Sub

    Protected Overrides Sub OnStop()

        EventLog.WriteEntry("Recipe14_06 Service stopping...")
        serviceTimer.Stop()

        ' Free system resources used by the Timer object.
        serviceTimer.Dispose()
        serviceTimer = Nothing

    End Sub
```

```vb
        Protected Overrides Sub OnPause()

            If serviceTimer IsNot Nothing Then
                EventLog.WriteEntry("Recipe14_06 Service pausing...")
                serviceTimer.Stop()
            End If

        End Sub

        Protected Overrides Sub OnContinue()

            If serviceTimer IsNot Nothing Then
                EventLog.WriteEntry("Recipe14_06 Service resuming...")
                serviceTimer.Start()
            End If

        End Sub

        Protected Overrides Sub OnSessionChange(ByVal changeDescription As ➡
System.ServiceProcess.SessionChangeDescription)

            EventLog.WriteEntry("Recipe14_06 Session change..." & ➡
changeDescription.Reason)

        End Sub

        Public Shared Sub Main()

            ' Create an instance of the Recipe14_06 class that will write
            ' an entry to the Application event log. Pass the object to the
            ' shared ServiceBase.Run method.
            ServiceBase.Run(New Recipe14_06)

        End Sub

    End Class
End Namespace
```

Usage

If you want to run multiple services in a single process, you must create an array of ServiceBase objects and pass it to the ServiceBase.Run method. Although service classes have a Main method, you can't execute service code directly. Attempting to run a service class directly results in Windows displaying the Windows Service Start Failure message box, as shown in Figure 14-2. Recipe 14-7 describes what you must do to install your service before it will execute.

Figure 14-2. *The Windows Service Start Failure message box*

14-7. Create a Windows Service Installer

Problem

You have created a Windows service application and need to install it.

Solution

Add a new class to your Windows service project that extends the System.Configuration.Install. Installer class to create an installer class containing the information necessary to install and configure your service class. Use the Installer tool (Installutil.exe) to perform the installation, which is installed as part of the .NET Framework.

■**Note** You must create the installer class in the same assembly as the service class for the service to install and function correctly.

How It Works

As stated in recipe 14-6, you cannot run service classes directly. The high level of integration with the Windows operating system and the information stored about the service in the Windows registry means services require explicit installation.

If you have Microsoft Visual Studio, you can create an installation component for your service automatically by right-clicking in the design view of your service class and selecting Add Installer from the context menu. This will generate a class called ProjectInstaller. ServiceProcessInstaller and ServiceInstaller components will be added to the class and configured for your service automatically. You can call this installation class by using deployment projects or by using the Installer tool to install your service.

You can also create installer components for Windows services manually by following these steps:

1. In your project, create a class derived from the Installer class.

2. Apply the attribute System.ComponentModel.RunInstallerAttribute(True) to the installer class.

3. In the constructor of the installer class, create a single instance of the System.ServiceProcess. ServiceProcessInstaller class. Set the Account, Username, and Password properties of ServiceProcessInstaller to configure the account under which your service will run. The Account property is set to one of the values of the ServiceAccount enumerator that represents the type of account the service will run under: LocalService, LocalSystem, NetworkService, or User. The default is User and means that you must specify an account to be used via the Username and Password properties.

4. In the constructor of the installer class, create one instance of the System.ServiceProcess. ServiceInstaller class for each individual service you want to install. Use the properties of the ServiceInstaller objects to configure information about each service, including the following:

   - ServiceName, which specifies the name Windows uses internally to identify the service. This must be the same as the value assigned to the ServiceBase.ServiceName property.

   - DisplayName, which provides a user-friendly name for the service. This property will use the value of ServiceName by default.

- StartType, which uses values of the System.ServiceProcess.ServiceStartMode enumeration to control whether the service is started automatically or manually or is disabled.
- ServiceDependsUpon, which allows you to provide a string array containing a set of service names that must be started before this service can start.

5. Add the ServiceProcessInstaller object and all ServiceInstaller objects to the System.Configuration.Install.InstallerCollection object accessed through the Installers property, which is inherited by your installer class from the Installer base class.

The Code

The following example is an installer for the Recipe14_06 Windows service created in recipe 14-6. The sample project contains the code from recipe 14-6 and for the installer class. This is necessary for the service installation to function correctly. To compile the example, you must reference two additional assemblies: System.Configuration.Install.dll and System.ServiceProcess.dll.

```
Imports System.Configuration.Install
Imports System.ServiceProcess
Imports System.ComponentModel

Namespace Apress.VisualBasicRecipes.Chapter14

    <RunInstaller(True)> _
    Public Class Recipe14_07
        Inherits Installer

        Public Sub New()

            ' Instantiate and configure a ServiceProcessInstaller.
            Dim ServiceExampleProcess As New ServiceProcessInstaller
            ServiceExampleProcess.Account = ServiceAccount.LocalSystem

            ' Instantiate and configure a ServiceInstaller.
            Dim ServiceExampleInstaller As New ServiceInstaller
            ServiceExampleInstaller.DisplayName = "Visual Basic 2005 Recipes " & ➥
"Service Example"
            ServiceExampleInstaller.ServiceName = "Recipe 14_06 Service"
            ServiceExampleInstaller.StartType = ServiceStartMode.Automatic

            ' Add both the ServiceProcessInstaller and ServiceInstaller to
            ' the installers collection, which is inherited from the
            ' Installer base class.
            Installers.Add(ServiceExampleInstaller)
            Installers.Add(ServiceExampleProcess)

        End Sub

    End Class
End Namespace
```

Usage

To install the Recipe14_06 service, build the project, navigate to the directory where Recipe14-07.exe is located (bin\Debug by default), and execute the command Installutil Recipe14-07.exe. You will see output similar to the following:

```
Microsoft (R) .NET Framework Installation utility Version 2.0.50727.42
Copyright (c) Microsoft Corporation.  All rights reserved.

Running a transacted installation.

Beginning the Install phase of the installation.
See the contents of the log file for the C:\Recipe14-07\Recipe14-07.exe assembly's
progress.
The file is located at C:\Recipe14-07\Recipe14-07.InstallLog.
Installing assembly 'C:\Recipe14-07\Recipe14-07.exe'.
Affected parameters are:
   logtoconsole =
   assemblypath = C:\Recipe14-07\Recipe14-07.exe
   logfile = C:\Recipe14-07\Recipe14-07.InstallLog
Installing service Recipe 14_06 Service...
Service Recipe 14_06 Service has been successfully installed.
Creating EventLog source Recipe 14_06 Service in log Application...

The Install phase completed successfully, and the Commit phase is beginning.
See the contents of the log file for the C:\Recipe14-07\Recipe14-07.exe assembly's
progress.
The file is located at C:\Recipe14-07\Recipe14-07.InstallLog.
Committing assembly 'C:\Recipe14-07\Recipe14-07.exe'.
Affected parameters are:
   logtoconsole =
   assemblypath = C:\Recipe14-07\Recipe14-07.exe
   logfile = C:\Recipe14-07\Recipe14-07.InstallLog

The Commit phase completed successfully.

The transacted install has completed.
```

■**Note** You can use your ServiceInstaller instance automatically with a Visual Studio Setup project. Details on how to do this can be found at http://support.microsoft.com/kb/317421.

You can then see and control the Recipe14_06 service using the Windows Computer Management console. However, despite specifying a StartType of Automatic, the service is initially installed unstarted. You must start the service manually (or restart your computer) before the service will write entries to the event log. Once the service is running, you can view the entries it writes to the Application event log using the Event Viewer application. To uninstall the Recipe14_06 service, add the /u switch to the Installutil command as follows: Installutil /u Recipe14-07.exe. You will get output similar to the following:

```
Microsoft (R) .NET Framework Installation utility Version 2.0.50727.42
Copyright (c) Microsoft Corporation.  All rights reserved.

The uninstall is beginning.
See the contents of the log file for the C:\Recipe14-07\Recipe14-07.exe assembly's
progress.
The file is located at C:\Recipe14-07\Recipe14-07.InstallLog.
Uninstalling assembly 'C:\Recipe14-07\Recipe14-07.exe'.
Affected parameters are:
   logtoconsole =
   assemblypath = C:\Recipe14-07\Recipe14-07.exe
   logfile = C:\Recipe14-07\Recipe14-07.InstallLog
Removing EventLog source Recipe 14_06 Service.
Service Recipe 14_06 Service is being removed from the system...
Service Recipe 14_06 Service was successfully removed from the system.

The uninstall has completed.
```

■**Note** If you have the Service application from the Control Panel open when you uninstall the service, the service will not uninstall completely until you close the Service application. Once you close the Service application, you can reinstall the service; otherwise, you will get an error telling you that the installation failed because the service is scheduled for deletion.

14-8. Create a Shortcut on the Desktop or Start Menu

Problem

You need to create a shortcut on the user's Windows desktop or Start menu.

Solution

Use COM Interop to access the functionality of the Windows Script Host. Create and configure an IWshShortcut instance that represents the shortcut. The folder in which you save the shortcut determines whether it appears on the desktop or in the Start menu.

How It Works

The .NET Framework class library does not include the functionality to create desktop or Start menu shortcuts; however, this is relatively easy to do using the Windows Script Host component accessed through COM Interop. Chapter 12 describes how to create an interop assembly that provides access to a COM component. If you are using Visual Studio, add a reference to the Windows Script Host Object Model listed in the COM tab of the Add Reference dialog box. If you don't have Visual Studio, use the Type Library Importer (Tlbimp.exe) to create an interop assembly for the wshom.ocx file, which is usually located in the Windows\System32 folder. (You can obtain the latest version of the Windows Script Host from http://www.microsoft.com/downloads/details.aspx?FamilyId= C717D943-7E4B-4622-86EB-95A22B832CAA. At the time of this writing, the latest version is 5.6.)

Once you have generated and imported the interop assembly into your project, follow these steps to create a desktop or Start menu shortcut.

1. Instantiate a `WshShell` object, which provides access to the Windows shell.

2. Use the `SpecialFolders` property of the `WshShell` object to determine the correct path of the folder where you want to put the shortcut. You must specify the name of the folder you want as an index to the `SpecialFolders` property. To create a desktop shortcut, specify the value `Desktop`; to create a Start menu shortcut, specify `StartMenu`. Using the `SpecialFolders` property, you can obtain the path to any of the special system folders. If the specified folder does not exist on the platform you are running on, `SpecialFolders` returns an empty `String`. Other commonly used values include `AllUsersDesktop` and `AllUsersStartMenu`. You can find the full list of special folder names in the section on the `SpecialFolders` property in the Windows Script Host documentation.

3. Call the `CreateShortcut` method of the `WshShell` object, and provide the fully qualified filename of the shortcut file you want to create. The file should have the extension .lnk. `CreateShortcut` will return an `IWshShortcut` instance.

4. Use the properties of the `IWshShortcut` instance to configure the shortcut. You can configure properties such as the executable that the shortcut references, a description for the shortcut, a hotkey sequence, and the icon displayed for the shortcut.

5. Call the `Save` method of the `IWshShortcut` instance to write the shortcut to disk. The shortcut will appear either on the desktop or in the Start menu (or elsewhere), depending on the path specified when the `IWshShortcut` instance was created.

The Code

The following example class creates a shortcut to Notepad.exe on both the desktop and Start menu of the current user. The example creates both shortcuts by calling the `CreateShortcut` method and specifying a different destination folder for each shortcut file. This approach makes it possible to create the shortcut file in any of the special folders returned by the `WshShell.SpecialFolders` property.

```
Imports System
Imports System.IO
Imports IWshRuntimeLibrary

Namespace Apress.VisualBasicRecipes.Chapter14
    Public Class Recipe14_08

        Public Shared Sub CreateShortcut(ByVal destination As String)

            ' Create a WshShell instance through which to access the
            ' functionality of the Windows shell.
            Dim hostShell As New WshShell

            ' Assemble a fully qualified name that places the Notepad.lnk
            ' file in the specified destination folder. You could use the
            ' System.Environment.GetFolderPath method to obtain a path, but
            ' the WshShell.SpecialFolders method provides access to a wider
            ' range of folders. You need to create a temporary object
            ' reference to the destination string to satisfy the requirements of
            ' the item method signature.
            Dim destFolder As Object = DirectCast(destination, Object)
            Dim fileName As String = ➥
```

```vb
Path.Combine(DirectCast(hostShell.SpecialFolders.Item(destFolder), String), ➥
"Notepad.lnk")

            ' Create the shortcut object. Nothing is created in the
            ' destination folder until the shortcut is saved.
            Dim shortcut As IWshShortcut = ➥
DirectCast(hostShell.CreateShortcut(fileName), IWshShortcut)

            ' Configure the fully qualified name to the executable.
            ' Use the Environment class for simplicity.
            shortcut.TargetPath = ➥
Path.Combine(Environment.GetFolderPath(Environment.SpecialFolder.System), ➥
"notepad.exe")

            ' Set the working directory to the Personal (My Documents) folder.
            shortcut.WorkingDirectory = ➥
Environment.GetFolderPath(Environment.SpecialFolder.Personal)

            ' Provide a description for the shortcut.
            shortcut.Description = "Notepad Text Editor"

            ' Assign a hotkey to the shortcut.
            shortcut.Hotkey = "CTRL+ALT+N"

            ' Configure Notepad to always start maximized.
            shortcut.WindowStyle = 3

            ' Configure the shortcut to display the first icon in Notepad.exe.
            shortcut.IconLocation = "notepad.exe,0"

            ' Save the configured shortcut file.
            shortcut.Save()

        End Sub

        Public Shared Sub Main()

            ' Create the Notepad shortcut on the desktop.
            CreateShortcut("Desktop")

            ' Create the Notepad shortcut on the Windows Start menu of
            ' the current user.
            CreateShortcut("StartMenu")

            ' Wait to continue.
            Console.WriteLine(Environment.NewLine)
            Console.WriteLine("Main method complete.  Press Enter.")
            Console.ReadLine()

        End Sub

    End Class
End Namespace
```

CHAPTER 15

■■■

Language Integrated Query (LINQ)

Akey element of almost any application is data. Inevitably, data needs to be listed, sorted, analyzed, or displayed in some fashion. It is the nature of what we, as programmers, do. We accomplish this by manually performing the appropriate operations and relying on the current functionality provided by the existing .NET Framework. We also rely heavily on the use of external data sources, such as SQL Server or XML files.

Chapter 9 covers writing applications that use SQL Server as the data source. If you look at the recipes in that chapter, you will notice that there is a major flaw in how applications are forced to handle data: a separation of functionality and control between the application and the data source. ADO.NET makes things fairly painless, but it requires that developers have intimate knowledge of the data source and its respective query language to be able to accomplish their goals.

We have all become used to working with data in this manner and have adapted appropriately. We have been doing it for years. Well, that's all about to change, thanks to Language Integrated Query, or LINQ (pronounced *Link*). LINQ is part of .NET Framework 3.5, which will be included with the next release of Visual Studio (code-named Orcas) and VB 9.0. VB 9.0 is currently in beta, but Microsoft hopes to have a final release available by the end of 2007.

■**Note** The contents of this chapter are based on the Beta 1 release of Visual Studio, code-named Orcas. This is available as a Microsoft Virtual Server image or standard install version, which can be downloaded from `http://msdn2.microsoft.com/en-us/vstudio/aa700831.aspx`. While much care was taken to ensure the overall accuracy of the information, it is subject to change in the final release of the product.

LINQ, at its core, is a set of features which, when used together, provide the ability to query any data source. Data can be easily queried and joined from multiple and varying data sources, such as joining data gathered from a SQL Server database and an XML file. The initial release of VB 9.0 includes several APIs that extend LINQ and provide support for the most common data sources, as listed in Table 15-1. LINQ was designed to be easily extended, which you can take advantage of to create full query support for any other data sources not covered by the included APIs.

Table 15-1. *APIs That Extend LINQ*

Name	Namespace	Supported Data Source
LINQ to Objects[a]	`System.Linq`	Collections that implement `IEnumerable(Of T)`
LINQ to XML	`System.Xml.Linq`	XML documents
LINQ to SQL	`System.Data.Linq`	SQL Server databases

Table 15-1. *APIs That Extend LINQ (Continued)*

Name	Namespace	Supported Data Source
LINQ to DataSet	`System.Data`	ADO.NET datasets
LINQ to Entities	`System.Data.Objects`	Entity Data Model (EDM) objects[b]

[a] *LINQ to Objects does support querying collections that implement IEnumerable rather than IEnumerable(Of T). However, this requires extra steps, which are demonstrated in recipe 15-6.*

[b] *EDM is new to Visual Studio (code-named Orcas) and provides the ability to easily design and model the data layer of an application.*

The first several recipes of this chapter cover some of the new features of VB 9.0 that make LINQ possible and which you will need to understand to use LINQ. The rest of the recipes concentrate on the LINQ to Objects API.

The recipes in this chapter describe how to do the following:

- Understand the basics of using LINQ (recipes 15-1, 15-2, 15-3, and 15-4)

- Query data in a collection (recipes 15-5 and 15-6)

- Sort and filter data in collections (recipes 15-7 and 15-8)

- Query data in multiple collections (recipe 15-9)

- Perform aggregate functions on collections (recipe 15-10)

- Retrieve a subset of data from a collection (recipe 15-11)

- Use paging to display the contents of a collection (recipe 15-12)

15-1. Use Implicitly Typed Variables

Problem

You need to create a strongly typed variable without explicitly declaring its type.

Solution

Ensure `Option Infer` is `On`, and then create a variable and assign it a value without using `As` and specifying a type.

How It Works

VB 9.0 allows you to create strongly typed variables without explicitly setting their data type. You could do this in previous versions of VB .NET, if `Option Strict` was set to `Off`, but the variable was always typed as an `Object`. In this case, its type is automatically inferred based on its value.

To use this new functionality, `Option Infer` must be set to `On`. You can specify this setting in the project settings dialog box or by adding `Option Infer On` to the top of your code. If you create a new project in the new version of Visual Studio, the project settings will have `Option Infer` set to `On` by default. Any projects that you migrate from previous Visual Studio versions will have `Option Infer` set to `Off`. If you are compiling your code using the VB compiler (`vbc`), you can use the `/optioninfer` option.

The following example demonstrates the use of type inference or implicit typing.

```
Dim name = "Todd"
Dim birthDay = #7/12/1971#
Dim age = 35
Dim people = New Person() {New Person("Todd"), New Person("Robb"), ➥
New Person("Alex")}
```

If you hover your cursor over any of the variables in the preceding example in the Visual Studio IDE, you will see a tool tip that shows that they are actually being strongly typed. name is *inferred* as a String, birthday is a Date, age is an Integer, and, as shown in Figure 15-1, people is an array of Person objects.

```
Imports System
Imports System.Linq
Public Class Samples

    Public Class Person
        Private m_Name As String
        Public Sub New(ByVal name As String)
            m_Name = name
        End Sub
    End Class
    Public Shared Sub Main()
        Dim name = "Todd"
        Dim birthDay = #7/12/1971#
        Dim age = 35|
        Dim people = New Person() {New Person("Todd"), N
    End Sub   Dim people() As Recipe1.Samples.Person

End Class
```

Figure 15-1. *A tool tip showing inferred type*

When your code is compiled to Microsoft Intermediate Language (MSIL), all variables are strongly typed. (See recipes 1-3 and 2-6 for more information about MSIL.) If you looked at this compiled MSIL code, using the MSIL Disassembler tool (Ildasm.exe), you would see that it has explicitly and correctly typed each variable. The following output was taken from the Ildasm.exe results for the sample code shown previously.

```
.locals init ([0] int32 age,
              [1] valuetype [mscorlib]System.DateTime birthDay,
              [2] string name,
              [3] class Recipe1.Samples/Person[] people,
              [4] class Recipe1.Samples/Person[] VB$t_array$S0)
```

Implicitly typing variables is an important part of creating and using LINQ queries. It keeps the query statement concise and less cluttered. Also, you may not know the exact data type being retrieved from a given data source. Without the ability to infer the type of a data source field, it might be impossible to efficiently query on that data source. It is also a required component of *anonymous types*, which are discussed in recipe 15-3.

15-2. Use Object Initializers

Problem

You need to initialize the properties of a class when it is first instantiated, without relying on the class constructor or default values.

Solution

Instantiate a new class instance and initialize any writable public fields or properties using the With keyword.

How It Works

VB 9.0 includes the ability to initialize the writable public fields or properties of a class when it is first instantiated. When you use object initializers, the default constructor of the class is called automatically. This means any class you wish to use object initializers for *must* have a default constructor. Any properties or fields that you do not initialize retain their default values.

Object initialization is made possible by the use of the With keyword. With is not new to VB .NET but was not previously usable in this manner. Here is a simple example of a class:

```
Public Class Person

    Private m_FirstName As String
    Private m_LastName As String

    Public Sub New()
        m_FirstName = String.Empty
        m_LastName = String.Empty
    End Sub

    Public Property FirstName() As String
        Get
            Return m_FirstName
        End Get
        Set(ByVal value As String)
            m_FirstName = value
        End Set
    End Property

    Public Property LastName() As String
        Get
            Return m_LastName
        End Get
        Set(ByVal value As String)
            m_LastName = value
        End Set
    End Property

End Class
```

In previous versions of VB .NET, you would instantiate and set property values like this:

```
Dim todd = New Person

With todd
    .FirstName = "Todd"
    .LastName = "Herman"
End With
```

The other option, if you had access to modify the class, is to use constructors to pass the property values. However, this method can become cumbersome quickly if you have a class with many properties. You further complicate things if you use an array, like this:

```
Dim people As Person() = New Person(2) {New Person, New Person, New Person}

With people(0)
    .FirstName = "Todd"
    .LastName = "Herman"
End With

With people(1)
    .FirstName = "Alex"
    .LastName = "Hughes"
End With

With people(2)
    .FirstName = "Robb"
    .LastName = "Zinn"
End With
```

Object initializers simplify this by allowing you to specify values during instantiation, like this:

```
Dim todd = New Person With {.FirstName = "Todd", .LastName = "Herman"}
```

or like this:

```
Dim people = New Person() {New Person With {.FirstName = "Todd", _
                                            .LastName = "Herman"}, _
                           New Person With {.FirstName = "Alex", _
                                            .LastName = "Hughes"}, _
                           New Person With {.FirstName = "Robb", _
                                            .LastName = "Zinn"}}
```

■**Note** Both of the preceding examples of object initialization use type inference (see recipe 15-1), rather than rely on explicit typing. This is not required but fits with the overall purpose of the chapter.

As the examples show, you use the With keyword followed by a comma-delimited list of fields or properties and their values. The objects being initialized and their values should be surrounded by curly braces ({}). As shown in Figure 15-2, the VB 9.0 IDE provides IntelliSense for all objects that can be initialized.

```
        Set(ByVal value As String)
            m_LastName = value
        End Set
    End Property
End Class
Public Shared Sub Main()
    Dim name = "Todd"
    Dim birthDay = #7/12/1971#
    Dim age = 35
    Dim people = New Person() {New Person With {.}}
End Sub
End Class
```

FirstName
LastName

Figure 15-2. *IntelliSense for object initializers*

Object initializers are a key component to using anonymous types (see recipe 15-3) and making LINQ queries concise and efficient.

15-3. Use Anonymous Types

Problem

You need to use a basic type class that doesn't exist, and you don't want to define it yourself.

Solution

Instantiate a class as you would normally, using the New keyword, but do not specify a type. You must also use object initialization (see recipe 15-2) to specify at least one property.

How It Works

When you use the New keyword to instantiate an object, you typically specify the name of the type you wish to create. In VB 9.0, when you omit this name, the compiler automatically generates the class for you. This class inherits from Object and overloads the ToString, GetHashCode, and Equals methods. The overloaded version of ToString returns a string representing all of the properties concatenated together. The overloaded Equals method returns True if all property comparisons are True and there are the same number of properties in the same order with the same names.

Figure 15-3 shows the MSIL Disassembler tool (Ildasm.exe) displaying the MSIL that the compiler would automatically generate for the following example (see recipes 1-3 and 2-6 for more information about MSIL):

```
Dim person = New With {.FirstName = "Todd", .LastName = "Herman"}
```

Figure 15-3. *MSIL Disassembler tool view of an anonymous type*

Creating anonymous types relies on several other new features of VB 9.0. As the name implies, the real name of an anonymous type is unknown. You will not be able to access it directly by its name and must rely on the variable used to first instantiate the class. This means you can't explicitly cast the person variable using As; you must rely on type inference (see recipe 15-1). Furthermore, an anonymous type *must* have at least one property. Properties for anonymous types are created by using object initializers (see recipe 15-2). The new version of Visual Studio fully supports the use of anonymous types by correctly displaying appropriate IntelliSense, as shown in Figure 15-4.

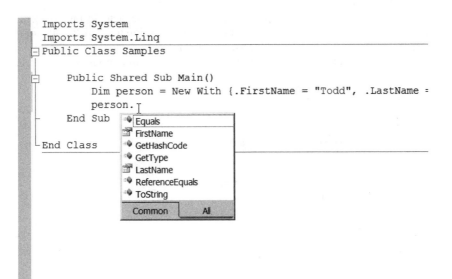

Figure 15-4. *IntelliSense support for anonymous types*

Anonymous types can also infer property names from object initializers, as in this example:

```
Dim person = New With {DateTime.Now, .FirstName = "Todd", .LastName = "Herman"}
```

In this case, the anonymous type created by the compiler would have the FirstName, LastName, and Now properties.

Anonymous types are a powerful new feature available in VB 9.0 and are used extensively in LINQ queries (see recipe 15-5) for returning strongly typed data.

15-4. Create Extension Methods

Problem

You need to extend the functionality of a class without relying on inheritance.

Solution

Create the method (a Sub or Function) that you wish to add, and then apply the ExtensionAttribute attribute to it.

How It Works

The key to using extension methods is the attribute ExtensionAttribute, which is new to VB 9.0 and located in the System.Runtime.CompilerServices namespace. You must apply this attribute to any method that you wish to use as an extension method. Furthermore, you can apply the attribute only to methods defined within a Module.

An extension method *extends* the functionality of a specific class without actually modifying it. The class being extended is referenced by the first parameter of the extension method. Because of this, all extension methods *must* have at least one parameter, and it *must* refer to the class being extended. Let's revisit the code that reverses a string (shown in recipe 2-1) and turn it into an extension method.

```
<System.Runtime.CompilerServices.Extension()> _
Public Function Reverse(ByVal s As String) As String

    Dim reversed As New Text.StringBuilder(s.Length)
    Dim chars As Char() = s.ToCharArray

    For count As Integer = chars.Length - 1 To 0 Step -1
        reversed.Append(chars(count))
    Next

    Return reversed.ToString()

End Function
```

The Reverse method is an extension method because it has the ExtensionAttribute attribute applied to it. You also know that it extends the String class because the first parameter is a String. Using an extension method is the same as calling any other method, and the Visual Studio IDE supports this via IntelliSense, as shown in Figure 15-5.

```
            Return reversed.ToString

        End Function

End Module
Public Class Samples

    Public Shared Sub Main()
        Dim blah As String = "This is a test message!"
        blah.r
    End Sub
```

```
ReferenceEquals
Remove
Replace
Reverse              Public Function Reverse() As String
  Common      All
```

```
End Class
```

Figure 15-5. *IntelliSense support for extension methods*

In the case of the preceding example, you would create a String and then call the Reverse method, like this:

```
Dim testString As String = "This is a test message!"
Console.WriteLine(testString.Reverse)
```

This would produce the following result:

```
!egassem tset a si sihT
```

It is perfectly legitimate to call an extension method directly. When used in this manner, the first parameter of the method is used as an actual parameter. For example, you would get the same results if you changed the example to this:

```
Console.WriteLine(Reverse(testString))
```

The preceding example is fairly simple but demonstrates how easy it is to extend the functionality of a class without directly modifying it. What makes extension methods even more powerful is that they can also be used to extend base classes or even interfaces.

Extension methods are another key component of LINQ queries. Most of the operators used to form a LINQ query, such as Select (see recipe 15-5) and Where (see recipe 15-8) are actually extension methods of the Enumerable type.

15-5. Query an IEnumerable(Of T) Collection

Problem

You need to query data that is stored in a collection that implements IEnumerable(Of T).

Solution

Create a LINQ query that iterates through the data stored in the target collection and returns the appropriate information.

How It Works

LINQ provides SQL-like functionality for querying virtually any data source. VB 9.0 incorporates several APIs that extend the core LINQ framework. LINQ to Objects, found in the System.Linq namespace, provides the support for querying collections that implement IEnumerable or IEnumerable(Of T). Querying IEnumerable collections is a special case and is covered in recipe 15-6.

If you have any familiarity with SQL, you will quickly recognize the standard query operators used by LINQ. A basic query uses the most recognizable operators: From and Select. While these operators are virtually identical to their SQL counterparts, LINQ orders them differently by requiring the From to come before the Select. The main reason for this is that the data source must be known prior to selecting any return data, or IntelliSense wouldn't work. Here is an example query, assuming names is an IEnumerable(Of String):

```
Dim query = From name In names Select name
```

The first part of this query, From name In names, is responsible for designating the source of the data. In this case, it is the names collection. This is structured in the same way as a For. . .Next loop. name is the iterator, and its type is inferred (see recipe 15-1) as a String. It is possible to use multiple data sources in a single From clause, which would allow you to query on each source or the combination of both (see recipe 15-9).

The second part of the sample query, Select name, is responsible for specifying what data is returned. In this case, an instance of the iterator object, name, is returned. You are not forced to return just the iterator or a single field of the iterator, if it was a class. You can return calculated data or even an anonymous type that contains properties based on data from the iterator (see recipe 15-3). If multiple items are used in the Select clause, then a new anonymous type is created and returned, with each item being a property of the new class. If the Select clause is omitted from a query, the query defaults to returning all iterators that were part of the From clause. For example, if you removed Select from the preceding query, it would still return the same information; Select name would be the default.

Like name, the data type for query is also being inferred. The data type depends on what is returned by the Select operator. In this case, that would be IEnumerable(Of String). When creating queries, you are not required to use type inference. You could have used:

```
Dim query As IEnumerable(Of String) = From name As String In names Select name
```

While that would work, type inference makes the query appear much cleaner and easier to follow. Furthermore, if you happened to return an anonymous type from the Select clause, you couldn't use the previously discussed method, because you wouldn't know the name of the type.

Queries can return a sequence of values, such as in the previous examples, in which case the query does not actually execute until you iterate through its results. They can also return a single value, in which case the query syntax would specify an aggregate operator, such as Count or Max (see recipe 15-10).

Since the example returns a sequence of values, you execute the query by iterating through it using a For ... Next loop, as shown here:

```
For Each name in query
    ...
Next
```

The Code

The following example calls three methods that each use LINQ to query a list of Employee objects. The EmployeeList method returns all of the objects and displays information. The EmployeeNames method returns and displays only the FirstName. The EmployeeInfo method returns an anonymous type that has the properties DaysSinceHired and FullName. DaysSinceHired is calculated by subtracting the employee's HireDate from the current date, and FullName is calculated by combining the employee's FirstName and LastName.

The Employee class is a simple class that represents an employee. HelperMethods.GetEmployees simply generates some sample employees, which are returned as IEnumerable(Of Employee), to use with the code. Both of these belong to the SampleData namespace. This namespace is not shown here; its purpose is only to provide sample data for the recipe. It is provided with the downloadable source code.

```vb
Imports System
Imports System.Linq

Public Class Recipe15_5

    ' Load sample data to be used for this recipe.
    Private Shared employees As List(Of SampleData.Employee) = ➥
SampleData.HelperMethods.GetEmployees

    ' Show a list of employees.
    Private Shared Sub EmployeeList()

        Console.WriteLine("List of employees:")

        ' Create a query that will simply return all
        ' employee objects. In this case, query is
        ' inferred as IEnumerable(Of SampleData.Employee).
        Dim query = From emp In employees
                    Select emp

        ' Execute the query and iterate through each
        ' employee object returned and display the
        ' information.
        For Each emp In query
            Console.WriteLine("  [{0}] {1} {2} {3} {4}", emp.EmployeeID, ➥
emp.FirstName, emp.LastName, emp.WorkGroup, emp.HireDate.ToString("MM/dd/yyyy"))
        Next

        Console.WriteLine(Environment.NewLine)

    End Sub

    ' Show a list of employee names.
    Private Shared Sub EmployeeNames()

        Console.WriteLine("List of employee first names:")
```

```vb
        ' Create a query that will return just the name
        ' for the employee object. In this case, query
        ' is inferred as IEnumerable(Of String).
        Dim query = From emp In employees _
                        Select emp.FirstName

        ' Execute the query and iterate through each
        ' employee name returned and display the
        ' information.
        For Each name In query
            Console.WriteLine(name)
        Next

        Console.WriteLine(Environment.NewLine)

    End Sub

    ' Show a list of employee full names (first and
    ' last) and how long (in days) since each was
    ' hired.
    Private Shared Sub EmployeeInfo()

        Console.WriteLine("List of employee full names and how long since " & ➥
"they were hired:")

        ' Create a query that will return the full name and
        ' number of days since hired for each employee. In
        ' this case, query is inferred as IEnumerable(Of
        ' <anonymous type>).
        Dim query = From emp In employees _
                        Select DaysSinceHired = _
                        DateTime.Now.Subtract(emp.HireDate).Days, _
                        FullName = emp.LastName & ", " & emp.FirstName

        ' Execute the query and iterate through each
        ' object returned and display the information.
        For Each emp In query
            Console.WriteLine("  {0} was hired {1} day(s) ago.", emp.FullName, ➥
emp.DaysSinceHired)
        Next

        Console.WriteLine(Environment.NewLine)

    End Sub

    Public Shared Sub Main()

        ' Call each sample method that demonstrates basic
        ' LINQ query expressions.
        Call EmployeeList()
        Call EmployeeNames()
        Call EmployeeInfo()
```

```
        Console.WriteLine("End of samples reached.  Press Enter.")
        Console.ReadLine()

    End Sub

End Class
```

Usage

When you run the preceding code, you will receive the following results:

```
List of employees:
   [1] Todd Herman Developer 02/21/2007
   [2] Robb Smith Developer 05/18/2006
   [3] Dick Edwards Manager 03/18/2001
   [4] Kevin Jones Technical Support Engineer 02/21/2007
   [5] Mike Newtron Developer 10/18/2005
   [6] Harry Dresden Technical Support Engineer 01/12/2007
   [7] Jason Holmes Supervisor 03/17/2007
   [8] Dave Turner Engineer 08/18/2002
   [9] Alex Simpson Engineer 03/13/2007
   [10] Vicky Bobby Technical Support Engineer 05/22/2006
   [11] Ardy Reznor Technical Support Engineer 03/18/1992

List of employee first names:
   Todd
   Robb
   Dick
   Kevin
   Mike
   Harry
   Jason
   Dave
   Alex
   Vicky
   Ardy

List of employee full names and how long since they were hired:
   Herman, Todd was hired 25 day(s) ago.
   Smith, Robb was hired 304 day(s) ago.
   Edwards, Dick was hired 2191 day(s) ago.
   Jones, Kevin was hired 25 day(s) ago.
   Newtron, Mike was hired 516 day(s) ago.
   Dresden, Harry was hired 65 day(s) ago.
   Holmes, Jason was hired 1 day(s) ago.
   Turner, Dave was hired 1673 day(s) ago.
   Simpson, Alex was hired 5 day(s) ago.
   Bobby, Vicky was hired 300 day(s) ago.
   Reznor, Ardy was hired 5478 day(s) ago.

End of samples reached.  Press Enter.
```

15-6. Query a Nongeneric Collection

Problem

You need to query data that is stored in a collection that implements IEnumerable, such as an ArrayList, rather than IEnumerable(Of T).

Solution

Create a standard LINQ query, as described in recipe 15-5, but strongly type the iterator variable used in the From expression.

How It Works

LINQ queries support collections that implement IEnumerable(Of T) by default. Nongeneric collections, such as ArrayList collections, are not supported by default. A typical query, assuming names implements IEnumerable(Of T), looks something like this:

```
Dim query = From name In names Select name
```

If names were an ArrayList, the query would not function properly because name is not strongly typed. This is due to the inability to infer the type of a collection that implements IEnumerable rather than the generic version, IEnumerable(Of T). You can make the query work by ensuring it is strongly typed, like this:

```
Dim query = From name As String In names Select name
```

The Code

The following example calls the EmployeeNames method. This method uses LINQ to query an ArrayList of Employee objects and returns a list of their names.

The Employee class is a simple class that represents an employee. HelperMethods.GetEmployees2 simply generates some sample employees, which are returned in an ArrayList, to use with the code. Both of these belong to the SampleData namespace. This namespace is not shown here; its purpose is only to provide sample data for the recipe. It is provided with the downloadable source code.

```
Imports System
Imports System.Linq

Public Class Recipe15_6

    ' Load sample data to be used for this recipe.
    Public Shared employees As ArrayList = SampleData.HelperMethods.GetEmployees2
    Public Shared Sub EmployeeNames()

        Console.WriteLine("List of employee names:")

        ' Create a query that will simply return all
        ' employee objects. In this case, query is
        ' inferred as IEnumerable(Of String).
        ' For LINQ to work with an ArrayList, you need to
        ' ensure you strongly type the iterator.
        Dim query = From emp As SampleData.Employee In employees
```

```
                    Select FullName = emp.LastName & ", " & emp.FirstName

            ' Execute the query and iterate through each
            ' employee object returned and display the
            ' information.
            For Each name In query
                Console.WriteLine("  {0}", name)
            Next

            Console.WriteLine(Environment.NewLine)

        End Sub
        Public Shared Sub Main()

            ' Call the method that demonstrates using basic
            ' LINQ query expressions over nongeneric IEnumerable
            ' collections.
            Call EmployeeNames()

            Console.WriteLine("End of samples reached.  Press Enter.")
            Console.ReadLine()

        End Sub

End Class
```

Usage

When you run the preceding code, you will receive the following results:

```
List of employee names:
  Herman, Todd
  Smith, Robb
  Edwards, Dick
  Jones, Kevin
  Newtron, Mike
  Dresden, Harry
  Holmes, Jason
  Turner, Dave
  Simpson, Alex
  Bobby, Vicky
  Reznor, Ardy

End of samples reached.  Press Enter.
```

15-7. Sort Data Using LINQ

Problem

You need to sort the data returned by a LINQ query.

Solution

Create a LINQ query (as shown in recipe 15-5) and use the Order By operator followed by a field name to ensure the data is properly ordered.

How It Works

If you are familiar with query languages, you should recognize the Order By operator. This is used to specify how the data returned from a query is sorted. The Order By operator supports the optional Ascending and Descending keywords, which specify in which direction the data is sorted. If omitted, Ascending is used by default. An Order By clause might look something like this:

```
Order By emp.FirstName Ascending
```

The Order By operator always comes after the From operator, but it can come before *or* after the Select operator. You use Order By before Select when you want to sort on data related to the iterator used by the From operator. If you want to sort on the data returned by the Select operator, then Order By must come after Select.

You can sort on multiple fields by separating them with commas, like this:

```
Order By emp.FirstName, emp.LastName Descending
```

The Code

The following example calls two methods that each uses LINQ to query and sort a list of Employee objects. The SortByLastName method returns all of the objects, sorts them in ascending order by the LastName property, and displays the information. The SortByFullName method returns an anonymous type that has the properties DaysSinceHired and FullName. DaysSinceHired is calculated by subtracting the employee's HireDate from the current date, and FullName is calculated by combining the employee's FirstName and LastName. The data is sorted in descending order by the DaysSinceHired property.

The Employee class is a simple class that represents an employee. HelperMethods.GetEmployees simply generates some sample employees to use with the code. Both of these belong to the SampleData namespace, which is not shown here; its purpose is only to provide sample data for the recipe. It is provided with the downloadable source code.

```
Imports System
Imports System.Linq

Public Class Recipe15_7

    ' Load sample data to be used for this recipe.
    Public Shared employees As List(Of SampleData.Employee) = ➡
SampleData.HelperMethods.GetEmployees

    ' Show a list of employees ordered by their last
    ' names.
    Private Shared Sub SortByLastName()

        Console.WriteLine("List of employees:")
        Console.WriteLine(" - Ordered by LastName (Ascending)")
        Console.WriteLine(Environment.NewLine)
```

```vb
        ' Create a query that will simply return all
        ' employee objects and sort them by the
        ' LastName property. In this case, query is
        ' inferred as IEnumerable(Of SampleData.Employee).
        Dim query = From emp In employees _
                    Order By emp.LastName Ascending
                    Select emp

        ' Execute the query and iterate through each
        ' employee name returned and display the
        ' information.
        For Each emp In query
            Console.WriteLine("  [{0}] {1} {2} {3} {4}", emp.EmployeeID, ➥
emp.FirstName, emp.LastName, emp.WorkGroup, emp.HireDate.ToString("MM/dd/yyy"))
        Next

        Console.WriteLine(Environment.NewLine)

    End Sub

    ' Show a list of employee full names (first and
    ' last) and how long (in days) since each was
    ' hired.
    Private Shared Sub SortByFullName()

        Console.WriteLine("List of employee full names and how long since " & ➥
"they were hired:")
        Console.WriteLine("  - Ordered by DaysSinceHired (Descending)")
        Console.WriteLine(Environment.NewLine)

        ' Create a query that will return the full name and
        ' number of days since hired for each employee and sort
        ' them by the DaysSinceHired property. In this case,
        ' query is inferred as IEnumerable(Of <anonymous type>).
        Dim query = From emp In employees _
                    Select DaysSinceHired = _
                    DateTime.Now.Subtract(emp.HireDate).Days, _
                    FullName = emp.LastName & ", " & emp.FirstName
                    Order By DaysSinceHired Descending

        ' Execute the query and iterate through each
        ' object returned and display the information.
        For Each emp In query
            Console.WriteLine("  {0} was hired {1} day(s) ago.", emp.FullName, ➥
emp.DaysSinceHired)
        Next

        Console.WriteLine(Environment.NewLine)

    End Sub
```

```
    Public Shared Sub Main()

        ' Call each sample method that demonstrates sorting
        ' with LINQ expressions.
        Call SortByLastName()
        Call SortByFullName()

        Console.WriteLine("End of samples reached.  Press Enter.")
        Console.ReadLine()

    End Sub

End Class
```

Usage

When you run the preceding code, you will receive the following results:

```
List of employees:
 -  Ordered by LastName (Ascending)

  [10] Vicky Bobby Technical Support Engineer 05/23/2006
  [6] Harry Dresden Technical Support Engineer 01/13/2007
  [3] Dick Edwards Manager 03/19/2001
  [1] Todd Herman Developer 02/22/2007
  [7] Jason Holmes Supervisor 03/18/2007
  [4] Kevin Jones Technical Support Engineer 02/22/2007
  [5] Mike Newtron Developer 10/19/2005
  [11] Ardy Reznor Technical Support Engineer 03/19/1992
  [9] Alex Simpson Engineer 03/14/2007
  [2] Robb Smith Developer 05/19/2006
  [8] Dave Turner Engineer 08/19/2002


List of employee full names and how long since they were hired:
 - Ordered by DaysSinceHired (Descending)

  Reznor, Ardy was hired 5478 day(s) ago.
  Edwards, Dick was hired 2191 day(s) ago.
  Turner, Dave was hired 1673 day(s) ago.
  Newtron, Mike was hired 516 day(s) ago.
  Smith, Robb was hired 304 day(s) ago.
  Bobby, Vicky was hired 300 day(s) ago.
  Dresden, Harry was hired 65 day(s) ago.
  Herman, Todd was hired 25 day(s) ago.
  Jones, Kevin was hired 25 day(s) ago.
  Simpson, Alex was hired 5 day(s) ago.
  Holmes, Jason was hired 1 day(s) ago.

End of samples reached.  Press Enter.
```

15-8. Filter Data Using LINQ

Problem

You need to apply some constraint, or a filter, to a LINQ query.

Solution

Create a LINQ query (as shown in recipe 15-5) and use the `Where` operator followed by one or more Boolean expressions.

How It Works

While the `Select` operator is responsible for transforming or returning data from a LINQ query, the `Where` operator is responsible for filtering what data is available to be returned. If you are familiar with SQL, the LINQ `Where` operator is virtually indistinguishable from the like-named operator in SQL. A Boolean expression, which performs the filtering on the data, comes after the `Where` operator. The operator itself must come between the `From` and `Select` clauses.

```
Dim names() As String = {"Todd", "Tom", "Mike", "Archie", "Veronica", "Jughead"}
Dim query = From name In names Select name
```

The preceding example creates a strongly typed array. You are able to query arrays because they implement `IEnumerable`. However, as discussed in recipe 15-6, you must ensure the `IEnumerable` data being queried is strongly typed. As the example stands now, `name` is inferred as a `String`, and `names` is an array of `Strings`. If you attempted to infer the type of `names()` by removing the `As String`, you would break the strong typing, unless the iterator used in the query were strongly typed. If you executed the preceding query, you would get back every name stored in the array.

Now, let's change the query to use the `Where` operator.

```
Dim query = From name In names Where name.StartsWith("T") Select name
```

If you executed this new query, you would get back only the first two names in the array: `Todd` and `Tom`.

The Code

The following example calls two methods that each uses LINQ to query a list of `Employee` objects. The `ListManagers` method returns information only for the employees who have a `WorkGroup` value of `Manager`. The `ListTechEngineers` method returns information only for employees who have a `WorkGroup` value of `Technical Support Engineer` and were hired during the current year.

The `Employee` class is a simple class that represents an employee. `HelperMethods.GetEmployees` simply generates some sample employees to use with the code. Both of these belong to the `SampleData` namespace, which is not shown here; its purpose is only to provide sample data for the recipe. It is provided with the downloadable source code.

```vbnet
Imports System
Imports System.Linq

Public Class Recipe15_8

    ' Load sample data to be used for this recipe.
    Public Shared employees As List(Of SampleData.Employee) = ➥
SampleData.HelperMethods.GetEmployees

    ' Show a list of employees that belong to the
    ' "Manager" workgroup.
    Private Shared Sub ListManagers()

        Console.WriteLine("List of Managers:")

        ' Create a query that will return employee objects
        ' that have a WorkGroup value of "Manager". In this
        ' case, query is inferred as IEnumerable(Of
        ' SampleData.Employee).
        Dim query = From emp In employees
                    Where emp.WorkGroup = "Manager"
                    Select emp

        ' Execute the query and iterate through each
        ' employee name returned and display the
        ' information.
        For Each emp In query
            Console.WriteLine("  [{0}] {1} {2}", emp.EmployeeID, emp.FirstName, ➥
emp.LastName)
        Next

        Console.WriteLine(Environment.NewLine)

    End Sub

    ' Show a list of employees that belong to the
    ' "Technical Support Engineer" workgroup and
    ' were hired this year.
    Private Shared Sub ListTechEngineers()

        Console.WriteLine("List of Technical Support Engineers hired in {0}:", ➥
DateTime.Now.Year.ToString)

        ' Create a query that will return employee objects that
        ' have a WorkGroup value of "Technical Support Engineer"
        ' and were hired sometime this year. In this case,
        ' query is inferred as IEnumerable(Of SampleData.Employee).
        Dim query = From emp In employees _
                    Where emp.WorkGroup = "Technical Support Engineer"
                    And emp.HireDate.Year = DateTime.Now.Year
                    Select emp
```

```
    ' Execute the query and iterate through each
    ' employee name returned and display the
    ' information.
    For Each emp In query
        Console.WriteLine("  [{0}] {1} {2} - Hired on {3}", emp.EmployeeID, ➥
emp.FirstName, emp.LastName, emp.HireDate.ToString("MM/dd/yyyy"))
    Next

    Console.WriteLine(Environment.NewLine)

  End Sub

  Public Shared Sub Main()

    ' Call each sample method that demonstrates sorting
    ' with LINQ expressions.
    Call ListManagers()
    Call ListTechEngineers()

    Console.WriteLine("End of samples reached.  Press Enter.")
    Console.ReadLine()

  End Sub

End Class
```

Usage

When you run the preceding code, you will receive the following results:

```
List of Managers:
  [3] Dick Edwards

List of Technical Support Engineers hired in 2007:
  [4] Kevin Jones - Hired on 02/22/2007
  [6] Harry Dresden - Hired on 01/13/2007

End of samples reached.  Press Enter.
```

15-9. Query Data from Multiple Collections

Problem

You need to query and combine data from multiple collections.

Solution

Create a LINQ query that references all required data sources in the From clause (see recipe 15-5). Then use the Where clause (see recipe 15-8) to merge the data based on a common element.

How It Works

The From operator allows you to specify more then one iteration statement. All listed collections will be queried, and all properties are available to be used as part of the query syntax.

```
Dim words() As String = {"Apple", "Bat", "Cat", "Dog", "Egg", "Frog"}
Dim searchCriteria() As String = {"C", "D"}

Dim wordSearch = From word In words, crit In searchCriteria _
                Where word.StartsWith(crit) _
                Select Word = word, Crit = crit

For Each match In wordSearch
    Console.WriteLine("{0} matches the search criteria of {1}.", match.Word, ➥
match.Crit)
Next
```

The preceding example creates two arrays: words contains a list of words, and searchCriteria contains a list of letters. The query collects data from both sources but uses the Where clause to return only the words that start with the letters specified in the searchCriteria array. The Select clause creates and returns an anonymous type that includes the Word and Crit properties. If you ran this example, it would produce the following output:

```
Cat matches the search criteria of C.
Dog matches the search criteria of D.
```

If the data sources queried have a common element, you can use the Where clause to more tightly join the data (as demonstrated in this recipe's code). In previous versions of VB, performing actions like this took a lot of code—so much that it was more common to move data into a data source that would support querying, such as SQL Server.

■**Note** Using multiple data sources in a From clause works for joining data, but it is somewhat limited. It is important to note that, like SQL, LINQ supports Join On and Group By. These query operators provide the necessary functionality to perform advanced joins and data grouping. However, these operators are not usable in the release of Visual Studio used for this chapter. They should work in the version available by the time this book is published.

The Code

The following example calls two methods that demonstrate how to use LINQ to join data from two related sources. The EmployeeTasks method joins a collection of Employee objects to a collection of Task objects based on the EmployeeID property. The employee's name and task title are displayed in the console. The OpenTasksForThisYear method performs the same join, but it returns only data for employees who were hired this year and have open tasks.

The Employee and Task classes are simple classes that represent an employee and a specific task, respectively. HelperMethods.GetEmployees generates some sample employees to use with the code, and HelperMethods.GetTasks generates tasks. These classes and methods belong to the SampleData namespace, which is not shown here; its purpose is only to provide sample data for the recipe. It is provided with the downloadable source code.

```vb
Imports System
Imports System.Linq

Public Class Recipe15_9

    Public Shared employees As List(Of SampleData.Employee) = ➥
SampleData.HelperMethods.GetEmployees
    Public Shared tasks As List(Of SampleData.Task) = ➥
SampleData.HelperMethods.GetTasks

    Private Shared Sub EmployeeTasks()

        Console.WriteLine("List of employees and their tasks:")
        Console.WriteLine(Environment.NewLine)

        ' Create a query that will join employee and task data,
        ' returning the first name and task title for each employee.
        Dim query = From emp In employees, task In tasks
                    Where emp.EmployeeID = task.EmployeeID
                    Select emp.FirstName, task.Title
                    Order By FirstName

        For Each rec In query
            Console.WriteLine("  {0} - {1}", rec.FirstName, rec.Title)
        Next

        Console.WriteLine(Environment.NewLine)

    End Sub

    Private Shared Sub OpenTasksForThisYear()

        Console.WriteLine("List of employees hired this year with open tasks:")
        Console.WriteLine(Environment.NewLine)

        ' Create a query that will join employee and task data,
        ' returning the first name and task title for each employee.
        Dim query = From emp In employees, task In tasks
                    Where emp.EmployeeID = task.EmployeeID And
                          emp.HireDate.Year = DateTime.Now.Year And
                          task.Status = SampleData.Task.TaskStatus.Open
                    Select FullName = emp.LastName & ", " & emp.FirstName,
                           task.Title
                    Order By FullName

        For Each rec In query
            Console.WriteLine("  {0} - {1}", rec.FullName, rec.Title)
        Next

        Console.WriteLine(Environment.NewLine)

    End Sub
```

```
    Public Shared Sub Main()

        Call EmployeeTasks()
        Call OpenTasksForThisYear()

        Console.WriteLine("End of samples reached.  Press Enter.")
        Console.ReadLine()

    End Sub

End Class
```

Usage

When you run the preceding code, you will receive the following results:

```
List of employees and their tasks:

  Alex - Sample Task 11
  Ardy - Sample Task 7
  Dave - Sample Task 9
  Dick - Sample Task 2
  Harry - Sample Task 15
  Kevin - Sample Task 5
  Mike - Sample Task 4
  Mike - Sample Task 13
  Robb - Sample Task 8
  Robb - Sample Task 10
  Todd - Sample Task 1
  Todd - Sample Task 3
  Todd - Sample Task 6
  Todd - Sample Task 12
  Vicky - Sample Task 14

List of employees hired this year with open tasks:

  Dresden, Harry - Sample Task 15
  Herman, Todd - Sample Task 1
  Herman, Todd - Sample Task 6
  Herman, Todd - Sample Task 12
  Simpson, Alex - Sample Task 11

End of samples reached.  Press Enter.
```

15-10. Perform Aggregate Operations on Collections

Problem

You need to perform basic aggregate operations (such as Max or Min) on data stored in a collection.

Solution

Call one of the aggregate methods, available to all IEnumerable(Of T) collections, to perform the required calculation.

How It Works

.NET Framework 3.5 offers several methods that perform aggregate calculations on a group of data. Table 15-2 shows the most commonly used methods.

Table 15-2. *Common Aggregate Operators*

Method	Description
Count	Returns the number of items
Sum	Returns the sum of the specified field
Max	Returns the maximum value in the specified field
Min	Returns the minimum value in the specified field
Average	Returns the average value in the specified field

These methods are defined in System.Linq.Enumerable and are actually extension methods (see recipe 15-4) of the IEnumerable(Of T) class. Any object that derives from IEnumerable(Of T) will have access to these methods. Here is an example:

```
Dim numbers() As Integer = {1, 2, 3, 4, 5, 6, 7, 8, 9, 10}

Console.WriteLine("There are {0} numbers in the array.", numbers.Count.ToString)
Console.WriteLine("The MIN is {0}.", numbers.Min.ToString)
Console.WriteLine("The MAX is {0}.", numbers.Max.ToString)
Console.WriteLine("The AVG is {0}.", numbers.Average.ToString)
Console.WriteLine("The SUM is {0}.", numbers.Sum.ToString)
```

This example creates an array of Integers called numbers. Since numbers derives from Enumerable, you have access to the desired extension methods. The code would produce the following results:

```
There are 10 numbers in the array.
The MIN is 1.
The MAX is 10.
The AVG is 5.5.
The SUM is 55.
```

A typical LINQ query returns some type of collection. The query is executed only when you attempt to iterate through that collection. Since any collection returned by a LINQ query derives from IEnumerable(Of T), the .NET Framework 3.5 aggregate methods are available. The form is to surround the query in parentheses and use dot notation to access the required method. You can convert part of the previous example into a LINQ query like this:

```
Dim numbers() As Integer = {1, 2, 3, 4, 5, 6, 7, 8, 9, 10}
Dim avg = (From num In numbers
           Select num).Average
```

Using aggregate methods in this manner forces the LINQ query to execute immediately, and only a single value, the aggregate value, is returned.

The Code

The following example calls five methods that demonstrate how to use LINQ to perform each of the aggregate operations listed in Table 15-2.

The Employee class is a simple class that represents an employee. HelperMethods.GetEmployees simply generates some sample employees to use with the code. Both of these belong to the SampleData namespace, which is not shown here; its purpose is only to provide sample data for the recipe. It is provided with the downloadable source code.

```
Imports System
Imports System.Linq

Public Class Recipe15_10

    Public Shared employees As List(Of SampleData.Employee) = ➥
SampleData.HelperMethods.GetEmployees

    Private Shared Sub ShowMaxWage()

        ' Create a query that executes immediately and returns
        ' the maximum hourly wage.
        Dim wageMax = (From emp In employees
                       Select emp.HourlyWage).Max

        Console.WriteLine("Maximum Hourly Wage: {0}", wageMax.ToString("$###.#0"))

    End Sub

    Private Shared Sub ShowMinWage()

        ' Create a query that executes immediately and returns
        ' the minimum hourly wage.
        Dim wageMin = (From emp In employees
                       Select emp.HourlyWage).Min

        Console.WriteLine("Minimum Hourly Wage: {0}", wageMin.ToString("$###.#0"))

    End Sub

    Private Shared Sub ShowWageSum()

        ' Create a query that executes immediately and returns
        ' the sum of all wages.
        Dim wageSum = (From emp In employees
                       Select emp.HourlyWage).Sum

        Console.WriteLine("Total Wage: {0}", wageSum.ToString("$###.#0"))

    End Sub
```

```vb
    Private Shared Sub ShowAvgWage()

        ' Create a query that executes immediately and returns
        ' the average hourly wage.
        Dim wageAvg = (From emp In employees
                        Select emp.HourlyWage).Average

        Console.WriteLine("Average Wage:  {0}", wageAvg.ToString("$###.#0"))

    End Sub

    Private Shared Sub HiredThisYear()

        ' Create a query that executes immediately and returns
        ' the number of employees that were hired in the current
        ' year.
        Dim cnt = (From emp In employees
                    Where emp.HireDate.Year = DateTime.Now.Year
                    Select emp).Count

        Console.WriteLine("{0} employees were hired this year.", cnt.ToString)

    End Sub

    Public Shared Sub Main()

        Call ShowMaxWage()
        Call ShowMinWage()
        Call ShowWageSum()
        Call ShowAvgWage()
        Call HiredThisYear()

        Console.WriteLine(Environment.NewLine)
        Console.WriteLine("End of samples reached.  Press Enter.")
        Console.ReadLine()

    End Sub

End Class
```

Usage

When you run the preceding code, you will receive the following results:

```
Maximum Hourly Wage:  $200.00
Minimum Hourly Wage:  $10.75
Total Wage:  $778.94
Average Wage:  $70.81
5 employees were hired this year.

End of samples reached.  Press Enter.
```

15-11. Retrieve a Subset of Data from a Collection

Problem

You need to retrieve specific elements or groups of elements from a collection.

Solution

Call one of the methods (such as First or Last), available to all IEnumerable(Of T) collections, to partition the data as required.

How It Works

Similar to the aggregate methods discussed in recipe 15-10, .NET Framework 3.5 also offers several methods that assist in retrieving certain data from a collection. Table 15-3 shows the most commonly used methods.

Table 15-3. *Common Partitioning Methods*

Method	Description
Take	Returns the specified number of items from the beginning of the collection
TakeWhile[a]	Returns the specified number of items from the beginning of the collection while the specified condition is True
Skip	Skips the specified number of items from the beginning of the collection and returns the rest
SkipWhile[a]	Skips the specified number of items from the beginning of the collection and returns the rest while the specified condition is True
ElementAt	Returns the item at the specified index in the collection; since the collection is zero-based, the first element is at index 0
First	Returns the first item in the collection
Last	Returns the last item in the collection

[a] *This method is not currently supported in the version of Visual Studio used for this chapter.*

These methods are defined in System.Linq.Enumerable and are actually extension methods (see recipe 15-4) of the IEnumerable(Of T) class. Any object that derives from IEnumerable(Of T) will have access to these methods. Here is an example:

```
Dim grades() As Integer = {95, 85, 90, 72, 60, 89, 94, 99, 87, 100}

Console.WriteLine("First five grades:")
Dim firstFiveGrades = grades.Take(5)
For Each grade In firstFiveGrades
    Console.WriteLine("  {0}", grade.ToString)
Next
```

This example creates an array of Integers called grades. Since grades derives from IEnumerable(Of T), you have access to the desired extension methods. This example uses Take to return the first five elements of the collection:

```
First five grades:
   95
   85
   90
   72
   60
```

Here is an example that uses the Skip method:

```
Console.WriteLine("All other grades:")
Dim lastFiveGrades = grades.Skip(5)
For Each grade In lastFiveGrades
    Console.WriteLine("  {0}", grade.ToString)
Next
```

Skip is the opposite of Take. It skips the first five elements in the collection and returns the remaining elements:

```
All other grades:
   89
   94
   99
   87
   100
```

The Take (or TakeWhile) and Skip (or SkipWhile) methods work using deferred execution. This means that the query does not execute until you attempt to iterate through the collection subset returned by the method. Some partitioning methods (such as First, Last, and ElementAt) force the query to execute immediately and return only a single value. Here is an example of using the same grades array shown in the preceding examples:

```
Dim firstGrade = grades.First
Dim lastGrade = grades.Last
Dim seventhGrade = grades.ElementAt(7)

Console.WriteLine("First grade:  {0}", firstGrade)
Console.WriteLine("Last grade:  {0}", lastGrade)
Console.WriteLine("The 7th grade:  {0}", seventhGrade)
```

Running this new example would produce the following results:

```
First grade:  95
Last grade:  100
The 7th grade:  99
```

Since any collection returned by a LINQ query derives from IEnumerable(Of T), the partitioning methods are available. The form is to surround the query in parentheses and use dot notation to access the required method. You would convert the previous example of using Take to a LINQ query like this:

```
Dim firstFiveGrades = (From grade in grades).Take(5)
```

15-12. Display Collection Data Using Paging

Problem

You need to segment data from a collection into *pages*.

Solution

Combine and use the Skip and Take extension methods (discussed in recipe 15-11) of an IEnumerable(Of T) instance to segment the data into a page. Call the Skip and Take methods in a loop, changing the parameter used with Skip to get and display each page.

How It Works

It is common to divide large amounts of data into manageable chunks, or *pages*. This is accomplished with LINQ by using a combination of the Skip and Take methods. As discussed in recipe 15-11, Skip and Take are extension methods of IEnumerable(Of T). Since Skip returns an IEnumerable(Of T) instance, Take can be used in conjunction with it, as shown here:

```
Dim page1 = procs.Skip(0).Take(10)
```

Assuming procs is an IEnumerable(Of T) collection, this statement would return the first ten items. For paging purposes, the parameter passed to Skip can be thought of as the starting point for a given page, and the parameter passed to Take represents the page size. With this in mind, if you wanted the second page of data, you would use this:

```
Dim page2 = procs.Skip(10).Take(10)
```

The Code

The following example uses LINQ to query the processes that are using more than 5 MB of memory. ToList, another IEnumerable(Of T) extension method, is used to force the query to execute immediately and return a List(Of Process) collection. A page, which consists of ten items, is retrieved by using Skip and Take as described in this recipe. The example loops through each page, displaying the data until there is no more.

```
Imports System
Imports System.Linq
Imports System.Diagnostics

Public Class Recipe15_12

    ' This constant holds the size of each page.
    Private Const PAGE_SIZE = 10
```

```vb
    ' A constant to hold a number representing 5 MB (in
    ' bytes). This is used in the LINQ query to check
    ' memory usage.
    Private Const FIVE_MB = 5 * (1024 * 1024)

    Public Shared Sub Main()

        ' Use LINQ to retrieve an IEnumerable(Of Process) List of
        ' processes that are using more than 5 MB of memory. The
        ' ToList method is used to force the query to execute immediately.
        Dim procs = (From proc In Process.GetProcesses.ToList
                     Where proc.WorkingSet64 > FIVE_MB
                     Order By proc.ProcessName
                     Select proc).ToList

        ' Calculate the total number of pages by dividing the count of
        ' processes by the page size.
        Dim totalPages As Integer = procs.Count / PAGE_SIZE

        Console.WriteLine("LIST OF PROCESSES WITH MEMORY USAGE OVER 5 MB:")
        Console.WriteLine(Environment.NewLine)

        ' Loop and display each page of data.
        For i = 0 To totalPages - 1
            Console.WriteLine("PAGE {0} OF {1}", i + 1.ToString(), ➥
totalPages.ToString())

            ' Loop through all of the process records for this page.
            ' A combination of the Skip and Take methods is used to
            ' accomplish paging on our data.
            For Each proc In procs.Skip(i * PAGE_SIZE).Take(PAGE_SIZE)
                Console.WriteLine("{0,-20} - {1,5} MB", proc.ProcessName, ➥
(proc.WorkingSet64 / 1048576).ToString("##.##"))
            Next

            ' Check if there are any more pages.
            If Not i = totalPages - 1 Then
                Console.WriteLine("Press Enter for the next page.")
                Console.ReadLine()
            End If
        Next

        Console.WriteLine(Environment.NewLine)
        Console.WriteLine("No more data available.  Press Enter to end.")
        Console.ReadLine()

    End Sub

End Class
```

Usage

When you run the preceding code, you will receive results similar to the following:

```
LIST OF PROCESSES WITH MEMORY USAGE OVER 5 MB:

PAGE 1 OF 5
Apache            -  8.28 MB
Apache            - 14.68 MB
Apache            -  6.55 MB
backupserver      -  7.21 MB
bagent            - 16.27 MB
csrss             -  5.11 MB
ctfmon            -  5.23 MB
CTHELPER          -  6.78 MB
CTSysVol          -  5.55 MB
devenv            - 79.44 MB
Press Enter for the next page.

 .  .  .

PAGE 5 OF 5
svchost           -  5.56 MB
svchost           - 13.51 MB
taskmgr           -  6.07 MB
TimounterMonitor  -  5.72 MB
wcescomm          -  6.81 MB
WDEzLink          - 18.77 MB

No more data available.  Press Enter to end.
```

Acronyms

ACL
    access control list

API
    application programming interface

ASCII
    American Standard Code for Information Interchange

CA
    certificate authority

CAS
    code access security

CCW
    COM callable wrapper

CLR
    common language runtime

COM
    Component Object Model

CPU
    central processing unit

CSP
    cryptographic service provider

CSS
    Cascading Style Sheets

CTP
Community Technology Preview

DCOM
Distributed Component Object Model

DLL
dynamic link library

DNS
Domain Name System

DOM
Document Object Model

DPAPI
Data Protection Application Programming Interface

EDM
Entity Data Model

FTP
File Transfer Protocol

GAC
global assembly cache

GC
garbage collection

GDI
Graphics Device Interface

GUI
graphical user interface

HTML
Hypertext Markup Language

HTTP
Hypertext Transfer Protocol

HTTPS
Hypertext Transfer Protocol over Secure Sockets Layer (HTTP over SSL)

I/O
input/output

ICMP
Internet Control Message Protocol

IIS
Internet Information Services

IL
intermediate language

ILDASM
Intermediate Language Disassembler

IMAP
Internet Message Access Protocol

IP
Internet Protocol

JIT
just in time

LINQ
Language Integrated Query

MAPI
Messaging Application Programming Interface

MBR
marshal by reference

MBV
marshal by value

MDI
Multiple Document Interface

MIME
Multipurpose Internet Mail Extensions

MSDN
Microsoft Developer Network

MSIL
Microsoft Intermediate Language

OS
operating system

PIA
primary interop assembly

PID
process identifier

POP3
Post Office Protocol 3

RBS
role-based security

RCW
runtime callable wrapper

RFC
Request For Comment

RID
role identifier

RPC
remote procedure call

SCM
Service Control Manager

SDK
software development kit

SID
security identifier

SMTP
Simple Mail Transfer Protocol

SOAP
Simple Object Access Protocol

SPC
software publisher certificate

SQL
Structured Query Language

SSL
Secure Sockets Layer

TCP
Transmission Control Protocol

TLBEXP
Type Library Exporter

TLBIMP
Type Library Importer

TSQL
Transact-SQL

UDP
User Datagram Protocol

URI
uniform resource identifier

URL
uniform resource locator

URN
uniform resource name

UTF
Unicode Transformation Format

W3C
World Wide Web Consortium

WMI
Windows Management Instrumentation

WSDL
Web Service Description Language

XML
Extensible Markup Language

XSD
XML Schema Definition

XSL
Extensible Style Language

XSLT
Extensible Style Language Transformation

Index

Find it faster at http://superindex.apress.com

Find it faster at http://superindex.apress.com

Find it faster at http://superindex.apress.com

Find it faster at http://superindex.apress.com

You Need the Companion eBook